AF696123

AILA's IMMIGRATION LITIGATION TOOLBOX

Essential Materials for Administrative and Federal Court Practice

Related Titles from AILA Publications

General Reference

Kurzban's Immigration Law Sourcebook, by Ira J. Kurzban
AILA's Asylum Primer, by Regina Germain
Immigration Consequences of Criminal Activity, by Mary E. Kramer
Immigration & Nationality Law Handbook

Statutes, Regulations, and Case Law

AILA's Immigration Case Summaries
Immigration & Nationality Act (INA)
Immigration Regulations (CFR)

Government Reprints

BIA Practice Manual
Immigration Judge Benchbook
Affirmative Asylum Procedures Manual
Immigration Law in the Ninth Circuit

Tables of Contents and other information about these and other AILA publications can be found at ***www.ailapubs.com***. Orders may be placed at that site or by calling 1-800-982-2839.

AILA's Immigration Litigation Toolbox

Essential Materials for Administrative and Federal Court Practice

Editor-in-Chief
Charles H. Kuck

Associate Editor
C. Lynn Calder

Contributors

Cynthia A. Aziz
Brian K. Bates
Kerry William Bretz
Robert H. Cohen
Susan H. Colussy
Stuart I. Folinsky
Tammy Fox-Isicoff
Anna M. Gallagher
Alice S. Glover
Karen T. Grisez
Philip Hornik
Anwen Hughes
Jeff Joseph
Mary A. Kenney
Mary E. Kramer
Ira J. Kurzban
Peter N. Larrabee
Martin J. Lawler
David W. Leopold
Oscar Levin
Laura L. Lichter
Cheryl Little
Elihu S. Massel
Elaine Veatch Morley
Thomas E. Moseley
Mark J. Newman
Zachary Nightingale
Robert Pauw
Trina Realmuto
Leonard M. Roos
Linda Rose
Kristen B. Rosati
T. Douglas Stump
Helena Tetzeli
Stacy Tolchin
Marc Van der Hout
Joseph A. Vail
David K. Wenger
Nadine K. Wettstein
Peter D. Williamson

Managing Editor
Stephanie L. Browning

Production Assistant
Natalie C. Simpson

Contributing Editors
Randy P. Auerbach
Tatia L. Gordon-Troy
Silvia S. Wang

AMERICAN IMMIGRATION LAWYERS ASSOCIATION
918 F Street NW, Washington DC 20004 ◆ (202) 216-2400 ◆ *www.aila.org*

Website for Corrections and Updates

Corrections and other updates to AILA publications can be found online at ***www.aila.org/BookUpdates***. If you have any corrections or updates to the information in this book, please let us know by sending a note to the address below, or e-mail us at ***books@aila.org***.

This publication is designed to provide accurate and authoritative information in regard to the subject matter covered. It is distributed with the understanding that the publisher is not engaged in rendering legal, accounting, or other professional service. If legal advice or other expert assistance is required, the services of a competent professional should be sought.

—from a Declaration of Principles jointly adopted by a Committee of the American Bar Association and a Committee of Publishers

Copyright © 2001, 2005 by the American Immigration Lawyers Association

All rights reserved. This book may be used in the normal course of the practice of law, including photocopying pages (or copying data from the CD) for individual cases or for the user's personal library, but not for redistribution. Other than that, no part of this publication may be reproduced or transmitted in any form or by any means, electronic or mechanical, including photocopy, recording, or any information storage retrieval system, without written permission from the publisher. No copyright claimed on U.S. government material.

Requests for permission to make electronic or print copies of any part of this work should be mailed to Director of Publications, American Immigration Lawyers Association, 918 F Street NW, Washington, DC 20004, or e-mailed to *books@aila.org*.

Printed in the United States of America

ISBN 1-57370-183-1
Stock No. 81-83

Dedicated to the memory of the man who led the way—

Sam Williamson

"Sue the Bastards"

Sam, thank you!

CAVEAT

The sample documents in the *Immigration Litigation Toolbox* are just that—samples. Read each one *carefully* before adapting it to the facts of your specific case, and don't forget to Shepardize all cases completely; the law can change quickly.

Also, be sure you are familiar with and in compliance with your local court rules, including the proper format for the pleadings. The formatting used in this *Toolbox* (and the accompanying CD), while approximating a typical pleading format, will by necessity vary from the actual layout any individual jurisdiction requires.

TABLE OF CONTENTS

I. Preparatory and Ancillary Material

II. DHS Pleadings and Requests

III. Immigration Court Motions and Briefs

IV. BIA Motions and Briefs

V. District Court Pleadings and Memoranda

Habeas Relief

PREFACE

Since the publication of the updated *AILA Litigation Toolbox* in 2001, we have witnessed an explosion of immigration litigation, one that has been a long time building. For this, we say thank you, and, it's about time! As immigration attorneys, we have historically been reluctant to litigate against the Department of Homeland Security (including USCIS, ICE, and CBP), the Department of Labor, and the Department of State, mostly because of the "I will need their help on this other case" syndrome.

Of course, there have always been those among our membership who have shrugged off this defeatist attitude and have charged ahead, in many ways leading us to a better place—a place where respect is earned because victories have been won. These victories have changed hundreds of thousands of lives and have sharpened the skills of those willing to fight for the rights our clients possess. You know the names of these men and women. You know their tenacity, their will, and their refusal to settle for less than the constitutionally protected rights of their clients. The motto of these attorneys is simple: "We would rather have the government fear us than like us."

We believe that if you are reading this, you are about to join those attorneys. Recent changes in immigration law have focused our concerns on the lack of due process, lack of equal protection, and the not-so-subtle and very clear intent of Congress to strip all remaining discretion from those charged with enforcing these laws. We also continuously run into those government employees who, rather than exercise the limited discretion granted to them to keep families together or allow our clients to grow their businesses, seek to use the immigration laws to further "punish" our clients by denying them access to counsel, timely access to the courts, and family unifying relief.

These words are not sour grapes; they are borne of experience and frustration at the increasing insensitivity to the U.S. Constitution. For these reasons, we have compiled and updated *AILA's Immigration Litigation Toolbox*. We seek to arm all attorneys with the sword of justice, and to allow immigration practitioners to make litigation a part of their everyday practices. We can no longer be afraid to bring to light the injustices against our clients simply because we need the help of DHS/DOL/DOS in cases for our other clients. We have no business representing anyone as attorneys if we are unwilling to use all of the tools at our disposal to seek justice for all of our clients. Much good can be accomplished by shining a light on the dark corners of injustice. *Be Not Afraid.*

The *Immigration Litigation Toolbox* is divided into separate sections; each section deals with a separate part of our judicial system. Each section contains sample motions, pleadings, and memoranda, along with a brief cover memo explaining when and how to use that particular sample. Of necessity, the *Immigration Litigation Toolbox* is more of a tome than a light piece of reading material. Motions, pleadings, and memoranda take up space. We have tried to consolidate these materials as much as possible, while at the same time making this volume easy to use. The *Immigration Litigation Toolbox* itself comes with a CD-ROM containing all of the samples, in Microsoft Word format (which can be read by other programs as well), to make it easy for attorneys to adapt and use the samples in their everyday practices.

The various sections of the *Immigration Litigation Toolbox* address, in order, the numerous administrative and judicial procedures with which we as immigration lawyers deal on a daily basis. This, of course, starts with DHS itself. The sub-agencies of DHS—USCIS, ICE, and CBP—all handle, in one respect or another, various provisions of Title 8 of the Code of Federal Regulations and the Immigration and Nationality Act (INA). Each of these agencies has set up various procedures for enforcing "its" part of the immigration laws. These procedures, if mastered by the attorney, can be used to effectively fight for our clients' rights. Along with the Administrative Appeals Office, USCIS's own internal review procedures require that certain types of pleadings and procedures be followed prior to granting certain benefits under the INA. Following along this natural progression, the *Immigration Litigation Toolbox* contains sections on the immigration court, the Board of Immigration Appeals, the federal district courts, and the circuit courts of appeal.

These sample motions, pleadings, and memoranda all come with two very simple caveats. First, the law changes constantly. Do not *ever* use one of these samples without first verifying that all cases, laws, and regulations cited in the sample have not been overruled, set aside, or modified by a subsequent ruling. To ignore this very simple rule, learned by all first-year law students, would be foolish. Second, read the local rules of procedure pertaining to the court in which you are filing. These include the Immigration Court Operating Procedures, the new *BIA Practice Manual*, the Federal Rules of Civil Procedure, and the Federal Rules of Appellate Procedure, and their local caveats. Local rules are dramatically different in every court included in this book. Ignore them at your client's risk!

Obviously, a volume of this size and detail does not come into existence on its own. Numerous individuals have contributed sample pleadings, and many of these individuals have served as senior and associate editors of this and the past volume of the publication. Continuing thanks and praise should be given to Cynthia A. Aziz, Robert H. Cohen, Alice S. Glover, Anwen Hughes, Jeff Joseph, Mary A. Kenney, Mary E. Kramer, Ira J. Kurzban, Peter N. Larrabee, Martin J. Lawler, Laura L. Lichter, Zachary Nightingale, Trina Realmuto, Leonard M. Roos, Linda Rose, Stacy Tolchin, Marc Van der Hout, Joseph A. Vail, and Nadine K. Wettstein.

The *Immigration Litigation Toolbox* is not the first effort by AILA to educate its members on the joys of litigating against DHS. The first such comprehensive effort was an excellent book edited by Lory D. Rosenberg, now the director of Immigration Defense & Expert Assistance (IDEA), and formerly a member of the Board of Immigration Appeals. She wrote her book, *Fair Hearings Pleadings Manual*, while serving as the first director of the AILF's Legal Action Center. It is her book that gave impetus to this larger volume, and some of those original pleadings are found in these pages. Previously, Stuart I. Folinsky and Bonnie Stern-Wasser developed the idea of what has become *AILA's Immigration Litigation Toolbox*. To them we owe a debt of gratitude. Without the base of wisdom and tenacity found in the work of the pioneers in immigration litigation, we would have had a much more difficult time preparing this book for you.

We must, of necessity and sincere gratitude, acknowledge the tremendous work of Stephanie L. Browning, Senior Legal Editor, in pushing this work to its completion. She is the driving force behind this volume and is a dedicated member of the AILA Publications team. It is quite clear to us that without her prodding, cajoling, long-suffering, and, lastly, sternness, this project would still be sitting on the floor next to our desks. If you in any way find use in the *Immigration Litigation Toolbox*, please send a note of gratitude to Stephanie. Additionally, sincere thanks and appreciation also go to Randy P. Auerbach, Director of Publications, Tatia L. Gordon-Troy, Associate Director of Publications, and Sharon Cook Poorak, Director of Education, for their own exertions and service in completing this work.

We hope you find the sample motions, pleadings, and memoranda in the *Toolbox* helpful in your practice. If you do, we ask you to do us one favor. Take a pro bono immigration case this year—please. Help out the private organizations whose workloads are staggering and whose funding is minimal. Ask them if there is one case you can take to lighten their load. We promise you that you will not regret the time you put into preparing, presenting, and hopefully winning a case on behalf of someone who cannot pay you. Those victories taste the sweetest.

Charles H. Kuck
Lynn Calder
September 2005

ABOUT THE EDITORS

Charles H. ("Chuck") Kuck (Editor-in-Chief) is the second vice president of AILA (2005–06). Mr. Kuck is the managing partner of the Kuck, Casablanca & Howard, LLC, an Atlanta- and Miami-based immigration law firm, and he is also an adjunct professor of law at the University of Georgia, where he teaches advanced immigration law seminars each year. He has been named a Georgia "Super Lawyer" in the field of immigration law by *Atlanta Magazine*, is listed in *Who's Who of International Corporate Immigration Attorneys*, and served as the editor-in-chief of the previous edition of the *AILA Litigation Toolbox*. He has litigated extensively against the government on a variety of immigration issues for more than 15 years, and is a passionate advocate for the use of litigation in seeking to hold the government accountable for its actions (or inactions) against foreign nationals.

C. Lynn Calder (Associate Editor) is a principal in the Raleigh, North Carolina, law firm of Allen and Pinnix, P.A., where as a North Carolina board-certified specialist in immigration law, she focuses her practice solely on immigration and naturalization law. She is former chair of the AILA Carolinas Chapter and the North Carolina Bar Association Immigration and Nationality Law Committee. Ms. Calder is a speaker, writer, and editor on immigration issues for AILA, the North Carolina Bar Association, the North Carolina Academy of Trial Lawyers, Wake Forest University School of Law Continuing Legal Education program, local bar associations, and other groups. She also is an adjunct professor of immigration law at North Carolina Central University School of Law. She is very proud to be a trustee emeritus of the American Immigration Law Foundation.

CHAPTER 1
PREPARATORY AND ANCILLARY MATERIAL

[Document No. 101]

FREEDOM OF INFORMATION ACT REQUEST

Description:

This letter is used in conjunction with DHS Forms G-639 and G-28 to request non-exempt information contained in an alien's file pursuant to the Freedom of Information Act (FOIA).

The FOIA request is especially important to use in cases where the client is in deportation proceedings or is detained in a location where the practitioner will have difficulty meeting with the client. The government will give practitioners most of what is contained in the client's file. The envelope conveying the requisite should be clearly marked "FREEDOM OF INFORMATION/PRIVACY REQUEST."

Generally, DHS will send an acknowledgment of the request. The information is supposed to be furnished within a 30-day period of the acknowledgment, but this timeframe seldom is honored by DHS. The time the request will take to fulfill will vary from office to office and with the actual location of the file. If the practitioner knows the location of the file, it is a good idea to mention that location in the cover letter. *See* Document No. 102, *infra*, for a form to use to appeal from either a refusal to furnish the copy of the file within the 30-day statutory period or to appeal from the deletion of portions of the file.

Advantages:

The FOIA is intended to make identifiable agency records available upon request and offers practitioners a method to obtain information regarding the alien in the possession of DHS.

Limitations:

DHS may decline to disclose information sought by a FOIA request. Nine exceptions to the duty to disclose are set forth in the FOIA. The significant exceptions are for those documents secret by executive order, confidential information obtained from persons outside the government, intra-agency and interagency documents not normally available in litigation, and law enforcement investigatory records.

Notes:

Practitioners should use the FOIA liberally. The FOIA provides an essential discovery tool in removal and federal court proceedings.

Citations:

5 USC §552; 6 CFR Part 5; 8 CFR §103.10

[Date]

FOIA Clerk
National Records Center
[Address]
[City, State, and Zip Code]

Re: Freedom of Information Act Request for [Alien, "A" Number]

Dear FOIA Clerk:

This letter is a formal request under the Freedom of Information Act (FOIA), as amended (5 U.S.C. §522), for all nonexempt portions of the information described below:

All document, forms or other written, photographic, electronic, computer or recorded materials and all printouts pertaining to the referenced request from the CIS, DACS, NCIC, CLAIMS, NIIS, and NAIL/IBIS databases, in the files of **[Alien and "A" Number]**.

I enclose my Form G-28 for **[Alien]**.

As you are aware, the FOIA permits fees to be charged only for search and copying costs and not for review of the material. As an alternative to being assessed copying fees in excess of $50.00, I wish to be contacted about the prospective amount of copying costs, and given the option of access to the requested documents that are responsive to my request so that I might review them without incurring duplication costs, and select those documents I wish copied. Section (a)(3) of the FOIA requires agencies to make documents and information promptly available. Section (a)(4) permits "recovery of only direct costs of such search and duplications." Therefore, agencies are required by law to make documents available for inspection and may not require the purchase of copies of documents.

I respectfully ask that you respond within 20 working days. If you have any questions regarding this request, please telephone me directly at (____) ____-______.

If the request is not stated with sufficient specificity, or if the request refers to documents or information not available in your office, I request a conference with you to remedy any defects in the request, pursuant to 8 C.F.R. §103.10(a)(2).

Thank you for your anticipated cooperation.

Very truly yours,

[Attorney]

Enclosure [Forms G-28 and G-639]

[Document No. 102]

NOTICE OF APPEAL OF FOIA REQUEST DENIAL OR PARTIAL DENIAL

Description: Frequently, DHS will withhold parts of the respondent's file or other information sought in a Freedom of Information Act request. The appeal is simple and direct, as shown by this letter.

Advantages: This appeal will often get you the documents withheld by DHS in the initial request.

Limitations: DHS officially has only a short timeframe in which to process the appeal (by regulation it is 10 days), but suggests waiting 20 days. It is rare that DHS responds to the appeal within this 20-day period.

Notes: The appeal must predate any action taken in federal court to obtain the requested information, to ensure that you can show exhaustion of administrative remedies.

If the practitioner is entitled to the information sought and DHS continues to withhold it, or simply does not process the request within the statutory or regulatory timeframe, he or she can proceed to federal court with a Petition for Writ of Mandamus to obtain the requested information. Do not forget to request attorneys' fees under the Equal Access to Justice Act.

Citations: 5 USC §552; 8 CFR §103.10(c)(2) and (d)(3); 28 CFR §16.8.

[Date]

[Via Certified Mail, Return Receipt Requested]

FOIA Appeals Office
Department of Homeland Security
[Address]
[City, State, and Zip Code]

Re: Appeal of FOIA Request; FOIA Case Number __________

Dear Sir or Madam:

I represent **[Alien]** in all immigration matters and enclose Form G-28. We filed a request for records pertaining to **[Alien]** on **[Date]**, and recently received the enclosed response, denying our request for all information pertaining to **[Alien]**. The letter indicates that there are **[__]** pages being withheld in full, and **[__]** in part. We hereby appeal the decision to withhold information and ask that you disclose all information contained in **[Alien's]** file, including the omitted pieces of the **[__]** partial-pages that were sent to us.

Disclosure of these records would not "interfere with law enforcement proceedings," as the letter states. Disclosure of Department of Homeland Security (DHS) records is a common practice for cases before the Immigration Court. It does not interfere with immigration proceedings, but, in fact, expedites matters by providing immigrants with information vital to their case. The judge, the DHS trial attorney, and the public all benefit from better-prepared respondents.

Furthermore, the exceptions under FOIA preventing disclosure are to be narrowly construed. *Dep't of the Interior v. Klamath Water Users Protective Ass'n*, 532 U.S. 1 (2001). In creating the FOIA, Congress intended "full agency disclosure unless information is exempted under clearly delineated statutory language." *Dep't of Air Force v. Rose*, 425 U.S. 352, 360–61 (1976). Because **[Alien's]** immigration file is not clearly exempted, it *must* be disclosed.

[Alien] received a Notice to Appear from DHS, and is now in removal proceedings. **[His/Her]** removal hearing is approaching and in order to defend **[himself/herself]**, **[he/she]** needs to know the information that may be used against **[him/her]**. **[Alien]** therefore asks that **[his/her]** request under FOIA be granted *immediately*.

Very truly yours,

[Attorney]

Enclosures [Form G-28 and FOIA Denial Letter]

[Document No. 103]

NOTIFICATION OF WRIT OF MANDAMUS TO USCIS COUNSEL

Description: This letter is used in conjunction with mandamus application forms found in Chapter 5 of this book.

The letter communicates to the counsel for the government agency, not only the serious nature of practitioner's intent to sue, but that he or she is making every effort to resolve the agency inaction in good faith.

Advantages: One of the key elements of a successful mandamus action is the documentation of notice to the government agency involved that the practitioner is doing everything in his or her power to ensure that the agency adjudicates the application in a timely fashion. In addition to documenting Infopass appointments and letters, faxes, and e-mails to the agency, it is important to put the agencies' counsel on notice. Many times, agency counsel will be able to secure a decision, or even give information that the practitioner has been unable to obtain through other means. However, even if agency counsel cannot resolve the client's issue, the practitioner has now shown the district court judge that he or she has taken every good faith effort to secure adjudication before going to federal court.

Limitations: The agency counsel may decline to assist, even if approached in this manner. As the saying goes, it is easier to catch a bear with honey.

[Date]

[Attorney]
Office of Chief Counsel, U.S. Citizenship and Immigration Services
Department of Homeland Security
[Address]
[City, State, and Zip Code]

Re: [Alien, "A" Number]

Dear Chief Counsel, USCIS:

We represent **[Alien]** in **[his/her]** immigration matters. **[Alien]** has patiently waited to have **[his/her]** application to be adjudicated since **[date]**. It has now been **[amount of time]** since **[Alien]** filed **[his/her]** application, and it has yet to be adjudicated. This unreasonable delay has impaired **[Alien's]** ability to make important decisions in **[his/her]** personal and professional life, and has deprived **[him/her]** of the right to permanent residency and the peace of mind to which **[he/she]** is entitled.

We have tried on numerous occasions to resolve this delay without success; therefore, we currently are preparing to file a Writ of Mandamus in federal district court. I have attached a copy of the Writ of Mandamus that we are preparing to file for your convenience. If we do not receive a response from you within 15 days, we will have no choice but to file a Writ of Mandamus with the U.S. District Court on **[date]**. We will also seek payment for attorneys' fees upon our prevailing on the motion.

Thank you for your prompt attention to this matter.

Very truly yours,

[Attorney]

Enclosures: [Copy of Application/Petition/Receipt]

[Document Nos. 104–05]

FBI FINGERPRINT AND CRIMINAL HISTORY REQUEST LETTERS

Description: These letters contain the basic format to forward a completed Form FD-258 (Fingerprint Chart) and notarized Authorization for Release of Records to the Federal Bureau of Investigation (FBI), in order to obtain the FBI printout of a client's arrest history and criminal background.

Advantages: Clients forget what they have been charged with, convicted of, or even if they have ever been arrested. These documents are invaluable tools in finding out about a client has forgotten (or poorly remembered) criminal history, and can save a client from subjecting him- or herself to removal when he or she files for relief for which he or she may not be entitled. The FBI usually responds with either the printout of a client's arrest history, or a stamp on the back of the FD-258 (which they return to the practitioner) indicating that no arrest records exist. It is also an excellent way to recover forgotten or lost alien numbers (*e.g.*, if the client was "turned around" at a port of entry but given no documents showing what happened).

Limitations: Some of the information on the arrest record may be inaccurate; attempt to verify all arrests with the reporting agency.

Citations: 28 CFR Part 16. Fee (currently at $18) is provided at 28 CFR §16.33.

[Date]

FBI—CJIS Division
Attn: SCU, Mod. D-2
1000 Custer Hollow Road
Clarksburg, WV 26306

Re: [Alien's Name]

To Whom It May Concern:

Enclosed please find a fingerprint chart for the above-named individual whom I am representing. I have also enclosed an authorization for release of records signed by **[Alien]** in order to have his/her records mailed directly to me at:

[Attorney Name]
[Firm Name]
[Address]
[City, State, and Zip Code]

In the event that you determine that your office is unable to send the report directly to me, please forward the fingerprint results to **[Alien]** at his/her home address.

[Alien's Name]
[Address]
[City, State, and Zip Code]

A money order in the amount of $18.00 is enclosed to cover the cost of the report. Please do not hesitate to contact me at **(___) ___-____** if you require additional information. Thank you for your attention in this matter.

Sincerely,

[Attorney]

Enclosures [Authorization for Release, Fingerprint Card]

[Date]

FBI—CJIS Division
SCU MOD D-2
1000 Custer Hollow Road
Clarksburg, WV 26306

Re: Request for Criminal History

Dear Sir or Madam:

I am writing to request a report of complete criminal history for the individual whose biographic information appears below. Please send this report directly to the following address:

[Name of Attorney]
[Firm Name]
[Address]
[City, State, and Zip Code]

Enclosed please find:

1. A G-28 form giving me permission to obtain this information as the attorney representing this individual in their immigration matters;
2. Authorization to Release executed by **[Alien]**;
3. A set of fingerprints;
4. A money order payable to the Treasury of the United States in the amount of $18.

The identifying information is as follows:

Name: ____________________ AKA: ____________________

DOB: ____________________ SS#: ____________________

POB: ____________________ A #: ____________________

Thank you for your assistance.

Very truly yours,

[Attorney]

Enclosures [G-28, Authorization to Release, Completed FBI Fingerprint Card, Check]

[Document No. 106]

AUTHORIZATION TO RELEASE DOCUMENTS

Description: This rather simple form would typically be used to secure the return of documents from former counsel or, in conjunction with a request to the FBI, to furnish a copy of its files on the client.

Notes: The client should execute this form upon the initiation of representation in any case in which the practitioner needs information in the client's FBI file. In conjunction with this form, the client will need to complete a fingerprint card. The FBI typically responds to these requests in 90 days.

RELEASE

I, **[Alien]**, hereby authorize the release of any and all records held by you concerning any details of my relationship with you, your agents, or your company. I authorize this release to **[Attorney]** of **[Firm Name]**, or any of **[his/her]** representatives.

____
[Alien]

STATE OF __________

:ss

COUNTY OF __________

SUBSCRIBED and sworn to before me this ___ day of ____, ____, by **[Alien]**.

____
Notary Public

My Commission Expires On: __________________

[Document No. 107]

AUTHORIZATION TO RELEASE MEDICAL RECORDS (HIPAA COMPLIANT)

Description: This form would be used to request copies of records from health care providers that are subject to the privacy provisions of the Health Insurance Portability and Accountability Act of 1996 (HIPAA) and implementing Privacy Rule regulation at 45 CFR Parts 160, 164.

Notes: The Privacy Rule does not dictate any particular format for the authorization request but does require that certain information be provided. The Authorization form may be prepared by a third party. The covered health care provider may impose reasonable cost-based fees to cover the copy of copying the records requested, including supplies and labor, and postage. Additional information regarding HIPAA and the Privacy Rule may be found at *www.hhs.gov/ocr/hipaa*.

[Date]

Re:

Dear Sir or Madam:

This law firm represents the above-referenced individual. Enclosed is a HIPAA Compliant Authorization for Release of Information. I would appreciate you forwarding to my attention copies of **[Name's]** medical records pursuant to the enclosed release.

If you have questions or need additional information, please contact me.

Sincerely,

[Attorney]

Enclosure

HIPAA COMPLIANT AUTHORIZATION FOR RELEASE OF INFORMATION

Patient Name:

Provider/Facility Name:

Dates of Treatment:

1. I, **[Patient]**, authorize the above-named provider/facility to release the following information to **[Law Firm Name and Address]**.

2. Information to be released (check all that apply):

☐Complete medical records	☐Admission Notes	☐Consultation Notes
☐Evaluations & Summaries	☐EKG's,Fetal Monitor Strips	☐History & Physical
☐Lab Reports	☐Progress Reports	☐Social History
☐X-Ray Reports	☐X-Ray Films	☐Catheterization Films
☐CT Scans	☐Echocardiogram Tapes	☐MRI Scans
☐Radiation Records	☐Psychiatric Records	☐Substance Abuse Records
☐Ultrasounds	☐Videos	☐Tissue Blocks or Slides
☐Pathology Specimens	☐Billing Information	☐Education Reports
☐Referral Documents		

☐Notes, correspondence, or records of any nature made by physicians, nurses, or other persons or facilities.

☐Other (specify): ____

3. I understand that if my record contains information relating to HIV infection, AIDS or AIDS-related conditions, alcohol abuse, drug abuse, psychological or psychiatric conditions, or genetic testing this disclosure will include that information. I also understand that I may refuse to sign this authorization and that my refusal to sign will not affect my ability to obtain treatment, payment for services, or my eligibility for benefits.

4. The purpose of this authorization is for full disclosure of all records for use in providing legal advice regarding immigration matters.

5. I understand that this consent may be revoked by me in writing at any time except to the extent that disclosure of information has already occurred prior to the receipt of revocation by the above-named provider. If written revocation is not received, authorization will be considered valid for the duration of my representation by **[Law Firm]**. To initiate revocation of this authorization, notification may be mailed to **[Law Firm Name and Address]**. If not revoked, this authorization will automatically become void when the undersigned's representation by **[Law Firm]** is concluded.

6. A photocopy of this authorization is to be considered as valid as the original.

7. The information used or disclosed pursuant to this authorization may be subject to re-disclosure by the recipient and may no longer be protected by Federal Law/HIPAA Privacy Rules.

Signed, this _____day of _______________, 200_.

[Patient]

[Witness]

THIS AUTHORIZATION REVOKES ALL PRIOR AUTHORIZATIONS

[Document No. 108]

CERTIFICATE OF TRANSLATION

Description: This document is the basic format for a certificate of translation, which must accompany every document written originally in another language. Both DHS and the EOIR require all documents to be translated into English and accompanied by a certificate of translation.

Notes: The certificate of translation need not be notarized, but must include the name and address of the translator. Be aware that some translations must be accompanied by a certificate of authenticity from the U.S. consulate in the home country of the individuals (also called an Apostille).

Citations: 8 CFR §§1003.33, 287.6, 1287.6.

CERTIFICATE OF TRANSLATION

I, **[Translator]**, being first duly sworn, on oath depose and say that I am thoroughly familiar with both **[Language]** and **[Language]**; that I am a qualified and experienced translator from each of the said languages into the other; that I have prepared the **[Language]** translation from the attached document(s), written in **[Language]**, as set forth and as corresponds with the attached; and that to the best of my knowledge and belief the translation attached hereto is a true and accurate version of the aforesaid originals.

____
(Signature)

STATE OF __________________
COUNTY OF __________________

Sworn to and subscribed before me,

this the ______ day of ____________________, 2005.

____
Notary Public

My Commission expires: ______________________

[Document No. 109]

CERTIFICATE OF SERVICE

Description: This is a sample form of a "certificate of service" of papers on opposing counsel. It can be used for the service of papers on trial attorneys.

CERTIFICATE OF SERVICE

I hereby certify that a copy of the foregoing **[Name and Title of Document]** was served by first-class mail [*or* hand-delivery, expedited courier, etc.], postage prepaid on:

Chief Counsel
U.S. Immigration and Customs Enforcement
[Address]
[City, State, and Zip Code]

on this ____ of ________, 20__.

[Dated:]

[Attorney]

[Document No. 110]

REQUEST FOR NOTIFICATION OF TRANSFER OF CLIENT

Description: This letter would be used to specifically notify U.S. Immigration and Customs Enforcement Chief Counsel's Office and Detention and Removal officers of practitioner's representation of a client in detention and request notification of transfer of the client to another detention facility or of the client's imminent removal from the United States.

Notes: This letter and accompanying G-28 should be sent to any government officer who may have authority over, or contact with, the client, including appropriate officer(s) at the detention facility. 8 CFR §241.4(d) requires that ICE forward to the attorney of record (G-28 filed) a copy of any notice or decision that is being served on the detained alien. Although an ICE officer may not comply with the attached request, having served it provides counsel additional equitable complaint if client is transferred or removed.

REQUEST FOR NOTIFICATION OF TRANSFER OF CLIENT

[Date]

[Name]
Chief Counsel
U.S. Immigration and Customs Enforcement
[Address]
[City, State, and Zip Code]

Re: [Alien, "A" Number]

Dear Chief Counsel:

Please find enclosed a G-28 regarding **[Alien]**. **[Alien]** currently is detained in **[location]**. He has a final order of deportation due to a 1994 cocaine related conviction. The final order was issued by the Board on **[date]**.

[Alien] appears to be eligible to file a Motion to Reopen for a waiver under the new Sec. 212(c) regulation. I am in the process of preparing the Motion to Reopen with an Emergency Request for a Stay of Deportation. I will forward those documents to you as soon as possible.

As his attorney of record, I would very much appreciate your notifying me if **[Alien]** is moved from **[location]** or if arrangements are made for his immediate removal. If I am not in my office or it is after regular business hours, please try to contact me on my cell phone (___) ___-____ or home phone (___) ___-____. My law partner, **[Name]**, or legal assistant, **[Name]**, also may be reached at my office regarding **[Alien]**.

By copy of this letter, I am notifying Deportation Officer **[Name]** of my Notice of Appearance and request that I be notified if **[Alien]** is to be moved.

Thank you for your attention to this request.

Sincerely,

[Attorney]

CHAPTER 2
DHS PLEADINGS AND REQUESTS

[Document No. 201]

Letter in Support of Application for Permission to Reapply for Admission after Expedited Removal (Form I-212)

Description: This letter should be sent in support of Form I-212, Application for Permission to Reapply for Admission after Deportation or Removal, when the client has been removed through expedited removal.

Advantages: The letter supports an application for admission by an individual who is in possession of a nonimmigrant visa and who was previously removed by expedited removal because he or she applied for admission within five years of removal. This letter carefully explains the events leading up to the removal and the equities in the individual's favor. It also details the district director's discretion, under the regulations, to approve the application retroactively, or *nunc pro tunc*, thereby permitting the client, upon approval of the application, to apply for admission using the nonimmigrant visa stamp in his or her passport.

Limitations: The letter offers the practitioner a basic structure for requesting approval of the application under these circumstances. However, it is case specific. Practitioners should take care to outline the facts of their client's specific circumstances. Further, this particular letter applies only to applicants for admission under circumstances *other than* aliens applying to a consular officer for a nonimmigrant visa or nonresident alien border crossing card, applicants for fiancé(e) or other K visas, applicants for immigrant visas, applicants for adjustment of status, or applicants for admission at a port of entry.

Notes: Aliens who have been removed from the United States, even under the most technical of circumstances, have a large burden of persuasion when requesting advance permission to reapply for admission. It is for this reason that the letter in support of such an application should offer the district director as much detail as possible about background of the case and why the alien merits favorable discretion.

Citations: INA §§212(a)(9)(A)(iii), 235(b)(1); 8 CFR §§212.2, 212.2(g); 1212.2, 1212.2(g). Procedures for Reapplying for Admission for aliens in other circumstances may be found at 8 CFR §§212.2(b)–(f); 1212.2(b)–(f).

[Date]

VIA HAND DELIVERY

[Attorney]
Deputy District Director
U.S. Immigration and Customs Enforcement
U.S. Department of Homeland Security
[Address]
[City, State, and Zip Code]

Request Accompanying Form I-212, Application for Permission to Reapply for Admission into the United States After Deportation or Removal Pursuant to INA §212(A)(9)(A)(iii), Filed on Behalf of [Alien]

Dear Deputy District Director:

As we discussed yesterday, I am filing directly with you a request under INA §212(a)(9)(A)(iii) and 8 CFR §§212.2(g) and 1212.2(g), seeking the consent of the U.S. Department of Homeland Security, U.S. Citizenship and Immigration Services, for Mr. **[Alien]**'s readmission into the United States. Thank you for the opportunity to present this information to you. We attach a new signed Form G-28 entering our appearance in this case.

On July 11, 1997, Mr. **[Alien]** was granted permission to withdraw his recent application for admission into the United States. He is departing the United States on **[date]**, at 4:00 p.m. He now seeks permission to reapply for admission to the United States. INA §212(a)(9)(A)(iii) gives him this opportunity. The regulations found in 8 CFR §§212.2(g) and 1212.2(g) specify the process for applications for consent to reapply for admission not found elsewhere in the regulations. This section directs applicants seeking consent to reapply for admission to file Form I-212 with the district director having jurisdiction over the place where the removal occurred. The regulations also allow for retroactive approval such that if you granted the application, it could be made retroactive to the date on which Mr. **[Alien]** embarked outside the United States, thus allowing him to enter the United States now under the H-1B visa stamp in his passport. 8 CFR §§212.2(i) and 1212.2(i).

A brief history of Mr. **[Alien]**'s case is in order. Mr. **[Alien]**'s most recent entry was under the auspices of an H-1B visa issued by the U.S. consulate in Athens, Greece. We understand that you have a copy of the Form DS-156 that Mr. **[Alien]** presented to the consular officer. That form DS-156 should indicate that Mr. **[Alien]** disclosed his expedited removal from the United States to the consular officer. In my conversation with the chief consular officer of the U.S. Embassy in Athens on **[date]**, she indicated that Mr. **[Alien]** and the deputy chief consular officer who interviewed him had discussed the circumstances of Mr. **[Alien]**'s removal from the United States. The chief consular officer and her deputy concluded that Mr. **[Alien]** could be issued an H-1B visa and advised him that he could return to the United States. She also told me that she could have been mistaken in doing this, but that the law was unclear. She said that in her opinion Mr. **[Alien]** had been completely forthcoming about his prior removal and that there had been no misrepresentations in connection with the application. She also said that she would be happy to speak with you or anyone else from the Immigration Service about the case. Her direct phone number is [________].

Mr. **[Alien]** attempted entry into the United States so soon after his removal because he did not understand that there was a mandatory five-year bar that results from an INA §235(b)(1) order. In fact, the Form I-296 (copy attached) does *not* indicate that he was subject to the five-year bar, lending to the confusion. Obviously, a clear reading of the INA §235(b)(1) requires the five-year bar. However, as noted above, the statute also allows for the U.S. Department of Homeland Security to "consent" to the readmission. This consent was not obtained because neither the consular officer nor Mr. **[Alien]** understood the need to obtain this consent because the I-296 did not indicate a five-year bar.

As you can see in the order of Expedited Removal (Form I-860), the only ground for removal was that Mr. **[Alien]**'s H-1B visa extension petition had been denied *after* he sought admission. The reason for the denial of the H-1B visa was procedural; the employer failed to include a certified Labor Condition Application in the H-1B submission. Counsel for his employer, Mr. **[Name]**, then ably interceded and the Texas Service Center of U.S. Citizenship and Immigration Services reopened the petition and approved it. We have previously submitted copies of his correspondence to the Texas Service Center and its subsequent approval of the H-1B visa extension petition.

Our reason for requesting consent for readmission under INA §212(a)(9)(A)(iii) and 8 CFR §§212.2(g) and 1212.2(g) is quite simple. If Mr. **[Alien]** leaves the United States now, he cannot return to the job in which he has been working for the last three years. During the time Mr. **[Alien]** will be outside the United States, he will be unable to return to his H-1B position with **[Employer]**, where he works as a producer. This will obviously hamper his employer's ability to carry out the job duties Mr. **[Alien]** was doing prior to his departure in **[date]**. A letter from Mr. **[Alien]**'s employer submitted to Officer **[Name]** on **[date]** verified this. Further, it serves no real purpose to have Mr. **[Alien]** suffer under the condition of this expedited removal order. He committed no crime and only entered in **[date]** with the mistaken understanding that because his extension application was pending he could return. Obviously, he bears the burden of this mistake, but he seeks your consideration in overcoming this mistake and what will turn into a very difficult situation for him and his employer should he be required to remain outside the United States for five years because of a procedural error that has now been corrected.

If you were to consider and approve the Form I-212, you could also approve it retroactively pursuant to 8 CFR §§212.2(i) and 1212.2(i). This retroactive approval would permit Mr. **[Alien]** to apply for admission using the H-1B visa stamp in his passport and, hopefully, be admitted to the Untied States.

Not only is there regulatory authority for granting retroactive or *nunc pro tunc* relief, but the Board of Immigration Appeals and the Attorney General have also recognized this authority. This is especially true where the grant of such relief would completely resolve the inadmissibility problem, such as in this case.

The Board of Immigration Appeals has authorized the *nunc pro tunc* approval of applications to reapply for admission. *Matter of Roman*, 19 I&N Dec. 855 (BIA 1988); *Matter of Ducret*, 15 I&N Dec. 620 (BIA 1976). The Board of Immigration Appeals has recognized the right to grant *nunc pro tunc* correction on a record of entry. *Matter of Arias-Uribe*, 13 I&N Dec. 696 (1971). The Operations Instructions also permit *nunc pro tunc* grants of relief of voluntary departure. OI 243.1(a).

There is nothing new in the grant of administrative relief *nunc pro tunc.* As far back as 1940, Attorney General Robert H. Jackson approved the retroactive grant of relief under the old Seventh Proviso to §3 of the Immigration Act of 1917, predecessor to INA §212(c). *Matter of L–*, 1 I&N Dec. 1 (AG 1940). Referring to the unjust result that would otherwise occur, the then–Attorney General stated, "I cannot conclude that Congress intended the immigration laws to operate in so capricious and whimsical a fashion." 1 I&N Dec. at 5. The power of the Attorney General to grant relief retroactively has long been recognized. *See* BIA memo dated April 6, 1990, to Attorney General Dick Thornburgh relating to *Matter of Hernandez-Casillas*, Int. Dec. 3147, reproduced in 67 *Interpreter Releases* 480 (Apr. 23, 1990). Retroactive relief has been awarded in granting permission to reapply for admission after prior deportation. *See Matter of S–N–*, 6 I&N Dec. 73 (BIA 1954; AG 1954); *Matter of Vrettakos*, 14 I&N Dec. 593 (BIA 1973, 1974); *Matter of Ducret*, 15 I&N Dec. 620 (BIA 1976). This power is based on regulations directing the Department of Homeland Security and its officials, officers or employees to exercise such discretion and authority conferred upon the Secretary of Homeland Security by law as is appropriate and necessary for the disposition of the case. 8 CFR §2.1.

In logic and fairness, there appears to be no reason why this power to grant relief retroactively should not also be applied in this particular case. Here the grant of relief under INA §212(a)(9)(A)(iii) and 8 CFR §§212.2(g) and 1212.2(g) would completely resolve the situation, without the delay and hardship resulting from an indefinite stay outside the United States. Even if this meant Mr. **[Alien]** leaving on Friday and re-entering the United States the following Monday with the consent to readmission in hand, it would still be a tremendous act of justice on the part of the Service, as well as great blessing for Mr. **[Alien]** and his U.S. employer.

Again, we thank you for your consideration of this application. We remain available to answer any questions or assist in any way you deem necessary.

Very truly yours,

[Attorney]

Enclosures

[Document No. 202]

APPLICATION FOR WAIVER UNDER INA §212(a)(9)(B)(V) (THREE- AND TEN-YEAR BARS)

Description: DHS still has not developed regulations pertaining to the request for a waiver of the three- and ten-year bars for immigrants created by INA§212(a)(9)(B) for unlawful presence in the United States. This letter outlines documentation submitted with an immigrant visa application and request for waiver under INA §212(a)(9)(B)(v). Form I-601 must be submitted to request the waiver, and the immigrant visa applicant must establish that refusal of admission would result in extreme hardship to his or her U.S. citizen or LPR spouse or parent. (Note that the waiver cannot be based on hardship to the alien's U.S. citizen or permanent resident child.) Also attached is an example of a "hardship" statement written by a U.S. citizen spouse. Obviously, the facts of each case will differ and emphasis will need to be given to the truly extreme hardship in the particular case. Last, attached is a letter from the USCIS officer responsible for waivers at the U.S. Consulate in Ciudad Juarez, Mexico. This provides an example of the types of information sought by USCIS when applying for a waiver.

Limitations: Different consulates and the various DHS offices around the world may have different aspects of each case on which they desire the applicant to focus. Ascertain from the particular office with which you are dealing, who will review and decide the application, and tailor the request to that audience.

Notes: Many consulates are liberally reviewing these requests for waiver particularly as they apply to spouses of U.S. citizens and other immediate relatives. Do not dismiss a client who may need this waiver. It is a "doable" process for many clients, as long as they are made fully aware of the consequences. Although the basis of the hardship cannot be to the alien's U.S. citizen or LPR child, the hardship to that child of losing the foreign national parent will certainly contribute to the hardship of the U.S. citizen or LPR spouse requesting the waiver and may be documented with that emphasis in mind. Psychological evaluations documenting hardship also have been found to be useful.

Waivers of the three- or ten-year bar may be requested for nonimmigrants as provided in INA §212(d)(3).

Citations: INA §212(a)(9)(B)(v). See also INA §212(d)(3) for the nonimmigrant waiver.

[Date]

American Consulate General
[Address]

Re: IR1 Case for: [Alien], Case Number:

Dear Sir or Madam:

I am enclosing the Immigrant Visa Package for my client, **[Alien]** who is being sponsored by his U.S. citizen wife, **[Wife]**. I am respectfully requesting that this matter be resolved as quickly as possible as **[Wife]** and the couple's U.S. citizen daughter, **[Daughter]** (age 4) are emotionally dependent upon **[Alien]** and a lengthy separation will have a dramatic effect on their family life.

If you have any questions, please do not hesitate to call me at **[number]**. I can also be reached on my cell telephone at **[number]** or at home **[number]**. Additionally, I regularly check my e-mail and that address is: **[Address]**.

We are enclosing the following documents:

A. IMMIGRANT VISA DOCUMENTS:

1. Copy of the DS-230 Part I and Part II
2. Original, copy, and translation of **[Alien]**'s birth certificate
3. Original and copy of couple's marriage license/certificate
4. Original and copy of **[Wife]**'s final divorce judgment
5. I-864 Affidavit of Support including 3 years of Federal Income Tax Returns, including W-2 forms as well as recent pay stubs for both **[Wife]** and **[Alien]**, since **[Alien]** is related by blood and has lived in the household for at least 6 months (see 8 CFR §213a.2(c)(2)(i)(C), copy attached).
6. Original and copy of the I-797 USCIS approval notice for the I-130 Alien Relative Petition
7. Original and copy of **[Wife]**'s birth certificate
8. Certified copies of **[Alien]**'s criminal record reports indicating no criminal record
9. Copy of I-693 Medical Examination conducted by DHS approved physician in VA
10. Copy of Medical Examination conducted in Mexico
11. Four photographs of applicant taken within the last 3 months
12. Copy of Mexican Passport

B. MARITAL EVIDENCE:

1. Copy of the birth certificate for **[Daughter]**, **[Alien]**'s U.S. citizen child with **[Wife]**
2. Bank statements and supporting letter from **[Bank]** showing a joint account since 2001
3. Insurance beneficiary designation showing **[Alien]** as the primary beneficiary
4. Medical Insurance cards for **[Alien]** and **[Wife]** showing they are covered by their respective employers

5. Medical Insurance information showing their child, **[Daughter]**, is covered under **[Alien]**'s policy
6. Covenants signed in 2001 by both **[Alien]** and **[Wife]** for the Mobile Home Park in which they reside
7. Driver's licenses for **[Alien]** and **[Wife]**
8. Cards and Photographs of the couple over the past four years they have been together

C. I-601 WAIVER EVIDENCE

In anticipation of the need to file an I-601 waiver based on INA §212(a)(9)(B), we are submitting the following documents to prove the extreme hardship that will be suffered by **[Alien]**'s U.S. citizen wife and daughter if he is not allowed to return to the United States:

1. G-28 Notice of Representation
2. I-601 Application for Waiver of Ground of Excludability
3. Statement of Extreme Hardship from **[Wife]**, the U.S. Citizen Spouse
4. Copy of the birth certificate for **[Daughter]**, **[Alien]**'s U.S. citizen child with **[Wife]**
5. Letter from **[Wife]**'s mother emphasizing **[Alien]**'s importance to their family
6. Letter from **[Wife]**'s father in support of **[Alien]**'s immigration case
7. Letter from **[Wife]**'s sister supporting **[Alien]**'s efforts to gain status in the U.S.
8. Letter from the couple's daycare provider
9. Evidence of couple's good-faith attempt to adjust **[Alien]**'s status by retaining the services of a Washington, DC-based attorney. As you can see by the documentation and the couple's statements and notations attached to the tax returns, the attorney clearly accepted the case without understanding immigration law or the regulations. The couple literally paid thousands of dollars in both legal and filing fees only to find that their case could not be processed in the United States. Additionally, the attorney neglected to correct the I-130 petition to reflect petitioner's prior immigration filing for her first spouse, as well as the birth information for **[Daughter]**. By maintaining this filing, prior counsel improperly obtained an Employment Authorization Card for **[Alien]**. Finally, the couple has stated that this same attorney advised the couple to file their income tax returns representing themselves as single-filing separately and he told **[Alien]** not to file any taxes until he received a social security number. The couple is investigating the filing of a claim against this attorney with the Virginia State Bar.
10. Letter from **[Alien]** regarding his history with **[Wife]** and evidence of his physical presence in the U.S. since 1997.

Please contact me if there is additional information you require in this matter.

Sincerely,

[Attorney]

Enclosures a/s

STATEMENT OF HARDSHIP BY [WIFE]

To Whom It May Concern:

My name is **[Wife]**. I am a United States citizen who is twenty-six years old, a mother of one, and a loving wife to my one and only soul mate, **[Alien]**, a Mexican citizen. I was born and raised right here in Virginia and except for a few years of living in North Carolina, I've never lived any place else. **[Alien]** is twenty-eight years old and originally from Oaxaca, Mexico and he is trying to get permission to return to our family here, in Virginia. I hope you will read this letter all the way through to see how extremely difficult not only my life, but the life of our daughter and the rest of my family will be if **[Alien]** is not allowed to return to us.

Background

[Alien] and I met by accident; however, I thank God everyday for this little "accident." I was still married to my first husband, **[First Husband]**, when I first saw **[Alien]**. **[First Husband]** and I had been having problems and I had been traveling back and forth from North Carolina to Virginia every other weekend. In January of 1999, I was home visiting my parents and I decided to go visit a friend of mine. I walked into her home and I saw the most attractive looking man I had ever seen. My friend was dating **[Friend]** and his best friend, **[Alien]**, was with him there at her house. I just talked a little with **[Alien]**, because I was still married and I knew I should not have such feelings for another man besides my husband.

Over time, I was coming home more and more and I knew it was really to see **[Alien]**. He knew I was married and he respected my marriage; but as we grew closer, I knew I could not continue things with my husband since I had such strong feelings for **[Alien]**. In March of 1999, I was still living in North Carolina; but I decided to get an apartment by myself. Still coming home to see my family and of course to see **[Alien]**, I felt better since I made the move to live alone. After two weeks of living in my apartment alone, I found out that I was pregnant. I knew right away that **[Alien]** was the father. My husband and I had not had a physical relationship since I started having strong feelings for **[Alien]**. I moved back to Virginia in October of 1999, after having spent time training someone new to take over my job in North Carolina.

On **[date]**, **[Daughter]** was born. Our daughter is now four years old and her name is **[Daughter]**; she was named after my great-grandmother and **[Alien]**'s aunt. She is the center of my and my husband's world. Although we were not planning on her coming into our lives at first, after she did, she brightened up both of our lives. **[Alien]**, **[Daughter]**, and I moved into an apartment together in January of 2000. We started our life as a family, something I always wanted. We had talked about getting married, but I was still legally married to **[First Husband]**. It wasn't necessary for us to get married right away, so we just lived together for a while.

[Alien] has been there every step of the way. In fact he was the one who was there when **[Daughter]** took her first steps. Unfortunately, I was taking a night class at the local Community college. **[Alien]** and **[Daughter]** have spent lots of bonding time together over the years while I was in school. He is an ideal father to her and loves her deeply. **[Daughter]**'s first word was "Da Da." It may not seem that important, but it meant the world to **[Alien]**. She is and always will be "Daddy's girl." Now that she is four years old, she actually sings to him as he used to do to her.

My divorce was finally granted in April of 2001. On June 9, 2001, **[Alien]** and I were married. It was a beautiful wedding. It was at a ranch in Virginia. He always loved horse ranches, and I thought it would be a great place to get married. We were married by my old school bus driver who was also a preacher of the church we were attending at the time. The ceremony was in the stables of the ranch. My mother, father, brothers, sister, and my close friends were there. **[Alien]**'s brother was his best man, and some of his friends were there also. It was truly the second happiest day in my life; the first was the day I gave birth to our daughter.

Months before we married, we had decided to purchase a mobile home to start our life together as the **[Alien]** family. So after our honeymoon, we came back to our home where we have been happily living together as a family ever since.

How We Tried To Get [Alien] Status in the U.S.

I knew **[Alien]** was not a U.S. citizen, but at the time it did not seem like such a big deal. We would just go about things the way we had before. Then I told him after time, he would have to become a citizen. In April 2002, we went to speak to an attorney in Virginia (five hours away). This attorney, **[Attorney]**, said he knew about immigration law. We trusted him with our case; we paid all the fees he requested. We believed he would give us correct information. Two years later, we learned we had an appointment with the Immigration and Naturalization Service in Virginia. Our attorney wanted to prepare us for the interview, so he told us to meet with him one week prior to the interview. After driving another five hours to meet with our attorney, we had to wait another hour to actually speak to him. We finally saw him and ONLY THEN did he inform us that it would be best for **[Alien]** and me not to go to the interview and if we did, INS would force **[Alien]** to go back to Mexico! **[Attorney's]** best suggestion was for us to wait even longer and just maybe the laws would change and **[Alien]** could stay in the country. Then he said even if the laws did not change, **[Alien]** had already been here seven years; after three more, he would be here for ten years and after being here for ten years he should not have anything to worry about. I was outraged to learn that after all this time, all this money, he was telling us to wait even longer, and we may or may not have anything to worry about? This was unacceptable, so I decided to find another legal representative. I am so mad that I have looked into filing something against him with the Virginia State Bar!

We met **[New Attorney]** from North Carolina. She did have more experience than our previous attorney and she has helped us more in the last four months than our previous attorney did in the entire two years he "helped" us. However during the first appointment with **[New Attorney],** she did tell us that we had been given the wrong information. Since we were not married until June of 2001, and nothing was ever filed in **[Alien]**'s behalf prior to April 30 2001, **[Alien]** would not be allowed to process his case here, in the U.S.; he would have to go back to Mexico if we were to pursue his status. **[New Attorney]** also told me that it is not guaranteed that **[Alien]** can return and that I have to show you how it would be an extreme hardship to me if he is not allowed to return. All of this devastated me. But we got through the appointment and returned home.

After writing the US consulate in Ciudad Juarez, Mexico, we were given another interview appointment set for July 15, 2004. Now, we are preparing **[Alien]** for his trip. His flights are booked, we are getting everything in order. I hope by this letter you can see what an extreme hardship it will be if **[Alien]** can't come home.

I know he has to go, but how do I explain to our four year old that her Daddy is going to another country and we can not afford to go with him? How can I tell her that he may never come back, no matter how much we love him? How can she adapt from being a Daddy's girl to not having her Daddy around possibly for years? When she asks me when Daddy is coming home and I have to look into her deep brown eyes and tell her that I don't know, how can I hold back the tears? How do I tell myself that I can get through this situation with half of my heart in another country thousands of miles away? How do I make ends meet, when I have been used to having a husband to share my financial responsibility? When the finance company for the home we are trying to purchase asks me why my payment is late, how do I explain my husband was forced to go into another country where he can not even make enough money to put food on the table? I am afraid that without **[Alien]**'s income, I will be forced to make late payments and I could possibly lose the home that **[Alien]**, **[Daughter]**, and I have come to love as we have been building our family and life together. How can I tell my heart to stop breaking? How can I hold my tears back when all I think about is him not being able to return home to me?

Having **[Alien]** leave is going to be extremely difficult on me and our daughter for financial, educational and family reasons. So you can better understand, I am dividing the rest of this letter up into those categories.

Educational Extreme Hardship

Since starting our life together, we have wanted to live the American Dream as best we can and to provide a good life for our daughter. I know this means more education, so I am working a full-time job and I have been enrolled part-time at Community College since the spring of 2001. I have been trying to get an Associate's Degree in legal assisting. Unfortunately, with the recent news of my husband leaving I will be forced to take at least the summer and probably the fall semesters off. I am not able to pay for the classes with just my income and I can't afford the extra childcare fees I would have to pay for **[Daughter's]** care. If we moved to Mexico to be with **[Alien]**, how could **[Daughter]** ever expect to get the kind of education she needs to make it in the United States? How could I continue my own education?

Not only is my education suffering, but my daughter's education and really her quality of life will suffer. She has been attending a daycare, learning so many things, with hopes of entering a public school pre-school program in the fall. For financial reasons I will not be able to afford her daycare costs anymore. I will have to find someone who can care for her at a much cheaper rate and this will likely affect her ability to continue learning in an enriching environment. Even if she is able to get into the public pre-school in the fall, I will have to start working more hours to make ends meet and I will not be able to pick her up in the afternoons; so she will have to stay with someone then, too. I am very afraid that this loving, funny and sensitive little girl will feel abandoned by her father and her mother. This thought deeply pains me.

Financial Extreme Hardship

Education and quality of life issues are just two of many things that are going to make **[Alien]**'s separation an extreme hardship to us. The financial hardship could be devastating. If I moved to Mexico to be with **[Alien]**, how could I even get a job? I know that **[Alien]** won't be able to find a job and how would we support our U.S. citizen daughter?

We have already had to sell a car to be able to afford **[Alien]**'s trip to Mexico and since he won't be able to find work down there, I will have to find a way to make it on one income. **[Alien]** and I have been together for quite some time now, and we have become accustomed to a certain lifestyle. We now have a monthly mortgage payment of $349.37 for a mobile home and the lot space rental is $115.00 per month. Telephone calls are going to be much more expensive and all this is on top of childcare costs, food, gas, utilities, a car payment, automobile and medical insurance for **[Daughter]** (she is covered under his work policy, but if he's not able to return, that won't be an option for very long). While I work full time at **[Job]**, my pay is not that great. Most people say that and don't mean it but I KNOW it's true in my case. My gross pay is only $1,525.00 per month. After Uncle Sam takes his cut, and after insurance is taken out, I am lucky to bring home a thousand dollars a month. Not nearly enough to pay the bills. I am not sure yet if I am eligible to receive any assistance from the state but I know if **[Alien]** is not allowed to come back we'll probably end up on welfare and that is something I could not bear.

Family Extreme Hardship

I was born and raised in Virginia and all of my family lives there as we have for many generations. Over the years, we have tried to be there to support each other and if I had to leave to live in Mexico, my family would suffer from my absence. **[Alien]** and I are the most responsible of my siblings and we are often the ones who are called to help out when my mother, father or siblings need anything. **[Alien]** often helps around my mom's house by fixing things or simply doing yard work. He has become a big part of our family and everyone would miss him if he could not return to the U.S.

My father recently came home from the hospital and is living alone. **[Alien]** and I have been trying to help him. Not only have we been there for him, but we've tried to give him a little financial help because he is out of work. He knows our situation and does not expect me to be able to help much longer since **[Alien]** is leaving, but I don't know how he'll make it now. My father suffers from depression and I know without him having anyone around for a while, he'll get worse. It breaks my heart I can not help my father in this time of need. My sister suffers from depression as well so I know she is not a strong person for my father to lean on. While I have never been diagnosed with extreme depression, I do have a history of anxiety and migraines caused by stress and I frequently go to the doctor for medical treatment. I have never felt as stressed as I am right now. Lately, I have been lying awake at night, when I should be sleeping, wondering what in this world I would do without **[Alien]** here with me. Sometimes, I look at him sleeping, listening to him snore trying to capture every moment I can because I know how much I will miss him. For him not to be allowed to come back would be like him dying to me.

Our daily lives are going to be changed for so many reasons. When I'm not in class, a normal week starts on Monday mornings with **[Alien]** waking up getting ready to go to work.

Sometimes, we try to ride to work together, first taking our daughter to daycare, then I drop him off at work and I am on my way to work. At home, we work together to do the household chores. I usually start preparing dinner for the three of us while **[Alien]** does other jobs, and **[Daughter]** usually watches television. After dinner is wash up time. I clean the kitchen and **[Alien]** gives **[Daughter]** a bath. Her bath time gives them a chance to bond as fathers and daughters usually do. We all usually sit down around eight o'clock and watch our favorite show. Then its bed time and **[Alien]** and I go into **[Daughter's]** room together to tuck our child snuggly in her bed. Then we settle down in our bed and end another hardworking day. Friday nights we all usually go out to dinner and rent some movies and come back home and watch them. Saturdays we always wake up a little later than during the week and start cleaning our home. **[Alien]** has the outside duties, while **[Daughter]** and I have the inside duties. Sundays are our "resting" days.

Soon all this will change. While my husband is in Mexico for whatever time he is must be there, I will have to raise our child alone. Mentally and physically this is going to be the most challenging time of my life. Working more than fifty hours per week, maintaining a home, and of course being both mother and father to our four year old daughter will be next to impossible.

My husband completes my family unit and while I do not understand the entire logistics of why he has to return to Mexico, I am willing to do whatever it takes to bring him back home legally. Our daughter has never been away from either of us for any considerable length of time, and I am positive that this tragedy of her father being away from her will indeed affect her for the rest of her life, as will it affect my life for as long as I live. So, please I am begging whoever may read this letter, to return my husband, the father of my child, the head of my family back to me as quickly as possible.

Thank You,

[Wife]

[Notary Statement and Signature]

I-601 LETTER FROM USCIS WAIVER OFFICE

U.S. Department of Homeland Security
American Consulate General
Ciudad Juarez, Chih., Mexico
P.O. Box 9896
El Paso, Texas 79905-9896

[Date:]

Re: CDJ [_____]
[Applicant Name]

This is in reference to your Application for Waiver of Grounds of Excludability. This waiver is provided for under Section 212 of the Immigration and Nationality Act, as amended. Approval of such application requires a finding that the refusal of admission to the United States of such immigrant alien would result in **extreme hardship to the United States citizen or lawful permanent resident ( ) spouse ( ) parent or ( ) child of such alien**. Approval also requires a favorable exercise of discretion from the Attorney General. This requires a weighing of all factors, the favorable against the unfavorable, in each case.

All claims of hardship **must** be supported by documentary evidence or explanation specifying the hardship. Family separation and financial inconvenience, in and of themselves, do not necessarily constitute extreme hardship. Therefore, it is important for your spouse or parent to describe and document any other claim that might be a hardship. The above-requested information is necessary to render an equitable and fair decision on your Application for Waiver of Grounds of Excludability (I-601).

Any response or evidence should be submitted to enable receipt by this office at the above address no-later-than 30 days from the date of this letter. Should you choose not to reply, the case will be decided on the basis of the information already at hand. A waiver of section 212 of the Immigration and Nationality Act is dependent first upon a showing that the bar imposes an extreme hardship on a qualifying family member. Congress provided this waiver but limited its application. By such limitation it is evident that it did not intend that a waiver be granted merely due to the fact that a qualifying relationship existed. The key term in the provision is "extreme" and thus only in cases of real actual or prospective injury to the United States national or lawful permanent resident will the bar be removed. Common results of the bar, such as separation, financial difficulties, etc., in themselves are insufficient to warrant approval of an application unless combined with much more extreme impacts. Matter of Ngai, 19 I & N Dec. 245. With this qualification in mind, furnish documentary evidence proving that failure to receive the waiver requested would result in extreme hardship to your US citizen spouse or parent.

Extreme hardship can be demonstrated in many aspects of your spouse or parent's life such as:

a. HEALTH—Ongoing or specialized treatment requirements for a physical or mental condition; availability and quality of such treatment in your country, anticipated duration of the treatment; whether a condition is chronic or acute, or long-or short-term.

b. FINANCIAL CONSIDERATIONS—Future employability; loss due to sale of home or business or termination of a professional practice; decline in standard of living; ability to recoup short-term losses; cost of extraordinary needs such as special education or training for children; cost of care for family members (i.e., elderly and infirm parents).

c. EDUCATION—Loss of opportunity for higher education; lower quality or limited scope of education options; disruption of current program; requirement to be educated in a foreign language or culture with ensuing loss of time for grade; availability of special requirements, such as training programs or internships in specific fields.

d. PERSONAL CONSIDERATIONS—Close relatives in the United States and /or your country; separation from spouse/children; ages of involved parties; length of residence and community ties in the United States.

e. SPECIAL FACTORS—Cultural, language, religious, and ethnic obstacles; valid fears of persecution, physical harm, or injury; social ostracism or stigma; access to social institutions or structures.

f. Any other situation that you feel may help you meet the burden of extreme hardship.

Please be very detailed as to how you meet the "extreme hardship" burden. Keep in mind that the hardship must be to your qualifying family member—not to you.

ATTACH A COPY OF THIS LETTER TO YOUR REPLY

Sincerely,

[Officer in Charge]

[Document No. 203]

LETTER BRIEF TO ASYLUM OFFICE IN SUPPORT OF APPLICATION FOR ASYLUM AND WITHHOLDING

Description: This letter brief is a basic format that can be used to supplement Form I-589, Application for Asylum and Withholding of Removal and Convention against Torture submitted to the Asylum Office. The Asylum Office adjudicates all affirmative asylum applications and also conducts all credible fear interviews.

Advantages: Form I-589 does not ask for, nor does it provide sufficient room to explain, the background, history, and overview of your client's asylum application. This letter provides an example of how a practitioner can supplement the asylum application. In addition, many individuals file asylum applications themselves, or use unqualified nonlawyers to assist them. This letter brief is an excellent sample document that one can use to supplement such a previously filed application prior to or at the interview.

Limitations: As an attorney-written document, this letter brief will not serve as evidence in a client's case, but rather as background material. Practitioners can also supplement their client's actual asylum application with a client-signed, but attorney-drafted affidavit, or an expert affidavit.

Notes: This letter should be very fact-specific and should be accompanied with exhibits, including an affidavit of support.

[Date]

Officer **[Name]**
ZAR Room #___
[Place] Asylum Office
[Address]
[City, State, and Zip Code]

Re: [Alien, "A" Number]

Dear Officer **[Name]**:

Applicant, **[Alien]**, respectfully submits this memorandum in support of **[his/her]** application for asylum and withholding of removal.

STATEMENT OF FACTS

Nepal faces significant civil unrest, bordering at times on lawlessness. As summarized by the State Department, in its Country Reports for Human Rights Practices, for 2003, Maoist guerillas "continued their campaign of torturing, killing, bombing, forcibly conscripting children, extorting, forcing closures of schools and businesses, and committing other serious and gross human rights abuses." U.S. Department of State Nepal Country Report on Human Rights Practices 2003 at 1. The State Department's report states, "an estimated 2,380 persons were killed in insurgency-related violence including 156 members of the national police..." *Id.*

The Department of State Reports go on to list scores of killings and human rights abuses by Maoists, explaining that

> Maoists rebels clashed with security forces during the year and engaged in targeted killing of individual members of security forces, government officials and civilians. For example, on July 30, the rebels abducted, tortured, and killed an unarmed RNA soldier in Kaski District. On August 4, rebels shot and killed a police officer in Jhapa District after abducting him several days earlier. *Id.*

The factual background below is a summary of Applicant's affidavit and **[his/her]** account of the events leading to **[his/her]** application for asylum which **[he/she]** gave in the asylum interview on May 19, 2005. **[Alien]** was born in Pipaldhara, Nepal, on June 19, 1965. From January 1993 to December 1996, **[Alien]** attended Tribhuvan University in Katmandu, Nepal, attaining a Master's degree. Before beginning **[his/her]** studies at the University, during **[his/her]** time in school, and after finished **[his/her]** education, **[Alien]** worked as a police officer for the National Police. **[Alien]** explained in **[his/her]** interview that **[he/she]** was the only member of **[his/her]** family to join the Nepal Police Force; **[he/she]** joined because **[he/she]** wanted to help **[his/her]** countrymen and improve conditions in Nepal. **[Alien]** attended school to advance further in the police force, and eventually was ranked as an Inspector. **[Alien]** also worked for the United Nations as a Police Monitor from August 1991 to July 1992, and **[he/she]** was stationed in Cambodia.

During **[his/her]** asylum interview, **[Alien]** gave a detailed account of **[his/her]** many police details—where **[he/she]** was assigned to various dangerous outposts around Nepal after the Maoists began to be a significant problem for the Nepali government. **[Alien]** accounted several instances where **[he/she]** was forced to defend **[his/her]** life, and the lives of fellow policemen and civilians from Maoist attack. **[Alien]** served fourteen years on the police force, from 1987 to 2001.

[Alien] accounted four attacks on police details that **[he/she]** personally served on. The first was November 24, 1999. During this attack, **[Alien]** was commanding approximately 100 policemen who were marching between two villages in order to patrol and protect the villagers from the Maoist guerillas. Approximately twenty men, as far as **[Alien]** could estimate, began firing on **[Alien]**'s force from a vantage point at the top of a hill. **[Alien]** was speaking to **[his/her]** commanding officer via satellite telephone when the shooting began. **[His/Her]** commanding officer gave **[Alien]** permission to fight back, and **[he/she]** did. **[His/Her]** force of 100 men succeeded in routing the Maoists and killed two of them including one of their District Commanders with local villagers witness to the battle. **[Alien]** knew the attackers to be Maoists because they were wearing uniforms, and they were later able to identify the men. **[Alien]** believes villagers who witnessed this incident understood **[he/she]** was the commander of the unit (normally all National Police officers dress the same so that rank cannot be differentiated by enemy attackers). **[Alien]** was given an award for valor after this attack, and sent off to protect even more dangerous outposts. **[He/she]** believes this incident led **[him/her]** to be targeted personally by guerillas.

On September 25, 2000, **[Alien]** suffered minor injuries from falling debris when Maoists attacked the police district headquarters at Dunai of Dopla District (this is in the far west of Nepal) in massive numbers. The Maoists threw an explosive at the outpost, and a wall fell on **[Alien]**. Fourteen policemen were killed and thirteen injured.

On May 29, 2001, **[Alien]** was stationed at the Area Police Post Kalitar (Kalikot) when hundreds of Maoists attacked them suddenly. Seven officers were killed, and the rest were forced to abandon the post. When the post was overrun, **[Alien]** hid by lying next to a dead body and pretending **[he/she]** had been killed. **[Alien]** was discovered and taken prisoner. They did not kill **[him/her]** because they believed **[he/she]** could provide useful information.

[Alien] was led a long way into the jungle with **[his/her]** eyes covered over with black tape, and finally held in a hut. There, **[he/she]** was held for two days. **[Alien]** was beaten and hit in the face. The Maoists wanted information. They held a gun to **[his/her]** head. They interrogated **[him/her]**. **[Alien]** explained in **[his/her]** asylum interview, that at that time **[he/she]** said whatever **[he/she]** could to stay alive, and there were several times when **[he/she]** thought **[he/she]** would certainly be killed. **[He/She]** was made to crawl on **[his/her]** knees and elbows in the hut for an extended period of time. The terrorists struck one of **[Alien]**'s knees, which has a scar. **[Alien]** provided a photo of this. **[Alien]** also explained that the Maoists who held **[him/her]** captor knew who **[he/she]** was, and knew **[his/her]** family was politically active and loyal to the government.

[Alien] finally escaped when the men guarding him both fell asleep late at night. **[Alien]** slipped out of the hut and walked approximately twelve hours through the jungle. **[He/She]** reached a village that was friendly to the government of Nepal. **[He/she]** explained to the villagers what had happened, and they gave **[him/her]** food, water, and money for bus fare to Katmandu.

[Alien] arrived in Katmandu and reported to the hospital for **[his/her]** injuries as well as the police headquarters. Once **[Alien]** had recovered, **[he/she]** was sent to an even more remote outpost in Kalikot District. **[He/she]** remained there from March 20, 2001 to July 6, 2001.

It was at this point in time that **[Alien]** began to experience a heightened fear for **[his/her]** life. The death threats continued against **[Alien]** and **[his/her]** family, and **[Alien]** knew that even though **[he/she]** was able to escape the place where **[he/she]** was detained and beaten, the Maoist terrorists would know **[him/her]** if caught a second time, and that **[he/she]** would never again be able to feign sympathy to their cause in order to stay alive, as **[he/she]** would be killed immediately. On July 2, 2001, Maoists attacked **[Alien]** and **[his/her]** men in the evening in the jungle. **[Alien]** thought **[he/she]** would be killed and could not see how many Maoists there were. The policemen were forced to counter fire. Two terrorists were killed, and three policemen injured.

[Alien] was stationed last in Naumula Dailekh District on July 6, 2001, where the previous outpost had been completely destroyed by the Maoists and about thirty policemen killed on April 7 of the same year. **[Alien]** was sent to re-establish the post as **[he/she]** had received a lot of recognition from **[his/her]** superiors after the events in Kalikot District. **[Alien]** remained at this post approximately one month before departing to the United States, due to the fact that **[his/her]** life and the lives of **[his/her]** spouse and children were in great danger.

Due to all of these events, **[Alien]** was identified individually by the Maoist terrorists. **[He/she]** received letters and phone calls threatening **[his/her]** life. The government was unable to protect **[Alien]** and **[his/her]** family, and the situation became increasingly dangerous. **[Alien]** and **[his/her]** spouse finally left Nepal on August 20, 2001. Their two children were left behind with **[Alien]**'s sister-in-law. They stopped in England for approximately one month because **[Alien]** has a heart condition and had a visa to seek treatment in England. **[Alien]** explained in the interview that the treatment proved too expensive, and **[he/she]** eventually departed England without receiving it.

[Alien] explained in the interview that **[he/she]** considers **[himself/herself]** a gentle person, and **[he/she]** has never harmed another person, except when attacked in order to defend **[his/her]** own life. **[He/she]** explained that every time Maoists attacked, **[he/she]** simply did what **[he/she]** could to defend **[his/her]** position. **[Alien]** attested that **[he/she]** has never taken the law into **[his/her]** own hands and harmed another person. **[Alien]** also attested that although **[he/she]** heard of abuses by members of the police force on occasion, **[he/she]** has no personal knowledge of any such occurrences. **[Alien]** did not personally know anyone who had committed abuses nor did **[he/she]** ever witness such occurrences. **[Alien]** testified clearly that under fire, **[he/she]** did not even attack until ordered to do so by a superior officer. **[Alien]** explained that Maoist terrorists are often on a suicide mission, which could explain why there were not many Maoist prisoners taken. **[Alien]** also served and received training as a United Nations police officer. **[Alien]** was therefore likely acutely aware of proper ethical behavior and international rules of combat during fighting with guerilla groups.

SUMMARY OF ARGUMENT

[Alien]'s Application for Asylum and Withholding of Removal, Form I-589, and **[his/her]** credible and consistent account of the events in **[his/her]** application during **[his/her]** asylum interview clearly establishes that the **[he/she]** has been persecuted by the Maoists, a group the government cannot protect **[Alien]** from, and that **[he/she]** will face persecution if the United States government removes **[Alien]** to Nepal.

[Alien] qualifies for asylum and withholding of removal based on past persecution due to **[his/her]** political opinion, both imputed and actual. Because **[Alien]** can establish that **[he/she]** suffered persecution in the past, **[he/she]** is entitled to a presumption that it is more likely than not that **[his/her]** life or freedom will be threatened upon **[his/her]** return to Nepal. **[Alien]** has further established that there is more than a ten percent chance that **[he/she]** will be subject to future persecution if returned to Nepal. *See INS v. Cardoza-Fonseca*, 480 U.S. 421 (1987). **[Alien]** has fulfilled **[his/her]** burden of proof, and the conditions in Nepal have not changed. **[Alien]** will suffer persecution if returned to Nepal.

Additionally, **[Alien]** has clearly established that it is more likely that not that **[he/she]** will be persecuted if forced to returned to Nepal on account of political beliefs, qualifying **[him/her]** for withholding of removal. Because **[Alien]** has never been convicted of a particularly serious crime, or any crime for that matter, **[he/she]** should also be granted withholding of removal.

ARGUMENT

I. Applicable Legal Standards

A. Asylum

To be granted asylum, an applicant must establish that he or she is a refugee under the laws of the United States. INA §§208(a)(1) (stating that any person physically present in the United States may apply for asylum) and 208(b)(1) (providing that an asylum applicant may be granted asylum if he or she establishes that he or she is a "refugee" as defined by INA §101(a)(42)(A)). Section 101(a)(42)(A) of the Immigration and Nationality Act defines a refugee as:

> Any person who is outside any country of such person's nationality . . . and who is unable or unwilling to return to, and is unable or unwilling to avail himself or herself of the protection of that country because of persecution or a well-founded fear of persecution on account of race, religion, nationality, membership in a particular social group, or political opinion.

The individual, organization, or entity that inflicts the actual, threatened or feared harm or suffering must be either the government or an actor that the government is unable or unwilling to control. *See Matter of Tan*, 12 I&N Dec. 564 (BIA 1967). An applicant for asylum must demonstrate that there is no safe place within the country, and the persecutor has the ability to carry out their threat countrywide. *Matter of Acosta*, 19 I&N Dec. 211 (BIA 1985).

An asylum applicant may establish a well-founded fear of persecution by demonstrating that a "reasonable possibility" of persecution exists in the country from which they are seeking asylum. *See INS v. Cardoza-Fonseca*, 480 U.S. 421 (1987). The term "reasonable possibility" means that the likelihood of persecution may be less than 50 percent likelihood, may be even as low as a 10 percent chance. *Id.*

An applicant's fear may be well-founded without the need for corroboration if it is based on credible subjective evidence. *Id.* An asylum applicant's testimony, if credible, may be sufficient by itself to sustain the applicant's burden of proof without the need for corroboration. *Id.*; 8 CFR §§208.13(a), 1208.13(a) (2003). To establish a well-founded fear of persecution, an applicant need only show that "a reasonable person in his circumstances would fear persecution." *Matter of Mogharrabi*, 19 I&N Dec. 439 (BIA 1987); *Matter of T–M–B–*, 21 I&N Dec. 775 (BIA 1997).

An asylum applicant may be granted asylum based on past persecution or a well-founded fear of future persecution. 8 CFR §§208.13(b), 1208.13(b). Once an applicant establishes past persecution, future persecution may be presumed unless the Department of Homeland Security (DHS) can demonstrate by a preponderance of evidence that conditions have changed to such an extent that the applicant no longer has a well-founded of being persecuted if forcibly returned to the country. 8 CFR §§208.13(b)(1), 1208.13(b)(1); *Matter of O–Z– & I–Z–*, 22 I&N Dec. 23 (BIA 1998).

B. Withholding Of Removal

To be eligible for withholding of removal under INA §241(b)(3), an Applicant must demonstrate a "clear probability of persecution." *INS v. Stevic*, 467 U.S. 407 (1984); *Velarde v. INS*, 140 F.3d 1305 (9th Cir. 1998). To qualify for withholding of removal, the applicant must establish that his or her life or freedom would be threatened in the proposed country of removal on account of race, religion, nationality, or membership in a particular social group or political opinion. 8 CFR §§208.16(b), 1208.16(b).

An applicant may sustain his/her burden of proof through his/her own testimony, if credible, without further corroboration. 8 CFR §§208.16(b), 1208.16(b). An applicant may also meet his/her burden by showing that it is more likely than not that he/she would be persecuted on account of race, religion, nationality, membership in a social group, or political opinion. 8 CFR §§208.16(b)(1), 1208.16(b)(1). An applicant may create a presumption that his/her life or freedom would be threatened in the country to which the DHS seeks to remove him or her by establishing past persecution. 8 CFR §§208.16(b)(2), 1208.16(b)(2); *Matter of O–Z– & I–Z–*, 22 I&N Dec. 23 (BIA 1998).

II. [Alien] Qualifies for Political Asylum and Withholding of Removal

[Alien] qualifies for political asylum because **[he/she]** has a well founded fear of persecution based on **[his/her]** political opinion. **[Alien]** was clearly singled out by Maoists because **[he/she]** was a police officer. However, **[he/she]** was specifically singled out (as is consistent with the Department of State Report) because **[he/she]** was a particular police officer. **[His/Her]** individual identity was known to the Maoist guerillas. **[Alien]** led a unit that was forced to defend itself against Maoist attack, killing two Maoists, including a district leader. **[Alien]** explained that the villagers who witnessed the shooting, were able to identify **[him/her]** as in charge, and likely notified Maoists. **[Alien]** explained that **[he/she]** and **[his/her]** spouse received death threats in letter form by regular mail. **[Alien]** also received phone calls threatening **[his/her]** life. **[Alien]** accounted being kidnapped by Maoists, that **[he/she]** was questioned extensively and violently, and that the Maoists were acutely aware of the political activities of **[his/her]** family, which was loyal to the government and active in politics.

Because **[Alien]** fought Maoists, **[he/she]** necessarily would have been identified by the Maoists as having a political opinion contrary to their own. Thus, **[Alien]** was persecuted, not only because **[he/she]** was defending Nepal against Maoists, but because the Maoists imputed a political opinion to **[Alien]** that was contrary to their opinion and their objectives of destroying the Nepal government. Every time **[Alien]** defended **[his/her]** life, the life of **[his/her]** fellow officers, and the people in Nepal from the Maoist terrorists, **[he/she]** was speaking out against Maoist political views and policies, whether **[he/she]** intended to or not. **[Alien]**'s employment told Maoists **[he/she]** was against them. No matter how outnumbered **[Alien]** was, and **[he/she]** would not sabotage **[his/her]** own government by switching **[his/her]** loyalties, and **[he/she]** would not quit the police force. **[Alien]** explained in the interview that **[he/she]** worked for the police force because **[he/she]** wanted to change what was wrong in **[his/her]** country and make it a better and safer place to live for everyone. This clearly establishes an imputed political opinion.

The fact that Maoists have not stopped their intimidation of **[Alien]** or **[his/her]** family illustrates that the Maoists' intentions were to maliciously persecute **[him/her]** for **[his/her]** beliefs. To this day, **[Alien]**'s children, who are still in Nepal, receive threats against their lives and are afraid to go out in public. (See letters from children and family submitted with the application.)

It is true the Maoist motives in **[Alien]**'s case were multifaceted. Maoists guerillas viewed **[Alien]** as an enemy militarily; however, that was only a *small* aspect of their motives and actions. As previously discussed, Maoists were also motivated by the political opinion **[Alien]** conveyed, actually and imputed, classifying this as a mixed-motive case. Mixed motive cases are well-defined by *Matter of S–P*, which explains:

> Persecutors may have differing motives for engaging in acts of persecution, some tied to reasons protected under the Act and others not. Proving the actual, exact reason for persecution or feared persecution may be impossible in many cases. An asylum applicant is not obliged to show conclusively why persecution has occurred or may occur. Such a rigorous standard would largely render a nullity the Supreme Court's decision in *INS v. Cardoza-Fonseco*, 480 U.S. 421 (1987) and would be inconsistent with the "well-founded fear" standard embodied in the "refugee" definition. 21 I&N Dec. 486 (BIA 1996).

The BIA has further stated:

> [A]n applicant does not bear the unreasonable burden of establishing the exact motivation of a 'persecutor' where different reasons for actions are possible. Rather, an asylum applicant bears the burden of establishing facts on which a reasonable person would fear that the danger arises on account of his race, religion, nationality, membership in a particular social group, or political opinion. *Id.* at 489–90 (quoting *Matter of Fuentes,* 19 I&N Dec. 658, 662 (BIA 1988).

Matter of S–P goes on to explain that the applicant does need to establish that this is one of the motives, either by documentary evidence, or in some cases, by testimony alone. *Id.* (citing *Matter of Dass*, 20 I&N Dec. 120 (BIA 1989).

In this case, **[Alien]** has presented threatening letters from the terrorist themselves, correspondence from the police forces verifying and listing **[his/her]** numerous assignments, lists of policemen who were in fact killed by Maoists, a photo of a scar on **[his/her]** knee, where **[he/she]** was struck by Maoists when **[he/she]** was kidnapped, and the credible testimony of himself and **[his/her]** spouse regarding the events in question. It is not easy to prove the exact motives behind the actions of a diabolical person who takes someone to a remote area and threatens their life, perpetrates violent attacks on that person and others, and makes death threats, not only against **[him/her]**, the policeman, but against **[his/her]** innocent spouse and children. There is no logical rationale for this type of insane behavior that can be rationally understood. However, the asylum law allows for, and understands this exact impossible quandary. As outlined in *Matter of S–P*, there are special rules for mixed motive cases. **[Alien]** has met **[his/her]** burden to establish that this was at least part politically motivated for a variety of reasons. **[Alien]** has also met **[his/her]** burden of establishing that there is greater than a ten percent chance that he will be killed or otherwise harmed if **[he/she]** and **[his/her]** spouse are forced to return to Nepal.

[Alien] was kidnapped, interrogated, harassed, and nearly killed by Maoist guerillas. The kidnappers indeed knew of **[Alien]**'s identity. They knew about **[his/her]** family and their political affiliations. **[Alien]**, a policeman nonetheless, was powerless to defend himself against such a great threat that is so poorly controlled by the Nepali government. **[Alien]** explained that **[he/she]** and **[his/her]** spouse took the threatening letters to the police. They believed **[him/her]** as a fellow officer, but failed to investigate the threats. Maoist guerillas run rampant and control all parts of the country. The Nepali government can do little to protect its own citizens, and **[Alien]** and **[his/her]** spouse will be in eminent peril if forced to return to Nepal.

A. [Alien] credibly established that [he/she] has never persecuted another person

[Alien] presented extremely detailed, specific, credible accounts of all parts of **[his/her]** claim to the asylum officer down to pointing out each one of **[his/her]** duty assignments on a large map of Nepal which the officer had on **[his/her]** computer screen. **[He/She]** answered all questions in an extremely detailed way down to the number of men at each conflict. **[Alien]** did not embellish the events and forthrightly admitted being afraid for **[his/her]** life, and being grossly outnumbered on many occasions. **[Alien]** was clear and consistent, and **[his/her]** detailed testimony was consistent with being an individual with police training and long history of serving on the police force.

[Alien] also credibly explained that **[he/she]** would never harm another human being unless it was absolutely necessary to defend **[his/her]** life and the life of those around **[him/her]** that **[he/she]** was obligated to protect. **[Alien]** testified clearly and convincingly that **[he/she]** has never disrespected human life or taken matters into **[his/her]** own hands.

[Alien] accounted events where **[he/she]** was in charge specifically and Maoists were firing on **[his/her]** unit. **[Alien]** received orders via satellite phone before firing back or simply fired back in response to keep from being killed. **[Alien]** also accounted events where **[his/her]** forces were greatly outnumbered by Maoists in which **[he/she]** did not shoot anyone and did not fight back at all. **[Alien]** accounts even lying next to a dead body to protect **[his/her]** life when fleeing was not an option. **[Alien]** explains that sometimes many more Maoists were killed than taken prisoner because Maoist guerillas were on a suicide mission and did not have high regard even for their own lives.

[Alien] credibly stated that **[he/she]** would never harm another person except where **[he/she]** had no choice. **[Alien]** also explained that **[he/she]** did not know anyone personally who would do such a thing, though **[he/she]** has heard, simply by being an informed citizen, of such instances. It should be noted that the Department of State Reports do not specifically give any examples of the National Police Force committing extrajudicial acts. It does, however, give example after example of Maoists groups committing such acts, killing many people.

Finally, **[Alien]** was a trained United Nations policeman at one point in **[his/her]** life. Surely **[he/she]** would not have been chosen for that job if **[he/she]** did not have ethical behavior as an officer. **[He/she]** also must have been taught respect for the Geneva Convention and human life and a United Nations policeman.

[Alien]'s fear is real, and **[his/her]** children are in continuing danger. Policemen in **[Alien]**'s exact situation in Nepal have been and continue to be killed and specifically targeted. **[Alien]** has been through quite an ordeal during **[his/her]** long-standing service on the police force. **[Alien]** has been kidnapped, and attacked numerous times. **[Alien]** and **[his/her]** family have also been threatened viciously and repeatedly by Maoists guerillas. **[Alien]** has met **[his/her]** burden to establish it would not be safe for **[him/her]** to return to Nepal.

[Alien] and **[his/her]** spouse had absolutely no reason to leave Nepal save a real fear of persecution. They do not fit the profile of individuals coming to the United States simply to make money or stay here. **[Alien]** waited two years for **[his/her]** asylum interview, and specifically requested our office send a letter to the asylum office requesting an interview. If **[he/she]** did not have a legitimate claim, **[he/she]** would not have been so anxious to adjudicate it.

[Alien] and **[his/her]** spouse had good jobs and a high standard of living in Nepal. **[Alien]** would have been able to retire and received a nice pension from the police force one **[he/she]** had been there twenty years; **[Alien]** had already served fourteen years on the force. **[Spouse]** worked as a school teacher. Both enjoyed a large house in Katmadu and a good standard of living. Now, **[Alien and Spouse]** are struggling to make ends meet. **[Alien]** works at A & R Market and Grocery, and **[Spouse]** works at Dunkin Donuts, even though they were highly educated people in Nepal. **[Alien]** has a Master's degree. They would not have taken such a step down in lifestyle and left the country if there was not a real danger. **[Alien]** dedicated fourteen years of **[his/her]** life to defending **[his/her]** country and **[his/her]** way of life; **[he/she]** would not leave unless **[he/she]** felt it was absolutely necessary.

[Alien]'s father passed away on January 18, 2002. It grieved **[him/her]** greatly that **[he/she]** could not be there for the funeral. According to Hindu tradition and custom, the child must attend the funeral in order for the father to go to heaven. **[Alien]** feels **[he/she]** disappointed the entire family by not returning to Nepal for this event. However, **[he/she]** could not because the danger to **[his/her]** life was too great and too real.

CONCLUSION

Because **[Alien]** has met **[his/her]** burden to show **[he/she]** has suffered past persecution and that **[he/she]** has a well-founded fear of future persecution on account of **[his/her]** political opinion, imputed and actual, **[Alien]** should be granted political asylum and withholding of removal by the United States.

Respectfully submitted this _____day of ________, 20___.

[Attorney]

[Document No. 204]

MOTION TO THE DISTRICT DIRECTOR TO REINSTATE AND EXTEND VOLUNTARY DEPARTURE

Description: The attached sample motion is used to request that the district director reinstate and extend voluntary departure granted by an immigration judge at the conclusion of removal proceedings. The purpose of the extension is to allow the client to proceed abroad to apply for an immigrant visa.

Advantages: If granted, the extension of voluntary departure will allow the client to leave voluntarily and protect him- or herself from the ramifications of departure under a final order of removal—inadmissibility for 10 years. Thus, the client may apply for the immigrant visa and, if granted, immediately return to the United States.

Limitations: The extension of voluntary departure may solve the problem of inadmissibility due to departure under a final order of removal. However, upon departure, the alien may still be inadmissible on other grounds, such as unlawful presence.

Notes: Clearly, it is better for an alien to depart under an order of voluntary departure than under a final order of removal. However, IIRAIRA's introduction of unlawful presence as a ground for inadmissibility makes voluntary departure, in many instances, a hollow remedy.

Citations: INA §240B; 8 CFR §240.25(c).

U.S. DEPARTMENT OF HOMELAND SECURITY
U.S. CITIZENSHIP AND IMMIGRATION SERVICES
[CITY, STATE] DISTRICT

	)
IN THE MATTER OF:	)
	)
	)
[Alien]	)
A[Number]	)
	)
Respondent	)
______________________	)

MOTION TO REINSTATE AND EXTEND VOLUNTARY DEPARTURE

[Alien] through undersigned counsel, pursuant to 8 C.F.R § 240.25(c), moves to reinstate and extend voluntary departure so that **[he/she]** may proceed abroad and apply for an immigrant visa before the **[United States Consul/United States Embassy]** in **[City/Country]**.

In support of **[her/his]** motion, **[Alien]** states, through counsel, as follows:

1. **[Alien], a [Country]** national is the beneficiary of an approved and current **[Type of Petition]** petition. (Ex. 1, copy of petition.)
2. **[Alien]** did not attend **[his/her]** visa appointment in **[Country]** because of **[his/her]** genuine fear of persecution in **[Country]**. A copy of **[his/her] [Type of Appointment]** appointment date is attached hereto as Exhibit 1.
3. The United States Vice Consul in **[City/Country]** has confirmed their agreement to process **[Alien's]** application in that country. *See* Exhibits 2 and 3 (correspondence of **[Name]** and **[Name]** confirming acceptance of **[Alien's]** case).
4. On **[date]**, **[Alien]** filed a petition, Case No.______, with the _____ Circuit Court of Appeals for review of a final order of removal (including the denial of political asylum and withholding of removal) entered by the Board of Immigration Appeals on **[date]**.
5. **[Alien's]** petition for review is meritorious and was not filed for the purpose of delay; said petition was filed during the period of voluntary departure granted **[him/her]** by the Board.
6. **[Alien]** is willing to withdraw their petition of review before the ____ Circuit before the government is required to devote any resources to briefing and arguing this matter.

WHEREFORE, [Alien] moves that you reinstate and extend their privilege of voluntary departure until and including the date set by the **[United States Consul/United States Embassy]** in **[City/Country]** for **[his/her]** immigrant visa interview.

Respectfully submitted, this ___ day of _______, 20___.

[Attorney]

[Document No. 205]
LETTER REQUESTING EXTENSION OF VOLUNTARY DEPARTURE

Description: The attached letter is used to request an extension of voluntary departure.

Advantages: Voluntary departure permits an alien to depart the United States in lieu of being subject to removal proceedings and/or a final order of removal and deportation. This may allow the alien to remain in the United States for an additional period of time and avoid the ten-year bar of inadmissibility applicable to aliens who have been previously removed under INA§240 or who have departed while an order of removal was outstanding.

Limitations: The total period allowed for voluntary departure may not exceed 120 days including extensions.

Notes: Practitioners requesting voluntary departure on behalf of clients should also advise the client regarding the applicability of unlawful presence. An alien who departs under an order of voluntary departure may be inadmissible due to a previous period of unlawful presence.

Citations: INA §240B; 8 CFR §1240.26.

[Date]

District Director
U.S. Citizenship and Immigration Services
[Address]
[City, State, and Zip Code]

Re: Request for 30-Day Extension of Voluntary Departure, for [Alien, "A" Number]

Dear District Director,

Pursuant to 8 C.F.R. § 1240.26(f), I am writing on behalf of our client, **[Alien]**, to request an extension of time for **[his/her]** voluntarily departure from the United States. On **[date]**, the Immigration Judge denied **[Alien's]** application for **[Name of Application]**, a copy of which is attached; however the Immigration Judge found **[Alien]** eligible for voluntary departure, and granted **[Alien] [X days]** to depart, until **[date]**. **[Alien]** has appealed this decision to the Board of Immigration Appeals, and the Board of Immigration Appeals denied **[his/her]** appeal on **[date]**. The Board of Immigration Appeals has allowed **[Alien] [X days]** days, until **[date]**, to voluntarily depart from the United States.

[Alien] has filed a Motion to Reopen and Reconsider, as well as a Motion to Stay Removal and a Motion to Stay or Extend Period of Voluntary Departure, with the Board of Immigration Appeals. I enclose a complete copy of **[Alien's]** Motions with this letter. **[Alien]** respectfully requests a 30-day extension of **[his/her]** Voluntary Departure so that **[he/she]** may pursue **[his/her]** motions before the Board of Immigration Appeals.

Since the Board of Immigration Appeals' decision, **[Alien]** has married **[Name]**, who is a United States citizen. They were married on **[date]**, in **[City/County/State]**. **[Alien]** and **[Name]** had already been involved in a serious relationship for quite some time, and had already been planning their marriage prior to **[Alien's]** order of removal. (See **[Alien's]** Affidavit, which is enclosed). They continue to reside in the **[City/State]** vicinity.

On **[date]**, **[Alien's Spouse]** filed an I-130 Petition on behalf of **[Alien]**. As the spouse of a United States citizen, **[Alien]** will be immediately eligible to apply for Adjustment of Status. A complete copy of the I-130 Petition is included with the Motion to Reopen. **[Alien]** filed the Motion to Reopen with the Board of Immigration Appeals because of this new material fact which could not have been presented at any prior hearings before the Immigration Judge.

[Alien] also filed a Motion to Stay Removal and a Motion to Stay or Extend Period of Voluntary Departure with the Board of Immigration Appeals because the Board will be prevented from rendering a decision on **[his/her]** Motion to Reopen if **[his/her]** Voluntary Departure period expires prior to a decision by the Board on the Motion to Reopen.

In addition to presenting a request for extension of Voluntary Departure from the Board of Immigration Appeals, **[Alien]** now also requests an extension from you, as the District Director. As the District Director, you have the power to grant **[Alien]** such an extension.

[Alien] has a strong likelihood of success on the merits of **[his/her]** adjustment of status application if **[his/her]** case is reopened and **[he/she]** is provided the opportunity to appear once again before the Immigration Judge. In addition, **[Alien]** continues to be eligible for Voluntary Departure as **[he/she]** continues to be a person of good moral character and has not been arrested or charged with any crimes.

We would be extremely grateful for your expeditious handling of **[Alien's]** request. Should you need any further information or documentation, please contact me at **(___) ___-____.**

Thank you in advance for your cooperation with this matter.

Very truly yours,

[Attorney]

Enclosures

[Document Nos. 206–07]

REQUESTS FOR JOINT MOTION TO REOPEN/TERMINATE BEFORE ICE CHIEF COUNSEL

Description: These sample letters provide the basic format to seek the filing of a Joint Motion to Reopen or Terminate with ICE chief counsel in the district office where the client's immigration court case was adjudicated. Practitioners would use this letter as a means to reopen or terminate the client's removal/deportation case, typically where a client has been ordered removed/deported, for a cause that the client can now overcome.

Advantages: This type of document is usually the only option available to clients who have been ordered removed/deported and who have undergone a change in circumstances that renders their prior removal order unfair, if not unjust.

Limitations: ICE chief counsel are usually quite circumspect in agreeing to joint motions to reopen/terminate.

Notes: These letters should be very fact-specific and should be accompanied with exhibits and supporting documentation.

Citations: 8 CFR §1003.23(b)(4)(iv).

[Date]

VIA FEDERAL EXPRESS

Chief Counsel
U.S. Immigration and Customs Enforcement
[Address]
[City, State, and Zip Code]

Re: [Alien, "A" Number]
Request for Joint Motion to Reopen

DETAINED ALIEN
EXPEDITED CONSIDERATION REQUESTED

Dear Chief Counsel:

Our firm represents **[Alien]** before U.S. Citizenship and Immigration Services (G-28 on file). **[Alien]** is the beneficiary of an approved I-130 Immigrant Relative Petition filed by her U.S. citizen husband, **[Spouse]**. **[Alien]** is also the subject of an absentia order of deportation stemming from her 1994 entry without inspection; as such, she was detained at the couple's adjustment interview on June 3, 2002 and currently remains in custody.

BRIEF PROCEDURAL HISTORY

A Request for Stay of Deportation was submitted on June 4, 2002, by prior counsel and amended by our office on June 5, 2002. As of this writing, the stay remains unadjudicated.

This letter is submitted in connection with our request that your office join in a Motion to Reopen and Rescind the absentia order entered against **[Alien]**, allowing her to adjust status based on her marriage to **[Spouse]**, a United States citizen. Were the case to be reopened, **[Alien]** would be adjustable under INA §245(i) and admissible under all relevant portions of INA §212.[1] We note that your office has previously joined in such a motion on behalf of **[Alien]**'s sister, **[Sister and A#]**. Her matter is currently pending before the Immigration Judge.

Finally, as noted above, **[Alien]** remains detained at the ICE facility in Aurora, Colorado, and has not yet received action on her request for stay. We urge you to take this into account in expediting your consideration of this request.

SUMMARY OF FACTORS IN SUPPORT OF JOINT MOTION

A more detailed history is contained in our June 5 letter to Officer **[Name]**, Denver Deportation, Detention and Removal (WCC/ICE), referring to the as-yet-pending application for stay (attached), however the relevant factors for your consideration are summarized below:

- **[Alien] and her husband have a bona fide marriage and long-term relationship; the couple was misdirected by prior immigration counsel and has been devastated by her detention**

[1] The complete adjustment packet is already part of the USCIS file; a copy of the receipt for filing is attached.

After her entry in 1994, **[Alien]**, a native and citizen of Peru, and her sister traveled to New York to join their mother, now a U.S. citizen. Although raised a Protestant, once in New York, **[Alien]** continued her prior spiritual path, immersing herself in Judaism and Jewish culture. Beginning in 1995, **[Alien]** studied Hebrew, Jewish law and religion; in June 2000, she completed the arduous conversion process and today practices as an Orthodox Jew.

In 1997, **[Alien]** was introduced to **[Spouse]** by her future mother-in-law; the initial meeting was anything but promising. The couple was politely disinterested in each other until **[Spouse]**'s trip to Peru later that year. Soon, the two discovered many things in common and a relationship blossomed. When **[Alien]** was formally adopted into the Jewish community, **[Spouse]** proposed; the couple was married in November 2000.

[Alien] and her husband duly investigated her status prior to filing for adjustment of status. After finding out about the absentia order, the couple was overjoyed to find out from their immigration attorney, **[Attorney]**, that they would be able to apply for status under INA §245(i). Even though the couple informed **[Attorney]** of the prior proceedings, he did not advise them of its implications or even note the matter on the applications submitted.[2]

[Alien]'s sister, **[Sister, A#]**, was in the identical factual and procedural posture (EWI, absentia order and married to a United States citizen), however the **[Sister and Spouse]** were represented by a different attorney who was more familiar with the implications of the absentia order. The **[Sister and Spouse]** filed an Immigrant Petition under INA §245(i), which was later approved; their attorney then successfully approached the Phoenix District Counsel's Office for a Joint Motion to Reopen; she is currently in proceedings in New York on the adjustment of status.

A copy of our proposed Joint Motion is attached in triplicate, per EOIR Phoenix guidelines.

- **[Alien] has no criminal history and her only immigration violation relates to her unlawful entry**

[Alien] has never committed any crime here or abroad, but for the immigration violation. A review of ICE's file indicates that **[Alien]**'s fingerprint results show no hits but for her arrest by ICE at entry. Notably, **[Alien]** has never used false documents or claimed any status she did not have.

- **[Alien] did not understand her legal position after her arrest and release**

[Alien] was the victim of unscrupulous smugglers on her entry from Mexico. The journey lasted three days on foot, with little food or water, and none at all for approximately 24 hours prior to her arrest. Immediately prior to her (fortunate) discovery by the Border Patrol, **[Alien]** and the others had collapsed after a 17-hour overnight forced march. They awoke dazed and confused in a field, to the sound of the Border Patrol approaching on horseback; the women were driven a short distance to a CBP office but, perhaps because the women were too scared to tell of the hardship they had suffered, the group was not provided any special attention.

[Alien] recalls that there was a water fountain in the room where she and approximately 12 others were processed; she states that she could not swallow without pain and felt ill after ingesting water. She could not understand the officer's Spanish (she did not speak any English at the time) and was unable to obtain clarification as she felt pressured to move forward with the process (another 10–15 people had arrived while **[Alien]**'s group was being processed).

ICE was apparently having difficulty finding a facility which would accept women for detention: **[Alien]** recalls that attempts were made at three separate facilities, but again there was no room for female detainees. At last the group was told they were being taken to see a judge; but apparently, being late in the day, the

[2] Please note that **[Alien]** readily disclosed the issue at the adjustment interview.

Judge refused to see them. Soon after, **[Alien]** and the others were released without bond (despite a $1000 bond indicated on her papers). **[Alien]** thought the matter had simply been dropped.

[Alien] had provided the address of a friend in Phoenix and expected any paperwork to be sent on to her in New York. Unfortunately no mail—including the notice of hearing or the absentia order itself—was forwarded. While **[Alien]** realized she was in the United States unlawfully, she and her husband were devastated to find out later that she had been the subject of an absentia order and its serious consequences.

- **[Alien]'s strong ties to the community and unique situation are deserving of a Joint Motion**

[Alien] has close family ties in the United States: her mother is a United States citizen, her brother is an LPR, her sister (as mentioned above) is in the process of obtaining permanent residence. Her husband and his family are all U.S. citizens and part of the tight-knit Orthodox Jewish community. **[Spouse's]** parents, **[Name]**, were working in schools near Ground Zero and have been traumatized by that experience. They are devastated and re-traumatized by the threat of **[Alien's]** deportation. **[Spouse]**, her husband, has barely slept or eaten since her arrest and detention.

Although relatively new to the Denver area, community support has been overwhelming. **[Spouse]** is a science teacher at a local public school; **[Alien]** is employed pursuant to work authorization as a secretary at a local Jewish school, the Hillel Academy. **[Alien]** has so many people wanting to see her at the Detention Center that a volunteer is coordinating the line up of concerned visitors. The community has organized a letter-writing campaign: attached are letter from family, friends, students, parents of students, religious and business leaders, politicians and concerned community members on **[Alien]**'s behalf.

Although the staff at WCC/ICE have been very accommodating, **[Alien]** is an Orthodox Jew whose religious practice is significantly impacted by her detention. The detention center has been able to bring in kosher food and recently allowed **[Alien]** to wear a hat to replace the towel she initially used to keep her head covered, however there are some aspects of Jewish practice that cannot be accommodated in detention.

For example, as an Orthodox Jewish woman, she must "dress modestly," which means no pants (obviously an impossibility given the uniforms available at the detention center). Further, it is customary for a married woman to attend a *mikvah* seven days after completion of menstruation, a purifying bath which by Jewish law must take place in "living waters" (a natural spring or moving water). This ritual obviously cannot be accommodated in detention. Also, **[Alien]** is expected to light candles on Sabbath which must be left to burn naturally throughout the evening; the Detention Center will not allow a detainee access to matches or open flame.

- **[Alien] has a well-founded fear of persecution based on her family's political activity**

The I-246 submitted by prior counsel makes the claim that **[Alien]** fears for her life due to her conversion to Judaism. As made clear in our amendment to that form, while practicing as an Orthodox Jew in Peru would entail many hardships, **[Alien]** does not fear for her life on this basis. **[Alien]** does have a well-founded fear of persecution related to her imputed political opinion: her uncle, **[Uncle]**, once a powerful political figure in Peru, has fallen out of favor in the recent machinations in that country and has been imprisoned for the past year; many other family members have either fled Peru or faced harassment for their affiliation. Please note that while there is no asylum claim pending at this time; however, such an application may form the basis for a Motion to Reopen if ICE denies this request.

CONCLUSION

In short, **[Alien]** and her husband are meritorious of ICE's exercise of discretion: the couple has a five-year long relationship, and has been married for approximately 19 months. **[Alien]** is adjustable under INA §245(i) and admissible under INA §212. Other than her illegal entry and failure to appear for the initial deportation hearing (which is well-mitigated by her confusion at the time), there are no adverse factors to consider in this application.

Thank you for your time and attention; please do not hesitate to contact our office if we may provide you with any further information to assist you in your decision.

Very truly yours,

[Attorney]

INDEX OF SUPPORTING EVIDENCE

[Alien]
[“A” Number]

1. Affidavit of **[Spouse]**
2. Affidavit of **[Alien]**
3. Amendment to Request to Stay, Letter to Officer **[Name]**, Denver Detention, Deportation and Removal and previously submitted I-246 Request for Stay of Deportation or Removal
4. Copy of receipt for filing Immigrant Petition/Adjustment of Status Application
5. Copy of conversion certificate
6. Copy of Naturalization Certificate for **[Alien’s Mother]**
7. Copy of I-551 Alien Registration Card for **[Alien’s Brother]**
8. “Community comforts Jewish INS detainee,” *Intermountain Jewish News*, June 7, 2002
9. Letters from family, friends, students, politicians, religious and business leaders and community members (over 350)

[Date]

Office of Chief Counsel
Department of Homeland Security
[Address]
[City, State, and Zip Code]

Re: Joint Motion to Terminate for [Alien, "A" Number]

Dear Chief Counsel:

I represent **[Alien]** in **[his/her]** immigration matters. I am writing to ask if you would agree to a Joint Motion to Terminate **[Alien's]** removal proceedings.

[Alien's] U.S. citizen spouse filed a Form I-130 on behalf of **[Alien]** on **[date]**. On **[date]**, U.S. Citizenship and Immigration Services (USCIS) erroneously denied **[Alien's]** I-130. On **[date]**, **[Alien and Spouse]** moved from **[Place]** to **[Place]**, and notified USCIS of their move; however, the change of address was not reflected in the Service's file and an interview notice was sent to the couple's old address, which they did not receive until after the scheduled time of the interview. As a result of this confusion, the couple's Form I-130 was denied, and removal proceedings were commenced against **[Alien]**.

[Alien and Spouse] were married on **[date]** and started a life together. On **[date]**, **[Spouse]**, a naturalized U.S. citizen, filed a Form I-130 petition on **[Alien's]** behalf. Concurrently, **[Alien]** filed Form I-485, Application to Adjust Status.

On or about **[date]**, **[Alien and Spouse]** moved to their current address. They promptly submitted a Form AR-11 at the Kentucky Change of Address Center of the Immigration Service; however, the local office of USCIS was not aware of the new address and on **[date]** sent out an interview notice scheduling them to appear for an adjustment interview on **[date]**. The Interview notice was sent to their old address. Due to delays in forwarding, the interview notice was not delivered to them until **[date]**, five days after the interview date.

The decision to deny **[Alien's]** Form I-130 is dated **[date]**; however, because it was sent to their old address, too, the decision did not reach **[Alien and Spouse]** until **[date]**. Immediately upon the receipt of the decision, **[Alien and Spouse]** filled out and submitted a Form I-290B, appealing the erroneous decision. In a letter that they attached to the Form I-290B, **[Alien and Spouse]** explained the circumstances surrounding the change of address and the inadvertently missed interview. The appeal was filed on **[date]** and is currently pending at the Atlanta Office of USCIS.

On **[date]**, your office issued a Notice to Appear to **[Alien]**. Again, the notice was sent to their old address and did not reach **[Alien and Spouse]** until some time later.

[Spouse's] petition on behalf of **[Alien]** is approvable as the couple is lawfully married and live in a bona fide marital relationship. We would be grateful if you would consider jointly terminating the proceedings against **[Alien]** and allow the Service to reopen **[his/her]** case based on the appeal filed by **[Alien and Spouse]**.

[Alien] is scheduled for a Master Calendar Hearing on **[date]**, and we would like to submit the enclosed I-471 before the hearing. I have also enclosed copies of all available supporting documents to assist you in terminating this court case.

Please do not hesitate to contact me if you desire to discuss this matter further.

Very truly yours,

[Attorney]

Enclosures [Form I-471, Supporting Documentation]

[Document Nos. 208–11]

REQUESTS FOR RELEASE FROM DHS PREHEARING DETENTION

Description: These letters are a standard format to request that DHS release an alien being detained pending a hearing as an arriving alien, or as an alien who is deportable/removable.

Advantages: Some DHS districts do not routinely release individuals. Consequently, the only way to bring a releasable alien to the attention of DHS is to formally request his or her release in writing.

Limitations: In many circumstances, DHS considers an individual ineligible for release (*e.g.*, an aggravated felon); it is up to counsel to convince DHS that the client is somehow eligible for release.

Notes: This letter should be very fact-specific and should be accompanied with exhibits, including an affidavit of support and supporting documentation to verify the twin pillars of DHS's release decision: flight risk and danger to the community. If DHS believes that the client will not show up for a hearing, it simply will not give a bond to the client. Also, because DHS has started setting substantial bonds in many cases, practitioners should include a reasonable suggested bond amount—one that the client can afford.

Citations: 8 CFR §§236.1, 1236.1.

[Date]

VIA HAND DELIVERY

[District Director]
Detention and Deportation
U.S. Immigration and Customs Enforcement
[Address]
[City, State, and Zip Code]

Re: Request for Release for [Alien, "A" Number]

Dear **[District Director]**:

We represent **[Alien]**. Our Form G-28 is on file.

Ms. **[Alien]** is a native and citizen of Guatemala. She attempted to enter the United States on **[date]** at the Atlanta International Airport. Ms. **[Alien]** was seeking to join her husband and three daughters in New York.

Ms. **[Alien]** remains detained at the Dekalb County Jail. On **[date]**, she appeared before an asylum officer for a Credible Fear interview. Ms. **[Alien]** was found to have met the credible fear standard. *See* Form I-870, Record of Determination/Credible Fear Worksheet, attached. Therefore, she is now entitled to present her asylum claim before the immigration judge.

Ms. **[Alien]** has three young daughters, ages 13, 11, and 3 years old, who need their mother immensely. The youngest daughter is a U.S. citizen. Ms. **[Alien]** is eligible for release from ICE custody and is the lowest priority level of incarceration under the new custody guidelines. She is not a criminal alien. She has never been charged with any crime. Ms. **[Alien]** needs to care for her daughters, particularly her youngest one.

We would ask you to exercise your discretion in this regard and parole Ms. **[Alien]** during the pendency of her request for asylum before the immigration judge. We would be happy to provide you with any other information about Ms. **[Alien]** and her family that would help you make a determination about her release on bond. The ICE file contains Ms. **[Alien]**'s true Guatemalan passport; therefore, her identity has been clearly established.

There really is no reason to continue detaining Ms. **[Alien]**, given the mandate to fill ICE custody slots with criminal aliens and those with final orders of deportation.

We very much appreciate your consideration in this matter. We look forward to a follow-up conversation with you later today regarding your decision.

Very truly yours,

[Attorney]

Enclosures

[Date]

VIA FACSIMILE AND HAND DELIVERY

[District Director]
Detention and Deportation
U.S. Immigration and Customs Enforcement
[Address]
[City, State, and Zip Code]

Re: Request for Release for [Alien, "A" Number]

Dear **[District Director]**:

We represent **[Alien]**. Our Form G-28 is attached.

Mr. **[Alien]** was arrested at his workplace and is currently in your custody. He has come to the attention of ICE due to a November 11, 1999, conviction for possession with intent to distribute cocaine. For that offense, Mr. **[Alien]** was sentenced to five years' probation.

We hereby request that you release Mr. **[Alien]** on a reasonable bond. He is 34 years of age and has been a lawful permanent resident since 1990. Mr. **[Alien]** is in a common law marriage and his wife is one month pregnant.

Mr. **[Alien]**'s wife is in great need of his support, care, and companionship. He has not been convicted of a crime of violence and is not a threat to the community. We would ask you to exercise your discretion in this regard and permit Mr. **[Alien]** to be released on his own recognizance or on a reasonable bond. We would be happy to provide you with any other information about Mr. **[Alien]** or his family that would help you make a determination about his release on bond.

We very much appreciate your consideration in this matter. We look forward to a follow up conversation with you later today regarding your decision.

Very truly yours,

[Attorney]

Enclosure

[Date]

VIA HAND DELIVERY

DETAINED JUVENILES

[District Director]
Detention and Deportation
U.S. Immigration and Customs Enforcement
[Address]
[City, State, and Zip Code]

Re: Request for Release on Bond for:
[Child 1] [Surname] (A# not assigned yet),
[Child 2] [Surname] (A00-000-000), and
[Child 3] [Surname] (A00-000-000)

Dear **[District Director]**:

We represent the **[Surname]** children. Our Forms G-28 signed by their father, **[Father] [Surname]**, are attached. The **[Surname]** children, ages 17, 15, and 12, remain in ICE custody at the [**Children's Home**]. Their parents, **[Father]** and **[Mother] [Surname]**, are detained at the **[Name of County]** County Jail, as well as their older sister **[Sister] [Surname]**.

The **[Surname]** children are Ethnic Albanian natives of Montenegro. The entire family will be applying for asylum in the United States because of the existing and increasing persecution of Ethnic Albanians in Montenegro. The **[Surname]** family attempted entry at the JFK airport in New York last week using a passport from a visa waiver country. They have been transported to Atlanta, Georgia, due to lack of detention space in New York. They have not, to this day, been scheduled for a hearing before the immigration judge.

We hereby request the immediate release of these children to their close blood relatives in New York. We are filing a separate request for the release of their parents and adult sister.

The **[Surname]** family will be supported by the **[Surname]** family, who resides in New York. Mr. **[Surname]**, **[Mother] [Surname]**'s brother and the children's uncle, will be sponsoring the children. The children's oldest sister, **[Sister]** is a lawful permanent resident living in New York; she will also help to care for her siblings (see her identity documents, attached). In support of this request for release, we include the following documents for each child:

1. Copy of each child's Birth Certificate from the Socialist Republic of Yugoslavia, Republic of Montenegro;
2. Copy of each child's passport from the Federal Republic of Yugoslavia;
3. Form I-134, Affidavit of Support, completed by the children's uncle, **[Uncle]**, reflecting an annual income of $_____ and stable employment with **[Company]** in the maintenance department;
4. Copy of Mr. **[Surname]**'s Resident Alien Card, New York State Driver License, and Social Security Card;
5. Copy of **[Mother] [Surname]**'s birth certificate, with translation, showing that her maiden name is **[Name]**;

6. Copy of photograph showing Mr. **[Surname]** (far right) with the children's mother, **[Mother]**, in Yugoslavia;
7. Copy of photograph showing Mr. **[Surname]** with **[Mother]** **[Surname]** and one of the children, **[Child 3]**, as an infant (photo taken in Yugoslavia);
8. Copy of photograph of the **[Surname]** family in Yugoslavia several years ago;
9. U.S. Income Tax Returns for **[Sister and Husband]** **[Surname]** for the years 1999 and 1998, as well as W-2 Forms for 1997; and
10. Resident Alien Card and Birth Certificate for the children's sister, **[Sister]** **[Surname]**; and
11. Letter from **[Sister]** **[Surname]** attesting to the identity of her parents and siblings.

Mr. **[Name]** is absolutely clear in his intent and ability to provide a home, as well as financial support, to his nieces and nephew. Mr. **[Surname]**'s Affidavit of Support and tax records clearly show that the children have close family in the United States, a family who is ready, willing, and most important, able to financially support them. *After what they have endured in Montenegro, these children deserve the opportunity to be in the loving care of their family, including their oldest sister* **[Sister]**, *as soon as possible.*

We reiterate that the **[Surname]** children, irrespective of their attempted entry under the Visa Waiver Pilot Program, are credible asylum applicants currently awaiting an asylum hearing before the immigration judge. The children are eligible for release from ICE custody and are the lowest priority level of incarceration under the new custody guidelines.

These children are not criminal aliens and have come to the United States after enduring the persecution of Ethnic Albanians in Montenegro.

We would ask you to exercise your discretion in this regard and permit the **[Surname]** children to be paroled into the United States to apply for asylum with their parents. We would be happy to provide you with any other information about the **[Surname]** and the **[Name]** families that would help you make a determination about their release.

We are very confident that you will give these cases the utmost priority. We do not believe it is or should be the policy of the ICE to separate and detain families seeking the protection of the United States in asylum proceedings, including those with young children, and particularly those who have close relatives willing to support them here in the United States. We look forward to your prompt decision in this matter.

Very truly yours,

[Attorney]

Enclosures

[Date]

VIA FACSIMILE AND HAND DELIVERY

[District Director]
Detention and Deportation
U.S. Immigration and Customs Enforcement
[Address]
[City, State, and Zip Code]

Re: Request for Release on Bond for [Alien, "A" Number]

Dear **[District Director]**:

Our office represents Mr. **[Alien]**. We enclose our signed Forms G-28, Notice of Entry of Appearance as Attorney or Representative before ICE.

Mr. **[Alien]** is a long-time lawful permanent resident. He was convicted of committing "larceny," and sentenced to 11 months' suspended confinement. Mr. **[Alien]** was detained by ICE upon his return to the United States and is now charged with excludability as an "arriving alien."

Mr. **[Alien]**'s conviction is not an aggravated felony because he was not sentenced to at least one year confinement. See INA §101(a)(43)(G). Moreover, Mr. **[Alien]** is not subject to mandatory detention under INA §236(c) because he was released from state custody prior to October 31, 1998.

We ask that you release Mr. **[Alien]** immediately on a reasonable bond. He is the spouse of a U.S. citizen, as well as the father of a U.S. citizen child and a lawful permanent resident child, ages 8 and 14. His unnecessary detention is causing great emotional and financial suffering to his wife and two young children. We attach a letter from Mr. **[Alien]**'s wife, **[Name]**, for your consideration. In addition, Mr. **[Alien]** is the owner of an export company.

We would ask you to exercise your discretion in this regard and permit Mr. **[Alien]** to be released on his own recognizance or on a reasonable bond. We would be happy to provide you with any other information about Mr. **[Alien]** or his family that would help you make a determination about his release on bond. There really is no reason to continue detaining Mr. **[Alien]** as he has not been convicted of a violent crime, and does not constitute a danger to the community. In addition, it will be in Mr. **[Alien]**'s best interest to report to both ICE and the immigration court. His family is here in the United States and he is prepared and eager to seek relief from removal before the immigration judge. Therefore, he is not a flight risk.

We very much appreciate your consideration in this matter. We look forward to a follow up conversation with you later today regarding your decision.

Very truly yours,

[Attorney]

Enclosure

[Document Nos. 212–15]

VEHICLE SEIZURE PETITIONS

Description: This set of forms is handy in the rare event that a vehicle is seized by DHS for use in an attempt to bring unauthorized aliens into the United States. The particular set of forms is aimed at situations where the driver and occupants of the vehicle were not the owners of the vehicle. This is also useable where there are liens against the vehicle or in the situation of a leased vehicle.

[Date]

Area Port Director
U.S. Customs and Border Patrol
[Address]
[City, State, and Zip Code]

PETITION FOR MITIGATION AND PETITION FOR REMISSION [FOR VEHICLE FORFEITURE]

Re: Seizure of:
Vehicle ID Number:
Asset Identification:
Asset Description:
Asset Value:

Dear Area Port Director:

I am writing you on behalf of **[Petitioner]**, owner of the vehicle identified above, which was seized by U.S. Customs and Border Patrol on **[date]**. **[Petitioner]** hereby submits this letter and supporting documents as a Petition for Remission, or in the alternative, a Petition for Mitigation.

Attached hereto is a certified Statement of **[Name]**, Vice President, together with (1) the vehicle registration establishing **[Petitioner's]**ownership of the seized vehicle; (2) the declaration of **[Name]**; (3) the declarations of **[Names]** describing the facts and circumstances relating to the seizure of the vehicle; (4) Canadian and U.S. business licenses establishing that **[Business]** is a registered motor vehicle wholesaler; (5) statements of several members of the **[type or place]** and **[type or place]** business communities, attesting that **[Business]** is a business in good standing.

In adjudicating this Petition for Mitigation or in the alternative Petition for Remission, please take into account that **[Business]** is a legitimate business that exports vehicles to the United States on a regular basis, at the rate of approximately [____] vehicles per month. The company regularly employs [____] people. The owners, **[Names]**, have no prior records of any criminal or immigration violations.

The **[Business]** employees involved in the **[date]** seizure did not intend to deceive U.S. Customs and Border Patrol border officers to that the drivers of the vehicle involved could enter the United States for an illegal purpose. **[Names]** involved in this incident were completely unaware that point-to-point hauling in these circumstances was in violation of the Immigration and Naturalization Act. **[Names]** believed that since the vehicle located in Tacoma, Washington, belonged to **[Name]**, it was lawful to deliver the vehicle to the purchaser in Spokane.

[Petitioner] recognizes and acknowledges that suggesting that the drivers give a misleading answer to border officials was wrong. However, please understand that the suggestion was made not to cover up activity they knew or belief to be illegal. **[Petitioner]** understands that it is completely unacceptable to give false or misleading information to the U.S. Customs and Border Patrol officials under any circumstances. After consulting with immigration attorneys, they now also know that point-to-point hauling within the United States, performed by individuals not authorized to work in this country, is in violation of U.S. immigration laws. The owners of company, **[Names]** have taken steps to ensure that all of their employees understand this and to ensure that an incident like this will not happen in the future.

[Petitioner] recognizes and accepts responsibility for its conduct. **[Name]** and **[Name]** are eager to settle this matter expeditiously. Based on the foregoing factors, we request that the penalty be mitigated or remitted as soon as possible so that this matter can be settled and the vehicle returned to **[Business]**.

If you need any additional information, please do not hesitate to contact me.

Sincerely,

[Attorney]

Enclosures

STATEMENT OF COUNSEL

I, **[Name]** hereby attest that I am duly authorized counsel for the **[Petitioner]**, and I attest, upon information and belief that the information contained in this Petition is true and correct.

____
[Attorney]

STATE OF __________________
ss.
COUNTY OF _________________

On this day, personally appeared before me, **[Name]**, to me known (or proven on the basis of satisfactory evidence) to be the individual who executed the within and foregoing instrument, and acknowledged that he signed the same as his free and voluntary act and deed, for the uses and purposes therein mentioned.

GIVEN UNDER my hand an official seal this ______ day of _____, ____.

____
Notary's Printed Name
Residing at _______

____
NOTARY PUBLIC in and for _____,

My appointment expires:
____

CERTIFIED STATEMENT REGARDING OWNERSHIP OF VEHICLE

Re: Conveyance:
Vehicle Identification Number:
Date and Place of Seizure:
Seizure Number:

1. I, **[Name]**, hereby submit the following statements to support the attached application for return of the vehicle identified above, which was seized by U.S. Customs and Border Patrol on **[date]**.
2. **[Petitioner]** is the owner of the vehicle identified above. This ownership interest is established by the vehicle registration, attached.
3. Attached to this Certified Statement are my statement and the statements of **[Business]** employees, describing the facts and circumstances relating to the seizure of our vehicle on **[date]**.
4. I certify, under penalty of perjury, that all of the statements contained in the attached letters and documents, and all of the statements in this Certified Statement, are true and correct to the best of my knowledge and ability.

Executed on this ______ day of ______, ____, at _____

Signed,

[Petitioner]

UNITED STATES DEPARTMENT OF HOMELAND SECURITY
U.S. CUSTOMS AND BORDER PATROL

IN THE MATTER OF:) **File No.: "A" Number**

[ ]

LIC. # [ ]

VIN. # [ ]

____

PETITION FOR RELIEF FROM FORFEITURE

I **[Attorney]**, hereby swear and state that the following is true and correct to the best of my knowledge, upon information and belief:

1. I am an attorney licensed to practice law in the State of **[Name of State]**.
2. I represent **[Alien]** in matters pending before U.S. Customs and Border Patrol.
3. **[Alien]** resides at **[address]**. She is the owner of the above-captioned **[vehicle]**, which has become subject to forfeiture pursuant to 8 USC §1324(b) and 8 CFR §274.
4. **[Alien]** respectfully requests remission of forfeiture, or in the alternative, mitigation of forfeiture, in the above-captioned case currently pending before the Regional Commissioner of U.S. Immigration and Customs Enforcement in **[Place]**. In support of her request, states through her attorney the following:
5. **[Alien]** married a **[Nationality]** citizen, **[Name]**, in **[Place]** on **[date]**.
6. **[Alien]** traveled to **[Country]** the end of **[date]** to celebrate their marriage with family who had been unable to attend the ceremony in **[Place]**.
7. On **[date]**, the **[Alien]**s planned to return for one week to **[Alien]**'s home in **[Place]**, before returning to **[Country]** where they intended to initiate immigration proceedings in order to apply for lawful permanent residence for **[Spouse]**. Upon presenting themselves to CBP inspectors at the border on **[date]**, at **[place]**, Mr. **[Spouse]** was refused entry to the U.S. by CBP, who contended that he was not in fact destined to the U.S. for a week visit but was rather intending to return to the U.S. to reside with his U.S. citizen spouse.
8. Mrs. **[Alien]**'s automobile was seized as the result of alleged use in the commission of a violation of 8 USC §1324(a).
9. At no time did Mrs. **[Alien]** intend to circumvent U.S. immigration laws. In fact, Mrs. **[Alien]** was misinformed about the proper procedures for filing an immediate relative visa petition for her husband **[Spouse]**, and believed that she must in fact return to **[Country]** to file such papers.

10. The full and honest intention of both **[Alien]** and **[Spouse]** was to remain in the U.S. for one week and then return to **[Country]** to file the proper immigration papers for **[Spouse]**. No violation of U.S. immigration laws would be involved in a one-week visit by Mr. **[Spouse]** to the U.S. In fact, he had traveled back and forth between his home and **[Alien]**'s home frequently over the course of several months up until his marriage on **[date]**, but maintained his residence in **[Country]** (see attached copies of mail addressed to Mr. **[Spouse]**).

11. **[Alien]** subsequently consulted an immigration attorney and learned that in fact she must file papers for **[Spouse]** in **[Place]**. She has filed the required I-130 petition. (See attached copy.) **[Spouse]** is waiting for his visa processing in **[Country]**, as he had planned.

12. Furthermore, **[Alien]** is employed by the **[Employer]** as a **[position]** . She works in the area of **[employment]** and is required on a daily basis to [transport children to their prospective pre-adoptive homes and the appointments, and to make home visits to foster and adoptive parents]. Mrs. **[Alien]** cannot perform her job without an automobile. She lives in a rural area of **[Place]** where there is minimal public transportation. Her place of employment is 12 miles from her home, and her clients live anywhere from two to one hundred miles from her office.

13. The seizure of Mrs. **[Alien]**'s vehicle would impose an extreme hardship not only on her, but also on the many clients whom she serves. Mrs. **[Alien]**'s program manager has submitted a letter verifying these facts to CBP. (see copy herein attached)

14. Mrs. **[Alien]** has already incurred expenses in excess of **[amount]** as the result of the seizure of her automobile. Her automobile was purchased with a loan from the **[Company],** which holds a lien on the vehicle. Four years of monthly payments of **[amount]** remain to be paid by Mrs. **[Alien]**.

15. For all of the foregoing reasons, **[Alien]**, through her attorney, respectfully requests that the Regional Commissioner grant remission of forfeiture in the above-captioned case.

16. At no time did **[Alien]** have any reason to believe that her vehicle was being used in violation of the law. Return of the vehicle to **[Alien]** will promote the interest of justice and will not diminish the deterrent effect of §274(b) of the Act.

Respectfully submitted, by her attorney,

[Attorney]

Dated: __________

Sworn to and subscribed before me this _____ day of ______, 20__.

____

Notary Public

My Commission Expires: ____________________

[Date]

Area Port Director
U.S. Customs and Border Patrol
[Address]
[City, State, and Zip Code]

Re: Seizure #______, [Vehicle Name; Vehicle Identification Number (VIN)];
License Number _________
Date of Seizure: [Date]

Dear Area Port Director:

This letter is a Remission Petition filed by the **[Petitioner]** for return of the **[vehicle]** described above and registered to **[Petitioner]**. Evidence supporting remission is set forth in the following paragraphs.

The **[Petitioner]** has a valid lien against the above described vehicle which pre-existed seizure of the vehicle on or about **[date]**. Evidence of the lien is attached as Exhibit A, and consists of a copy of our Chattel Mortgage dated **[date]**. A copy of our official registration confirmation from Victoria, British Columbia authorities showing this Chattel Mortgage was registered under **[number]** and registered **[date]** is attached as Exhibit B. Further, the **[Petitioner]** attaches a letter and financial statement as Exhibit C hereto which reveals the bank's current outstanding principal balance in the seized vehicle to be $15,387.41 (Canadian), which equals $13,151.63 (U.S.). The **[Petitioner]** understands that the U.S. Customs and Border Patrol Seizure Officer and its attorney in this matter, **[Name]**, have agreed that the value of the seized vehicle is $10,000 (U.S.). We do not know the value of the vehicle in question and ratify this agreement.

The **[Petitioner]** has no knowledge of the particular violation which subjected the vehicle to seizure and forfeiture. The **[Petitioner]** has no knowledge that the registered owner of the seized vehicle had any record of violations of the laws of the United States or any state or foreign country or had any intent to violate the laws of the United States or any state or foreign country and would not have participated in any scheme by **[Name]** to do so.

The **[Petitioner]** understands that following the granting of this Remission Petition, it may obtain permission of the vehicle, after paying costs and expenses incident to the seizure and forfeiture. It will do so.

The **[Petitioner]** also understands that upon the granting of this petition it may be required to furnish an instrument executive by the registered owner and other know claimant of an interest in the pretty releasing their interest in the property, or furnish an agreement to hold the United States government, as agents and employees harmless from any and all claims which might result form the grant or remission. It agrees to do so as required. The **[Petitioner]** also understands that it may be required by U.S. authorities to agree not to return the seized vehicle to **[Name]**, and will execute such an agreement if required to do so.

Lastly, this letter serves to confirm that the writer, **[Name]**, is an employee of the **[Business]** and is duly authorized to make the representation contained in this notarial letter.

Sincerely,

[Attorney]

Subscribed and Sworn to before me this ____ day of________, _______.

____
Notary Public

FINANCIAL STATEMENT

Case Selling Price		______
Added Misc. Charges (Tax, transfer fees, etc.)		______
Total Selling Price		______
Less Trade-in	______	
Less Cash Down Payment	______	
Total Deductions		______
Unpaid Balance of Selling Price		______
Plus Finance Charges	______	
Plus Insurance Premium	______	
Total of Charges to be Added to Selling Price		______
Total		______
Less Total Payments	______	
Less Unearned Financial Charges	______	
Less Unearned Insurance Premium	______	
Total Deductions		______
Petitioner's Recognized Equity		______

I certify that the accounting in this financial statement is true and correct to the best of my knowledge and belief and that the payment or credits are correct as shown.

Signature ______________

[Date]

[Date]

[Address]

SUBMISSION OF CLAIM AND COST BOND

Re: Vehicle:
Vehicle Identification Number:
Date of Seizure:
Place of Seizure:
Seizure Number:

Dear **[Name]**,

I am writing to you concerning the vehicle identified above, which was seized by U.S. Customs and Border Patrol on **[date]**.

Enclosed with this letter is a certified check in the amount of $__________, which is submitted as the claim and cost bond required under 8 CFR §274.10. I request that this case be handled in judicial forfeiture proceedings.

I am the owner of the vehicle identified above. See attached documentation establishing my ownership interest. I believe that my vehicle is not subject to seizure for the following reasons:

* * * * * * * * *

If you need additional information, please contact me.

Sincerely,

[Attorney]

CHAPTER 3
IMMIGRATION COURT MOTIONS AND BRIEFS

[Document No. 301]

MOTION TO WAIVE APPEARANCE OF RESPONDENT AT MASTER CALENDAR HEARING

Description: This motion requests the immigration court to waive the respondent's presence for a master hearing at which pleadings will be taken and relief sought through counsel.

Advantages: Allows counsel to take action for the client who is far from the hearing location and saves the client's funds for more crucial appearances.

Limitations: Most immigration courts will not waive a respondent's appearance before granting voluntary departure, due to the warnings that must be given.

U.S. DEPARTMENT OF JUSTICE
EXECUTIVE OFFICE FOR IMMIGRATION REVIEW
IMMIGRATION COURT
[LOCATION]

IN THE MATTER OF:	)	
	)	
[Alien]	)	
A[Number]	)	IN REMOVAL PROCEEDINGS
	)	
Respondent	)	
______________________________	)	

MOTION TO WAIVE APPEARANCE OF RESPONDENT

I, **[Attorney]**, hereby respectfully move that the Executive Office for Immigration Review waive the appearance of **[Alien]**, Respondent, at **[his/her]** Master Calendar Hearing schedule for **[date]**. In support of this Motion, I swear and state the following:

1. Respondent is a native and citizen of **[Country]**.

2. I represent respondent in all matters before the Executive Office for Immigration Review, as indicated by the attached Form EOIR-28.

3. Respondent has executed and signed an affidavit in which **[he/she]** admits to the allegations on the Order to Show Cause and concedes removability.

4. Respondent presently resides in **[Location]**, where **[he/she]** has accepted a **[position]** at **[Employer]**. Respondent's **[employment]** responsibilities begin the week of **[date]**, presenting Respondent with an unforeseen difficulty in traveling to **[Location]** to be present at **[his/her]** Master Calendar hearing.

5. Respondent wishes to continue with asylum and suspension cases in the **[Place]** District, as **[his/her]** witnesses reside there and in order that **[he/she]** can continue to be represented by **[his/her]** her present counsel.

6. The Department of Homeland Security Trial Attorney has agreed to this request for a waiver of Respondent's appearance.

For the forgoing reasons, Respondent respectfully request that this Motion to Waive Respondent's Appearance be granted.

Respectfully submitted this ___ day of __________, 20__.

[Attorney]

[ADD CERTIFICATE OF SERVICE]

[Document No. 302]

MOTION TO SUBSTITUTE COUNSEL AND FOR CONTINUANCE OF HEARING

Description: This pleading seeks the substitution of new counsel and a continuance for additional time to prepare.

Advantages: The motion sets forth specific facts as to the need for new counsel—here a substitution of one *pro bono* counsel for another. The motion provides the specific bases for available relief and then provides the particular reasons for the unavailability of counsel for the upcoming hearing.

Limitations: The pleadings call for the court both to allow substitution of counsel and grant a continuance based on the unavailability of new counsel, which presupposes that the court will grant the first part of the motion. This motion is limited to its own facts.

Notes: Motions of this nature should be filed well in advance of the hearing date. Be sure to make a timely filing. The most common motion for substitution of counsel involves a client who terminated counsel and has selected new counsel or, more likely, present counsel has determined his or her inability to continue to represent the client for any of a variety of reasons and has likely been granted permission to withdraw as counsel. As an alternative format, one may prepare a motion to substitute counsel and upon its granting, file a separate motion for continuance.

U.S. DEPARTMENT OF JUSTICE
EXECUTIVE OFFICE FOR IMMIGRATION REVIEW
IMMIGRATION COURT
[LOCATION]

IN THE MATTER OF:	)	
	)	
[Alien]	)	
A[Number]	)	IN REMOVAL PROCEEDINGS
	)	
Respondent	)	
______________________________	)	

MOTION TO SUBSTITUTE COUNSEL AND FOR CONTINUANCE

Respondent, through undersigned counsel, moves the Immigration Judge to allow **[him/her]** to substitute counsel and to continue these proceedings.

In support of this motion, Respondent, through undersigned counsel, states as follows:

1. Prior counsel was representing the Respondent **[on a pro bono basis in cooperation with Agency]**, and counsel to be substituted is the new, private pro bono representative.

2. New counsel, whose Entry of Appearance, Form EOIR-28, is attached hereto, will be away on professional business from **[date]** to **[date],** and is unavailable to appear on behalf of Respondent at Respondent's merits hearing, which is currently scheduled for **[date and time].**

3. To the best of counsel's knowledge and information, Respondent is presently incarcerated at **[Jail]** as the result of convictions entered on **[date]** and **[date],** on criminal charges of **[charges]** arising from a related series of incidents in which Respondent participated with others, and in which, apparently, mitigating circumstances are present. On information and belief, Respondent is serving a sentence of **[X years]**, and may be eligible for release prior to that time.

[and/or];

4. Respondent reasserts **[his/her]** fear of political persecution in **[Country]** and **[his/her]** desire to seek the protection of withholding of removal and of political asylum in the United States. Respondent does not abandon **[his/her]** claim, but seeks to pursue it, and asserts **[his/her]** rights to a hearing on the merits of **[his/her]** claim, notwithstanding **[his/her]** incarceration.

5. Respondent has a constitutionally protected right to apply for asylum in the United States. *Chun v. Sava*, 708 F.2d 869, 877 (2d Cir. 1983); *Haitian Refugee Ctr. v. Smith*, 676 F.2d 1023, 1038 (5th Cir. 1982); *Jean v. Nelson*, 472 U.S. 846 (1985). Similarly, due process guarantees attach to the determinations of whether Respondent is entitled to withholding of removal under §243(h) of the INA. *Carvajal-Munoz v. INS*, 743 F.2d 562 (7th Cir. 1984); *Augustin v. Sava*, 735 F.2d 32, 37 (2d Cir. 1984); *Kovac v. INS*, 407 F.2d 102, 108 (9th Cir. 1969).

6. Moreover, as the federal courts have recognized, due process requires that Respondent be able to submit and substantiate [his/her] asylum claim, *Haitian Refugee Center*, at 1038, inasmuch as, "[T]he United States has by treaty, statute and regulations, manifested its intention of hearing the pleas of aliens who come to this country claiming a fear of being persecuted in their homelands." *Nunez v. Boldin*, 537 F. Supp. 578, 584 (S.D. Tex. 1982). Consequently, due process requires that Respondent have an opportunity to present [his/her] case with the assistance of counsel and have its merits fully judged.

WHEREFORE, Respondent prays the Immigration Judge allow substitution of Counsel and order these proceedings adjourned temporarily.

Respectfully submitted this ____ day of _________, 20__.

[Attorney]

[ADD CERTIFICATE OF SERVICE]

[Document Nos. 303–04]

MOTION TO WITHDRAW REPRESENTATION BEFORE THE EOIR

Description: These are sample motions requesting permission to be relieved from representation of a client before the Executive Office for Immigration Review.

Notes: After a Notice of Appearance (E-28) is filed with the immigration court, counsel is responsible for all aspects of the case before the immigration court until there is a final order in the case or counsel is relieved from representation by the immigration judge. Counsel is required to appear for all scheduled court appearances and is responsible for notifying the respondent of all future appearances. Until an order granting withdrawal is signed, counsel may still be responsible for the case and bear liability for preparing it.

A request to withdraw representation would be made when the client is not cooperating in preparing his or her case, which impacts counsel's effective representation, or the client expressly requests that counsel withdraw representation. If a practitioner does not document his or her efforts to assist the client, he or she runs the risk of a claim of ineffective assistance of counsel if the respondent eventually suffers negative consequences. A request to withdraw representation should be put in writing as would be done with any other formal motion.

The motion should include the reasons for withdrawing. If the problem is a lack of cooperation, then any correspondence to the client documenting the attorney's efforts to contact the client should be attached. The client should be informed in writing that counsel intends to withdraw from the case. Serve a copy of the motion on the client.

The attorney should appear at the next hearing if he or she has not received a response from the court dismissing the firm from the case. It is advised to include an Order to be signed by the immigration judge. In some jurisdictions, the immigration judge will not relieve counsel until the subsequent hearing and this is usually done in person.

Citations: 8 CFR §1003.17(b).

U.S. DEPARTMENT OF JUSTICE
EXECUTIVE OFFICE FOR IMMIGRATION REVIEW
IMMIGRATION COURT
[LOCATION]

IN THE MATTER OF:	)	
	)	
[Alien]	)	
A[Number]	)	IN REMOVAL PROCEEDINGS
	)	
Respondent	)	
______________________	)	

MOTION TO WITHDRAW REPRESENTATION AS ATTORNEY

I, **[Attorney]**, hereby request that this Honorable Court allow me to withdraw my appearance on behalf of the above-named Respondent, pursuant to 8 C.F.R. §§ 1003.17(b).

In support of this motion I state the following:

1. Respondent has a hearing set for **[date]** before this court.
2. I have been unable to contact Respondent through written or telephonic correspondence and have been informed by ______ of ______ that Respondent has left **[his/her]** home and that they have no knowledge of Respondent's whereabouts at present.
3. In lieu of contact from Respondent, Respondent's **[Husband/Wife/Relative, Name]**, has formally requested that I discontinue my representation of Respondent and formally withdraw my appearance as counsel in this matter.
4. I have written the Respondent at **[his/her]** last known address concerning this situation; however, I have received no response to date. (*See* Ex. 1, copy of letter sent to Respondent.)
5. To the best of my knowledge the Respondent's last known address is as stated on Form EOIR-28 and on Exhibit 1.

Respectfully submitted this ______ day of __________, 20__.

[Attorney]

[ADD CERTIFICATE OF SERVICE]

UNITED STATES DEPARTMENT OF JUSTICE
EXECUTIVE OFFICE FOR IMMIGRATION REVIEW
IMMIGRATION COURT
[LOCATION]

IN THE MATTER OF:)
)
[Alien])
A[Number]) MOTION TO WITHDRAW
) AS ATTORNEY OF RECORD
Respondent)
_______________________________)

The undersigned, **[Attorney]**, hereby requests that the Immigration Judge allow her to withdraw her appearance on behalf of the above named respondent pursuant to 8 C.F.R. §§ 1003.17(b) and 292.4(a). In support of this Motion, she hereby states as follows:

1. **[Alien]**, a citizen and national of Liberia, is married to a U.S. citizen, **[Wife]**. **[Wife]** filed an I-130 Petition on behalf of the Respondent which was to be adjudicated after interview of the couple by USCIS. The undersigned has appeared before this Court by telephone with the Respondent on a number of occasions in which the hearing was continued pending the outcome of the I-130 adjudication. The next Master Calendar Hearing is scheduled **[date]**.
2. The I-130 filed in **[Alien]**'s behalf was approved on **[date]**. A copy is attached hereto as Exhibit A.
3. Undersigned counsel advised the Respondent of the conditions of her representation. Respondent, however, has not complied with those conditions even though the undersigned has indicated that she would have no choice but to request to withdraw from this matter.
4. The undersigned has consistently advised the Respondent of the progress of this matter and the date and time of his next Master Calendar Hearing. The undersigned has advised the Respondent that he must appear for the hearing on **[date]** or risk an *in absentia* removal order. The undersigned will, however, be available in her office at the time of the hearing if the Court wishes to speak with her. She can be reached on that date at **[number]**.

WHEREFORE, the undersigned counsel respectfully requests that she be allowed to withdraw her appearance as attorney for the Respondent, **[Alien]**.

This the _____ day of ________, 20__.

[Attorney]

[ADD CERTIFICATE OF SERVICE]

UNITED STATES DEPARTMENT OF JUSTICE
EXECUTIVE OFFICE FOR IMMIGRATION REVIEW
IMMIGRATION COURT
[LOCATION]

IN THE MATTER OF:)
)
[Alien])
A[Number])
)
Respondent)
)

ORDER

Upon consideration of the request by counsel of record in this matter, **[Attorney]**, this Court hereby allows her Motion to Withdraw as Counsel.

This the _____ day of ________, 20__.

[Immigration Judge]

[Document Nos. 305–08]

MOTION FOR BOND HEARING/REDETERMINATION

Description: These are four versions of a simple bond motion requesting the immigration judge to schedule a hearing to set a bond or to review a bond determination by U.S. Immigration and Customs Enforcement (ICE).

Advantages: The motion is one of the prescribed procedures to schedule a hearing on a bond determination before an immigration judge. Most immigration judges prefer that a written motion be used to make scheduling of the hearing easier for clerical staff. However, oral motions for a bond hearing are proper under 8 CFR §1003.19. Bond hearings are considered separate and apart from the merits hearing on the case and most immigration judges do not record bond hearings. For this reason, it is recommended that a written motion be prepared with supporting documents. Bond hearings can also be requested even before formal proceedings have commenced. The detained individual or his or her representative may request a bond redetermination hearing by simply filing a motion for bond redetermination with the clerk of the court along with the warrant from ICE that sets forth ICE's original bond determination.

Limitations: Not all detained individuals are eligible for bond redetermination. The immigration judge has no jurisdiction to redetermine bond for arriving aliens or those subject to mandatory detention under INA §236(c). In those cases, a bond redetermination motion would not result in a bond hearing. If however, counsel is contesting that the client is properly charged as an arriving alien or improperly charged as being subject to a mandatory detention category, he or she can request a hearing to determine if the judge lacks jurisdiction to determine bond by filing a Motion Requesting a *Matter of Joseph* Hearing. See Document No. 316.

Notes: This motion need not include anything but a request for a bond hearing, but it is advisable to set out the reasons that bond should be granted or lowered, and should include supporting evidence. The two key factors the court will consider are danger to the community and flight risk. If counsel is requesting a second bond hearing, he or she must show a change in circumstances from the first bond hearing that warrants a subsequent bond hearing, and such request must be in writing.

Citations: 8 CFR §1003.19

U.S. DEPARTMENT OF JUSTICE
EXECUTIVE OFFICE FOR IMMIGRATION REVIEW
IMMIGRATION COURT
[LOCATION]

IN THE MATTER OF:	)	
	)	
[Alien]	)	
A[Number]	)	IN REMOVAL PROCEEDINGS
	)	
Respondent	)	
______________________________	)	

MOTION FOR BOND HEARING

Respondent, through undersigned counsel, requests that a bond hearing be set as soon as possible. Respondent is currently detained by U.S. Immigration and Customs Enforcement.

Respondent respectfully request that a bond hearing be set as soon as possible so that **[he/she]** can be provided an opportunity to demonstrate why **[he/she]** should be released on **[his/her]** own recognizance, or at the lowest possible bond.

RESPECTFULLY submitted this _____day of __________, 20___.

[Attorney]

[ADD CERTIFICATE OF SERVICE]

UNITED STATES DEPARTMENT OF JUSTICE
EXECUTIVE OFFICE FOR IMMIGRATION REVIEW
IMMIGRATION COURT
[LOCATION]

IN THE MATTER OF:	)	
	)	
[Alien]	)	
A[Number]	)	IN REMOVAL PROCEEDINGS
	)	
Respondent	)	
______________________	)	

MOTION FOR BOND HEARING

Comes now **[Attorney]**, counsel of record for the above referenced respondent, **[Alien]**, and pursuant to 8 C.F.R. § 1003.19, requests that a bond redetermination hearing in this matter be set as soon as possible. In support of this request, respondent shows as follows:

1. The respondent, **[Alien]** has been married to **[Spouse]**, a lawful permanent resident, since December 2000. The couple lives together in a home located at **[Address]**. They have a two and one-half year old U.S. citizen son together, **[Son]**. The Respondent's husband filed an I-130 in her behalf on or about January 27, 2004.

2. U.S. Immigration and Customs Enforcement (ICE) has alleged in the Notice to Appear, dated June 24, 2004, that **[Alien]** is "an alien present in the United States who has not been admitted or paroled" and "you falsely represented yourself to be a United States citizen for the following purpose or benefit: To obtain a United States passport." (See Exhibit 1.)

3. **[Alien]** has been charged in the U.S. District Court, Eastern District of North Carolina with a violation of 18 U.S.C. § 1542. She was granted pre-trial release by U.S. Magistrate Judge **[Judge]** on June 9, 2004. After appeal by the U.S. Attorney, U.S. District Court Judge **[Judge]** reaffirmed the Magistrate's release conditions, and specifically found as follows:

   > Based on the defendant's family status, former employment and community support, the court finds that the defendant is *not a flight risk nor a danger to the community.* (Emphasis added.) (See Exhibit 2.)

4. **[Alien]** secured the required $20,000.00 bond with her home (Exhibit 3). Due to the ICE detainer filed with the U.S. Marshal's office, ICE was notified upon the posting of the bond. **[Alien]** was picked up by ICE officers and is being detained in **[Location]**.

5. ICE officers have refused to set a bond.

6. A non-citizen detained and charged with being removable may be released on bond or parole. INA § 236. **[Alien]** is not subject to INA § 236(c) mandatory detention as she has no criminal convictions. The provisions of § 236(a) therefore apply in this matter; and pursuant to § 236(a), **[Alien]** should

not be detained by the Department of Homeland Security unless there is a risk she will abscond, she poses a danger to the community, or she poses a risk to national security. *Matter of Adeniji*, 22 I&N Dec. 1102 (BIA 1999); *Matter of Patel*, 15 I&N Dec. 666 (BIA 1976).

7. **[Alien]** has significant ties to the **[City and State]** community in which she lives. She and her husband are buying their home and regularly participate in church activities at Our Lady of Perpetual Help in **[City]** (Exhibits 4 and 5.) **[Alien]** has worked for a catering business in **[City]** for the past three years and she and her husband file taxes together (Exhibits 6 and 7). Aside from the charge at issue (there is no conviction), she has no criminal history of any kind. As evidenced by the attached letters, she is well respected in the community. (Exhibits 8.)

8. **[Alien]**'s most important community ties are to her husband and son. Her son, **[Son]**, has now been without his mother for over two months. As indicated in the Affidavit of the child's father,

> Although I am devastated by my wife being detained and not being with us, **[Son]** is suffering the most. He cannot understand any of what is happening, as at least I can. He is sleeping with me while his mother has been gone and he wakes up in the middle of every night pushing me away and asking for mama. He also roams around the house at times during the day looking and calling for her. (Exhibit 9.)

Further, although **[Son's]** grandmother has helped to care for him over the past two months, she is preparing to return to Mexico for approximately half a year.

9. While she is waiting for removal proceedings to go forward, **[Alien]** needs to be able to consult with her undersigned attorney, **[Attorney]**, regarding her defense to the criminal charge. **[Attorney]**, who has been appointed as **[Alien]**'s Public Defender, has offices in **[Location]**, a short 40 minute drive from **[City]**. **[Location 2]** is more than a five hour drive from **[Attorney's]** offices. She also needs to be available to consult with counsel regarding the removal charges.

10. **[Alien]** has no intention of fleeing from immigration authorities if she is released from detention prior to the resolution of removal proceedings. All of her ties are to her home in **[City]**. She has no history of flight even though questioned by federal authorities months prior to the arrest. She wants only to return home and care for her two and a half year old son, receive support from her husband and community, and have access to counsel to assist her with the criminal and immigration charges. Furthermore, she has pledged to appear in the criminal proceedings in **[Location]** and has posted a $20,000 bond secured by her home. **[Alien]** is not a threat to national security, is not likely to abscond and is not a poor bail risk.

WHEREFORE, Respondent requests that she be scheduled for a bond redetermination hearing before an Immigration Judge at the earliest available date. Respectfully submitted, this the______ day of __________, ______.

By:______________________________

[Attorney]

[ADD CERTIFICATE OF SERVICE]

UNITED STATES DEPARTMENT OF JUSTICE
EXECUTIVE OFFICE FOR IMMIGRATION REVIEW
OFFICE OF THE IMMIGRATION JUDGE
[LOCATION]

IN THE MATTER OF:	)	
	)	
[Alien]	)	
A[Number]	)	IN REMOVAL PROCEEDINGS
	)	
Respondent	)	
______________________	)	

MOTION TO REDETERMINE BOND

Respondent, **[Alien]**, by and through counsel, **[Attorney]**, hereby moves this Honorable Court to redetermine bond in this matter. As grounds for this Motion, Counsel states as follows:

1. Respondent is a native and citizen of Cambodia who entered the United States as a K-1 fiancée of **[Fiancé]**, a United States citizen. The couple already established the bona fides of their initial engagement.
2. Although the couple had some limited marital difficulties in relation to **[Alien's]** failure to disclose information to his wife regarding a child born out of wedlock, and his less than stellar employment and financial history, the couple resolved to continue their relationship and did lawfully enter into marriage. The couple cohabitated until her detention and in all respects lived as husband and wife.
3. Despite apparent allegations that **[Spouse]** was extorting money from Respondent to continue his support of her application for permanent residence, counsel has investigated the matter further and will present at hearing both written and testimonial evidence in support of the bona fides of the marriage.
4. This information was unavailable at the last hearing due to errors made by prior counsel and the failure of **[Spouse]** to adequately communicate his position. Specifically, the Court's apparent concern that **[Spouse]** intended to testify under oath as to his complicity in a marriage fraud scheme was appropriate but unfounded.
5. **[Spouse]** submits his affidavit with this motion; he will be available to testify at hearing.
6. **[Individual]** will appear as a witness; he was unable to testify at the prior hearing; **[Individual]** has relevant testimony as he is related to the mother of **[Spouse]'s** out of wedlock child and a family friend of both **[Spouse]**, his ex-girlfriend, and Respondent's aunt.
7. Respondent will submit additional evidence of character and bona fides at hearing.

WHEREFORE, in light of the significant developments in evidence available in this matter since the initial bond hearing, Respondent respectfully requests reconsideration of release on bond.

DATED: _______________, 20___

Respectfully submitted,

[Attorney]
ATTORNEY FOR RESPONDENT

[ADD CERTIFICATE OF SERVICE]

UNITED STATES DEPARTMENT OF JUSTICE
EXECUTIVE OFFICE FOR IMMIGRATION REVIEW
OFFICE OF THE IMMIGRATION JUDGE
[LOCATION]

IN THE MATTER OF:	)	
	)	
[Alien]	)	
A[Number]	)	IN REMOVAL PROCEEDINGS
	)	
Respondent	)	
______________________	)	

MOTION FOR BOND REDETERMINATION AND BRIEF IN SUPPORT OF BOND REDETERMINATION

Respondent, through counsel, moves the Immigration Judge to grant a personal recognizance bond or, in the alternative, low cash, bond to ensure Respondent's appearance at future proceedings, and to secure his release from custody.

In support of his motion, Respondent, through the undersigned counsel, asserts the following:

1. On Thursday, June 16, 2005, Respondent was taken into custody by Immigration & Customs Enforcement (ICE) officials. He is currently being held without bond at the ICE detention facility in **[Location]**.
2. A Notice to Appear (NTA) was issued on December 31, 2003, setting forth the allegations as to why Respondent is removable pursuant to INA §212(a)(6)(i).
3. Specifically, the NTA alleges that Respondent is subject to removal as an alien present in the United States without having been admitted or paroled. There are no other allegations on the Notice to Appear.
4. The standard for setting an immigration bond was declared in *Matter of Patel*, 15 I&N Dec. 666 (BIA 1976):

> An alien generally is not and should not be detained or required to post bond except on a finding that he is a threat to the national security, *Carlson v. Landon*, 243 U.S. 524 (1952), or that he is a poor bail risk, *Matter of Moise*, 12 I&N Dec. 102 (BIA 1967); *Matter of S–Y–L–*, 9 I&N Dec. 575 (BIA 1962).

This standard has been reaffirmed consistently, without modification.

> We have held that an alien generally should not be detained or required to post bond pending a determination of deportability unless there is a finding that he is a threat to the national security or is a poor bail risk. *Matter of Andrade*, 19 I&N Dec. 488 (BIA 1987), citing *Matter of Patel*, 15 I&N Dec. 66 (BIA 1976).

The standard was followed in *Matter of Shaw*, 17 I&N Dec.177, 178 (BIA 1979); *Matter of Vea*, 18 I&N Dec.171 (BIA 1981) and *Matter of Spiliopoulos*, 16 I&N Dec. 561, 563 (BIA 1978).

5. It is within the discretion of the Attorney General to release an alien, who is not subject to mandatory detention, on bond. INA §236(a)(2)(A). The Immigration Judge has authority and jurisdiction to re-determine bond and release an alien if the alien is not precluded from release under section 236(c) of the Immigration and Nationality Act. 8 U.S.C. § 1226(c). Respondent is not subject to mandatory detention under INA § 236(c).

6. Respondent should be released on a low bond. He does not pose a high flight risk and will not fail to appear before the Immigration Court when required to do so. He has not been convicted of a crime of violence, and he presents no threat to the safety or security of the community. Given the charges listed on the NTA, holding Respondent without bond is disproportionate.

7. In determining the necessity for, and the amount of bond, such factors as a stable employment history, length of residence in the community, the existence of family ties, a record of non-appearance at court proceedings, and previous criminal or immigration law violations are properly considered. *Matter of Spiliopoulos*, 16 I&N Dec. 561, citing *Matter of Patel*, 15 I&N 666 (BIA 1976); *Matter of San Martin*, 15 I&N Dec. 167 (BIA 1974); *Matter of Moise*, 12 I&N Dec. 102; *Matter of S–Y–L–*, 9 I&N Dec. 575 (BIA 1962). Identical standards have been reaffirmed and adopted consistently. See *Matter of Andrade*, 19 I&N Dec. at 489.

8. Respondent does not have a record of any non-appearances at any court proceedings.

9. Furthermore, to this date there is no evidence that Respondent presents a threat to national security.

10. Respondent's family ties in the United States are substantial. His mother, stepfather and siblings are in **[Location]**, as are his aunts, uncles, and cousins.

11. Respondent had a criminal case pending in **[Location]**. The charges in this case were dismissed after trial and the Respondent was acquitted of all charges. *(Exhibit 1, Court Dispositions, **[Location]**.)*

12. At the conclusion of his case, Respondent was transferred to the ICE Detention Facility in **[Location]**, where he is currently being held.

13. Until being taken into custody, Respondent lived with his parents in **[Location]**, on whom he has always depended for care and support. Respondent has severe Cerebral Palsy (CP), and requires a great deal of assistance in his daily life. *(Exhibit 2, Acceptance Letter, **[Name of]** Health Care Program for Children with Special Needs; Letter from **[Witness]**, Cognitive Needs Teacher & Denise Jones Ed.S., School Psychologist; Letter from Respondent's cousin; Letter from **[Witness]** teacher, **[High School]**.)* Please also see *Tutorial for Cerebral Palsy,* University of Virginia Health System *(Exhibit 3)*

14. Although Respondent faces limitations as a result of his condition, he graduated with his class from Battle Mountain High School in 1999. *(Exhibit 4, Official Transcript, **[High School]**.)* Furthermore, he has chosen to rise above his physical and mental limitations to hold a job in the community. *(Exhibit 5, Letters from **[Witness]**, **[Witness]**, and **[Witness]**.)*

15. Respondent is a benefit to his community and well-loved by his friends, co-workers, and teachers in **[Location]**. This motion is supported by numerous character references for Respondent that speak to the fact that he is well-respected and trustworthy. *(Exhibit 6)*

16. Respondent does not have the ability to drive, nor the resources to travel by any other means. He also requires a great deal of care from his family, who would not wish him to travel any great distance on his own. Therefore, Respondent does not pose an increased flight risk or a greater threat to the community, or raise any of the other issues in *Matter of Patel*, 15 I&N Dec. 666 (BIA 1976).

17. Respondent has an extremely caring and supportive network of family and friends who will look after him and ensure that he makes all of his future court appearances.
18. Holding Respondent without bond is inappropriate considering he has not committed a crime of violence and since there is no evidence that he is a threat to national security or that he is a flight risk.

WHEREFORE, Respondent prays the court to order his release from ICE custody for a low cash pending completion of removal proceedings.

Respectfully submitted,

[Attorney]

Dated this _____ day of ______, 20__

[ADD CERTIFICATE OF SERVICE]

[Document No. 309]
MOTION FOR CHANGE OF VENUE

Description: The motion is to request a change of venue in an immigration proceeding.

Advantages: A change of venue may be advantageous especially where the matter is heard in the jurisdiction in which the alien and/or critical witnesses reside. A new venue may also reduce the cost of litigation for the alien.

Limitations: The decision to change venue is discretionary. The respondent has the burden of demonstrating good cause. No change of venue shall be granted without identification of a fixed street address, including city, state, and zip code, where the respondent may be reached for further hearing notification.

Notes: Practitioners should consider seeking a change of venue where the alien has moved to a new jurisdiction after the commencement of proceedings or where the majority of critical witnesses reside in one jurisdiction.

Citations: 8 CFR §1003.20.

UNITED STATES DEPARTMENT OF JUSTICE
EXECUTIVE OFFICE FOR IMMIGRATION REVIEW
IMMIGRATION COURT
[LOCATION]

IN THE MATTER OF:	)	
	)	
[Alien]	)	
A[Number]	)	MOTION TO CHANGE VENUE
	)	
Respondent	)	
______________________________	)	

Respondent, **[Alien]**, by and through counsel, **[Attorney]**, hereby requests this Court to change the venue of these proceedings to the Immigration Court in Atlanta, Georgia, pursuant to 8 C.F.R. § 1003.20(b); and in support thereof, Respondent shows unto the Court as follows:

1. Respondent is a native and citizen of Mexico and lawful permanent resident of the United States.

2. Respondent has a Master Calendar Hearing scheduled in this court on **[date]** at **[time]**.

3. Respondent currently resides at **[Address]**. His telephone number is **[number].** He owns and operates a business in Chapel Hill, NC, called **[Name of Business]**.

4. Respondent admits the factual allegations numbered 1 through 3 in the Notice to Appear dated September 14, 2003. Respondent was personally served with the Notice to Appear on September 14, 2003, after arrival at the **[Airport]**. The admitted allegations are as follows:

   1. are not a citizen or a National of the United States.

   2. are a Native and citizen of Mexico.

   3. are ineligible for admission to the United States because you were, on May 26, 1989, convicted in the 17th Circuit Court at Grand Rapids, Michigan for the offense of breaking and entering, with intent, in violation of MCL 750.110-A, a crime involving moral tupitude *[sic]*.

[**[Alien]** was found guilty on April 5, 1989, upon a plea of guilt. *See* Exhibit A.]

5. Respondent concedes the charge of removal in the Notice to Appear, stated as follows:

   Section 212(a)(2)(A)(i)(I) of the Immigration and Nationality Act, as amended, in that you are an alien who has been convicted of, or who admits having committed, or who admits committing acts which constitute the essential elements of a crime involving moral turpitude (other than a purely political offense).

6. In case removal becomes necessary, Respondent designates Mexico as the country of removal.

7. Respondent's status was adjusted to lawful permanent resident on January 6, 1987. (*See* Exhibit B.) As stated above, he entered a plea of guilty to the criminal offense charged. He therefore is eligible to apply for a waiver under former Section 212(c) of the INA pursuant to *I.N.S v. St. Cyr*, 533 U.S. 289 (2001).

8. The undersigned counsel has discussed this motion with Assistant Chief Counsel, **[Government Attorney]**. **[Government Attorney]** does not oppose the change of venue.

9. This motion is being made for good cause and not for purposes of delay.

WHEREFORE, based on the foregoing and for good cause shown, Respondent respectfully requests that venue of these proceedings be changed to Atlanta, Georgia.

This the _____ day of _________, 20__.

[Attorney]

[ADD CERTIFICATE OF SERVICE]

UNITED STATES DEPARTMENT OF JUSTICE
EXECUTIVE OFFICE FOR IMMIGRATION REVIEW
IMMIGRATION COURT
[LOCATION]

IN THE MATTER OF:)
)
[Alien])
A[Number])
)
Respondent)
________________________________)

ORDER

Upon consideration of the Motion by Respondent to change venue of these proceedings to Atlanta, Georgia and it appearing that Respondent has shown good cause for the change of venue pursuant to 8 C.F.R. §1003.20.

IT IS HEREBY ORDERED that venue in this matter shall be changed to Atlanta, Georgia.

This the _____ day of _____________, 20__.

[Immigration Judge]

[County]
NORTH CAROLINA

VERIFICATION AND AFFIDAVIT

I, **[Alien]**, being first duly sworn, hereby depose and state as follows:

1. I have read the foregoing Motion to Change Venue and know the content thereof and that the same is true of my own knowledge except as to those matters and things stated upon information and belief and as to those matters, I believe them to be true.

2. I am a native and citizen of Mexico and lawful permanent resident of the United States.

3. I currently live at **[Address]**. My telephone number is **[number]**.

4. I was personally served with a Notice to Appear on September 14, 2003, after arrival at the **[Airport]**.

5. I admit the following:

   A. I am not a citizen or a national of the United States.

   B. I am a native and citizen of Mexico.

   C. I was, on May 26, 1989, convicted in the 17th Circuit Court at Grand Rapids, Michigan for the offense of breaking and entering, with intent, in violation of MCL 750.110-A, a crime involving moral turpitude. I was found guilty on April 5, 1989 upon a plea of guilt.

6. I concede the charge of removal in the Notice to Appear, stated as follows:

7. Section 212(a)(2)(A)(i)(I) of the Immigration and Nationality Act, as amended, in that you are an alien who has been convicted of, or who admits having committed, or who admits committing acts which constitute the essential elements of a crime involving moral turpitude (other than a purely political offense).

8. In case removal becomes necessary, I designate Mexico as the country of removal.

9. I last entered the United States by flying into **[Airport]** on September 14, 2003. I have lived in Chapel Hill, North Carolina for about the past 9 years and have owned a business, **[Name of Business]**, for about the past 5 years.

10. My attorney and all potential witnesses who may testify for me during removal proceedings reside in North Carolina. I have no connection to **[City, State]** other than the entry on September 14, 2003.

11. I have directed my attorney to request that removal proceedings be moved to Atlanta, Georgia.

This the ______ day of ___________, 20__.

[Alien]

Sworn to and subscribed before me

this the ____ day of _____________, 20__.

____
Notary Public

My Commission expires:

[Document No. 310]

MOTION TO RECALENDAR HEARING AND FOR CHANGE OF VENUE

Description: The motion is to request that a hearing be calendared by the immigration court in proceedings previously administratively closed and venue be changed.

Advantages: The respondent now has relief available in deportation proceedings so needs to have a hearing scheduled in order to proceed to apply for such relief. A change of venue is required as respondent has moved to a different area of the country since the prior close of proceedings.

Limitations: The motion to recalendar must be filed in the venue where the last hearing took place. The decision to change venue is discretionary. The respondent has the burden of demonstrating good cause. No change of venue shall be granted without identification of a fixed street address, including city, state, and zip code, where the respondent may be reached for further hearing notification.

Notes: Practitioners should consider seeking a change of venue where the alien has moved to a new jurisdiction after the commencement of proceedings or where the majority of critical witnesses reside in one jurisdiction.

Citations: 8 CFR §§1003.18(a) and 1003.20.

UNITED STATES DEPARTMENT OF JUSTICE
EXECUTIVE OFFICE FOR IMMIGRATION REVIEW
IMMIGRATION COURT
[LOCATION]

IN THE MATTER OF:)
)
[Alien])
A[Number])
)
Respondent)
_________________)

MOTION TO RECALENDAR DEPORTATION HEARING AND CHANGE VENUE

Respondent, **[Alien]**, by and through counsel, **[Attorney]**, hereby requests this Court to recalendar a Master Calendar Hearing in Deportation Proceedings and change the venue of these proceedings to the Immigration Court in Atlanta, Georgia, pursuant to 8 C.F.R. § 1003.20(b). In support thereof, Respondent shows unto the Court as follows:

1. Respondent is a native and citizen of El Salvador.
2. As stated in the attached Affidavit of the Respondent (Exhibit 1), the Respondent entered the United States without inspection in or about April, 1986. On or about September 16, 1988, while living in Westbury, New York, the Respondent applied for political asylum, assisted by a "notario."
3. The address given on the asylum application was **[Address]**. The Respondent never lived at that address and was unaware that it was the address submitted. At the time of the asylum application, he was unable to read, write or understand English. His correct address was **[Address]**.
4. Since the time of the asylum application, a legal representative obtained a copy of the Respondent's immigration file. For the first time, **[Alien]** learned that the notice of the asylum interview, asylum denial and Order to Show Cause had been issued. He never personally received any of these documents from legacy INS or the Immigration Court. The documents apparently were sent to **[Address]**. (See Exhibits 2 through 4.)
5. On July 12, 1989, the Immigration Judge ordered that due to failure of the Respondent to appear at his deportation hearing on that date, the case be "administratively closed until such time as a motion to recalendar is filed with this court." (Exhibit 5.)
6. Pursuant to former 8 C.F.R. § 242.1(c), service of the Order to Show Cause could be accomplished by either personal service or routine service. However, if routine service was used and the respondent did not appear for the hearing, personal service was required. As stated above, the Respondent did not receive personal service of the Order to Show Cause.

7. **[Alien]** currently resides at **[Address],** and he is employed in **[City, State]**. His telephone number is **[Number]**.
8. Respondent's undersigned counsel of record has offices in **[City, State]**.
9. **[Alien]** was married to **[Spouse]**, a U.S. citizen, on October 10, 1998. An I-130 petition was approved on September 14, 2000 (see copy attached as Exhibit 6). **[Alien]**'s application for adjustment of status, however, was denied on July 7, 2003, due to the pending deportation proceedings. (See copy of adjustment denial attached as Exhibit 7.)
10. Once a hearing in deportation proceedings is recalendared, **[Alien]** will pursue adjustment of status in Immigration Court on the basis of the approved I-130. For purposes of adjustment of status, **[Alien]** is "grandfathered" under INA § 245(i).
11. **[Alien]** and his wife have two U.S. citizen children together: **[Child]** born January 30, 2001; and **[Child]**, born September 19, 2002. Because of the stress of these immigration issues, **[Alien]** and his wife have experienced some difficulty in their marriage and are currently are not living together. They are still married and do not have a separation agreement.

WHEREFORE, based on the foregoing and for good cause shown, Respondent respectfully requests that his Master Calendar Hearing be recalendared and that venue be changed to Atlanta, Georgia so that he may pursue adjustment of status before the Court.

This the _____ day of ___________, 20__.

[Attorney]

[ADD CERTIFICATE OF SERVICE]

EXHIBIT LIST

[ALIEN], [A NUMBER], RESPONDENT

1. Affidavit of the Respondent
2. Notice of Asylum Interview
3. Denial of Asylum Application
4. Order to Show Cause
5. Immigration Court Order of July 12, 1989
6. I-130 Approval Notice
7. Denial of Adjustment of Status

UNITED STATES DEPARTMENT OF JUSTICE
EXECUTIVE OFFICE FOR IMMIGRATION REVIEW
IMMIGRATION COURT
[LOCATION]

IN THE MATTER OF:)
)
[Alien])
A[Number])
)
Respondent)
______________________________)

ORDER

Upon consideration of the Motion by Respondent to recalendar his Master Calendar Hearing in Deportation Proceedings and Change Venue to Atlanta, Georgia, and it appearing that Respondent has shown good cause for the change of venue pursuant to 8 C.F.R. § 1003.20(b);

IT IS HEREBY ORDERED that venue shall be changed to Atlanta, Georgia, for recalendaring of Respondent's hearing in Deportation Proceedings.

This the _____ day of ________, 20____.

[Immigration Judge]

[Document Nos. 311–13]

MOTION TO CONTINUE MERITS/MASTER CALENDAR HEARING

Description:

The following sample motions can be filed with the immigration court for a continuance of a merits or master calendar hearing. The most useful of these motions will likely be the "*Garcia*" continuance: the Board of Immigration Appeals, in *Matter of Garcia*, 16 I&N Dec. 653 (BIA 1978), and *Matter of Arthur*, 20 I&N Dec. 475 (BIA 1992), held that it is appropriate for an immigration judge to continue a master calendar hearing while an I-130 is pending before INS (or, now, USCIS), *if* the marriage occurred prior to proceedings. In *Matter of Velarde*, 23 I&N Dec. 253 (BIA 2002), the BIA held that a marriage after initiation of proceedings may also establish the basis of seeking a continuance, *if* the parties can prove the marriage is bona fide.

Advantages:

The bottom line is this—practitioners are not always ready to proceed with cases at the scheduled hearing. A variety of intervening factors, *e.g.*, marriage, job loss, change of country conditions, unavailability of witnesses, all can lead to a need for more time to prepare for the hearing. Generally, motions to continue filed in a timely manner according to local rules (and not abusively) are granted.

Limitations:

The motion intended for political asylum is limited to political asylum relief situations. In the instance of the respondent seeking additional time for new counsel, if the foreign national has changed attorneys more than once, the immigration judge may deny this motion. Further, changing attorneys on the eve of a merits hearing will generally not get a continuance.

Notes:

Motions for continuance need to be filed as early as possible (usually at least 10 days prior to a hearing). Moreover, it is helpful to request a specific amount of time for the continuance or a date certain for the new hearing, and to seek the approval of ICE counsel when doing so.

UNITED STATES DEPARTMENT JUSTICE
EXECUTIVE OFFICE FOR IMMIGRATION REVIEW
OFFICE OF THE IMMIGRATION JUDGE
[LOCATION]

IN THE MATTER OF:	)	
	)	
[Alien]	)	
A[Number]	)	IN REMOVAL PROCEEDINGS
	)	Next Individual Hearing Date:
Respondent	)	**[Date/Time]**
______________________________	)	

MOTION TO CONTINUE MERITS HEARING

Respondent, through undersigned counsel, moves to reschedule the individual hearing set for **[date/time]** for the reason that Respondent is awaiting a final decision of USCIS on his wife's Petition for Asylee Relative, Form I-730. (Ex. 1, copy of Receipt Notice.) Respondent and his wife have been common law spouses since September 15, 1992. (Ex. 2, copy of Certificate of Common Law Marriage.) They have two children together. If USCIS approves this Petition (Form I-730), Respondent will be considered an asylee and this Court will be able to terminate this matter without the need for a formal hearing on the merits of the case. If USCIS denies this Petition, this hearing could then go forward. However, given the likelihood that this Petition will be approved, it would seem a waste of judicial resources and the time of counsel for ICE and the Respondent to go forward with the merit hearing at this time.

A prior continuance of the merit hearing permitted Respondent time to obtain the certificate of common law marriage, thus confirming that Respondent was married prior to the initiation of removal proceedings to an individual eligible to petition for him to remain lawfully in the United States. This request is much like the situation where a respondent is married to a U.S. citizen prior to initiation proceedings (where an immediately available immigrant visa would likely be approved) and continuances are granted for USCIS to adjudicate the Form I-130. See Matter of Garcia, 16 I. & N. Dec. 623 (BIA 1978) (stating an immigration judge may grant a continuance to permit the Service to adjudicate an I-130 petition); see also Matter of Arthur, 20 I. & N. Dec. 475 (BIA 1992). If the Form I-730 is approved, this would obviate the need for a hearing on the merits in this case. This in turn will save valuable Court time. Respondent, who is not detained, respectfully requests that the Court reset this Individual Hearing to a time frame slightly longer than that anticipated for adjudication of the Form I-730 (after **[date]**).

RESPECTFULLY submitted this ____ day of _____, 20___.

[Attorney]

[ADD CERTIFICATE OF SERVICE]

UNITED STATES DEPARTMENT JUSTICE
EXECUTIVE OFFICE FOR IMMIGRATION REVIEW
OFFICE OF THE IMMIGRATION JUDGE
[LOCATION]

IN THE MATTER OF:	)	
	)	
[Alien]	)	
A[Number]	)	IN REMOVAL PROCEEDINGS
	)	Next Individual Hearing Date:
Respondent	)	**[Date/Time]**
______________________________	)	

MOTION TO CONTINUE MERITS HEARING

Pursuant to 8 C.F.R. § 1003.29, Respondent, through undersigned counsel, hereby moves the court to re-schedule **[his/her]** merits hearing that is currently scheduled for **[date/time]**. Respondent has recently retained new local counsel to assist with this case, and local counsel needs additional time to prepare for this complex asylum hearing. A continuance of the merit hearing will allow for Respondent's counsel to gather additional supporting documentation, which, in turn, will save valuable Court time.

Therefore, Respondent, who is not detained, respectfully requests that the current hearing be continued and that a new merits hearing date be set in this matter.

RESPECTFULLY submitted this _____ day of _________, 20___.

[Attorney]

[ADD CERTIFICATE OF SERVICE]

UNITED STATES DEPARTMENT OF JUSTICE
EXECUTIVE OFFICE FOR IMMIGRATION REVIEW
IMMIGRATION COURT
[LOCATION]

IN THE MATTER OF:)
)
[Alien])
A[Number])
)
Respondent)
_______________________________)

"*GARCIA*" MOTION TO CONTINUE MASTER CALENDAR HEARING

Respondent, by and through the undersigned counsel, respectfully moves this Court to continue the Master Calendar Hearing scheduled **[date and time]** pursuant to 8 C.F.R. § 1003.29, and shows unto the court as follows:

1. Respondent is a citizen and national of **[Country]**. He was served with a Notice to Appear dated **[date]** alleging that he entered the United States on or about August 9, 2001, as a nonimmigrant student but did not attend the proper institution. As such, he was charged with removal based on INA § 237(a)(1)(C)(i) for failure to maintain or comply with the conditions of the nonimmigrant status under which he was admitted.

2. Said Notice to Appear was issued and served as a result of Respondent's appearance for registration in Newark, New Jersey, under "Call-in Special Registration" under the National Security Entry-Exit Registration System (NSEERS).

3. Previously, on April 10, 2002, **[Alien]** married **[Spouse]**, a U.S. citizen. The couple resides together at **[Address]**. Upon information and belief, they filed an I-130 and I-485 on or about May 2, 2002, with (legacy) Immigration and Naturalization Service. (See Exhibit A, response to status inquiry.)

4. **[Alien]** and his wife were interviewed by the Charlotte, NC (legacy) INS sub-office in late 2002. **[Alien]** received a notice to be fingerprinted and was fingerprinted in July 2003. They have not yet received a decision on the I-485.

5. Upon inquiry by counsel, USCIS in Charlotte advised that **[Alien's]** file had been transferred to Atlanta in June 2003.

6. Respondent requests a continuance of his Master Calendar Hearing so that the I-130 pending in this matter may be adjudicated and the I-485 considered or remanded by this Court. As the spouse of a U.S. citizen who was last admitted after being inspected, **[Alien]** is prima facie eligible for adjustment of status under INA § 245 once the I-130 is approved by USCIS. **[Alien]** was married and the application for adjustment of status was filed prior to the initiation of removal proceedings. Pursuant to *Matter of Garcia*, 16 I. & N. Dec. 653 (BIA 1978) and *Matter of Arthur*, 20 I. & N. Dec. 475 (BIA 1992), it is appropriate for the Court to continue proceedings so that the I-130 may be adjudicated by USCIS.

7. This motion is made for good cause and not for purposes of delay.

WHEREFORE, Respondent, respectfully requests that this Court continue his Master Calendar Hearing so that the adjudication of the I-130 filed by his U.S. citizen wife may be completed.

This the _____ day of __________, 20____.

By:________________________________

[Attorney]

[ADD CERTIFICATE OF SERVICE]

UNITED STATES DEPARTMENT OF JUSTICE
EXECUTIVE OFFICE FOR IMMIGRATION REVIEW
IMMIGRATION COURT
ATLANTA, GEORGIA

IN THE MATTER OF:)
)
[Alien])
A[Number])
)
Respondent)
______________________________)

ORDER

Upon Motion by Respondent in this matter for a continuance of his Master Calendar Hearing scheduled January 25, 2004, and upon showing of good cause,

IT IS HEREBY ORDERED that the Master Calendar Hearing shall be continued until **[date and time]**.

This the ____ day of _____________, 20__.

[Immigration Judge]

[Document No. 314]

MOTION TO SET HEARING BEFORE IMMIGRATION JUDGE

Description: The motion is to request that a hearing be calendared by the immigration court in removal proceedings.

Advantages: If a respondent is being detained, or has a need to present his or her meritorious claim to the court as soon as possible, it may be in his or her best interest to request the court to schedule a hearing on the merits expeditiously.

Limitations: The time frame in which the court will calendar hearings is in the discretion of the court. 8 CFR §1003.18(a).

Notes: This motion is a practical device that *may* expedite the scheduling of hearings in some immigration courts.

UNITED STATES DEPARTMENT OF JUSTICE
EXECUTIVE OFFICE FOR IMMIGRATION REVIEW
OFFICE OF THE IMMIGRATION JUDGE
[LOCATION]

IN THE MATTER OF:)
)
[Alien])
A[Number]) IN REMOVAL PROCEEDINGS
)
Respondent)
)

RESPONDENT'S MOTION TO SET HEARING

Respondent, **[Alien]**, by and through his attorney, **[Attorney]**, respectfully moves this Court to set a hearing in this matter.

As grounds for this Motion, Respondent states as follows:

1. Respondent was taken into custody by ICE on May 27, 2004.
2. Respondent wishes to expedite this matter, both in terms of a review of the initial custody determination and resolution of the merits of the case.

WHEREFORE, Respondent respectfully requests this Court grant this Motion to set a hearing in this matter.

[Datcd:]

Respectfully submitted,

[Attorney]

[ADD CERTIFICATE OF SERVICE]

[Document No. 315]

MOTION TO WAIVE MASTER CALENDAR HEARING AND SCHEDULE INDIVIDUAL CALENDAR HEARING

Description: Similar to the motion to set hearing before the immigration judge also included herein, the purpose of this motion is to avoid waiting for the master calendar hearing to be scheduled and completed and immediately move to the hearing on the merits of the case.

Advantages: In some jurisdictions, the time between a master calendar hearing and individual hearing may be up to a year or more. Therefore, it may be in the best interest of the respondent to move forward as quickly as possible to a resolution of the case and hearing on his or her claim for relief.

Limitations: Many courts will require a previous determination or admission of deportability and sufficient explanation of grounds for relief before waiving a master calendar hearing. If a plea regarding the facts alleged and ground(s) of removal charged has not previously been made, such a plea should be a part of the motion. In some courts, an affidavit by the respondent regarding the plea also will be required. Evidence of eligibility for the relief being sought also may be required by the particular court. Because the respondent will forgo the opportunity during the master calendar hearing for specific instructions from the immigration judge regarding the relief being sought, counsel must be thoroughly familiar with the local immigration court procedures for that relief. The time frame in which the court will calendar hearings is in the discretion of the court.

Notes: This motion is a practical device that may expedite the scheduling of the merits hearing.

U.S. DEPARTMENT OF JUSTICE
EXECUTIVE OFFICE FOR IMMIGRATION REVIEW
IMMIGRATION COURT
[LOCATION]

IN THE MATTER OF:)
)
[Alien])
A[Number])
)
Respondent)
)

MOTION TO WAIVE MASTER CALENDAR HEARING AND SCHEDULE INDIVIDUAL CALENDAR HEARING

COMES NOW, Respondent, **[Alien]**, by and through the undersigned counsel, **[Attorney]**, and moves this Court to waive the Master Calendar Hearing scheduled **[date]** and schedule the Individual Calendar Hearing to consider Respondent's I-485, Application for Adjustment of Status. In support of this motion, Respondent shows unto the Court as follows:

1. **[Alien]** is a native and citizen of Pakistan. Upon information and belief (a copy of the record is not available at this time),[1] **[Alien]** applied for asylum soon after entering the United States in 1994. The application ultimately was denied by the Immigration Court in New York and **[Alien]** appealed that decision to the Board of Immigration Appeals. The Immigration Court apparently did allow some period of time for voluntary departure.

2. By summary decision of January 27, 2003, the Board of Immigration Appeals affirmed the Immigration Judge's decision. In accordance with the decision in *Matter of Chouliaris*, 16 I. & N. Dec. 168 (BIA 1977), the Board allowed the Respondent 30 days voluntary departure until February 26, 2003.

3. **[Alien]** married a U.S. citizen, **[Spouse]**, on December 4, 1998, and the couple has lived together in **[City, State]** since that date. The marriage took place after the order of the Immigration Court denying the asylum application.

4. **[Spouse]** filed an I-130 Petition on or about February 9, 1999; the I-130 was approved by the Charlotte INS (formerly) Sub-office in Charlotte, North Carolina on February 26, 2003. (*See* Exhibit A.) Voluntary departure was extended by Charlotte INS until April 25, 2003. (*See* Exhibit B.)

5. Upon Motion to the Board of Immigration Appeals to reopen the Deportation Proceedings to consider an I-485, the Board granted said Motion to Reopen on April 8, 2003. (*See* Exhibit C.)

[1] **[Previous Counsel]**, the attorney who previously represented **[Alien]** before the Immigration Court in New York and initially before the Board of Immigration Appeals, reportedly moved from New York to California. Some time after the move, **[Previous Counsel]** passed away. **[Previous Counsel's]** New York employer does not have a copy of **[Alien]**'s file regarding the deportation proceedings and the undersigned counsel has not yet been able to locate old files of **[Previous Counsel]**. **[Alien]** does not have a copy of the documents related to the prior proceedings.

6. Venue initially was set in New York, the venue of the prior proceedings; venue was changed to Atlanta by Order of the New York Immigration Court on April 11, 2003. (*See* Exhibit D.)

7. The Master Calendar Hearing has been scheduled by the Atlanta Immigration Court for September 11, 2003 at 9:00 a.m. (*See* Exhibit E.)

8. The I-485 was previously submitted to the Board of Immigration Appeals with the Motion to Reopen. It therefore should be included in the remanded Record of Proceedings. The INS (formerly) New York District Counsel's Office was served with a copy. A copy of the I-485 is attached for the convenient reference of the Court and Atlanta District Counsel. (*See* Exhibit F.)

9. Although **[Alien]** entered the U.S. without inspection, he is eligible to apply for adjustment of status under INA § 245(i). His adjustment would be "grandfathered" due to the I-130 having been filed in 1999.

10. This Motion is being made so that the Individual Calendar Hearing may be scheduled as soon as possible. Deportability was determined during prior proceedings before the New York Immigration Court and the relief now being pursued is adjustment of status under INA § 245(i).

11. Prior to the Individual Calendar Hearing, Respondent will pay the necessary fee to USCIS for adjudication of the I-485 and will obtain a medical examination by an appropriate authorized physician.

12. Respondent requests that the Immigration Court instruct the Office of the District Counsel to take necessary steps to schedule a fingerprint appointment.

WHEREFORE, Respondent respectfully requests that this Court schedule the Individual Calendar Hearing for consideration of his I-485 Application for Adjustment of Status as soon as possible.

Respectfully submitted, this the ____ day of ________, 20__.

[Attorney]

[ADD CERTIFICATE OF SERVICE]

U.S. DEPARTMENT OF JUSTICE
EXECUTIVE OFFICE FOR IMMIGRATION REVIEW
IMMIGRATION COURT
[LOCATION]

IN THE MATTER OF:)
)
[Alien])
A[Number])
)
Respondent)
_______________)

ORDER

Upon consideration by this Court of the Respondent's Motion to Waive Master Calendar Hearing and Schedule Individual Calendar Hearing, the Court hereby finds and orders as follows:

1. This Court has appropriate venue and jurisdiction to consider this matter.
2. Respondent's Master Calendar Hearing is scheduled for September 11, 2003.
3. Respondent has previously submitted an I-485 to the Board of Immigration Appeals and said I-485 is a part of the Record of Proceedings in this matter. Deportation Proceedings have been reopened by the Board of Immigration Appeals so that this Court may consider Respondent's I-485.
4. The Individual Calendar Hearing shall be scheduled for **[date and time]**.
5. The Office of the District Counsel shall take appropriate action to ensure that the Respondent receives an appointment to have fingerprints taken by the Application Support Center in Charlotte, North Carolina. Said appointment shall be scheduled by **[date]**.
6. Respondent shall submit the receipt for payment of the filing fee for the I-485 by **[date]**.
7. Respondent shall submit any and all proposed exhibits and witnesses to be considered by this Court at the Individual Calendar Hearing by **[date]**.
8. The Office of the District Counsel shall submit any and all proposed exhibits and witnesses to be considered by this Court at the Individual Calendar Hearing by **[date]**.

This the _____ day of _______________, 20__.

[Immigration Judge]

[Document No. 316]

MOTION FOR *MATTER OF JOSEPH* HEARING

Description: This motion requests that the judge conduct a hearing to see if the respondent is properly included in a category of individuals subject to mandatory detention under INA §236(c). The Board of Immigration Appeals (BIA) has held in *Matter of Joseph*, 22 I&N Dec. 799 (BIA 1999), that the immigration judge is not bound by DHS's initial determination that an individual is removable under one of the mandatory detention grounds; and that the immigration judge may release an individual on bond if the immigration judge finds, on the basis of the bond record as a whole, that it is substantially unlikely that DHS will prevail on the charge of removability.

Advantages: The motion is helpful when a respondent is being held without bond under §236(c) and counsel has a legal argument that the individual is not properly classified under one of the mandatory detention grounds of §236(c). For example, DHS may be charging the respondent as an aggravated felon for a crime that arguably is not an aggravated felony. The *Matter of Joseph* motion would allow the respondent to have a hearing on the legality of detention.

Limitations: Often, the issue of whether the respondent is subject to mandatory detention also will resolve the issue of removability in and of itself. In other words, if the respondent is not properly charged with an offense that renders him or her removable, then the case will be terminated. If this is the case, the *Matter of Joseph* motion may be the quickest way to achieve termination of the proceedings. DHS retains the ability to file an automatic stay of the immigration judge's custody decision in conjunction with any appeal. 8 CFR §1003.19(i).

Notes: Although this motion need not include anything but a legal or factual argument as to why the respondent is not properly included in a mandatory detention category under INA §236(c), it is advisable also to address granting or lowering bond and include supporting evidence. The two key factors the court will consider regarding bond are danger to the community and flight risk. This way, if the judge agrees that the respondent is not subject to mandatory detention, the judge will be prepared to proceed to an immediate bond hearing.

Citations: *Matter of Joseph*, 22 I&N Dec. 799 (BIA 1999).

UNITED STATES DEPARTMENT OF JUSTICE
EXECUTIVE OFFICE FOR IMMIGRATION REVIEW
OFFICE OF THE IMMIGRATION JUDGE
[LOCATION]

IN THE MATTER OF:	)	
	)	
[Alien]	)	
A[Number]	)	IN REMOVAL PROCEEDINGS
	)	
Respondent	)	
	)	

MOTION REQUESTING A *MATTER OF JOSEPH*[1] HEARING

Respondent, through counsel, moves the Court hold a *Joseph* hearing for the purpose of determining whether or not Respondent is properly included in a mandatory detention category under section 236 of the Immigration and Nationality Act and 8 C.F.R. section 1003.19(h)(1)(ii). In support of this motion, Respondent states:

1. Respondent, a citizen of Turkey, is a Lawful Permanent Resident of the United States. He appeared for deferred inspection at Denver International Airport on June 17, 2004. On that date, he was arrested and served a Notice to Appear (NTA).

2. Immigration and Customs Enforcement (ICE) is alleging in the Notice to Appear that Respondent is an arriving alien.

3. ICE is also alleging in the Notice to Appear that Respondent was, "on February 11, 1981 convicted in Baltimore, Maryland court for the offense of Possession with the intent to Distribute Cocaine to wit: drug dealing, in violation of State of Maryland law."

4. Finally, ICE is alleging in the Notice to Appear that Respondent was, "on May 01, 2001, convicted in county Court at Eagle, County, Colorado for the offense of C.R.S. 18-18-422, to wit: Possession with Intent to Distribute an Imitation Controlled Substance, Class (F4)."

5. Alternatively, ICE is alleging that Respondent "admitted committing the following acts: Possession with Intent to Distribute an Imitation Controlled Substance, which constitute the essential elements of a violation of (or conspiracy or attempt to violate) any law or regulation of a State, the United States, or a foreign country relating to a controlled substance, to wit: Possession with Intent to Distribute an Imitation Controlled Substance."

6. Based on the allegations in the NTA, ICE is charging that Respondent is subject to removal from the United States pursuant to Section 212(a)(2)(A)(i)(I) of the Immigration and Nationality Act in that Respondent is an alien who has been convicted of, or who admits having committed, or who admits committing acts

[1] *Matter of Joseph*, 22 I&N Dec. 799 (BIA 1999).

which constitute the essential elements of (or a conspiracy or attempt to violate) any law or regulation of a State, the United States, or a foreign country relating to a controlled substance (as defined in Section 102 of the Controlled Substances Act (21 U.S.C. §802).

7. The Immigration and Nationality Act prescribes mandatory detention for certain aliens, including those who are inadmissible for having committed any offense in section 212(a)(2), including controlled substance violations. INA §236(c)(1)(A).

8. "The regulations generally do not confer jurisdiction on Immigration Judges over custody or bond determinations respecting those aliens subject to mandatory detention" *Matter of Joseph*, 22 I&N Dec. (BIA 1999) *citing* 8 C.F.R. section 1003.19(h)(2)(i)(D). The regulations, nevertheless, specifically allow an alien to seek a determination from an Immigration Judge "that the alien 'is not properly included within' certain of the regulatory provisions which would deprive the Immigration Judge of bond jurisdiction." *Matter of Joseph*, 22 I&N Dec. 799 (BIA 1999); *citing* 8 C.F.R. section 1003.19(h)(2)(ii).

9. The Board of Immigration Appeals determined in *Matter of Joseph* that "the Immigration Judge may make a determination on whether a lawful permanent resident 'is not properly included' in a mandatory detention category, in accordance with 8 C.R.S. section 1003.19(h)(2)(ii), either before or after the conclusion of the underlying removal case." *Matter of Joseph*, 22 I&N Dec. 799 (BIA 1999).

10. Respondent is not properly included in the mandatory detention category.

11. First, Respondent is a lawful permanent resident of the United States having obtained his permanent residency on January 27, 1959. [See Exhibit 1, Copy of front and back of Resident Alien Card].

12. Having been conferred the benefit of lawful permanent residence, Respondent is presumed to be a lawful resident, and maintains his lawful permanent residence unless and until there is a final administrative order of exclusion, deportation or removal. 8 C.F.R. §1001.1(p).

13. Generally, as a lawful permanent resident, Respondent is presumed to be admissible to the United States and shall not be regarded as an arriving alien seeking entry into the United States. INA §101(a)(13)(C).

14. There are certain enumerated exceptions to the rule that a lawful permanent resident is not to be regarded as an arriving alien seeking entry. These exceptions are enumerated in the statute at INA §101(a)(13)(C)(i–vi).

15. ICE is alleging that Respondent is an arriving alien seeking admission pursuant to INA §101(a)(13)(C)(v), based on the allegations noted in the Notice to Appear.

16. ICE cannot substantiate these allegations, and therefore, the NTA should be terminated and the case dismissed.

Respondent is not inadmissible based on the alleged conviction from February 11, 1981, in that the ground of inadmissibility triggered by that offense was previously waived by an Immigration Judge under INA §212(c)

17. On March 22, 1981, Respondent was issued an Order to Show Cause and deportation proceedings were commenced based on an alleged plea of guilty on June 4, 1981, "in the Circuit Court for Baltimore County, Towson, Maryland to possession of a controlled substance, to wit: cocaine, in violation of Article 27, Section 287 of the Annotated Code of Maryland." [See Attached Exhibit 2, Order to Show Cause, dated March 22, 1982].

18. On the basis of this allegation, it was charged that Respondent is deportable based on Section 241(a)(11) of the Immigration and Nationality Act, "in that, you at any time have been convicted of a viola-

tion of any law or regulation relating to the illicit possession of a controlled dangerous substance, to wit: cocaine, in violation of Article 27, Section 287 [sic] of the Annotated Code of Maryland." [See Exhibit 2, Order to Show Cause].

19. On December 21, 1983, Respondent submitted form I-191 Application for Advance Permission to Return to Unrelinquished Domicile to the Immigration Court requesting a waiver of deportability under INA section 212(c). [See Attached, Exhibit 3, Form I-191 Application for Advance Permission to Return to Unrelinquished Domicile].

20. On April 25, 1984, Immigration Judge **[Judge]**, sitting in the Immigration Court in Baltimore, Maryland granted the 212(c) waiver and ordered that the respondent continue in the status of a lawful permanent resident of the United States. [See Attached, Exhibit 4, Order from **[Judge]**, granting 212(c) relief; See also, Attached Exhibit 5, Record of Action Sheet from the Trial Attorney indicating that the a 212(c) hearing was held and that the waiver was granted].

21. Upon information and belief, this offense that was waived in 1982, is the same offense that is now alleged in the new Notice to Appear.

22. Having been previously granted 212(c) relief, on the basis of this offense, the offense is waived for all time. 8 C.F.R. §212.3(d); *Matter of Przygocki*, 17 I&N Dec. 361 (BIA 1980). *See also Matter of Gordon*, 20 I&N Dec. 52 (BIA 1989).

23. An Immigration Judge may not reconsider the grant of a 212(c) waiver based on allegations of later criminal activity. *Matter of Gordon*, 20 I&N Dec. 52 (BIA 1989).

24. Because Respondent has been previously granted a waiver of inadmissibility for the conviction alleged in the Notice to Appear, this allegation should be dismissed and the charge of inadmissibility based on that allegation dismissed as well.

Respondent is not inadmissible for an alleged conviction on May 01, 2001, in that Possession of an Imitation Controlled Substance is not an inadmissible offense "relating to a controlled substance (as defined in Section 102 of the Controlled Substances Act (21 U.S.C. 802))"

25. The Notice to Appear alleges that Respondent was convicted of (or admits committing the act of) Possession with Intent to Distribute an Imitation Controlled Substance and cites C.R.S. 18-18-422. On the basis of this allegation, the NTA charges that Respondent is inadmissible to the United States under section 212(a)(2)(A)(i)(I) for giving been convicted of or admitting the essential elements of any law or regulation of a State, the United States, or a foreign country relating to a controlled substance (as defined in Section 102 of the Controlled Substances Act, 21 U.S.C. §802).

26. In order to support this charge and allegation, ICE must not only prove the admission or the conviction of the crime, but must also show that the crime is a crime relating to a controlled substance as defined in Section 102 of the Controlled Substances Act.

27. Colo. Rev. Stat. section 18-18-422 provides, "it is unlawful for any person to manufacture, distribute, or possess with intent to distribute an immigration controlled substance." Colo. Rev. Stat. §18-18-422(1)(a). [See attached, Exhibit 6, Colo. Rev. Stat. §18-18-422].

28. "Imitation Controlled Substance" is defined as "a substance that is not the controlled substance that it is purported to be but which, by appearance, including color, shape, size, and markings, by representations made, and by consideration of all relevant factors as set forth in section 18-18-421, would lead a reasonable person to believe that the substance is the controlled substance that it is purported to be." Colo. Rev. Stat. §18-18-420(3). [See attached Exhibit 7, Colo. Rev. Stat. §18-18-420(3)].

29. In order for ICE to prevail on the allegation and charge, they must prove that the conviction for the offense defined above is an offense relating to a controlled substance under federal law.

30. There is no federal felony defined in Section 102 of the Controlled Substances Act, 21 U.S.C. §802 that relates to possession of an imitation controlled substance. Possession of an imitation controlled substance is not a violation punishable under federal law. [See attached exhibit 8, Section 102 of the Controlled Substances Act, 21 U.S.C. §802].

31. Section 102 of the Controlled Substances Act, 21 U.S.C. §802 provides the definitions for the offenses in the Controlled Substances Act.

32. "Controlled Substance is defined as, "a drug of other substance, or immediate precursor, included in Schedule I, II, III, IV, or V of part B of this title (21 U.S.C. §802). The term does not include distilled spirits, wine, malt beverages, or tobacco, as those terms are defined or used in subtitle E of the Internal Revenue Code of 1954." 21 U.S.C. §802(6). The definition of controlled substance does not include imitation controlled substances. [See attached exhibit 8].

33. While not providing for a violation regarding imitation controlled substances, Section 802 does provide for a violation involving "counterfeit" controlled substances. Counterfeit controlled substance is defined as, "*a controlled substance* which, or the container or labeling of which, without authorization, bears the trademark, trade name, or other identifying mark, imprint, number, or device, or any likeness thereof, of a manufacturer, distributor, dispense other than the person or persons who in fact manufactured, distributed, or dispensed such substance and which thereby falsely purports or is represented to be the product of, or to have been distributed by, such other manufacturer, distributor or dispenser." 21 U.S.C. §802(7). [See attached exhibit 8].

34. At first blush, this may seem to be an offense that is related to imitation controlled substances. However, the case law and Colorado Statute provide otherwise.

35. First, the Fourth Circuit has concluded that in instances where a criminal defendant is attempting to pass an imitation substance (wax and flour) as a controlled substance (crack cocaine), that such act does not constitute a violation of federal narcotics laws.

36. In *United States v. Sampson*, 140 F.3d 585 (4th Cir. 1998) [Attached as Exhibit 9], the Fourth Circuit held, that "flex" a combination of flour, wax and baking soda passed off as cocaine was not a "counterfeit substance" within the meaning of 21 U.S.C. §802(7). The Court stated, "Simply because a substance looks like cocaine, and the defendant represents to his unsuspecting purchaser that the substance is cocaine, does not make the mere distribution of that substance a violation of the federal narcotics laws." *Id.* at 589.

37. The Third Circuit agreed with *Sampson* stating, "We share the *Sampson* Court's common sense skepticism of the District Court's outcome. The treatment of candle wax and flour, no matter how it is marketed, as a Schedule I controlled substance is an 'absurd' result of the kind our canons of construction instruct us to avoid." *United States v. Hodge*, 321 F.3d 429, 439 (3d Cir. 2003) [Attached as exhibit 10].

38. The fact that possession of a "counterfeit" substance is not the same as possession of an "imitation" substance is also proven by examining the Colorado Statute. The Colorado Statute provides a separate and distinct offense for possession of a counterfeit substance. Colo. Rev. Stat. §18-18-423. [See attached exhibit 11 Colo. Rev. Stat. 18-18-423].

39. The language of section 18-18-423 tracks the language of the federal offense almost identically: "It is unlawful for any person knowingly or intentionally to manufacture, deliver, or possess with intent to manufacture or deliver, a controlled substance which, or the container or labeling of which, without authorization, bears the trademark, trade name, or other identifying mark, imprint, number, or device, or any likeness thereof, of a manufacturer, distributor, or dispenser, other than the person who in fact manufactured, distributed, or dispensed the substance." Colo. Rev. Stat. §18-18-423. It is clear that had Respondent been con-

victed under this statute, his offense would have been one "relating to" a controlled substance defined in section 102. However, this is not the offense for which Respondent is allegedly convicted.

40. In an unpublished decision out of the Third Circuit, the Court addressed the question of whether a conviction under the Pennsylvania controlled substance act which prohibited the delivery of a counterfeit controlled substance was an offense relating to a controlled substance so as to render someone removable under INA section 241(a)(2)(B)(i). *Clarke v. Ashcroft*, 2004 U.S.App. LEXIS 12028 (3d Cir. June 16, 2004) [See attached exhibit 12].

41. The Third Circuit looked to the language of the Pennsylvania statute for delivery of a counterfeit controlled substance to determine whether the state offense was related to a crime as defined in section 102.

42. Section 780-102(b) of the Pennsylvania controlled substance act defined "counterfeit" as a controlled substance . . . which or the container or labeling of which, without authorization, bears the trademark, trade name, or other identifying mark, imprint, number, or device, or any likeness thereof, of a manufacturer, distributor, or dispenser other than the person or persons who in fact manufactured, distributed, or dispensed such substance and which thereby is falsely purported or represented to be the product of, or to have been distributed by, such other manufacturer, distributor, or dispenser." *Id. citing* Pa. Cons. Stat. §780-102(b).

43. Significantly, in upholding the decision of the BIA, the Third Circuit found: "Based on this language, the BIA found that the term 'counterfeit controlled substance' refers to a substance that includes at least some substance that is prohibited. This interpretation is reasonable, particularly in light of the fact that the Pennsylvania controlled substance statute includes a separate section to cover ordinary substances that, although they may resemble a controlled substance, do not actually contain any prohibited controlled substances." *Clarke v. Ashcroft*, 2004 U.S. App. LEXIS 12028 at *8 (underlining added). Thus, the Court found that the conviction under Pennsylvania law was an offense relating to a controlled substance as defined in section 102 for two reasons. First, the offense of possession of a counterfeit substance included possession of some substance that is prohibited. Second, the Pennsylvania code had a separate section dealing with offenses that, while resembling a controlled substance, do not actually contain a prohibited substance.

44. This case is on all fours with the present matter. Colorado, like Pennsylvania, has two separate offenses for possession of imitation controlled substances and for possession of counterfeit controlled substances. This Court should find that possession of an imitation controlled substance is a separate offense from possession of a counterfeit substance and find that possession of an imitation controlled substance is not an offense "related to" any controlled substance or controlled substance offense as defined in section 102 of the Controlled Substances Act.

45. While not providing an offense for possession of an imitation controlled substance, section 102 also provides for an offense related to possession of a "controlled substance analogue." 21 U.S.C. §802(32)(A). [See attached exhibit 8]. Controlled substance analogue is defined as: "A substance—(i) the chemical structure of which is substantially similar to the chemical structure of a controlled substance in schedule I or II; (ii) which has a stimulant, depressant, or hallucinogenic effect on the central nervous system that is substantially similar to or greater than the stimulant, depressant, or hallucinogenic effect on the central nervous system of a controlled substance in schedule I or II; or (iii) with respect to a particular person, which such person represents or intends to have a stimulant, depressant, or hallucinogenic effect on the central nervous system that is substantially similar to or greater than the stimulant, depressant or hallucinogenic effect on the central nervous system of a controlled substance in schedule I or II." 21 U.S.C. §802(32)(A).

46. Again, when examining the elements, it is clear that this offense is different from the offense of which Respondent is alleged to be convicted. The Third Circuit agreed in *United States v. Hodge*, 321 F.3d 429 (3d Cir. 2003). In *Hodge*, a federal agent purchased from the defendant a package containing a mixture of candle wax and flour, which the defendants told the agent was crack cocaine. *Id.* The defendants were indicted and convicted in the District Court for possession of a controlled substance analogue under 21 U.S.C.

802(32)(A)(i–iii). *Id.* In overturning the decision of the District Court and dismissing the conviction, the Third Circuit held, "We conclude that Congress did not intend to include substances such as wax and flour within its definition of controlled substance analogues. Moreover, even if we were not sure, we would be compelled to reverse the appellants' drug convictions. *See Government of Virgin Islands v. Knight*, 989 F.2d 619, 633 (3d Cir. 1993) (counseling that "any ambiguity concerning the meaning of a criminal statute be resolved in favor of the criminal defendant"). *Id.* at 439.

47. When consulting the definition section at Section 102 of the Controlled Substances Act, it is clear that possession of an imitation controlled substance does not relate to any offense as defined in such section. The offense of possession of an imitation controlled substance has been found to be different in substance and form from possession of a counterfeit controlled substance and from possession of a controlled substance analogue.

48. Counsel can state to a reasonable degree of certainty that neither the Federal Courts, nor the BIA have ever held that possession of an imitation controlled substance is an offense covered under 212(a)(2)(A)(i)(II).

ICE is substantially unlikely to establish at the merits hearing, the charge that subjects Respondent to mandatory detention under 236(c), and in such circumstances, Respondent is eligible for release

49. In *Matter of Joseph*, 22 I&N Dec. 799 (BIA 1999), the Board found that the Service was "substantially unlikely to establish the charge of deportability it is appeal of the underlying removal case. Under such circumstances, we find it inappropriate to continue to treat the respondent as an alien who is subject to mandatory detention." *Id.*

50. The Board concluded, "[W]e determine that a lawful permanent resident will not be considered 'properly included' in a mandatory detention category when an Immigration Judge or the Board is convinced that the Service is substantially unlikely to establish at the merits hearing, or on appeal, the charge or charges that would otherwise subject the alien to mandatory detention." *Id.*

51. "The regulations . . . allow this determination to be made by the Immigration Judge at a very early stage of the overall proceedings." *Id.*

WHEREFORE, Respondent prays the court to immediately release the client on his own recognizance or immediately set this matter for a bond hearing under INA section 236(a). *Matter of Adeniji*, 22 I&N Dec. 1102 (BIA 1999).

Respectfully submitted,

[Attorney]

[Dated:]

[ADD CERTIFICATE OF SERVICE]

[Document No. 317]

MOTION TO APPEAR TELEPHONICALLY AT MASTER CALENDAR HEARING

Description: This motion is to request the opportunity for counsel and respondent to appear by telephone at a master calendar hearing rather than appear in person before the immigration judge.

Advantages: In some jurisdictions, counsel and respondents who reside some distance from the immigration court are permitted to appear together by telephone. The benefit is obvious—both counsel and respondent avoid the need to travel at some distance and expense.

Limitations: Telephonic appearance is permitted in a limited number of courts. In those venues where it is permitted, not all judges within the same venue may allow such an appearance; or they may require that the respondent personally appear even if counsel appears by phone. It is therefore necessary to determine local procedures. In most circumstances, Immigration and Customs Enforcement counsel appears personally in the courtroom. When allowed, telephonic appearance is best used for master calendar appearance in matters without unusual circumstances or where complicated and prolonged legal argument to the immigration judge is not anticipated.

Citations: 8 CFR §1003.25(c).

UNITED STATES DEPARTMENT OF JUSTICE
EXECUTIVE OFFICE FOR IMMIGRATION REVIEW
IMMIGRATION COURT
[LOCATION]

IN THE MATTER OF:)
)
[Alien])
A[Number])
)
Respondent)
)

MOTION TO APPEAR TELEPHONICALLY

Respondent, **[Alien]**, by and through counsel, **[Attorney]**, hereby requests this Court to allow him and counsel to appear telephonically at the Master Calendar Hearing scheduled **[date]** at **[time]** in Atlanta, Georgia; and in support thereof, Respondent shows unto the Court as follows:

1. Respondent is a native and citizen of Mexico and a lawful permanent resident of the United States.

2. On or about September 14, 2003, Respondent was served personally with a Notice to Appear upon entry into the United States at **[Airport]** from Mexico. He previously appeared at a Master Calendar Hearing in Immigration Court in Houston on April 5, 2004, at which time he requested that venue be changed to Atlanta, Georgia.

3. In pleadings submitted prior to the Master Calendar Hearing in Houston, Respondent admitted factual allegations 1 through 3 in the Notice to Appear, as follows:

   1. are not a citizen or a National of the United States.

   2. are a Native and citizen of Mexico.

   3. are ineligible for admission to the United States because you were, on May 26, 1989, convicted in the 17th Circuit Court at Grand Rapids, Michigan for the offense of breaking and entering, with intent, in violation of MCL 750.110-A, a crime involving moral tupitude (*sic*).

4. Respondent also conceded the charge of removal in the Notice to Appear, stated as follows:

   Section 212(a)(2)(A)(i)(I) of the Immigration and Nationality Act, as amended, in that you are an alien who has been convicted of, or who admits having committed, or who admits committing acts which constitute the essential elements of a crime involving moral turpitude (other than a purely political offense).

5. Respondent resides and works in Chapel Hill, North Carolina. The undersigned counsel has offices in **[City, State]**. Due to the distance, attending the hearing in Atlanta would require Respondent and counsel to either travel by air to Atlanta at undue expense, or to travel overnight to Atlanta, thereby causing two days loss of work.

6. Respondent, however, would be able to be present at the hearing telephonically with counsel in her office in **[City, State]** with little travel required.

7. This Motion is being made in good faith and not for purposes of delay.

WHEREFORE, Respondent respectfully requests that he be allowed to appear at his Master Calendar Hearing, scheduled **[date]** at **[time]**, telephonically through counsel's office in **[City, State]**, telephone number **[number]**.

This the _____day of ______________, 20__.

[Attorney]

[ADD CERTIFICATE OF SERVICE]

UNITED STATES DEPARTMENT OF JUSTICE
EXECUTIVE OFFICE FOR IMMIGRATION REVIEW
IMMIGRATION COURT
[LOCATION]

IN THE MATTER OF:)
)
[Alien])
A[Number])
)
Respondent)
_______________________________)

ORDER

Upon consideration of the Respondent's Motion to Appear Telephonically at his Master Calendar Hearing scheduled **[date]** at **[time]**, the Court hereby allows Respondent to appear telephonically with counsel at the office of **[Firm Name, Address, and Phone Number]**.

This the _____ day of ___________, 20__.

[Immigration Judge]

[Document No. 318]

REQUEST FOR ORAL ARGUMENT BEFORE IMMIGRATION COURT

Description: This is a request for oral argument regarding a motion to reopen filed with the immigration court.

Advantages: Often, motions filed with the immigration court are determined based on the pleadings with no argument presented to the court. For example, pursuant to 8 CFR §1003.23(b)(iv), the immigration judge may set and extend time limits for replies to motions to reopen or reconsider and a motion will be considered unopposed unless a timely response is filed. There may be situations where counsel would prefer the opportunity to more fully argue the points of the motion and answer any questions the court may have. It may also be beneficial or necessary to present testimony from witnesses in support of the motion. If advisable, a request for oral argument could be included with any motion; it is within the discretion of the immigration judge to grant or deny the request.

Notes: Local rules of the immigration court must be consulted for any specific requirements regarding filing and responding to motions and the availability of oral argument and presentation of testimony before the court.

Citations: 8 CFR §1003.23(b)(iv); 8 CFR §1003.31(c) (regarding the authority of the immigration judge to set time limits for filing of documents and responses thereto).

EXECUTIVE OFFICE FOR IMMIGRATION REVIEW
IMMIGRATION COURT
[LOCATION]

IN THE MATTER OF:)
)
[Alien])
A[Number]) IN REMOVAL PROCEEDINGS
)
Respondent)
_________________________)

REQUEST FOR ORAL ARGUMENT

Respondent, **[Alien]**, hereby requests oral argument for the reason that the resolution of the novel, varied and complex issues presented in the Motion to Reopen will be aided by oral argument. The facts are complicated and may need further explanation by counsel. There are important statutory and constitutional issues addressed in the Motion that must be decided by this Court.

Dated this _____ day of __________________, 20__.

[Attorney]

[ADD CERTIFICATE OF SERVICE]

[Document No. 319]
MOTION TO DISMISS CERTAIN ALLEGATIONS

Description: This motion seeks to dismiss certain allegations and charges lodged on the Notice to Appear. Specifically, in this motion, Department of Homeland Security (DHS) has alleged various grounds of removability related to misrepresentation upon entry into the United States from Canada, violation of the terms of the respondent's nonimmigrant status, and grounds of removal related to a conviction that had been withdrawn on constitutional grounds. This motion is helpful in that it raises several charges of removability that counsel may often encounter in immigration court and provides an example of how counsel can seek to narrow the issues on which DHS may seek removal of a client.

Advantages: In a removal proceeding, DHS has the burden of establishing by clear, unequivocal, and convincing evidence that, in the case of an alien who has been admitted to the United States, the alien is deportable. This burden cannot be met by a mere accusation in the Notice to Appear, but can be satisfied only by production of the required evidence, unless the alien admits the charge or charges.

This motion seeks to force DHS to prove all of the allegations and charges in the Notice to Appear.

Limitations: The inclination in immigration proceedings may be to admit the charges and allegations and move immediately to the "relief" stage. On the other hand, there will be times where it is in the client's best interest to aggressively litigate every issue. This needs to be weighed on a case-by-case basis. Also, be advised that termination of the case altogether may not assist the client. If a client is applying for adjustment of status, counsel needs the client to remain in removal proceedings so that he or she may adjust status and receive permanent residence. For that reason, counsel may want to litigate some of the charges while admitting others.

Citations: Burden of proof: INA §240(c)(3)(A); *Woodby v. INS*, 285 U.S. 276, 286 (1966); *Matter of Pichardo-Sufren*, 21 I&N Dec. 30 (BIA 1996); *Matter of Lam*, 14 I&N Dec. 168 (BIA 1972).

UNITED STATES DEPARTMENT OF JUSTICE
EXECUTIVE OFFICE FOR IMMIGRATION REVIEW
OFFICE OF THE IMMIGRATION JUDGE
[LOCATION]

IN THE MATTER OF:	)	
	)	
[Alien]	)	
A[Number]	)	IN REMOVAL PROCEEDINGS
	)	
Respondent	)	
______________________	)	

MOTION TO DISMISS CHARGES AND ALLEGATIONS IN NOTICE TO APPEAR

Respondent, through counsel, moves the immigration judge to dismiss allegations four and five, and charges one, three, four, five and six of the Notice to Appear. In support of this motion, Respondent states:

1. Respondent was issued a Notice to Appear on December 5, 2002. The Notice to Appear issued by U.S. Immigration and Customs Enforcement (ICE) charges that Respondent is subject to removal from the United States pursuant to six provisions of law. Out of the six charges being brought against Respondent, the only charge that can be substantiated is charge two, section 237(a)(1)(B), in that Respondent has remained in the United States longer than permitted. All other charges against Respondent should be dismissed.

2. In addition, allegations four and five of the Notice to appear should be dismissed.

CHARGE I. SECTION 237(a)(1)(A) OF THE IMMIGRATION AND NATIONALITY ACT

1. ICE charges that respondent is removable pursuant to section 237(a)(1)(A) of the Immigration and Nationality Act (Act) in that at the time of entry into the United States, Respondent was "within one or more of the classes of aliens inadmissible by the law existing at such time, to wit: aliens who seek to procure of have sought to procure, or who have procured a visa, other documentation, or entry into the United States, or other benefit provided under the Act, by *fraud or by willfully* misrepresenting a *material fact* under section 212(a)(6)(C)(i) of the act." (Emphasis added).

2. The principal elements of the ground of excludability contained in this section of the Act are fraud or willfulness and materiality.

3. Fraud requires that the respondent make false representations of a *material* fact with knowledge of its falsity, *intend to deceive* the Government official, and succeed in the deception. *Matter of G–G–*, 7 I. & N. Dec. 161 (BIA 1956) (emphasis added).

4. Fraud is defined as "the *intentional* perversion of the truth in order to induce another to part with something of value or to surrender a legal right." *The Merriam-Webster On-Line Dictionary*, *www.m-w.com/*

cgi-bin/dictionary, 1/28/03 (emphasis added). The definition of fraud in *The Oxford American Dictionary* is "A deception deliberately practiced *in order to secure unfair or unlawful gain*" (emphasis added).

5. Furthermore, as stated above, the Act itself states that the misrepresentation must be done "willfully." INA §212(a)(6)(C)(i); 8 U.S.C. §1182(a)(6)(C)(i).

6. ICE has the burden of proof in substantiating the charges brought against the Respondent, in its claim that she is removable under section 237(a)(1)(A). Therefore, ICE has the burden of proof in establishing that Respondent was inadmissible at the time of entry when she committed a misrepresentation of a material fact by fraud of willfulness. INA §240(c)(3)(A); 8 U.S.C. §1229a(c)(3)(A).

7. In an attempt to substantiate the charge brought against the Respondent, ICE alleges that when the Respondent entered the United States on or about May 6, 1998, she failed to disclose the fact that she was intending to reside permanently in the United States. To date, ICE has not provided respondent or counsel any evidence establishing that Respondent intended to permanently reside in the United States when she entered the country from Canada.

8. In addition, when the Respondent entered the United States from Canada via automobile, on or about May 6, 1998, she was not questioned by an immigration officer/border inspector. She was stopped by an inspector who asked to see her identification. She provided the inspector with her passport and photo identification. She was not questioned but was given authorization to enter the United States. Because Respondent was not questioned and she volunteered no information to the inspector, Respondent made <u>no</u> fraudulent or willful material misrepresentations regarding her intent to temporarily visit the United States. A failure to disclose information is not fraud or willful misrepresentation of a material fact.

9. The Foreign Affairs Manual Section 40.63 is instructive on how a consular officer or border official is to handle cases involving misrepresentation or false claims to United States Citizenship. Notes 4.1 and 4.2 explain clearly that failure to volunteer information does not constitute fraud or misrepresentation under INA section 212(a)(6)(C)(i). Section 4.1 states, "As used in INA 212(a)(6)(C)(i), a misrepresentation is an assertion or manifestation not in accordance with the facts. Misrepresentation requires an affirmative act taken by the alien." Section 4.2 elaborates, "In determining whether a misrepresentation has been made, it is necessary to distinguish between misrepresentation of information and information that was merely concealed by the alien's silence. Silence or the willful failure to volunteer information does not itself constitute a misrepresentation for purposes of INA section 212(a)(6)(C)(i)."

10. Respondent married her United States citizen husband, **[Husband]**, nine months after entering the United States from Canada. It was approximately one and a half years later that she and her husband submitted an I-130 Petition for Alien Relative and I-485 Application to Register as Legal Permanent Resident to the Immigration and Naturalization Service.

11. The Foreign Affairs Manual also sets out a "30/60 day rule." FAM §40.63 N4.7. The rule states, that "When violative conduct occurs more than 60 days after entry into the United States, the Department does not consider such conduct to constitute a basis for an INA 212(a)(6)(C)(i) ineligibility." Here the conduct in question occurred nine months after Respondent's entry into the United States and her application for permanent residence occurred one and a half years later.

CHARGE II. SECTION 237(a)(1)(B) OF THE IMMIGRATION AND NATIONALITY ACT

1. ICE charges that respondent is removable pursuant to section 237(a)(1)(B) of the Immigration and Nationality Act (Act) in that after admission as a nonimmigrant under section 101(a)(15) of the Act, Respondent remained in the United States for a time longer than permitted.

2. When Respondent entered the United States on or about May 6, 1998 she did not receive a visa or an I-94. Although she was inspected by a legacy INS officer and legally entered the United States, she was not

questioned regarding her travel to the United States. A Department of State Cable on Inspected Canadian Entrants Should Be Treated Same As Duration-of-Status Cases states, "a Canadian…admitted following inspection, who has not been issued an I-94, should be treated in the same manner as a duration of status case, similar to an F or J." Ref: (a) Montreal 1497, (b) Victars E57819, (c) 97 State 23545, (d) State 60539 (attached).

3. "As in duration of status cases, a Canadian…, who is found to have violated status and be removable by an Immigration Judge, or found to have violated status, by an INS officer, in the course of adjudicating a benefit, such as an extension of stay or a change of adjustment of status, is unlawfully present. *The unlawful presence commences on the date when the immigration judge, or INS officer, makes the ruling, not the date the status violation began.*" (emphasis added). Ref: (a) Montreal 1497, (b) Victars E57819, (c) 97 State 23545, (d) State 60539.

4. Respondent formally was "found" out of status when her adjustment application was improperly denied. She was placed back in a period of stay authorized by the attorney general when she renewed her application before the immigration judge, and remains in a period of stay authorized while the adjustment application remains pending. Michael A. Pearson, Executive Associate Comm'r, Memorandum for Regional Directors, "Period of stay authorized by the Attorney General after the 120-day tolling period for purposes of 212(a)(9)(B) of the Immigration and Nationality Act," HQADN70/21.1.24-P, AD 00-07 (March 3, 2000) (attached).

CHARGE III. SECTION 237(a)(1)(C)(i) OF THE IMMIGRATION AND NATIONALITY ACT

1. ICE charges that respondent is removable pursuant to section 237(a)(1)(C)(i) of the Immigration and Nationality Act (Act) in that after admission as a nonimmigrant under section 101(a)(15) of the Act, Respondent failed to maintain or comply with the conditions of the nonimmigrant status under which she was admitted, in that she plead guilty to two felony controlled substance offenses.

2. The dismissal of the case and charges against Respondent was based on a stipulation between the prosecutor and Respondent's defense counsel. The prosecutor stipulated to the removal of Respondent's guilty plea. (See Transcript at pg. 7, line 5).

3. Respondent's guilty plea was not withdrawn for rehabilitative purposes, nor was the conviction expunged after a plea was entered. In this case, the plea was withdrawn upon agreement by all parties. As such this case is not within the purview of *Matter of Roldan*, 22 I&N Dec. 512 (BIA 1999) or *Matter of Pickering*, 23 I&N Dec. 621 (BIA 2003), and there is no conviction for immigration purposes under INA section 101(a)(48); 8 U.S.C. §1101(a)(48).

4. Respondent plead guilty to a controlled substance offense on January 5, 1993, in the State of Michigan. Respondent did not appear for sentencing on the case and a bench warrant was issued before any sentence was imposed. Her guilty plea was withdrawn and the case dismissed on December 21, 2001, without prejudice.

5. Because the case was dismissed against Respondent by the Judicial Court Judge, in the State of Michigan, Respondent does not have a conviction for immigration purposes resulting from her prosecution for a controlled substance offense. Therefore, ICE cannot substantiate this charge against the Respondent. (See Order of Criminal Court).

CHARGE IV. SECTION 237(a)(2)(A) OF THE IMMIGRATION AND NATIONALITY ACT

1. ICE charges that respondent is removable pursuant to section 237(a)(1)(A) of the Immigration and Nationality Act (Act) in that any alien who at any time after admission is convicted of two or more crimes involving moral turpitude.

2. The Notice to Appear issued by the Bureau on December 5, 2002 makes no allegations that would substantiate the charge that Respondent has been convicted of two or more crimes involving moral turpitude. Without proper allegations to support his claim, Respondent is not removable from the United States based on this charge.

3. As noted above, Respondent does not have a conviction to a controlled substance violation nor has she admitted the essential elements of a controlled substance violation or crime involving moral turpitude.

4. Furthermore, the statute at issue in this case, the Public Health Code of the State of Michigan, section 333.7401 is a divisible statute which provides:

> Manufacturing, creating, delivering, or possessing with intent to manufacture, create or deliver controlled substance, prescription form, or counterfeit prescription form; dispensing, prescribing, or administering controlled substance
>
> (1) Except as authorized by this article, a person shall not manufacture, create deliver, or possess with intent to manufacture, create or deliver a controlled substance, a prescription form, or a counterfeit prescription form. . . .

Mich. Comp. Laws §333.7401 (2003).

5. Taking the statute at its minimum, one can be convicted under this statute without intent or knowledge. In the absence of intent or knowledge as an element of the statute, possession or distribution of drugs is not a crime involving moral turpitude. *Matter of Khourn*, 21 I&N Dec. 1041 (BIA 1997).

CHARGE V. SECTION 237(a)(2)(B)(i) OF THE IMMIGRATION AND NATIONALITY ACT

1. ICE charges that respondent is removable pursuant to section 237(a)(1)(B)(i) of the Immigration and Nationality Act (Act) in that any alien who at any time after admission has been convicted or a violation of or conspiracy or attempted to violate any law or regulation of a State, the United States, or a foreign country relating to a controlled substance.

2. As previously stated, Respondent plead guilty to a controlled substance offense on January 5, 1993, in the State of Michigan. A sentence was never imposed on Respondent and her guilty plea was withdrawn and the case dismissed on December 21, 2001, without prejudice.

3. Because the case was dismissed against Respondent before any sentence was imposed, Respondent does not have a conviction for immigration purposes resulting from her prosecution for a controlled substance offense. Therefore, ICE cannot substantiate this charge against Respondent.

CHARGE VI. SECTION 237(a)(2)(B)(ii) OF THE IMMIGRATION AND NATIONALITY ACT

1. ICE charges that respondent is removable pursuant to section 237(a)(1)(B)(ii) of the Immigration and Nationality Act (Act) in that any alien who is, or at any time after admission has been a drug abuser or addict is deportable.

2. The International Center for the Advancement of Addiction Treatment defines addition as: A primary, chronic neurobiological [sic] disease, with genetic, psychosocial, and environmental factors influencing its development and manifestations. It is characterized by behaviors that include one or more of the following: impaired control over drug use, compulsive use, continued use despite harm, and craving." Available at: *www.opiateaddictionrx.info/facts/facts01.htm* (attached).

3. *FamilyPracticeNotebook.com* defines drug abuse as: Recurrent use over a 12-month period despite physically hazardous situations, legal problems and negative social and interpersonal consequences. Available at: *www.fpnotebook.com/PSY26.htm* (attached).

4. Respondent displays no patters or symptomatic and chronic drug abuse.

5. Determining whether a person is a drug abuser or addict requires a medical diagnosis. ICE has not provided any examination or evidence from a trained medical professional indicating that Respondent is or has been a drug abuser or addict. Unless ICE intends to demonstrate this charge by having Respondent examined by a medical professional, it is unable to substantiate this charge.

6. In addition, Respondent previously submitted to a medical evaluation prior to filing an I-130/I-485 Application with ICE. Respondent passed her medical evaluation and there was no indication in the medical examination report that Respondent was a drug abuser or addict.

CONCLUSION: MOTION TO DISMISS CHARGES AND ALLEGATIONS IS WARRANTED

WHEREFORE, Based on the fact that ICE has not and is unable to substantiate the charges that they have brought against Respondent in the Notice to Appear dated December 5, 2002, Respondent, through counsel, requests that this court terminate the said charges and allegations against Respondent.

Respectfully Submitted,

[Attorney]

[ADD CERTIFICATE OF SERVICE]

[Document Nos. 320–22]

MOTION FOR ISSUANCE OF SUBPOENAS

Description: The purpose of these motions are to obtain subpoenas issued by an immigration judge for witnesses and documents subsequent to commencement of immigration proceedings, from both government and nongovernment entities. One motion to the immigration judge seeks to compel the presence of DHS officials for purposes of testifying at a merits hearing or on a motion to suppress evidence.

Advantages: It should come as no surprise that DHS may make certain individual officers "unavailable" for testimony at a hearing in immigration court. A motion may be the only way to secure the testimony of an adverse DHS witness. 8 CFR §287.4(n)(2)(ss) also authorizes subpoenas for depositions, which offer the advantage of allowing the respondent's attorney to obtain the information prior to the hearing from unavailable witnesses.

Limitations: In certain limited circumstances, the immigration judge will typically be reluctant to issue this subpoena, as it may require the travel of a DHS employee form a distant city. Nonetheless, such a subpoena is clearly permitted under regulation and should be strenuously argued should DHS oppose it.

Notes: Counsel may not use these motions very much in practice, but the one time he or she needs it is the one time counsel doesn't know how to word it! Be judicious in its use, but this motion and the actual compelling of documents or the physical presence of a DIIS officer may be the only way to prevail in a particular case.

Citations: 8 CFR §§287.4(a)(2)(ii), 1287.4, 1003.35(b).

UNITED STATES DEPARTMENT OF JUSTICE
EXECUTIVE OFFICE FOR IMMIGRATION REVIEW

IN THE MATTER OF:	)	
[Alien]	)	
A[Number]	)	IN REMOVAL PROCEEDINGS
Respondent	)	

RESPONDENT'S MOTION FOR ISSUANCE OF SUBPOENAS AND MOTION FOR CONTINUANCE

Now comes respondent in the above captioned matter, pursuant to 8 CFR §§287.4(a)(2)(ii), 1287.4(a)(2)(ii), and 1003.35(b) and requests that subpoenas be issued for **[Individuals]**.

In support of this motion, respondent says:

1. The testimony of **[Individual]** is absolutely necessary in order for respondent to present his defense in the above-captioned matter. Respondent has made the following diligent efforts without success to obtain the requested information without a subpoena. See attached affidavit of respondent's attorney regarding these efforts, incorporated hereto.
2. On **[date]** agents from ICE entered the **[Business]** and began questioning various persons present as to their immigration status.
3. Upon information and belief these agents did not have any arrest warrant. The respondent hereby incorporates by reference his Motion to Suppress; and
4. That a continuance until these documents are produced is necessary, fair, and consistent with the interest of justice.

Respondent,
By his attorney,

[Attorney]

[Dated]:

UNITED STATES DEPARTMENT OF JUSTICE
EXECUTIVE OFFICE FOR IMMIGRATION REVIEW

IN THE MATTER OF:	)	
[Alien]	)	
A[Number]	)	IN REMOVAL PROCEEDINGS
Respondent	)	

RESPONDENT'S MOTION FOR ISSUANCE OF SUBPOENAS

NOW COMES respondent in the above-captioned matter and requests, pursuant to 8 CFR §§287.4(a)(2)(ii), 1287.4(a)(2)(ii), and 1003.35(b), that subpoenas be issued to the following persons:

a) **[Individual]** or his agent, custodian of documents, to produce the following:

i. Copy of any search warrant including copies of any and all affidavits in support thereof, obtained, regarding the arrest of respondent at **[Location]**;

ii. Copy of any arrest warrant issued regarding respondent, including copies of any and all affidavits in support thereof;

iii. The names of all ICE agents who participated in the arrest of respondent and other aliens at **[Location]** on **[date]** located at **[Address]**.

iv. A copy of any and all **[Name]**'s, Area Control record cards, for **[Individual]**.

v. Any and all forms or statements or other documents completed by or concerning respondent's investigation, interrogation, detention, arrest, and processing by ICE.

b) **[Individuals]**, who were agents of the Investigations Unit at ICE, on **[date]**.

c) Any other DHS agents, officers, employees, interpreters, and supervisory personnel who participated in the investigation and subsequent arrest of respondent at **[Location]** in **[City and State]** on **[date]**.

In support of this motion, respondent states and argues as follows:

1. The testimony of these individuals is relevant to and necessary for Respondent's Motion to Suppress. **[Individuals]** have signed Forms I-213, I-214, I-215(b), I-263A, and I-221S, some of which ICE has attempted to, or tends to introduce into evidence at Respondent's deportation hearing in an attempt to prove the allegations in the Order to Show Cause.

Although an I-213 cannot be accepted into evidence unless the ICE officer who completed it is present to authenticate it, *see, e.g.*, *Iran v. INS*, 656 F.2d 469 (9th Cir. 1981), Respondent also has a statutory right to cross-examine witnesses pursuant to constitutional right, *see Ganzalez v. Zubrick*, 45 F.2d 934 (6th Cir. 1930), and that the denial of such a right renders the hearing unfair. *Navarette-Navarette v. Landon*, 223 F. 2d 234 (9th Cir. 1955). In *Matter of Martinez*, 16 I&N Dec. 723 (BIA 1979), the Board of Immigration Appeals held that any evidence gathered by INS (now DHS), whether oral or written, should not be permitted to become part of the record if the respondent had been denied the right to cross-examination.

2. The manner of arrest is a central issue for Respondent's Motion to Suppress, which Respondent thereby incorporates as if fully set forth at this point. Respondent has made diligent efforts without success to discover the names of the ICE officers who carried out any investigation and subsequent arrest of respondent at **[Location]** on **[date]**. See attached affidavit of Respondent's attorney regarding these efforts, incorporated hereto.

Respondent, in this Motion to Suppress, alleges egregious Fourth Amendment violations that offend notions of fundamental fairness. *See Matter of Toro*, 17 I&N 240, 343 (BIA 1980); *INS v. Lopez-Mendoza*, 468 U.S. 1032 (1984). In a court of appeals decision, the Ninth Circuit stated in evaluating the Supreme Court's *Lopez-Mendoza* decision, "the court, however, expressly left open the questions whether exclusion of evidence might be appropriate if the evidence were obtained by egregious violations of the Fourth Amendment or other liberties that might transgress notions of fundamental fairness and undermine the probative value of the evidence obtains." *Id.* at 3490. *Arguelles-Vasquez v. INS*, 786 F.2d 1433 at 1434 (9th Cir. 1986).

In denying Respondent's instant request to subpoena, the arresting officers and documentary evidence, the court would be denying respondent his statutory right pursuant to INA §242(b)(3) to present witnesses on his behalf to show that this initial arrest was in violation of his constitutional rights and that any subsequent statements taken from Respondent were fruits of an unlawful seizure.

WHEREFORE, FOR THE ABOVE REASONS, Respondent request that subpoenas be issued to the above-mentioned individuals.

Respectfully submitted this _____ day of _____ at ____________.

[Attorney for Respondent]

[Dated:]

UNITED STATES DEPARTMENT OF JUSTICE
EXECUTIVE OFFICE FOR IMMIGRATION REVIEW
OFFICE OF THE IMMIGRATION JUDGE

IN THE MATTER OF:)
)
[Alien])
A[Number]) IN REMOVAL PROCEEDINGS
)
Respondent)
____________________)

RESPONDENT'S MOTION FOR ISSUANCE OF SUBPOENAS (DHS OFFICIALS)

Now comes Respondent in the above captioned matter, pursuant to 8 CFR §§287.4(a)(2)(ii), 1287.4(a)(2)(ii), and 1003.35(b), and requests that subpoenas be issued to the following officers, agents, and employees of the Department of Homeland Security:

1. _________ _________
2. _________ _________
3. _________ _________

In support of this motion, Respondent says:

1. The testimony of the above persons is absolutely necessary in order for Respondent to present his defense in the above-captioned matter.
2. On **[date]** agents from ICE entered the **[Location]** and began questioning various persons present as to their immigration status.
3. Upon information and belief these agents did not have any arrest warrant but at most only an administrative search warrant whose validity is subject to questions.
4. Respondent was arrested at **[Location]** on **[date]**.
5. Respondent has filed a Motion to Suppress alleging that all property, evidence, and statements obtained from him were illegally obtained in violations of his constitutional rights, his rights under DHS statutes and regulations, and his rights pursuant to **[Law/Regulation]**.
6. A number of questions, including but not limited to the question of whether ICE agents had the reasonable suspicion required by the statute and regulations when they approached, questioned and arrested the Respondent, and the question of whether Respondent's right to avoid self-incrimination and coerced statements under the Fifth Amendment was violated, depend upon a careful determination of the facts.

7. The testimony of the above witnesses is absolutely necessary to establish the facts of what transpired in the above-captioned matter, to determine whether ICE had reasonable suspicion to act as it did, and whether respondent was subject to coercive and other fundamentally unfair treatment by ICE.

8. The above witnesses have refused to appear voluntarily.

WHEREFORE, respondent prays that this court issue a subpoena directed to **[Individual]**, **[Individual]**, and **[Individual]** commanding that they be present at Respondent's hearing on his motion to suppress.

Respondent,
By his attorney,

[Attorney]

[Dated:]

[Document Nos. 323–25]

MOTION TO SUPPRESS AND EXCLUDE EVIDENCE

Description: These motions are designed to exclude evidence and statements in removal proceedings, possibly as a basis for termination of proceedings.

Advantages: If a client is facing removal because of evidence obtained by the Department of Homeland Security (DHS) in a way that offends the Constitution, counsel has an obligation to attempt to have that evidence not considered by the immigration court in its deliberations.

Limitations: The rules of evidence are virtually nonexistent in immigration court. The Federal Rules of Evidence only apply as a possible equitable argument. Consequently, unless counsel can point to a constitutional violation in the obtaining of the evidence, it is likely that the immigration judge will consider any and all evidence presented by DHS.

Notes: In most removal cases, a motion like this would not be necessary, but DHS still conducts investigations and interrogations and proceedings result from these activities. If a practitioner represents a respondent in such a case, analyze the evidence to be presented by DHS to see if the obtaining of the evidence was lawful and constitutional.

Citations: *Matter of Toro*, 17 I&N Dec. 240 (BIA 1980); 8 CFR §287.3. See also citations included in the following motions.

UNITED STATES DEPARTMENT OF JUSTICE
EXECUTIVE OFFICE FOR IMMIGRATION REVIEW
OFFICE OF THE IMMIGRATION JUDGE
[LOCATION]

IN THE MATTER OF:	)	
	)	
[Alien]	)	
A[Number]	)	IN REMOVAL PROCEEDINGS
	)	
Respondent	)	
______________________________	)	

MOTION TO SUPPRESS EVIDENCE UNDER BEST EVIDENCE RULE AND FOR PRODUCTION OF DOCUMENTS RELATED TO FALSE CLAIM TO UNITED STATES CITIZENSHIP

Respondent, through counsel, hereby submits this Motion to Suppress Evidence.

TABLE OF CONTENTS

I. Statement of Case and Facts

Respondent entered the United States without inspection in 1991 at the age of six. He has never left the United States since his initial entry in 1991. Respondent's father, **[Father]**, filed an I-130 petition on his behalf in 1998. He is now eligible to receive a V visa. In addition, Respondent is eligible for 10 year cancellation of removal.

Respondent was arrested based on criminal charges in December of 2003. Because he was unlawfully present in the United States, he was also interrogated by a U.S. Immigration and Customs Enforcement officer. During the course of this interrogation, Respondent told the officer that he had last entered the United States through El Paso in August of 2000, and that upon entry had told the inspector at the border that he was a United States citizen. Respondent signed a sworn statement to this effect on December 2, 2003.

Based on his sworn statement and undocumented status in the United States, Respondent was issued a Notice to Appear (NTA) and placed into removal proceedings. The NTA alleges that the Respondent arrived in the United States at or near El Paso, Texas, on or about August 1, 2000. The NTA further alleges that he was not admitted or paroled after inspection by an Immigration Officer, and that on or about August 1, 2000, Respondent falsely represented himself to be a United States citizen for the following purpose or benefit: to gain entry for residence to the United States.

Based on these allegations, the NTA charges that Respondent is subject to removal from the United States pursuant to Section 212(a)(6)(C)(ii) of the Act as an alien who falsely represents, or has falsely represented, himself or herself to be a citizen of the United States for the purpose or benefit under the Act or any other Federal or State law.

In an effort to prove the allegations and charges against the Respondent, Immigration and Customs Enforcement is relying exclusively on Form I-263W Record of Sworn Statement signed by the Respondent on December 2, 2003. There is no evidence or exhibits that have been submitted by ICE to the court or counsel, other than the Respondent's sworn statement, to establish that the Respondent did in fact leave the United States and attempt to reenter the United States in August of 2000.

Respondent admits to having made a sworn statement to ICE officers on December 2, 2003, but he maintains that his sworn statement was not the truth, and that he had in reality never made a false claim to U.S. citizenship at the border in August of 2000, or at any other time.

On August 16, 2004, **[Expert]**, a Polygraph Specialist, administered a polygraph examination to Respondent.[1] **[Expert]** received his undergraduate degree from the University of Colorado in 1962. He later graduated from the United States Department of Defense Polygraph Institute in 1983. In 1987, he graduated from the University of Virginia Advanced Polygraph Studies Program. From 1965 to 1995, **[Expert]** worked as a Special Agent with the FBI. He was a certified FBI polygraph examiner from 1983 to 1995. Since leaving the FBI in 1995, **[Expert]** has been a private consultant and polygraph expert.

On the polygraph examination, Respondent was asked, "Other than in the sworn statement, have you ever actually told any U.S. Immigration authorities that you were a United States Citizen?" Respondent's response to this question was NO. Second, Respondent was asked, "Did you lie in your sworn statement about telling El Paso immigration authorities in August of 2000 that you were a U.S. Citizen?" Respondent's response to this question was YES.[2]

In his report, **[Expert]** states, "It is the opinion of this examiner that the recorded responses are not indicative of deception, and that Respondent was being truthful in his assertions that he had never actually told any U.S. Immigration authority that he was a U.S. citizen and that he had lied about having done so in his sworn statement."

At a Master Calendar hearing on **[date]**, this matter was set for an individual hearing on **[date]** at 10:30AM for a hearing on the allegations. Based on the polygraph results obtained by **[Expert]**l and review of the proposed exhibits that ICE intends to enter into evidence to prove the conviction, counsel hereby requests the suppression of Form I-263W Record of Sworn Statement based on the following grounds:

II. Argument

a. ICE Has Not Met the Burden of Proof

i. In a Removal Proceeding, ICE Has the Burden of Proving Removability

[1] *See attached CV of* **[Expert]**.

[2] *See attached Letter from* **[Expert]** *regarding the results of his polygraph examination of Respondent.*

In a removal proceeding, ICE has the burden of establishing by clear, unequivocal and convincing evidence that, in the case of an alien who has been admitted to the United States, that the alien is removable.[3] This burden cannot be met by a mere accusation or charge in the Notice to Appear. It can be satisfied only by evidence produced which is clear, unequivocal and convincing, unless the alien admits the charge or charges.[4] Respondent denies the allegations and charge that would, according to the Notice to Appear, render him deportable without the possibility of relief in the form of 10 year cancellation of removal. The documents submitted by ICE to prove the charges in the Notice to Appear are inadmissible and violate the best evidence rule.[5]

ii. The Documents ICE Offers as Evidence are Inadmissible in this Removal Proceeding as Evidence of the Respondent's Alleged False Claim to United States Citizenship

Black's Law Dictionary defines the Best Evidence Rule as a "Rule which requires that best evidence available be presented in lieu of less satisfactory evidence."[6] The best evidence rule provides that the original of a "writing, recording, or photograph" is required to prove the contents thereof.[7] A writing or recording includes a "mechanical or electronic recording" or "other form of data compilation."[8] Where the rule applies, the proponent must produce the original or a duplicate or explain its absence.[9]

In *Matter of M–*, the Board of Immigration Appeals determined that the best evidence rule applies in removal proceedings and should be considered.[10] Although the BIA found that there was no violation of the best evidence rule in *Matter of M–*, it did consider the matter in the context of removal proceedings.[11]

In order for ICE to establish by clear, unequivocal and convincing evidence that the Respondent was admitted to the United States in August of 2000, and that he made a false claim to United States citizenship and is therefore removable, ICE must present the best evidence to establish their allegations and charges. In this case, the best evidence that an individual entered the United States and made a false claim to United States citizenship would be the border inspector's report in August of 2000, or testimony from the actual inspector at the border that was told directly by Respondent in August of 2000, that he was a United States citizen. If the Respondent had made a false claim to United States citizenship upon his entry into the United States, he would have been expeditiously removed or placed into removal proceedings that that time under INA section 235.

The only evidence that ICE has that Respondent entered the United States or attempted to enter the United States in August of 2000, and made a false claim to United States citizenship is Respondent's sworn statement taken in December of 2003, during his arrest and interrogation. Respondent asserts that the sworn statement that he provided to ICE officer in December of 2003, is incorrect and contains false statements. Respondent's assertion that the sworn statement contains false statements has been confirmed by a polygraph expert, **[Expert]**. "It is the opinion of this examiner that the recorded responses are not indicative of deception, and that the Respondent was being truthful in his assertions that he had never actually told any U.S. Immigration authority that he was a U.S. citizen and that he had lied about having done so in his sworn statement."[12] Given that the performance of a polygraph examination has revealed that the sworn statement given by Respondent in December of 2003 is unreliable, the sworn statement cannot be considered the best evidence in proving the allegations and charges against

[3] *See* Immigration and Nationality Act, § 240(c)(3)(A), 8 U.S.C. §1229(a)(c)(3)(A) (hereinafter "The Act" or "INA"); *Woodby v. INS*, 385 U.S. 276, 286 (1966); *In re Aricio Pichardo-Sufren*, Int. Dec. 3275 (BIA 1996); *In re Madrigal*, Int. Dec. 3274 (BIA 1996).

[4] *See Matter of Lam*, Int. Dec. 2157 (BIA 1972); *In re Pichardo-Sufren*, Int. Dec. 3275 (BIA 1996).

[5] Fed. R. Evid. 1002.

[6] BLACK'S LAW DICTIONARY 160 (6th ed. 1994).

[7] Fed. R. Evid. 1002.

[8] Fed. R. Evid. 1001(1).

[9] Fed. R. Evid. 1002, 1003, 1004.

[10] *Matter of M–*, 5 I.&N. Dec. 484 (BIA 1953).

[11] *Id.*

[12] See attached Letter from **[Expert]** regarding the results of his polygraph examination of Respondent.

Respondent. ICE must produce evidence other than that obtained directly from the Respondent, that he in fact made a false claim to United States citizenship. Anything less would violate the best evidence rule and would be unclear and unconvincing evidence of Respondent's alleged false claim to United States citizenship.

In *United States. v. Bennett*, the Ninth Circuit Court of Appeals found that the best evidence rule applied in Mr. Bennett's case. In this case there was a boarding and search of Bennett's boat by members of a joint task force targeting smuggling activity from Mexico into Southern California. Officer James was the officer to first spot Bennett's boat near the U.S.-Mexico border. Officer James never actually saw Bennett's boat cross the border. Bennett challenged evidence regarding the global positioning system that the government attempted to use in establishing Bennett's journey from Mexico to California. The Ninth Circuit determined in this case that the best evidence rule applies. The court concluded that "the government did not produce the GPS itself—or a printout or other representation of such data, *see* Fed. R. Evid. 1001(3)—which would have been the best evidence of the data showing Bennett's travels. Instead, the government offered only . . . GPS-based testimony about an event—namely, a border-crossing—that he never actually saw."[13]

In *United States v. Rivera-Carrizosa*, the government attempted to establish Rivera's alienage through testimony of an agent regarding Rivera-Carrizosa's birth certificate. In response to the fact that the birth certificate was never introduced into evidence, the Ninth Circuit Court of Appeals stated, "This poses an obvious problem for the government. The agent's testimony violated the 'best evidence' rule, Fed. R. Evid. 1002."[14] The court found that, "Here neither the writing nor a copy was provided. The agent's testimony, unsupported by such documentation, was inadmissible."[15]

Although the fact in *United States v. Bennett* and *United States v. Rivera-Carrizosa* are different than the facts in Respondent's case, the same legal analysis regarding the best evidence rule should apply. The best evidence of Respondent's alleged false claim to United States citizenship would be a document provided by ICE that an immigration inspector had actually contacted the Respondent at the border or that the Respondent actually made a statement to an officer claiming to be a United States citizen at the border in August of 2000. In this case, the Respondent made a sworn statement three years after the alleged event occurred indicating that he had previously told immigration officers that he was a United States citizen. He did not claim to be a United States citizen in 2003 and his sworn statement has been shown to be unreliable.

Other evidence of the contents of a writing, recording, or photograph is admissible if the original is lost, destroyed or otherwise unobtainable.[16] ICE has made no showing that evidence, other than the sworn statement, is available to establish that Respondent did in fact make a false claim to United States citizenship.

In addition to violating the best evidence rule, use of a Respondent's own testimony to establish removability is prohibited.[17] In *Picardo-Sufren*, the Board of Immigration Appeals considered "whether the respondent's deportation hearing testimony regarding the incident which gave rise to his 1988 conviction . . . constitutes clear, unequivocal, and convincing proof of his deportability."[18] The Board of Immigration Appeals found that "If we were to make an exception here and accept the respondent's testimony as proof of his deportability . . . there would be no clear stopping point where this Board could limit the scope of seemingly dispositive but extrinsic evidence bearing on the respondent's deportability."[19] Therefore, the BIA found that the Service's charge of deportability was not proven in this case based solely on Respondent's own admissions.

---

[13] *United States v. Bennett*, 363 F.3d 947 (9th Cir. 2004).

[14] *United States v. Rivera-Carrizosa*, No. 93-10642, 1994 U.S. App. LEXIS 25488 at *6 (9th Cir. Aug. 8, 1994).

[15] *Id.*

[16] Fed. R. Evid. 1004.

[17] *Picardo-Sufren*, 21 I.&N. Dec 330 (BIA 1996).

[18] *Id.*

[19] *Id.*

In *Tokatly v. Ashcroft*, the Ninth Circuit Court of Appeals found that the "Immigration Judge erred in relying on testimonial evidence adduced at the immigration proceeding, including the petitioner's own admissions regarding the nature of his relationship with the victim, and in finding him removable."[20]

As in *Pichardo-Sufren* and *Tokatly v. Ashcroft*, the Immigration Court should preclude ICE from relying on Respondent's own testimony, in the form of his sworn statement, to find him removable. Even if the government is allowed to use such testimony, such testimony cannot be the government's sole evidence to establish removability. The government has the burden of introducing evidence, not obtained directly from Respondent, in proving the allegations and charges against him.

III. Prayer for Relief

WHEREFORE, Respondent, through counsel, prays the court to suppress the sworn statement provided by Respondent in December of 2003, which has been found to be unreliable, unclear and unconvincing through polygraph examination.

[Dated:]

Respectfully submitted,

[Attorney]

[ADD CERTIFICATE OF SERVICE]

[20] *Tokatly v. Ashcroft*, 371 F.3d 613, at *2 (9th Cir. 2004).

UNITED STATES DEPARTMENT OF JUSTICE
EXECUTIVE OFFICE FOR IMMIGRATION REVIEW
OFFICE OF THE IMMIGRATION JUDGE
[LOCATION]

IN THE MATTER OF:	)	
	)	
[Alien]	)	
A[Number]	)	IN REMOVAL PROCEEDINGS
	)	
Respondent	)	
	)	

MOTION TO PRECLUDE THE USE OF ALL EVIDENCE CONTAINED IN THE PRESENTENCE REPORT OR OBTAINED BY THE PROBATION DEPARTMENT'S PERSONNEL IN PREPARING THE REPORT

SUMMARY OF THE ARGUMENT

1. The presentence investigation is a process whereby a defendant, and others with knowledge of the defendant, engage in a critical evaluation of the defendant's entire persona: his or her family relationships, religious and ethical views, past proven or suspected criminal activity, emotional and sexual attitudes, and a wide range of other matters. The ultimate goal of the investigation is not to prove any specific act, but instead to understand the motivating forces underlying the defendant's conduct.

2. Given the wide-ranging nature and purpose of the inquiry, and the relaxed evidentiary standards governing it, the presentence investigation is more closely akin in degree of intimacy to psychiatric or spiritual counseling than to the public, adversarial cast of the trial of the guilt phase of a criminal proceeding. This court should prohibit the use of the presentence report prepared by the probation department, (sometimes referred to herein as the "probation report" or "PSIR"), and the information contained therein[1] because: the information contained in a presentence report is inherently unreliable; and the disclosure of the information will violate significant and long standing public policy concerns; the disclosure of the information will violate the HIPAA provisions; the disclosure of the information will violate the provisions of the Federal Rules of Criminal Procedure relating to the confidentiality of presentence reports; and the disclosure of the information will violate the ABA Standards for Criminal Justice.

[1] All argument concerns both the evidentiary use of the report itself and the evidentiary use of testimony by the probation officer(s) who gathered the information contained in the report: any distinction between the two would be a hyper-technical distinction straining credibility and unworthy of consideration.

ARGUMENT

I. Information Contained Within a Probation Reports Is Inherently Unreliable

1. Because the factual narratives contained in the probation report are prepared by a probation officer on the basis of interviews with numerous persons including prosecuting attorneys, police officers, law enforcement agents, etc., they contain unsubstantiated and unverified hearsay that is frequently inaccurate. *Dickson v. Ashcroft*, 346 F.3d 44 (2d Cir. 2003); *United States v. Charmer*, 711 F.2d 1164, 1175–76 (2d Cir. 1983).

2. There are no formal limitations on what can be included in a probation report and the report may contain unsubstantiated hearsay and information unrelated to the offense charged. *Gregg v. United States*, 394 U.S. 489, 492 (1969)("no limitation shall be placed on the information concerning the background, character, and conduct of a person convicted of an offense which a court of the United States may receive and consider for the purpose of imposing an appropriate sentence."); *Gore v. United States*, 357 U.S. 386, 393 (1958) ("There are no formal limitations on their contents, and may rest on hearsay and contain information bearing no relation whatsoever to the crime with which the defendant is charged.")

3. The Colorado Rules of Criminal Procedure permits the use of hearsay that would not have been admissible at trial in a probation report and does not require a hearing to determine the veracity or even the reliability of statements made in the presentence report. Rule 32, Colorado Rules of Criminal Procedure; see also, *People v. Padilla*, 907 P.2d 601 (Colo. 1995).

4. Hearsay statements contained in presentence reports and psychological evaluations need only contain minimal indicia of reliability to be used at sentencing. *U.S. v. Browning*, 61 F.3d 752, 755 (10th Cir. 1995). And conclusions in a presentence report, unsubstantiated by actual facts, do not meet the "preponderance of the evidence" standard. *U.S. v. Gomez-Arrellano*, 5 F.3d 464, 467 (10th Cir. 1993).

5. Probation reports may include allegations that were not proven at trial, as well as alleged facts that would have been inadmissible at trial had the prosecution attempted to present them. *See Hili v. Sciarrotta*, 140 F.3d 210, 216 (2d Cir. 1998) (noting that the inclusion of hearsay statements and inaccurate information in a PSR is "virtually inevitable"); *Dorman v. Higgins*, 821 F.2d 133, 138 (2d Cir. 1987) (noting that verification of the information contained in a PSR is "desirable . . . [but] not always possible").

6. A sentencing judge may consider allegations (even if supported only by hearsay or illegally obtained evidence) that the defendant has committed other, uncharged crimes; the court may even consider prior acquittals, or crimes committed by the defendant as a juvenile, for limited purposes. See *United States v. Agyemang*, 876 F.2d 1264, slip op. at 12–14 (7th Cir. 1989) (approving sentencing court's extensive reliance on hearsay); *United States v. Nowicki*, 870 F.2d 405, 406–07 (7th Cir. 1989) (sentencing court may consider allegation, even if based on hearsay, that defendant threatened co-defendant or witness); *United States v. Gardner*, 860 F.2d 1391, 1399 (7th Cir. 1988); *United States v. Perez*, 858 F.2d 1272, 1275, 1277–78 (7th Cir. 1988).

7. A defendant has the right to challenge the accuracy of factual statements contained in the presentence report. See, e.g., *United States v. Brown*, 870 F.2d 1354, slip op. at 11–14 (7th Cir. 1989); *United States v. Perez*, 858 F.2d 1272, 1276–77 (7th Cir. 1988); *United States v. Eschweiler*, 782 F.2d 1385, 1387–91 (7th Cir. 1986); *United States v. Rone*, 743 F.2d 1169, 1171–76 (7th Cir. 1984). However, the sentencing court need not make a finding as to all matters which the defendant contests. Instead, the court may simply disregard contested facts, in which case the challenged statements remain in the report. *Levesque v. Brennan*, 864 F.2d 515, 518–20 (7th Cir. 1988).

8. Further, the defendant does not have the right to challenge "evaluations", as opposed to "facts", contained in the report; thus, some of the most subjective, and potentially unreliable, material in the report is immune to challenge. *United States v. Manso-Portes*, 867 F.2d 422, 428 (7th Cir. 1989) (defendant may not challenge statement that he had "managerial position" in drug conspiracy); *cf. United States v. Atehortua*, 875 F.2d 149, slip op. at 4 (7th Cir. 1989). Even if the district court accepts the defendant's version of disputed facts, the inaccurate material is not excised from the report; instead, the district court's contrary finding is simply attached to the report as an appendix.

9. Thus, there is a strong possibility that the report will contain material which is untrustworthy or simply incorrect, or which the defendant has not been given a full opportunity to rebut. See Fennell & Hall, Due Process at Sentencing: An Empirical and Legal Analysis of the Disclosure of Presentence Reports in Federal Courts, 93 Harv.L.Rev. 1613, 1628–30 (1980) (documenting instances of inaccuracies and "subtle distortions" in presentence reports).

10. Hearsay is admissible in immigration proceedings. However, the evidence that is submitted must still be clear, unequivocal and convincing, unless the alien admits the charge or charges. *Matter of Lam*, Int. Dec. 2157 (BIA 1972); *In re Aricio Pichardo-Sufren*, Int. Dec. 3275 (BIA 1996). The Ninth Circuit confirmed this in *Abreu-Reyes*, when they stated, "the test for admissible hearsay in removal proceedings is whether the hearsay statement is probative and whether its admission is fundamentally fair." *Abreu v. Reyes v. INS*, 292 F.3d 1029, 1032 (9th Cir. 2002).

11. Factual statements contained in a probation report are not a highly reliable basis for a decision of such importance as deportation. *Dickson v. Ashcroft*, 346 F.3d 44 (2d Cir. 2003). The introduction of such unreliable statements in order to establish the grounds of removal necessary to deport a lawful permanent resident from the United States is fundamentally unfair. *United States v. Charmer*, 711 F.2d 1164, 1175–76 (2d Cir. 1983).

12. The use of a presentence report to establish removability has been specifically rejected by two different Circuit Courts, one of which was an *en banc* decision. *United States v. Corona-Sanchez*, 291 F.3d 1201, 1211–12 (9th Cir. 2002) *(en banc); Dickson v. Ashcroft*, 346 F.3d 44, 53–54 (2d Cir. 2003).

II. Information Contained Within a Probation Reports Has Traditionally Been Considered Confidential and Prosecutorial Use of the Information Violates Significant Public Policy Concerns

1. It is clear that presentence reports have traditionally been confidential—indeed, it is only in the past 25 years that the defendant has had access to the presentence report, either as a discretionary matter or as of right. *See, Williams v. New York*, 337 U.S. 241 (1949) (no denial of due process where sentencing judge considered presentence report which was not disclosed to defendant). See also history of amendments to Fed. Rules of Criminal Procedure 32 described below.

2. As stated by the Supreme Court: "In both civil and criminal cases the courts have been very reluctant to give third parties access to the pre-sentence investigation report prepared for some other individual or individuals. . . . One reason for this is the fear that disclosure of the reports will have a chilling effect on the willingness of various individuals to contribute information that will be incorporated into the report. A second reason is the need to protect the confidentiality of the information contained in the report. Accordingly, the courts have typically required some showing of special need before they will allow a third party to obtain a copy of a presentence report." *U.S. Dep't of Justice v. Julian*, 486 U.S. 1 (1988).

3. This court should be mindful of the fact that the use of the information contained in a PSIR whether disclosed through the report itself or the probation officer necessitates a public disclosure if it is a basis for removal since the basis for removal is (generally) public information.

4. The general factors justifying the secrecy of presentence reports include: (1) the privacy interests of the defendant, the defendant's family and the victim; (2) the interest of the court in full disclosure of information relevant to sentencing; and (3) the interest of the government in the secrecy of information related to ongoing criminal investigations. Each of these factors will be considered in turn.

A. Privacy Interests of the Defendant and Others

1. The criminal defendant has a strong interest in maintaining the confidentiality of his or her presentence report. Sentencing proceedings, and particularly the presentence investigation, often involve a broad-ranging inquiry into a defendant's private life, not limited by traditional rules of evidence. *See, e.g.*, 18 U.S.C. § 3661 ("No limitation shall be placed on the information concerning the background, character, and conduct of a person convicted of an offense which a court of the United States may receive and consider for the purpose of imposing an appropriate sentence.").
2. The probation report may contain: a listing of juvenile adjudications involving the defendant (which are normally confidential under state law); allegations concerning the defendant's involvement in other, uncharged offenses; the defendant's physical and mental health (including the defendant's I.Q., results of psychiatric tests, history of substance abuse problems and unusual fears, hostilities, obsessions, compulsions, depressions, or sexual deviations); any history of child abuse or neglect; details of the defendant's relationship with his or her spouse or significant other; and details of the defendant's financial condition. *See Gregg v. United States*, 394 U.S. 489 (1967) (there are no formal limitations on the contents of presentence reports, and they may rest on hearsay and contain information bearing no relation whatever to the crime with which the defendant is charged); *Williams v. New York*, 337 U.S. 241 (1949) (sentencing judge's consideration of presentence report containing wide range of information concerning defendant's personal life and past criminal behavior does not deny due process, even though defendant not allowed to examine report or challenge its contents); Model Penal Code § 7.07(3) (presentence report should contain, inter alia, "the defendant's history of delinquency or criminality, physical and mental condition, family situation and background, economic status, education, occupation and personal habits").
3. The prosecutorial use of personal information contained in a probation report results in the invasion of Respondent's personal privacy. This is an unprecedented and unwarranted intrusion unjustified in the law.

B. Possible Adverse Effects of Disclosure on the Free Flow of Information to the Sentencing Judge

1. The considerations discussed below demonstrate that, the subsequent prosecutorial use of information contained in a presentence report interferes with the proper functioning of probation office(s) and sentencing court(s) throughout the United States.
2. Frequently information disclosed to probation officers during the presentence investigation is given to the investigators in confidence. For example, a defendant may disclose his income but not wish to have those figures made public. A psychiatrist may provide an evaluation whose availability would best be restricted to the court and those involved in the defendant's rehabilitation. Law enforcement agencies frequently wish to protect the sources of information in their records and will sometimes exact a promise of confidentiality from the probation officer. In order to ensure the availability of as much information as possible to assist in sentencing, the courts have generally determined that presentencing reports should be held confidential. *See, e.g., United States v. Martinello*, 556 F.2d 1215, 1216 (5th Cir. 1977) (per curiam); *United States v. Greathouse*, 484 F.2d 805, 807 (7th Cir. 1973); *United States v. Fischer*, 381 F.2d 509, 511-13 (2d Cir. 1967), cert. denied, 390 U.S. 973 (1968).

3. In affirming a refusal to disclose to a defendant the presentence report on a codefendant, the court in *Martinello* stated as follows: "Presentence reports are not public records but rather confidential reports to the trial judge for use in his effort to arrive at a fair sentence. *United States v. Greathouse*, 188 F. Supp. 765 (M.D. Ala. 1960).

4. As other courts have held, requiring disclosure of a presentence report is contrary to the public interest as it may adversely affect the sentencing court's ability to obtain data on a confidential basis from the accused, and from sources independent of the accused, for use in the sentencing process." *Martinello*, 556 F.2d at 1216.

5. Maintaining the confidentiality of the probation report insures citizens will be more forthcoming with information concerning a defendant. There exists a legitimate fear that disclosure of probation reports will have a chilling effect on the willingness of various individuals to contribute information that will be incorporated into the report. *United States Department Justice Et Al. V. Julian Et Al.*, 486 U.S. 1 (1988). Persons with negative information about a defendant may feel threatened not just by a defendant learning of the contents but equally from the public at large. *See United States v. Charmer Indus., Inc.*, 711 F.2d 1164, 1174–75 (2d Cir. 1983); *Hancock Bros., Inc. v. Jones*, 293 F. Supp. 1229, 1234 (N.D.Cal. 1968) ("Reprisal by the defendant is only one event to guard against in promoting free and untrammeled disclosures by persons who have information necessary for sentencing or grand jury purposes.").

6. Moreover, the desire to avoid being publicly associated with a convicted criminal (by supplying information for the presentence report) applies equally to individuals who have favorable impressions of the defendant. It is in the best interests of the defendant, and society at large, that this information be disclosed to the court before sentence is imposed.

7. Governmental use of information within a probation report will affect the information received by a sentencing court from the most important source of presentence information: the defendant. Defendants will be reluctant to disclose details of their private life due to the possibility that the contents of the presentence report might one day be used in a 'quasi-criminal' proceeding such as this or otherwise open for other public inspection.

8. The sentencing court has a substantial interest in insuring that all information relevant to the sentencing decision is made available to the court. The Supreme Court has long recognized that "conscientious judges" seek "to sentence persons on the best available information rather than on guesswork and inadequate information." *Williams v. New York*, 337 U.S. 241, 249 (1949).

9. Permitting administrative, civil use of the information contained in the PSIR will jeopardize the "free flow of information" and the quality and quantity of presentence information courts receive at sentencing. *United States v. Greathouse*, 484 F.2d 805, 807 (7th Cir. 1973) ("requiring disclosure of a presentence report is contrary to the public interest as it would adversely affect the sentencing court's ability to obtain data on a confidential basis from the accused and from sources independent of the accused for use in the sentencing process."); *see also United States v. Anderson*, 724 F.2d 596, 598 (7th Cir. 1984); *United States v. Cyphers*, 553 F.2d 1064, 1069 (7th Cir.), cert. denied, 434 U.S. 843 (1977); *United States v. McKnight*, 771 F.2d 388, 390 (8th Cir. 1985), cert. denied. 475 U.S. 1014 (1986); *United States v. Charmer Indus., Inc.*, 711 F.2d 1164, 1171 (2d Cir. 1983); *United States v. Martinello*, 556 F.2d 1215, 1216 (5th Cir. 1977) (per curiam); *United States v. Dingle*, 546 F.2d 1378, 1381 (10th Cir. 1976); *United States v. Boesky*, 674 F. Supp. 1128, 1130 (S.D.N.Y. 1987); *Hancock Bros., Inc. v. Jones*, 293 F. Supp. 1229, 1232 (N.D.Cal. 1968).]

10. Permitting prosecutorial use of the information contained in the PSIR also interferes with the presentence report as a correctional tool in the important rehabilitative process. The presentence investigation can be an important first step in the rehabilitation of the defendant. During the presentence in-

vestigation the defendant may be amenable to personal change. The investigation may have both a salutary and traumatic effect on the defendant. The crisis of the situation often brings about a re-evaluation of the offender's personal situation. Thus, it is an excellent time to develop a positive atmosphere for the subsequent supervisory relationship.

11. It is frequently through the presentence report that the court determines what types of rehabilitative services are appropriate for a defendant. Frequently drug addiction is an underlying cause in many different crimes. If a defendant is afraid to admit his drug dependency to a probation officer because his "admissions" can be used in a future removal proceeding, the court will not impose the correct rehabilitative programs, the defendant's problem will not be fixed and future criminal activity becomes more likely.

12. Prosecutorial use of a presentence report is incompatible with the purpose of the report as a sentencing and correctional tool. Candor and openness on the part of the report's primary source, the defendant, will be stifled if the report is available for prosecutorial or investigative use. Prosecutorial use of the contents of the presentence report will not promote the effective functioning of the probation office, or, by extension, the sentencing court; rather, prosecutorial use will be a positive hindrance to the probation office's performance of its obligation to provide the sentencing court with a comprehensive analysis of the defendant's character.

13. The government also has an interest in preventing the disclosure of presentence reports. The presentence report will often contain information regarding the defendant's past or future cooperation with the government. The report may also include information conveyed by informants or cooperating co-defendants regarding the defendant's relative culpability for the offense for which he has been convicted, and the defendant's involvement in other crimes which may be under investigation. Especially where the defendant was a member of an organized, ongoing criminal enterprise, disclosure may pose a substantial risk to the safety of government informants, even though the defendant is incarcerated. And disclosure of the defendant's cooperation with the government may increase the risk of retaliation against the defendant, both during his or her imprisonment, and upon release. Therefore widespread disclosure of the presentence report may obstruct the government's ability to investigate crimes. *See United States v. Boesky*, 674 F. Supp. 1128, 1129-30 (S.D.N.Y. 1987) (fact that presentence report would reveal defendant's involvement in ongoing criminal investigation justifies non-disclosure).

III. Disclosure of the Probation Report Will Violate the HIPAA Provisions

1. The HIPAA provisions mandate that protected health information from a "covered entity" may be disclosed in a legal proceeding only if the defendant consents, the production is pursuant to a lawful subpoena or valid court order; or otherwise required by law. 45 C.F.R. Section 164.512(e) (relevant provision attached hereto as Appendix A). Even if legally produced in a criminal proceeding, the use of that information is strictly limited to that proceeding and further use of the information is precluded under a qualified protection order. 45 C.F.R. Section 164.512(e)(1)(iv) and (v) (any disclosure from a covered entity for a judicial or administrative proceeding provides for a qualified protective order that prohibits disclosure of the Protected Health Information for purposes other than the proceeding, and requires the return or destruction of the PHI at the end of the proceeding).

2. The defendant has not affirmatively consented, and in fact objects to the disclosure of any and all protected health information in these proceedings. The probation report and any protected health information contained therein have not been produced in response to a court order, a valid subpoena or other discovery request. The probation report and any protected health information contained therein has been produced without any attempt to notify Respondent that this material was being produced

and used in a prosecutorial manner. The probation report and any protected health information contained therein have been produced without any attempt to secure a qualified protective order.

3. The use of the probation report without regard to the protections and in violation of the HIPAA provisions violated statutory law and public policy and renders the proceedings fundamentally unfair.

IV. Disclosure of the Information Will Violate the Provisions of the Federal Rules of Criminal Procedure Relating to the Confidentiality of Presentence Reports

1. Rule 32 of the Federal Rules of Criminal Procedure mandates the confidentiality of presentence reports. Admittedly, the probation report that is the subject of this motion was prepared in a state proceeding and is governed by the Colorado Rules of Criminal Procedure. However, the Federal Rules of Criminal Procedure, as pertaining to third party disclosure of information in a probation report, provide useful guidance and ample support for the position that this information should not be used in a prosecutorial manner.

2. The circumstances under which presentence investigation reports are to be made, their content, and the circumstances under which they may be disclosed, are governed by Rule 32 of the Federal Rules of Criminal Procedure. Under Rule 32 of the Federal Rules of Criminal Procedure a presentence report was traditionally treated as such a highly confidential document that even the defendant who was the subject of the report could not get access to the information contained therein. Over time there has been a gradual relaxation of Rule 32's restraints on disclosure to allow access by the defendant but not third-parties. *See generally United States Dep't of Justice v. Julian*, 486 U.S. 1 (1988) (outlining history of, and reasons for, successive amendments of Rule 32). However, while the bonds of secrecy surrounding the presentence report were loosened to permit defense access, the framers of the Federal Rules remained sensitive to the concerns of law enforcement officials that unlimited access to the report might discourage full disclosure of relevant information to the sentencing judge, and might jeopardize ongoing criminal investigations.

3. Thus, unless the court directs otherwise, Rule 32(c)(3)(E) requires that "copies of the presentence investigation report made available to the defendant . . . shall be returned to the probation officer immediately following the imposition of sentence." The Advisory Committee Notes to the 1974 amendment of Rule 32 make clear that this return requirement is meant "to insure that [presentence reports] do not become available to unauthorized persons. 'Such reports shall be part of the record but shall be sealed and opened only on order of the court.'" 62 F.R.D. 271, 325 (citation omitted); *see also United States Dep't of Justice v. Julian*, 108 S. Ct. at 1615 (Scalia, J., dissenting) (quoting letter of Chief of Probation Division, indicating that main concern with defendant's retention of presentence report is that "there would be no way of effectively prohibiting further disclosure of the information to third parties").

4. The successive amendments of Rule 32, culminating in an extremely broad right of access for defendants, are based on compelling considerations of fairness to the person most directly affected by the contents of the presentence report—the defendant. These considerations have no relevance to third-party requests for access.

5. If this were a probation report prepared in a federal court, ICE would have no legal right to access the information contained within the probation report without a court order. Federally prepared probation reports are strictly confidential and the information contained therein is jealously protected. The use of the probation report without regard to the protections and in violation of the Federal rules of Criminal Procedure renders the proceedings fundamentally unfair.

V. The ABA Standards for Criminal Justice Mandates the Confidentiality of Presentence Reports

1. The American Bar Association's Standards for Criminal Justice, while mandating disclosure of the presentence report to the defendant based on considerations of "[fundamental] fairness," Standard 18-5.4(a), also state quite emphatically that the report should not be disclosed to third parties, except the sentencing and appellate courts, and persons having a "legitimate professional interest" in the report's contents. Standard 18-5.3. The commentary notes: "[These] standards take the position that the presentence report should not be a matter of public record. No legitimate interests are served by public disclosure. The incentive both for the offender and for sources close to the offender to cooperate candidly in the presentence investigation might be lessened if they knew that their statements could become part of the public record. Alternatively, the desire to protect sources from harassment and revenge might lead to the preparation of presentence reports that fail to convey candidly the information gathered. . . . In turn, such evasive phrasings might also make effective rebuttal of the report impossible. Finally, the offender has a continuing right to privacy in matters in his or her life and background that are not connected with the offense for which the offender stands convicted. An obvious social interest exists in minimizing unnecessary stigmatization of the offender, since any failure to facilitate the eventual reentry of offenders into society is in turn a likely cause of recidivism." Id. at 18-362.

2. Under the ABA standards of Criminal Justice probation reports are strictly confidential and the information contained therein is jealously protected. The use of the probation report without regard to the protections and in violation of the Federal rules of Criminal Procedure renders the proceedings fundamentally unfair.

CONCLUSION

1. This court should prohibit the use of the presentence report prepared by the probation department, (sometimes referred to herein as the "probation report" or "PSIR"), and the information contained therein because: the information contained in a presentence report is inherently unreliable; and the disclosure of the information will violate significant and long standing public policy concerns; the disclosure of the information will violate the HIPAA provisions; and the disclosure of the information will violate the provisions of the Federal Rules of Criminal Procedure relating to the confidentiality of presentence reports; the disclosure of the information will violate the ABA Standards for Criminal Justice.

Administrative agency use of a presentence report in civil removal proceedings is incompatible with the purpose of the report as a sentencing and correctional tool. Candor and openness on the part of the report's primary source, the defendant, may be stifled if the report is available for prosecutorial or investigative use. The American Bar Association also has recommended that presentence reports be maintained as confidential documents, and it apparently would limit their disclosure, insofar as third persons are concerned, to persons or agencies dealing with the defendant's rehabilitation.

[Dated:]

Respectfully submitted,

[Attorney]

[ADD CERTIFICATE OF SERVICE]

EXECUTIVE OFFICE FOR IMMIGRATION REVIEW
OFFICE OF THE IMMIGRATION JUDGE
[LOCATION]

IN THE MATTER OF:	)	
	)	
[Alien]	)	
A[Number]	)	IN REMOVAL PROCEEDINGS
	)	
Respondent	)	
______________________	)	

BRIEF IN SUPPORT OF MOTION TO SUPPRESS AND TERMINATE PROCEEDINGS

Counsel for Respondent, **[Attorney]**, respectfully moves this Court to terminate these proceedings or alternatively to suppress any and all statements or other evidence arising from the ICE's unlawful stop, detention and arrest of Respondent.

As grounds for this Motion, Respondent through Counsel proffers the following (affidavit or testimony to be provided at hearing pursuant to the Court's determination):

1. That on February 12, 2002, Respondent left his workplace in Commerce City at approximately 5:00 p.m., and was driving in his own vehicle to visit his cousin, who was then in jail in Brighton;
2. That traffic was heavy but moving on the roadway and Respondent was keeping pace with other cars and maintaining a safe distance from the vehicle in front of him in the left lane;
3. That about three miles from the jail, Respondent noticed that there was a white, late-model van driving aggressively behind his vehicle; that at times the van would tailgate Respondent's vehicle. Specifically, the van would speed up to within less than 10 feet of Respondent's truck, and then fall back;
4. That due to the van driver's aggressive and dangerous driving behind Respondent for several minutes in rush-hour traffic, Respondent believed the van driver was dangerous and wanted to pass;
5. That Respondent then changed from the left lane to the right lane to allow the van to pass, but which instead changed lanes and continued to follow Respondent's vehicle in an aggressive and close manner;
6. That Respondent continued to maintain pace with other vehicles in his lane (observing all traffic rules and well within the speed limit due to the congestion), and observe the van in order to maintain safety; that despite his continued observation of the van and its driver immediately behind him, Respondent did not notice any markings or lights on the vehicle or gestures or other attempts to communicate with him;
7. That upon reaching the appropriate place, Respondent used his turn signal, turned off of the highway, and pulled into the Adams Country Jail parking lot; that the driver of the van accelerated in order to stay immediately behind Respondent, maintaining an unsafe and threatening distance;

8. That after Respondent pulled into the parking lot, the van pulled sharply into a parking space on the driver's side of Respondent's vehicle; that the driver got out of the van rather quickly, came around the back of the van, and approached Respondent's vehicle on the driver's side.
9. That although Respondent was fearful that the driver was angry and aggressive, he rolled down his window in order to be able to communicate with the man as he approached; that as he approached, the agitated man told Respondent to "Turn off the engine! Turn off the car!"
10. That because the man had not identified himself or what he wanted, and given his prior dangerous and aggressive driving, Respondent was in fear and did not immediately turn off the engine;
11. That when Respondent asked the man why he should do so, the man angrily said that he was with ICE, and simultaneously reached through Respondent's window, turned off the engine, and took the keys out of the ignition and out of the car into the Agent's possession;
12. That the Agent then opened Respondent's car door and ordered him our of his vehicle; that Respondent did not feel as though he could disobey him and exited the vehicle; that as Respondent was getting out of the vehicle, the Agent again said he was with ICE and for the first time showed Respondent a government-issued badge;
13. That the Agent asked Respondent for "papers," and Respondent indicated that he could show him a valid driver's license; that the Agent asked if he was from Mexico and whether he had a green card; that Respondent handed the Agent his driver's license.
14. That the Agent then told Respondent to turn around and face his vehicle; that as Respondent turned, the Agent roughly grabbed his hands, put them behind his back, and placed him in handcuffs; that the Agent patted Respondent down, and told him he was under arrest;
15. That the Agent was very rough and put the handcuffs on very tightly; that the Agent jerked Respondent's hands upward behind his back hard enough to hurt and make the Respondent cry out in pain and tell the Agent he was hurting him; that the Agent did not respond and continued to treat Respondent in an aggressive and rough manner;
16. That the Agent told Respondent that he had been following him for 20 miles and demanded to know why Respondent hadn't pulled over; that the Agent also made comments about the sign on the back of his truck, saying that Respondent was a "stupid Mexican" and reminding Respondent that he "was not in Mexico."
17. That the Agent took Respondent's wallet from his person and told him that he would be deported for 20 years and taunted Respondent, telling him he had no right to go to court, to see or judge or to get a bond;
18. That the Agent communicated almost entirely in English; that Respondent has difficulty communicating in English, but responded to the Agent's questions in a combination of mostly Spanish and some English;
19. That during this time, the Agent repeatedly told Respondent that he would be deported and had no right to see a judge; that the Agent continued to make fun of Respondent for "being stupid enough" have the "Piss on La Migra" sign on Respondent's truck;
20. That the Agent then took Respondent into the jail building through the front door, inquiring with a jail official or employee if there was space to keep Respondent there overnight; that the jail employee informed the Agent that there was no room;
21. That at this point, the Agent became visibly upset, and walked Respondent back out to the van and placed him in the rear, making another two to three cell phone calls;

22. That after about 5–8 minutes, the Agent pulled him out of the van, and took Respondent to the back door of the jail, speaking with a female jail employee or official; that Respondent was placed in a holding room where his boots and handcuffs were removed;
23. That after approximately 15 minutes, Respondent heard the Agent and a female jail employee outside the holding cell making fun of him, saying derogatory things about Mexicans, such as "Mexicans are so stupid," "they think that they are in Mexico and this is definitely not Mexico," and again making fun of Respondent for having the "Piss on La Migra" sign on his vehicle;
24. That although Respondent did not understand all of what was said, nor did he hear every single word, it was clear that they were making fun of Respondent and making disparaging remarks about his Mexican nationality; that Respondent observed the Agent make most of the derogatory comments, with the jail employee mostly just laughing and agreeing;
25. That after making additional telephone calls, the Agent left without informing Respondent of his status or how long he would remain in the jail; that Respondent stayed overnight in the jail holding cell and was not informed regarding his custody or fate until at approximately 2:00 p.m. the next day, when a different ICE Agent picked him up and transported him to the DHS Denver District Office;
26. That this Agent brought Respondent inside the building and proceeded to take his picture and fingerprints; that the transporting Agent also directed Respondent to sign many documents, which he read to him in English and which Respondent did not fully understand; that Respondent was not advised by either Agent that any statements could be used against him; that at no time was he advised in Spanish or provided with a translator;
27. That while being processed at the Denver District Office, Respondent recognized the arresting Agent, who told the processing agent that he "knew" that Respondent would immediately cross the border back from Mexico after he was deported; that the two Agents began discussing the "Piss on La Migra" sign on Respondent's vehicle and the arresting officer again made derogatory remarks, stating "Mexicans are so stupid;"
28. That approximately an hour later, Respondent was transferred to the ICE Detention Center in Aurora.

Respondent's NTA was filed with the Court and a custody hearing was held, after which Respondent posted bond and later appeared at a continued master calendar. At that master calendar hearing, Respondent was represented by counsel, **[Attorney]**, who admitted that it was her first appearance in immigration court and that she did not know how to proceed. Further, **[Attorney]** was waiting for production of materials from DHS in response to her FOIA request and was not in possession of the information regarding the unlawful stop and arrest at the time of the initial master calendar.

The tape of hearing indicates that the Court suggested that **[Attorney]** enter pleadings, which she did. At a subsequent hearing, represented by undersigned counsel, Respondent indicated that he would stand mute in these proceedings in light of the egregious violations of his rights and withdrew the pleadings entered by **[Attorney]** as improvidently made.

ARGUMENT

The government has the burden of establishing alienage and removability by clear and convincing evidence. *Woodby v. INS*, 385 US 276, 285 (1966). The evidence obtained by ICE to establish alienage and removability was the fruit of an unlawful stop, further tainted by ICE's failure to follow its own arrest procedures. The Agent's words and actions demonstrate bias and general animus toward the Respondent. These egregious violations transgress notions of fundamental fairness requiring the exclusion and suppression of the fruits of that stop and arrest.

Not only did the arresting Agent lack the required reasonable suspicion to make an immigration stop, the Agent's conduct of the arrest itself was in violation of ICE's own regulations designed to protect Respondent. Further, the Agent's facially biased, unsafe and unprofessional actions, his many disparaging and racially-charged derogatory remarks and punitive conduct unlawfully harmed Respondent.[1]

In light of ICE's unlawful conduct in its stop, arrest and custody of Respondent, no evidence obtained by ICE as a result of these unlawful acts may be admitted into evidence in these proceedings; without untainted, independent evidence of alienage, these proceedings may not go forward and must properly be terminated.

A. ICE Lacked "Reasonable Suspicion" to Make an Immigration Stop

Immigration enforcement-related stops require a showing of "reasonable suspicion" to comply with the protections of the Fourth Amendment. *U.S. v. Brignoni-Ponce*, 422 U.S. 873 (1975). The Tenth Circuit has held that legacy INS/DHS agents "may stop vehicles only if they are aware of specifically articulable facts, together with rational inferences from those facts, which reasonably warrant suspicion." *U.S. v. Monsisvais*, 907 F.2d 987, 989–90 (10th Cir. 1990) (*quoting Brignoni-Ponce*, 422 U.S. at 884). These standards mirror the language and requirements in the Service's own regulations. *See* 8 C.F.R. 287.8(b)(2). In reviewing whether reasonable suspicion exists, "a court must consider the totality of the circumstances." *U.S. v. De La Cruz Tapia*, 162 F.3d 1275, 1277 (10th Cir. 1998). Although a court may not isolate and reject individual factors, "the officer must articulate more than an inchoate and unparticularized suspicion or hunch." *Id.*; *see also U.S. v. Arvizu*, 534 U.S. 266 (2002). The government bears the burden of demonstrating reasonable suspicion to justify the immigration stop and the admissibility of the evidence gained therefrom. *Arvizu*, 534 U.S. 266.

According to the government's own records, Respondent only came to the arresting Agent's attention because of a sign reading "Piss on La Migra" in the back window of Respondent's vehicle. The agent apparently "ran" Respondent's plates, which informed him only that Respondent was not in the DHS database. There are no other elements indicated in the DHS file to support the Agent's interest in Respondent other than his exercise of free—if somewhat inflammatory—speech.

The agent's lack of reasonable suspicion (and apparent animus) was such that he claims to have followed Respondent for 20 miles before contact was made in the parking lot of the Adams County Jail. That "contact" was at minimum an unlawful stop (as Respondent had not yet turned off his engine); further, the agent's actions (reaching in to Respondent's vehicle, turning off the engine and removing the keys and identifying himself as an immigration agent) resulted the restraint of Respondent's freedom of movement to the degree associated with formal arrest. This action was closely followed by a formal arrest without benefit of the protections provided in 8 C.F.R. §§287.3 and 287.8 and under the Fourth and Fifth Amendment.

B. ICE Violated Respondent's Rights in Failing to Follow Arrest Procedures in the Encounter

To determine the validity of an interrogation, a court must first determine whether the encounter was merely a stop or a seizure. A stop is tantamount to a seizure where a "reasonable person would have believed he was not free to leave." *U.S. v. Mendenhall*, 446 U.S. 544 (1980); see also *INS v. Delgado*, 466 U.S. 210 (1984); *U.S. v. Alarcon-Gonzalez*, 73 F.3d 289 (10th Cir. 1996) (police officer yelling freeze turns stop into seizure). The Tenth Circuit has held that a routine traffic stop is a seizure under the Fourth Amendment. *U.S. v. Baron-Cabrera*, 119 F.3d 1454, 1458 (10th Cir. 1997). The agent's stop clearly rose to the level of a seizure.

[1] In addition to the conduct described in Respondent's proffer above, the agent classified Respondent as a flight risk who would flee if given bond without any apparent rational basis for the decision.

Further, the BIA has held that any evidence resulting from an egregious arrest would necessarily be excluded by the application of the exclusionary rule. *See Matter of Cervantes Torres*, 21 I & N Dec. 351, 353 (BIA 1996) (*citing INS v. Lopez-Mendoza*, 468 U.S. 1032 (1984) (exclusionary rule applies in deportation proceedings involving egregious violations which transgress notions of fundamental fairness)); for a discussion of the Board's historical adherence to the exclusionary rule in immigration proceedings, *see Matter of Sandoval*, 17 I&N 170, (Applemen, concurring in part and dissenting in part).

Interrogation, detention and arrest procedures are detailed in ICE's regulations at 8 C.F.R. §§287.3 and 287.8(b), (c). Interrogation is defined in the regulations as "questioning designed to elicit specific information. An immigration officer, like any other person, has the right to ask questions of anyone as long as the immigration officer *does not restrain the freedom* of an individual, not under arrest, to walk away." 8 C.F.R. §287.8(b)(1) (emphasis added). Only if the immigration officer "has reasonable suspicion, based on specifically articulable facts, that the person being questioned is, or is attempting to be engaged in an offense against the United States or is an alien illegally in the United States, the immigration officer may briefly detain the person for questioning." 8 C.F.R. §287.8(b)(2).

For warrantless arrests, such as Respondent's, the procedures under 8 C.F.R. §287.3(c) specify that, inter alia, the examining officer must advise the alien of the reasons for the arrest, the right to counsel, and that any statement made may be used against him in a subsequent proceeding. Notably, "[t]he use of threats, coercion, or physical abuse by the designated immigration officer to induce a suspect to waive his or her rights or to make a statement, is prohibited." 8 C.F.R. §287.8(c)(2)(vii).

Immigration officers have the right to stop and question a person "only for the purpose of determining whether he or she has a right to be or remain in the U.S." *Lau v. INS*, 445 F.2d 217 (D.C. Cir.), *cert. denied*, 404 U.S. 864 (1971); 8 U.S.C. §1357(a). However, even this "statutory provision is limited by the Fourth Amendment." *Murillo v. Musegades*, 809 F.Supp. 487, 498 (W.D. Tex. 1992).

DHS must have reasonable suspicion based upon articulable facts that the individual questioned is an illegal alien unless consent is given by the person whom the officer seeks to question. *Matter of King and Yang*, 16 I&N Dec. 502 (BIA 1978) (Oriental appearance, in conjunction with past history of illegal employment at restaurant and anonymous tip, deemed sufficient for only *consensual, non-custodial* questioning). Race or alienage alone (even in conjunction with anti-INS/DHS sentiment) is insufficient to establish the "specifically articulable facts together with rational inferences from those facts" that suggest an illegal alien is present, notwithstanding ICE' broad authority under INA §287(a).[2] Subjective factors such as avoid-

[2] *U.S. v. Sigmond-Ballesteros*, 247 F.3d 943 (9th Cir. 2001) [Reversed district court's denial of motion to suppress where defendant pulled off the road, attempted to obscure his face from the officer's shining light, was driving on a route notorious for alien smuggling, was driving a vehicle (pick up truck) typically used for smuggling without a back seat, was driving at 4:20am when the route was normally used for commercial traffic and was on a route to the border but not near the border]; *United States v. Lopez-Valdez*, 176 F.3d 282 (5th Cir. 1999) [Reversed district court denial of suppression motion notwithstanding vehicle's proximity to border, numerous passengers in the vehicle, and the road the vehicle was traveling on could be used to circumvent an immigration checkpoint]; *United States v. Rodriguez-Rivas*, 151 F.3d 377 (5th Cir. 1998) [Reversed district court denial of suppression motion where vehicle stopped by Border Patrol because it had no front license plate]; *United States v. Jones*, 149 F.3d 364 (5th Cir. 1998) [Reversed district court finding of reasonable cause and held that under totality of circumstances the stop of the vehicle was unconstitutional]; *Gonzalez-Rivera v. INS*, 22 F.3d 1441 (9th Cir. 1994); *Illinois Migrant Counsel v. Pilliod*, 540 F.2d 1062 (7th Cir. 1976), modified, 548 F.2d 715 (7th Cir. 1977); *U.S. v. McDaniel*, 463 F.2d 129 (5th Cir. 1972); *Nicacio v. U.S. INS*, 797 F.2d 700 (9th Cir. 1985) [Mexican or Latin appearance alone are insufficient. "Articulable facts" forming the basis of reasonable suspicion are "measured against an objective reasonable man standard, not by the subjective impressions of a particular officer"]; *U.S. v. Mendoza-Carrillo*, 107 F.Supp.2d 1098 (D. S.D. 2000) [No probable cause to detain passenger in car where minor traffic stop]; *U.S. v. Lopez-Valdez*, 102 F. Supp. 2d 728 (W.D. Tex. 2000) [An anonymous tip was insufficient basis for investigative stop; evidence suppressed]; *U.S. v. Alvarado-Ramirez*, 975 F. Supp. 906 (W.D. Tex. 1997) [No probable cause or reasonable suspicion on stop]; *U.S. v. Covarrubia,* 911 F. Supp. 1409 (D.N.M. 1994) [Where officer listed a series of factors but could not demonstrate how they related to his and fel-

continued

ing eye contact or suspicious looks are insufficient; stopping a U.S. citizen without objectively reasonable suspicion is considered unlawful detention.

A stop may ripen into a lawful seizure only when there is probable cause. *Dunaway v. New York*, 442 U.S. 200, 215 (1979); *Murillo*, 809 F. Supp. at 499 (W.D. Tex. 1992) ("A search or seizure will never be considered reasonable if the officer stops the vehicle solely because of the Mexican ancestry of the occupant"). The refusal to answer questions cannot be considered in determining whether there is probable cause to arrest. *Florida v. Royer*, 460 U.S. 491 (1983); *Ramirez v. Webb*, 719 F. Supp. 610, 616 (W.D. Mich. 1989).

The arresting Agent violated Respondent's due process rights by failing to advise Respondent that his statements could be used against him. The Agent further harmed Respondent by taking his statement personally instead of transporting him to the District Office for processing or calling another Agent to assist. 8 C.F.R. § 287.3(a) (arresting officer should not take statement unless no other officer available or it would result in unnecessary delay). The failure to contact another agent or transport should also be looked at in light of the Agent's exhibited animosity toward Respondent.

By regulation, the examining officer (or arresting officer if the ICE is able to establish no other officer available and/or unnecessary delay) must provide advice of rights in the context of that interrogation. This advice should have included: (1) the reason for Respondent's arrest; (2) notice of right to be represented by counsel of Respondent's choice; (3) a list of available free legal services; (4) advice of the right against self-incrimination; (5) notice that a decision on proceedings would be made within twenty-four hours or less; (6) advice regarding whether Respondent will continue in custody or be released on bond. ICE's failure to provide notice of these right until after Respondent's arrest (and even then, read to him in English and conducted without a translator) is a clear violation of Respondent's Due Process rights, as well as the Fourth and Fifth amendments to the Constitution.

No advice of rights, verbal or otherwise, was presented to Respondent upon his arrest. It was not until after he was processed at the Denver District Office that he was provided with form I-214, which even then was not read to him in his native language. Further aggravating the egregious facts of the arrest and interrogation was the arresting Agent's continuous affirmative misinformation of the Respondent's rights: telling him he would be deported for 20 years; telling him he would not be released on bond; telling him he would not be given the opportunity to see an immigration judge. Not only did such actions violate Respondent's rights as noted above, they are clear evidence of the climate of duress and coercion created by the arresting agent, in direct violation of ICE's own regulations.

The information taken by the arresting officer in the process of the unlawful stop and flawed arrest cannot be characterized as a later admission freely or voluntarily given. While there is no explicit "but for" rule, the taint of original illegal arrest can carry over to such evidence. *Wong Sun v. U.S.*, 371 U.S. 471 (1963). The burden is on the government to show that a later admission was an act of free will, unaffected by any initial Fourth Amendment illegality. *Brown v. Illinois*, 422 U.S. 590, (1975). Factors to be considered include (1) whether any required warnings were made; (2) the temporal proximity of the arrest and statements; and (3) the purpose and flagrancy of the official misconduct.

The applicability of the exclusionary rule is not limited to criminal proceedings and its use in civil proceedings is well-established. The reasoning is well-stated in *U.S. v. Blank*:

---

low officer's experience in fighting transportation of illegal aliens, reasonable suspicion was not established]; Murillo, 809 F. Supp. at 498–99 [The failure to answer an INS officer's questions or the refusal to cooperate with the officer cannot be the basis to draw an inference for probable cause or reasonable suspicion]; *U.S. v. Ramos*, 753 F. Supp. 75 (W.D.N.Y. 1990) [Hispanic appearance alone insufficient]; *Ramirez v. Webb*, 719 F. Supp. 610 (W.D. Mich. 1989) [INS illegally detained and used excessive force against USCs based upon their Hispanic appearance]; *McElrath v. Goodwin*, 713 F. Supp. 299, 303 n.3 (E.D. Ark. 1988) (citations from Kurzban, *Kurzban's Immigration Law Sourcebook* (9th ed. 2004).

> Where as here there is a correlative civil action open to the Government which imposes a penalty . . . commensurate with the criminal sanctions to which an accused, victimized by an illegal search, would be exposed, then we see no distinguishable difference between the two forms of punishment which excuses the Government from complying with Constitutional mandates when prosecuting their action in a civil forum.

261 F. Supp 180, 182 (N.D. Ohio 1966). There is nothing about a removal proceeding which makes the application of the rule less compelling or less effective.

> The exclusionary rule . . . links the power to search and seize with the use of incriminatory evidence. Its purpose is to insure that abuse of one takes the profit out of the acquisition of the other. It prevents the violation by penalizing the violator. Aborting the consequences of the violation is only an incidental result, or better stated, a means to the primary end of curbing Fourth amendment violations.
>
> . . . .
>
> So long as an abuse of a power to invade privacy and arrest and search, might be an integral part of the gathering of incriminatory evidence for use in either a civil or criminal proceeding, as is possible in deportation cases, it would seem to make little difference, so far as the violation is concerned, if the end result is the use of the evidence in a civil, or criminal, proceeding, or both. If anything, looking to the need for the rule, it would seem to follow that the less significant the objective sought to be obtained by the breach of the constitutional imperative, the more reprehensible and needful of restraint or deterrence, is the violation.

Matter of Sandoval, 17 I&N 170, 186 (Applemen, concurring in part and dissenting in part).

WHEREFORE, Respondent through Counsel respectfully requests this Court to suppress any and all evidence arising from the unlawful stop and arrest, and terminate these proceedings.

[Dated:]

Respectfully submitted,

[Attorney]

[ADD CERTIFICATE OF SERVICE]

[Document Nos. 326–30]

MOTION TO TERMINATE REMOVAL PROCEEDINGS

Description: This motion is used to request termination of an immigration removal proceeding. The five versions that follow reflect various situations in which a motion to terminate would be appropriate. In the first, Immigration and Customs Enforcement (ICE) placed someone in proceedings while the individual had a pending I-130/I-485 with U.S. Citizenship and Immigration Services (USCIS), while the foreign national was in valid status. This would be an "improvidently issued" Notice to Appear (NTA) case. The second involves an argument that a person was in valid status during the pendency of an I-539, which was approved subsequent to the issuance of the NTA. The third motion relates to an argument that the alleged foreign national is actually a U.S. citizen. Following that, a brief in support of a motion to terminate argues that a domestic violence conviction is not a deportable offense because it is not, in this case, a crime of violence. Finally, the fifth motion to terminate is based on a defective NTA and on ICE's failure to meet its burden of proof regarding respondent's removability.

Advantages: Termination of removal proceedings protects the respondent from the expense of protracted litigation and the risk of a final order of removal or deportation.

Limitations: There are very few limitations. DHS may recharge if there are other applicable grounds for removal. If filing this motion on the grounds of derivative citizenship, make sure to provide the evidence statutorily required for derivative citizenship. Also, note that filing in advance may give DHS an opportunity to mount a rebuttal prior to final decision by the immigration judge.

Notes: Practitioners should consider filing motions to terminate where there are no facts upon which DHS can sustain its burden of proof.

Citations: 8 CFR §1003.40; 8 USC §§320, 321, and 322.

UNITED STATES DEPARTMENT OF JUSTICE
EXECUTIVE OFFICE FOR IMMIGRATION REVIEW
ATLANTA, GEORGIA

IN THE MATTER OF:	)	
	)	
[Alien]	)	
A[Number]	)	IN REMOVAL PROCEEDINGS
	)	
Respondent	)	
______________________________	)	

MOTION TO TERMINATE REMOVAL PROCEEDINGS

Respondent, through undersigned counsel, requests that **[his/her]** removal proceedings be terminated. In support of this request, Respondent states:

1. Respondent was admitted into the United States in valid **[type of status]** on or about **[date]**. (*See* Ex. 1, copy of Respondent's I-94 and passport);

2. On **[date]**, Respondent married a United States citizen, **[Spouse]**. (*See* Ex. 2 and 3, copy of marriage certificate, and copy of Respondent's spouse's U.S. birth certificate);

3. Respondent's U.S. citizen spouse subsequently submitted Form I-130, Petition for Alien Relative, on behalf of Respondent, and Respondent concurrently filed Form I-485, Application to Adjust Status to Permanent Residence. (*See* Ex. 4, copy of I-130 and I-485 applications);

4. U.S. Citizenship and Immigration Services (hereafter "USCIS") received Respondent's applications on **[date]**. (*See* Ex. 5, copy of I-130 receipt notice, and Ex. 6, copy of I-485 receipt notice);

5. On **[date]**, Respondent was placed in removal proceedings. (*See* Exhibit 7, copy of Notice to Appear). Respondent was charged with removal because respondent remained in the United States longer than authorized;

6. Respondent is not removable from the United States; rather, Respondent is eligible to adjust **[his/her]** status to permanent residence pursuant to INA §§ 245(a) and (c) and § 201(b). INA § 245(a) states:

> The status of an alien who was inspected and admitted…into the United States…may be adjusted by the Attorney General, in his discretion and under such regulations as he may prescribe, to that of an alien lawfully admitted for permanent residence if
>
> 1. the alien makes an application for such adjustment,
> 2. the alien is eligible to receive an immigrant visa and is admissible to the United States for permanent residence, and
> 3. an immigrant visa is immediately available to him at the time his application is filed.

7. Respondent filed an application for adjustment, as evidenced by her I-485 receipt notice (Ex. 6);

8. Respondent is eligible to receive an immigrant visa because of Respondent's marriage to a United States citizen, and Respondent is otherwise admissible to the United States for permanent residence;

9. An immigrant visa was immediately available to the Respondent at the time Respondent filed **[his/her]** application for adjustment of status. (Exhibit 5);

10. Respondent is also eligible to adjust status to permanent residence, despite any subsequent lapses in lawful immigration status, under INA § 245(c)(2). INA § 245(c)(2) states:

> Subsection (a) [of INA § 245] shall not be applicable to… (2) an alien **(other than an immediate relative as defined in section 201(b)…)** who is in unlawful immigration status on the date of filing the application for adjustment of status or who has failed…to maintain continuously a lawful status since entry into the United States.

INA § 245(c)(2) (Emphasis added)

11. Even if Respondent has failed to maintain **[his/her] [type of status]** after admission, Respondent remains eligible for adjustment of status under INA §§ 245(a) and (c) because **[he/she]** is an immediate relative as defined by INA § 201(b). Pursuant to INA § 201(b)(2)(A)(i), an spouse of a U.S. citizen is an immediate relative of that individual. As such, Respondent is an immediate relative according to the immigration laws because **[he/she]** is the spouse of a U.S. Citizen.

WHEREFORE: Because Respondent was lawfully inspected and admitted into the United States, is married to a citizen of the United States, is eligible for an immediately available immigrant visa, has made an application for adjustment of status ,and is otherwise admissible to the United States for permanent residence, Respondent requests the termination of **[his/her]** removal proceedings so that **[he/she]** may continue to pursue **[his/her]** application for adjustment of status which is now pending with the Bureau of Citizenship and Immigration Services.

RESPECTFULLY submitted this ____ day of _______, 20__.

[Attorney]

[ADD CERTIFICATE OF SERVICE]

UNITED STATES DEPARTMENT OF JUSTICE
EXECUTIVE OFFICE FOR IMMIGRATION REVIEW
IMMIGRATION COURT
ATLANTA, GEORGIA

IN THE MATTER OF:	)
	)
[Alien]	)
A[Number]	)
	)
Respondent	)
______________________________	)

MOTION TO TERMINATE PROCEEDINGS; *IN THE ALTERNATIVE,* MOTION TO APPEAR BY TELEPHONE AT MASTER CALENDAR HEARING

Respondent, **[Alien]**, by and through counsel, **[Attorney]** of **[Law Firm and Location]**, hereby requests this Court to terminate removal proceedings; *IN THE ALTERNATIVE*, Respondent requests that she and counsel be permitted to appear by telephone at her Master Calendar Hearing scheduled **[date]** at **[time]**; and in support thereof, Respondent shows unto the Court as follows:

1. Respondent, **[Alien]**, is a native and citizen of Columbia. This is the first setting of her Master Calendar Hearing.
2. **[Alien]** entered the United States in B-2 visitor status on December 13, 1999; her I-94 was valid until June 13, 2000. (Exhibit 1.)
3. **[Alien]** was served with a Notice to Appear, dated April 22, 2002, alleging that she was admitted as a B-2 visitor "on or about December 13, 1999, as a nonimmigrant VISITOR with authorization to remain in the United States for a temporary period not to exceed *June 13, 1999*" (emphasis added). The Notice to Appear further alleges that "You remained in the United States beyond June 13, 1999 without authorization from the Immigration and Naturalization Service." **[Alien]** did not enter the United States until December 13, 1999. These allegations obviously are in error and an act impossible to commit.
4. **[Alien]** is charged with being subject to removal from the United States pursuant to "Section 237(a)(1)(B) of the Immigration and Nationality Act (Act), as amended, in that after admission as a nonimmigrant under Section 101(a)(15) of the Act, you have remained in the United States for a time longer than permitted."
5. **[Alien]** timely applied to extend her B-2 status prior to June 13, 2000; the extension was approved for B-2 status until December 13, 2000. (Exhibit 2.)
6. **[Alien]** timely applied for a change of status from B-2 to F-1; the Notice of Receipt indicates that the application was received on December 11, 2000. (Exhibit 3.) The extension was finally ap-

proved a year later, on December 10, 2001, valid for duration of status (D/S). (Exhibit 4.) The I-20 indicates the course of study should last from January 8, 2001 to August 31, 2003. (Exhibit 5.)

7. **[Alien]** also filed an Application for Asylum and received notification that it was received October 22, 2001. She received an interview notice dated November 14, 2001. (Exhibit 6.) By letter of November 15, 2001 sent to the INS Asylum Office in Arlington, VA, **[Alien]** submitted a request to withdraw the application from further consideration. (Exhibit 7.)

8. **[Alien]** received a notification dated April 4, 2002 from the Arlington Asylum Office that, pursuant to her request, her case was terminated. (Exhibit 8.)

9. It is impossible for **[Alien]** to have remained in the U.S. beyond the time authorized as stated in the Notice to Appear. Furthermore, because **[Alien]** properly and timely applied for extension of her B-2 status and for change of status to F-1, she is currently in lawful nonimmigrant status despite the termination of her asylum application. There is therefore no basis for the charge of removal as indicated.

10. This motion is being made in good faith and not for purposes of delay.

WHEREFORE, based on the foregoing and for good cause shown, Respondent respectfully requests that the Removal Proceedings pending against her be terminated; *IN THE ALTERNATIVE*, she requests that she be permitted to appear with counsel by telephone at her Master Calendar Hearing, scheduled July 17, 2002.

This the _____ day of _________, 20__.

[Attorney]

[ADD CERTIFICATE OF SERVICE]

UNITED STATES DEPARTMENT OF JUSTICE
EXECUTIVE OFFICE FOR IMMIGRATION REVIEW
IMMIGRATION COURT
[LOCATION]

IN THE MATTER OF:	)
	)
[Alien]	)
A[Number]	)
	)
Respondent	)
______________________________	)

ORDER

Upon consideration of the Motion by Respondent to Terminate Removal Proceedings and it appearing that Respondent has shown good cause for termination of these removal proceedings;

IT IS HEREBY ORDERED that this matter shall be terminated.

This the _____ day of _________, 20__.

[Immigration Judge]

UNITED STATES DEPARTMENT OF JUSTICE
EXECUTIVE OFFICE FOR IMMIGRATION REVIEW
IMMIGRATION COURT
[LOCATION]

IN THE MATTER OF:)
)
[Alien])
A[Number])
)
Respondent)
_______________________________)

MOTION TO TERMINATE REMOVAL PROCEEDINGS; *IN THE ALTERNATIVE,* MOTION TO APPEAR TELEPHONICALLY

Respondent, by and through undersigned counsel, hereby requests this Court to terminate removal proceedings, or *in the alternative*, allow him and counsel to appear telephonically at the Master Calendar Hearing scheduled December 8, 2004 at 9:00 a.m. in Atlanta, Georgia; and in support thereof, Respondent shows unto the Court as follows:

1. Respondent was served with a Notice to Appear, dated December 22, 2003, on December 22, 2003 by personal service at Charlotte Douglas International Airport in Charlotte, NC. This is the first setting of his Master Calendar Hearing.

2. In his Notice to Appear, Respondent is alleged to be an arriving alien, a native and citizen of Yemen and to have been convicted of two crimes in Volusia County, Florida, in 1996 and 1997. He is charged with being subject to removal pursuant to INA § 212(a)(2)(A)(i)(I), related to crimes involving moral turpitude.

3. Pursuant to INA § 321, Respondent derived citizenship through the naturalization of his father. Respondent was born on June 1, 1978, and acquired lawful permanent residence on November 18, 1994, at the age of 16. His father, **[Father]**, naturalized on October 2, 1979 (Respondent was 1 year old); and his mother died on March 3, 1989 (Respondent was 10 years old). (*See* the N-600 Application for Citizenship and supporting documents attached hereto.)

4. Respondent has not been able to obtain a U.S. passport because he is required to submit an original copy of his father's naturalization certificate, which is not available to him. He has therefore filed the Application for Citizenship, which is pending with the USCIS office in Charleston, South Carolina.

5. As Respondent is a U.S. citizen as evidenced by the attached documentation, the Respondent requests that these proceedings be terminated.

ALTERNATIVE REQUEST FOR RELIEF

6. In the event the Immigration Judge does not grant continuance prior to the Master Calendar Hearing scheduled December 8, 2004, Respondent respectfully requests that he be allowed to appear telephonically with counsel from her office in **[City, State]**. Respondent resides and works in Charleston, South Carolina. The undersigned counsel has offices in **[City, State]**. Due to the distance, attending the hearing in Atlanta would require Respondent to travel a greater distance than to **[City, State]**; counsel would be required to either travel by air to Atlanta at undue expense, or to travel overnight to Atlanta, thereby causing two days loss of work.

7. Respondent, however, would be able to be present at the hearing telephonically with counsel in her office in **[City, State]**.

WHEREFORE, Respondent respectfully requests that these proceedings be terminated. *In the alternative*, Respondent respectfully requests that he be allowed to appear at the Master Calendar Hearing telephonically through counsel's office in **[City, State]**, telephone number **[number]**.

This the ____ day of ____________, 20__.

[Attorney]

[ADD CERTIFICATE OF SERVICE]

UNITED STATES DEPARTMENT OF JUSTICE
EXECUTIVE OFFICE FOR IMMIGRATION REVIEW
IMMIGRATION COURT
[LOCATION]

IN THE MATTER OF:)
)
[Alien])
A[Number])
)
Respondent)
______________________________)

ORDER

Upon consideration of the Respondent's Motion to Terminate Remove Proceedings, or *In the Alternative*, Appear Telephonically at his Master Calendar Hearing scheduled December 8, 2004 at 9:00 a.m., the Court hereby

_________ terminates these proceedings; OR

_________ allows Respondent to appear telephonically with counsel at the office of **[Office Name, Address, and Phone Number]**.

This the _____ day of ___________, 20__.

[Immigration Judge]

UNITED STATES DEPARTMENT OF JUSTICE
EXECUTIVE OFFICE FOR IMMIGRATION REVIEW
OFFICE OF THE IMMIGRATION JUDGE
DENVER, COLORADO

IN THE MATTER OF:	)	
	)	
[Alien]	)	
A[Number]	)	IN REMOVAL PROCEEDINGS
	)	
Respondent	)	
____________________	)	

PREHEARING BRIEF IN SUPPORT OF MOTION TO TERMINATE

ISSUE PRESENTED

1. Whether a state felony conviction under C.R.S. §18-3-302(1) for second degree kidnapping can support a ground of deportability for a crime of domestic violence under in INA §237(a)(2)(E)(i).

ARGUMENT

I. The categorical and modified categorical methods of statutory analysis apply to the evaluation of deportability under INA §237(a)(2)(E)(i)

In examining whether a conviction for domestic violence is a deportable offense under INA §237(a)(2)(E)(i), the categorical and modified categorical approach to statutory interpretation should be used. *Tokatly*, 371 F.3d 613, 615 (9th Cir. 2004). This methodology for examining criminal convictions is well-established. *See Taylor v. United States*, 495 U.S. 575 (1990).

When a statute is non-divisible, the court should examine the minimum conduct necessary to satisfy the elements of the offense and should not resort to the record of conviction. *Matter of Short*, 20 I. & N. 136, 137–38 (BIA 1989). Where any such minimum conduct under the offense falls outside of the ground of deportation, the respondent is not deportable. *Hamdan v. INS*, 98 F.3d 183 (5th Cir. 1996). However, where the statute covering the offense is divisible, a "modified" categorical approach must be used to determine deportability, one in which the Court is limited to examining the record of conviction in order to determine if the offense is a deportable one. *Tokatly*, 371 F.3d at 615. The Court is not to look behind the record of conviction to examine the particularized facts. *Id.* If the record of conviction is insufficient to support a basis for removal under a divisible statute, then the government has not met its burden of proving removability. *Id.* This divisible statute analysis applies to all grounds of deportation. See *Matter of Sweetser*, Int. Dec. 3390 (BIA 1999).

The BIA also adheres to a categorical and modified categorical methodology in order to determine whether a prior conviction constitutes a basis for removal under the INA. *See, e.g.*, *In re Teixeira*, 21 I & N Dec. 316, 318–19 (BIA 1996). While the Court may look to probative evidence outside of the record of conviction in determining whether or not to exercise judicial discretion relating to a grant of relief under the Act, for purposes of establishing a conviction for immigration purposes, "the Immigration Judge and this Board may not go beyond the record of conviction to determine the guilt or innocence of the alien." *In re Mendez-Moralez*, 21 I & N Dec. 296, 303 n. 1 (BIA 1996).

This analysis was affirmed by the Seventh Circuit, which held that the BIA is not entitled to look beyond the elements of the petitioner's state battery offense to his actual conduct in order to determine whether his crime was a crime of violence under 18 U.S.C. 16, as incorporated in INA §237(a)(2)(E)(i). *Flores v. Ashcroft*, 350 F.3d 666 (7th Cir. 2003). Applying the statutory methodology of analysis outlined in *Taylor*, the court held that the prior conviction failed to constitute a "crime of violence" under the provision and reversed the BIA's finding of removability on this basis. *Id.* at 672.

A. Legal definition of a domestic violence offense under INA §237(a)(2)(E)(i)

A crime constitutes a domestic violence offense for immigration purposes only if (1) it is a crime of violence as defined by 18 U.S.C. §16, and (2) the victim was a "protected person" within the meaning of 8 U.S.C. §1227(a)(2)(E). *Tokatly v. Ashcroft*, 371 F.3d 613, 619 (9th Cir. 2004); *Sutherland v. Reno*, 228 F.3d 171 (2d Cir. 2000). Under the domestic violence ground of deportability found at INA §237(a)(2)(E)(i), a crime of domestic violence directly incorporates the definition of a "crime of violence" found at 18 U.S.C. §16. That provision states that a crime of violence is:

a. An offense that has an element the use, attempted use, or threatened use of physical force against the person or property of another, or

b. Any other offense that is a felony and that, by its nature, involves a substantial risk that physical force against the person or property of another may be used in the course of committing the offense.

Thus, the analysis of whether a criminal offense constitutes a deportable crime of domestic violence under INA §237(a)(2)(E)(i) hinges upon an analysis of whether the offense is considered a crime of violence as outlined at 18 U.S.C. §16.

B. Applicability of section 16(a) and section 16(b) to INA §237(a)(2)(E)(i)

The statute at 18 U.S.C. §16 makes clear that there are two prongs under which a conviction can be considered a "crime of violence." Under the first prong of section 16(a), the actual elements of the crime must signify the use, attempted use, or threatened use of physical force against persons or property. In the case at bar for Respondent's offense for second degree kidnapping, the Colorado statute contains no such set of elements relating to force. Therefore, 18 U.S.C. §16(a) does not apply to the analysis of whether his conviction is a deportable offense for domestic violence under the INA.

The second prong of analysis under 18 U.S.C. §16(b) requires that (1) the offense be a felony; and that (2) the offense, by its nature, involves a substantial risk that physical force against the person or property of another may be used in the course of committing the offense. Here, Respondent was convicted under Colorado state law of C.R.S. §18-3-302(1), a class four felony. His conviction is also a felony under federal law because the potential sentence for the crime is greater than one year. 18 U.S.C. §3559(a)(5). Therefore, the analysis of section 18 U.S.C. §16(b) relating to the "substantial risk of force" is controlling in the analysis of Respondent's conviction.

II. C.R.S. §18-3-302(1) is not a crime of violence under 18 U.S.C.§16 because the statute contains no elements of force or domestic violence against protected persons

In order to determine whether C.R.S. §18-3-302(1) constitutes a crime of domestic violence for immigration purposes, the Court should examine the statutory elements of the offense, not underlying facts or conduct. *Matter of Pichardo*, 21 I. & N. 330, 335 (BIA 1996). Where the statute at issue is a divisible one that contains both domestic violence offenses and non-domestic violence offenses, the Court may look to the record of conviction in order to determine under which part of the statute the defendant was convicted. *Matter of Sweetser*, 22 I. & N. Dec. 709 (BIA 1999). This divisibility analysis applies to all grounds of deportation. See *Matter of Sweetser*, 22 I. & N. Dec. 709 (BIA 1999) (aggravated felony); *Matter of Short*, 20 I. & N. 136 (BIA 1989) (crimes involving moral turpitude); *Matter of Teixiera*, Int. Dec. 3273 (BIA 1996) (firearms offenses); *Matter of Mena*, 17 I. & N. Dec. 38 (BIA 1979) (controlled substance offenses).

However, where the statute is not divisible, the categorical approach must be used in order to examine the nature of the crime as defined by statute. In such situations, the Court should not look to the record of conviction. *Short*, 20 I. & N. at 137-138. Additionally, where the minimum conduct sufficient to satisfy all the elements of the statute falls outside of a ground of deportability, a person convicted of that offense is not deportable. *Hamdan v. INS*, 98 F.3d 183 (5th Cir. 1996).

Under the statute at issue, C.R.S. §18-3-302(1), there are simply no elements of the offense that relate to force or to domestic violence against a "protected person" within the meaning of INA §237(a)(2)(E)(i). Therefore, the Court should not look past the statutory elements to the record of conviction in order to determine deportability. On this basis alone, a conviction under C.R.S. §18-3-302(1) cannot support a ground of deportability for domestic violence under INA §237(a)(2)(E)(i).

The second degree kidnapping statute found at C.R.S. §18-3-302(1) states:

a. Any person who knowingly seizes and carries any person from one place to another, without his consent and without lawful justification, commits second degree kidnapping.

The Colorado statute for second degree kidnapping contains only one set of elements and one offense. That offense is kidnapping. Because the plain language of the statute reveals that it is not divisible, the Court's inquiry into Respondent's deportability should be confined to an analysis of the statutory elements constituting the offense, and not involve an examination of the record of conviction. Additionally, the Colorado statute in no way mentions force or domestic violence as elements of the offense of second degree kidnapping. While a conviction under C.R.S. §18-3-302(1) might sustain another ground of deportability under the INA, the elements of the offense simply cannot support a finding that second degree kidnapping is a crime of domestic violence for immigration purposes.

III. C.R.S. §18-3-302(1) is not a crime of violence under 18 U.S.C. §16(b) because the offense does not, by its nature, involve a substantial risk of physical force

A. Judicial interpretation of the term "force" in 18 U.S.C. §16(b), and the elements of the offense do not suggest a substantial risk of physical force

Respondent's conviction does not meet the second prong of analysis under 18 U.S.C.§16(b) for a "crime of violence" because the acts prohibited by C.R.S. §18-3-302(1) do not, by their nature, involve a substantial risk of physical force. The Tenth Circuit has examined the meaning of "force" under 18 U.S.C. §16(b) in *United States v. Venegas-Ornelas*, 348 F.3d 1273 (10th Cir. 2003). In reviewing section 16(b) of the federal statute relating to crime of violence, the Court noted:

> "Force," as used in the definition of a "crime of violence," is "synonymous with destructive or violent force," *United States v. Landeros-Gonzales*, 262 F.3d 424,, 426 (5th Cir. 2001)

(quoting *United States v. Rodriguez-Guzman*, 56 F.3d 18, 20 n. 8 (5th Cir. 1995); see also *United States v. Lucio-Lucio*, 347 F.3d 1202 (10th Cir. 2003) (explaining that §16(b) calls to mind "active violence"); *Bazan-Reyes v. INS*, 256 F.3d 600, 611 (7th Cir. 2001) ("We found the term 'physical force' in 18 U.S.C.§16(b) refers to actual violent force.").

An application of the Tenth Circuit's interpretation of "force" to C.R.S. §18-3-302(1) shows that the offense does not involve a substantial risk of force as defined by the Tenth Circuit. The operative elements of C.R.S. §18-3-302(1) that punish a person who "seizes and carries" another person do not contemplate the concepts of "destructive or violent force" or "active violence" mandated by the Tenth Circuit in *Venegas-Ornelas* and *Lucio-Lucio*. The Colorado criminal statute encompasses criminal acts that fall far below such a definition of force.

Colorado courts have also interpreted C.R.S. §18-3-302(1) to include acts that in no way involve force or the substantial risk of force. In *People v. Metcalf*, the Colorado Court of Appeals held that for purposes of second degree kidnapping under C.R.S. §18-3-302(1), the word "seize" in the statute encompasses a *mere taking* and does not imply the use of force. 926 P.2d 133, 137 (Colo. App. 1996) (emphasis added)(attached). The Colorado Court of Appeals further interpreted the issue of force under C.R.S. §18-3-302(1) in *People v. Maass*. 981 P.2d 177 (Colo. App. 1988) (attached). In that case, the court expanded the reach of criminal behavior covered by the second degree kidnapping statute in holding that the taking of a person *through the use of deceit* falls within the term "seize" because it is a taking without the consent of the victim. *Id*. at 185-186 (emphasis added).

Likewise, the Colorado Supreme Court has held that under C.R.S. §18-3-302(1), there is no requirement that "force" be an element of the crime, nor any indication of legislative intent that "force" must be an element of second degree kidnapping. *People v. Powell*, 716 P.2d 1096, 1102 (Colo. 1986). Additionally, the Colorado Supreme Court ruled that assault is not a necessary element of second degree kidnapping under the statute. *People v. Caldwell*, 510 P.2d 317 (1973). Colorado courts have uniformly rejected the idea that a substantial risk of force is inherent in the nature of the offense of second degree kidnapping under C.R.S. §18-3-302(1). The act of taking and the mere use of deceit is conduct that cannot be synonymous with the definition of force required by the Tenth Circuit.

B. Force is included in the Colorado offense of first degree kidnapping under C.R.S. §18-3-301

The legislative intent that force, or the substantial risk of force, not apply to the offense of second degree kidnapping is further reinforced by comparing the language of second degree kidnapping in C.R.S. §18-3-302(1) to that of first degree kidnapping under C.R.S. §18-3-301. Under the offense of first degree kidnapping, force is both explicitly found as an element of the offense and capable of sustaining the substantial risk of physical force. In particular, the first degree kidnapping statute outlines conduct that would certainly fall within designation under 16(a) and 16(b) of 18 U.S.C. as a crime of violence, as the statute states:

> Any person who does any of the following acts with the intent thereby to force the victim or any other person to make any concession or give up anything of value in order to secure the release of a person under the offender's actual or apparent control commits first degree kidnapping:
>
> a. Forcibly seizes and carries any person from one place to another;
> b. Imprisons or forcibly secretes any person

The noteworthy difference between a conviction for first and second degree kidnapping is that under first degree kidnapping, "force" is an element of the offense under subsection (a). More importantly, the substantial risk of force can also be found under the statutory language of subsection (c) in the acts of imprisonment or forcible secretion of any person. The offenses of first and second degree kidnapping can be distinguished from one another since first degree kidnapping involves either the explicit use or the substantial risk of the use of physical force.

WHEREFORE, Respondent prays the Court to find that his conviction for second degree kidnapping under C.R.S. §18-3-302(1) cannot support a ground of deportability for domestic violence pursuant to INA §237(a)(2)(E)(i).

Date this ______ day of_____, 20__.

Respectfully submitted,

[Attorney]

[ADD CERTIFICATE OF SERVICE]

UNITED STATES DEPARTMENT OF JUSTICE
EXECUTIVE OFFICE FOR IMMIGRATION REVIEW
IMMIGRATION COURT
[LOCATION]

IN THE MATTER OF:	)	
	)	
[Alien]	)	
A[Number]	)	IN REMOVAL PROCEEDINGS
	)	
Respondent	)	
___________________________	)	

RESPONDENT'S MOTION TO TERMINATE PROCEEDINGS

COMES NOW the Respondent, **[Alien]**, by and through her undersigned counsel, and files the respondent's Motion to Terminate Proceedings. In support of this motion, the Respondent, by and through the undersigned counsel, states as follows:

1. After the commencement of the removal proceedings only the Immigration Judge may terminate proceedings upon request by either party. *See Matter of G-N-C-*, 22 I&N Dec. 281 (BIA 1988).

2..The respondent may request termination on grounds such as: (1) the Notice to Appear is defective; (2) incongruity between the charge and the allegations; or (3) U.S. Immigration and Customs Enforcement (ICE) has not met its burden of proof as outlined in *Woodby v. INS*, 385 U.S. 276 (1966) (ICE must prove by "clear, unequivocal, and convincing evidence" the alien's deportability); 8 C.F.R. § 240.8(a). *See United States Department of Justice Immigration Judge Benchbook*, 4th Edition, Volume 2, p. 605.

3. In the instant case, the Notice to Appear ("NTA") is defective because it fails to allege with any specificity regarding the basis of the Respondent's removal. ICE alleges that the respondent is removable under Section 212(a)(2)(A)(i)(I) of the Immigration and Nationality Act ("INA"), for having been convicted of, admitted having committed, or admitted committing acts which constitute the essential elements of a crime involving moral turpitude (other than a purely political offense) or an attempt or conspiracy to commit such a crime. See Exh. A (Notice to Appear). The only factual basis of the allegations is that the Respondent was convicted for Food Stamp Fraud and Money Laundering on March 13, 1998. The NTA, however, does not indicate whether the conviction was for a state or federal crime, or provide any statute under which the Respondent was convicted. *Id.*

4. ICE also has failed to prove by "clear, unequivocal, and convincing evidence" that the Respondent is removable, as required. In removal proceedings in which ICE alleges Respondent's removability based on her criminal conviction, ICE has a high burden to produce certified criminal record and to prove that Respondent is removable by virtue of her criminal conviction. *See Matter of Bahta*, 22 I&N Dec. 1381, 1393 (BIA 2000). *See also Matter of Beckford*, 22 I&N Dec. 1216, 1218 (BIA 2000) (the Service has the initial burden of proof in removal proceedings); *Matter of Pichardo*, 21 I&N Dec. 330 (BIA 1996) (holding that a respondent's testimony concerning his violation of the law is not admissible and does not relieve the Service of its burden of proving that the respondent is subject to deportation or removal based on a particular convic-

tion); INA § 240(c)(3)(A) (burden of proof on ICEe to prove Respondent's removability); 8 C.F.R. § 1240.8 (same); INA § 243B (ICE's burden to produce certified record of conviction); 8 C.F.R. § 1003.41 (same).

5. Assuming ICE produces the Respondent's certified criminal record, as required, the record will indicate that, on March 19, 1998, the Respondent was convicted of the following crimes: (1) Illegal Possession of Food Stamp Coupons, in violation of 7 U.S.C. § 2024(b)(1); and (2) False Statements in Redemption of USDA Food Stamp Coupons, in violation of 18 U.S.C. §§ 2, 1001.[1] The record will also indicate that, for these convictions, the Respondent was sentenced to 24 months' probation, $450 assessment and $6,018 restitution, however, that no sentence of imprisonment or fine was imposed. The record will further indicate that, upon the Government's motion for "Satisfaction of Restitution," Respondent's judgment as to the restitution portion of the sentence was vacated on the ground that she paid the full amount of the restitution. Finally, the record will indicate that, on December 22, 1999, pursuant to the district court's order, the Respondent's probation was terminated early.

6. In addition, assuming ICE produces Respondent's certified criminal records, as required, her plea agreement will indicate the following. First, as to the Illegal Possession of Food Stamp Coupons, in violation of 7 U.S.C. § 2024(b)(1), required elements for conviction were: (1) Defendant knowingly used, possessed, or acquired food stamp coupons; and (2) Defendant did so in any manner not authorized by the statute or the regulations issued pursuant to its authority. Second, as to the False Statements in Redemption of USDA Food Stamp Coupons, in violation of 18 U.S.C. §§ 2, 1001, the required elements for conviction were: (1) Defendant knowingly made a false statement in relation to a matter within the jurisdiction of a department or agency of the United States, as charged; (2) the false statements related to a material matter; and (3) Defendant acted willfully and with knowledge of the falsity.

7. In the instant case, Respondent is not removable based on her criminal convictions because none of her convictions constitutes a crime of moral turpitude ("CMT").

8. First, Respondent's conviction under 7 U.S.C. § 2024(b)(1) does not involve a CMT. There is no BIA or circuit case law on whether a conviction under 7 U.S.C. § 2024(b)(1) constitutes a CMT. In absence of any precedents on whether a specific crime is a CMT, courts first look to the statutory elements of the crime. *See Matter of Esfandiary*, 16 I&N Dec. 659 (BIA 1979); *Matter of Ghunaim*, 15 I & N Dec. 269 (BIA 1975).

9. In *Liparota v. United States*, 471 U.S. 419 (1985), the Supreme Court held that 7 U.S.C. § 2024(b)(1) which prohibits the knowing acquisition or possession of food stamps in any manner not authorized by the statute or regulations, required proof of: (1) the defendant's knowledge of his acquisition or possession of the food stamps; and (2) his knowledge that his possession or acquisition of the food stamps was not authorized by the regulation. *Id.* at 433–34. The Court's holding was based on its reasoning that the statute covered a wide range of unauthorized food stamp transactions, including innocent transfers and, as such, elements of crime under the statute must be construed to protect the innocent. *Id.* at 425. Accordingly, for CMT purposes, 7 U.S.C. § 2024(b)(1), which was a divisible statute prior to *Liparota*, is now a non-divisible statute by the Supreme Court's judicial construction of that statute.

10. Here, a crime under 7 U.S.C. § 2024(b)(1) is not a CMT because it does not contain any element that involves moral turpitude. Under this statute, a person can be convicted under 7 U.S.C. § 2024(b)(1) as long as she knows that she is possessing or acquiring food stamp and that she is doing so in violation of food stamp regulations. Thus, the minimum conduct required for a conviction under the statute is merely a violation of food stamp regulations. That conduct in and of itself does not involve any moral turpitude, especially in light of the fact that the statute punishes individuals for violating any part of its chapter, or "in any manner contrary to [the] chapter or the regulations issued pursuant to [the] chapter." *See Matter of P–*, 6 I & N Dec

[1] Without admitting any of the allegations in the NTA, Respondent makes reference to her criminal record for the sole purpose of informing the court that, as a matter of law, none of the crimes of which she had been convicted constitutes a removable offense, including crimes of moral turpitude.

193, 198 (1954) ("[I]t is the nature of the act itself and not the statutory prohibition of it which renders a crime one of moral turpitude").

11. In addition, Respondent's conviction may not constitute a CMT because the plea agreement only attaches knowledge to the first element (possession or acquisition of food stamp), but not to the second element (violation of food stamp regulations) of the crime under 7 U.S.C. § 2024(b)(1) offense. *See, e.g., Ciambelli ex rel. Maranci v. Johnson*, 12 F.2d 465 (D. Mass. 1926) (holding that assault and battery upon a police officer does not involve moral turpitude where intent is not charged); *Matter of Lopez*, 13 I & N Dec. 725, 726–27 (BIA 1971) (finding no moral turpitude where statute does not distinguish between voluntary and involuntary manslaughter and indictment does not reveal intent).

12. Respondent is not removable based on her conviction under 18 U.S.C. § 1001 because this statute does not involve CMT. The statute, entitled, "Making a false statement to a Government Agency," provides in pertinent parts:

> a. Except as otherwise provided in this section, whoever, in any matter within the jurisdiction of the executive, legislative, or judicial branch of the Government of the United States, knowingly and willfully -- (1) falsifies, conceals, or covers up by any trick, scheme, or device a material fact; (2) makes any materially false, fictitious, or fraudulent statement or representation; or (3) makes or uses any false writing or document knowing the same to contain any materially false, fictitious, or fraudulent statement or entry; shall be fined under this title or imprisoned not more than 5 years, or both.

13. Under the controlling BIA precedents, a conviction under 18 U.S.C. § 1001 is not a CMT, because a person can be convicted under 18 U.S.C. § 1001 for making either "false" or "fraudulent" statement, without proof of any "fraudulent intent." *See Matter of B–M–*, 6 I & N Dec 806 (1955) (a violation of 18 U.S.C. § 1001 is not a CMT unless the minimum conduct underlying the crime involves "inherent fraud element."); *Matter of Espinoza*, 10 I & N Dec. 98 (BIA 1962) (abetting nonimmigrant visitor in executing false application for extension of stay, resulting in the abettor's conviction under 18 U.S.C. § 1001(3), was not a CMT, since conviction under the statute would be possible without the element of fraudulent intent, and any ambiguity must be viewed in light most favorable to the respondent); *Matter of Marchena*, 12 I & N Dec. 355 (BIA 1967) (conviction under 18 U.S.C. § 1001 (2) not a CMT for the same reasons provided in *Matter of Espinoza*).

14. Here, none of the elements defined in the plea agreements indicates that the crime to which the Respondent had agreed to enter a guilty plea included an element of fraud. As indicated earlier, the plea agreement defines the elements of crime under 18 U.S.C. § 1001 as (1) knowingly and willfully making false statements to a federal government agency, (2) which is related to a material matter, and (3) with knowledge of the falsity. As in *Matter of B–M–*, this definition only falls under subsection (2) of the statute, which does not contain any fraud element. Therefore, under the controlling BIA precedents, Respondent is not removable by virtue of her conviction under 18 U.S.C. § 1001.

15. Therefore, the Respondent is not removable by virtue of her criminal convictions since the crime in which she was convicted does not constitute a CMT under INA § 212(a)(2)(A)(i)(I).

WHEREFORE, Respondent, by and through her undersigned counsel, prays that this Honorable Court terminates the instant removal proceedings based on the fact that the Service failed to meet its burden to prove that the Respondent is removable by virtue of her criminal convictions and that the Notice to Appear is defective.

Respectfully submitted,
[Attorney]

[ADD CERTIFICATE OF SERVICE]

[Document Nos. 331–34]

MOTION TO REOPEN REMOVAL PROCEEDINGS AND REQUEST FOR STAY OF DEPORTATION

Description: The motion to reopen varies by the facts of each case. Two of these particular motions are based on a removal order against someone who was never served with a hearing notice from the immigration court (*in absentia* removal). In *in absentia* cases, generally, the filing of a motion to reopen acts as an automatic stay. 8 CFR §1003.23(b)(1)(v). In the third motion, the foreign national had departed prior to the start of the Notice to Appear (NTA), and is now seeking to reopen his case so he can adjust status and not have to seek a waiver of his prior removal. In the fourth motion, the motion to stay was required, as the motion to reopen is based upon an "after-acquired" spouse, *e.g.*, marrying someone after the close of removal proceedings, and in this case, during the period of voluntary departure.

Advantages: The motion and request for stay, when required, are essential in stopping the Department of Homeland Security from removing the client from the United States during the pendency of the motion. This stay will be in place during the time the immigration judge is deliberating the motion.

Limitations: The stay created by the granting of the latter motion is temporary only. More important, the stay must be granted; it is not automatic, except in cases of *in absentia* removals. If the immigration judge rules against this motion, an emergency appeal and request for stay from the Board of Immigration Appeals would be required.

Notes: This is a tool practitioners will frequently use. According to U.S. Immigration and Customs Enforcement, there are more than 300,000 individuals with outstanding removal orders, many of whom have actual relief from removal available to them. If removal is imminent, be insistent on obtaining the actual grant of the stay from the immigration judge at or near the time of filing, if this is not an automatic stay (*in absentia* hearing) type of case.

Citations: 8 CFR §1003.23(b)(1)(v) and (4).

U.S. DEPARTMENT OF JUSTICE
EXECUTIVE OFFICE FOR IMMIGRATION REVIEW
IMMIGRATION COURT
[LOCATION]

IN THE MATTER OF:)
)
[Alien])
A[Number]) IN REMOVAL PROCEEDINGS
)
Respondent)
)

MOTION TO REOPEN

Respondent, **[Alien]**, through undersigned counsel, has respectfully moved that this Court to reopen her removal proceedings pursuant to 8 C.F.R. § 1003.23. Respondent was ordered removed *in absentia* by this Immigration Court on August 5, 2004. Because Respondent did not receive proper notice of her hearing, she is requesting this Court to rescind the *in absentia* order pursuant to INA § 240(b)(5)(C); INA § 242B(c)(3) (pre-IIRAIRA, April 1997); 8 C.F.R. § 1003.23(b)(4)(ii), (iii)(A)(2); Matter of G-Y-R-, 23 I. & N. Dec. 181 (BIA 2001); Matter of M-S-, 23 I. & N. Dec. 349 (BIA 1998); Matter of Grijalva, 21 I. & N. Dec. 27, 34 (BIA 1995); Matter of Haim, 19 I. & N. Dec. 641 (BIA 1988).

RESPONDENT RECEIVED INEFFECTIVE ASSISTANCE OF COUNSEL

As stated in Respondent's affidavit, she was ineffectively assisted by **[Purported Attorney]** in New York, New York. Respondent and her husband went to **[Purported Attorney]** to do their I-140, believing him to be a lawyer. **[Purported Attorney]** advised **[Alien]** to write a letter to immigration withdrawing her previous I-130 application, but did not advise her that this could result in a notice to appear or to update her address with immigration. **[Purported Attorney]** did not assist **[Alien]** in writing the letter, nor was it prepared on any type of letterhead from a law firm. **[Purported Attorney]** also did not list either his name and address on the preparer section of Respondent's husband's form I-140 or Respondent's name and address as the wife. When Respondent and her husband asked him why she was not listed, he told them he would list her later. We cannot find any evidence that **[Purported Attorney]** is licensed to practice law in New York State, nor did he list his name and address on the forms he prepared. All we have been able to locate for **[Purported Attorney]** is a phone number at some type of company that is not a law firm. When **[Attorney]** called and left him a message regarding **[Alien]** and told him she was being detained and it was extremely urgent, he did not return her call. (Ex. 1, affidavit of **[Attorney]**.) Likewise he does not return calls from **[Alien]** and her husband. This seems to fall under the definition for ineffective assistance of counsel, though it would be extremely difficult to report since **[Purported Attorney]** appears not to be licensed.

RESPONDENT IS ELIGIBLE TO ADJUST HER STATUS UNDER VISA LOTTERY

Respondent's husband has won the diversity visa lottery for 2005. Both Respondent and her husband are immediately eligible to adjust their status under diversity visa lottery and have paid the fees and filed form I-485 with the Atlanta USCIS. **[Spouse]** is the principal, and **[Alien]** is the dependant applicant. Only **[Spouse]** as the principal is required to have a high school education or two years work experience under 22 C.F.R. § 42.33, but both do. **[Spouse]** works as a landscaper for **[Business]**, which had filed an I-140 on his behalf before he won the diversity visa lottery. **[Alien]** is a medical assistant by profession. Respondent is also required to adjust her status, under diversity visa lottery 2005, by September 30, 2005. USCIS transferred both **[Alien]** and **[Spouse's]** cases to the Atlanta office for adjudication. They paid the fees for adjustment of status, filing form I-485 on October 18, 2004. **[Alien and Spouse]** had their interviews together on January 4, 2005. **[Spouse's]** case was recommended for approval at that time. (Ex. 2, interview packet for **[Spouse]**.) He will be called back for a stamp in his passport as soon as his file is transferred to Atlanta. **[Alien]**'s case was denied because of her *in abstentia* deportation order. However, since her husband is the principal applicant and he was approved, she is still eligible to be re-scheduled for interview and adjust her status, if she can do so before September 30, 2005.

RESPONDENT WILL SOON BE ELIGIBLE TO ADJUST UNDER HER HUSBAND'S APPROVED FORM I-140

Respondent's husband has a form I-140 filed on his behalf. (Ex. 4, Form I-140 and online status notification.) Although we are unable to get a receipt notice from **[Purported Attorney]** who filed it, this filing is being handled by **[Attorney]**. **[Attorney]** explained that there was a request for evidence issued on this case to the attorney's office that **[Purported Attorney]** was using the name of but not working with named **[Attorney]**. (Ex. 5, G-28 from **[Attorney]**.) The request for evidence was returned to immigration as undeliverable and **[Attorney]** was eventually able to get a copy of it and respond late with an explanation of why the response was late. USCIS should be making an adjudicatory decision on the I-140 within the very near future.

CONCLUSION

Based on all these factors, the Respondent respectfully requests a rescission of her *in absentia* order of deportation and a reopening of her removal proceedings.

Respectfully submitted this ____day of ________, 20__.

[Attorney]

[ADD CERTIFICATE OF SERVICE]

U.S. DEPARTMENT OF JUSTICE
EXECUTIVE OFFICE FOR IMMIGRATION REVIEW
IMMIGRATION COURT
[LOCATION]

IN THE MATTER OF:	)	
	)	
[Alien]	)	
A[Number]	)	IN REMOVAL PROCEEDINGS
	)	
Respondent	)	
	)	

MOTION TO REOPEN REMOVAL PROCEEDINGS

[Alien], through undersigned counsel, hereby moves the Immigration Court to reopen her removal proceedings in order to allow **[Alien]** to file for adjustment of status.

FACTUAL AND PROCEDURAL HISTORY

[Alien] is a national and citizen of Russia. **[Alien and Spouse]** were married on February 9, 2002, in Moscow, Russia, and on **[date]**, **[Alien]** entered the United States at Laredo, Texas, where she immediately requested political asylum. **[Alien]** was not in possession of a valid Immigrant Visa; therefore, **[Alien]** was detained by ICE, and given a credible fear interview by an asylum officer. (See Ex. 1, Notice to Appear.) The asylum officer determined that **[Alien]** had a credible fear of future persecution or torture, (Ex. 1), and on **[date]**, **[Alien]** was paroled and released from custody. (Ex. 2, copy of **[Alien]**'s parole card).

After being released from custody, **[Spouse]** took **[Alien]** home to live to **[Address]**, (see Ex. 2); however, when completing the Notice to EOIR: Alien Address, Deportation Officer **[Officer]** mistakenly reported **[Alien]**'s address as **[Address]**. (Ex. 3, copy of Notice to EOIR: Alien Address). Due to this mistake, **[Alien]** never received notice of the removal hearing held on March 25, 2005. (Ex. 4, copy of Notice of Hearing in Removal Proceedings mailed to an incorrect address). In an *in absentia* removal hearing held on March 25, 2005, a result of **[Alien]** not being notified of the hearing, Immigration Judge **[Judge]** ordered **[Alien]** removed from the United States to Russia. (Ex. 5, copy of Immigration Judge's order of removal).

[Spouse] is a member of the United States Army, and was stationed in Tennessee when **[Alien]** entered the United States. **[Spouse and Alien]** lived in their home at **[Address]**, until March 6, 2003, when **[Spouse]** was deployed to Iraq to support Operation IRAQI FREEDOM. After **[Spouse's]** deployment, **[Alien]** moved to New York to be with family, and on September 30, 2003, **[Alien and Spouse]** gave birth to their daughter, **[Daughter]**. **[Alien]** notified DHS of her change of address, and believed that she was still awaiting a decision on her asylum application. (Ex. 6, Affidavit of **[Alien]**).

On February 1, 2004, **[Spouse]** returned from Operation IRAQI FREEDOM, and Mr. and **[Alien]** moved to Kentucky. Once again **[Alien]** reported her change of address, and received no response regarding her asylum application. (Ex. 6.) On February 19, 2004, **[Spouse]** became a naturalized United States citizen. (Ex. 7.) On

February 19, 2004, **[Spouse]** also personally drove to the immigration office in Memphis, Tennessee, and filed a Petition for Alien Relative, Form I-130, (Ex. 8, copy of Form I-130), and inquired as to the status of **[Alien]**'s asylum application. **[Spouse]** was informed that **[Alien]**'s asylum application was still pending. (Ex. 6.)

On July 30, 2004, Mr. and Mrs. **[Alien]** personally drove to the immigration offices in Louisville, Kentucky. Once again, Mr. and Mrs. **[Alien]** inquired as to the status of **[Alien]**'s asylum application, and were informed that it was still pending. (Ex. 6.) **[Alien]** then applied for employment authorization. (Ex. 9, copy of receipt of **[Alien]**'s application for employment authorization). On November 23, 2004, **[Alien]** was fingerprinted in connection with her application for employment authorization. (Ex. 6.)

On December 22, 2004, Mr. and Mrs. **[Alien]** moved to **[Address]**, in connection with a duty reassignment that **[Spouse]** received from the Army. **[Alien]** immediately notified immigration services regarding her change of address. (Ex. 6.) On May 18, 2005, Mr. and Mrs. **[Alien]** attended an interview at the USCIS office in Charlotte, North Carolina, and **[Spouse's]** Petition for Alien Relative, Form I-130, which he had filed for **[Alien]**, was approved. (Ex. 10, Notice of Approval of Relative Immigrant Visa Petition).

ARGUMENT

An Immigration Judge may rescind an *in absentia* order of removal upon a motion to reopen, *filed at any time*, when the alien demonstrates that the alien did not receive notice in accordance with 8 U.S.C. § 1229. 8 U.S.C. § 1229a(b)(5)(C)(ii). 8 U.S.C. § 1229(a) requires that an alien in removal proceedings be given written notice either through personal service or by mail, if personal service is not practicable.

Judicial review of an *in absentia* order of removal is "confined to (i) the validity of the notice provided to the alien, (ii) the reasons for the alien's not attending the proceeding; and (iii) whether or not the alien is removable." *Nazarova v. I.N.S.*, 171 F.3d 478, 482 (7th Cir. 1999). **[Alien]** was never provided notice of the hearings which resulted in the order of removal against her on March 25, 2003. On February 26, 2003, a Notice of Hearing in Removal Proceedings was mailed to **[Alien]**; however, it was mailed to the incorrect address. (Ex. 4.) As Immigration Judge **[Judge]** clearly indicated in her order of removal, the Notice to Appear was mailed to **[Alien]** at **[Address]**, (Ex. 5), as provided by Detention Officer **[Officer]** when he submitted Notice to EOIR: Alien Address, Form I-830. (Ex. 3.) This was not **[Alien]**'s address. When **[Alien]** was detained on **[date]**, and subsequently released on **[date]**, she correctly reported her address as **[Address]**, (Ex. 6), as further indicated on her parole card. (Ex. 2.) As **[Alien]** never received notice of the hearing, the Notice of Hearing in Removal Proceedings did not comply with 8 U.S.C. § 1229, and was therefore, invalid.

[Alien]'s failure to appear on March 25, 2003, was the direct result of not being provided notice of the hearing. The only reason that **[Alien]** did not attend the removal proceedings on March 25, 2003, when Immigration Judge **[Judge]** ordered **[Alien]** removed to Russia, was because she was not notified of the proceedings. (Ex. 6.) Furthermore, **[Alien]** is not at fault for the failure to be notified. **[Alien]** provided Detention Officer **[Officer]** with her correct address, (Ex. 6), as illustrated on her parole card. (Ex. 2.) It was Detention Officer **[Officer]** that incorrectly reported **[Alien]**'s address, when he submitted Notice to EOIR: Alien Address, Form I-830, with both **[Alien]**'s name spelled incorrectly and an incorrect address for **[Alien]**. (Ex. 3.)

[Alien] had a bona fide application for asylum based upon persecution she faced due to her political beliefs. As indicated by the asylum officer that interviewed her, **[Alien]**'s fear of persecution is credible. (Ex. 1.) **[Alien]** diligently awaited a decision on her application for asylum, reporting her changes of address every time she moved. (Ex. 6.) It was not until after **[Alien]**'s husband filed a Petition for Alien Relative, and his petition was approved, that **[Alien]** even became aware that an order of removal had been issued in her case.

CONCLUSION

[Alien] respectfully requests that this Court grant her Motion to Reopen and rescind the order of removal issued on March 25, 2003, in accordance with 8 C.F.R. § 1229a(b)(5)(C)(ii), so that she may apply for adjustment of her status. **[Alien]** was never properly notified of the removal proceedings that lead to an *in absentia* order of removal to Russia, and now is the beneficiary of an approved Petition for Alien Relative, Form I-130, making her eligible to apply for adjustment of her status.

Respectfully submitted this _____ day of __________, 20__.

[Attorney]

[ADD CERTIFICATE OF SERVICE]

UNITED STATES DEPARTMENT OF JUSTICE
EXECUTIVE OFFICE FOR IMMIGRATION REVIEW
IMMIGRATION COURT
[LOCATION]

IN THE MATTER OF:)
)
[Alien])
A[Number]) IN REMOVAL PROCEEDINGS
)
Respondent)
)

MOTION TO RESCIND *IN ABSENTIA* REMOVAL ORDER, REOPEN, AND TERMINATE PROCEEDINGS

Pursuant to INA § 240(b)(5)(C)(ii) and 8 C.F.R. §§ 1003.23(b)(4)(ii), Respondent, **[Alien]**, by and through his attorney, respectfully moves this Court to rescind the *in absentia* order of removal entered against him, reopen his case and terminate the proceedings against him as the Notice to Appear was improvidently issued after his departure from the United States 8 C.F.R. §§ 239.2(a)(4), 239.2(c) and 1239.2(c).

As grounds for this motion, Petitioner states the following:

STATEMENT OF CASE AND SUMMARY OF RELEVANT FACTS

1. Respondent is a native and citizen of Nigeria who entered the United States on or about June 23, 2001, pursuant to a valid B-2 nonimmigrant visa and re-entered on September 30, 2002, after filing an application for adjustment of status, pursuant to advanced parole.
2. After his 2001 entry, **[Alien]** met and married a United States citizen. Although the couple began the process of applying for **[Alien]**'s residency on that basis, their relationship deteriorated. When the couple determined that their marriage was no longer viable, **[Alien]** abandoned his pending applications and departed the United States.
3. Because **[Alien]** and his now ex-wife had failed to prosecute the immigrant petition and application for permanent residence, the adjustment was denied. Despite **[Alien]**'s prior departure in 2002, an NTA was generated on April 5, 2004, referring the matter for removal, and service attempted upon Respondent via certified mail. The NTA, as well as a notice of denial of the I-485 were also sent by certified mail to Respondent's prior counsel, **[Attorney]**, on or about that time. Because **[Attorney]** understood his client to be outside the United States, with no interest in pursing status on the basis of the marriage, he did not respond to the NTA.
4. The Notice alleged that Respondent was removable on two grounds, citing INA §§ 237(a)(1)(B) & (C), as a nonimmigrant who had overstayed his period of admission and failed to comply with the conditions of his status. The factual allegations were in fact deficient, in that a material and fatal fact—Respondent's departure—was not noted.

5. As noted above, prior to issuance of both the I-485 Denial and Notice to Appear, **[Alien]** had already abandoned the application and departed the United States on his own accord. Indeed, he had actually left the country approximately eighteen months earlier, on October 8, 2002. *See* Airline Boarding Pass, and other evidence of travel attached as Exhibit 1; see also SwissAir Travel Club Gold account activity Third Quarter 2002, Exhibit 2. This final departure followed his return to the U.S. from a brief trip abroad for which he had obtained advanced parole. *See* Advanced Parole Travel Document, attached as Exhibit 3.
6. Based upon his departure in October of 2002, the one-step application that he had filed would already have been considered to have been abandoned, by operation of law, when he failed to return prior to the expiration of his advanced parole authorization, which was valid only through September 30, 2003. *See* 8 C.F.R. § 1245.2(a)(4).
7. **[Alien]** did not return to the United States from October 2002, until his attempted entry in August 2004. The stamps in his passport reveal that throughout 2003 (and 2004), **[Alien]** traveled extensively between Nigeria and South Africa; and when he did actually attempt to enter the U.S. as a visitor in August of 2004, he was denied admission, notwithstanding the fact that he had applied for, and been granted, a new visitor's visa prior to his trip. *See* Copy of Passport, attached as Exhibit 4.
8. Thus, both the Notice to Appear, which was issued approximately *a year and a half after Respondent left the United States*, was essentially without legal or factual basis and proceedings resulting from its filing with EOIR were improvidently initiated.
9. The *in absentia* order of removal which was issued against Respondent has resulted in significant prejudice, barring him from travel to the U.S. As a senior executive in a multi-national telephony company which does extensive business with the U.S., his ability to travel to the U.S. for business meetings is critical.
10. Respondent's order of removal has not been the subject of any prior motions or litigation before the Immigration Court, the Board of Immigration Appeals, or any of the federal courts.
11. Based upon the foregoing, Respondent contests the validity of the removal order entered against him insofar as it was entered without basis in fact and such proceedings were in fact improvidently begun. Further, Respondent notes that, due to his absence from the United States at the time the proceedings were initiated and conducted, his absence prevented him from the opportunity to appear or respond to these charges.

ARGUMENT

a. Proceedings Against Respondent Were Improvidently Begun as Respondent had Already Abandoned His Application and Departed the United States

It is somewhat axiomatic that a removal proceeding be undertaken to remove a person who is already outside the United States. Where a person is no longer in the United States, proceedings can only be commenced if that individual presents themselves as an arriving alien and applicant for admission. See 8 C.F.R. § 1003.14(a) ("Jurisdiction vests, and proceedings commence, when a charging document is filed with the Immigration Court by the Service."); see also, 8 C.F.R. § 1003.13 (defining the charging document as the "written instrument which initiates a proceeding before an immigration judge); and 8 C.F.R. 1003.15(c).

Where an alien has already departed the United States, prior to the filing of the charging document, such proceedings are considered improvidently begun. See 8 C.F.R. 239.2(a); *Matter of Vicarra-Delgadillo*, 13

I&N Dec. 51 (BIA 1968). The charging document should be cancelled, or at a minimum, the proceedings dismissed because the respondent is not in the United States. See 8 C.F.R. § 239.2(a)(4).

Further, an *in absentia* removal order requires a showing by DHS that the person is, not surprisingly, *removable.* 8 C.F.R. § 1003.26(c)(1). Logically, a person who is neither presenting themselves as an applicant for admission nor present in the United States can be considered properly the subject of proceedings. Because proceedings were improvidently begun, they fail to properly start the "clock" under 8 C.F.R. 1003.23((b)(4)(iii)(A)(1). Alternatively, because DHS had an obligation to dismiss the case on their own motion, such a Motion to Reopen should be reviewed by the court under its *sua sponte* authority.

b. Notice of Hearing Was Ineffective Based on Respondent's Prior Abandonment of His Application and Departure from the United States

Pursuant to INA § 240(b)(5)(C)(ii), a removal order may be rescinded "upon a motion to reopen filed at any time if the alien demonstrates that the alien did not receive notice in accordance with paragraph (1) or (2) of section 239(a) . . . ." *Id.* (Emphasis added).

Section 239(a) begins with the statement that "[i]n removal proceedings under section 240, written notice . . . shall be given in person to the alien (or, if personal service is not practicable, through service by mail to the alien or to the aliens' counsel of record, if any) . . .." *Id.* (Emphasis added). A straightforward reading of the language would seem to suggest that a two-tiered approach is called for: (1) personal service is required; but (2) if such service is not practicable, service by mail is sufficient. Logically, one would then look to the regulations to identify parameters which define when personal service is not practicable.

The regulations that define "personal service" and "service by mail" first review the phrase, "personal service," which includes "[m]ailing a copy by certified or registered mail, return receipt requested, addressed to a person at his last known address," 8 C.F.R. § 103.5a(a)(2)(iv). The regulation proceeds to identify more specifically those situations in which "personal service" is required:

> In any proceeding which is initiated by the Service, with proposed adverse effect, service of the initiating notice and of notice of any decision by a Service officer shall be accomplished by personal service, except as provided in section 239 of the Act.

8 C.F.R. §103.5a(c)(1).

While the "adverse effect" of initiating removal proceedings against an individual is largely self-evident, in the case of an alien who has already departed, the prejudice is even more obvious. Until the person is properly notified of the obligation, it is inappropriate to enter an *in absentia* order. See *Matter of G-Y-R-* , 23 I & N Dec. 181 (BIA 2001). In the instant case, Respondent never received the Notice to Appear (NTA) that was issued by the Department and was therefore never properly apprized of his duty to inform the Department (or Court) of a change in his address. His counsel did not provide that information to him, as he had already indicated that he would not pursue the matter and had departed the United States several months earlier, abandoning any application for status. As a result, no error was committed by prior counsel and no filing under *Matter of Lozada* is required.

WHEREFORE, Respondent asks this Court to set aside the *in absentia* order of removal, reopen and then terminate the proceedings against him in order to remove the bar to his entry as a visitor.

Respectfully submitted this ____day of __________, 20__.

[Attorney]

[ADD CERTIFICATE OF SERVICE]

U.S. DEPARTMENT OF JUSTICE
EXECUTIVE OFFICE FOR IMMIGRATION REVIEW
IMMIGRATION COURT
[LOCATION]

IN THE MATTER OF:)
)
[Alien])
A[Number]) IN REMOVAL PROCEEDINGS
)
Respondent)
__________________________)

RESPONDENT'S MOTION TO STAY REMOVAL AND MOTION TO STAY OR EXTEND PERIOD OF VOLUNTARY DEPARTURE PENDING DECISION ON MOTION TO REOPEN

Mr. **[Alien]**, through undersigned counsel, hereby moves the Immigration Court to stay his removal case while his Motion to Reopen is pending, and Respondent moves this Court to **stay** or **extend** his period of voluntary departure.

The Immigration Judge granted Mr. **[Alien]** voluntary departure until **November 29, 2004**. Exhibit 1. If he does not depart the United States by that date, his removal will be imminent. Just as importantly, if the Court does not stay or extend Respondent's current period of voluntary departure, the Court will be prevented from making a decision on Respondent's Motion to Reopen. Once reopened, however, the Court has the authority to reinstate and extend a Respondent's period of voluntary departure. 8 C.F.R. § 240.26(h).

This court has jurisdiction to grant this stay under 8 C.F.R. 1003.2(f) while the Motion to Reopen is pending. The Respondent meets the requirements of applicable law by showing that (1) he is likely to succeed on the merits of his case; (2) he would suffer irreparable harm if the stay is not granted; (3) the potential harm to Mr. **[Alien]** in being removed while his motion is pending outweighs the harm to the United States government in allowing Mr. **[Alien]** to stay in the United States during this time; and (4) granting the stay would serve the public interest.

I. RESPONDENT IS ELIGIBLE FOR A STAY OF REMOVAL

The Immigration Court may grant a Motion to Stay Removal when Respondent can show that he is likely to succeed on the merits of the case, he would suffer irreparable harm if the stay were not granted, that the potential harm to him if the stay is not granted exceeds the potential harm to the government if the stay is granted, and that the stay would serve the public interest. Mr. **[Alien]** can demonstrate all of this.

A. Respondent is Likely to Succeed on the Merits of his Motion

Respondent is likely to succeed on his motion to reopen because he is eligible to adjust status to permanent residence once USCIS approves Form I-130 filed on his behalf by his U.S. citizen wife. At the time the Immigration Court first considered Mr. **[Alien]**'s asylum claim, he was not eligible for adjustment of status. Now that his wife, **[New Wife]**, has filed Form I-130, Petition for Alien Relative, on her husband's behalf making Mr. **[Alien]** eligible to adjust status to that of a permanent resident once it has been approved by the Service. Mr. **[Alien]**'s Motion to Reopen is not time barred because he presents new, materials facts which were not available at trial 8 C.F.R. §1003.23(b)(3).

B. Mr. [Alien] Will Lose His Right to Have His Motion Heard on Its Merits If This Stay Is Not Granted or His Voluntary Departure Is Not Stayed or Extended.

If Mr. **[Alien]** is not given a stay while his motion is pending, he will be subject to immediate removal from the United States to Pakistan. In addition, if Mr. **[Alien]**'s period of voluntary departure is not stayed or extended, the Immigration Court will not be able to make a decision on his Motion to Reopen. The Immigration Judge has granted voluntary departure to Mr. **[Alien]** until **[date]**. If Mr. **[Alien]** does not leave the United States by this date, he will be subject to immediate removal. If the Court, however, either stays Mr. **[Alien]**'s period of voluntary departure or grants an extension of voluntary departure, it will then have the legal authority to make a decision on his Motion to Reopen and Remand. 8 C.F.R. §1240.26(h).

If Mr. **[Alien]** is leaves the United States, his Motion to Reopen will be deemed abandoned. He will lose his right to have his Motion considered on its merits by this Court. The consequences of <u>not</u> staying his removal while his Motion to Reopen is pending would be the same as denying the Motion without considering its merits.

More significantly, Mr. **[Alien]**'s deportation will prevent him from returning to his family in the United States for ten years. Having been ordered removed, he will be subject to a ten-year bar before he can apply for admission to the United States. Although Mr. **[Alien]** may apply for a waiver of inadmissibility, there is no guarantee that it will be granted.

Moreover, if Mr. **[Alien]** is not granted either a stay of his voluntary departure or is not granted an extension of voluntary departure, he will be unable to depart the United States by November 29, 2004. This will result in Mr. **[Alien]**'s having remained in the United States beyond a grant of voluntary departure and will prevent him from being eligible to apply for any further relief under Section 240B and Sections 240A, 245, 248, and 249 of the Immigration and Nationality Act. INA § 240B(d).

Mr. **[Alien]** has roots in the United States as he has lived and worked here for four years. He is now married and would like to start a family in the United States.

C. The United States Government Would Not Be Harmed by the Stay

Granting the stay of removal and stay or extension of voluntary departure while Mr. **[Alien]**'s Motion is pending would cause little harm to the government. Mr. **[Alien]** has never been arrested nor committed any crimes during his eight years in the United States, and he is a person of good moral character. He is not currently detained so granting the Stay or extending his voluntary departure would not be an expense to the United States government but, in fact, it would save the United States government money. If the Stay were denied or his voluntary departure were not stayed or extended, however, the U.S. government would bear the expense of jailing Mr. **[Alien]** until his travel to Pakistan is arranged and paying for his airline ticket to Pakistan.

Even if, after the Stay or extension of voluntary departure is granted, and the Motion to Reopen is denied, Mr. **[Alien]** will still not be an expense to the United States government. Mr. **[Alien]**'s wife will get him a flight on the next plane out of the country rather than allow her husband to be jailed like a common criminal.

Mr. **[Alien]** is not a flight risk because he and his wife know that if he does not leave the United States he will probably never be allowed to return, even after the ten-year bar.

D. Granting the Stay Would Serve the Public Interest

Granting a stay or extending Mr. **[Alien]**'s voluntary departure in this case would be in everyone's best interest, including the public. It would save the tax payers the expense of jailing Mr. **[Alien]** and removing him to Pakistan. It would allow his case to be heard on the merits, rather than be dismissed as involuntarily abandoned because the stay was not granted or the voluntary departure was not extended, which preserves the integrity of our justice system.

II. CONCLUSION

Because Mr. **[Alien]**'s Motion to Reopen is likely to be granted, he would suffer irreparable damage if the stay is denied or his period of voluntary departure is not stayed or extended, and the United States government will not suffer harm if he remains in the United States while the Motion to Reopen is pending, Mr. **[Alien]** respectfully requests that his Motion for Stay of Removal and Motion for Stay or Extension of Voluntary Departure be granted.

Respectfully submitted this _____ day of _____, 20__.

[Attorney]

[ADD CERTIFICATE OF SERVICE]

[Document Nos. 335–36]

JOINT MOTION TO REOPEN REMOVAL/DEPORTATION PROCEEDINGS

Description: This is the motion to use when the chief counsel is in agreement with the respondent in seeking the immigration court's reopening of deportation or removal case.

Advantages: This is the easiest method in which to secure a reopening of a removal or deportation matter. Unless extremely negative circumstances exist, no immigration judge will deny a joint motion to reopen. In many cases, it is the only way to secure a reopening of a case; *e.g.*, when the regulatory timeframe for the respondent's filing of a motion to reopen has passed.

Limitations: The key limitation is obtaining the chief counsel's agreement. Many times, the facts of a particular case do not strike the chief counsel as meriting a reopening of a removal case, despite the ramifications of a removal or deportation order.

Notes: Plan the approach to the chief counsel carefully. Document the hardships the client is seeking to avoid by the filing of the joint motion to reopen. Distinguish client's case from the rest. Typically, chief counsel has a stack of such motions sitting on his or her desk. To be successful, counsel has to be persistent, but also communicative of the extreme nature of the hardship meriting the joint motion to reopen in the case.

Citations: 8 CFR §1003.23(b)(4)(v).

U.S. DEPARTMENT OF JUSTICE
EXECUTIVE OFFICE FOR IMMIGRATION REVIEW
IMMIGRATION COURT
[LOCATION]

IN THE MATTER OF:	)	
	)	
[Alien]	)	
A[Number]	)	IN REMOVAL PROCEEDINGS
	)	
Respondent	)	
______________________________	)	

JOINT MOTION TO REOPEN REMOVAL PROCEEDINGS

Respondent, through undersigned counsel, and the Department of Homeland Security, through District Counsel **[Attorney]**, respectfully move to reopen Respondent's Removal Proceedings, pursuant to 8 C.F.R. § 1003.23(b)(4)(ii). Respondent is a(n) **[Country]** national. **[Alien]** was granted voluntary departure on **[date]** by this Court. (Ex. 1, copy of Order of Immigration Judge.) At that time, **[Alien]** expected that her attorney would file a Motion to Reopen (under the regular, permissible method) within 90 days if the Form I-130 was granted. (Ex. 2, copy of Notice of Approval.) In fact, the Form I-130 was approved within the 90 days, but former counsel failed to file a timely Motion to Reopen. Subsequently, **[Alien's]** father was granted asylum by an Immigration Judge in Boston (Ex. 3, copy of Order granting asylum.)

The Respondent and ICE now move to reopen **[Alien's]** removal proceedings to serve the cause of justice, directly relating to the approved Form I-130 and the subsequent grant of asylum to **[Alien's]** father.

Accordingly, Respondent and ICE jointly request that the Court reopen these proceedings and grant the attached Joint Motion to Terminate (Form I-471), permitting **[Alien]** to proceed to adjustment of status with USCIS.

Respectfully submitted this _____ day of _________, 20__.

[Alien's Attorney]

[Counsel, Department of Homeland Security]

[ADD CERTIFICATE OF SERVICE]

UNITED STATES DEPARTMENT OF JUSTICE
EXECUTIVE OFFICE FOR IMMIGRATION REVIEW
IMMIGRATION COURT
[LOCATION]

IN THE MATTER OF:)
)
[Alien])
A[Number])
)
Respondent)
______________________________)

JOINT MOTION TO REOPEN DEPORTATION PROCEEDINGS

COMES NOW, the undersigned, **[Attorney and Address]**, and District Counsel, U.S. Immigration and Customs Enforcement, **[Address]**, and jointly move this Court to reopen to above-captioned deportation proceedings, pursuant to 8 C.F.R. § 1003.2(c)(3)(iii), showing unto the Court as follows:

1. Respondent, **[Alien]**, born October 22, 1966, is a citizen and national of Vietnam.

2. Respondent's mother, **[Mother]**, is married to **[Step-Father]**, a U.S. citizen. When U.S. military troops left Vietnam, **[Mother]** immigrated to the United States in 1971 based on her marriage to **[Step-Father]**; the couple is still married. She left her 4-year old son with his grandmother in Vietnam and began seeking reunification with him in 1974.

3. **[Mother]** was naturalized as a U.S. citizen on August 9, 1974 (Exhibit 1). She filed an I-130 Petition for **[Alien]** on October 16, 1974 (hereinafter referred to as "First Petition"); the First Petition was approved on February 12, 1975 (Exhibit 2). The First Petition was approved for **[Name] [a name that was technically incorrect, although the same person as Alien]**. (See Exhibit 3.)

4. Although the First Petition and Approval could have been amended to reflect the proper name of her son, **[Mother]** filed another I-130 which was approved for **[Alien]** on July 10, 1986 (hereinafter "Second Petition") (Exhibit 4).

5. **[Alien]** was processed through the Orderly Departure Program and after 20 years of waiting, entered the United States on August 12, 1994. **[Alien]** had married on August 8, 1991, and was still married when he entered the U.S.

6. After **[Alien]** attempted to sponsor his wife and child for immigrant visas, the (former) INS initiated deportation proceedings on August 1, 1996 due to **[Alien]**'s entry in 1994 "as an unmarried son of a citizen of the United States" although he was married (Exhibit 5).

7. On March 18, 1997, the Immigration Judge ordered Voluntary Departure until November 18, 1997. Legacy INS/ICE has extended **[Alien]**'s voluntary departure status yearly; currently it is granted until **[date]** (Exhibit 6).

8. **[Alien]** cannot return to Vietnam. His wife divorced him on October 28, 1997, and he has no other family there (Exhibit 7). **[Alien]**'s father died in 1972 and his grandmother died in 1981.

9. **[Mother]** filed a third I-130 Petition on behalf of **[Alien]** on April 10, 1997 (hereinafter "Third Petition"); the Third Petition was approved on July 22, 1999 (Exhibit 8).

10. If deportation proceedings were reopened, **[Alien]** would qualify to apply for adjustment of status under INA Sec. 245(i):

    a. He is the beneficiary of an approved I-130;

    b. His priority date, April 10, 1997, is current for the First Preference family category (Exhibit 9);

    c. He is eligible to apply under Sec. 245(i) because the Third Petition was filed prior to January 14, 1998 and is therefore "grandfathered."

11. The following are factors to be considered in this matter:

    a. **[Alien]** has presented new evidence unavailable at his 1997 deportation hearing, to wit: he now has another approved I-130 and current priority date;

    b. He is eligible to apply for relief, to wit: adjustment of status under INA Sec. 245(i);

    c. After entering the United States, **[Alien]** immediately obtained a full-time job and then a second, part-time job (Exhibit 10). He has purchased his own home. He has no family in Vietnam and is the only child of his mother in the United States.

    d. **[Alien]**'s mother has been a U.S. citizen for over 25 years. Her husband is 71 years old and she has no other family, other than her son, in the United States. She suffers from asthma and high blood pressure and is on daily medication. The stress of her son's immigration situation adversely affects her medical conditions (Exhibit 11).

    e. **[Alien]** has no arrests or criminal record.

    f. **[Alien]** has no sponsor for return to Vietnam.

WHEREFORE, based on the foregoing, the undersigned counsel for the Respondent and for U.S. Immigration and Customs Enforcement respectfully request that the deportation proceedings in this matter be reopened.

[Date:]

[Attorney]

[Date:]

[ICE District Counsel]

[ADD CERTIFICATE OF SERVICE]

[Document No. 337]

MOTION AND ARGUMENT FOR VOLUNTARY DEPARTURE

Description: This is a motion designed to seek voluntary departure without the need for attending a master calendar hearing.

Advantages: This motion would be necessary in the case of an individual in proceedings who has overstayed his or her visa by not longer than six months, and who by remaining in the United States to attend a master calendar hearing would become subject to the three-year bar.

Limitations: As noted, this motion would be filed in limited circumstances in seeking to preempt the master calendar hearing and conclude the proceedings in the most expedient manner possible.

Notes: The timing of this motion is important, as is the insistence on a prompt decision. Rare is the circumstance when the client is in the situation where he or she is in proceedings, but has not yet acquired the six months of overstay that would subject him or her to the three-year bar. Filing this motion will keep the client eligible to return to the United States without having to file and have approved a waiver of the three-year bar.

Citations: 8 CFR §1003.25(b).

UNITED STATES DEPARTMENT OF JUSTICE
EXECUTIVE OFFICE FOR IMMIGRATION REVIEW
OFFICE OF THE IMMIGRATION JUDGE

IN THE MATTER OF: **[Alien]** **A[Number]** Respondent	))))))))	IN REMOVAL PROCEEDINGS

MOTION AND ARGUMENT FOR VOLUNTARY DEPARTURE IN LIEU OF DEPORTATION

Respondent, through his attorney, hereby moves this Immigration Court to grant him the privilege of voluntary departure under §244(e) of the Immigration and Nationality Act (INA), in lieu of deportation. In support of this Motion, Respondent states through counsel as follows:

1. Respondent entered the United States legally as a nonimmigrant visitor on **[date]** and was authorized to remain until **[date]**.

2. During this visit Respondent stayed in **[Location]** with family, and in **[Location]** with his sister, a lawful permanent resident of the United States; and visited friends and relatives in **[Location]**. Respondent's activities were consistent with his B-2 status.

3. In **[Month]**, prior to his departure date, Respondent applied to USCIS for a one-month extension of his B-2 status, stating on his application for extension of nonimmigrant stay that his desire for an extension was on account of the possibility his sister might be pregnant and require his temporary assistance because of a history of problem pregnancies. See, Receipt No. **[#]** for form I-539, fee'd in on **[date].**

4. According to the fee receipt, he was to wait 45 days before making any inquiry concerning the adjudication of his request for an extension. To date, **[number]** days later, Respondent has not received any response from USCIS. Respondent's sister was pregnant and in **[date]** went to **[Location]** to be with her family.

5. On or about **[date]**, during the 45-day period Respondent was awaiting adjudication of the I-539, he traveled by train with a friend to see family in **[Location]** and to visit another friend he had known previously in **[Location]**, now residing in **[Location]**. During their brief visit, **[Individual]** left the house and went to the airport where he was arrested. Federal agents then returned to **[Individual]**'s house and arrested Respondent and his friend.

6. Respondent remained in pre-trial detention for approximately **[number]** months, and on **[date]**, the charges against him were dropped for lack of evidence, and an Order of dismissal entered by the Court. See, Order, attached. Respondent was released and taken into custody by ICE on **[date]** and he was charged with having overstayed his nonimmigrant visit.

ARGUMENT

As argument in support of his Motion, Respondent states through counsel as follows:

Respondent is statutorily eligible for voluntary departure pursuant to INA §244(e). He can demonstrate good moral character pursuant to INA §101(f) in that he has never been convicted of, nor does he admit the commission of, any crime either of moral turpitude or relating to controlled substances; he has not been incarcerated for more than 180 days; he has not given false testimony to obtain immigration benefits; and he comes within no other statutory preclusion contained in INA §101(f).

Respondent is deserving of voluntary departure as a matter of discretion based upon the following considerations:

First, Respondent has observed the immigration laws, entering the country for the true and lawful purpose of visiting with family here. He was inspected and admitted as a B-2 visitor. Respondent filed for a one month extension within the authorized period of stay. Respondent has never been employed in the United States.

Second, although, on a prior occasion, Respondent entered the United States, he was given the privilege of departing voluntarily and did so depart. He did not re-enter the United States unlawfully but came lawfully and was inspected and admitted in B-2 status. He sought an extension during his authorized period of stay. To the best of his knowledge he has never been granted voluntary departure in relation to this entry, as he has never received any notice of USCIS action on his **[dated]** request for an extension.

Third, Respondent intends and always had intended to return to **[Location]** at the end of his visit here. He was employed as a **[Position]** at **[Business]**, a cooperatively owned bar of which his brother is President, from **[date]** to **[date]**. He was trained and employed previously for **[number]** years from **[date]** to **[date]** as an auto mechanic. Respondent can return to either occupation in **[Location]** either directly or after visiting with family on his father's side in **[Location]**.

Fourth, Respondent has numerous family ties with lawful residents in the United States, including siblings on his mother's side, and his natural father who is a United States citizen.

Fifth, with the exception of the charges lodged and dismissed in **[date]**, respondent has never been arrested by state or federal authorities either in the U.S. or in **[Location]**. While Respondent was arrested, he always has claimed to be innocent, and the Order of Dismissal is consistent with his denial of any involvement in any criminal activity.

Sixth, Respondent wishes only to depart the United States, and after being cleared of any criminal charges, he has remained only to seek this relief in deportation proceedings. He overstayed his present period of stay only because he was seeking an extension of stay and was arrested and held in pre-trial detention. Respondent does not wish to jeopardize his future opportunities to enter the United States to see family. Respondent is ready, willing, and able to depart, and can pay for his airline ticket.

Whether discretion should be exercised in favor of an alien requesting voluntary departure initially depends upon the particular facts in that individual's case. *Matter of Blas*, 15 I&N Dec. 626, 628 (BIA 1974). The Immigration Judge is entrusted with the duty of exercising discretion, and must consider all relevant factors present in the case and base his decision thereon. *Matter of Tsang*, 14 I&N Dec. 294, 296 (BIA 1973); *Matter of Vega*, 11 I&N Dec. 337, 339 (BIA 1965) ("[the immigration judge] must base his conclusion where a matter of discretion is concerned on an evaluation of all the facts and circumstances of the particular case . . . ."). This case is distinguishable from *Matter of Rojas*, 15 I&N 492 (BIA 1975). *Matter of Rojas* concerned a native and citizen of Colombia and who used a professional smuggler to gain illegal entry into the United States and could demonstrate no outstanding equities in her behalf other than a lawful permanent resident sister.

In the instant case, Respondent entered and remained in the United States legally pursuing his status under the immigration laws and regulations. He has many family ties here. He has acted consistently with the terms of his admission. He never received notification of the disposition of his application for an extension of stay. He did not knowingly remain after any grant of voluntary departure. Respondent is a person of good moral character who has always been gainfully employed and resides with his mother in his home country. Respondent does not use alcohol or drugs, nor has he been involved in any criminal activity. While evidence of criminal conduct without a conviction may be considered in the exercise of discretion, the charges against Respondent were dropped for insufficient evidence. Moreover Respondent asserts his innocence as substantiated by the Order of Dismissal.

For the foregoing reasons, Respondent moves this court to grant him voluntary Departure for a period of thirty days or as otherwise deemed appropriate.

Respectfully submitted
by his attorney,

[Attorney]

[Dated:]

[ADD CERTIFICATE OF SERVICE]

[Document No. 338]

MOTION FOR RECONSIDERATION OF VOLUNTARY DEPARTURE

Description: This motion requests that the immigration court reconsider and clarify its decision granting the respondent voluntary departure in lieu of removal. In this case, respondent's counsel disagrees with the ICE interpretation and implementation of the court's order of voluntary departure "under safeguard" conditions. ICE has refused to release the respondent so that he may voluntarily depart on his own volition. The motion is filed pursuant to 8 CFR §1003.14 (jurisdiction of the immigration judge); 8 CFR §1003.19(b) and (c)(1) (bond redetermination made by immigration judge); and 8 CFR §1003.23(b)(1) (jurisdiction of the immigration court to reopen or reconsider any case in which it has made a decision, unless jurisdiction is vested with the Board of Immigration Appeals (BIA).

Advantages: Although especially useful for requesting release of an alien improperly detained under an order of voluntary departure, this motion illustrates a procedure for bringing the misapplication of any order to the attention of the immigration judge. The same type of motion could be used for any order counsel believes is not being implemented properly by the government. In this case, the motion does not violate any of the time and number limitations on motions to reopen/reconsider found in 8 CFR §1003.23. An alternative argument in the motion is that the judge should reconsider and amend the order.

Notes: Local immigration court rules regarding the filing of motions should be consulted and followed.

Citations: 8 CFR §§1003.14; 1003.19(b) and (c)(1); 1003.23; and 1003.23(b)(1).

UNITED STATES DEPARTMENT OF JUSTICE
EXECUTIVE OFFICE FOR IMMIGRATION REVIEW
IMMIGRATION COURT
[LOCATION]

IN THE MATTER OF:)
)
[Alien])
A[Number]) IN REMOVAL PROCEEDINGS
)
Respondent)
)

RESPONDENT'S MOTION FOR RECONSIDERATION OF AND CLARIFICATION OF THIS COURT'S NOVEMBER 30, 2004 ORDER GRANTING VOLUNTARY DEPARTURE PURSUANT TO SECTION 240B(a)(1) OF THE IMMIGRATION AND NATIONALITY ACT

COMES NOW the Respondent, **[Alien]**, by and through his undersigned counsel, and files Respondent's Motion for Reconsideration pursuant to 8 C.F.R. § 1003.14, 8 C.F.R. §§ 1003.19(b) and (c)(1), and 8 C.F.R. § 1003.19. In support of this motion, Respondent, by and through the undersigned counsel, states as follow:

PROCEDURAL HISTORY AND STATEMENT OF FACTS

1. On November 17, 2004, the U.S. Department of Homeland Security ("DHS" or "Service") issued a Notice to Appear ("NTA"), charging **[Alien]** as removable for failing to maintain his nonimmigrant status, in violation of Section 237(a)(1)(C)(i) of the Immigration and Nationality Act ("INA" or "the Act"). *See* Exhibit A (copy of NTA).

2. On the same date, the Service also issued a Notice of Custody Determination, finding that, pursuant to INA § 236 and 8 C.F.R. § 236, **[Alien]** "shall be detained in the custody of the Service." *See* Exhibit B (copy of Notice of Custody Determination). Additionally, said notice established that **[Alien]** "may request a review of this [custody] determination by an Immigration Judge." *Id.*

3. On November 30, 2004, following a Master Calendar Hearing in which **[Alien]** conceded his removability, this Court granted **[Alien]** relief of Voluntary Departure pursuant to INA § 240B(a)(1). *See* Exhibit C (Copy of this Court's November 30, 2004 Order). However, the Court imposed a condition upon the relief, namely, that voluntary departure be granted "under safe guards from the Krome Detention Center." *Id.* at 7. The Court also indicated that there would be no final order of removal unless Respondent "fails to depart as required." *Id.*

4. Despite the grant of voluntary departure, Respondent has been detained at the Krome Service Processing Center since November 19, 2004, in the custody of the DHS. The government has taken the position that they will keep **[Alien]** in detention until the "decide" whether or not they will appeal this Court's order. At the same time, they have taken the position that **[Alien]** can only leave Krome "under safeguard," which

they interpret to mean that even if they comply with the Court's order, **[Alien]** will not be released and must leave directly from Krome.

5. By this motion, **[Alien]** by and through the undersigned counsel, formally requests that this Court reconsider and clarify its November 30, 2004 Order and: (1) eliminate any direct or implied "departure under safeguard" condition imposed upon **[Alien]**'s voluntary departure; (2) clarify that **[Alien]**'s voluntary departure order does not become a final order of removal by December 17, 2004, if his departure is beyond his control because the DHS insists on continuing to detain him in violation of this Court's order while they decide whether they will appeal his case or ignore the Court's order; and (3) direct the DHS to release **[Alien]** today so that he may comply with the voluntary departure order and leave the United States as ordered by this Court.

DISCUSSION

6. This Court may upon its own motion at any time, or upon motion of the Service or the alien, reopen or reconsider any case in which the Court has made a decision, unless jurisdiction is vested with the BIA. 8 C.F.R. § 1003.23(b)(1). A non–sua sponte motion to reconsider must be filed within 30 days. *Id.* The instant motion to reconsider is timely as this Court entered the order on November 30, 2004 and there is no final order of removal.

7. Where, as here, the Court has granted voluntary departure prior to completion of removal proceedings pursuant to INA § 240B(a)(1), the Act only confers upon the Court a discretionary authority to impose a "voluntary departure bond." INA § 240B(a)(3). No other condition is authorized under the statute.

8. In granting the Respondent voluntary departure, this Court imposed a condition not authorized by the Act, namely, "under safe guards (sic) from the Krome Detention Center." Exhibit C at 7. Although the Court indicated in its order that Respondent agreed to such condition, it should be noted that the Respondent did not agree to such condition.

9. Nor is the condition authorized by the regulations. Even a cursory comparison of the regulations of DHS and EOIR demonstrate that departure under safeguards is a condition that only the *Service* may impose if it grants voluntary departure. 8 C.F.R. §240.25(b). Under the regulations: "The Service may attach to the granting of voluntary departure *any conditions* it deems necessary to ensure the alien's timely departure from the United States, including the posting of a bond, *continued detention pending departure, and removal under safeguards."* (emphasis added). In contrast, the immigration judge's regulation governing the grant of pre-hearing voluntary departure is far more circumscribed. 8 C.F.R. §1240.26(b)(3). The regulation does *not* specify "removal under safeguards" as a condition the IJ may impose. It further does not allow the imposition of "any conditions" but only those conditions as the IJ "deems necessary to ensure the alien's timely departure." *Id.*

10. Here, the imposition of "safeguards" achieves a result directly contrary to the "alien's timely departure" and therefore the condition is contrary to the regulation, itself. By attaching a "safeguards" condition, the Court *prevents* **[Alien]** from leaving immediately and leaves it solely to the discretion of the DHS has to how, when and "if" they will permit those "safeguards." Because such a condition has the opposite effect from ensuring his "timely departure" it is not authorized under the regulation even if the regulation itself could be read to include safeguards—a condition not specified under 8 C.F.R. §1240.26(b)(3) as it is under 8 C.F.R. §240.25 for the Service.

11. This Court also imposed the condition that if **[Alien]** does not depart by December 17, 2004, his voluntary departure order will become a final order of removal. However, **[Alien]**, due to the Court's decision to require "safeguards" is not permitted to depart when he wants and cannot leave Krome of his own volition. As his physical detention remains in the whim of DHS he cannot comply with this Court's order unless DHS allows him to depart.

12. In addition, there is no reason to further detain the Respondent as he poses no flight risk. The sole purpose of imposing a bond as a condition to voluntary departure of aliens such as the Respondent is to ensure their timely departure. *See* INA § 240(a)(3). Here, there is no basis to believe that Respondent will not timely depart. As this Court duly noted in its November 30, 2004, Respondent "has never violated immigration laws of this country." Exhibit C at 7. In fact, as soon as Respondent learned that this Court granted him voluntary departure, he purchased a one-way airplane ticket to Mexico to comply with this Court's order. *See* Exhibit D (Copy of One-way Airplane Ticket to Mexico). As such, further detention of Respondent will defeat the very legislative purpose behind voluntary departure under INA § 240(a) to ensure timely departure of Respondent. Therefore, the Court should strike its "departure under safeguard" provision and allow **[Alien]** to voluntarily depart immediately.

WHEREFORE, Respondent, by and through his undersigned counsel, prays that this Honorable Court reconsider and clarify it November 30, 2004 Order and: (1) eliminate any direct or implied "departure under safeguard" condition imposed upon **[Alien]**'s voluntary departure; (2) clarify that **[Alien]**'s voluntary departure order does not become a final order of removal by December 17, 2004, if his departure is beyond his control because the DHS insists on continuing to detain him in violation of this Court's order while they decide whether they will appeal his case or ignore the Court's order; and (3) direct the DHS to release **[Alien]** today so that he may comply with the voluntary departure order and leave the United States as ordered by this Court.

Respectfully submitted,

On this ___ day of _______, 20__.

[Attorney]

[ADD CERTIFICATE OF SERVICE]

[Document No. 339]

MEMORANDUM OF LAW IN SUPPORT OF ASYLUM, WITHHOLDING OF REMOVAL, AND CAT RELIEF

Description: This memorandum of law and proposed order is a comprehensive discussion of asylum relief, or in the alternative, withholding of removal under INA §241(b)(3) and under the Convention Against Torture (CAT). Applying the testimony and evidence presented during the removal hearing, this post-removal hearing memorandum discusses applicable law and burden of proof issues and the specific facts qualifying the applicant, a citizen of Rwanda, for the relief sought. The memorandum also addresses disqualifying acts that would preclude relief and why none of these acts occurred.

The memorandum is presented as a proposed order. Even if an immigration judge would not use a comprehensive document such as this for reproduction as an order, submission of the memorandum could assist the court in drafting its own order.

Advantages: A post-hearing memorandum in any type of removal case can help persuade the court that the applicant's testimony and evidence proved the relief sought, and it serves as an outline for the court's order. It could also be used as the draft of an appellate brief if the respondent is not successful and chooses to appeal. Prehearing memoranda also may be beneficial in presenting a road map for the court of how the case will be proved. (Counsel may choose not to present such a road map, however, as it could give the case away to the other side.)

Notes: Relief under the Convention Against Torture is the only relief available for certain applicants with serious criminal convictions.

UNITED STATES DEPARTMENT OF JUSTICE
EXECUTIVE OFFICE FOR IMMIGRATION REVIEW
IMMIGRATION COURT
[LOCATION]

IN THE MATTER OF:	)	
[Alien]	)	
A[Number]	)	IN REMOVAL PROCEEDINGS
Respondent	)	[Judge]
	)	U.S. Immigration Judge

MEMORANDUM OF LAW IN SUPPORT OF [ALIEN]'S APPLICATION FOR ASYLUM, AND IN THE ALTERNATIVE, FOR WITHHOLDING OF REMOVAL UNDER INA §241(b)(3) AND UNDER THE CONVENTION AGAINST TORTURE (CAT), AND PROPOSED ORDER

I. INTRODUCTION

[Alien] is entitled to asylum and, alternatively, withholding of removal under INA §241(b)(3) and under the Convention Against Torture (CAT). He has shown past persecution, as well as a well-founded fear of future persecution, as well as that it is more likely than not that he would be tortured upon his return to Rwanda. *See* INA §208(a); 8 U.S.C. §1158(a); 8 C.F.R. §208.13(b); 8 C.F.R. §208.16. As has been shown through the presentation of substantial evidence, including the testimony expert and lay witnesses, if returned **[Alien]** would face unjust incarceration at best, or, at worst, extrajudicial killing, torture, or simply "disappearing" at the hands of the ruling Kagame regime. Moreover, the evidence demonstrates that, contrary to the assertions of the government, **[Alien]** has not engaged in fraud or any criminal activity whatsoever. Rather, it is unrebutted that Respondent is a well-known and well-respected humanitarian who has worked tirelessly throughout the years to protect the human rights of all citizens of Rwanda, whether Tutsi or Hutu. In fact, **[Alien]** has always worked toward racial and political unification in Rwanda and has been instrumental in fostering peace in that country.

II. [ALIEN] HAS SUFFERED PAST PERSECUTION

Pursuant to the Immigration and Nationality Act (INA), and the pertinent federal regulations relating to asylum, **[Alien]** is able to show he suffered past persecution in the Republic of Rwanda. *See* INA §§101(a)(42) and 208(a); *see also* 8 C.F.R. §§208.13(b) (past persecution and burden of proof). Under INA §208(a), an asylee is a person who meets the "past persecution" or "well founded fear" definition of a refugee under INA §101(a)(42), but who is physically present in the U.S. or is at a land border or port of entry of the U.S. at the time he is seeking refuge in this country. Under 8 C.F.R. §208.13(b),

The applicant may qualify as a refugee either because he or she has suffered past persecution or because he or she has a well-founded fear of future persecution.

> (1) Past persecution. An applicant shall be found to be a refugee on the basis of past persecution if the applicant can establish that he or she has suffered persecution in the past in the applicant's country of nationality or, if stateless, in his or her country of last habitual residence, on account of race, religion, nationality, membership in a particular social group, or political opinion, and is unable or unwilling

> to return to, or avail himself or herself of the protection of, that country owing to such persecution. An applicant who has been found to have established such past persecution shall also be presumed to have a well-founded fear of persecution on the basis of the original claim. That presumption may be rebutted if an asylum officer or immigration judge makes one of the findings described in paragraph (b)(1)(i) of this section. If the applicant's fear of future persecution is unrelated to the past persecution, the applicant bears the burden of establishing that the fear is well-founded.

Id. (emphasis added).

Under 8 C.F.R. §208.13(b)(1)(i), the IJ, in the exercise of his discretion, "shall deny the asylum application of an alien found to be a refugee on the basis of past persecution if any of the following is found by a preponderance of the evidence:

> A) There has been a fundamental change in circumstances such that the applicant no longer has a well-founded fear of persecution in the applicant's country of nationality or, if stateless, in the applicant's country of last habitual residence, on account of race, religion, nationality, membership in a particular social group, or political opinion; or
>
> B) The applicant could avoid future persecution by relocating to another part of the applicant's country of nationality or, if stateless, another part of the applicant's country of last habitual residence, and under all the circumstances, it would be reasonable to expect the applicant to do so.

Id.

Similarly, under the provisions regarding withholding of removal, see 8 C.F.R. §208.16(b), the initial burden is on the applicant for withholding of removal under INA §241(b)(3) "to establish that his or her life or freedom would be threatened in the proposed country of removal on account of race, religion, nationality, membership in a particular social group, or political opinion." *Id.* The regulation further provides that "[t]he testimony of the applicant, if credible, may be sufficient to sustain the burden of proof without corroboration." *Id.* Of particular importance is the following provision found in the Regulation concerning "past threat to life or freedom:"

> (i) If the applicant is determined to have suffered past persecution in the proposed country of removal on account of race, religion, nationality, membership in a particular social group, or political opinion, it shall be presumed that the applicant's life or freedom would be threatened in the future in the country of removal on the basis of the original claim. This presumption may be rebutted if an asylum officer or immigration judge finds by a preponderance of the evidence:
>
> > (A) There has been a fundamental change in circumstances such that the applicant's life or freedom would not be threatened on account of any of the five grounds mentioned in this paragraph upon the applicant's removal to that country; or
> >
> > (B) The applicant could avoid a future threat to his or her life or freedom by relocating to another part of the proposed country of removal and, under all the circumstances, it would be reasonable to expect the applicant to do so.
>
> (ii) In cases in which the applicant has established past persecution, the Service shall bear the burden of establishing by a preponderance of the evidence the requirements of paragraphs (b)(1)(i)(A) or (b)(1)(i)(B) of this section.
>
> (iii) If the applicant's fear of future threat to life or freedom is unrelated to the past persecution, the applicant bears the burden of establishing that it is more likely than not that he or she would suffer such harm.

8 C.F.R. §208.16(b)(1)(i)-(iii) (emphasis added).

[Alien] has presented a plethora of substantial evidence clearly showing past persecution against himself and his family members. **[Alien]** first faced persecution prior to the genocide in Rwanda, when his life was threatened by the ruling Hutu government. **[Alien]** testified that as early as 1970–73, he made attempts to bridge Hutus and Tutsis. During the reign of the Hutu president, Habaryimana, government militia raided and searched his house and office. He also testified that there was widespread discrimination of Tutsis under the Habaryimana regime. In 1990, **[Alien]** pushed Habaryimana for the return of Tutsi refugees but the president rejected **[Alien]**'s pleas, and instead said that the only way the refugees could return is if they fought their way back in. After **[Alien]**'s attempted intercession for the refugees, Habaryimana was very angry with **[Alien]**

In April 1990, men attacked **[Alien]**'s house. In May 1990, soldiers attacked **[Alien]** again and sent someone to poison him and his family. Military and paramilitary surrounded Respondent's house; *i.e.*, placed him under house arrest. Between May and August 1990, he was under house arrest. He was finally able to leave in Aug. 1990, with the help of Bizimungu. Bizimungu was a high-ranking Hutu who later became president of the country. **[Alien]** testified that he and his son sat in the backseat of Bizimungu's car and wore a big hat, and the uniform of electro-gas company so they could be disguised and leave the house undetected. **[Alien]** left the country of Rwanda on August 25, 1990, and did not go back until November 1994.

As will be discussed, after the genocide the testimony presented at the hearings in this case revealed the following instances of past persecution: (1) **[Alien]** was administered electric shocks repeatedly by Kagame's henchman; (2) **[Alien]**'s children were falsely arrested and kept in a military camp against their will for three months in order to intimidate and silence Respondent; (3) **[Alien]** and his family were repeatedly threatened by Kagame's men both directly and indirectly; (4) all his property and wealth was seized including Respondent's petroleum business and his bank, BACAR, of which he was a majority shareholder. Each of these instances is discussed further below.

A. [Alien] was administered electric shocks repeatedly by Kagame's henchman

First, **[Alien]** testified that he was subjected to physical shocks at the hands of Kagame and his men, as punishment for speaking out in Parliament. The physical shocks were also mentioned by **[Alien]**'s wife and **[Witness 1]**, former Speaker of the National Assembly. The form of the shocks came from a device, a stun-gun, in English, which delivered voltage and left **[Alien]** feeling weak and disoriented. *See* testimony of **[Alien]**; *see also* corroborating testimony of **[Witness 1]** and Mrs. **[Alien]**.[1]

As **[Alien]** discussed on the witness stand, and in his own affidavit attached to the Amended I-589, and as confirmed by Expert Witness **[Expert Witness 1]**, in 1997 while a member of Parliament the Respondent criticized the leadership of Rwanda. The shocks began after **[Alien]** began speaking out against the Kagame regime. As **[Expert Witness 1]** confirmed by his expert testimony, the opposition activities of Respondent including his oral speech to the Rwandan Assembly against the Rwandan government accusing them of "bad governance" on Oct. 1, 1997. The criticisms made by **[Alien]** in open parliament were consistent with statements he subsequently made in an open letter to Kagame on Aug. 7, 2001. People close to President Kagame told **[Alien]** that Kagame was convinced that **[Alien]** was campaigning for the presidency, and so the threats against his family and his person increased. *See* Affidavit ¶ 2. Lt. Col. **[Name]**, a close collaborator of Kagame, threatened his son, **[Son]**, by saying, "Tell your father that he will shortly deal with RPF and General Kagame." Exh 14-B; i.e., Exh. B to Nov. 30th Filing (**[Alien]**'s Affidavit).

B. [Alien]'s sons were falsely arrested and kept in a military camp against their will for three months in order to intimidate and silence Respondent.

Mrs. **[Alien]** testified that her sons were kidnapped for a period of three (3) months by Kagame and kept in a military camp even though they were civilians and then released without a trial. There was no legitimate reason to arrest the sons. The people who arrested them were military soldiers sent by Kagame in 1995. This was to intimi-

---

[1] The existence of the shocks was confirmed by Mrs. **[Alien]** in her testimony in that she remembers her husband describing the shocks to her. Mrs. **[Alien]** further testified that there were many political opponents who were persecuted by the Kagame regime for opposing the government, just like her husband. Mrs. **[Alien]** confirmed that she had been told by Respondent about the physical shocks used by Kagame to punish Respondent.

date their father. When **[Son]**'s wife tried to find out why they had been arrested, she was told by Kagame's men that "this is just the beginning."

C. [Alien] and his family were repeatedly threatened by Kagame's men both directly and indirectly

Mrs. **[Alien]** also testified that her sons were threatened with death by Kagame's men after a birthday party given for their son **[Son]**. According to Mrs. **[Alien]**, the birthday party was thought (incorrectly) by the regime to be a gathering to work on propaganda to help Bizimungu or to start a new political party. Moreover, **[Son]**went to see a Colonel **[Name]**, a member of Kagame's military after the party. The colonel called **[Son]** into his office and threatened Respondent's son by saying that "we can kill you at any time." Mrs. **[Alien]** testified that both their sons, **[Son]** and **[Son]**, left Rwanda and escaped Kagame's threats in 2001.

Further testimony by Mrs. **[Alien]** revealed that in 2001, a Lt. Colonel **[Name]** in Kagame's army told **[Son]** that Kagame and the RFP are going to hurt their father. They reportedly wanted to silence him so he could not run for president. By April 2001, groundless rumors were circulating that **[Alien]** had stolen money from BACAR. (See further discussion in Respondent's affidavit and his testimony.) At the end of July 2001, while outside the country on a business trip, a friend of Respondent's sons who was close to Kagame told them that Kagame gave him orders to kill them both and to kill Respondent when he returned from the trip. Both of his sons managed to escape. **[Son]**went to South Africa, while **[Son]**was forced into hiding. **[Son]**was able to warn **[Alien]** just before he left for Kigali. Instead of going home, **[Alien]** came to the United States on July 29, 2001, because he feared he would be killed if he returned to Rwanda. *Id.*

The past persecution of **[Alien]** is further supported by the close connection between Respondent and former president Bizimungu. *See* Testimony of Expert **[Expert Witness 1]**; **[Alien]**, Mrs. **[Alien]** and **[Witness 1]**. As recounted above, Bizimungu and the Respondent were close friends after Bizimungu helped **[Alien]** to flee the Hutu-dominated country in 1990. Although Bizimungu was the titular head of the government following the genocide when the RPF took control of the country, the real person in charge was Paul Kagame; he was in control of the military and also Vice President of the country. Kagame had Bizimungu jailed for alleged "corruption" following the latter's resignation. Bizimungu was charged with corruption and financial improprieties, according to **[Expert Witness 1]**, and was a close friend of Respondent's. It is commonly reported and believed that Bizimungu's trial and arrest did not meet minimum standards of fairness under international law. *See also* Dep't of State (DOS) Letter, Exh 14-G attached to Nov. 30th Filing (confirming that **[Alien]** and Bizimungu are "close friends" and stating significantly that "We are not aware that the charges against Bizimungu and his codefendants were supported by the presentation of material evidence.")

D. The existence of the threats and past persecution must be understood against the larger backdrop of [Alien]'s relationship to the Kagame regime including the fact that Kagame wanted to appropriate Respondent's petroleum business and his bank, BACAR

The existence of the threats and past persecution must be understood against the larger backdrop of **[Alien]**'s long relationship with the Kagame regime. In 1995, after the genocide the government wanted to take control of BACAR bank. However, on August 1, 1995, **[Alien]** outbid the regime for control of the shares of the bank and acquired 51 percent of the shares of the bank. *See* Testimony of **[Alien]**. As a result of Kagame's frustration with being outbid, he raided the bank in 1995, and all the computers and records were taken. After the raid, a commission was set up to determine the opening balances. *Id.* A report was issued by Laurent Rurtayisire which established that the bank had been robbed. The commission, according to **[Alien]** established a balance sheet and made it public. They gave their report to the Minister of Finance and it was published. Importantly, from 1995 until 2000, **[Alien]** received no notice of any kind that he was accused of any impropriety, despite the existence of the governmental commission.

On July 31, 2001, the offices of BACAR as well as Respondent's home in Kigali and the homes of his family were stormed by Rwandan police. No evidence was found that implicated the **[Alien]** in any wrongdoing at BACAR or anywhere else. Members of the Board of Directors, including Respondent's brother, **[Brother]**, were arrested. Despite the fact that he was ordered released freed by all the Rwandese courts—the Tribunal of the First Instance of Kigali, the Court of Appeal of Kigali and the Supreme Court of Rwanda—**[Brother]** is still in jail just because he is Respondent's brother. These facts were confirmed in a State Department letter which also supports the fact that Respondent's close ally, past-President Bizimungu, also suffered persecution at the hands of Kagame's regime. *See* Exh. 14-G; i.e., Exh. G to Nov. 30th Filing (Dept. of State Letter of Oct. 14, 2004).

Mrs. **[Alien]** testified extensively regarding the unlawful detention and arrest of members of BACAR bank, and the fact that there was one member of the group who was refused proper medical treatment after having metal rods inserted in his arms in 2001 because of a previous unrelated automobile accident. The metal rods are still in despite having been inserted in 2001. Another one of the detainees died of advanced hepatitis. He was left untreated and died. Mrs. **[Alien]** has documents which show that the other members of BACAR have been ordered released by the courts in Rwanda. (Since her testimony, undersigned attorneys have obtained these documents which have been certified and authenticated by the United States Embassy in Rwanda.) Despite these lawful orders none of the detainees has been released, in contravention of the lawful orders of the courts of Rwanda.

After **[Alien]** left Rwanda in 2001, fearing for his life, Kagame seized **[Alien]**'s petroleum company, as well as the BACAR bank. **[Alien]** testified that there was never any formal judicial or legal process which was used to legitimately seize these properties. In fact, **[Alien]** has learned that the BACAR bank has since been "sold" unlawfully to another bank in Kenya, outside of Rwanda. **[Alien]** has not agreed to the sale, nor was he ever consulted.

E. Government's Lack of Rebuttal Evidence Regarding Past Persecution

It is important to note that the government has not offered *any* evidence whatsoever which would contradict or rebut any of the incidents of past persecution about which **[Alien]** and the other witnesses have testified. A perusal of the documents submitted by the government shows that these documents are either not relevant to Respondent's claims of past persecution or they are aimed at supporting the Rwandan government's false claims that **[Alien]** is connected with bank fraud. As will be fully discussed below, the so-called Ernst & Young reports, marked as Exh. 10-7 and not admitted into evidence, do not show that **[Alien]** was involved in any wrongdoing. Moreover, other documents presented, such as Exh. 11-1, discussing allegation of human rights abuses by Kagame, actually help **[Alien]**'s case in that it shows why **[Alien]** came to oppose Kagame and his abusive regime. In addition, for example, the government has submitted an article by Respondent's *own* expert witness, **[Expert Witness 1]**, Exh. 15-1, which merely shows his expertise and qualifications for testifying about Rwanda and its judicial and social systems.

III. [ALIEN] HAS A WELL-FOUNDED FEAR OF FUTURE PERSECUTION

Under 8 C.F.R. §208.13(b)(2)(i), an applicant has a well-founded fear of [future] persecution if:

> (A) The applicant has a fear of persecution in his or her country of nationality . . . on account of race, religion, nationality, membership in a particular social group, or political opinion;
>
> (B) There is a reasonable possibility of suffering such persecution if he or she were to return to that country; and
>
> (C) He or she is unable or unwilling to return to, or avail himself or herself of the protection of, that country because of such fear.

Id. The regulation further provides that [a]n applicant does not have a well-founded fear of persecution if

> the applicant could avoid persecution by relocating to another part of the applicant's country of nationality . . . if under all the circumstances it would be reasonable to expect the applicant to do so.

8 C.F.R. §208.13(b)(2)(ii). "In evaluating whether the applicant has sustained the burden of proving that he or she has a well-founded fear of persecution, the asylum officer or immigration judge shall not require the applicant to provide evidence that there is a reasonable possibility he or she would be singled out individually for persecution if:

> (A) The applicant establishes that there is a pattern or practice in his or her country of nationality . . . of persecution of a group of persons similarly situated to the applicant on account of race, religion, nationality, membership in a particular social group, or political opinion; and

(B) The applicant establishes his or her own inclusion in, and identification with, such group of persons such that his or her fear of persecution upon return is reasonable.

8 C.F.R. §208.13(b)(2)(iii) (emphasis added).

The following evidence has been submitted supporting **[Alien]**'s well-founded fear of future persecution. The evidence shows both that Respondent has a well-founded fear of persecution on account of his race/membership in a particular social group (*i.e.*, being a Tutsi) and based on his political opinion (*i.e.*, his criticism and opposition to the current political regime, the RPF, headed by President Kagame). Moreover, under 8 C.F.R. §208.13(b)(2)(iii), **[Alien]** is able to show there is a "pattern or practice" in Rwanda of persecution of a group of persons similarly situated to him on account of race, religion, nationality, membership in a particular social group, or political opinion.

In his testimony, **[Alien]** discussed his well-founded fear of future persecution in that the authorities have jailed BACAR employees, including Director of Internal Audit, **[Director]**, his deputy, **[Brother]** (Respondent's younger brother), the Director of the Legal Matters Department, **[Director]**, and the Head of the Computer Department. They ransacked the offices and took the videotape of the commission meetings where the opening balances were reconstructed. The very next day, a warrant was issued for Respondent's arrest on bank fraud and embezzlement charges in spite of the fact that his accusers had not yet had time to do even a cursory review of the bank's records. Those arrested the day before were charged as his accomplices. Both of Respondent's sons were also charged as accomplices even though only one of them had ever worked for BACAR.

A. The Kagame Regime has a pattern and practice of widespread human rights abuses and of persecuting political opponents and critics

The testimony of **[Witness 1]**, **[Expert Witness 1]**, the other witnesses clearly showed that Kagame has committed human rights abuses and effectuated a pattern and practice of persecuting political opponents and critics as a strategy for gaining and maintaining power. Even the documents submitted by the government in this very case support the conclusion that Kagame has committed human rights abuses, and is not hesitant to engage in extra-judicial killings or kidnapping to effectuate his ends. *See, e.g.*, Exh. 11-1 (RWANDA, Talking peace, waging war, Human Rights Since the October 1990 Invasion). This exhibit discusses alleged abuses by the RPF, <u>and it is unrebutted that Kagame was the strongman who controlled the RPF at that time in the early 1990s</u>. *See* Testimony of **[Alien]**; Testimony of **[Expert Witness 1]**.

Furthermore, **[Witness 1]**, the former Speaker of the National Assembly in Rwanda, testified as to Respondent's well-founded fear. **[Witness 1]** testified that the judiciary in Rwanda is controlled by the Executive Branch, i.e., by Kagame's regime. **[Witness 1]** further stated that human rights abuses by Kagame are very well-known by the Parliament and the citizens and well-documented. **[Witness 1]** testified extensively regarding the persecution suffered by past-President Bizimungu at the hands of Kagame and his regime, including the fact that Kagame had advisors of Bizimungu killed.

[Witness 1]'s testimony made clear that Respondent was vocal in Parliament and that in 1997 Respondent vocally opposed Kagame and called into question his leadership. Specifically, some people said it was "suicide" to say this. **[Witness 1]** made clear that any charges for corruption/fraud against **[Alien]** only were lodged after Respondent left Rwanda in 2001. BACAR was considered well-managed during the entire time **[Alien]** was in charge of the bank.

Importantly, **[Witness 1]** stated that President Kagame had a special way to discipline opponents or critics, like **[Alien]**. <u>If you were Hutu, Kagame would allege that the opponent was involved in the genocide and therefore have him placed in jail or killed. If you were a Tutsi, like Respondent, Kagame would charge the person with "corruption," including bank fraud or other alleged financial improprieties</u>. The use of false charges was a widespread basis for persecution. **[Witness 1]** also stated that the governmental regime of Kagame had <u>oversight</u> over the financial institutions in Rwanda, and that, despite this oversight there never was any issue of corruption with respect to BACAR or **[Alien]** during the time during the time Respondent ran BACAR.

In addition to the testimony of **[Witness 1]**, Mr. **[Expert Witness 1]** provided his expert testimony at the hearing held January 26, 2005. **[Expert Witness 1]** testified as to the likelihood of future persecution against

[Alien]. Specifically, **[Expert Witness 1]** testified to the political context in post-genocide Rwanda, where dissidents are killed, jailed or "disappeared" supporting **[Alien]**'s well-founded fear of future persecution. **[Expert Witness 1]** detailed the state of the judiciary in Rwanda as subject to executive influence. **[Expert Witness 1]** began to discuss prison conditions but was prevented by the Court, although the Court did allow limited testimony of this topic. **[Expert Witness 1]** discussed the opposition activities of Respondent, including his book and speech in Parliament in 1997, and his open letter to Kagame alleging threats against himself and his children. **[Expert Witness 1]** concluded that he is prepared to submit that it is more likely than not that **[Alien]** would be persecuted if sent back to Rwanda. **[Expert Witness 1]** further maintained that he believes **[Alien]** was a popular critic and opponent of the Kagame, the president of Rwanda and his political party, and that Respondent has a well-founded fear of persecution by the government or individuals acting on behalf of the government if returned to Rwanda.

B. Well-Founded Fear is also supported by the fact that Kagame has already falsely arrested [Alien]'s sons and brother

As discussed in the previous section regarding past persecution, Mrs. **[Alien]** stated that Kagame had both of her sons arrested and sent to a military camp for three months despite a lack of charges or other valid reason for their arrest and detention. Also, with respect to the later charges of bank fraud in 2001, the fact that both Respondent's sons were charged—although only one works at the bank—supports the claim that the charges were politically motivated and that President Kagame is behind these groundless accusations. As stated above, on November 23, 2001, the Supreme Court of Rwanda ordered the release of those arrested in the BACAR scandal, but they have yet to be released. *See* Exh. 14-B; i.e., Exh. B to Nov. 30th Filing (**[Alien]**'s Affidavit); *see also* Dep't of State (DOS) Letter, Exh 14-G. attached to Nov. 30th Filing; *see also* Exh. 13; previously Exh. 14-I, attached to Nov. 30th Filing (Affidavit of Mr. **[former Prime Minister]**, former Primer Minister of Rwanda) (identifies **[Alien]** as a political rival to Kagame and discusses Kagame's opposition to Respondent's business dealings including preventing the foreclosure of over 300 residential houses and commercial real properties in Rwanda and creating fictitious companies as competitors of Respondent's companies.) Another of the BACAR employees arrested was Respondent's brother, **[Brother]**.

The letter from the U.S. Department of State, Exh. 14-G, <u>confirms</u> Respondent's testimony that in July 1997, he spoke out against Parliament and accused the new RPF-government of corruption and human rights abuses and that in Nov 2001, 4 BACAR employees were ordered released and the Kigali Court of Appeals affirmed the release order on Oct 23, 2003 and again on Nov 19, 2003, <u>but all 4 remained in detention without trial until Sept 17, 2004</u>. On that date, one of the four was released due to terminal cirrhosis of the liver on humanitarian grounds. On Sept 30, 2004 one of three employees remaining in detention requested release on medical grounds for treatment of injuries sustained in an unrelated car accident which occurred years earlier. <u>To date the three employees remain in detention.</u> The DOS letter strongly supports Respondent's well-founded fear of persecution in that the letter suggests that past-President Bizimungu suffered persecution at the hands of Kagame's regime. The letter states, significantly, that "We are not aware that the charges against Bizimungu and his co-defendants were supported by the presentation of material evidence." *Id.*; *see also* extensive testimony of Mrs. **[Alien]**.

C. [Alien] has shown that there is a "pattern or practice" in Rwanda of persecution of a group of persons similarly situated to him on account of race, religion, nationality, membership in a particular social group, or political opinion, most especially former President Bizimungu

As discussed, Mr. Bizimungu and **[Alien]** were close friends and shared many of the same political views concerning unification between Hutu and Tutsi in Rwanda. *See* Testimony of **[Alien]**; Testimony of **[Witness 1]**; Testimony of **[Expert Witness 1]**. **[Expert Witness 1]** testified that incidents of persecution, including Bizimungu's trial, were indicative of a pattern of persecution of political opponents and critics by the government of Rwanda, led by Kagame. Although Bizimungu was the titular head of the government following the genocide when the RPF took control of the country, the real person in charge was Paul Kagame; he was in control of the military and also Vice President of the country. Kagame had Bizimungu jailed following the latter's resignation. Bizimungu was charged with corruption and financial improprieties, according to **[Expert Witness 1]**, and was a close friend of Respondent's. It is commonly reported and believed that Bizimungu's trial and arrest <u>did not meet minimum standards of fairness under international law</u>. *See also* Dep't of State (DOS) Letter, Exh 14-G attached to Nov. 30th Filing (confirming that **[Alien]** and Bizimungu are "close friends" and stating significantly that "We are not aware that the charges against Bizimungu and his codefendants were supported by the presentation of material evidence.") [2]

---

[2] Respondent has also submitted many documents supporting his claim of well-founded fear of future persecution. *See* Exh. 12-3 in the Binder (ADMITTED); Article entitled What Hope For Justice? Detailing 130,000 prisoners incarcerated for several years without trial. Discusses Silas Munyagishali, former prosecutor, who was publicly executed on Apr. 24, 1998; Exh. 12-4 in the Binder (ADMITTED); Article entitled Rwanda: 23 public executions will harm hope of reconciliation. Discussing fact that "significant portion" of 130,000 detained are believed to be innocent; Exh. 12-7 in the Binder (ADMITTED); Article entitled Analysis: Why Bizimungu Mattered.. Discussing Bizimungu and accusations made against the ex-president. Also, Bizimungu complains about unfair accusations against Mr **[former Prime Minister]**, the former Prime Minister. These two individuals are both friends of **[Alien]**; Exh. 9 in the Binder (ADMITTED); Article entitled RPF threatened by schism. Stating that **[Alien]** among the cited leaders of disgruntled RPF members; Exh. 11 in the Binder (ADMMITED); Article entitled Rwanda ex-president under arrest. Discussing Bizimungu's arrest and marginalization by Kagame; Exh. 12 in the Binder (ADMITTED); BBC News Article entitled Rwandan bank fraud suspects arrested. Stating that **[Alien]** who resigned as a member of parliament, after a falling out with ruling the RPF, claims legal action is politically motivated; Exh. 13 in the Binder (ADMITTED); Article entitled Rwanda: Opposition repressed; country in ebullition. Stating that Bizimungu was placed under arrest for attempts to create a political party; Stating that RPA (Rwandan Patriotic Army) is divided, within the RPA there is a serious rift: Those who are ready to die for Kagame, and those who are tired of war; Exh. 15 in the Binder (ADMITTED); Declaration 005/2001: Alarming human rights situation in Rwanda issued by the Rwandan Alliance for the Renaissance of the Nation. Calling for Kagame regime to stop its continual and overbearing interference with the judicial system in Rwanda; Mentioning **[Alien]** by name as one of the citizens persecuted by Kagame; Exh. 17 in the Binder (ADMITTED); Article entitled ARENA, Imbaga and FDLR create an alliance to overthrow General Kagame published by the Observatoire de l'Afrique Centrale; Mentioning **[Alien]** by name as a former high ranking official within RPF and one who may continue to play the major role of mediator and sage; Exh. 18 in the Binder (ADMITTED); Report on political situation, security and human rights in Rwanda. A report by the British-Danish mission to Brussels and Antwerp, Belgium. 19-20 Feb. 2002; On pg 25, the report lists the following persons as being particularly at risk of persecution by the government and security forces in Rwanda: Persons with a prominent, strong, political or economic base in Rwanda. Generally the government fears such persons as they are beyond the government's control; A western embassy in Kigali confirmed that those most at risk of persecution from the authorities were prominent opposition politicians and their financiers. . .who are overly critical of the government. See Pages 25-26; Exh. 20 in the Binder (ADMITTED); Report of International Crisis Group (ICG) entitled Rwanda at the end of the Transition: A necessary political liberalisation; Page 28: Listing **[Alien]** as RPF Opponent who have gone into exile since 1995; Exh. 22 in the Binder (ADMITTED); Article from Human Rights Watch entitled Rwanda: RPF Seeks to Eliminate, Opposition Election Set to Solidify Power; Human Rights Watch quotes a recent speech by Kagame, in which he says the outcome of the elections is already known. Kagame also threatens to "wound" dissidents who oppose the governments; Exh. 23 in the Binder (ADMITTED); Article by Amnesty International, entitled Opposition silenced in run-up to elections in Rwanda, dated Aug. 2003; Noting that former president Bizimungu and former government minister Charles Ntakirutinka and six of their supposed supporters have been in prison since May 2002 for attempting to form a political party; Amnesty International considers them prisoners of conscience; Exh. 24 in the Binder (ADMITTED); Report by Peace Negotiations Watch containing an article by our own expert, **[Expert Witness 1]**; On page 10, he discusses "Gacaca," the traditional justice ritual which he says is an affront to human rights; Provides further background on the inadequacies of the judicial system in Rwanda and the 100,000 pretrial detainees languishing in Rwandan prisons; Exh. 25 in the Binder (ADMITTED); Amnesty International report discussing the "disappearances," arbitrary arrests, unlawful detentions, and ill-treatment of detainees, and abuses of criminal justice system; Exh. 27 in the Binder (ADMITTED);US Dept of State country report of 2003. Discussing arbitrary and unlawful deprivation of life as well as reports of politically motivated disappearances; Also discusses torture and other cruel and inhuman or degrading treatment; arbitrary arrest and detention; denial of a fair public trial in Rwanda; Exh. 28 in the Binder (ADMITTED);Report of the Committee to Protect Journalists, discussing the fact that a reporter, **[Journalist]** said that top security officials threatened to kill him and his colleagues or detain them and throw away the keys. On Feb 26 [2004], armed men came to his home took them to a nearby forest and told them they were going to die; **[Journalist]** another journalist fled the country in fear for his life; Exh. 30 in the Binder (ADMITTED); Boston Globe article dated 4/5/2004, reporting that 2,671 senior government officials had drawn bank loans of about $5.1 million but had declined to repay them; As a result of the scandal, Attorney General Gerald Gahima was forced to resign; NOTE: Mr Gahima was the person who was named as the signatory on the Interpol Red Notice. The Interpol Notice was attached as Exh. 4 to the government's filing dated Dec. 30, 2004; Exh. 31 in the Binder (ADMITTED); Article dated 4/6/2004, entitled Rwanda, Ten Years Later: Justice is Elusive, Despite Peace Reporting that Kagame rules Rwanda with an iron fist. Critics charge there is no freedom of the press or association. Opposition parties have been outlawed; Exh. 32 in the Binder (ADMITTED); Article from Great Lakes News dated May 7, 2004, entitled Kampala: **[Alien]**says he will ally himself with the FDLR against General Kagame; Exh. 33 in the Binder (ADMITTED); Amnesty International Public Statement, entitled Rwanda: Government slams door on political life and civil society; Discussing underlying political motives for arrest and detention of Bizimungu; Describing them as falling far short of international standards of fairness; Exh. 34 in the Binder (ADMITTED); Article from Human Rights Watch dated July 2, 2004, discussing fact that Rwandan parliament seeks to abolish rights group, League for the Promotion and Defense of

continued

IV. [ALIEN] HAS A VALID CLAIM UNDER THE CONVENTION AGAINST TORTURE (CAT) BECAUSE IT IS MORE LIKELY THAN NOT HE WOULD BE TORTURED IF RETURNED TO RWANDA

Under international law, as domesticated under United States law, a person may not be returned to a country where he or she will be tortured. *See* United Nations Convention Against Torture and Other Cruel, Inhuman or Degrading Treatment or Punishment (CAT), opened for signature Feb. 4, 1985, G.A. Res. 39/46, 39 U.N. GAOR Supp. No. 51 at 197, U.N. Doc. A/Res/39/708 (1984), *reprinted in* 23 I.L.M. 1027 (1984), *modified* in 24 I.L.M. 535 (1985). The Convention was enacted into U.S. law on Oct. 21, 1998 by Fiscal Year 1999 Omnibus Consolidated and Emergency Supplemental Appropriations Act, P.L. 105-277, Division G, Subdivision B, Title XXI §2242 of the Foreign Affairs Reform and Restructuring Act of 1998, 112 Stat. 2681-822, 105th Cong. 2d Sess. (1998) [FARRA]; 144 Cong. Rec. H11044-03; 136 Cong. Rec. S17486, 36198 (1990); *Committee on Foreign Relations, Convention Against Torture and other Cruel, Inhuman or Degrading Treatment or Punishment,* S. Exec. Rep. 101-30 (1990).

The Department of Justice has published regulations to effectuate the Convention. *See* 8 C.F.R. §208.16 to 208.18, 64 Fed. Reg. 8478 (Feb. 19, 1999), *reprinted in* 76 No. 7 *Interpreter Releases* 275, 288-305 (Feb. 22, 1999). Section 208.16 concerns withholding of removal under §241 (b)(3)(B) of the INA and under CAT, and provides, *inter alia*, that "[t]he burden of proof is on the applicant for withholding of removal under this paragraph to establish that it is more likely than not that he or she would be tortured if removed to the proposed country of removal." 8 C.F.R. §208.16(c)(2). The regulation provides that the testimony of the applicant, if credible, may be sufficient to sustain the burden of proof without corroboration. *Id.* "In assessing whether it is more likely than not that an applicant would be tortured in the proposed country of removal, all evidence relevant to the possibility of future torture shall be considered, including, but not limited to:

> (i) Evidence of past torture inflicted upon the applicant;
>
> (ii) Evidence that the applicant could relocate to a part of the country of removal where he or she is not likely to be tortured;
>
> (iii) Evidence of gross, flagrant or mass violations of human rights within the country of removal, where applicable; and
>
> (iv) Other relevant information regarding conditions in the country of removal.

8 C.F.R. §208.16(c)(3)(i)-(iv).

Torture is defined as "any act by which severe pain or suffering, whether physical or mental, is intentionally inflicted on a person for such purposes as obtaining from him or her or a third person information or a confession, punishing him or her for an act he or she or a third person has committed or is suspected of having committed, or intimidating or coercing him or her or a third person, or for any reason based on discrimination of any kind. . . ." 8 C.F.R. §§208.18(a)(1), 1208.18(a)(1). In order for acts which constitute mental pain or suffering to be considered torture, they must be caused by or result from: (i) intentional or threatened infliction of severe physical pain or suffering; (ii) administration or threat of mind altering substances or other procedures to disrupt profoundly senses or personality; (iii) threat of imminent death; or (iv) threat that another will be subject to (ii) or (iii) above. 8 C.F.R. §§208.18(a)(4), 1208.18(a)(4).[3]

Human Rights; Exh. 35 in the Binder (ADMITTED); Article from Amnesty International dated July 6, 2004, Rwanda: Deeper into the abyss-Waging war on civil society; Discussing how the RPF is manipulating the concept of genocide to silence organizations and individuals critical to the government, including religious institutions such as Catholic Church, among others, and many NGOs; Exh. 37 in the Binder (ADMITTED); Article dated Aug. 27-29, 2004, by The New Times, entitled **[Alien]** arrested…to be extradited from the US; Significant because it shows Rwandan position that **[Alien]** is to be extradited, despite existence of extradition treaty; Also acknowledges that **[Alien]** claims he fled Rwanda due to political persecution.

[3] It should be noted that torture does not include (i) lesser forms of cruel and inhumane treatment; (ii) acts that result in unintended severity of pain and suffering; or (iii) lawful sanctions judicially imposed including the death penalty. 8 C.F.R. §§208.18(a) (2), (3), & (5), 1208.18(a) (2), (3), & (5). In the instant case, however, the threatened unlawful arrest, detention, conviction and extra-judicial killing or disappearance which **[Alien]** faces if returned to Rwanda are not "lawful sanctions." It is well-settled that unlawful arrest, detention and

continued

To bring a successful CAT claim, the applicant must show that the act of torture will be done "by or at the instigation of or with the consent or acquiescence of a public official or other person acting in an official capacity." 8 C.F.R. §§208.18(a)(1), 1208.18(a)(1). Acquiescence must include awareness of the torture and failure to intervene in breach of a legal responsibility to do so. 8 C.F.R. §§208.18(a)(7), 1208.18(a)(7). Acquiescence does not necessarily require actual knowledge of the torture but may include "willful blindness." S. Exec. Rep. 101-30 at 9 (1990). In *Matter of S–V–*, 22 I&N Dec. 1306 (BIA 2000), the BIA set the standard for "acquiescence" and determined that an applicant's burden of proof must include either actual knowledge or proof that government officials "are willfully accepting" the non-governmental torture.

The evidence cited above, supporting **[Alien]**'s well-founded fear of future persecution, may also be used in addition to support **[Alien]**'s CAT claim. Specifically, the extra-judicial killing as threatened by Kagame to **[Alien]** and his family members is enough to constitute torture under the Convention. The evidence is clear that the penal and judicial systems of Rwanda are controlled by the executive branch. *See* **[Expert Witness 1]**'s Expert Testimony, **[Witness 1]**'s Testimony, Mrs. **[Alien]**'s Testimony, and Human Rights Reports. There is also ample evidence of unlawful arrests and prolonged illegal detentions of various political dissidents, including former President Bizimungu. *See* Dept. of State (DOS) Letter, Exh 14-G. attached to Nov. 30th Filing. The evidence also shows that **[Alien]** is an outspoken critic and opponent of the present regime, including a personal enemy of President Kagame. *See* **[Alien]**'s Testimony, **[Expert Witness 1]**'s Expert Testimony, **[Witness 1]**'s Testimony, and Mrs. **[Alien]**'s Testimony.

The case law and regulations are clear that torture under the Convention may be found where there is evidence of extra-judicial killings or disappearances perpetrated by the government or with governmental acquiescence. *See* 8 C.F.R. §208.18(a)(4) ("In order to constitute torture, mental pain or suffering must be prolonged mental harm caused by or resulting from: (i) The intentional infliction or threatened infliction of severe physical pain or suffering; . . .(iii) The threat of imminent death; or (iv) The threat that another person will imminently be subjected to death, severe physical pain or suffering. . ."); *Comollari v. Ashcroft*, 378 F.3d 694, 697 (7th Cir. 2004) (Posner, J.) (rejecting government's argument that assassination is not torture; "Even if death itself is painless. . .the anticipation of it can be a source of acute mental anguish; if the threat of imminent albeit painless death were deliberately employed to cause such anguish, it would be a form of torture) (citing 8 C.F.R. §208.18(a)(4)(iii)); *Khup v. Ashcroft*, 376 F.3d 898, 907 (9th Cir. 2004) (CAT claim granted where there was more than 51 percent chance that respondent would be tortured if returned to Burma; evidence showed military sought his arrest and his friend was arrested and tortured).

The BIA has defined torture as the following: (1) an act causing severe physical or mental pain or suffering that must be "an extreme form of cruel and inhuman treatment" and not lesser forms; (2) the act must be "specifically intended" to inflict severe physical or mental pain or suffering and an act that results in unanticipated or unintended severity of pain or suffering does not constitute torture; (3) the act must have an "illicit purpose" such as "obtaining information or a confession, punishment for a victim's or another's act, intimidating or coercing a victim or another or any discriminatory purpose;" (4) the act must be an intentional government act directed against a person in the offender's custody or control; and (5) the act "does not include pain or suffering arising only from, inherent in or incidental to lawful sanctions" such as a judicially imposed death penalty. *Matter of J–E–*, 23 I&N Dec. 291, 297–99 (BIA 2002) (Indefinite detention of criminal deportees by Haitian authorities in substandard prisons does not constitute torture because there is no intention to inflict pain or suffering). *Accord Cadet v. Bulger*, 377 F.3d 1173, 1181, 1186–96 (11th Cir. 2004) (followed *Matter of J–E–* and 5-part test for torture claim finding that cruel, degrading and inhumane treatment in Haitian prisons and/or by Haitian police officers does not amount to torture under CAT); *Settenda v. Ashcroft*, 377 F.3d 89, 95–96 (1st Cir. 2004) (applied analysis in *Elien* and *Matter of J–E–* to person facing detention in Uganda); *Elien v. Ashcroft*, 364 F.3d 392, 398–99 (1st Cir. 2004) (Following *Matter of J–E–* and holding that be-

conviction, especially in the context of the horrendous conditions of the Rwandan penal system and system of justice, as the evidence amply shows, constitutes torture under CAT. *See Zubeda v. Ashcroft*, 333 F.3d 463, 473–74(3d Cir. 2003) (The Convention does not require that the persecutor actually intend to cause the threatened result. It is enough if the persecutor causes severe psychological suffering by threatening beating). The standard of proof is more objective and the subjective elements if asylum and withholding are not applicable. *Ramsameachire v. Ashcroft*, 357 F.3d 169, 184–86 (2d Cir. 2004); *see also Camara v. Ashcroft*, 378 F.3d 361, 371–72 (4th Cir. 2004) (following *Ramsameachire* and other circuits and finding that credibility determinations as to asylum/withholding claims are not dispositive of a CAT claim because the latter is objective while the former applies to applicant's subjective state of mind).

cause there was no evidence that Haiti used torture pervasively or as a matter of policy on detainees, the IJ did not err in denying CAT claim).

The instant case is distinguishable from *Matter of J–E–*, 23 I&N Dec. 291, 297–99 (BIA 2002), because, here, there is no question that the threatened indefinite detention and/or extra-judicial killing at the hands of the Kagame regime would be intentional acts to inflict pain and suffering designed by Kagame and his regime to instill fear and suppress free speech in general and the political opposition, in specific, of **[Alien]**, and other political adversaries.

V. [ALIEN] DID NOT COMMIT ANY DISQUALIFYING ACTS WHICH WOULD PRECLUDE THE GRANTING OF ASYLUM OR ANY OTHER RELIEF

Under Section 208 of the INA, there are certain enumerated exceptions to the grant of asylum. The statute provides that "Paragraph (1) shall not apply to an alien if the Attorney General determines that--

> (i) the alien ordered, incited, assisted, or otherwise participated in the persecution of any person on account of race, religion, nationality, membership in a particular social group, or political opinion;
>
> (ii) the alien, having been convicted by a final judgment of a particularly serious crime, constitutes a danger to the community of the United States;
>
> (iii) there are serious reasons for believing that the alien has committed a serious nonpolitical crime outside the United States prior to the arrival of the alien in the United States;
>
> (iv) there are reasonable grounds for regarding the alien as a danger to the security of the United States;
>
> (v) the alien is inadmissible under subclause (I), (II), (III), (IV), or (VI) of section 1182(a)(3)(B)(i) of this title or removable under section 1227(a)(4)(B) of this title (relating to terrorist activity), unless, in the case only of an alien inadmissible under subclause (IV) of section 1182(a)(3)(B)(i) of this title, the Attorney General determines, in the Attorney General's discretion, that there are not reasonable grounds for regarding the alien as a danger to the security of the United States; or
>
> (vi) the alien was firmly resettled in another country prior to arriving in the United States.

INA §208(b)(2), 8 U.S.C. §1158(b)(2). As will be shown, none of these grounds is applicable in the instant case. The government has raised two bars to the grant of asylum: (b)(2)(i): "the alien ordered, incited, assisted, or otherwise participated in the persecution of any person on account of race, religion, nationality, membership in a particular social group, or political opinion; and (b)(2)(iii): "there are serious reasons for believing that the alien has committed a serious nonpolitical crime outside the United States prior to the arrival of the alien in the United States."

It should be further mentioned, that pursuant to 8 C.F.R. §208.13(c), regarding mandatory denials or asylum, the regulation provides that as to applications filed on or after April 1, 1997, "an applicant shall not qualify for asylum if section 208(a)(2) or 208(b)(2) of the Act applies to the applicant." Id. However, "the applicant shall also be considered for eligibility for withholding of removal under the Convention Against Torture if the applicant requests such consideration or if the evidence presented by the alien indicates that the alien may be tortured in the country of removal." *Id.* (emphasis added). Accordingly, even were **[Alien]** to be found ineligible for asylum under (b)(2), discussed above, he still is eligible for withholding of removal under CAT.

A. [Alien] Did Not Order, Incite, Assist, Or Otherwise Participate In The Persecution Of Any Person On Account Of Race, Religion, Nationality, Membership In A Particular Social Group, Or Political Opinion

The first issue concerns whether **[Alien]** participated in the persecution of others. The government argues that Respondent gave financial support to the RPF during the genocide and therefore must have "participated" or "assisted" in the genocide and human rights abuses perpetrated by the RPF in 1994. **[Alien]** admits in his affidavit attached to the amended I-589, Paragraph 4, that "I was not part of the military effort but I provided political and financial support. Similarly, in the original Chronology attached to the original I-589, **[Alien]** stated as follows: "I politically and financially took part in the war." See Chronology ¶ 2. The evidence discussed below proves that although **[Alien]** gave money to the RPF, this was coerced by the leadership of the RPF at the time and was required of all high-ranking Tutsis. *See* Dept. of State (DOS) Letter, Exh 14-G. attached to Nov. 30th Filing.

During **[Alien]**'s cross-examination, the government's attorney attempted to make much out of a passage in Respondent's book concerning the transport of military clothes, as if to suggest that this would somehow show that **[Alien]** had "participated in the persecution of others" by the mere transportation of military-style clothes. First, it should be pointed out that **[Alien]** fully explained the passage in that he stated that the clothes were for children, and not for any military purpose. This was fully explained also in his book. *See* Exh. 14-L , excerpted from Chapter 12, pp. 280-81 (explaining that the clothes were for orphaned Tutsis called "Kadogo" whose parents had been killed on the battlefield.) Second, even if assuming *arguendo* the clothes were for military troops—which Respondent denies—the mere delivery of clothing does not rise to the level of "persecution of others." **[Alien]** has always been forthcoming in admitting he supported the war effort financially and politically because that was the only way to stop the genocide. Furthermore, the testimony was also clear and uncontradicted that this was a common practice among elite Tutsi, and that they were expected and required to contribute their resources to the war effort. *See* Dept. of State (DOS) Letter, pp. 2-3, Exh 14-G. attached to Nov. 30th Filing.

Under pertinent BIA and federal court precedent, **[Alien]**'s actions can **not** be considered "inciting, assisting or otherwise participating" in persecution of others. In *Matter of Rodriguez-Majano*, 19 I & N Dec. 811 (BIA 1988), the BIA found that the applicant's conduct, assisting in propaganda trips and acting as a lookout for Salvadoran guerrillas during car bombings, were typical examples of military tactics not amounting to persecution. Furthermore, the BIA held that the motivations of guerrillas were not "on account of" a protected ground. The Board's finding that the respondent had not participated in the persecution of others is consistent with its reasoning in other cases that actions taken against individuals in furtherance of military objectives in the context of a civil war do not constitute persecution[4] *See Matter of Maldonado-Cruz*, 19 I & N Dec. 509 (BIA 1988), rev'd 883 F.2d 788 (9th Cir. 1989).

The finding that **[Alien]**'s financial support of the RPF's during the civil war in Rwanda cannot be considered to be "persecution of others" is further supported by the BIA's ruling in *Matter of McMullen*, 19 I & N Dec. 90 (BIA 1984), *aff'd on other grounds*, 788 F.2d 591 (9th Cir. 1986). In *McMullen*, the respondent was a former member of the Provisional Irish Republican Army (PIRA) and was precluded from asylum because he was effectively responsible for PIRA's acts, including assassination of political opponents. The Board found the political

---

[4] It should be pointed out that in *Rodriguez-Majano*, the Board stated that "[t]he participation or assistance of an alien in persecution need not be of his own volition to bar him from relief." *Id.* at 815 (citing *Fedorenko v. United States*, 449 U.S. 490 (1981)). **However**, the Board continued that "mere membership in an organization, even one which engages in persecution, is not sufficient to bar one from relief, but only if one's action or inaction furthers that persecution in some way. It is the objective effect of an alien's actions which is controlling." *Id.* (citing *Laipenieks v. INS*, 750 F.2d 1427, 1435 (9th Cir. 1985); *Matter of Fedorenko*, Interim Decision 2963, at 17 (BIA 1984); *see Fedorenko v. United States*, at 750 n.34) (emphasis added). Importantly, in *Rodriguez-Majano*, the Board found that the respondent was not a persecutor of others, in spite of his membership in a guerrilla group in El Salvador. The Board further held that "activities directly related to a civil war are not persecution" and furthermore, that "[a] finding of persecution requires some degree of intent on the part of the persecutor to produce the harm that the applicant fears in order that the persecutor may overcome a belief or characteristic of the applicant. *Id.* (citing *Matter of Acosta*, Interim Decision 2986 (BIA 1985) (modified by *Matter of Mogharrabi*, Interim Decision 3028 (BIA 1987)). **[Alien]**, just like Mr. Rodriguez-Majano, cannot be considered a persecutor of others because his activities—financial and political support for the RPF in late 1990 and 1991—were "activities directly related to a civil war" and in no way did he have any knowledge that the RPF had persecuted or would persecute others or engage in any human rights abuses.

opponents were directly affected by the respondent's actions and persecution was "on account of" the political opinion of the victims. In the instant case, **[Alien]**'s financial contributions toward the war effort of the RPF to reclaim Rwanda and put a stop to the genocidal actions of the Hutu-regime cannot be considered persecution of others. **[Alien]**'s actions did not "directly" result in the persecution of others; rather his actions brought about the end of the genocide.

In *McMullen*, furthermore, the BIA held that the applicant's membership in PIRA was "active and effective," citing his personal participation in special operations, training of other PIRA members, intelligence gathering and coordination of arms shipments to Northern Ireland. No such personal participation by **[Alien]** exists in the instant case. In addition, in *Rodriguez-Majano*, the Board ruled that the evidence must support a close nexus between the person and the acts of persecution, such that his "action or inaction furthers that persecution in some way, in order for the bar to apply." 19 I & N Dec. at 815. There is no such "close nexus" found in the present case.

Federal courts have also required some active involvement in specific acts of persecution. There is a requirement on the part of the applicant of some active leadership or managerial role whose actions make the direct persecutory conduct of others possible. *See Ofosu v. McElroy*, 933 F. Supp. 237, 244–46 (S.D.N.Y. 1995), *stay granted by* 98 F.3d 694 (2d Cir. 1996) (upholding bar to asylum where senior officer in Ghanaian president's security force reported anti-government activity, arrested political dissidents and delivered them to the army for indefinite detention and torture). *Id.* Most cases entail "particularized conduct", *i.e.*, the applicant actual commission of a persecutory act or active facilitation of persecution. *See U.S. v. Koreh*, 59 F.3d 431, 439–40 (3d Cir. 1995) (upholding denaturalization where application assisted in the persecution as editor of propaganda materials essential to the Nazis putting into effect policy of mass extermination).

Furthermore, the government may attempt to argue that **[Alien]** is ineligible for asylum due to the support through the payment of funds to a "terrorist organization," a ground of both inadmissibility and denial of asylum. *See* INA §212(a)(3)(B), 8 U.S.C. §1182(a)(3)(B) (ground of inadmissibility) and INA §208(a)(2), 8 U.S.C. §1182(a)(2) (ground for denial of asylum). This argument is flawed for several reasons. First, the RPF is not among the list of terrorist organizations recognized by the U.S. State Department. *See* Notices, Department of State, Office of Counterterrorism, Public Notice 3795, 66 FR 51088-01, 2001 WL 1172570 (Oct. 5, 2001); *see also* http://www.state.gov/s/ct/rls/ fs/2004/37191.htm. Second, **[Alien]** does not fall into any of the categories of inadmissible persons under the INA 212(a)(3)(B). For example, he has never engaged in a terrorist activity, nor is there grounds to believe he has engaged or is likely to engage in any such activity, nor has he incited terrorist activity under circumstances indicating an intention to cause death or serious bodily injury, under the statute, etc. *Id.*[5]

The lack of close nexus and other evidence supporting the fact that **[Alien]** is not a persecutor of other is found in the United States' own letter authored by a member of the United States State Department, Exh. 14-G, attached to Respondent's Nov. 30, 2004 Filing. As the letter provides:

> The applicant [**[Alien]**] claims to have donated $1.5 million to the RPF between 1991 and 1994. Numerous reports indicate there was an element of coercion involved in contributions by Rwandan Tutsis to the RPF in the early 1990s. Tutsi living in the near-diaspora [including Uganda]. . .

---

[5] Moreover, INA §212(a)(3)(B)(i)(IV), inadmissibility for being a representative of a terrorist organization, has been held not to apply if the Secretary of DHS determines that there are not reasonable grounds for regarding the applicant as a danger to the security of the U.S.; *see Matter of U–H–*, 23 I&N Dec. 355, 356 (BIA 2002) (finding that the USA PATRIOT Act §412 did not alter the "reasonable grounds to believe" standard); *Cheema v. INS*, 372 F.3d 1147, 1155–57 (9th Cir. 2004) (reversing BIA finding that persons who support terrorist activity in India are ineligible for asylum and rejected BIA's analysis as collapsing a finding of terrorism and a danger to security into one); *Perinpanathan v. INS*, 310 F.3d 594, 598–99 (8th Cir. 2002) (where applicant voluntarily participated in activities of the Liberation Tigers of Tamil Eelam, he was precluded from receiving asylum). Congress amended the statute to permit disqualification for asylum if the AG decides that there are reasonable grounds for regarding the person as a danger to the security of the U.S. *or* that the person is inadmissible or removable for terrorist activity. *Bellout v. Ashcroft*, 363 F.3d 975 (9th Cir. 2004) (upheld preclusion of asylum because there was substantial evidence that person was engaged in terrorist activity as defined under the INA and distinguished *Cheema* as a case under prior law).

> in the early 1990s were expected to donate 1/6 of their income to the RPF or were socially shunned by other Tutsis.

Exh. 14-G (emphasis added).

Furthermore, **[Expert W3itness 1]** in his expert testimony stated that he found no evidence in his research of **[Alien]** that he has ever been accused of genocide, war crimes, or crimes against humanity, either within Rwanda or in any international forum. Moreover, although **[Alien]** was allied with the RPF in its early years, he came out in opposition to Kagame and the RPF when the regime showed signs of corruption and repression. Now, **[Alien]** is RPF's opponent and critic, and has denounced the RPF's and Kagame's repressive practices.

B. [Alien] Did Not Commit A Serious Non-Political Crime Outside the United States Prior To His Arrival

The evidence further shows that **[Alien]** did not commit a serious non-political crime outside the United States. INA §208(b)(2)(iii), 8 U.S.C. §1158(b)(2)(iii). As will be discussed, *infra*, Expert Witness **[Expert Witness 2]**, C.P.A., testified in open court there is no question that the Ernst & Young reports have serious and fundamental flaws. Although the present Rwandan regime claims **[Alien]** committed "forgery, use of forgery, breach of trust, fraud, and corruption," the evidence shows that the allegations against **[Alien]** are groundless, trumped up charges which are politically motivated. *See* Arrest Warrant, Exh. 5 to government filing of Dec. 30, 2004. The Kagame regime is using the penal and judicial system to discredit and persecute Respondent due to his political statements and past criticism of Kagame. The charges have no basis in fact or law.

Case law has outlined what is the sufficient quantum of proof to determine whether "there are serious reasons for believing that the alien has committed a serious nonpolitical crime outside the United States prior to the arrival of the alien in the United States." In *McMullen v. INS*, 788 F.2d 591 (9th Cir. 1986), the Ninth Circuit analogized the standard to "probable cause." *Id.* at 599. Commentators have stated that the standard is one of "sufficient proof warranting the assumption of [the person's] guilt of such a crime." Deborah Anker, Law of Asylum in the United States 430 n.95 (citing Nehemiah Robinson, Convention Relating to the Status of Refugees 63 (1953)) (hereinafter "D. Anker"). In *McMullen*, proof of the applicant's "willing and material" involvement in an organization, the PIRA, was sufficient where the applicant engaged in terrorist acts of a serious non-political nature. The court employed the "totality of the circumstances" test, and stated as follows:

> We conclude that the "totality of the circumstances," *cf. Illinois v. Gates*, 462 U.S. 213, 230, 103 S.Ct. 2317, 2328, 76 L.Ed.2d 527 (1983), which include McMullen's willing and material involvement in a terrorist organization that carried out acts of violence against civilians, his assistance in training members of that organization and procuring arms shipments, support the BIA's conclusion that there are "serious reasons" to believe that McMullen committed some of these unprotected, serious nonpolitical crimes.

Id. at 599. Under the totality of the circumstances, there is no reasonable grounds to believe that **[Alien]** committed any serious non-political offense.

C. The Facts Do Not Support A Reason To Believe That [Alien] Committed a Serious Non Political Crime Outside The United States

There is no question that the facts of this case do not support a reason to believe that **[Alien]** committed a serious non-political crime outside the United States. During the period of the genocide, Respondent was not even in the country of Rwanda. He could therefore not have made the bank transfers or set up any phony accounts during this time period, which is the period when many of the alleged phony accounts were supposed to have been created. *See* Testimony of **[Expert Witness 2]**; of **[Witness 1]**; and of Mr. **[Alien]**; *see also* Exh. 10-7, Appx. 1, listing trial balances of accounts on two different dates: 06/04/94 [*i.e.*, April 6, 1994, the date the genocide began] and 12/07/94 [i.e., July 12, 1994, the date the genocide ended]. The fact that **[Alien]** was not in Rwanda during the genocide is also clearly supported by the testimony of **[Witness 1]** and other witnesses that if Respondent had been in Rwanda during that period he would have been killed as he was a very well-known and respected Tutsi.

Second, as **[Expert Witness 2]** pointed out, the purported fraud makes no sense. At the time **[Alien]** allegedly transferred the funds, he was also paradoxically placing money back into the bank and buying more equity in BACAR. As he already controlled a majority of shares at BACAR, his use of funds to buy a 92 percent share versus a 51 percent share of BACAR would make no sense if **[Alien]** was stealing funds from the bank. If he had any illicit designs, he could have stolen the funds and maintained the 51 percent interest and then taken the funds outside the country. As a sophisticated banker, **[Alien]** could definitely have hidden the funds in various ways outside of Rwanda, in bank accounts located in Europe, Latin America, or elsewhere.

Moreover, it would have been impossible to commit the fraud as alleged. The bank was audited by the Central Bank of Rwanda on a monthly basis, and there was a governmental commission set up to determine opening balances when the bank opened after the genocide. The bank not only had internal auditors but had Price Waterhouse as its external auditor. In fact, Price Waterhouse was hired to audit the bank by **[Alien]** himself. *See* Testimony of **[Alien]**. During the period 1995–2000 there was never any accusation or even hint of impropriety concerning **[Alien]** or his family. *See* Testimony of **[Alien]**; **[Witness 1]**, and **[Expert Witness 2]**.

Third, the U.S. Department of State letter dated October 14, 2004, casts serious doubt on the legitimacy of charges brought against **[Alien]** and other BACAR employees. *See* Exh. 14-G. In that letter, the State Department analyst writes as follows:

> In 2001, the applicant, the majority owner of Banque Continentale Africaine-Rwanda (BACAR), was accused along with several other employees of financial improprieties, and some of the employees were arrested. The applicant was out of the country at the time. In November 2001, four BACAR employees were ordered released. The Kigali Court of Appeal reaffirmed the release order on October 23, 2003, and again on November 19, 2003, but all four employees remained in detention without trial until September 17, 2004—when one of the four employees, suffering from terminal cirrhosis of the liver, was released for humanitarian reasons. On September 30, 2004, on e of the three employees remaining in detention requested provisional release for medical reasons, citing his need to travel to Belgium for periodic treatment of injuries sustained in an unrelated automobile accident that occurred years earlier. However, to date, the three employees remain in detention.

Id., p. 2. The U.S. State Department reinforces and confirms Mrs. **[Alien]**'s testimony concerning the unlawful continued incarceration of the BACAR employees, in spite of court orders releasing these individuals. This fact, in and of itself, shows the Kagame regime's executive branch opposition to, and thwarting of, the rule of law in Rwanda.

Fourth, the only document relied upon by the government to support a claim of bank fraud was the Ernst & Young reports. *See* proposed exhibit 10-7. This document has been the subject of a Motion to Exclude and the court has reserved its decision on admitting this document. Expert Witness **[Expert Witness 2]**, CPA, found that the reports were replete with serious flaws. Therefore, the reports cannot be used to support a reason to believe **[Alien]** committed any crime.

[Expert Witness 2] testified that it was highly irregular for the Ernst & Young reports not to contain any mention that the authors of the reports consulted or attempted to consult with **[Alien]** or anyone else involved with the running of the bank during the time period in question. **[Expert Witness 2]** stated that in many places the reports contain references to documents, but the documents themselves are not attached. Nor is there any mention that the authors consulted government reports or any governmental banking authorities, or internal or external auditors of the bank. As **[Alien]** testified, he hired Price Waterhouse as an external auditor in the late 1990s to audit the bank and to provide their independent assessment. Price Waterhouse was never consulted by the reports' authors.

Fifth, the charges against **[Alien]** do not make any sense. Although he had a lot of funds in his account at BACAR, this was normal as he was a wealthy businessman. **[Expert Witness 2]** testified there is nothing improper about a member of a bank having an account containing personal funds in the same bank where he works.

Moreover, **[Expert Witness 2]** found it unlikely that **[Alien]** would allegedly take money and then leave the money in the bank when he left the country. It does not make sense that **[Alien]** would steal money from customers and then leave the money in his account. When Respondent left the country of Rwanda he did not keep it with him nor did he have it wired to himself at another account outside Rwanda.

Sixth, the report does not square with the unrebutted fact that a governmental commission was appointed after the genocide to re-create accounts and to establish opening balances. As stated above, in 1995 the commission established a balance sheet and made it public. They gave their report to the Minister of Finance and it was published. Importantly, from 1995 until 2000, **[Alien]** received no notice of any kind that he was accused of any impropriety, despite the existence of the governmental commission. *See* Testimony of **[Alien]**.

Seventh, **[Alien]** has fully explained any uses of funds from his account in the BACAR bank. The account contained personal funds used for tuition purposes to educate his daughters in the United States. With respect to the Colette auditing agency, **[Alien]** explained that this was a firm he hired to oversee the change in management after the genocide and to audit the bank and report to the Board of Directors. There was nothing improper or unusual about hiring such an auditing firm.

Eighth, and perhaps most importantly, there was no supporting documentation regarding the movement of funds to **[Alien]**'s account. *See* **[Expert Witness 2]** Testimony. There are no "paper trails," just a list of account numbers which could have been forged or made up. There are no supporting documents.

Ninth, the Ernst & Young reports are so flawed as to be utterly useless in supporting any claim of fraud. As **[Expert Witness 2]** concluded, the reports appear to indicate that **[Alien]** or his family have been the ultimate beneficiaries of the movement of certain funds but nowhere does it say that **[Alien]** committed fraud. In fact, the Ernst & Young report itself, in several places, recognizes its own inherent limitations and provides explicit disclaimers regarding the permissible use of the report. See Exh. 10-7, Section 6.2, p. 9, Special Audit Report, Executive Summary, section entitled "The Lack of Support Documentation," and finding that "There is a distinct possibility, albeit remote, that the findings may change where new audit evidence becomes available." The report further acknowledges on the same page "The limited utilisation of sophisticated data interrogation techniques," finding as follows: "Sophisticated data interrogation techniques may provide more information on the transactions that have occurred in relation to the reduction in depositors' balances, the creation of new accounts and the subsequent movement of funds." The report also acknowledges that "Other account have not been investigated." The report also has a section explicitly entitled, "Restriction of Use." See Exh. 10-7, Special Audit Report, p. 5. In that section, the authors state as follows: "This report has been prepared for the sole use of BNR. <u>The report or is contents should not be disclosed, quoted, or relied upon to/by third parties without our written permission</u>. . . ." There is nothing to evidence that Ernst & Young has provided its consent for the report to be utilized as part of the instant proceedings.

Tenth, finally, the charges against **[Alien]** are directly contrary to how he has acted his whole life. These charges have come only <u>after</u> he has challenged the corruption and authority of the Kagame regime. **[Witness 1]** discussed at length **[Alien]**'s reputation throughout the country of Rwanda. **[Witness 1]** stated that **[Alien]** was well-known throughout the country as a Member of Parliament. His reputation was as a man who fought for what he believed in. He was known to challenge the RPF and highly regarded not only by Parliament itself but by the people of Rwanda. He was also known for challenging the Kagame regime by stating in 1997 that the regime was guilty of "bad governance." *See* Testimony of **[Witness 1]**, **[Expert Witness 1]**, and **[Alien]**.

D. Distinguishing Legitimate "Prosecution" from Prohibited "Persecution" of the Applicant

In the case at bar, as discussed above, there is no plausible reason for believing that **[Alien]** committed a serious non-political crime. Even if there were reason to believe he had committed such a crime, the <u>prosecution</u> of **[Alien]** must be distinguished from the impermissible <u>persecution</u> by governmental authorities of Respondent. There is a requirement that there be a balancing of the seriousness of the offense against the degree of persecution feared. *See* D. Anker, p. 199, 437. In the instant case, <u>even were there reason to believe</u> that **[Alien]** committed bank fraud, as alleged, the likely penalty imposed by the Kagame regime against Respondent, indefinite detention, torture, and/or extra-judicial killing, would be entirely disproportionate to the alleged offense.

If prosecution is motivated by political opinion or another enumerated factor and the punishment is sufficiently serious, prosecution under a law of general applicability can amount to persecution. *Hoque v. Ashcroft*, 367 F.3d 1190, 1197 (9th Cir. 2004) (IJ's determination that applicant's arrest for demonstration was simply prosecution was not supported by substantial evidence where applicant stated he was wrongly accused and government arresting opponents took power); *Lin v. INS*, 238 F.3d 239, 244 (3d Cir. 2001) (reversed BIA denial of withholding and asylum to Chinese student who demonstrated during Tiananmen Square era despite being sought through lawful subpoena for arrest); *see also Rodriguez-Roman v. INS*, 98 F.3d 416, 420 (9th Cir. 1996).

In *Rodriguez-Roman v. INS*, the court considered the question whether Cuba's severe penalties for illegal departure, including death, can be considered persecution and not prosecution. The court noted that labeling someone as a traitor and severe penalties for illegal departure ranging from three to twenty years in prison, indefinite sentences, or death, were indicative of political persecution rather than prosecution. As noted by the court in *Rodriguez-Roman*, the BIA has found that prison sentences of eight months and one year, confiscation of property among other factors were evidence that "what would await [the applicant] upon his return to Czechoslovakia would not be punishment for violation of an ordinary criminal statute. . .but persecution for the political offense which he has committed against the State." *Id.* at 428 (citing *Janus & Janek*, 12 I & N Dec. 866, 875 (BIA 1968).

There is ample evidence presented in the instant case that President Kagame is using the penal and judicial systems of Rwanda to suppress opposition, imprison dissenters like **[Alien]** to stifle free speech, and to terrify opponents into submission. Examples include the continued imprisonment of three BACAR employees and associates of **[Alien]**, the arrest and continued detention of ex-President Bizimungu for attempting to create a political party, and the threats against the lives of Respondent and his sons.

The following evidence has been produced supporting **[Alien]**'s claim that the charges of bank fraud and the other allegations against him are political persecution for his outspoken criticism of the regime and not "prosecution." First, as already discussed at length, **[Alien]**'s own testimony establishes that the Kagame regime arrested and incarcerated fellow BACAR employees, including **[Brother]**, **[Alien]**'s younger brother. Respondent's sons were also charged as accomplices even though only one of them had ever worked for BACAR. On November 23, 2001, the Supreme Court of Rwanda ordered the release of those arrested in the BACAR scandal, but they have yet to be released. *See* Exh 14-B, *i.e.*, Exh. B to Nov. 30th Filing (**[Alien]**'s Affidavit) (ADMITTED).

The illegitimacy of the bank fraud charges are also supported by the U.S. Department of State's own letter, affirming Respondent's position that in July 1997, he spoke out against Parliament and accused the new RPF-government of corruption and human rights abuses. Exh. 14-G; i.e., Exh. G to Nov. 30th Filing (Dept of State Letter of Oct. 14, 2004) (ADMITTED). The letter, as stated above, also confirms that in November 2001, four BACAR employees were ordered released and the Kigali Court of Appeals affirmed the release order on Oct 23, 2003 and again on Nov 19, 2003, but all 4 remained in detention without trial until Sept 17, 2004. On that date, one of the four was released due to terminal cirrhosis of the liver on humanitarian grounds. On Sept 30, 2004 one of three employees remaining in detention requested release on medical grounds for treatment of injuries sustained in an unrelated car accident which occurred years earlier. <u>To date the three employees remain in detention.</u> The DOS letter strongly support Respondent's credible fear of persecution in that the letter supports the fact that past-President Bizimungu suffered persecution at the hands of Kagame's regime. Again, the DOS states that "We are not aware that the charges against Bizimungu and his co-defendants were supported by the presentation of material evidence. See also Exh. 13; previously Exh. 14-I, attached to Nov. 30th Filing (Affidavit of **[former Prime Minister]**, former Primer Minister of Rwanda) (Discussing Kagame's opposition to Respondent's business dealings including preventing the foreclosure of over 300 residential houses and commercial real properties in Rwanda and creating fictitious companies as competitors of **[Alien]**'s companies).

PROPOSED ORDER

THEREFORE, in light of the foregoing and for the reasons stated above, IT IS HEREBY ORDERED that the Respondent, **[Alien]** be GRANTED asylum in the United States, as he has satisfied his burden of showing past persecution and a well-founded fear of future persecution as required under INA §208; 8 U.S.C. §1158; and 8 C.F.R. §208.13.

[Dated:]

____

[Judge]
Immigration Judge

[ADD CERTIFICATE OF SERVICE]

[Document No. 340]

MEMORANDUM OF LAW FOR LATE-FILED ASYLUM APPLICATION DUE TO CHANGED CIRCUMSTANCES

Description: The law requires that all applications for asylum (but not applications withholding of removal or Convention Against Torture (CAT) relief) be filed within one year of entry to the United States. This memorandum reflects a good-faith argument for an immigration judge (or an asylum officer) to accept a Form I-589, Application for Asylum, filed more than one year after entry to the United States.

Advantages: If granted, this will ameliorate time-counting errors or situations in which asylum applicants, particularly those traumatized by violence or those whose countries underwent violent change while they were gone, simply do not know about the one-year rule.

Limitations: This is a decision that is *completely* discretionary to the immigration judge. Counsel must make his or her strongest argument at that level.

Notes: The courts of appeal *cannot* overrule a decision to deny the opportunity to late-file an asylum application.

Citations: 8 CFR §§208.4(a)(1), (4); 1208.4(a)(1), (4).

UNITED STATES DEPARTMENT OF JUSTICE
EXECUTIVE OFFICE FOR IMMIGRATION REVIEW
IMMIGRATION COURT
[LOCATION]

IN THE MATTER OF:	)	
	)	
[Alien]	)	
A[Number]	)	IN REMOVAL PROCEEDINGS
	)	
Respondent	)	
______________________	)	

MEMORANDUM OF LAW FOR FILING AN APPLICATION FOR ASYLUM

I. APPLICABLE LAW

An applicant for asylum must demonstrate by clear and convincing evidence that she filed an application within one year of her arrival in the United States. 8 C.F.R. § 208.4(a)(2)(i)(A). Even if the applicant does not meet this one-year deadline, she may qualify for an exception. One of those exceptions is where an applicant can show "changed circumstances which materially affect the applicant's eligibility for asylum under section 208(a)(2)(D) of the Act." An applicant need only apply "within a reasonable period given those changed circumstances." 8 C.F.R. § 208.4(a)(4)(ii). "Changed circumstances" include changes in conditions in the applicant's country of nationality or changes in the objective circumstances relating to the applicant in the United States. 8 C.F.R. § 208.4(a)(4)(i)(A, B). These changes must materially affect her eligibility for asylum. 8 C.F.R. § 208.4(a)(4)(i).

Respondent arrived in the United States on May 27, 1998, but she did not file an application until after the one-year deadline passed. However she is still eligible for asylum because she filed her application within a reasonable period of those changed circumstances.

II. EXISTENCE OF CHANGED CIRCUMSTANCES

The change in circumstances need only create a "reasonable possibility that the applicant may qualify for asylum." *See* 8 C.F.R. § 208.4(a)(4)(i)(B). In the present case, the Respondent can demonstrate the existence of significant changed circumstances that create such a possibility. When Respondent departed for the United States, she had no intent to apply for asylum, nor was she fleeing an imminent threat of female genital mutilation (FGM). Because her father did not force her to undergo the procedure before, her belief that she was safe from FGM was objectively reasonable. Her father in Senegal decided to give her hand in marriage to his friend and that she would have to undergo FGM. *See* A of Tab I of Respondent's Documents in Support of Asylum.

Her father's decision to have her marry and then excised is a change in condition in the applicant's native country. *See* 8 C.F.R. § 208.4(a)(4)(i)(A). When she left her country, the condition in Senegal was that she did not have to undergo FGM, but now the condition in Senegal is that she will have to undergo this procedure. This change in her native country also indicates a change in the objective circumstances relating to the applicant in the United States. Furthermore, these changed circumstances materially affected her eligibility for asylum. *See Matter of Kasinga*, Int. Dec. 3278 at 17 (BIA 1996) (holding that female genital mutilation is persecution on account of membership in a particular social group). Based upon these changed circumstances, *i.e.*, she will undergo FGM, there is now a reasonable possibility that she qualifies for asylum which did not exist at the time of her admission.

III. RESPONDENT FILED WITHIN A REASONABLE TIME

Respondent has also demonstrated that she applied for asylum within a reasonable time of the changed circumstances. The INS Asylum Officer Training Manual states that in considering what constitutes a reasonable time, "asylum officers musk ask themselves if a reasonable person under the same or similar circumstances would have filed sooner." *See INS Asylum Officer Training Manual: One-year Filing Deadline*, 18 (1999) (found at Tab A of Attached Documents). The benefit of a doubt should be given in determining what constitutes a reasonable time. *See id.* (found at Tab A of Attached Documents). In this case, a reasonable person in the Respondent's circumstances would not have filed sooner. Although she received a letter from her father stating that she was to be married, she did not begin to believe that she might actually have to undergo FGM until she received her brother's letter in late August of 1998. *See* Tab B of Attached Documents. This was reasonable because her father had not yet forced her to undergo FGM during her childhood like he did with her older sisters and maybe she could change his mind.

Even when she felt FGM was certain, she was still unsure whether she would remain or go back to Senegal. After January of 1999, her brother made her realize that she should seriously consider remaining in the United States. *See* Tab C of Attached Documents. She believed that she did not have to make that final decision until April of 1999, the date her visa expired. Her decision was an extremely difficult one and could not be made instantly. The practice of Female Genital Mutilation has deep cultural roots and is mandated by the ancestors. Refusing to undergo excision is a rejection of her family and culture. To defy one's father and tradition is difficult, and a person making such a decision would carefully consider the consequences, including possible permanent banishment from family. One can not look at the horrors of FGM with western eyes and chastise her for not deciding sooner. We must look at the situation from the perspective of the Respondent. When she finally made the decision to stay, she did not have legal representation and did not know anything about United States asylum law. A friend told her in November of 1999 that she could apply for asylum. She was previously unaware of this. *See* Statement of **[Friend]** at Tab D of Attached Documents. Shortly afterward, she obtained an application for asylum and filed it shortly afterward in January 2000.

A reasonable person in Respondent's circumstances would not have filed any sooner. In any case, she should be given the benefit of a doubt. *See Asylum Training Manual*, at 18 (found at Tab A of Attached Documents). The fact that the one-year deadline contains exceptions like changed circumstances evidences the intent to give an applicant this benefit of doubt. Congress correctly refrained from mandating a designated length of time to file an application after there are changed circumstances. Instead, Congress chose a more lenient "within a reasonable time" standard. This standard recognizes that each person reacts differently upon discovering that they cannot return to their country because their life would be threatened. Each person will make a final decision about what to do and figure out how to do it according to his own time frame. Before denying asylum on other grounds beside the merits of the claim itself, one should also consider the humanitarian implications of asylum law. If her claim is valid, she will endure female genital mutilation and a significant chance of death. This consideration is evident when the UNHCR states that an applicant for asylum should be given a benefit of a doubt in proving the facts of their claim. *See* United Nations High Commission for Refugees, *Handbook on Procedures and Criteria for Determining Refugee Status*, at 48 (1979). If an applicant deserves discretion in proving up her claim, she must also deserve the same discretion in meeting any non-substantive hurdles to relief. The United States Supreme Court has stated that this Handbook is a valuable tool in determining asylum law. *See INS v. Cardoza-Fonseca*, 480 US 421 (1987). In doing so, it has apparently accepted this consideration to apply discretion to give an applicant the benefit of a doubt.

IV. CONCLUSION

Respondent is eligible for the exception to the one-year deadline. She has demonstrated a changed circumstance and has shown that she applied for asylum within a reasonable time of those changed circumstances.

Respectfully submitted,

[Attorney]

[Dated:]

[ADD CERTIFICATE OF SERVICE]

[Document No. 341]

EXPERT AFFIDAVITS FOR APPLICATION FOR ASYLUM

Description: These affidavits are samples of one used to support an application for asylum. Using an expert witness is many times essential to educating an immigration judge about both the general aspects of country conditions and the specific reasons why a client would suffer the requisite harm if returned (*e.g.*, medical reasons).

Advantages: In addition to educating the immigration judge, this type of document also serves to help focus the practitioner's arguments and typically contains a detailed factual outline of the case.

Limitations: The judge may not consider the affiant's expertise to be sufficient. Or, even if the judge considers the affiant to be an expert, he or she may totally disregard the expert's opinion.

SAMPLE EXPERT AFFIDAVITS FOR ASYLUM

Sample Expert Affidavit—Country Conditions

AFFIDAVIT

State of Illinois)

County of Cook)

I, Heather McClure, being duly sworn, state as follows:

1. I, Heather McClure, am Resource Director of the Midwest Human Rights Partnership for Sexual Orientation (MHRPSO) in Chicago, Illinois. MHRPSO is a human rights project of the Heartland Alliance for Human Needs & Human Rights (formerly Travelers & Immigrants Aid), also in Chicago, Illinois. MHRPSO investigates and documents human rights violations against gay men, lesbians, and people with HIV/AIDS in Guatemala, and other focus countries. On January 23, 1997, I testified in the court of **[Jurisdiction]** to the authenticity of the documents I gathered in Guatemala City during a fact-finding trip from **[dates]**. These documents were submitted to the court in **[date]**, by **[Attorney]**, lawyer for the **[Client]**.

2. It has been brought to my attention that on the day of the aforementioned hearing, the court raised questions as to what constitutes or determines gay male identity. To help the court make its determination, I refer it to Attorney General Order No. 1895-94, dated June 19, 1994 (as reprinted in the "Task Force Update: Newsletter of the Lesbian and Gay Immigration Rights Task Force, Inc.," Fall 1996, Attachment A), and Stephen O. Murray's *Latin American Male Homosexualities* (University of New Mexico Press, 1995), a collection of anthropological essays that examine different homosexual practices throughout Latin America in relation to issues of family, society, culture, politics, economics, and ethnicity. Additional clarification is offered by (1) a mission statement describing the services of OASIS, a prominent HIV/AIDS prevention center in Guatemala City directed by Dr. Ruben Mayorga (Attachment B), and (2) a presentation of cases of patients with HIV/AIDS compiled by physicians affiliated with the Guatemalan Association for the Prevention and Control of AIDS (admitted into evidence by Judge **[Name]** on **[date]**).

3. In Attorney General Order No. 1895-94, dated June 19, 1994, David A. Martin states legacy INS's position that "homosexuals do constitute a particular social group." Martin continues, "(a)ccordingly, our briefs should not pursue arguments that homosexuality fails to define a particular social group because it is not an immutable characteristic. Nor should the INS argue that homosexuals are too diverse and non-cohesive a group to qualify as a particular social group." As the documentation below illustrates, homosexuals in Guatemala do not share many of the cultural ways of life that, in large part, distinguish U.S. homosexuals. Guatemalan homosexuals, nevertheless, still should be regarded as a particular social group with their own particular characteristics that have adapted in response to a history, and an economic and political system that are very different from those of the United States.

4. Both Dr. Murray's research and Dr. Mayorga's work in Guatemala City demonstrate that in Guatemala a homosexual man cannot be determined by the extent to which his sexual orientation is known to family, friends, and doctor; by his lack of membership in a gay organization; or by his involvement in heterosexual relationships (including marriage).

   a. Dr. Stephen Murray's research in Guatemala City reveals that "one major difference between North American and Latin American men engaged in recurrent homosexual relations is that Latin Americans live with their family of origin until they marry. . . . In my 1980 sample of homosexually active men in Guatemala City, the only men who did not live with their parents lived with wives of their own."

b. Murray identifies reasons for the influence Latin American families exert over their children: "[B]esides greater centrality in socialization, the Latin American family retains economic functions. . . . In societies experienced by most as capricious and heartless, the family provides more than merely psychological shelter. If an individual is struck down by illness or injury and has no family to provide support, s/he will be reduced to begging in the streets. Examples of this horrific danger are readily visible." Continues Murray, "because revelation of homosexuality is a basis for expulsion from the home, and because of the economic as well as psychological security provided by the family, homosexually active Latin Americans cultivate family relations to a greater extent than do those who can take them for granted."

c. Further, Dr. Murray links the strong influence of the family to the lack of gay and lesbian organizations in Guatemala City (to date, none exists). Murray writes that the centrality of family is a long-enduring obstacle to gay self-identification and gay community-building because "[men's] residence with families scattered throughout cities precludes the development of gay neighborhoods." Without gay neighborhoods, such as those "gay ghettos" established in the United States after World War II, there exists in Guatemala tremendous obstacles to the formation of gay consciousness, culture, and community as these have developed in Anglo North America.

d. As I testified on **[date]**, there are currently no gay or lesbian organizations in Guatemala. Though lesbians and gay men are involved in many prominent human rights and HIV/AIDS prevention and treatment organizations, they are not open about their sexual orientation, nor do they use their common sexual preferences as a basis for establishing gay and/or lesbian organizations. When I interviewed Guatemalans (gays, lesbians, and individuals of unidentified sexual orientation) as to why gays and lesbians were not more visible, I was told repeatedly that they are afraid they will be victims of violence, in addition to losing their jobs and the support of their families and friends.

e. The likelihood of violence against gays and lesbians is increased by a common misconception in Guatemalan society that lesbians and gay men are also "AIDS carriers." Conversely, people with HIV/AIDS are assumed to be gay or lesbian. AIDS-phobia and homophobia reinforce one another. Thus, there is a two-fold danger of being perceived, or exposed, as HIV-positive and/or homosexual—status in one group strongly implies membership within the other.

f. The presentation of cases of patients' with HIV/AIDS compiled by physicians affiliated with the Guatemalan Association for the Prevention and Control of AIDS (admitted into evidence by Judge **[Name]** on **[date]**), attests to additional risks that persons with HIV/AIDS take when they seek out medical care for HIV/AIDS in Guatemala. Case #7 (page 4) records that "there was no confidentiality of [the patient's] diagnosis within this hospital. Almost all of the doctors and nurses were made aware [of her HIV-positive status] and they asked her questions about her sexual conduct." On **[date]**, the patient was approached by "a journalist and a camera person" who wanted an interview. The patient "believes that it was one of the nurses of the hospital that contacted the press and television with her name and other confidential facts."

This case, like others documented by the Guatemalan Association for the Prevention and Control of AIDS, testifies to the lack of confidentiality afforded patients with HIV/AIDS (*see* Case #2). Given the tremendous social stigma associated with homosexuality (*see* documents admitted into evidence by Judge **[Name]**) and HIV/AIDS in Guatemala (*see* all patient cases), and the violence directed against gay men, lesbians, and persons with HIV/AIDS (*see* Cases #1 and #8, and other documents admitted into evidence by Judge **[Name]**), a gay man who seeks medical treatment for HIV/AIDS runs the risk of having his sexuality exposed to other doctors and nurses not responsible for his care, other patients, and society at large through the media. The consequences of such exposure could be the increased likelihood that he will be a target of violence, and will suffer other types of social rejection (including loss of job, family, and colleagues). If a gay man has no other alternative but to seek medical treatment for AIDS-related symptoms, it is highly probable that he will not divulge his sexuality for fear of possible exposure or retribution.

g. Additionally, Dr. Mayorga testifies in his affidavit dated **[date]** (admitted into evidence on **[date]**), that "two gay men who have participated in OASIS' workshops were beaten upon leaving a gay bar (Metropolis) by a group of unknown men. They robbed them of a few personal items . . . and (the two men) suffered from bruises and cuts on their backs, necks and faces." Though it is not known whether the men's association with OASIS played a part in their perpetrators' motivations to attack them, it is evident that the general societal respect in the United States accorded gays and lesbians is not replicated in Guatemala. Instead, a gay Guatemalan man clearly endangers himself through his association with places deemed gay or lesbian (*e.g.*, bars), and may put himself at risk for affiliating himself with HIV/AIDS organizations perceived as sympathetic to gays and lesbians.

h. Thus, U.S. expectations that gay identity be defined through an individual's openness with his family about his sexual orientation, and membership in gay organizations, grows from the particular cultural and economic histories of Anglo-America. Similar criteria, when applied to Guatemalan gay men, obscures the very different family pressures, economic scarcity, and lack of a social safety net—as well as a dearth of institutions openly supportive of gay men, and risks of associating with those organizations—that help to define gay male identity in Guatemala.

i. Murray describes how gay men respond to severe homophobia and AIDS-phobia when he writes that gay men's association with like others is limited. He observes, "for fear of having their reputation 'burned' (*quemada*) and their security thereby endangered, many persons involved in homosexual behavior avoid being seen with or being acknowledged by males who might be judged effeminate and also avoid places where homosexuals are known to congregate. The same pattern existed among homosexual Anglo Americans in the mid-1960s, although then and there it was fear of losing jobs more than Latin Americans' fear of the family learning of stigmatizing association." Dr. Mayorga's letter attests the very real fear of violence adds to men's concern that their families or employers will learn of their sexual orientation as a result of their involvement in organizations that might be perceived as places "where homosexuals are known to congregate."

j. Additional survival mechanisms gay men may adopt to avoid repercussions include living "double lives." As Dr. Murray explains, "Latinos [and others] can compartmentalize homosexuality—in space or time. According to Goode (1960), compartmentalization of roles is a common response to role strain; by no means is it unique to managing masculine self-presentation while engaged in homosexual behavior in Latin America. In Latin America, as in Anglo North America, there is 'a traditional difference between that which people know and that which they agree to admit that they know, that which they see and that which they speak of.'" (Henry James, quoted in Murray). One survival mechanism for gay men is marriage, or involvement in highly visible heterosexual relationships.

k. Both men's and women's social and professional standing in Guatemala is highly determined by their marital status. Consequently, the great majority of Guatemalans marry in their early- to mid-20s. A Guatemalan man who is unmarried by the age of approximately 30 is often suspected of being gay and may be victimized in the ways described above.

l. Though there are no exact statistics as to how many gay men marry, the AIDS epidemic in the last 10 years in Guatemala illustrates that a greater proportion of married men are involved in gay relationships than previously believed. Dr. Mayorga admits that "very little is know[n] about the spread of HIV among this population of men who have sexual relations with other men in developing countries and, in general, there are no prevention programs nor special attention designed with this population in mind. And [i]t is estimated that sexual activity among men is more frequent than previously thought. As an example, in the HIV/AIDS clinic of the St. John of God General Hospital in Guatemala, of the 397 men with HIV/AIDS, 187 have had sexual relations with other men" (from OASIS Introduction). This same phenomenon, of married men having extramarital sex with other men (including gay sex workers), is prevalent enough that OASIS cites it as causally related to the increased transmission of HIV from husbands to their wives and to their children in utero.

5. In conclusion, the above demonstrates that a Guatemalan gay man's involvement in a marriage or other form of heterosexual relationship is not necessarily an indicator of his sexual practices or even his sexual identity. Instead, a gay man may choose to be married for the same reason he may decide never to reveal to his family or doctor the true nature of his sexual orientation: to avoid social and familial censure and, consequently, the risk of more serious repercussions, including physical violence, for being recognized as a gay man. Similarly, the failure of a gay man to involve himself in an organization that is sympathetic to gays and lesbians does not belie his sexuality; instead, it attests to the potential danger of association with such organizations. Indeed, the gap between sexual identity and sexual practice in Guatemala is a testament to the intensity and prevalence of homophobia and AIDS-phobia in that country, which can erupt into violence against individuals who are, or are perceived to be, gay and/or HIV-positive.

6. Finally, though **[Client]** is in the United States, it is very difficult to "shake off" deeply ingrained mechanisms that, in Guatemala, are necessary for a gay man's physical, emotional, and economic survival. It is even more likely that these mechanisms will continue to determine a gay man's life in the United States if he remains in contact with his family, and is dependent for emotional support on a Guatemalan immigrant community shaped by the same cultural values that oppressed the gay male when he lived in Guatemala.

7. The process of "coming out" for lesbians and gay men is a gradual one and can take many years, even decades. Many American lesbians and gay men never reveal their sexual orientation to their families, doctors, colleagues, or employers; do not belong to gay and lesbian organizations; and have been married or are currently choosing to end marriages due to their sexual orientation.

8. **[Client]** has had to struggle against additional obstacles, including the very real threat of state-sanctioned physical violence against those who are gay or lesbian (see MINUGUA, Report No. 22, Team No. 5, admitted into evidence) in a society whose judicial and security institutions have been identified as highly responsible for extensive human rights violations (documented by the U.S. Department of State and Amnesty International) against "undesirables" and "subversives," including homosexuals. In addition, widespread and severely debilitating social stigmas against gays, lesbians, and people with HIV/AIDS in Guatemala are realities most Americans never have to face. These challenges may have made **[Client]**'s ability to live as an openly gay man that much more difficult to achieve. Though these forces cannot erase his sexual orientation, they can define to a large extent the choices he feels he has, as a gay Guatemalan man, for expressing himself both in Guatemala and in the United States.

I declare under penalty of perjury that the foregoing is true and correct. Executed on this 3rd day of February 1997, in the City of Chicago, County of Cook, State of Illinois.

Subscribed and sworn to before me this ____ day of ________, 19___

____

Heather McClure

____

Notary Public

Sample Expert Affidavit—Medical

OFFICE OF THE IMMIGRATION JUDGE
EXECUTIVE OFFICE FOR IMMIGRATION REVIEW

In the Matter of the Application for Asylum and Withholding of Removal of __________________ a/k/a, ________________________	A # ________________ **AFFIDAVIT OF DOUGLAS SHENSON, MD, MPH**

STATE OF NEW YORK)
) ss.:
COUNTY OF THE BRONX)

DOUGLAS SHENSON, MD, MPH, being duly sworn, deposes and says:

1. I am an American physician licensed in the State of New York, currently working as an Assistant Professor in the Department of Epidemiology and Social Medicine, at Montefiore Medical Center/Albert Einstein college of Medicine. I am fully trained and board-eligible in the specialty of Internal Medicine.
2. I am a graduate of Tulane University School of Medicine and Tulane University School of Public Health and Tropical Medicine. In addition to holding medical and public health degrees, I have earned a bachelor's and a master's degree in Human Sciences from Oxford University in England. My clinical training was at the Residency Program in Social Internal Medicine at Montefiore Medical Center/Albert Einstein College of Medicine, where my last year I held the position of Chief Resident.
3. Since completing my clinical training, I have practiced in the Bronx. Because I speak French fluently, my colleagues have over the years referred to me a large number of West African and Haitian patients. I have been designated as an expert witness in the New York Eastern District court case of HIV-infected Haitian refugees seeking legal representation during their incarceration at Guantanamo U.S. Naval Base in Cuba.
4. I have a long-standing interest in medical human rights, and have published on the subject. I am on the Board of Directors of *Doctors of the World*, an American-based humanitarian and human rights group affiliated with the French organization, *Médecins du Monde*. I have received specialized postgraduate training in the use of medical skills for the documentation and treatment of human rights victims. Several human rights organizations have referred to me for evaluation individuals who have been subjected to torture or physical maltreatment in their homeland. These organizations include Physicians for Human Rights, Church World Services, The Lawyers Committee for Human Rights, and PEN.
5. **[Attorney]**, Esq. requested that I conduct a physical examination of Mr. **[Client]** in order to evaluate Mr. **[Client]**'s physical condition in light of his allegations that he was physically abused by government officials prior to this flight from **[Country]** to this country.
6. I have had the opportunity to review the medical records that were provided to Mr. **[Client]** through the Department of Homeland Security, by the Wackenhut Facility ("Wackenhut").

7. On January 19, 1993, I was able to visit Mr. **[Client]** at Wackenhut, where he is currently being detained, and conducted a thorough clinical examination. During the course of that examination, Mr. **[Client]** described the events surrounding his incarceration in **[Country]**. On **[date]**, four soldiers forcibly entered Mr. **[Client]**'s apartment and beat him severely. He was repeatedly hit in the face, on the head, and about the ears. He was kicked in the stomach when he fell to the ground. At one point, after getting up from the floor, he was pushed into a metal chair on which he gashed his right forearm. During the beating, one of the soldiers attacked him with a whip while another pinned his arms behind his back with a metal-buckled belt or cord. These beatings continued for approximately 15 minutes.

8. Mr. **[Client]** was then bodily carried (with his arms still pinned back) and tossed into the back of a waiting van. He landed on his head and shoulders, apparently dislocating his right shoulder. He was then taken to **[Location]** prison where he was held for 165 days. During his incarceration he received inadequate medical attention for his multiple injuries. His right shoulder was placed in a primitive cast, but was otherwise left unattended. He described to me the great fear he experienced during that period, not knowing when he would be released or what his fate might be.

9. Mr. **[Client]** also described a variety of changes in his health which began following his beatings in the **[Prison]**. He stated he now has great difficulty concentrating and is often forgetful. He suffers from frequent headaches, is unable to sleep at night and finds himself sleeping through much of the day. He is very sad and sometimes cries without any proximate cause. He is continuously anxious and has little appetite. He also states his hearing is impaired since his beatings.

10. On physical examination, Mr. **[Client]** exhibits numerous scars. I asked him to point out how he sustained each one, and my findings are as follows: He has a 6 cm circular scar on the superior aspect of his right shoulder which follows the form of a crude buckle; he has a trailing 4 cm scar on the anterior aspect of his left shoulder consistent with a whipping; he has a 4 cm poorly joined scar on the medial surface of his left arm consistent with the "tearing" wound of a tightly bound rope; he has a well-joined 4 cm scar on his right forearm consistent with a cut from a sharp object such as a metal chair; he has a 3 cm trailing scar on the anterior aspect of his left thigh, which is also consistent with a whipping wound; he has a 3 cm poorly healed scar on his right anterior shin, which he states resulted from an earlier sports accident.

11. Mr. **[Client]** also has an asymmetrical hearing loss, with apparent sensorineural damage to his right ear (positive Weber Test). His tympanic membranes have been damaged, with probably perforation.

12. Based on my examination and experience in diagnosing other victims of physical maltreatment and torture, my assessment is that his multiple sights and symptoms are entirely consistent with the story he recounts. The fact that Mr. **[Client]** attributes a rather dramatic scar to an unrelated sports accident persuades me further that he is telling the truth.

13. I would be willing to further explain my assessment, and answer any other questions relevant to this matter if requested to do so, whether in writing or orally.

Sworn to before me this ___ day of ________, ______

_____________________ _____________________

Notary Public DOUGLAS SHENSON, MD, MPH

[Document No. 342]

BRIEF IN SUPPORT OF RELIEF UNDER INA §212(c)

Description: This brief presents basic case law and arguments in support of a grant of relief under INA §212(c), which was restored to lawful permanent residents with pre-1996 convictions by the Supreme Court's decision in *INS v. St. Cyr*, 533 U.S. 289 (2001).

Advantages: This cogent brief contains a thorough review of the law concerning relief under INA §212(c).

Limitations: Remember to make the brief in support factually specific, and apply those facts to the factors supporting a grant of relief.

U.S. DEPARTMENT OF JUSTICE
EXECUTIVE OFFICE FOR IMMIGRATION REVIEW
IMMIGRATION COURT
[LOCATION]

IN THE MATTER OF:	)	
	)	
[Alien]	)	
A[Number]	)	IN REMOVAL PROCEEDINGS
	)	
Respondent	)	
______________________	)	

RESPONDENT'S OPENING BRIEF

FACTUAL BACKGROUND

[Alien] is a citizen and national of Mexico. **[Alien]** has resided in the United States since 1981. In 1986, **[Alien]** applied for, and was granted, amnesty and ultimately temporary resident status under INA §210, the Special Agricultural Workers provision of the Immigration Reform and Control Act of 1986 (IRCA). On December 1, 1990, **[he/she]** he was granted legal permanent residence.

On December 17, 1991, **[Alien]** plead guilty to federal charges of transporting an unauthorized alien within the United States. **[Alien]** was sentenced to 90 days in jail and two years probation. **[Alien]** was denied relief from removal by the Immigration Judge (IJ) on June 20, 1995. **[Alien]** appealed, and the Board of Immigration Appeals (BIA) remanded the case back to the IJ for relief after INS v. St. Cyr, 121 S. Ct. 2271 (2001). For this same offense, **[Similarly-Situated Individual]** was granted relief from deportation under §212(c) by the immigration judge in the hearing dated February 24, 2004.

On June 9, 1995, **[Alien]** pled guilty to possession of more than once ounce of marijuana in Colquitt County, Georgia. He was sentenced to four years probation and 160 to 200 days in jail. See Exhibit 6A, Tab 2. In 2002 and 2003, **[Alien]** was also convicted of driving while intoxicated. Tr. at 40-41 and 49-50. From this, **[Alien]** paid a fine, and his driver's license was taken away. On April 18, 2002, Respondent pled guilty to battery and was sentenced to twelve months in jail which was served on probation. See Exhibit 7A.

For this offense in 2002, the IJ found **[Alien]** ineligible for relief under INA §212(c) and ineligible for Cancellation of Removal under INA §240A because the twelve-month sentence constituted an aggravated felony. On February 24, 2004, the IJ therefore ordered **[Alien]** deported to Mexico, finding him ineligible for relief under INA §212(c) and never considering the merits of his application.

On March 5, 2004, the State Court in Colquitt County, Georgia, amended the sentence of April 18, 2002, from twelve months probation to eleven months probation by a Consent Order. See Exhibit 8A. This made **[Alien]**'s criminal charge neither a crime of moral turpitude nor an aggravated felony. It is therefore not an offense for which **[Alien]** can be removed from the United States. **[Alien]** is now eligible for relief under §212(c). A Notice of Appeal was timely filed on March 24, 2004, and a motion to re-open was filed with the Immigration Court on March 24, 2004.

ARGUMENT

Under INS v. St. Cyr, 121 S. Ct. 2271 (2001), the Supreme Court held that aliens whose convictions occurred before April 24, 1996, the enactment date of Antiterrorism and Effective Death Penalty Act of 1996 (AEDPA) §440 (d), are eligible to have their petitions for relief under §212 (c) adjudicated. The Court stated that even though Immigration and Naturalization Service did not commence deportation proceedings against the alien until after April 24, 1996, the alien should still be eligible for the discretionary relief under §212(c). Therefore, §212(c) relief remains available for aliens who, at the date of their conviction, would have been eligible for §212(c) relief. Id. at 2293 (June 25, 2001).

[Alien] is within the category of aliens eligible to have their applications for §212(c) relief adjudicated. At the time of all but his 2002conviction, **[Alien]** was eligible for relief under §212(c). After the amendment of his 2002 conviction, **[Alien]** became eligible for relief under §212(c). As an eleventh-month probation sentence, the 2002 crime of battery is neither a crime of moral turpitude nor an aggravated felony. **[Alien]** is not removable for this offense, though it can go toward the discretionary factors when the IJ considers **[Alien]**'s application on the merits. As stated in St. Cyr, the Supreme Court has held that §212(c) should be available to aliens who were convicted prior to the enactment of AEDPA and IIRAIRA. Under this reasoning, this Court has jurisdiction to consider **[Alien]**'s application for §212(c) relief for his two convictions prior to 1996.

A. [Alien] Meets the 7 Years Unrelinquished Domicile Requirement

Generally for an alien to be eligible for relief pursuant to INA §212(c), the lawful permanent resident alien must be returning to lawful unrelinquished domicile of seven consecutive years. See Monet v. INS, 791 F.2d 752 (9th Cir. 1986); Matter of Lok, 15 I&N Dec. 720 (BIA 1976). **[Alien]** became a lawful permanent resident on December 1, 1990. He departed the United States in July 1991 and returned in August 1991. Exhibit 5A. Since that date, he has not departed the United States. He has always maintained his status as a lawful permanent resident. Therefore, **[Alien]** has approximately 14 years of unrelinquished domicile in the United States as a lawful permanent resident.

B. [Alien]'s Many Positive Factors Which Outweigh His Prior Convictions

The positive factors that may be considered for a §212(c) waiver application are: (1) family ties within the United States; (2) residency of long duration in the U.S.; (3) evidence of exceptional and extreme hardship to the family should they be deported; (4) service in the armed forces; (5) history of employment; (6) existence of property or business ties; (7) existence of value and service to the community; (8) proof of genuine rehabilitation when a criminal record exists; and (9) evidence attesting to a respondent's good character. See Matter of Marin, 16 I&N Dec. 581 (BIA 1978); Matter of Wadud, Int. Dec. # 2980 (BIA 1984).

Clearly, **[Alien]** meets the first and second criteria above in that he has lived in the United States for approximately 24 years. **[Alien]** is married to a United States citizen. His United States citizen step-children all reside in the United States. The third factor to be considered is the hardship the family will face if **[Alien]** is ordered removed. **[Alien]** would not likely be able to support his family on a farmer's wage in Mexico, which would be considerable less than the $10.50 an hour he makes working for **[Employer]**. His wife and step-children are American-born and not proficient in Spanish. It would be extremely difficult for them to relocated with him. The family would be emotionally destroyed by that outcome.

[Alien] has shown responsibility toward his family and community. **[Alien]** has worked on a full time basis, often over 40 hours a week, for **[Employer]** packing boxes. He has been associated with **[Employer]** since the early 2001. Before that, **[Alien]** worked in the construction industry.

[Alien] has shown rehabilitation since his past criminal record. **[Alien]** realizes he has made mistakes and has behaved irresponsibly. He is sorry for his actions. It is clear that **[Alien]** is eligible for relief under INA §212(c). He has demonstrated that he has been contributing in a positive manner to his family and community. He has also demonstrated that he meets the criteria for relief under INA §212(c) in that he has been a lawful permanent resident of the United States for approximately 14 years and that his positive factors for relief greatly outweigh the negative. Therefore, we respectfully request that the Court grant his application for relief pursuant to INA §212(c).

CONCLUSION

Now that **[Alien]**'s 2002 criminal sentence has been amended to eleven months probation, his application for §212(c) relief should be remanded back to the IJ for consideration on the merits. He is categorically eligible for relief under §212(c). He should be entitled to have the IJ review his case for §212(c) relief on the merits.

Respectfully submitted this ___th day of _____, 20__.

[Attorney]

[ADD CERTIFICATE OF SERVICE]

[Document No. 343]

APPLICATION FOR CANCELLATION OF REMOVAL (RELIEF UNDER INA §240A(a)—LPRS)

Description: This brief presents basic case law and arguments in support of a grant of relief under INA §240A(a), which provides a means for a lawful permanent resident (LPR) to retain his or her status if he or she meets the necessary criteria.

Advantages: A brief helps to focus the immigration judge's attention on the factual issues of the case. It also can serve as an excellent starting point for an opening and/or closing statement.

Notes: Remember to make a brief in support factually specific, and apply those facts to the factors supporting a grant of relief. Also be sure to review current Board of Immigration Appeals case law.

Counsel should disclose *all* relevant facts. Don't hide the distasteful ones; rather, place them in the best possible light.

UNITED STATES DEPARTMENT OF JUSTICE
EXECUTIVE OFFICE FOR IMMIGRATION REVIEW
IMMIGRATION COURT

IN THE MATTER OF:)
)
[Alien])
A[Number])
)
Respondent)
______________________________)

APPLICATION FOR CANCELLATION OF REMOVAL BEFORE THE IMMIGRATION JUDGE

FACTUAL BACKGROUND

[Alien] is a native and citizen of Mexico, born on June 15, 1943 in Jalisco, Mexico. He first came to the United States in the late 1960s because it was very difficult to find work in Mexico. He obtained his permanent residency through his daughter, **[Daughter]**. **[Alien]** became a legal permanent resident as the immediate relative of a United States citizen on January 19, 1976. **[Alien]** has six children. Four are United States citizens from a previous marriage. Two are in the United States on V visas with his current wife. **[Alien]**'s United States citizen children are grown, but he is very close with his son, **[Son]**, who is mildly retarded. **[Alien]** helped his son obtain a job at the same place he works, **[Business]**. (Ex. 1.)

[Alien] has been treated by a U.S. doctor for a heart condition since 1999. (Ex. 2.) He also has a wife and two younger children from the second marriage here in the United States on V-visas. Their status is contingent on his. **[Alien]** arranged for his older child **[Child]** to work with him at **[Business]**. His youngest son, **[Child]**, is a star football player and would very much like the opportunity to go to college in the United States. (Ex. 2 and 3.)

The Department of Homeland Security (DHS) served **[Alien]** with a Notice to Appear (NTA) dated March 4, 2003. DHS charged him with removability under INA §237(a)(2)(A)(iii) and §237(a)(2)(c) in that he was "an alien convicted of an aggravated felony" for "selling firearms." (Ex. 4.) **[Alien]** is applying for cancellation of removal. Form EOIR 42A, Application for Cancellation of Removal for Certain Permanent Residents, and Addendum, are submitted to the court for consideration.

In September 1977, **[Alien]** pled guilty to aiding in the export of defense articles without a license under 22 U.S.C. §2778 and 18 U.S.C. §2. He served 6 months with 6 months suspended time and 2 years probation. (Ex. 5.) **[Alien]** had been selling rifles across the border in Mexico. **[Alien]** cooperated with the investigation fully, and even agreed to wear a wire. The United States attorney states in the plea agreement that **[Alien's]** cooperation in the investigation led to the arrest and prosecution of the other defendant who supplied the rifles.

In 1971, **[Alien]** was arrested for not paying a ticket. He served 30 days in jail and two years probation. In 1982, **[Alien]** switched cars with a friend because the friend was helping fix his car. He was pulled over. It turned out the car was stolen. **[Alien]** was convicted of a misdemeanor of driving the car without the owner's permission and was given three years probation.

ARGUMENT

[Alien] is within the category of aliens eligible to have their applications for §240 A(a) relief adjudicated. **[Alien]** has been a legal permanent resident for more than five years, has resided in the United States continuously for more than seven years, has not been convicted of an aggravated felony, and does not fall under any of the grounds of ineligibility under INA §240A(c).

[Alien] Has Been a Legal Permanent Resident for More than Five Years

Generally for an alien to be eligible for relief pursuant to INA §240A(a), the lawful permanent resident alien must have been a lawful permanent resident for five years. **[Alien]** meets this requirement. He has been in the United States more than twenty-nine years and a legal permanent resident for 29 years.

[Alien] Meets the Seven Years Unrelinquished Domicile Requirement

Generally for an alien to be eligible for relief pursuant to INA §240A(a), the lawful permanent resident alien must be returning to lawful unrelinquished domicile of seven consecutive years. See *Monet v. INS*, 791 F.2d 752 (9th Cir. 1986); *Matter of Lok*, 15 I&N Dec. 720 (BIA 1976). **[Alien]** became a lawful permanent resident on January 19, 1976. He traveled for short trips from the United States to Mexico to visit his family, but he always maintained his status as a lawful permanent resident. He always maintained a home in the United States. Therefore, **[Alien]** has approximately 30 years of unrelinquished domicile in the United States as a lawful permanent resident.

[Alien] Has Not Been Convicted of an Aggravated Felony

Although DHS alleges that **[Alien]** was convicted of an aggravated felony under §237(a)(2)(A)(iii), DHS has not met its burden to prove that **[Alien]**'s 28 year old conviction was an aggravated felony. Respondent has submitted his conviction record to the court, and he does not have a conviction that falls under INA §1101 (a)(43).

Although **[Alien]** did have a conviction related to firearms in 1977, this conviction does not fall under §1101(a)(43)(C) because it was not for "illicit trafficking in firearms" as specified in the Act. **[Alien]** was convicted under 22 U.S.C. §2778, which relates to licensing and registration with the U.S. government when importing or exporting defense articles. "Illicit trafficking" is not defined in 18 U.S.C. §921. The Board of Immigration Appeals ruled that all elements of a state criminal offense must meet the exact elements required by the aggravated felony definition to be an aggravated felony. *In re Vasquez-Muniz*, Int. Dec. 3440 (BIA 2000). In *Vasquez-Muniez*, the Board determined the respondent's conviction was not an aggravated felony because it did not have an effect on state commerce pursuant to 18 U.S.C. §922(g). Similarly, **[Alien]**'s conviction must meet the elements of §1101(a)(43)(C). There is no provision under the statute that requires trading in firearms in order for Respondent to be convicted. The statute itself simply speaks of export without license. "Export" is defined by 22 C.F.R. §120.17 in this case as sending a defense article outside the United States except by mere travel.

"Trafficking" is entirely different and must more narrowly construed. *Webster's Dictionary* defines it as "trading" or "bartering." Here, Respondent simply transported the goods. There is no evidence that they were traded or sold. **[Alien]** merely failed to obtain a license. **[Alien]**'s activity did not rise to the level of trafficking. This was a mere issue licensure.

[Alien] Has Many Positive Factors Outweighing His Prior Conviction

The positive factors that may be considered for a §240A(a) waiver application are whether the immigrant: (1) has been physically present in the United States for a continuous period of not less than 10 years immediately preceding the date of such application; (2) has been a person of good moral character during such period;

(3) has not been convicted of an offense under section 212(a)(2), 237(a)(2), or 237(a)(3) (except in a case described in section 237(a)(7) where the Attorney General exercises discretion to grant a waiver); and (4) establishes that removal would result in exceptional and extremely unusual hardship to the alien's spouse, parent, or child, who is a citizen of the United States or an alien lawfully admitted for permanent residence. See *Matter of Marin*, 16 I&N Dec. 581 (BIA 1978); *Matter of Wadud*, Int. Dec. # 2980 (BIA 1984).

Clearly, **[Alien]** meets the first and second criteria above in that he has lived in the United States for over 30 years, 29 as a legal permanent resident. He has had no arrest history since 1983, more than 20 years. Four of his children live in the United States and are United States citizens. His wife and two younger sons also live in the United States, and **[Alien]** has applied for their residency.

[Alien's] family will face extreme hardship if **[Alien]** is ordered removed. **[Alien]** and his wife have been married for 24 years. They own a house together in Dalton, Georgia. (Ex. 5.) They are raising two responsible, intelligent children. **[Child]** graduated from Northwest Whitfield High School in May 2004 and is now working with his father at **[Business]**. (Ex. 6.) Their youngest son is still in high school, is an excellent football player, and very much hopes to play football in college. **[Alien]** would not adequately be able to support himself or his family if he were sent back to Mexico. He would not be able to earn enough money to pay for his son's schooling or his family's expenses. He would not have access to his doctor here in the United States, who has been treating his heart condition for the past six years. **[Alien]**'s other four children were all born and raised in the United States. They have gone through American schools and are American, not Mexican. They would no longer be able to see their father, especially **[Child]**, who is mentally impaired and works with his father on a daily basis. Because they do not know Mexico's customs and culture, and would have a difficult time finding a job, they would not move to Mexico with their father.

[Alien]'s employment history and business ties are strong. He has always worked hard and provided well for his family. Since moving to Dalton in 1995, he has helped the economy grow, working hard at carpet factories. Practically **[Alien]**'s whole family has been employed with him in the carpet industry over the course of many years. **[Alien]**'s wife and two sons currently work with him. His other son worked with him at one time. **[Alien]** has worked hard, stayed out of trouble, and kept his family around him. **[Alien]** pays his taxes every year. (Ex. 6 and 7, copies of **[Alien's]** federal tax returns.). A letter from his employer is included as (Ex. 8.) He is also a member of St. Joseph's Catholic Church, and has been an active member of the congregation since 1996. (Ex. 9.)

The court should also consider rehabilitation when considering an application under §240A(a). **[Alien]** greatly regrets the mistakes he made in the past. He learned his lesson and has tried to be a good example to his children. **[Alien]** also aided federal investigators during his original conviction. (Ex. 10.)

Finally, the letters of support included in this application demonstrate **[Alien]**'s good moral character. They speak of his honesty, generosity, and hard work.

CONCLUSION

It is clear that **[Business]** is eligible for relief under INA §240A(a). He has demonstrated that he has been contributing in a positive manner to his family and community. He has also demonstrated that he meets the criteria for relief under INA §240A(a) in that he has been a lawful permanent resident of the United States for 29 years and that his positive factors for relief greatly outweigh the negative. Therefore, Respondent respectfully request that the Court grant his application for relief pursuant to INA §240A(a).

Respectfully submitted this ____ day of _________, 20______.

[Attorney]

[ADD CERTIFICATE OF SERVICE]

[Document No. 344]

APPLICATION FOR CANCELLATION OF REMOVAL (RELIEF UNDER INA §240A(b)—NON–LPRS)

Description: This brief presents basic case law and arguments in support of a grant of relief under INA §240A(b), which provides cancellation of removal and adjustment of status for certain non–permanent residents.

Advantages: A brief helps to focus the immigration judge's attention on the factual issues of the case. It also can serve as an excellent starting point for an opening and/or closing statement.

Notes: Remember to make a brief in support factually specific, and apply those facts to the factors supporting a grant of relief. Also be sure to review current Board of Immigration Appeals case law.

Counsel should disclose *all* relevant facts. Don't hide the distasteful ones; rather, place them in the best possible light.

UNITED STATES DEPARTMENT OF JUSTICE
EXECUTIVE OFFICE FOR IMMIGRATION REVIEW
IMMIGRATION COURT

IN THE MATTER OF:)
)
[Alien])
A[Number])
)
Respondent)
______________________________)

APPLICATION FOR CANCELLATION OF REMOVAL BEFORE THE IMMIGRATION JUDGE

INTRODUCTION

[Alien] requests that the this Court grant her request for cancellation of removal under the Immigration and Nationality Act (INA) §240A(b). **[Alien]** is statutorily eligible for cancellation of removal because she has been physically present in the United States since 1988, she is a person of good moral character, and she has not been convicted of any crimes. Her removal to Guatemala would result in exceptional and extremely unusual hardship to her United States citizen child. The Immigration Court should apply the standard for exceptional and extremely unusual hardship as articulated by this Board in Monreal-Aguinaga, 23 I. &N. Dec. 56 (BIA 2001), and grant **[Alien]**'s application for cancellation of removal.

PROCEDURAL HISTORY

[Alien] is a native and citizen of Guatemala. She last entered the United States on June 6, 1988, by crossing from Mexico into the U.S. near El Paso, Texas. **[Alien]** concedes removability, but asks the Court to grant her cancellation of removal for non–permanent residents.

STATUTORY ELIGIBILITY

United States immigration law provides that a foreign national seeking cancellation of removal for non–permanent residents must show that:

1. She has been physically present in the United States for a continuous period of not less than ten years immediately preceding the date of his application;
2. She is a person of good moral character for ten years;
3. She has not been convicted of an offense under INA §§212(a), 237(a)(2), or 237 (a)(3);
4. Removal would result in exceptional and extremely unusual hardship to her spouse, parent, or child, who is a United States citizen or lawful permanent resident.

INA §240A(b). **[Alien]** is statutorily eligible for relief because the meet all of the criteria under this section of law.

FACTUAL BASIS OF CASE

[Alien] is an upstanding member of her community, and has been since her arrival in the United States. **[Alien]** has four U.S. children, all of which have been raised and only know the U.S. None of the children can read, write, or speak Spanish, and **[Alien]** and her family have developed deep family roots in the U.S. Currently, **[Alien]** and her family live in a small town in rural North Carolina, where it is quiet and safe.

There is a great deal of poverty and civil unrest in Guatemala. According to the U.S. Department of State, the unemployment rate is 55 percent. **[Alien]** has no idea how she will support herself and her children were she forced to return to Guatemala. (Ex. 1, Consular Information Sheet.)

LEGAL STANDARD

The criteria for establishing hardship is "exceptional and extremely unusual." See Matter of Ching, 12 I. & N. Dec 710 (BIA 1968). The BIA has found that "relevant factors though not extreme in themselves, must be considered in the aggregate in determining whether extreme hardship exists." See Matter of IG, 20 I. & N. Dec. 880, 882 (BIA 1994); Matter of O-J-O, 20 I. & N. Dec. 381(BIA 1996).

The Courts and the BIA have addressed the question of hardship to United States citizen children of foreign nationals. The consideration of the impact on the children of leaving the U.S. must be "careful and individualized." See Jara-Navarrete v. INS, 813 F. 2d 1340, 1343 (9th Cir. 1986). The BIA cannot assume that the affected children will have no problem adjusting to life in their parent's native country. Id. at 1342–43; see also Watlkins v. INS, 63 F. 3d 844, 849 (9th Cir. 1995). The Court in Ramos v. INS, 695 F. 2d 181, 186 (5th Cir. 1983) stated:

> There is ample authority in other Circuits for the proposition that imposing on grade school age citizen children, who have lived their entire lives in the United States, the alternatives of either prolonged and geographically extensive separation from both parents or removal to a country of vastly different culture where they do not speak the language, is a matter which normally must be considered by the INS in determination of "whether extreme hardship" has been shown.

ARGUMENT

I. Standard of Review

The appropriate standard of review in **[Alien's]** case is to consider the hardship to **[Alien's]** children in the aggregate. The law requires that all the factors must be considered together in evaluating hardship. Singling out language difficulties or diminished educational opportunities of the children, without considering all the other factors which contribute to their hardship, is a misapplication of the law. Although individually no single factor rise to the level of exceptional and extremely unusual hardship, in conjunction with all the other serious conditions weighing on the children, they do rise to that level in this case.

The BIA in Monreal-Aguinaga, 23 I. & N. Dec. 56, 58 (BIA 2001), made clear that the "ages, health and circumstances of the . . . United States citizen relative" should be considered by the Immigration Judge in evaluating a cancellation case. The BIA further stated stated that "[a]s with extreme hardship, all hardship factors should be considered in the aggregate when assessing exceptional and extremely unusual hardship." Id. at 64 (emphasis added). The plain language of the statute, and its interpretation by the BIA, do not require a finding of catastrophic illness or unconscionable situation. Id. at 60. ("In fact, . . . that history suggests a standard that, although high, is clearly less than 'unconscionable.'") Such an interpretation would indeed result in a policy contrary to common sense. Instead, the law only requires that taken together, all of the factors must build up to exceptional and extremely unusual hardship. Id. at 64. For example, a lower standard of living, alone, may not be sufficient to support a finding of exceptional and extremely unusual hardship, but taken with other factors, it would. Id. at 63–64. In the instant case, exceptional and extremely unusual hardship exists.

II. [Alien's] Children Would Experience Exceptional and Extremely Unusual Hardship

[Alien's] children would have an exceptional and extremely difficult time if forced to move Guatemala. First, there is the problem of language. None of the children reads, writes, or speaks Spanish. The children would be unable to communicate with their teachers or their peers. They will be very frustrated by not being able to communicate and make new friends would not be easy. One child, **[Child]** is very shy and has a hard time making friends in the language and culture he grew up with. It will be even more difficult for him to socialize in a culture and language completely foreign to him. In Guatemala, **[Child]**'s adjustment to a school where he knows no one and cannot communicate would be harsh. He would also be lonely without his friends and his dog, and it is difficult to predict the extent of his loneliness.

Dr. Aldridge has examined the children and has concluded that **[Child]** would suffer long-term psychological effects from being removed form the United States at this stage of his psychological and emotional development. (Ex. 2.)

In addition to the social adjustment problems, the children's inability to write or speak Spanish will cause drastic academic problems. Because they will not be able to communicate in Spanish, they will not be able to progress at the appropriate grade level and will be held back. The As and Bs they are accustomed to receiving will no longer appear on their report cards. This will result in the children being forced to graduate a few years after the other children their age graduate, if at all. The social stigma of not being in the proper grade level for their age, getting poor grades, and not graduating with their peers will have a harmful psychological effect on these high-achieving children.

Dr. Aldridge has also concluded that based on her experience in working with children who have been maltreated and suffer from post-traumatic stress disorder, she believes the children would suffer similar shock and symptoms. The complete change in environment would be devastating and traumatic. Dr. Aldridge expects the transition to be so difficult for the children to make friends, if at all.

The likelihood that they will live in poverty, and experience its consequences, should not be easily dismissed. It will be very hard for **[Alien]** to find a job in Guatemala. More than half of the population is currently out of work. If she is able to secure employment, her income would decrease drastically. The effect of poverty is harsh in the United States, but its effect on a child growing up in middle-class America and then living in a third-world country, would be severe. These serious effects cannot be overlooked.

The court is also compelled to weigh **[Alien's]** and the children's safety in Guatemala. She will be likely a target for crime because it will be obvious to everyone that she and her family have returned from America. In Guatemala, unfortunately, theft and robbery are frequents means of obtaining money. People suspected of having wealth are often victims of crimes. Because **[Alien]** and her family dress and act like Americans, they very likely will be targets for crime. Even assuming **[Alien]** and her family somehow protect themselves from such a crime, the effort to do so, and the constant threat, would cause severe worry and anxiety. **[Alien]** and her family do not know about muggings, drugs, and gangs. The children have been living in a quiet, safe town in the rural south. They would be traumatized by the pressure to avoid being robbed.

CONCLUSION

Given the strength of these six factors—social and academic maladjustment, limits on higher education, difficulties in living in a foreign culture, hunger and illness resulting from poverty, increase in physical danger, separation from friends, family and community—**[Alien]** has met her burden of showing exceptional and extreme hardship as required by the INA. As such, **[Alien]**'s application for cancellation of removal and adjustment of status to that of an alien lawfully admitted should be granted.

Respectfully submitted this __ day of _______, 20___.

[Attorney]

[ADD CERTIFICATE OF SERVICE]

Chapter 4
BIA Motions and Briefs

[Document Nos. 401–05]

NOTICE OF APPEAL TO BIA

Description: The samples of various Notices of Appeal to the BIA address issues such as denial of a claim for asylum; denial of a claim for relief under the Convention against Torture; and an order of removal based on erroneous interpretation of the aggravated felony definitions.

Advantages: The Notice of Appeal, Form EOIR-26, is the only method of initiating an appeal with the BIA. If represented, this Notice of Appeal should be accompanied by a Form EOIR-27, Notice of Entry of Appearance. (The EOIR forms can be downloaded at *www.usdoj.gov/eoir/formslist.htm.*)

Limitations: Specificity, at least to one claim of error, must be indicated on the Notice.

Notes: It is important to detail, as much as possible, the reasons for the appeal. Complete details may not be available because the transcript will not be typed until long after the filing of the Notice of Appeal. Be sure to present factual reasons for the appeal along with the citations to legal authority, when available. It is always wise to also include a general averment of error by the immigration judge that will be detailed in the supporting brief.

Citations: 8 CFR §1003.3.

NOTICE OF APPEAL TO THE BOARD OF IMMIGRATION APPEALS

[Item 6 of Form EOIR-26]

6. State in detail the reason(s) for this appeal.

The Immigration Judge erred in denying Ms. **[Alien]**'s Application for Asylum and Withholding of Deportation when he found that she, as the mother of 5 children who have converted to Christianity (four of whom have been granted asylum, the other being an F-1 student), did not meet the burden of proof required of asylum and withholding of deportation applicants. Substantial, probative, and reliable uncontradicted evidence submitted by Ms. **[Alien]**, including expert testimony, clearly establishes that she would certainly face persecution, as defined in 8 CFR §§208.1, 1208.1 *et seq.* if forced to return to Pakistan. Further, the Immigration Judge erred in finding that Ms. **[Alien]** had a safe haven in Pakistan, inasmuch as she could live in a city far removed from her family, and far removed from her husband (who works in Saudi Arabia and to which she cannot travel), without a means to support herself or without family support. The Immigration Judge also made other substantive errors of law and fact which require this Board to reverse the decision. Further errors of fact and law will be discussed in detail in the brief that will be submitted with this case after receipt of the transcript of the testimony.

NOTICE OF APPEAL TO THE BOARD OF IMMIGRATION APPEALS

[Item 6 of Form EOIR-26]

6. State in detail the reason(s) for this appeal. * * *

1. The Immigration Judge made numerous errors of fact and law that require this Board to affirm this Appeal and grant asylum and withholding of deportation to the Respondent. The Immigration Judge constantly interrupted the questioning of Respondent by both counsel for the Respondent and by ICE counsel. These interruptions were not only disruptive of the questioning and intimidating to the witness, but they also served to confuse and harass the witnesses. For example, the Immigration Judge asked whether Respondent had requested a visa from Jordan and only allowed him a yes or no answer. In fact, such an answer was not complete because many factors went into the decision to not request such a visa. Therefore, this Board needs to remand this case for further testimony, uninterrupted by the Immigration Judge to allow for a clear presentation of the evidence. Although the Immigration Judge may desire to "have a clear record," Respondent and his counsel (and ICE) are also permitted and should be able to present the case as they see fit. This did not occur here. These interruptions were sufficient to cause a violation of Respondent's Due Process rights to a fair hearing.

2. The Immigration Judge failed to properly consider the facts concerning Respondent's claim as they pertain to the regulations governing a grant of asylum under either the terms of past persecution found at 8 CFR §§208.13(b)(1), 1208.13(b)(1) or under the terms of well-founded fear of persecution found at 8 CFR §§208.13(b)(2), 1208.13(b)(2). Particularly, the Immigration Judge failed to adequately address the testimony of the corroborating witness who confirmed the timing and reasons for Respondent's Incarceration in Saudi Arabia. The Immigration Judge also failed to properly consider the basis of Respondent's fear of return to Saudi Arabia, the physical impossibility of his return to Saudi Arabia, and the forced separation from Respondent's family that is caused by his fear of persecution in Saudi Arabia.

3. The Immigration Judge erred in finding that Respondent was only credible in part of his testimony. By interrupting the testimony at crucial junctures, the Immigration Judge deprived Respondent of the opportunity to explain his answers and reasons for requesting asylum in the United States. In fact, the Immigration Judge stated in his decision that he found part of the testimony not credible, but he did not identify any specific facts justifying such a conclusion. Therefore, the conclusion must be rejected.

4. The Immigration Judge erred in finding that Respondent was firmly resettled in Saudi Arabia. How can a person be firmly resettled in a country in which they were born? *Matter of Hung*, 12 I&N Dec. 178 (BIA 1987) (query is a person firmly resettled in a country other than the one in which they were born).

5. The Immigration Judge erred in finding that Respondent made generalized statements of his fear of persecution and claims of past persecution, when in fact the transcript will show that Respondent's testimony was clear, detailed and consistent with all known accounts of country conditions.

6. The Immigration Judge also erred in finding that no credible claim existed under the Convention against Torture, when the State Department's own 1998 Country Report speaks of valid claims of torture in Saudi Arabia.

7. The Immigration Judge also erred in finding that a claim of Withholding of Removal was not made, as Respondent presented sufficient facts and evidence to meet the burden of proof found at 8 CFR §§208.16(b), 1208.16(b).

8. The Immigration Judge also erred in finding that General Counsel's legal opinion on Palestinians not applicable to this case, as sufficient credible testimony was introduced to show that Respondent would not be allowed to return to his country of birth, Saudi Arabia, and that he was ineligible for entry into any other country.

9. There are also other errors of fact and law made by the Immigration Judge in his decision, which will be described in the brief that will be submitted with this appeal upon receipt of the transcript.

NOTICE OF APPEAL TO THE BOARD OF IMMIGRATION APPEALS

[Item 6 of Form EOIR-26]

6. State in detail the reason(s) for this appeal. * * *

The Immigration Judge erred in denying relief under the Convention against Torture. Further, the Immigration Judge erred in his decision by first granting deferral of removal, then denying deferral of removal in an amended written order, without providing counsel for Respondent the opportunity to present a brief or argument against the Court's reversal of its original decision. The Respondent presented sufficient documentary and testimonial evidence to sustain his burden of proving that it was likely that he would be tortured if returned to his country of nativity. Further, the Immigration Judge failed to adequately explain the basis of his denial of relief under the Convention against Torture, and was obviously confused over the standard of proof required. The Immigration Judge also erred in stating that the actions taken against Respondent, which actions the Immigration Judge admits occurred, were not torture. The Immigration Judge, while recognizing the credibility of Respondent, failed to note Respondent's testimony in the context of how and why he was tortured. The Immigration Judge erroneously held that Respondent was not "singled out" for torture and therefore Respondent was not eligible for relief under the Convention against Torture. This is obviously an erroneous standard. Respondent requests that this Board grant his application for relief under the Convention against Torture and that this Board grant him deferral of removal. Alternatively, Respondent requests that this Board remand this case to the Immigration Judge for further proceedings consistent with its decision.

NOTICE OF APPEAL TO THE BOARD OF IMMIGRATION APPEALS

[Item 6 of Form EOIR-26]

6. State in detail the reason(s) for this appeal. * * *

The Immigration Judge erred in finding that Appellant Mr. **[Alien]** was an aggravated felon pursuant to INA §§101(a)(43)(P) and (N). Consequently, the Immigration Judge erred in finding Mr. **[Alien]** ineligible for relief pursuant to INA §240(A)(a). If the Board finds the Immigration Judge erred in these matters, we are also appealing the Immigration Judge's factually and legally flawed reasoning in a discretionary denial of relief pursuant to INA §240(A)(a). The Immigration Judge misapplied the standard of discretionary relief that Mr. **[Alien]** was required to show and also failed to adequately consider the extreme and highly unusual hardship occurring to Mr. **[Alien]**'s family should be forced to depart the United States. The Court also erred in finding that Mr. **[Alien]** had not been rehabilitated, as substantial evidence was introduced proving rehabilitation. Finally, there are other errors of fact and law that will be detailed in brief that will be submitted in support of this Notice of Appeal.

NOTICE OF APPEAL TO THE BOARD OF IMMIGRATION APPEALS

[Item 6 of Form EOIR-26]

6. State in detail the reason(s) for this appeal. * * *

The Immigration Judge erred in finding that INA §101(a)(43)(G), includes a conviction under the Official Code of Georgia Annotated Section 16-8-18, Entering an Auto with the Intent to Commit a Theft. A theft offense as contemplated under INA §101(a)(43)(G), should, by the limiting nature of the language of the statute, actually have to involve a conviction for actual theft, as opposed to a conviction for "intent" to commit theft. By interpreting the language of INA §101(a)(43)(G) so broadly, the Immigration Judge has ignored congressional intent and unconstitutionally broadened the statute.

[Document Nos. 406–07]

MOTION FOR EXTENSION OF TIME TO FILE BRIEF WITH THE BIA

Description: The attached motions are used to request additional time in which to file a brief with the Board of Immigration Appeals.

Advantages: If granted, an extension of time will allow the busy practitioner more time to devote to the preparation of a detailed, comprehensive brief on behalf of his or her client.

Limitations: The BIA may extend the time for filing a brief up to 90 days for good cause shown. However, in most cases, the BIA will not grant an extension for more than 21 days. The BIA has discretion to grant or deny the motion. If the motion is denied, the brief must be filed within the same timeframe set by the BIA briefing schedule.

Notes: Practitioners should only request an extension of time in which to file an opening brief with the BIA for good cause.

Citations: 8 CFR §1003.3(c)(1).

EXECUTIVE OFFICE FOR IMMIGRATION REVIEW
BOARD OF IMMIGRATION APPEALS

IN THE MATTER OF:	)	
	)	
[Alien]	)	
A[Number]	)	IN REMOVAL PROCEEDINGS
	)	
Respondent	)	
______________________________	)	

RESPONDENT'S MOTION FOR EXTENSION OF TIME TO FILE BRIEF

Respondent, through undersigned counsel, hereby requests an extension of time in which to file his brief in this matter. Respondent's brief is currently due on **[date]**. Counsel for Respondent has had several other briefs and motions due in the local immigration court, as well as a brief in the 11th Circuit Court of Appeals during the past two weeks and next week. Consequently, in order to prepare a detailed, comprehensive brief in this matter, thoroughly covering the errors of fact and law by the Immigration Judge, Counsel seeks a three week extension in which to finish and submit the Opening Brief. In the interest of justice and fairness and to safeguard Respondent's right to representation, we pray that this motion is granted.

Respectfully submitted this ____ day of _______, 20__.

[Attorney]

[ADD CERTIFICATE OF SERVICE]

U.S. DEPARTMENT OF JUSTICE
EXECUTIVE OFFICE FOR IMMIGRATION REVIEW
BOARD OF IMMIGRATION APPEALS
FALLS CHURCH, VA

IN THE MATTER OF:)
)
[Alien])
A[Number]) IN REMOVAL PROCEEDINGS
)
Respondent)
________________________________)

MOTION FOR EXTENSION OF DEADLINE TO SUBMIT OPENING BRIEF

COMES NOW the Respondent, by and through his attorney, **[Attorney]**, to request an extension of the deadline for submitting a brief in support of his appeal for a period of 21 days, until **[date]**.

As grounds therefore, Respondent states the following:

1. Following timely appeals submitted by both parties from the Immigration Judge's decision, the Board forwarded a transcript of the proceedings and notice of briefing schedule which requires submission of briefs on or before **[date]**.

2. Although the Board's notice of briefing schedule is dated **[date]**, Counsel for Respondent did not receive the notice or transcript at her office until **[date]**. This has effectively left Counsel with a total of ___ days to prepare the brief.

3. Inasmuch as Counsel had no control over the date upon which the transcript and briefing schedule were generated, commitments which preceded receipt of the briefing schedule have made preparation of the brief during the period allotted next to impossible.

A) Counsel for Respondent had prior commitments to conduct out-of-town hearings and attend out-of-town Board meetings which significantly limited her time in the office.

B) In addition to the travel, Counsel had prior commitments to conduct numerous hearings and draft several appellate and trial briefs, in other cases.

4. Counsel anticipates that preparing a brief in support of **[Alien's]** appeal will entail substantially more work than is typically involved in a Board appeal because both parties have raised significant issues in their notices of appeal.

5. Counsel has not sought any prior extensions of the deadline and seeks this extension in good faith.

Based on the foregoing, Counsel respectfully asks for a 21-day extension of the deadline to submit the Opening Brief, until **[date]**.

Dated: ___________ ____, 20____

[Attorney]

[ADD CERTIFICATE OF SERVICE]

[Document No. 408]

MOTION TO ADMIT EVIDENCE ON APPEAL

Description:	A variation on a theme, this motion seeks to present new evidence to the Board of Immigration Appeals prior to the BIA's consideration of the case on its merits.
Advantages:	If the client acquires new evidence after a merit hearing on a matter, then this motion provides the method for introducing that evidence into the record at the BIA.
Limitations:	Any new facts to be presented must generally be newly discovered or unable to have been discovered at the time of the merit hearing. Such facts must be presented in the motion and must typically be accompanied by sworn affidavits.
Notes:	This motion provides excellent citations strongly supporting the submission of newly acquired evidence. Such a motion should rarely be used, as all factual evidence should be presented to the immigration judge to prevent the necessity of such an appeal. However, in those circumstances when an immigration judge denies a waiver, this motion provides the means to present the newly acquired evidence into the record.
Citations:	*BIA Practice Manual*, Section 5.2.

UNITED STATES DEPARTMENT OF JUSTICE
EXECUTIVE OFFICE FOR IMMIGRATION REVIEW
BOARD OF IMMIGRATION APPEALS

IN THE MATTER OF:)
)
[Alien])
A[Number]) IN REMOVAL PROCEEDINGS
)
Respondent)
______________________________)

MOTION TO ADMIT EVIDENCE ON APPEAL FROM DENIAL OF WAIVER

Respondent, **[Alien]**, through his attorney, moves the Board of Immigration Appeals to admit new evidence (submitted as Appendix A, with supporting documents, thereafter numbered) in support of his Motion to Reopen now pending before the Board on appeal from denial of the Immigration Judge. In support of his motion, Respondent argues that,

1. The Board has the power to review the record of deportation proceedings on appeal before it and to enter its judgment anew. *Matter Lok*, 18 I & N Dec. 101, 106 (BIA 1981); *Matter of Becerra-Miranda*, 12 I & N Dec. 358 (BIA 1967). *See also Goon Wing Wah v. INS*, 386 F. 2d 292, 293-94 (1st Cir. 1968) ("The Board is not bound by the [Immigration Judge's] order and may make its own determination").

2. The admission of new information or supplementary evidence is permissible in the context of the Board's *de novo* review power, and is authorized specifically by Board precedent, *see e.g., Matter of SS Captain Demosthenes* 13 I & N Dec. 345 (BIA 1969) (new information may be considered to avoid delay); *Matter of Godfrey*, 13 I & N Dec. 179 (BIA 1971) (in exceptional circumstances additional affidavits or documents may be considered); *Matter of N-*, 9 I & N Dec. 506) (BIA 1961) (Board may solicit and consider further information from State Department instead of remanding for consideration of new evidence). *See also* Gordon and Rosenfeld, *Immigration Law and Procedure*, §1.10e, 1-77, 1-78.

3. The evidence submitted is relevant and material to a showing of **[Alien]**'s proven rehabilitation over the fifteen year period since the commission of a crime of moral turpitude (as well as within the twenty year period since his infraction if the immigration laws in failing to depart voluntarily and not surrendering for deportation), and of the extensive equities and hardship to his United States citizen wife, all of which is central issue in this Board's finding of a prima facie eligibility and its exercise of discretion in reopening Mr. **[Alien]**'s deportation hearing to allow him to seek adjustment of status and a waiver of inadmissibility under INA §212(h). These factors were not adequately or fully considered below by the Immigration Judge who denied reopening. Moreover, these documents are inherently trustworthy, consisting of certificates, statements from correctional officers, employers, universities, physicians and other reliable third parties acting in

their professional capacities, who would have no interest in either falsifying or distorting the information contained therein.

4. The evidence contained in Appendix A would inform and facilitate the Board's decision in this appeal. Admission and consideration of the evidence in Appendix A is consistent with the principle of fundamental fairness and the interests of justice. Should this Board decide not to itself consider this evidence in the first instance, then Respondent respectfully seeks remand to the Immigration Judge so that all of the relevant factors in this case may be properly considered and addressed.

WHEREFORE, Respondent **[Alien]** urges this Board accept the proffered evidence and admit it into the record on appeal.

Respectfully submitted,

[Attorney]

[Date]

[ADD CERTIFICATE OF SERVICE]

[Document No. 409]

ASYLUM APPEAL BRIEF BEFORE BIA

Description: This brief to the Board of Immigration Appeals is an example of the text, legal argument, and formatting necessary for presenting factually specific and logically reasoned arguments to the BIA. This particular brief argues for asylum based on past persecution and a well-founded fear of future persecution.

Advantages: These briefs are required when one appeals to the BIA. The brief relies on the written record of the transcribed hearing. If counsel appeals a case for a client and does not file a brief, the case will most certainly be denied for that reason.

Limitations: There really are no limits in the brief, other than those found in the BIA's *Practice Manual*.

Notes: Be certain to review the *BIA Practice Manual* BEFORE filing your first brief, and every time before you file a brief thereafter. There are hidden gems of wisdom, and some rather obscure rules in the *Practice Manual*. Counsel needs to be familiar with them in order to file an effective brief.

Citations: 8 CFR §§1003.38(f). 1003.3(c).
www.usdoj.gov/eoir/bia/qapracmanual/apptmtn4.htm.

U.S. DEPARTMENT OF JUSTICE
EXECUTIVE OFFICE FOR IMMIGRATION REVIEW
BOARD OF IMMIGRATION APPEALS
FALLS CHURCH, VIRGINIA

IN THE MATTER OF:	)	
	)	
[Alien]	)	
A[Number]	)	IN REMOVAL PROCEEDINGS
	)	
Respondent	)	
______________________________	)	

RESPONDENTS' BRIEF ON APPEAL

TABLE OF CONTENTS

I. STATEMENT OF THE CASE

Respondents, **[Alien]** and his wife, **[Alien]**, are natives and citizens of Indonesia who entered the United States on or about June 19, 1999, pursuant to non-immigrant visitor's visas valid for a period of six months. The couple extended their authorized stays for an additional six months, until May 20, 2000. Hearing Transcript ("H.T.") at 21.

On or about November 27, 2000, **[Alien]** filed an affirmative application for asylum with (what was then) the Immigration and Naturalization Service. Following an interview on the application, they were referred to the Immigration Court based upon the issuance of a Notice to Appear ("NTA") dated April 9, 2001. The NTA alleged that **[Alien]** was subject to removal under section 237(a)(1)(B) of the Immigration and Nationality Act ("INA"), as an alien who had overstayed his authorized period of admission. See NTA.

At Respondent's first master calendar hearing conducted in San Francisco, California, on April 30, 2001, **[Alien]** appeared with counsel, admitted the allegations, conceded that he was subject to removal, declined to designate a country for deportation, and sought permission of the Court to pursue applications for asylum, withholding of removal and relief under the Convention against Torture. H.T. at 2. They were scheduled for an individual hearing on the merits of their applications for relief on April 2, 2003 H.T. at 3.

Following a change of venue to the Immigration Court in Denver, Colorado, the merits hearing was conducted on April 8, 2004. At the hearing, the Court admitted all evidence proffered by the parties into the record, H.T. at 9-11, and considered the testimony of both Respondents, H.T. at 12-52 (**[Alien]**),53-59 (**[Alien]**), before issuing a decision denying Respondents' applications for asylum but granting them withholding of removal. Oral Decision of the Immigration Judge ("IJ Dec'n") at 7. The Department filed a timely appeal of the decision and Respondents filed a timely cross-appeal. Following a motion to extend the deadline which was granted, Respondents are submitting their opening brief by express mail guaranteed for timely delivery.

II. SUMMARY OF THE ASYLUM CLAIM

[Alien]'s application for asylum is based upon the experiences he and members of his ethnic and religious groups endured in Indonesia before he came to the United States. **[Alien]**, both of his parents, his wife, and both of her parents, belong to the Chinese ethnic group. H.T. at 15, 44, 53. He testified that he is readily identifiable as a person of Chinese ethnicity based upon his physical appearance. H.T. at 28-29, 36. Although he owned a car, he typically preferred to ride a motorcycle because the helmet he wore obscured his features and afforded him a somewhat higher level of safety. H.T. at 35.

[Alien] and his wife are also members of the minority Christian faith, which comprises approximately ten percent of the Indonesian population. H.T. at 18-19, 45, 53; see also Ex. 2 (I-589) at 5. Though not necessarily apparent by appearance, members of the faith are readily identifiable through entries on the national identification cards they carry. H.T. at 19-20; see also Ex. 2 (I-589) at 5.

[Alien] was educated in private Christian schools but lived in a predominantly Muslim neighborhood, where he was pressured, ostracized and insulted as a part of his everyday life. H.T. at 30-32; Ex. 2 (Declaration in Support for Asylum) at 1. This type of treatment continued throughout the time he lived in Indonesia. H.T. at 34. He was frequently confronted by groups of Muslims and would either have to fight or flee, depending on the situation. H.T. at 35. On some occasions, he was prevented from going to church. H.T. at 47 (cross-examination); Ex. 2 (Declaration in Support for Asylum) at 4.

On one occasion in October of 1996, H.T. at 40, when **[Alien]**'s car had been cut off and blocked in a traffic jam, he got out to see what had happened and was attacked from behind by a bus driver who had exited his own vehicle. H.T. at 37. The driver hit **[Alien]** three or four times before he collapsed on the street. H.T. at 38; Ex. 2 (I-589) at 6. Rather than coming to his aid after witnessing the unprovoked assault, a large group of bystanders joined in, repeatedly hitting him and then looting his car. H.T. at 38 (direct examination), 51 (cross-examination); Ex. 2 (Declaration in Support for Asylum) at 4. A policeman also witnessed the assault and, instead of apprehending any of the assailants, advised **[Alien]** to just go home. H.T. at 38.

The traffic incident **[Alien]** described in detail was neither isolated nor rare. See also Ex. 2 (Declaration in Support for Asylum) at 3 (referring to the practice of stopping cars with Chinese occupants as "common"; relating another incident in which Respondent and his wife escaped an attack with only minor damage to their car); Ex. 2 (I-589) at 6. His wife related a similar encounter with a hostile Muslim crowd. Outside of a soccer match, she and her then-boyfriend had been stopped in their car by pan-handlers who saw that they were Chinese. When they turned down the request for money, a crowd descended on the car, scratching it, and ultimately shattering the rear windshield before the couple could speed away. H.T. at 54-55. **[Alien]** related yet another incident which took place right in front of her house. A hostile mob knocked down the gate to her home while they made three futile calls to the police for help. H.T. at 57.

Apart from the incidents **[Alien]** and his wife suffered themselves, the two witnessed the aftermath of countless other, more serious attacks. Ex. 2 (Declaration in Support for Asylum) at 3-5. On a visit to Situbando, Respondent saw shops and churches which had been burned to the ground, some of which involved fatalities among church members who could not get out. In another incident, triggered by the defecation of a stray dog, a hostile mob of Muslims broke out the windows of the "Loving Light" Church, before turning on the building next to the Church. The crowd beat the building's owner and burned his building. Ex. 2 (Declaration in Support for Asylum) at 4.

During one of **[Alien]**'s business trips to the island of Lombok, he was initially turned away by the police because of an "explosive" situation and after persisting, found that the warehouse he had come to visit had been burned to the ground. Ex. 2 (Declaration in Support for Asylum) at 5. The violence **[Alien]** and his wife described was not limited to petty assaults and crimes against property. Individuals with whom Respondents were personally familiar had been victimized, as well. Ex. 2 (Declaration in Support for Asylum) at 5 (briefly recounting victims of arson and rape).

Although **[Alien]**'s decision to leave Indonesia was based on his fear of persecution, he did not apply for asylum during his first year in the U.S. because he had hoped that "the situation in Indonesia would get better." H.T. at 22. After he learned that his wife had become pregnant, in June of 2000, however, **[Alien]** examined the situation in Indonesia, concluded that it would not be improving in the foreseeable future, and decided not to return to Indonesia. H.T. at 23-25. His concerns for the safety of the child he was expecting and the advice of his parents who continued to live in Indonesia contributed significantly to his decision. His parents "forbade" him from returning due to the continued climate of intolerance and violence against Chinese Christians in Indonesia. H.T. at 24-27. He discussed his decision with his pastor, Mr. **[Pastor]**, H.T. at 22, and retained an attorney to represent him in September of 2000. H.T. at 25.

[Alien]'s parents continue to live in Indonesia but "mostly stay at home" due to their fear of violence. H.T. at 40. The complex in which they live has a manned security perimeter and his family employs a private security guard, in addition. H.T. at 40-41.

The Chinese in Indonesia have suffered a long history of persecution. Perceived as a privileged and wealthy minority, H.T. at 52 (cross examination), ethnic Chinese have been the victims of numerous, serious waves of rioting, most recently in 1998 and 2000. The country is also racked by inter-religious strife between the majority Muslim population and the smaller, Christian minority (primarily Chinese). Leaders in the Muslim community have openly called for a Jihad, H.T. at 42; See also Ex. 2 (Declaration in Support for Asylum) at 2 (discussing constant announcements over the loudspeaker exhorting Muslims to wipe out infidels), while the government has failed to hold accountable the religious extremists who commit crimes. Ex. 4 (State Department's International Religious Freedom Report on Indonesia for 2003, at 1). President Bush's "War on Terrorism" has only exacerbated the situation in Indonesia, where support for Al Qaida is much stronger than that which the U.S. enjoys. H.T. at 58. The State Department acknowledges in its Travel Warning of

August 28, 2003, that "[s]ectarian, ethnic, communal (inter-intra group) and separatist strife, and violence are ongoing threats to personal safety and security in various areas." Id. at 2.

III. ARGUMENT

A. Under the traditional evidentiary burden, Respondents have established both past persecution and a well-founded fear of future persecution

1. Standards for Asylum & Withholding of Deportation

Consistent with international law, the United States has established three remedies for aliens who fear returning to their homeland, only two of which are relevant in this case. Section 208 of the Immigration and Nationality Act ("INA") allows the Attorney General to provide asylum to individuals who fall within the statutory definition of "refugee." Section 241(b)(3) of the INA, withholding of removal, prohibits the Attorney General from forcibly returning eligible aliens whose lives would be threatened upon return to their countries of nationality.

Withholding of removal is mandatory in nature, and prohibits only the return of the alien to the country from which he/she fled. Asylum, on the other hand, is discretionary. The Attorney General is prohibited from deporting asylees to any country. Under the regulations promulgated by the Attorney General, applications for asylum are treated as simultaneous applications for withholding of removal. See 8 C.F.R. § 208.3(b), § 1208.3(b).

An applicant for withholding of removal must establish that his/her "life or freedom would be threatened . . . on account of race, religion, nationality, membership in a particular social group or political opinion." INA § 241(b)(3) (emphasis added). This standard has been interpreted to require that aliens demonstrate a clear probability that they would face persecution. INS v. Stevic, 467 U.S. 407 (1984) ("more likely than not" standard).

To qualify for asylum, applicants must first establish that they qualify as "refugees" under the definition set forth in Section 101(a)(42) of the INA. Once an applicant has satisfied this requirement, the Attorney General (or her designate) may then grant asylum in the exercise of discretion. This discretion is not limitless, however. Hernandez-Ortiz v. INS, 777 F.2d 509 (9th Cir. 1985). Only "the most egregious of adverse factors" should preclude a grant of asylum to an otherwise qualified refugee. Matter of Pula, Int. Dec. 3033 (BIA 1987).

The evidentiary standard for asylum is less onerous than that for withholding of removal. See INS v. Cardoza-Fonseca, 480 U.S. 421 (1987). The Cardoza-Fonseca Court held that the clear probability standard used for withholding was more rigorous than that required to establish a well-founded fear for asylum. The Court echoed the Board's prior holding in Matter of Mogharrabi, 19 I & N Dec. 439 (BIA 1987), noting that a chance of persecution significantly less than a "clear probability" would suffice to establish eligibility for asylum. See Cardoza-Fonseca, 480 U.S. at 447 ("[O]ne can certainly have a well-founded fear of an event happening when there is less than a fifty percent chance of the occurrence taking place.").

The Cardoza-Fonseca Court emphasized that the statistical possibility of persecution is not determinative. 480 U.S. at 440 ("[t]here is simply no room in the United Nations' definition [essentially identical to the INA definition] for concluding that because an applicant only has a 10% chance of being shot, tortured, or otherwise persecuted, that he or she has no 'well-founded fear' of the event happening"). Accord Perez-Alvarez v. INS, 857 F.2d 23, 25 (1st Cir. 1988) (observing that if one of ten persons in the applicant's country is in danger, a well-founded fear exists). In summarizing its analysis, the Supreme Court concluded that an applicant for asylum "need not prove that it is more likely than not that he or she will be persecuted in his or her home country." Cardoza-Fonseca, 480 U.S. at 449. They need only show that future persecution is "a reasonable possibility." 8 C.F.R. § 208.13(b)(2), § 1208.13(b)(2).

2. Requirements for Demonstrating Eligibility as a Refugee

Applicants can establish that they are refugees by demonstrating that they have been persecuted in the past or by establishing that they have a well-founded fear of persecution in the future. 8 C.F.R. § 208.13(b)(1) (1993); See also Matter of Chen, Int. Dec. 3104 (BIA 1989). Either claim may be proven by the applicant's testimony alone, where that testimony is believable, consistent, and sufficiently detailed to provide a plausible and coherent account of the basis of the applicant's fear. Matter of Mogharrabi, 19 I & N Dec. 439 (BIA 1987).

In evaluating asylum claims, applicants must demonstrate not only a subjective fear of persecution but an objectively reasonable fear, as well. See, e.g., Matter of Acosta, Int. Dec. 2986 (BIA 1985); see also Office of the United Nations High Commissioner for Refugees, Handbook on Procedures and Criteria for Determining Refugee Status ¶¶ 40, 42 (Geneva, 1979). The subjective fear may be established simply by showing that the applicant's fear is genuine. Diaz-Escobar v. INS, 782 F.2d 1488, 1492 (9th Cir. 1986). The "reasonability" requirement may be satisfied by a showing that the applicant has a subjective fear with enough basis to be considered well-founded. Cardoza-Fonseca, 480 U.S. 421.

In Matter of Mogharrabi, 19 I. & N. Dec. 439 (BIA 1987), the Board adopted the Fifth Circuit's approach to determining whether an applicant for asylum has demonstrated the reasonability of his/her fear by requiring the applicant to show that a reasonable person in his circumstances would fear persecution. Applicants must show through "credible, direct, and specific evidence in the record," "facts that would support a reasonable fear that the alien faces persecution." Id.

a. Qualifying through past "persecution"

The BIA has defined persecution, in pertinent part, as "the infliction of suffering or harm upon those who differ in a way regarded as offensive." Matter of Sanchez & Escobar, 19 I&N Dec. 276 (BIA 1985). Persecution undoubtedly includes more than just restrictions on life and liberty. INS v. Stevic, 467 U.S. 407 (1984). In INS v. Cardoza-Fonseca, 480 U.S. 421 (1987), the Supreme Court declined to define the particular acts that might rise to the level of persecution and instead suggested that the well-founded fear could "only be given concrete meaning through a process of case-by-case adjudication." Id. at 448.

By practically any definition offered, Respondents have established persecution on account of their membership in minority ethnic and religious groups. **[Alien]** was violently assaulted on one occasion and only narrowly escaped serious physical harm numerous other times. Although the attacks he suffered were not at the hands of the government, evidence on the record clearly establishes that the Indonesian government has failed miserably in its limited attempts to protect its ethnic and religious minorities. Under such circumstances, the cumulation of attacks and restrictions on individuals' ability to practice their religion rises to the level of past persecution.

According to Matter of Chen, Int. Dec. 3104 (BIA 1989), past persecution, alone, satisfies the requirements of Section 101(a)(42)(A) of the INA. Under Chen, the burden of proof then shifts to ICE to prove that the conditions in the applicant's country have changed to such an extent that the likelihood of future persecution remains insignificant. Inasmuch as substantial evidence on the record establishes that anti-Chinese and anti-Christian violence still takes place at appalling levels, the Department is unable to rebut the presumption established. Accordingly, Respondent meets the definition of refugee as set forth in section 101(a)(42)(A) of the INA.

b. Standards for evaluating the well-founded fear of persecution

In Matter of Mogharrabi, the Board enunciated the following four elements which an applicant for asylum must show in order to establish a well-founded fear of persecution:

1. The alien possesses a belief or characteristic a persecutor seeks to overcome in others by means of punishment of some sort;

2. The persecutor is already aware, or could . . . become aware, that the alien possesses this belief or characteristic;
3. The persecutor has the capability of punishing the alien; and
4. The persecutor has the inclination to punish the alien.

Acosta, at 22.

Respondent has met the four requirements and has thereby established that his fear of persecution in the future is well-founded. The documentary evidence overwhelmingly demonstrates that the government of Indonesia has neither the will nor ability to put an end to the religious and ethnic violence that has plagued the nation for years.

[Alien] is readily identifiable as an ethnic (and religious) minority member and it is reasonable to conclude that, if returned, he would face a reasonable possibility of further persecution. Substantial evidence on the record in the form of human rights reports has established that members of the ethnic Chinese and Christian minorities are the targets of repeated violent attacks while the government stands by idly.

[Alien] has thus shown that he will, more likely than not, be persecuted if returned to Indonesia and is therefore entitled to withholding of removal. A fortiori, he has met the lower standard of asylum by showing that his fear of persecution is reasonable.

B. Pursuant to 8 C.F.R. § 208.13(b)(2)(iii), §1208.13(b)(2)(iii), Respondents are "category" aliens, entitled to a lower evidentiary burden to establish their well-founded fear of persecution

Section 208.13(b)(2)(iii), 1208.13(b)(2)(iii), provides that an individual need not establish that he or she would be "singled out individually for persecution" if alien can establish that he or she is included in and identified with a group of similarly situated persons who have experienced a pattern and practice of persecution such that the fear of persecution is reasonable.[1]

Substantial evidence on the record has established the existence of a pattern and practice of persecution in which members of the Chinese ethnic and Christian religious minority groups have been, and continue to be, persecuted on account of their ethnicity and religion. The documentary evidence demonstrates that members of these groups have repeatedly fallen victim to mob violence.

Respondent has met the second requirement of section 208.13(b)(2)(iii), 1208.13(b)(2)(iii), by establishing his inclusion in, and identification with, the group of ethnic and religious minorities. Thus, Respondent has also established that his fear of persecution is reasonable.

He has asserted through clear and detailed testimony that he has experienced past persecution. He was the victim of violent attacks and numerous near-misses. His freedom to worship has been restricted on a daily basis and denied, in total, on many occasions. Under the circumstances, it is clear that **[Alien]** maintains a well-founded fear of persecution upon return to Indonesia.

---

[1] 8 C.F.R. § 208.13(b)(2)(iii), § 1208.13(b)(2)(iii) reads as follows:

(i) In evaluating whether the applicant has sustained his burden of proving that he has a well-founded fear of persecution, the Asylum Officer or Immigration Judge shall not require the applicant to provide evidence that he would be singled out individually for persecution if: (A) he establishes that there is a pattern or practice in his country of nationality or last habitual residence of persecution of groups of persons similarly situated to the applicant on account of race, religion, nationality, membership in a particular social group, or political opinion; and (B) he establishes his own inclusion in and identification with such group of persons such that his fear of persecution upon return is reasonable. It also bears noting that eligibility for withholding of removal is governed by an almost identical provision in 8 C.F.R. § 208.16, § 1208.16.

C. Discussion of the Judge's decision

1. Exceptions to the One-Year Asylum Deadline

Section 208(a)(2)(D) of the INA provides important and significant exceptions to the requirement that applicants for asylum must submit their applications within one year of entering the United States. The regulations set forth at 8 C.F.R. § 208.4(a)(4), 1208.4(a)(4), refer to the "changed circumstances" which may justify an alien missing the one-year deadline, and specifically include: "[c]hanges in objective circumstances relating to the applicant in the United States," 8 C.F.R. § 208.4(a)(4)(i)(B), § 1208.4(a)(4)(i)(B).

The language of the regulation suggests that the circumstances noted are not meant to be an exhaustive list. More importantly, the regulatory and legislative histories support an expansive interpretation. The Chairman of the Judiciary Committee which passed the bill, commented on the exceptions, noting, "I am committed to ensuring that those with legitimate claims of asylum are not returned to persecution, particularly for technical deficiencies." 142 Cong. Rec. S 11838 (Sep. 30, 1996). The need for an expansive and flexible interpretation was echoed in the Department's (then INS's) Training Manual for asylum adjudications, which counseled that adjudicators "must be flexible and inclusive in examining changed circumstances or other filing deadline exceptions," Asylum Officer Training Manual, Apr. 9, 1997, § IV(A)(1)(d), and goes on to note specifically that "[i]n some cases an applicant's need of protection occurs by dint of changes in his or her individual circumstances." *Id.* § IV(A)(2).

If Respondent's particular fact pattern does not fall within the specific language of the examples set forth in the regulation, it clearly falls within an expansive interpretation thereof. Prior to the birth of his child, **[Alien]** was far from certain that he would apply for asylum. He had been monitoring the situation in Indonesia, hoping, and waiting to see positive changes. Such changes never materialized, however, and, if anything, the situation has deteriorated. In and of itself, that deterioration was not sufficient to compel **[Alien]** to seek asylum. The birth of their child, however, changed everything. Of all the events an individual experiences in their lifetime, arguably none can compare with bringing another life into the world and accepting responsibility for guiding a child to adulthood. The difficulties and dangers **[Alien]** and his wife (as well as his parents, for that matter) were willing to endure for themselves are markedly different than those to which they would expose their child. They had become accustomed to living in fear but, after "tasting" actual freedom to worship and live free from fear, they chose to seek asylum to give their child a better life than they expected for themselves.

Applicants who base their claims on changed circumstances may be "excused" from the one-year deadline but are still required to file their applications for asylum "within a reasonable period given those 'changed circumstances.'" 8 C.F.R. § 208.4(a)(4)(ii), 1208.4(a)(4)(ii). In the instant case, **[Alien]** filed his application for asylum within a few months of the life-changing event. Under the circumstances, he was justified in filing after the one-year deadline and should remain eligible for asylum.

Given the Judge's finding that Respondents face a clear probability of persecution upon return to Indonesia, there can be little doubt that they possess the "lesser," well-founded fear required to establish their eligibility for asylum, as refugees.

2. Fear of Persecution

Respondents agree fully with the Judge's conclusion that Respondents were persecuted in the past. To the extent that ICE is challenging that conclusion, it should be set out in its entirety:

> I find that **[Alien]** testified credibly and I find that he was persecuted in the past <u>because of</u> his religion and his nationality and that is on one occasion he was terrorized by a gang of young Muslim men. Another time he was beaten, his property, that is his car, was seriously damaged and as a result he went to the police and nothing was done about it.

> There are many cases arising out of Indonesia where the person did not suffer any damage or any personal injury, they are just afraid, but this respondent and his wife did suffer actual persecution.
>
> * * *
>
> The violence against Chinese has been horrific over the last five years and I believe that even though the Chinese Christians are not a group where they are automatically entitled to asylum because of being in this group, I find that where there is individual persecution, one is entitled here because the government is unable to protect them as shown in the previous violence that took place.

IJ Dec'n at 6-7 (emphasis added).

ICE boils its appeal down to one issue: (1) whether Respondent suffered past persecution on account of one of the five grounds enumerated at section 101(a)(42). Dept. Brf. at 4. Before arguing that point, ICE summarized and mischaracterized the Judge's decision as "expressly based upon the finding that he was terrorized by a gang of young Muslim men on one occasion; and, on another occasion, was beaten by a group of people and his car was seriously damaged," Dept. Brf. at 4. ICE's analysis apparently skipped over the Judge's findings of fact earlier in the decision, which noted that:

> [E]ven though there has been an abatement of religious violence in that country, there were still seven Christian churches that were either completely destroyed or bombed or at least damaged in that country. The State Department report shows that a few years ago there were riots in Indonesia where hundreds of Chinese women were raped in the streets, dozens of Chinese businesses were destroyed by fire and looting, dozens of Chinese, if not hundreds of Chinese homes were destroyed and there were many deaths and there was an enormous amount of property damage.

IJ Dec'n at 5.

ICE also failed to acknowledge the Judge's other findings of fact that noted Respondents' "relatives who were harmed or who lost property in the riots that took place a few years ago including the attempted rape of his sister-in-law . . ." IJ Dec'n at 4.

ICE does not apparently take issue with the Judge's finding that Respondents were persecuted in the past. Rather, it argues that the persecution Respondents' suffering was not "on account of" an enumerated ground. Dept. Brf. at 4. In this regard, ICE demands evidence "as to the perceived or actual motivation of the crowd." Dept. Brf. at 6; see also Dept. Brf. at 7 ("No motivation was given for throwing rocks at the car . . ."); Dept. Brf. at 8 ("No testimony was elicited from the Respondent concerning the motivation of the bus driver or the crowd."). ICE concludes its argument on this issue by stating that "[n]either of the two events detailed by the Respondent support the conclusion that the action of the persons involved was motivated by Respondent's ethnicity or religion." Dept. Brf. at 9.

Although applicants for asylum bear the burden of proof in establishing their eligibility as refugees, the refugee definition does not require an applicant to identify the particular motivation of his persecutors as long as the possible motivations are invidious under the statute. *Matter of Fuentes*, Int. Dec. 3065 (BIA 1988) (applicant "does not bear the unreasonable burden of establishing the exact motivation of a 'persecutor' where different reasons for actions are possible."). This particular holding was essentially an elaboration from its prior decision in *Matter of R-A-*, Int. Dec. 3403 (BIA 1999), which held that "there must also be some showing of how the characteristic is understood in the alien's society, such that we in turn may understand that the potential persecutors in fact see persons sharing the characteristic as warranting suppression or the infliction of harm." *Id.*

> If Respondents were not attacked "on account of" their ethnicity—the only readily identifiable characteristic they possessed which was different from their attackers, only "random" violence can account for the incidents. In a vacuum, this interpretation might be reasonable. However, the events Respondents described took place in Indonesia. They were subject to more than one such attack. They escaped more than one similar threat. And, countless other persons of Chinese ethnicity have been subject to similar attacks.

The Tenth Circuit specifically rejected the "random violence" theory in Velis v. INS, 1995 U.S. App. LEXIS 2941 (10th Cir. 1995), which noted that "[t]he tenuous "at random" theory becomes even less likely in view of the persecution that numerous of Petitioner's family members, also involved in SICAFE, suffered." See Hernandez-Ortiz, 777 F.2d at 516-17 ("Here, numerous incidents were all directed at members of the same family. . . . The inference that they were connected and politically motivated is an appropriate one."). Id. Given the significant backdrop against which the Respondents' attacks took place, attributing the violence to their ethnicity is a perfectly reasonable inference supported by substantial evidence on the record and ample precedent.

ICE's second argument is that the record does not support Respondent's claim that the Indonesian government is unable or unwilling to protect him . . ." Dept. Brf. at 9. In this regard, ICE notes that because the appearance of police at one incident apparently scared off the attackers (after the damage had been done), Respondents essentially have nothing to fear. Although the government's willingness to protect its minorities is a subject of significant controversy, the record amply establishes its inability. The Judge's findings explicitly acknowledged the horrific levels of violence to which Chinese citizens were subjected. He specifically noted the anti-Chinese riots and hundreds of rapes which took place recently enough to be reported in the State Department's annual report. The next-to-final sentence of the Judge's decision summarized: "[T]he government is unable to protect them as shown in the previous violence that took place." IJ Dec'n at 7.

IV. CONCLUSION

Through clear, consistent, and detailed testimony, found credible by the Judge, Respondents have established that they were the victims of past persecution and harbor not only a well-founded fear of persecution but remain subject to a clear probability of persecution. Respondents respectfully ask the Board to review the record in its entirety, and either grant them asylum or dismiss ICE's appeal from their grant of withholding of removal. In the alternative, Respondents ask the Board to remand the matter for consideration of a request for voluntary departure, which was never considered in the Judge's original decision.

Respectfully submitted this ____day of ___________ 20____, by:

[Attorney]

[ADD CERTIFICATE OF SERVICE]

[Document No. 410]

MOTION TO CONSIDER LATE-FILED BRIEF BEFORE BIA

Description: The motion seeks to have the BIA accept a brief that is filed after the date established by the BIA on its briefing schedule.

Advantages: The BIA will NOT accept a late filed brief, except in certain circumstances. The motion is a requisite to even have the BIA consider the brief.

Limitations: Simply put, the BIA does not grant these motions very often!

Notes: Hopefully, a practitioner will never have to use this motion. But when that one mistake happens, or when the client hires the practitioner after the briefing deadline, it is good to have an example from which to proceed.

Citations: *BIA Practice Manual*, Section 5.2.
www.usdoj.gov/eoir/vll/qapracmanual/apptmtn4.htm.

U.S. DEPARTMENT OF JUSTICE
EXECUTIVE OFFICE FOR IMMIGRATION REVIEW
BOARD OF IMMIGRATION APPEALS
FALLS CHURCH, VA

IN THE MATTER OF:	)	
	)	
[Alien]	)	
A[Number]	)	IN REMOVAL PROCEEDINGS
	)	
Respondent	)	
______________________________	)	

MOTION TO CONSIDER LATE-FILED BRIEF

Respondents, through undersigned counsel, hereby move the Board of Immigration Appeals ("BIA") to accept this late-filed brief, and render a decision based upon the merits of their case.

FACTS

Respondents, **[Aliens]**, are nationals and citizens of Colombia. In 2000, Respondents entered the United States at New York, New York as nonimmigrant visitors with authorization to remain in the United States for a temporary period of time. Respondents remained in the United States longer than authorized.

On November 5, 2003, Immigration and Naturalization Services initiated removal proceedings, and Respondents sought relief by filing applications for asylum, withholding of removal, and protection under the United Nations Convention against Torture. On May 4, 2004, Immigration Judge **[Name]** denied Respondents' applications for asylum, withholding of removal, and protection under the United Nations Convention against Torture, and ordered Respondents removed to Colombia. (Ex. 1., copy of Immigration Judge's order.)

On May 7, 2004, Respondents submitted their Notice to Appeal from a Decision of an Immigration Judge, Form EOIR-26, to the Board of Immigration Appeals ("BIA"). (Ex. 2 copy of filing receipt for appeal). On May 12, 2005, the BIA issued a Notice—Briefing Schedule to Respondents' representative, **[Attorney]**, with instructions for Respondents to submit a brief to the BIA by June 2, 2005. (Ex. 3 copy of briefing schedule notice). **[Attorney]** practices primarily in civil litigation; therefore, **[Attorney]** withdrew **[his/her]** representation of Respondents and referred Respondents to **[Attorney]** to assist them further in regards to their appeal. **[Attorney]** initially met with Respondents on March 7, 2005; however, Respondents did not retain the services of **[Attorney]** until June 3, 2005.

ARGUMENT

The Board of Immigration Appeals has the discretion to consider a late-filed brief. Respondents did not intend not to file a brief with the BIA, nor did Respondents intend to file a brief with the BIA late. However, due to financial hardship, Respondents were not able to retain the services of counsel until June 3, 2005. (See Ex. 4, affidavit of Respondent.)

Respondents fled Colombia for fear of persecution. In Colombia, **[Alien]** worked as a teacher, and Respondents enjoyed a high quality of life and were well respected in the community. Since fleeing Colombia for fear of persecution, Respondents have not been able to maintain the quality of life they had in Colombia, and **[Alien]** has only been able to find employment as a shipping and receiving clerk for a closet manufacturer. (Ex. 4.) Further, since arriving in the United States, **[Alien]**'s health has significantly deteriorated. **[Alien]** now suffers from severe high blood pressure, which causes **[him/her]** headaches, lower-back pain, and even blurred vision at times. (See Ex. 4, affidavit of **[Alien]** supported by medical records).

Respondents have diligently sought better employment; however, **[Alien]**'s teaching credentials from Colombia are not recognized in the United States, and **[Alien]** does not have the funds to receive the further education required in order to obtain a teaching certificate in the United States at this time. (Ex. 4.) Due to facts that **[Alien]**'s teaching credentials are not recognized in the United States and that **[his/her]** health is deteriorating, **[Alien]** has not been able to find better employment than that of a shipping and receiving clerk. As a shipping and receiving clerk, **[Alien]** barely makes enough money to support **[his/her]** family. This has resulted in Respondents consistently being late in their payments, an inability to afford necessary medical treatment, and an inability to obtain necessary education for **[Alien]** and their children. (See Ex. 4.) Recently, Respondents were even forced to leave the home because they were unable to make the payments. On June 3, 2005, Respondents received a personal loan that they had desperately been trying to obtain, and immediately retained counsel to assist them. (Ex. 4.)

Respondents are honest, hardworking individuals that have a genuine fear of persecution if forced to return to Colombia. In this regards, Respondents deeply regret having not filed their brief with the BIA within the allotted time, and now requests that the BIA use its discretionary power to consider this late-filed brief and render a decision based upon the merits of their case and not dismiss it based upon a procedural mishap, as Respondents will face certain persecution if forced to return to Colombia.

CONCLUSION

Respondents, through undersigned counsel, respectfully request that the Board of Immigration Appeals grant this Motion to Consider Late-Filed Brief, and render a decision based upon the merits of their case.

Respectfully submitted this _____ day of ______, 20___.

[Attorney]

[ADD CERTIFICATE OF SERVICE]

[Document Nos. 411–15]

MOTION TO RECONSIDER AND MOTION TO REOPEN AND REMAND (NEWLY DISCOVERED EVIDENCE)

Description: This is a formal motion to the Board of Immigration Appeals seeking reopening of a BIA decision based on new evidence and remand to the immigration court for further proceedings. These motions also are made to the BIA if an appeal is pending. If expedited consideration of the motion to reopen is desired, a separate motion to expedite should be filed with the BIA (see Document No. 415).

Advantages: If the client is faced with likely removal and did not have the newly discovered evidence at the original immigration court hearing, then this motion provides the method for introducing that evidence into the record and obtaining a remand to the immigration court to pursue a possible new basis for relief.

Limitations: Any new facts to be presented must generally be newly discovered or unable to have been discovered at the time of the merits hearing. Such facts must be presented in the motion and must be accompanied by sworn affidavits or other evidentiary material. The regulation limits filing certain motions to reopen and motions to reconsider by time and number. The BIA may at any time, however, reopen or reconsider on its own motion.

Notes: While motions to reopen are based on newly discovered evidence, motions to reconsider must specify error in fact or law made by the BIA or immigration judge. Motions to reopen proceedings to submit an application for relief must be accompanied by the application and necessary supporting documents. Furthermore, 8 CFR must be consulted for the specific requirements for motions to reopen or motions to reconsider regarding certain applications for relief, such as relief under INA §212(c) (8 CFR §1003.44).

Citations: 8 CFR §1003.2; also 8 CFR §1003.8 (regarding fees). See also *Board of Immigration Appeals Practice Manual*.

DETAINED

U.S. DEPARTMENT OF JUSTICE
EXECUTIVE OFFICE FOR IMMIGRATION REVIEW
BOARD OF IMMIGRATION APPEALS

IN THE MATTER OF:	)	
	)	
[Alien]	)	
A[Number]	)	IN REMOVAL PROCEEDINGS
	)	
Respondent	)	
	)	

VERIFIED MOTION FOR RECONSIDERATION OF BOARD DENIAL OF MOTION FOR EMERGENCY STAY OF DEPORTATION

COMES NOW, Respondent, **[Alien]**, by and through the undersigned counsel, **[Attorney]**, and requests this Court to reconsider the denial of his previously filed Motion for Emergency Stay of Deportation. Respondent hereby references the original Motion for Emergency Stay, filed December 30, 2004, as if fully set out; and in support of this Motion for Reconsideration, submits the following:

1. **Prior Motion:** For the Board's convenient reference, Respondent attaches as Exhibit 1 the previously filed Motion for Emergency Stay of Deportation with exhibits (hereinafter referred to as "original motion"). After office hours on Friday, January 14, 2005, the Clerk of the Board gave the original motion to a Board member for review. The Clerk later telephoned the undersigned to advise that the original motion had been denied with reasons cited that there was no Affidavit or conviction record. The written denial indicates that "the Board has concluded that there is little likelihood that the motion [to reopen] will be granted."

2. **Imminent Deportation:** Respondent has been detained by U.S. Immigration and Customs Enforcement (ICE) since his arrest on or about December 8, 2004. Respondent has been transferred to the Krome Detention Facility in Miami, Florida. The undersigned has been advised that ICE has obtained Respondent's travel document from the Embassy of Colombia and is preparing for his imminent deportation. For verification, the Krome ICE officer assigned to Respondent's file is Officer **[Name]**, **[phone number]**.

3. **Response by DHS:** The original motion and Special Motion to Seek Section 212(c) Relief were served on Department of Homeland Security (DHS) counsel on December 29, 2004. There has been no response filed by DHS.

RESPONDENT IS ELIGIBLE TO APPLY FOR 212(C) RELIEF ACCORDING TO 8 C.F.R. SEC. 1003.44

4. The emergency stay is being requested so that the Board may review Respondent's "Special Motion to Seek Section 212(c) Relief." The Respondent is eligible to apply for 212(c) relief according to 8 C.F.R. Sec. 1003.44, as follows:

A. Respondent was a lawful permanent resident and is now subject to a final order of deportation or removal.

For the first time, Respondent submits a copy of his Alien Registration Receipt Card (Exhibit 2). On the back, the card indicates that Respondent's temporary resident adjustment date was November 14, 1988, and his adjustment of status was December 1, 1990. The back and the front of the card apply to the same person: the name, **[Alien]**, and A number, **[A Number]**, are indicated on both sides.

As explained in the original motion, this Alien Registration Receipt Card was not available at the time the original motion was filed.

A copy of the May 30, 1996 deportation of the Immigration Judge was attached as Exhibit A to the original motion.

B. Respondent agreed to plead guilty to an offense rendering him removable pursuant to a plea agreement made before April 1, 1997.

As indicated in the attached Order from the Circuit Court, Fairfax County, Virginia (Exhibit 3), **submitted for the first time**, Respondent was found guilty on January 9, 1995, pursuant to a guilty plea to possession of a controlled drug in violation of Virginia Code. He was sentenced to five years, with two years suspended and three years probation from release. Documents submitted as Exhibit 3 include the True Bill of Indictment, November 21, 1994; Arraignment on the Indictment and conviction pursuant to the guilty plea, entered on January 11, 1995; Final Order entered on March 6, 1995.

As cited in the original motion; the Transcript of the Deportation Hearing and the Immigration Judge's Oral Decision indicates that on March 6, 1995, in Fairfax County, Virginia, Respondent was convicted of possession of a controlled drug with intent to distribute in violation of Virginia Code. He admitted and conceded deportability charged on the basis of INA Sec. 241(a)(2)(B)(i), conviction of and for a violation of a controlled substance act; and INA Sec. 241(a)(2)(A)(iii), conviction of and for an aggravated felony. (Exhibit A to original motion.)

In the attached Affidavit of the Respondent (Exhibit 4), **submitted for the first time**, Respondent states that he pled guilty to the offense of possession of a controlled drug with intent to distribute in violation of Virginia Code. He was not tried for the offense.

C. Respondent had seven consecutive years of lawful unrelinquished domicile in the United States prior to the date of the final administrative order of removal.

The final administrative order of removal was March 13, 1997. 8 C.F.R. Sec. 212.3(f), Sec. 1212.3(f), provides that lawful domicile includes time spent as a lawful temporary resident pursuant to section 245A or section 210 of the Act. The attached Alien Registration Receipt Card indicates that Respondent became a lawful temporary resident on November 14, 1988, more than seven years before the deportation order of the Immigration Judge (May 30, 1996) and eight years before the final Board order of March 13, 1997.

Respondent indicates in his attached Affidavit that after entering the United States in 1986, he departed on only two occasions, both short trips: once to Colombia to visit his family after he received his temporary card and once to accompany them to the United States as lawful permanent residents.

D. Respondent is eligible to apply for section 212(c) relief under the standards in effect at the time his plea was made.

Although Respondent was convicted of an aggravated felony, he did not serve more than 5 years for his offense, a requirement under the 212(c) provision which would apply to him. As stated above, the Fairfax County Circuit Court Order indicates that Respondent's sentence was five years with two years suspended and three years probation.

In her attached Affidavit (Exhibit 5), **submitted for the first time, [Daughter]**, the daughter of the Respondent, states that:

> In 1994, my father and brother were arrested in Fairfax County, Virginia and charged with cocaine related offenses. I have personal knowledge that my brother and father both pled guilty to charges against them. Although my family does not have a copy of the conviction records for my father, I know that he was not tried by a jury on his charges. **It is my personal knowledge that after being convicted, my father was incarcerated at the Fairfax County Jail and was released in less than one year.** Attached to this statement are copies of the only documents my mother or I could locate in our personal belongings regarding my father's charges. Although difficult to read, these are the best copies available to us at this time. (Emphasis added.)

The documents attached to the Affidavit indicate the following:

- "RECOGNIZANCE," dated October 24, 1994 indicating that **[Alien]** was charged with "Poss Cont Drug w/Int Dist" and was posting a $10,000.00 bond.

- Two Department of Corrections Legal Updates indicating a sentence start date of "17 DEC 1994" and a "TOTAL SENTENCE: 003 YEARS." The Discretionary Parole Eligibility Date and Anticipated Mandatory Parole Release Date appear to change over time.

Respondent also states in his Affidavit (Exhibit 4) that he served less than one year for the offense.

As further evidence that he served less than five years, he personally appeared at his deportation hearing on May 30, 1996, after having been convicted on March 6, 1995.

5. **Supporting Documents Previously Unavailable:** According to ICE policy, deportation officers may not disclose the date of deportation to Respondent or counsel. When the undersigned filed the original motion on behalf of the Respondent, she knew only that he was detained by ICE with a final order of deportation and that deportation was imminent. She proceeded to protect Respondent's interests as quickly as possible. She filed the original motion with documentation available at the time; and has since been able to obtain a copy of Respondent's Alien Registration Receipt Card (indicating his temporary residence adjustment date), his order of conviction (indication his plea of guilt and sentence) and the two affidavits.

6. **Verified Motion:** This Motion is being submitted as a verified motion so that any statements made by the undersigned may be considered as a sworn statement.

WHEREFORE, the Respondent, **[Alien]**, respectfully requests this Board to reconsider the denial of his Motion for Emergency Stay of Deportation and halt his deportation pending review of the Motion to Reopen. Newly obtained and previously unavailable documentation is attached hereto which clearly demonstrates that Respondent is eligible to apply for Section 212(c) relief under 8 C.F.R. Sec. 1003.44. DHS has not responded in any way to the motion for emergency stay or the motion to reopen. It would be an egregious and irrevocable injustice to the Respondent to allow his deportation, with no hope of ever returning to the United States as a lawful permanent resident, without allowing him to pursue the lawful relief available to him.

Respectfully submitted, this ____ day of _________, 20____.

[Attorney]

[ADD CERTIFICATE OF SERVICE]

VERIFICATION

[Attorney], of **[Firm]**, Counsel of Record in this matter, being first duly sworn, deposes and says that she has read the foregoing and knows the content thereof and that the same are true of her own knowledge except as to those matters and things stated upon information and belief and as to those matters, she believes them to be true.

This the ________ day of ____________, 20__.

[Attorney]

Sworn to and subscribed before me

this the ____ day of _________, 20__.

____

Notary Public

My Commission expires:

U.S. DEPARTMENT OF JUSTICE
EXECUTIVE OFFICE FOR IMMIGRATION REVIEW
BOARD OF IMMIGRATION APPEALS
FALLS CHURCH, VA

IN THE MATTER OF:	)	
	)	
[Alien]	)	
A[Number]	)	IN REMOVAL PROCEEDINGS
	)	
Respondent	)	
______________________________	)	

MOTION TO REOPEN

MOTION TO REOPEN PROCEEDINGS

[Alien], through undersigned counsel, hereby moves the Board of Immigration Appeals ("BIA") to reopen his removal proceedings and remand the proceedings back to the Immigration Court for a new hearing. This Motion to Reopen states new facts that will be proven at a hearing if this case is reopened and supported by material evidence that was not available and could not have been discovered or presented at the former hearing. See 8 C.F.R. § 1003.2 (2003).

STATEMENT OF FACTS

[Alien], a devote Shi'ite Muslim, is a national and citizen of Bangladesh. On August 23, 2001, **[Alien]** was admitted to the United States at Atlanta, Georgia, as a nonimmigrant B-2 visitor with authorization to remain in the United States for a temporary period of time, not to exceed six months. **[Alien]** remained in the United States beyond six months without authorization.

In compliance with 67 Fed. Reg. 77136 (2002), **[Alien]** "appear[ed] before, register[ed] with, and provide[d] requested information to the Immigration and Naturalization Service on or before February 21, 2003." **[Alien]**'s compliance with this Federal Regulation alerted the Government to **[Alien]**'s unlawful status, and on March 31, 2003, **[Alien]** was arrested for illegally being present in the United States. See Exhibit 1 (Notice of Rights and Request for Disposition). On April 1, 2003, the Department of Justice initiated removal proceedings by issuing **[Alien]** a Notice to Appear, Form I-862, alleging that **[Alien]** was in violation of section 237(a)(1)(B) of the Immigration and Nationality Act. See Exhibit 2 (Notice to Appear).

After removal proceedings were initiated, **[Alien]** sought the assistance of counsel to inform him of his rights and options. Upon consultation with counsel, **[Alien]** completed and filed an asylum application on September 23, 2003. See Exhibit 3. **[Alien]**'s application was not frivolous; however, on August 2, 2004, **[Alien]** withdrew his application for asylum. See Exhibit 4 (copy of Immigration Judge's order). **[Alien]** withdrew his application for asylum because his wife had recently received an approved Labor Certification Application and her employer had filed a Petition for Alien Worker, Form I-140, on her behalf. **[Alien]** believed that the probability of his ability to legally immigrate to the United States was greater through the Petition for Alien Worker, Form I-140, which had been filed on his wife's behalf, than through his asylum application.

At his hearing on August 2, 2004, **[Alien]** requested a continuance, based upon the fact that his wife had recently received an approved Labor Certification Application and that his wife's employer had filed a Petition for Alien Worker, Form I-140, on her behalf. The Immigration Judge denied **[Alien]**'s motion for continuance, and granted **[Alien]** voluntary departure. See Exhibit 4. On September 1, 2004, **[Alien]** timely field an appeal with the Board of Immigration Appeals ("BIA") seeking review of the Immigration Judge's denial of his motion for continuance. See Exhibit 5 (copy of **[Alien]**'s appeal to the BIA).

On September 23, 2004, the Petition for Alien Worker, Form I-140, which had been filed on **[Alien]**'s wife's behalf, was approved. See Exhibit 6 (I-140 approval notice). On May 10, 2005, **[Alien]**'s wife filed for Adjustment of Status, based on the approved Form I-140 that had been filed on her behalf, with a priority date of April 25, 2001, making her eligible to adjust her status under I.N.A. § 245(i), 8 U.S.C. § 1255(i). See Exhibit 7 (copy of Application to Register Permanent Residence or Adjust Status). This Motion to Reopen follows.

ARGUMENT

The BIA may grant a motion to reopen when the motion offers new material facts that were not available at trial and "could not have been discovered or presented at the former hearing." 8 C.F.R. § 1003.2(c)(1). The BIA has stated:

> [W]here an alien is seeking previously unavailable relief and has not had an opportunity to present h[is] application before the Immigration Judge, the Board will look to whether the alien has proffered sufficient evidence to indicate that there is a reasonable likelihood of success on the merits so as to make it worthwhile to develop the issues further at a full evidentiary hearing. *In Re M-S-*, 22 I. & N. Dec. 349 (BIA 1998); *See also Matter of L-O-G-*, 21 I. & N. Dec. 413 (BIA 1996).

[Alien] has proffered sufficient evidence to indicate that there is a reasonable likelihood of success on the merits so as to make it worthwhile to develop the issue further at a full evidentiary hearing. **[Alien]**'s wife is the beneficiary of an approved Petition for Alien Worker, Form I-140, see Exhibit 6, and has filed for Adjustment of Status. See Exhibit 7. As a direct beneficiary of an approved Petition for Alien Worker, Form I-140, that was filed before April 31, 2001, **[Alien]** is now eligible to adjust his status to that of a permanent resident of the United States pursuant to I.N.A § 245(i), 8 U.S.C. § 1255(i), too. **[Alien]**'s wife did not become the beneficiary of an approved I-140 until September 23, 2004; therefore, **[Alien]** did not have the opportunity to discover such evidence and present it to the court at his hearing on August 2, 2004. **[Alien]** can now prove these facts at a full evidentiary hearing, as demonstrated by the attached exhibits.

In *In Re Mario Eduardo Velarde Pacheco*, 23 I. & N. Dec. 253 (BIA 2002), the BIA stated:

> [A] motion to reopen may be granted, in the exercise of discretion, to provide an alien with an opportunity to pursue the application for adjustment of status where the following factors are present: (1) the motion is timely filed; (2) the motion is not numerically barred by the regulations; (3) the motion is not barred by *Matter of Shaar*, 21 I. & N. Dec. 541 (BIA 1996), or any other procedural grounds; (4) the motion presents a clear and convincing evidence indicating a strong likelihood that the respondent's marriage is bona fide; and (5) the Service either does not oppose the motion or bases its opposition solely on *Matter of Arthur* 20 I. & N. Dec. 475 (BIA 1992).

In the instant case, the Motion to Reopen has been timely filed. **[Alien]** filed an appeal with the BIA on September 1, 2004. See Exhibit 5. The BIA has yet to issue an order in this matter; therefore, 90 days from the date of entry of a final administrative order of removal has not passed, as a final administrative order has yet to be entered by the BIA, making this Motion to Reopen timely. See 8 C.F.R. §1003.2(c)(2).

[Alien]'s Motion to Reopen is not numerically barred. This is Respondent's first Motion to Reopen; therefore, this Motion to Reopen complies with the numerical limitations imposed by 8 C.F.R. § 1003.2(c)(2) on motions to reopen.

In *Matter of Shaar*, the BIA held that neither the filing of a motion to reopen to apply for suspension of deportation during the pendency of a period of voluntary departure, nor the Immigration Judge's failure to adjudicate the motion prior to the expiration of voluntary departure constitutes an "exceptional circumstance" that would prevent the harsh consequences of denial of relief. 21 I. & N. 541 (BIA 1996). **[Alien]** is not filing this Motion to Reopen in order to apply for suspension of deportation; therefore, **[Alien]**'s Motion to Reopen is not barred by *Matter of Shaar*, nor is **[Alien]**'s motion barred by any other procedural grounds.

[Alien] is eligible to adjust his status. In accordance with 8 C.F.R. § 1003.2(c)(1), **[Alien]** has submitted his Application to Register Permanent Residence or Adjust Status, Form I-485, with all necessary documentation concurrently with this Motion to Reopen. <u>See</u> <u>Exhibit 8</u> (copy of **[Alien]**'s adjustment of status application). **[Alien]** now asks that the Board of Immigration Appeals to grant his Motion to Reopen, thus enabling him to lawfully remain in the United States with his family.

CONCLUSION

[Alien]'s wife is the beneficiary of a Petition for Alien Worker, Form I-140, which has now made **[Alien]** eligible to file for adjustment of his status. **[Alien]** respectfully requests that the Board of Immigration Appeals reopen his removal proceedings and remand his case back to the Immigration Judge so that he may seek adjustment of his status.

Respectfully submitted this _____ day of _______, 20___.

[Attorney]

[ADD CERTIFICATION OF SERVICE]

U.S. DEPARTMENT OF JUSTICE
EXECUTIVE OFFICE FOR IMMIGRATION REVIEW
BOARD OF IMMIGRATION APPEALS
FALLS CHURCH, VIRGINIA

IN THE MATTER OF:	)	
	)	
[Alien]	)	
A[Number]	)	IN REMOVAL PROCEEDINGS
	)	
Respondent	)	
______________________________	)	

RESPONDENT'S MOTION TO REOPEN AND REMAND

[Alien], through undersigned counsel, hereby moves the Board of Immigration Appeals ("BIA") to reopen **[his/her]** deportation case and remand it to the Immigration Judge for a new hearing on **[his/her]** application for adjustment of status. This motion to reopen states new facts that will be proven at a hearing if this case is reopened, and is supported by affidavits and material evidence that was not available and could not have been discovered or presented at the former hearing. *See* 8 C.F.R. § 1003.2 (2003).

[Alien] is a native and citizen of Romania. **[Alien]** first came to the United States on September 3, 2000, as a visitor and filed an I-589 Request for Asylum application on September 20, 2000. On February 1, 2001, the Immigration Judge denied Respondent's request for asylum, and Respondent submitted **[his/her]** Notice of Appeal to the BIA on February 9, 2001. Respondent's appeal is still pending with the BIA.

> "Where an alien is seeking previously unavailable relief and has not had an opportunity to present her application before the Immigration Judge, the Board will look to whether the alien has proffered sufficient evidence to indicate that there is a reasonable likelihood of success on the merits so as to make it worthwhile to develop the issues further at a full evidentiary hearing." *In Re M-S-*, 22 I. & N. Dec. 349 (BIA 1998); *See also Matter of L-O-G-*, 21 I. & N. Dec. 413 (BIA 1996).

[Alien] is currently eligible for adjustment of status. On November 14, 2001, **[Alien]** married **[Spouse]**, a United States citizen. **[Spouse]** filed a Petition for Alien Relative, Form I-130, on September 15, 2002, on behalf of Respondent. On April 19, 2003, the **[Spouse]**'s I-130 petition was approved, thus conferring **[Alien]** an immediate relative visa as the spouse of a United States Citizen under section 201(b)(2)(A)(i) of the Immigration and Nationality Act (INA).

We have enclosed **[Alien's]** Application for Adjustment of Status, Form I-485, with supporting documents and proof of payment of the filing fee. **[Alien]** has roots in the United States as **[he/she]** has married a U.S. citizen, is of high moral character, and has never been convicted of a crime. **[Alien]** is clearly admissible as a lawful permanent resident.

At the time of **[his/her]** hearing **[Alien]** did not have this relief available; therefore, **[Alien]** did not have an opportunity to present **[his/her]** application to the Immigration Judge at that time. **[Alien]** clearly is eligible for adjustment of status to a lawful permanent resident.

For the reasons stated above, **[Alien]** respectfully requests that **[his/her]** removal proceedings be reopened and remanded to the Immigration Judge so that **[Alien]** may be permitted to adjust **[his/her]** status to that of a lawful permanent resident.

Respectfully submitted this _____ day of __________, 20___.

[Attorney]

[ADD CERTIFICATE OF SERVICE]

U.S. DEPARTMENT OF JUSTICE
EXECUTIVE OFFICE FOR IMMIGRATION REVIEW
BOARD OF IMMIGRATION APPEALS
FALLS CHURCH, VIRGINIA

IN THE MATTER OF:)
)
[Alien])
A[Number]) IN REMOVAL PROCEEDINGS
)
Respondent)
)

MOTION TO REOPEN AND REMAND AND REQUEST FOR EXPEDITED CONSIDERATION

COMES NOW, Respondent, by and through the undersigned counsel, and moves this Court to reopen the above-captioned deportation matter and remand it to the Immigration Judge for a new hearing on his application for adjustment of status. This motion to reopen states new facts that will be proven at a hearing if this case is reopened, and is supported by material evidence that was not available and could not have been presented at the former hearing. *See* 8 C.F.R. §§ 1003.2(c) and 1003.23(b)(3). Furthermore, pursuant to order of this Board (explained below), *[Alien] has voluntary departure until February 26, 2003. The Immigration and Naturalization Service [now Immigration and Customs Enforcement] has not agreed to any extension. As such, [Alien] is requesting expedited review of this Motion.*

1. **[Alien]** is a native and citizen of Pakistan. Upon information and belief (a copy of the record is not available at this time),[1] **[Alien]** applied for asylum soon after entering the United States in 1994. The application ultimately was denied by the Immigration Court in New York and **[Alien]** appealed that decision to the Board of Immigration Appeals. The Immigration Court apparently did allow some period of time for voluntary departure.

2. By summary decision, this Board affirmed the Immigration Judge's decision by order of January 27, 2003. In accordance with the decision in *Matter of Chouliaris*, 16 I. & N. Dec. 168 (BIA 1977), the Board further allowed the Respondent 30 days voluntary departure.

3. Respondent married a U.S. citizen, **[Spouse]**, on December 4, 1998, and the couple has lived together in Raleigh, North Carolina, since that date. The marriage took place after the order of the Immigration Court denying the asylum application.

[1] The undersigned counsel was retained to represent **[Alien]** and his U.S. citizen wife approximately 2 weeks ago, after they received the decision of the Board. **[Previous Counsel]**, the attorney who previously represented **[Alien]** before the Immigration Court in New York and before this Board, reportedly moved from New York to California. Some time after the move, **[Previous Counsel]** passed away. **[Previous Counsel's]** New York employer does not have a copy of **[Alien]**'s file regarding the deportation proceedings and the undersigned counsel has not yet been able to locate old files of **[Previous Counsel]**. **[Alien]** does not have a copy of the documents related to the prior proceedings.

4. **[Spouse]** filed an I-130 Petition which was received by the Texas Service Center on February 9, 1999. The couple was interviewed by the Charlotte Sub-office on January 21, 2001, and the decision is still pending there. Upon information and belief, within the past few weeks, the Charlotte adjudications officer assigned to the matter has been called to active duty as a member of the Reserves.[2]

5. Enclosed is **[Alien]**'s I-485, application for adjustment of status, with supporting documents.

6. At the time of his deportation hearing, **[Alien]** did not have the relief of adjustment of status available to him, and therefore did not have an opportunity to present his application to the Immigration Judge. Once the I-130 is approved, he clearly is eligible for adjustment of status to a lawful permanent resident. Although **[Alien]** entered the U.S. without inspection, he is eligible to apply for adjustment of status under INA § 245(i). His adjustment would be "grandfathered" due to the I-130 having been filed in 1999.

7. This Motion is being made in accordance with *In re Velarde-Pacheco*, 23 I. & N. Dec. 253 (BIA 2002), allowing a properly filed motion to reopen for adjustment of status based on a marriage entered into after the commencement of proceedings notwithstanding the pendency of a visa petition filed on the alien's behalf. As required pursuant to *Velarde-Pacheco*, (1) this motion is timely filed in that it is within 90 days of the date of the Board order; (2) the motion is not barred numerically by regulations in that no prior motion has been filed; (3) the motion is not barred by *Matter of Shaar*, 21 I. & N. Dec. 541 (BIA 1996), or on any other procedural grounds: Respondent's voluntary departure period has not expired; and (4) clear and convincing evidence is presented herein indicating that the marriage is bona fide.

8. Attached hereto are numerous exhibits as evidence that the marriage of **[Alien and Spouse]** is *bona fide*. In accordance with *Velarde-Pacheco* and *In re M-S-*, Int. Dec. 3369 (BIA 1998), this is sufficient evidence to indicate that there is a reasonable likelihood of success on the merits to make it worthwhile to develop the issues further at a full evidentiary hearing.

WHEREFORE, Respondent respectfully requests that his deportation proceedings be reopened and remanded to the Immigration Judge for consideration of his adjustment of status application.

Respectfully submitted, this ____ day of ___________, 20__.

[Attorney]

[ADD CERTIFICATE OF SERVICE]

[2] A request to extend the Board's grant of 30 days' voluntary departure has been requested of the Charlotte INS office. The undersigned has been advised that the office is having great difficulty locating **[Alien]**'s immigration file due to this officer being away. She has been told that the officer has "over 400 files" assigned to him and they do not know where **[Alien]**'s file is located. Charlotte INS does not want to consider extension of voluntary departure without review of the file.

NON-DETAINED

U.S. DEPARTMENT OF JUSTICE
EXECUTIVE OFFICE FOR IMMIGRATION REVIEW
BOARD OF IMMIGRATION APPEALS

IN THE MATTER OF:)
)
[Alien])
A[Number]) IN REMOVAL PROCEEDINGS
)
Respondent)
)

RESPONDENT'S MOTION TO EXPEDITE PREVIOUSLY FILED MOTION TO REOPEN

COMES NOW, Respondent, by and through the undersigned counsel, and renews his request for expedited review of his "Motion to Reopen," filed February 21, 2003, and his "Supplement to Motion to Reopen and Request for Expedited Review," filed on or about March 6, 2003. As more fully explained herein, ***Respondent's extended voluntary departure expires April 25, 2003.***

1. On February 21, 2003, **[Alien]** filed a timely Motion to Reopen in accordance with the Board's ruling in *Matter of Velarde*, 23 I. & N. Dec. 253 (BIA 2002). The motion was filed within 90 days of the Board's summary affirmance of the decision of the Immigration Judge and within a period of voluntary departure; the motion included evidence required by *Velarde*. At that time, an I-130 filed by Respondent's U.S. citizen wife was still pending.

2. On March 6, 2003, Respondent filed a Supplement to the Motion to Reopen, explaining that, after four years of waiting, the I-130 was approved by INS on February 26, 2003. (See Exhibit A attached hereto.)

3. In its summary affirmance, the Board had allowed **[Alien]** 30 days voluntary departure, which expired February 26, 2003. On February 25, 2003, INS approved **[Alien]**'s request for extension of voluntary departure to April 25, 2003. (See Exhibit B attached hereto.)

4. In accordance with *Matter of Arthur*, 20 I. & N. Dec. 475 (BIA 1992), **[Alien]** now has an approved I-130 which was not available at the time of his deportation hearing. He has provided the Board with an I-485 and extensive documentation in support of the bona fide nature of his marriage (submitted with the original Motion to Reopen). As discussed in the original motion, **[Alien]** is eligible to apply for adjustment of status under INA § 245(i) and an immigrant visa now would be immediately available to him. Furthermore, as his voluntary departure has been extended, this motion is not barred by *Matter of Shaar*, 21 I. & N. Dec. 541 (BIA 1996). These motions have been filed within 90 days of the Board's final decision.

5. If this matter is not reopened prior to the expiration of Respondent's voluntary departure, he will be forced to depart the U.S. and apply for an immigrant visa through the National Visa Center and U.S. Consulate in Pakistan. "Consular" processing in **[Alien]**'s home country of Pakistan would cause considerable and avoidable expense to both the Respondent and his wife and to the U.S. Government. Continuous delays would most certainly occur, especially in light of current volatile political conditions in that area of the world. Travel may indeed be dangerous to the Respondent.

WHEREFORE, Respondent respectfully requests that consideration of his Motion to Reopen removal proceedings be expedited.

Respectfully submitted, this ____ day of ___________, 20____.

[Attorney]

[ADD CERTIFICATE OF SERVICE]

[Document No. 416]

MOTION FOR STAY OF REMOVAL BEFORE BIA PENDING DECISION ON MOTION TO REOPEN

Description:

The motion seeks to have the BIA stay a client's removal pending the BIA decision on a previously filed motion to reopen. The motion for stay can be filed separately from the motion to reopen in those circumstances where removal has become imminent, but was not such when the initial motion was filed.

Advantages:

The motion and request for stay are essential in stopping DHS from removing a client from the United States during the pendency of the motion at the BIA. When granted, this stay will be in place during the time the immigration judge is deliberating the motion.

Limitations:

The BIA is usually not in any rush to rule on a motion for stay, so if the practitioner has an emergent need for a stay, it would be wise to contact the Clerk of the BIA to indicate such and ask for an emergency stay. These emergency stays are not typically treated as an emergency, so be sure to be diligent in following up with the Clerk.

Notes:

This is a tool practitioners will frequently use. According to ICE, there are more than 300,000 individuals with outstanding removal orders, many of whom have actual relief from removal available to them. If removal is imminent, be insistent on obtaining the actual grant of the stay from the BIA.

Citations:

BIA Practice Manual, Section 5.2.

U.S. DEPARTMENT OF JUSTICE
EXECUTIVE OFFICE FOR IMMIGRATION REVIEW
BOARD OF IMMIGRATION APPEALS
FALLS CHURCH, VIRGINIA

IN THE MATTER OF:	)	
	)	
[Alien]	)	IN REMOVAL PROCEEDINGS
A[Number]	)	
	)	
Respondant	)	
	)	

RESPONDENT'S MOTION TO STAY REMOVAL PENDING DECISION ON MOTION TO REOPEN

[Alien], through undersigned counsel, hereby moves the Board of Immigration Appeals ("BIA") to stay **[his/her]** removal proceedings while **[his/her]** Motion to Reopen is pending before this Board. The Motion to Reopen was filed with the BIA on April 29, 2004, and is still pending. (Ex. 1.) The Respondent <u>is being detained</u> and was transferred from Colquitt County Jail to Tensas Parish Prison on <u>June 3, 2004</u>. (Ex. 2.) **[His/her]** removal is imminent. This court has jurisdiction to grant this stay pursuant to 8 C.F.R. §1003.2(f). The Respondent meets the requirements of applicable law by showing that 1) **[he/she]** is likely to succeed on the merits of **[his/her]** case; 2) **[he/she]** would suffer irreparable harm if the stay is not granted; 3) the potential harm to **[Alien]** in being removed while **[his/her]** motion is pending outweighs the harm to the United States government in allowing **[him/her]** to stay in the United States during this time; and 4) granting the stay would serve the public interest.

I. FACTUAL AND PROCEDURAL HISTORY

[Alien] is a native of Thailand, and entered the United States as a visitor on or about May 25, 1986. **[Alien]** has remained in the Unites States since that time.

By 1992, **[Alien]** was living in California, and working at various jobs for temporary amounts of time. Sometime in 1992 or 1993, during a period of unemployment, **[Alien]** offered to drive some acquaintances to New Mexico so that they could apply for jobs there. While returning from New Mexico to California, they encountered a road block. Neither **[Alien]**, nor the passengers, could speak English well enough to explain the purpose of their travel to the officer.

When the officer asked about **[his/her]** immigration status, **[Alien]** was truthful and told the officer that **[he/she]** did not have a green card. **[Alien]** showed the officer **[his/her]** valid California driver's license and told the officer where **[he/she]** was living in California, which was the same address as indicated on **[his/her]** driver's license. The officer issued **[Alien]** some papers that **[he/she]** could not understand, because **[Alien]** cannot read English. When **[Alien]** tried to explain to the officer that **[he/she]** did not understand the papers, the officer told **[Alien]** to sign the papers and that **[he/she]** would receive further information in the mail. The officer did not give **[Alien]** any papers in return and, although **[he/she]** waited and anticipated their arrival, **[Alien]** received nothing in the mail regarding Immigration for as long as **[he/she]** remained at that address. Each time **[he/she]** moved, **[Alien]** updated **[his/her]** address with the California registry of motor vehicles.

On February 14, 2003, **[Alien]** married **[Spouse]**, a native of Thailand and citizen of the United States, in Marietta, Georgia. (Ex. 3.) After their marriage, **[Spouse]** filed applications with the Immigration Service so that **[Alien]** could receive **[his/her]** permanent residence. On February 9, 2004, U.S. Citizenship and Immigration Services ("USCIS") denied **[Spouse]**'s I-130 petition on behalf of **[Alien]**. (Ex. 4.) In its decision, USCIS stated that **[Alien]** had been ordered deported in an *in abesentia* hearing on December 7, 1993.

On February 10, 2004, before USCIS mailed its denial of **[Alien]**'s I-130 petition, it issued an appointment notice to **[Alien]**, indicating that **[he/she]** was to appear at their office for "Green Card Processing." (Ex. 5.) When **[Alien]** arrived for **[his/her]** processing appointment, **[he/she]** was arrested. Only after **[his/her]** arrest did **[Alien and Spouse]** learn that their Form I-130 had been denied and that **[Alien]** had been removed *in absentia* in 1993.

[Alien] did not receive notice of **[his/her]** proceedings, nor of **[his/her]** removal order. **[Alien]**'s spouse filed a second Petition for Alien Relative, Form I-130, with USCIS on March 12, 2004. (Ex. 6.) **[Alien]** then filed a Motion to Reopen with the Immigration Court in El Paso on March 16, 2004. On March 31, 2004, in a one-page decision, **[his/her]** Motion was denied. (Ex. 7.) **[Alien]** filed a timely Appeal to the Board of Immigration Appeals on April 29, 2004. (Ex. 1.)

[Alien] is married to a United States citizen who has severe health problems, and **[he/she]** is eligible to have **[his/her]** application for adjustment of status adjudicated.

II. RESPONDENT IS ELIGIBLE FOR A STAY OF REMOVAL

The Board of Immigration Appeals may grant a Motion to Stay Removal when Respondent can show that **[he/she]** is likely to succeed on the merits of the case, **[he/she]** would suffer irreparable harm if the stay were not granted, that the potential harm to **[him/her]** if the stay is not granted exceeds the potential harm to the government if the stay is granted, and that the stay would serve the public interest. **[Alien]** can meet their burden of proof in this regard.

A. Respondent Is Likely to Succeed on the Merits of [His/Her] Motion

Respondent is likely to succeed on **[his/her]** motion to reopen because **[he/she]** is eligible to adjust status to permanent residence. At the time of **[his/her]** removal *in absentia*, **[Alien]** was not eligible for adjustment of status. Now that **[his/her]** wife is a United States citizen and has filed an I-130, Petition for Alien Relative, on **[his/her]** behalf, **[Alien]** is eligible to adjust status to that of a permanent resident.

B. [Alien] Will Lose [His/Her] Right to Have [His/Her] Motion Heard on Its Merits if this Stay Is Not Granted.

If **[Alien]** is not given a stay while **[his/her]** motion is pending, **[he/she]** will be immediately removed from the United States to Thailand. ICE has recently moved **[Alien]** from Colquitt County Detention Center to Tensas Parish Prison. Counsel for **[Alien]** has hand delivered a request to the Acting District Director, asking him to exercise **[his/her]** discretion and refrain from removing **[Alien]** while the Motion to Reopen is pending. The request is currently under consideration.

If **[Alien]** is removed from the United States, **[his/her]** Motion to Reopen will be deemed abandoned. **[Alien]** will lose **[his/her]** right to have **[his/her]** Motion considered on its merits by the BIA. The consequences of not staying **[his/her]** removal while **[his/her]** Motion to Reopen is pending would be the same as denying the Motion without considering the merits at all.

More significantly, **[Alien]**'s removal will prevent **[him/her]** from returning to **[his/her]** family in the United States for ten years. Because **[Alien]** has been ordered removed, **[he/she]** will be subject to a ten-year bar before **[he/she]** can apply for admission to the United States. **[Alien]**'s spouse has severe kidney failure and requires a kidney transplant within the next year; however the physician has yet to find a donor that is the right match for **[Spouse]**. **[Spouse's]** health is failing and **[he/she]** depends upon **[Alien]** to assist with even the most basic of daily tasks. Although **[Alien]** may apply for a waiver of inadmissibility, there is no guarantee that it will be granted, and it will take time which will had adverse affects on **[Alien's]** family.

[Alien] has roots in the United States as **[he/she]** has lived and worker here for eighteen (18) years. **[Alien]** has grown children from **[his/her]** first marriage, and step-children from **[his/her]** marriage to **[Spouse]**.

C. The United States Government Would Not Be Harmed by the Stay

Granting the stay of removal while **[Alien]**'s Motion is pending would not cause harm to the government. **[Alien]** has never been arrested nor committed any crimes and is a person of good moral character. **[Alien]** is an asset to the United States. **[Alien]** has worked full-time for the same employer, **[Business]**, for almost six years. **[Alien]** and **[his/her]** spouse are both working hard to save money for a much-needed kidney transplant. **[Alien]** owns an automobile and has a bank account in the United States. **[Alien]** pays income tax and has invested in life insurance policies for both **[Alien and Spouse]**.

D. Granting the Stay Would Serve the Public Interest

Granting a stay in this case would be in everyone's best interest, including the public. It would allow **[Alien's]** case to be heard on the merits, rather than be dismissed as involuntarily abandoned because the stay was not granted, which preserves the integrity of our justice system.

III. CONCLUSION

Because **[Alien]**'s Motion to Reopen is likely to be granted, **[he/she]** would suffer irreparable damage if the stay is denied, and the United States government will not suffer harm if **[Alien]** remains in the United States while the Motion to Reopen is pending, **[Alien]** respectfully requests that **[his/her]** Motion for Stay of Removal be granted.

Respectfully submitted this _____ day of _____________, 20__.

[Attorney]

[ADD CERTIFICATE OF SERVICE]

[Document Nos. 417–18]

MOTION TO REOPEN AND REMAND (INEFFECTIVE ASSISTANCE OF COUNSEL)

Description: This is a formal motion to the Board of Immigration Appeals seeking remand of a case in immigration court for reasons relating to ineffective assistance of counsel.

Advantages: If a client is faced with likely removal and did not have the opportunity to present all of the evidence or did not have all possible claims pursued on his or her behalf at the immigration judge level, the motion to reopen and motion for remand may be a client's only option for remaining in the United States.

Limitations: Obviously, claims of ineffective assistance of counsel must be pursued with great care and must strictly comply with the requirements of the BIA's decision in *Matter of Lozada*, 19 I&N Dec. 637 (BIA 1998).

Notes: Claims of ineffective assistance of counsel generally require the filing of a bar complaint against the prior counsel, as well as providing prior counsel the opportunity to submit a written statement rebutting the claims of ineffective assistance. Typically, gross negligence would be a standard for setting aside a final decision of the BIA.

Citations: 8 CFR §§1003.2(c)(2) and (4).

U.S. DEPARTMENT OF JUSTICE
EXECUTIVE OFFICE FOR IMMIGRATION REVIEW
BOARD OF IMMIGRATION APPEALS

IN THE MATTER OF:)
)
[Alien])
A[Number]) IN REMOVAL PROCEEDINGS
)
Respondent)
)

MOTION TO REOPEN

[Alien], through undersigned counsel, and pursuant to 8 C.F.R. § 1003.2(c)(2) and (4), hereby moves the Board of Immigration Appeals ("BIA") to reopen his removal proceedings and remand this case to the Immigration Judge in Memphis, Tennessee. On March 9, 2000, the BIA denied and dismissed **[Alien]**'s appeal of the decision of the Immigration Judge denying his asylum claim. **[Alien]**'s motion is based on his claim of ineffective assistance of previous counsel of record, **[Attorney]**, while representing **[Alien]** before the BIA. As clearly established below, **[Alien]** has met all the requirements of *Matter of Lozada*, 19 I&N Dec. 637 (BIA 1998).

I. FACTUAL BACKGROUND

[Alien] is a native and citizen of Ukraine. He comes from a family of anti-communist convictions and political activism. **[Alien]**'s college education in the late 1970s was threatened by his reluctance to participate in the activities commemorating the Great October Socialistic Revolution in 1977. He was immediately threatened with expulsion from the college.

[Alien] began to be perceived as against the communist regime in Ukraine. During his military service in the USSR Army, **[Alien]** served one week in the military prison for standing up against the regime's abuses and corporal punishment on one of his fellow soldiers. **[Alien]** increased his involvement in the struggle for human rights and democracy in Ukraine. As a result of his activities, he was threatened by the KGB on numerous occasions. He was detained for writing and spreading anti-communist propaganda, and for concealing people pursued by the KGB. In 1985, **[Alien]** was held under house arrest for a period of three months. His mail was monitored, his telephone disconnected. **[Alien]**'s house was burglarized and ransacked on several occasions by the KGB. They constantly looked for hidden anti-communist materials.

While never a formal member, **[Alien]** began supporting the Ukrainian Social Group, later known as the Ukrainian Republican Party. In 1988, **[Alien]** and members of the group initiated a hunger strike to protest the arrest of fellow members. In July of that year, **[Alien]** was detained, interrogated, and severely beaten due to his support of the Ukrainian Social Group. His pro-democracy activities continued. In 1989–1990, **[Alien]** was again arrested and detained, this time for 72 hours; he was, again, severely beaten. **[Alien]** was always very vocal about his support for the independence of Ukraine.

In the years that followed, and prior to his departure for the United States in 1995, **[Alien]** endured the threats and abuse of high ranking communist leaders who had now achieved positions of power in the newly created "democratic" Ukrainian government. The leadership of former communist leaders, combined with the lawlessness and corruption infesting Ukraine, created a society where citizens like **[Alien]**, concerned and determined to obtain a true democracy, are persecuted and tortured. **[Alien]** was again detained and beaten to unconsciousness on March 8, 1993—this because he had received evidence linking a local political leader to the underground criminal world. **[Alien]** began to realize that his dreams for a safe and democratic life in Ukraine would never be realized. His political activities, and the ensuing conflicts with the KGB and with high ranking communist officials, had made **[Alien]** an enemy of a corrupt government and of their underground criminal cohorts.

[Alien] had no choice but to flee Ukraine. He arrived in the United States in March of 1995. Afraid of returning to Ukraine, he applied for asylum and withholding of deportation. On February 26, 1997, the Immigration Judge denied his applications for asylum and withholding of removal and granted him the privilege of 30-days voluntary departure. On March 9, 2000, the BIA upheld the decision of the Immigration Judge as to the relief of asylum and withholding of deportation, as well as the grant of voluntary departure.

II. [ALIEN] WAS PRIMA FACIE ELIGIBLE TO APPLY FOR RELIEF UNDER THE CAT

The BIA did not consider **[Alien]** for relief under the Convention against Torture (CAT). To be granted "withholding of removal" under CAT, the applicant must establish that it is more likely than not that the applicant would be tortured and that the applicant is not subject to any mandatory bars to withholding contained in section 241(b)(3)(B) of the Immigration and Nationality Act (INA) (based on persecution of others, conviction for a particularly serious crime, etc.). An individual who is barred from withholding of removal under section 241(b)(3)(B) of the INA, may apply for "deferral of removal" under CAT. To be granted "deferral of removal" under CAT, an individual must establish the likely of torture in the country to which he or she would be removed. "Deferral of removal" is a more limited form of relief than "withholding of removal" in that it may be terminated more easily. The regulations establish that for aliens who were ordered removed, or whose removal orders became final, before March 22, 1999, a motion to reopen proceedings to seek protection under CAT (8 C.F.R. § 208.16(c) (1999)) must have been filed within June 21, 1999—with evidence establishing a prima facie case that the applicant's removal must be withheld or deferred under CAT. Article 3 of CAT prohibits the return by the United States of individuals facing torture in their country of origin. The implementing legislation and regulations have made it clear that in any case where the removal of an individual has been ordered before March 22, 1999, a prima facie claim made pursuant to Article 3 must be heard and decided by the Immigration Courts. A motion to reopen and remand filed prior to June 21, 1999, was the only vehicle to accomplish such purpose.

Prior to and on June 21, 1999, the BIA had jurisdiction of this case as a result of the appeal that was filed by **[Alien]** in March of 1997. Consequently, as **[Alien]** had shown a prima facie claim for CAT relief, an order reopening and remanding the case to the Immigration Court for the purpose of presenting and adjudicating a CAT Article 3 claim would have been the appropriate remedy according to the regulations.

[Alien]'s attorney of record, **[Attorney]**, failed to file a motion to reopen and remand to seek relief under CAT before the Immigration Judge. As a result, **[Alien]** was barred from this important form of relief. **[Attorney]**, familiar with **[Alien]**'s genuine and well-founded fear of returning to Ukraine, should have protected his client from refoulement to a situation of torture in Ukraine. **[Attorney]**, in failing to file a motion to reopen and remand, and thus eliminating the possibility of non-refoulement of his client to Ukraine, has provided ineffective assistance to **[Alien]**.

III. [ALIEN] HAS COMPLIED WITH ALL ASPECTS OF *MATTER OF LOZADA*

A motion to reopen or reconsider based upon a claim of ineffective assistance of counsel requires: (1) that the motion be supported by an affidavit of the allegedly aggrieved respondent setting forth in detail the agreement that was entered into with counsel with respect to the actions to be taken and what representations counsel did or did not make to the respondent in this regard; (2) that counsel whose integrity or competence is being impugned be informed of the allegations leveled against him and be given an opportunity to respond, and (3) that the motion reflect whether a complaint has been filed with appropriate disciplinary authorities with respect to any violation of counsel's ethical or legal responsibilities, and if not, why not. Matter of Lozada.

[Alien]'s affidavit setting forth his agreement with **[Attorney]**, as well as his understanding of counsel's representations is attached as Exhibit 1. In compliance with *Matter of Lozada*, **[Alien]** hereby submits copy of the letter sent to **[Attorney]**, informing him of the allegations leveled against him and inviting a response. See Exhibit 2. Moreover, **[Alien]** hereby submits copy of the complaint drafted, but not filed, with the Tennessee Bar Association, the disciplinary authority overseeing attorney **[Attorney]** practice of law. See Exhibit 3. **[Alien]** did not file a complaint against **[Attorney]** because the regulations regarding the filing deadline for CAT motions to reopen are open to different interpretation.

The heading for 8 C.F.R. § 208.18(b)(2), § 1208.18(b)(2), reads: "*Aliens who were ordered removed, or whose removal orders became final before March 22, 1999.*" (Emphasis added). The text of 8 C.F.R. § 208.18(b)(2), § 1208.18(b)(2), reads in pertinent part: "*An alien under a final order of deportation, exclusion or removal that became final prior to March 22, 1999 may move to reopen proceedings to seek protection under § 208.16(c).*" (Emphasis added)

The heading of this relevant section of the Code of Federal Regulations clearly renders it applicable to aliens who were ordered removed, but whose removal orders were not yet final due to an appeal pending before the BIA. **[Alien]** clearly falls under this first category. The text of this section, however, allows the interpretation that only aliens whose removal, deportation, or exclusion orders had become final, were subject to the June 21, 1999, filing deadline.

An order of deportation is not final until the BIA rules on a pending appeal of the Immigration Judge's order. Therefore, because **[Alien]**'s appeal was pending before the BIA, he was not under a final order of deportation.

[Attorney] has responded to our letter. See Exhibit 4. In his letter, **[Attorney]** stated that, in his opinion, "a motion to reopen under CAT would them [sic] be timely under normal MTR [motion to reopen] rules on 90 days beyond March 9, 2000 [the date of the BIA order dismissing the appeal]." Id . **[Attorney]** makes reference to conversations with experts in the field, including Morton Sklar, Director of the World Organization Against Torture USA. The undersigned attorney recognizes the ambiguity created by the relevant regulations. In fact, this counsel has conferred with Mr. Sklar on this subject. See Affidavit of **[Attorney]**, attached as Exhibit 5. Whether the June 21, 1999, filing deadline applied to **[Alien]**'s pending appeal case remains unclear, even to experts such as Mr. Sklar, who advocated for the implementation of U.S. obligations under the Convention against Torture through these same regulations. We submit that **[Attorney]** should have exercised prudence and caution in light of the ambiguous regulations. His responsibility was to resolve the ambiguity within the regulations in the manner most responsible to his client—he should have filed a motion to reopen and remand prior to June 21, 1999. His failure to file the motion to reopen constitutes ineffective assistance because it has potentially barred **[Alien]** from presenting his CAT claim.

[Alien] recognizes the BIA's interest in having a method of monitoring those attorneys who practice before that body. *See Matter of Cecilia Rivera-Claros*, Int.Dec. 3296 (BIA 1996). He clearly understands that the BIA relies "on the disciplinary process of the relevant jurisdiction's bar as the first, and ordinarily the fastest, means of identifying and correcting possible misconduct." *Id.* A bar complaint serves various important purposes: (1) it increases the BIA's confidence in the validity of the particular claim; (2) it reduces the likelihood that an evidentiary hearing will be needed; (3) it serves the BIA's long-term interests in policing the immigration bar; and (4) in filing of a complaint, or adequately explaining why such a complaint has not been filed, it protects against possible collusion between counsel and the alien client. *Id.*

[Alien] prepared a detailed bar complaint for submission to the Tennessee Bar Association. See Exhibit 3. However, **[Alien]**, through the advice of undersigned counsel, has chosen not to file the bar complaint because of the ambiguity present in the relevant regulations. While undersigned counsel would have preserved **[Alien]**'s right to a CAT hearing by filing a motion to reopen and remand prior to June 21, 1999, counsel recognizes that 8 C.F.R. § 208.18(b)(2)(i), (ii), 8 C.F.R. § 1208.18(b)(2)(i), (ii), could be interpreted as applicable only to aliens under final orders of deportation, exclusion or removal. **[Alien]** thus submits that **[Attorney]**'s actions, while ineffective and potentially depriving him of a CAT hearing, were reasonable in light of the state of the regulations. Because other experts in the field, such as Mr. Sklar, have also had difficulty in assessing the meaning of the regulations, **[Alien]** will not file a bar complaint against **[Attorney]**.

IV. CONCLUSION

[Alien] was found to be credible by the Immigration Judge. (TR 6.) INS stipulated to the past persecution of **[Alien]** in Ukraine because of his political opinion. (TR 7.) The Immigration Judge made a vague determination that "any rebuttable presumption of a well-founded fear of future persecution based thereon is overcome by the fact that there has been a very dramatic change in conditions in the former Soviet Union related to the fall of the Soviet government." (TR 7-8.) He generally concluded that because Ukraine is now an independent country, "it is impossible to hold that [**[Alien's]**] fear of future persecution in the Ukraine, on account of political opinion. . . are objectively reasonable." *Id.* at 8.

The decision of the Immigration Judge well preceded the implementation of CAT. Consequently, it lacks a thorough determination of **[Alien]**'s eligibility for "withholding of removal" or "deferral of removal" under CAT. The regulations provide that **[Alien]** was entitled to such determination. His attorney's failure to file a motion to reopen and remand this case to the Immigration Judge eliminated such possibility.

Consequently, and within the statutory time limitations of 8 C.F.R. § 1003.2(c)(2), **[Alien]** begs the BIA to reopen his case due to the ineffective assistance of his prior counsel. **[Alien]** respectfully requests that his case be remanded to the Immigration Judge for consideration of relief under CAT.

Respectfully submitted this ___day of _______, 20__.

[Attorney]

[ADD CERTIFICATE OF SERVICE]

UNITED STATES DEPARTMENT OF JUSTICE
EXECUTIVE OFFICE FOR IMMIGRATION REVIEW
BOARD OF IMMIGRATION APPEALS
FALLS CHURCH, VIRGINIA

IN THE MATTER OF:	)	
	)	
[Alien][1]	)	
A[Number]	)	IN REMOVAL PROCEEDINGS
	)	
Respondent	)	
	)	

VERIFIED MOTION TO REOPEN DUE TO INEFFECTIVE ASSISTANCE OF COUNSEL SUBJECT TO EQUITABLE TOLLING AND/OR SUA SPONTE AUTHORITY

Respondent, **[Alien]**, by and through undersigned counsel, **[Attorney]**, hereby moves the Board to reopen its prior dismissal of Respondent's appeal of the Immigration Judge's denial of her Motion to Reopen, and remand this matter to the immigration court for consideration of adjustment of status or any other relief which the Board deems proper, based on prior counsels' and immigration consultant's ineffective assistance of counsel.

Respondent's deportation was interrupted by an action in the United States Court for the District of Colorado, halting her imminent exit during a layover in Newark, New Jersey. ***A Temporary Restraining Order is in effect until Monday, March 21, 2005, enjoining the Department of Homeland Security from proceeding with deporting her to Israel.*** *Respondent is currently in DHS custody in Elizabeth, New Jersey.*

While in general, Motions to Reopen are limited in time and number, 8 CFR § 1003.23(b)(1), those restrictions may be equitably tolled under circumstances where the alien is prevented from filing by deception, fraud, or error, so long as the Respondent acts with due diligence. Even where equitable tolling is recognized as a remedy, Respondent must still establish not only that there was ineffective assistance of counsel, but also prejudice.

In the instant case, Respondent was the victim of at least two, possibly three different attorneys and one immigration "consultant" who held himself out as an attorney, over a period spanning more than a decade. Despite her due diligence, Respondent has only recently, through counsel's efforts, discovered the depth and breadth of the prejudicial errors and misrepresentations made in her case, albeit almost too late to provide any hope of relief.

PROCEDURAL AND FACTUAL CASE HISTORY[2]

Respondent, a native of Uzbekistan and citizen of Israel, entered the United States in 1988 as a B-2 visitor and overstayed her authorized period of stay. Later, with the aid of an attorney, **[Attorney 1]**, she filed a bona fide application for asylum based in part on religious and ethnic discrimination that she suffered in Is-

[1] Although Respondent's family name is spelled "**[Name 1]**," all prior proceedings are listed under the misspelling "**[Name 2]**."
[2] *See generally*, Verification at close of this motion, Exhibit A, Declaration of Respondent's daughter, **[Daughter]**.

rael from the restrictive interpretations of the Orthodox Community there, which has a final say in matters of religious life. *See* Exhibit **[Attorney 1]** business card. **[Attorney 1]** collected a fee of over $12,000 for this representation.

The matter was referred to immigration proceedings, and in April 1994, **[Attorney 1]** accompanied Respondent to an initial master calendar hearing. **[Attorney 1]** did not speak Russian or Hebrew, Respondent's primary languages. She spoke little or no English, but was accompanied by her daughter, **[Daughter]**, whose English was better than Respondent's but far from fluent or adequate to translate matters of legal importance in deportation proceedings. Due to the obvious language difficulties presented at the hearing, the immigration judge requested that the Respondent's daughter translate the proceedings.

In his brief appearance before the immigration court, **[Attorney 1]** committed several prejudicial errors. After conceding deportability, **[Attorney 1]** apparently abandoned Respondent's asylum claim, failed to seek alternative relief such as requesting a hearing on suspension of deportation (or to seeking a brief continuance to allow her the time to establish eligibility), and requested the matter be set over for a hearing on voluntary departure, all without adequately conferring with, explaining to or obtaining the consent of his client.

[Attorney 1] also failed to advise his client that she had the right to request a court appointed translator so that she could understand the proceedings. **[Attorney 1]** did not explain any of the other rights guaranteed Respondent had before, during or after the hearing. It is also unclear whether **[Attorney 1]** entered an appearance or, if so, requested the permission of or even informed his client before withdrawing. Respondent was only told that **[Attorney 1]** would not continue to represent immediately after the hearing, and that she should retain other counsel before her hearing in two weeks on voluntary departure. Respondent was referred to **[Individual]**, an immigration consultant who represented himself to be an attorney. *See* Exhibit O, Affidavit and evidence of complaint against **[Individual]**, dated January 6, 2003; Exhibit P, **[Individual]** Associates business card. **[Individual]** verbally agreed to represent Respondent in the deportation proceedings, charging her $4,000 the scheduled hearing and any appeal, "if necessary." **[Individual]** compounded the errors previously committed by **[Attorney 1]**, failing to explain to Respondent what voluntary deportation was or provide any other information regarding her rights or alternate relief. **[Individual]** was also unable to communicate directly with Respondent: he did not speak any Russian or Hebrew and during the initial meeting communicated through her daughter.

On May 4, 1994, **[Individual]** accompanied Respondent to the continued hearing. Her daughter was unable to attend that day and no translator—court-appointed or otherwise—was present. Respondent attempted to proceed in English as best she could, and recalls agreeing that **[Individual]** was her attorney. She was apparently granted 30 days voluntary departure, but—both due to the lack of a translator and the failure of either **[Attorney 1]** or **[Individual]** to provide information—was never advised regarding either the consequences for failure to depart or opportunities to request an extension from the District Director.

After receiving notice from INS informing her that she was required to depart the United States, Respondent, accompanied by her daughter, immediately sought **[Individual]**'s advice. He informed Respondent that she did not need to leave and could ignore the INS notice because he had appealed the case. Respondent continued to make inquiries regarding the status of her case with **[Individual]**'s office on a regular basis, via telephone and in-person office visits through approximately 1997 or 1998. **[Individual]** consistently assured Respondent that her appeal had been filed and was pending.

Between 1996 and 1998, Respondent, with the aid of her daughter, sought independent legal consultations, speaking with approximately a half dozen attorneys via telephone, as well as paying for in-office consultations at least twice. Respondent was informed there was no way to verify the status of her appeal, but that it was common for cases to languish at the Board for years. Neither of the two attorneys she visited expressed interest in taking her case, advising her to wait until her daughter was a U.S. citizen and able to file for her permanent residence.

Again, in approximately 1997 or 1998, Respondent, accompanied by her daughter, twice made in-person inquiries at the New York INS office, waiting several hours to speak with an Information Officer. At the first inquiry, Respondent provided her name, A Number, and explained that she needed information regarding the status of her case. The officer informed Respondent that there was no information about her appeal on computer system, but that her file was most likely archived. Because the Service was in the process of transferring such information into their computer systems, the officer advised her to wait a few months to allow the information to be input.

Approximately two months later, Respondent again waited several hours in line and presented herself at the window. This time she was told that the computer system was temporarily unavailable and was again not provided any information. Because of her limited English, Respondent's daughter needed to accompany her to the INS office; however, the time required away from work and family obligations was a hardship. Respondent, with her daughter's assistance, attempted to contact INS through their 1-800 customer service number. She was unable to obtain any useful information from the automated system and never reached a live operator.

Respondent was frustrated by the lack of news regarding her case, but her daughter had recently become eligible for U.S. citizenship, which she understood would provide her status independent of her "pending" appeal. Due to INS processing delays, her daughter's citizenship application was pending for almost two years before she naturalized in July 2000. *See* Exhibit D, Respondent's daughter's Certificate of Naturalization, dated July 25, 2000.

While she was in New York for her naturalization proceedings in the summer of 2000, Respondent's daughter attempted to contact **[Individual]**, but discovered that his office was closed. Using "411" directory assistance, she was provided a business listing for **[Individual]**, of Los Angeles, California, who turned out to be **[Individual]**'s son. *See* Exhibit Q, Respondent's daughter's handwritten notes regarding attempts to contact **[Individual]** in 2000. The son indicated that his father was seriously ill and in a coma; client records were in storage and the son had no access to Respondent's file.

Respondent's daughter appeared in person at the INS District Office in Denver, explained her mother's situation and that she had recently naturalized. The Information Officer instructed her to file a "one step" application and provided her the appropriate forms to start the permanent residence process for both her parents. The I-130 Immigrant Petition, I-485 Application for Permanent Residence and I-765 Application for Employment Authorization were filed with the INS Denver District Office in October 2000. *See* Exhibit C, Form I-485, Application to Register Permanent Residence, with evidence of fee receipt, dated October 31, 2000. Respondent was fingerprinted, interviewed for and issued a work authorization card, and presented additional evidence as requested; she was scheduled for an interview in November 2001. *See* Exhibit F, Respondent's Fingerprint Information Worksheet, August 3, 2001.

At the adjustment interview, the INS examiner informed Respondent that Service records only showed the 1994 voluntary departure order, but did not reflect that an appeal had ever been filed. The examiner informed Respondent that he was required to deny the application and suggested that she file a Motion to Reopen. No formal denial was ever issued.

Having little faith in counsel after her prior experiences with attorneys, Respondent attempted to file a *pro se* Motion to Reopen in early 2002. Respondent was advised by a Denver District Information Officer that she would need to ask for INS to join in the case, and that she should provide information regarding the errors and misadvised to submit the request with the Denver District Office.

Apparently in response to her filing, on April 8, 2002, Respondent was informed by letter from the District Director that his office did not have jurisdiction over her application to adjust status. Her original I-485 was returned to her; however, no refund of the filing fee was made. *See* Exhibit G, INS correspondence "returning" Respondent's I-485, dated April 8, 2002.

On April 25, 2002, again acting on advice from the Information Officers at the Denver District Office, Respondent re-filed her *pro se* Motion to Reopen with the Immigration Court in New York on May 2, 2002. On June 13, 2002, the Immigration Judge denied the motion citing only the time restrictions in 8 CFR 1003.23(b)(1). In a footnote to the decision, the Immigration Judge noted that Respondent's claims might have supported a late filing under *Matter of Lozada*, 19 I&N Dec. 637 (BIA 1988), but that she had failed to show prejudice. *See* Exhibit H, Order the Immigration Judge, denying Respondent's *pro se* Motion to Reopen, dated June 13, 2002.

On July 12, 2002, Respondent filed a *pro se* appeal to the Board of Immigration Appeals. On July 23, 2002, she also fee'd in and re-submitted a *pro se* Request for Joint Motion to Reopen, but this time with the INS Trial Counsel in New York. *See* Exhibit I, Respondent's *pro se* Request for Joint Motion to Reopen, dated July 23, 2002, with $110 filing fee stamp (filed with INS, not NY Immigration Court). In August 2002, Respondent then hired attorney **[Attorney 2]**[3] to assist with her case which she now believed was too complex to handle on her own. **[Attorney 2]** also committed numerous prejudicial errors. **[Attorney 2]** failed to conduct even the most rudimentary file review or interview of Respondent or her daughter, simply assuring them that he would brief the appeal and attempt to seek a joint motion to reopen. *See* Exhibit T, Fee Agreement, dated August 14, 2002 and Receipt for $3,000 Fee, dated August 13, 2002. He never identified the issues related to **[Attorney 1]**'s representation, nor did he even inquire as to whether Respondent was properly advised of her rights or provided competent translation during the deportation hearing itself.

On August 6, 2002, Respondent's previously submitted *pro se* request to NY Trial Counsel to join in her motion to reopen was denied. *See* Exhibit J. **[Name]**, Assistant District Counsel, informed her that the Service could not join at that time because she had failed to comply with *Matter of Lozada*, 19 I&N Dec. 637 (BIA 1988) or to explain why she hadn't left under the voluntary departure order. *Id.*

In September 2002, **[Attorney 2]** filed a factually incorrect and legally deficient brief in support of the appeal. Although he identified that strict compliance with *Lozada* was not necessary because **[Individual]** wasn't an attorney, **[Attorney 2]** failed to identify prejudice, failed to substantiate Respondent's eligibility for relief, provide or even assert that she was the beneficiary of an approved (or even pending) immigrant petition,[4] visa petition with a current priority date of application for adjustment of status. *All this information was readily available and/or in [Attorney 2]'s own files.*

The Board, citing the failure to provide evidence of prejudice and/or eligibility for relief, denied the appeal on October 29, 2002. **[Attorney 2]** did not attempt to cure these defects and/or file a Motion to Reopen the Board's October 29, 2002 Decision. Instead, **[Attorney 2]** inexplicably and unnecessarily filed a second I-130 on or about November 18, 2002. Despite the fact that Respondent had retained **[Attorney 2]** after an adjustment interview, he did not take any concrete or effective steps to determine the status of the I-130 petition until June 30, 2003. *See* Exhibit U, Letters from **[Attorney 2]**, Esq. to **[Name]**, Denver USCIS District Director, showing **[Attorney 2]** unaware of previously approved I-130, or relief currently available to Respondent, dated June 18, 2003 and September 9, 2003. He continued to prosecute the redundant I-130 through early Fall 2004, responding to Service requests for additional evidence despite having received a reissued notice of the November 2001 approval a full year earlier, in November 2003. *See, e.g.*, Exhibit W, Letter from **[Attorney 2]**, Esq. to Respondent, regarding Request for Evidence on second (redundant) I-130, dated August 16, 2004.

---

[3] Please note that **[Attorney 2]**'s license to practice law has been suspended by the State of Colorado for numerous violations of attorney ethics and competence rules. See attached Exhibits W-AA.

[4] **[Attorney 2]**'s file shows evidence that he was unaware that Respondent's I-130 had long since been approved, however, given the importance of this fact his efforts to do more than write two letters (at nine months and a full year after being retained) were clearly insufficient.

In November 2003, **[Attorney 2]** informed Respondent of the anticipated sale of his law practice to attorney **[Attorney 3]**. *See* Exhibit X, Letter from **[Attorney 2]**, Esq. to Respondent, regarding sale of practice to **[Attorney 3]**, Attorney at Law; dated November 12, 2003. As his successor, Respondent elected to have **[Attorney 3]** retain the file in hopes of some continuity in her representation. **[Attorney 3]** conducted a relatively detailed if inaccurate and legally incorrect evaluation of her case that same month. *See* Exhibit V, Letter from **[Attorney 3]** to Respondent, regarding case evaluation and estimated fees, dated November 14, 2003. **[Attorney 3]** estimated that his fee to continue with the case would range from $15,000 to $30,000. *Id.* It is unclear whether the sale or transfer actually took place: **[Attorney 2]** continued to represent Respondent and at no point in time made a formal withdrawal.

[Attorney 2] also inexplicably waited well over a year after he was initially retained, until January or February 2004, to pursue a Joint motion to reopen, committing still more errors along the way. *See* Exhibit R, Transmittal of Respondent's second Request for Joint Motion to Reopen, filed by **[Attorney 2]**, Esq., dated January 6, 2004, with FedEx shipment record, dated February 4, 2004. In November 2004, **[Attorney 2]** was suspended from practice, though there is no record in the file provided that Respondent was properly advised of his suspension. *See* Exhibit Y, Colorado Supreme Court Attorney Information regarding **[Attorney 2]**, Esq.; Exhibit Z, Colorado Supreme Court Disciplinary History for **[Attorney 2]**; and Exhibit AA, Colorado Supreme Court case summary regarding **[Attorney 2]**'s suspension from the practice of law in the State of Colorado, effective November 15, 2004, for a period of 18 months. **[Attorney 2]**'s practice and certain files appear to have been assumed by The Law Office of **[Attorney 3 & Attorney 4]**.

Although **[Attorney 3]** never formally accepted Respondent's case, he was a former associate of **[Attorney 2]** and the newly formed practice was located in the exact same space as **[Attorney 2]** had occupied. Respondent understandably believed that **[Attorney 3]** was continuing to represent her in her immigration matters; however, **[Attorney 3]** only entered an appearance after Respondent was detained by DHS, specifically limiting his counsel to the potential that Respondent would be a material witness for the U.S. Attorney's Office on a pending criminal investigation. *See* Exhibit CC, Letter from **[Attorney 3]**, to **[Name]**, Assistant United States Attorney, regarding his representation of Respondent in any criminal investigation as a potential material witness, dated February 3, 2005; Exhibit DD, Letter from **[Attorney 3]** to Field Office Director, **[Name]**, requesting Respondent's release from Aurora Detention Facility as a potential material witness, dated February 3, 2005.

By failing to properly investigate, **[Attorney 2]** failed to discover the myriad errors and substantial prejudice resulting from both **[Attorney 1]**'s and **[Individual]**'s representation. He failed to properly identify the equitable tolling issue and as a result, failed to investigate Respondent's due diligence in pursuing her case. In short, **[Attorney 2]** continued with his misidentification of the issues, seeking a joint motion to reopen, without providing the full facts surrounding Respondent's case (which failure directly led to the denial of such request), and then failed to adequately protect Respondent's interests both at the point where he sold his law practice, and later (after having rescinded the sale), failing to inform Respondent of any further steps to be taken or the details regarding the transfer of any cases to **[Attorney 3]**.

ARGUMENT

1. Respondent suffered prejudice as the result of ineffective assistance of counsel

Respondent, having demonstrated that she suffered at the hands of two (possibly three) attorneys and an immigration "consultant," has demonstrated sufficient prejudice to support reopening under *Matter of Lozada*, the doctrine of equitable tolling, or alternatively the Board's own *sua sponte* powers to reopen.

Respondent is entitled to Due Process of law under the Fifth Amendment to the Constitution of the United States. A long line of cases, including Supreme Court precedents, have established that deportable non-citizens—even those who are unlawfully present in the United States, are protected by the Constitution. *See Yamataya v. Fisher*, 189 U.S. 86 (1903); *Plyler v Doe*, 457 U.S. 202 (1982); *Mathews v. Diaz*, 426 U.S. 67 (1976). The *Plyler* Court explicitly stated that "the Fifth Amendment protects aliens whose presence in this country is unlawful." 457 U.S. at 210.

Although noncitizens do not possess a Sixth Amendment right to assistance of counsel at government expense in immigration proceedings, they do have a right to competent representation at their own expense. *See* INA §§ 242(b)(2) & 292, 8 U.S.C. §§ 1252(b)(2) & 1362; 8 C.F.R. §§ 238.1(b)(2)(i), 1003.102; *See also Olvera v. INS*, 504 F.2d 1372 (5th Cir. 1974). This fundamental right is considered a part of the Due Process guarantees under the Fifth Amendment to the Constitution. *See Orantes-Hernandez v. Thornburgh*, 919 F.2d 549, 554 (9th Cir. 1990).

In the instant case, Respondent first appeared before the Immigration Court with an attorney who failed her in almost every manner imaginable; she later returned with an individual who fraudulently held himself out to her (and apparently, the Court) as an attorney. In circumstances such as the instant case where a non-citizen has been the victim of not only ineffective assistance of counsel but outright fraudulent representation, courts have granted relief even absent a showing of prejudice. *See, e.g., Waldron v. INS*, 17 F.3d 511, 518 (2d. Cir. 1994).

In the instant case, prejudice is clearly present. Petitioner would have been eligible for relief through an application for suspension of deportation under former INA § 244 within a matter of months. Had she sought to prosecute such an application and schedule a merits hearing, it is extremely likely that the Court would not have been able to find a hearing date prior to which she would become eligible.[5] Although suspension of deportation has been eliminated as a form of relief from deportation and its replacement, cancellation of removal, includes a "stop-time" rule which cuts off accrual of residency upon service of a charging document, at the time of her hearing, it was common practice to continue cases for a few months until an applicant could meet the seven-year requirement. But for **[Attorney 1]**'s and **[Individual]**'s deception, fraud and errors, and the immigration court's own lack of concern for her rights or due process, she would have had the opportunity to present a meritorious claim for relief in suspension.

Further, Respondent would have been eligible to continue with her application for asylum, yet no one advised her of this right. No competent attorney would have abandoned a meritorious claim to relief, even without a guarantee of success, before advising her client of her rights to pursue the application. Further, where in the course of pursuing the application the Respondent would have become eligible for alternative relief, such a decision to abandon the application without the advice to or consent of the Respondent was severely prejudicial at the time of the 1994 hearing.

A continuance was available to Respondent for "good cause shown," which includes accumulating time towards eligibility for relief. *See* 8 CFR § 1003.29. Even if the immigration judge had refused to continue the matter for such relief, Respondent would have the right to appeal that refusal. In the time that an appeal would have been pending, Respondent would certainly have accrued the necessary time for suspension, and could have moved to remand for consideration of her application. Based on the substantial equities in her case and the extensive family ties she has in the U.S., **[Alien]** would have presented a quite compelling case.

2. Respondent has a Due Process right to a fundamentally fair hearing

Both statutes and regulations require that individuals placed in immigration proceedings be informed of their right to counsel, their right to examine the evidence against them, their right to present testimony on their own behalf, and their right to appeal the Immigration Judge's decision (among other rights). See 8

[5] As the Board is aware, in most jurisdictions, merits hearings are scheduled at least six months from the date of a calendar due to the volume of cases on an individual Judge's docket.

C.F.R. § 1240.10 (current regulations governing advisals which are essentially identical to those in effect at the time of **[Alien]**'s hearing).

Whether the Judge attempted to inform Respondent of any of these rights (as required) is difficult to determine because a transcript of the proceeding was never generated. Fortunately, in the instant case, no transcript is necessary because whatever attempts the Judge may have made would have been entirely futile without an interpreter. To this day Respondent's English skills are fairly limited. At the time she appeared before the Court, her skills were practically non-existent. She first appeared before the Immigration Court, with her prior attorney, who apparently abandoned her in the hallway immediately after her initial appearance. No translator was present (only her daughter—whose English was also fairly limited at the time—was present); the attorney did not speak either Russian or Hebrew, Respondent's primary languages. Respondent's case was apparently set over for a hearing on voluntary departure.

New "counsel" turned out to be an unaccredited immigration consultant, fraudulently presenting himself as an attorney. When she appeared at the next court proceeding, neither she, the consultant, nor the court, could communicate or interpret the proceedings. In and of itself, the failure to provide an interpreter constitutes a denial of due process. *See, e.g., He v. Ashcroft*, 328 F.3d 593, 598 (9th Cir. 2003) ("Due process requires that an applicant be given competent translation services."); *Amadou v. INS*, 226 F.3d 724 (6th Cir. 2000) (finding denial of due process for incompetent interpretation); *see also Matter of Exilus*, 18 I & N Dec. 276 (BIA 1982) (holding that although due process does not require translation of an entire administrative hearing, certain portions of the hearing must be translated in order for the proceeding to be fair). Equally important, any advisals which might have been provided by the Court would have been totally ineffectual and Respondent was denied an explanation of any of the rights to which she was entitled. *See Accardi v. Shaughnessy*, 347 U.S. 260 (1954) (holding that compliance with its own regulations is an essential safeguard of an alien's right to due process).

In a similar vein, any waiver of rights which may have been asserted or deemed to have been asserted by Respondent could not have been considered either knowing or intelligent. She had absolutely no idea of whether she eligible for any relief, whether she could ask for more time, or whether she could appeal the Judge's decision. *See U.S. v. Ahumada-Aguilar*, 295 F.3d 943 (9th Cir. 2002) (finding prejudice where an alien had not been advised of right to appeal the Judge's decision in order to gain sufficient time to qualify for alternative relief); *U.S. v. Arrieta*, 224 F.3d 1076, 1079 (9th Cir. 2000) (holding that *pro se* alien's waiver of the right to appeal his deportation order was invalid where the IJ failed to inform him about his eligibility for relief from deportation).

Under ordinary circumstances, an individual is bound by the representations of their chosen counsel. In the instant case, however, where counsel and later, the immigration consultant, were so clearly ineffective, any representations which may have been made should be given no effect.

Apart from the lack of an interpreter and the ineffective assistance of counsel, the hearing which ultimately determined Respondent's fate suffered from another significant flaw: she was never advised of her right to prosecute the application for asylum which had prompted her referral to immigration proceedings in the first place. While Immigration Judges are not required to advise every respondent before them of their eligibility to file for asylum, they are required to explain such rights in cases where an individual has either expressed a fear or otherwise manifested the intent to seek asylum. *Opoku v. INS*, 1989 U.S. Dist. LEXIS 7011 (S.D. N.Y. 1989).

In the instant case, the file in front of the Immigration Judge undoubtedly included a completed Form I-589 application for asylum; if the form had not been provided to the court, then it was at least part of her attorney's file or known to INS trial counsel. It would be hard to contemplate a more effective means of conveying such a desire than a previously filed I-589. Nevertheless, Respondent was not advised of her right to "renew" the application and have the Judge consider it on the merits.[6]

Finally, in cases where *pro se* respondents appear to be eligible for forms of discretionary relief from deportation, the Immigration Courts do have an obligation to determine whether the respondents are aware of their eligibility and wish to prosecute an application. See former 8 C.F.R. § 242.17 (1997) (in effect at the time of Respondent's hearing); *Matter of Cordova*, 22 I & N Dec. 966 (BIA 1999) (noting Immigration Judge's "duty to inform aliens of potential forms of relief for which they are apparently eligible"); *Bui v. INS*, 76 F.3d 268 (9th Cir. 1996) (immigration judge must inform an alien in a deportation hearing of an alien's "apparent eligibility" to seek relief). There is no indication in the (limited) record (or Respondent's recollection) that the Court ever informed her that she would be eligible for suspension of deportation within a few months.

Between the ineffective assistance of counsel, the lack of interpreter, and the failure to be advised of her rights (to seek relief and appeal), it could hardly be any clearer that Respondent's rights to a fundamentally fair hearing were denied. But for the infringement of these rights, she would have had an opportunity to pursue her asylum application and undoubtedly within months, present a compelling case for suspension of deportation.

[Attorney 2] failed to properly prosecute the appeal of the later-filed *pro se* Motion to Reopen, mislead Respondent as to her eligibility for relief, mischaracterized her case in presenting a request for a joint motion to reopen and failed to adequately protect Respondent during the contemplated sale of his practice and as a result of his later suspension from the practice of law. In almost every conceivable aspect, **[Attorney 2]**'s representation was woefully inadequate and prejudicial, and Petitioner should be allowed the opportunity to pursue the matter being filed with the Board of Immigration Appeals.

3. Respondent's failure to timely file her Motion to Reopen and the necessity for a second filing are the result of "Exceptional Circumstances" caused by ineffective assistance of prior counsel

A. Respondent's Claims Comply with *Matter of Lozada*

The Board has held that any claim of ineffective assistance as an exceptional circumstance meriting reopening should comply with the requirements of *Matter of Lozada, supra. Lozada* requires that: (1) any motion be supported by Respondent's affidavit or verification setting forth the agreement and representations of counsel; (2) demonstrate that Respondent has informed counsel of his error and given opportunity to respond; and (3) reflect whether any bar complaint or grievance against counsel has been initiated, or explain any failure to do so.

Respondent has been detained by DHS in a different state and has only been able to communicate regarding this motion via limited telephone contact; it was impractical given the time considerations to obtain her signature on these pleadings, however, the substance and factual allegations contained in this motion were read and/or summarized to Respondent via telephone, using her daughter, **[Daughter]** as interpreter. Respondent has authorized counsel to execute her verification of these pleadings on her behalf.

Further evidence of Respondent's compliance with the three prongs of *Lozada* and evidence thereof is attached to this Supplement. Specifically:

---

[6] It should be noted that Respondent is not asserting that she presented a claim which would have entitled her to asylum. She is simply asserting, however, that had she been informed of her right to a hearing on the application, she would have pursued the application, and as a result, would have accrued sufficient time to qualify for alternative relief, including suspension of deportation.

Ineffective Assistance of Attorney [Attorney 1]

Undersigned counsel outlined the errors committed by **[Attorney 1]** in a letter to the Grievance Committee for the Departmental Disciplinary Committee for the First Department for New York and Bronx Counties, submitted on behalf of Respondent. See Exhibit N, Letter from Respondent's counsel to Grievance Committee for the Second and Eleventh Judicial Districts regarding request for investigation of **[Attorney 1]**, dated March 12, 2005. A copy of that complaint, with a request for response, was mailed concurrently to **[Attorney 1]** at **[Address]**. See Exhibit M, Letter from Respondent's counsel to **[Attorney 1]**, regarding *Lozada* Complaint, dated March 12, 2005. Due to the recent nature of this filing (March 12, 2005), no response has yet been received from **[Attorney 1]**.

Ineffective Assistance of Immigration Consultant, [Individual]

Respondent previously filed an affidavit and written complaint with the New York State Department of Law, Office of the Attorney General, Department of Legal Practice Complaints, citing the consultant, **[Individual]**'s errors, fraud and misrepresentation. See Exhibit O, Affidavit and evidence of complaint against **[Individual]**, dated January 6, 2003. Although Respondent diligently attempted to contact **[Individual]**, she has learned that he is in ill health and incapacitated in a coma. See attached Declaration of Respondent's daughter, **[Daughter]**, business card for **[Individual]**; notes from Respondent's daughter, regarding phone and contact numbers for **[Son]**, son of **[Individual]**.

Further, pursuant to *Rabiu v. INS,* 41 F.3d 879 (2d Cir. 1994), as cited in the Board's own decision, certain elements of compliance with *Lozada* may be inappropriate where the error was committed by a person not licensed to practice law. Inasmuch as Respondent has demonstrated prejudice and also filed a complaint against **[Individual]**.

Ineffective Assistance of [Attorney 2]

Respondent, through counsel, has contacted the Colorado Supreme Court Attorney Regulation Counsel via telephone (as required) to initiate the process of filing a formal request for investigation against **[Attorney 2]**, despite his current suspension from the practice of law. While **[Attorney 2]** is not currently allowed to practice as an attorney, it is known that he maintains a presence at his former office, and a letter outlining his errors has been sent to him for comment at that address.

B. Time and number limitations on Motions to Reopen may be equitably tolled upon a showing of ineffective assistance of counsel.

Where counsel or a person purporting to act as counsel act in a fraudulent, ineffective manner to the Respondent's prejudice, time and number limitations on motions to reopen may be equitably tolled on a showing of due diligence. The circumstances surrounding Respondent's representation clearly support a finding of exceptional circumstances, but due to the continuing and egregious nature of the violations, equitable tolling, allowing consideration of this motion is warranted.

The doctrine of equitable tolling has been recognized by several Circuits, including the Tenth (the location of Respondent's application for residence, her detention and the custodian who is seeking to deport her), as well as the Second (the court of original jurisdiction in this matter), Fourth and Ninth Circuits. *See, e.g., Riley v. INS*, 310 F.3d 1253 (10th Cir. 2002); *Iavorski v. INS*, 232 F.3d 124 (2d Cir 2000) ("In a situation where fraud or concealment of the existence of a claim prevents an individual from timely filing, equitable tolling of a statute of limitations is permitted until the fraud or concealment is, or should have been, discovered by a reasonable person in the situation.").

The prejudice suffered by Respondent—failure to file an appeal, failure to be allowed to proceed with applications for relief, failure to timely depart, failure to make an effective submission of her own motion to reopen or the appeal of that motion—is clearly within the scope of the harm contemplated by the doctrine of equitable tolling. *See, e.g., Singh v. Ashcroft*, 367 F.3d 1182 (9th Cir. 2003) ("Where an alien is prevented from filing an appeal in an immigration proceeding due to counsel's error, the error deprives the alien of the appellate proceeding entirely. And this error mandates a presumption of prejudice because the adversary process itself has been rendered presumptively unreliable"). After prejudice, the analysis turns to Respondent's due diligence in correcting the error. *See, e.g., Riley*.

Respondent was deprived of any fundamental understanding of her legal rights by a combination of factors in her deportation proceedings. First, her attorney, **[Attorney 1]**, did not advise her and acted without authorization in abandoning her asylum application, failing to pursue suspension or a request for a continuance, and setting the matter for a hearing on voluntary departure. Her next appearance with **[Individual]** compounded those error when the matter proceeded without an interpreter, and through his deceitful and fraudulent acts, including holding himself out as an attorney, misrepresenting and lying to Respondent about whether he had filed an appeal and later, that the appeal was pending, as well as that she had no obligation to depart the U.S. or appear before INS.

Respondent diligently kept in contact with **[Individual]** for years; he continued to avoid and deceive her. Respondent also clearly exercised due diligence in her numerous efforts to contact other counsel and obtain second opinions, check with the government via phone and in person, even while it had been represented to her that her appeal was still pending. Despite having presented herself in person before the Service on at least four occasions, Respondent first learned of the deceit, fraud and error in her adjustment interview in November 2001.

Within a matter of several weeks, she compiled and filed—as directed by INS—a *pro se* motion to reopen with the Denver INS office. When that request was essentially rejected and her I-485 application to adjust returned to her, within a few days she again inquired of the INS how to resolve the matter. According to their instructions, she filed a motion to reopen with the immigration court in New York. Although INS had advised her to include certain information, they had not provided her a roadmap to establishing compliance under *Lozada*, and to expect such a level of legal competence from a layperson is unwarranted.

Respondent timely filed a *pro se* appeal and submitted a *pro se* request to the Service to join in her motion. A few weeks later, she hired **[Attorney 2]**, whose errors previously chronicled did little to advance her case. When **[Attorney 2]** was suspended in November 2004, there was every indication that Respondent had reason to believe that successor firm, **[Attorney 3 & Attorney 4]**, were continuing to represent her interests vis-à-vis her immigration case, rather than the limited appearance regarding her potential value as a material witness. It only approximately ten days prior to the drafting of this motion that Respondent, through her daughter, contacted undersigned counsel and she was able to understand the full extent of this tragedy. Far from having "slept on her case" as **[Attorney 2]** erroneously characterized Respondent's situation, she has at all times diligently pursued her case, seeking our experienced and competent counsel, as well as maintaining contact with counsel (at an aggressively annoying level at times).

4. Respondent is not barred from relief for failing to timely depart after the 1994 voluntary departure order, based on former INA § 242B(e)(2).

Prior to the changes wrought by IIRIRA, voluntary departure was a more flexible form of relief. Under former INA § 244(e), there was no statutory or regulatory limit to the duration, and INS District Directors more freely allowed extensions of voluntary departure, even on a *nunc pro tunc* basis where a Respondent appeared to merit such relief. The penalties for failing to depart after a grant of voluntary departure still included a bar to most discretionary forms of relief; however, the bar did not apply in all circumstances.

Failure to depart was without penalty where the Respondent could demonstrate that the failure was caused by "extraordinary circumstances" or in the alternative, after more that five years had passed since the scheduled date of departure. INA § 242B(e)(2)(A). Further, written notice in English and Spanish, as well as "*oral notice* either in either the alien's native language or another language the alien understands of the consequences . . . of the alien's remaining in the United States after the scheduled date of departure, other than because of exceptional circumstances." INA § 242B(e)(2)(B).

The record clearly demonstrates that it has been more than five years since the original order of voluntary departure has expired. More importantly, Respondent was not merely "waiting out" the order, but the victim of unscrupulous, deceitful and fraudulent behavior of both her initial immigration attorney, as well as the individual who purported to be representing her best interests but who was only an immigration consultant.

Respondent was not provided sufficient notice as there was no official or even informal translator present when she was granted voluntary departure. Further, given that **[Individual]**'s deceitful and fraudulent misrepresentations (that he had filed the appeal and that she need not depart the United States or appear at immigration) are a classic example of exceptional circumstances.

5. Respondent is eligible for relief in the form of adjustment of status under INA § 245(c)

Respondent is eligible and deserving of the relief she seeks upon reopening, adjustment of status. Respondent is the beneficiary of an approved I-130 Relative Petitioner filed by her U.S. citizen daughter, providing her with an immediately available visa. *See* Exhibit B, approved I-130; Exhibit D, Petitioner's naturalization certificate. Further, Respondent has already submitted and fee'd in a complete application for adjustment of status, demonstrating her eligibility to adjust and showing that she is not inadmissible under INA § 212. *See* Exhibit C, Fee-Paid I-485; Exhibit E, Respondent's I-94.

Counsel notes that while ICE and DHS have not yet joined in Respondent's motion, they have not opposed. Such failure to respond under the regulations, as well as the Board's prior holding in *Matter of Velarde*, further support the Board's reopening of its consideration of this matter.

[Dated:]

Respectfully submitted,

[Attorney]

VERIFICATION

Pursuant to 28 U.S.C. § 1746, I hereby verify under penalty of perjury that the factual allegations contained in the foregoing Motion are true and correct to the best of my knowledge. Because I cannot sign this motion in person due to my incarceration and transfer to New Jersey, I hereby authorize my attorney to sign this Verification on my behalf.

[Date]

[Alien] (by counsel on oral authorization)

[ADD CERTIFICATE OF SERVICE]

[Document No. 419]

MOTION FOR PANEL RECONSIDERATION OR *EN BANC* RECONSIDERATION

Description: This motion seeks panel or *en banc* reconsideration by the BIA of a denied motion to remand. The motion could also be used for reconsideration of the denial of an appeal or the denial of a motion to reopen.

Advantages: The advantage of this motion is that it seeks to have the case reviewed more closely by the initial panel (or judge) that rendered the decision, but also, alternatively seeks reconsideration *en banc*. Although the opportunity to have *en banc* review is rare, it is worth asking for.

Limitations: There is a 30-day statute of limitations on motions to reconsider. 8 CFR §1003.2(b)(2). A motion to reconsider does not toll removal, so it is advisable to seek a stay from the BIA if the client is facing imminent removal.

Citations: 8 CFR §1003.2 *et seq.*

UNITED STATES DEPARTMENT OF JUSTICE
EXECUTIVE OFFICE FOR IMMIGRATION REVIEW
BOARD OF IMMIGRATION APPEALS

IN THE MATTER OF:	)	
	)	
[Alien]	)	
A[Number]	)	IN REMOVAL PROCEEDINGS
	)	
Respondent	)	

MOTION FOR PANEL RECONSIDERATION OF DENIAL OF MOTION TO REMAND OR *EN BANC* RECONSIDERATION

Respondent, through undersigned counsel, respectfully requests that the Board reconsider its decision of August 3, 2004 denying the Motion to Remand for Consideration of an Application for Adjustment of Status. Respondent requests that the Board reconsider the decision by referral to a panel or *en banc*.

This motion for reconsideration is timely filed within 30 days of the Board decision. 8 C.F.R. §1003.2(b)(2). **Oral argument is requested**. 8 C.F.R. §1003.3(h).

The Board's decision should be reconsidered for several reasons.

ARGUMENT

I. The Board's Decision that the Respondent Fabricated His Asylum Claim Is Not Supported in the Record

First, the Board holds that the Motion to Remand must be denied "because the Respondent's motion is opposed by DHS on a separate basis." Specifically, DHS opposed the Motion to Remand on the basis that the Respondent is not "deserving of adjustment of status because the respondent fabricated elements of his asylum claim." There is no basis for such a finding in the record. The Immigration Judge, while finding inconsistencies in the Respondent's testimony and making a negative credibility determination never made a finding that the application was frivolous, fabricated or fraudulent.

The Board, in its decision, never addresses the references to the record made by DHS in its motion in opposition to remand, and never makes any finding regarding whether the references to the Immigration Judge's findings constitute fabrication or whether such statements are simply inconsistencies which go to the Respondent's credibility as a witness. Absent such analysis by the Board, there is no means of judicial review by a Circuit Court as to what, if anything, the Board found to be fabricated elements.

II. The Board's Decision Provides No Basis for Determining if the Board Engaged in Meaningful Review

A case of fabrication cannot be made just because DHS says it is so. Furthermore, the Board cannot simply "react" to the arguments of DHS without a reasoned analysis of the arguments presented by both sides. Individuals have a right to a reasoned, individualized and articulated opinion that clearly announces that the reviewing administrative court has reviewed the record and has adopted the decision of the immigration judge. *Turri v. INS*, 997 F.2d 1306, 1310 (10th Cir. 1993). This decision must be articulated with sufficient analysis to allow the Court of Appeals to perform judicial review. *Panrit v. INS*, 19 F.3d 544, 546 (10th Cir. 1994).

In *Panrit*, the Tenth Circuit laid out the requirements that must be included in an opinion such that it is clear to the appellant that the reviewing agency has engaged in an independent analysis. Since *Panrit* was decided, eight other Circuit Courts have followed the rationale of *Panrit.* See *Gandarillas-Zambrana v. BIA*, 44 F.3d 1251, 1255 (4th Cir. 1995); *Maashio v. INS,* 45 F.3d 1235, 1238 (8th Cir. 1995); *Alaelua v. INS*, 45 F.3d 1379, 1382–83 (9th Cir. 1995); *Urokov v. INS*, 55 F.3d 222, 227–28 (7th Cir. 1995); *Gomez-Mejia v. INS*, 56 F.3d 700, 702 (5th Cir. 1995); *Prado-Gonzalez v. INS*, 75 F.3d 631, 632 (11th Cir. 1996); *Bing Feng Chen v. INS*, 87 F.3d 5, 8 (1st Cir. 1996).

In *Panrit*, the Tenth Circuit held that the Board of Immigration Appeals is not required to "write an exegesis on every contention." *Id.* at 545. However, the BIA must "consider the issues and announce its decision in terms sufficient to enable . . . a reviewing Court to perceive that it has heard and considered the arguments rather than merely reacted." *Id.* The Court also requires, at a minimum, that the decision of the Board specifically recite that it has "reviewed the record and the immigration judge's decision and that it is content to rest its decision on the immigration judge's reasoning." *Id.* at 546. But clarifying this point, the Court held that this does not grant the Board "unrestricted license to summarily adopt immigration judges' decisions without examining those decisions to ensure that all of the factors urged by the alien were in fact fully considered by the immigration judge." *Id.* Otherwise, the Board would be "effectively remove[d] . . . as a separate reviewing body." *Id.*

In this case, the Board does not even get to the Immigration Judge's findings regarding credibility. Rather, the Board simply relies on the statements made by the DHS in their response brief and concurs with the statements made by DHS without any analysis or explanation as to why the statements made by DHS were correct as a matter of law.

III. The Board's Decision Denying the Motion to Remand Based on the Mere Statements of DHS Violates Due Process

It is well-settled that aliens have the right to due process in removal proceedings. In *Bridges v. Wixon*, the Supreme Court emphasized the importance of strictly protecting the alien's right to procedural due process in removal proceedings:

> Here the liberty interest of an individual is at stake . . . We are dealing here with procedural requirements prescribed for the protection of the alien. Thought deportation is not technically a criminal proceeding, it visits a great hardship on the individual and deprives him of the right to stay and live and work in this land of freedom. That deportation is a penalty—at times a most serious one—cannot be doubted. Meticulous care must be exercised lest the procedure by which he is deprived of that liberty not meet the essential standards of fairness.

Bridges v. Wixon, 326 U.S. 135, 154 (1945). A due process violation occurs if the alien can demonstrate prejudice which implicates the fundamental fairness of the proceeding. *Michelson v. INS*, 897 F.2d 465, 468 (10th Cir. 1990); *See also Lozada v. INS*, 857 F.2d 10, 13–14 (1st Cir. 1988); *Castillo-Perez v. INS*, 212 F.3d 518, 526–27 (9th Cir. 2000); *Lu v. Ashcroft*, 259 F.3d 127, 131 (3d Cir. 2001); *Huicochea-Gomez v. INS*, 237 F.3d 696, 699 (6th Cir. 2001).

The fundamental requirement of due process is the ability to be heard in a meaningful time and in a meaningful manner. *Llana-Castellon v. INS*, 16 F.3d 1093, 1096 (10th Cir. 1994), citing *Mathews v. Eldridge*, 424 U.S. 319, 333 (1976).

This Court has held that, in the context of an administrative proceeding, due process requires, at a minimum, "fact-finding based on the record produced before the decisionmaker, and disclosed to that person, and an individualized determination of his interests." *Llana-Castellon*, 16 F.3d at 1096. It also requires that the decisionmaker actually consider the evidence and arguments that a party presents in an appeal. *Id.* The failure of the Board to review all of the evidence is reviewable for procedural irregularity. *Panrit v. INS*, 19 F.3d 544, 546 (10th Cir. 1994).

IV. The Board's Finding that Elements of the Asylum Application Were Fabricated Is Clear Error

Respondent did not submit a frivolous asylum application. Applicable regulations provide that "an asylum application is frivolous if any of its material elements is deliberately fabricated." 8 C.F.R. §208.20, §1208.20. The IJ based his denial of asylum heavily on the fact that he found the Respondent's account of persecution implausible as opposed to any deliberate fabrication of a material element.

Although 8 C.F.R. §208.20, §1208.20, refers to a frivolous application, it is understood to refer to a fraudulent application. *Barreto-Clara v. U.S. Attorney General*, 275 F.3d 1334, 1339 (11th Cir. 2001). The Respondent did not commit fraud in his application for asylum. The BIA has held that "fraud" should be defined "in the commonly accepted legal sense, that is, as consisting of false representations of a material fact made with knowledge of [their] falsity and with intent to deceive the other party. The representation must be believed and acted upon by the party deceived to his disadvantage." *Matter of G-G-*, 7 I&N Dec. 161, 164 (BIA 1956).

There is no hint in the IJ's decision of a frivolous application, since he makes no mention that any material elements were deliberately fabricated. The IJ also did not make an explicit finding that the Respondent's application was frivolous as specifically required under 8 C.F.R. §208.20, §1208.20.

As the DHS argues in its Motion Opposing Remand, the IJ refused to grant asylum because he found certain elements of the Respondent's account of persecution in Algeria implausible. An unsupported implausibility finding, in and of itself, is not necessarily grounds for a negative credibility finding of certain details is not even a ground for a negative credibility finding, much less a finding that the asylum application was fabricated. To find that an asylum applicant is incredible, the Immigration Judge must provide "specific, cogent reasons" for disbelieving the witness' testimony. *Sviridov v. Ashcroft*, 358 F.3d 722, 727 (10th Cir. 2004). This standard of review is a deferential one, but the BIA cannot blindly accept an IJ's determination that an alien seeking asylum or restriction on removal is not credible, or the DHS' unsupported statements that an application is fabricated. *Osorio v. INS*, 99 F.3d 928, 931 (9th Cir. 1996); *see also Aguilera-Cota v. INS*, 914 F.2d 1375, 1381 (9th Cir. 1990) ("The fact that an IJ considers a petitioner not to be credible constitutes the beginning not the end of our inquiry.").

An IJ's adverse credibility determination may appropriately be based upon such factors as inconsistencies in the witness' testimony, lack of sufficient detail, or implausibility. *See Capric v. Ashcroft*, 355 F.3d 1075, 1085 (7th Cir. 2004); *Dia v. Ashcroft*, 353 F.3d 228, 249 (3d Cir. 2003) (en banc). Additionally, an IJ may find a witness not to be credible because of his or her testimonial demeanor. *See Mendoza Manimbao v. Ashcroft*, 329 F.3d 655, 662 (9th Cir. 2003) ("[W]e grant special deference to the IJ's eyewitness observations regarding demeanor evidence."). In this case, the IJ did not fault Respondent's testimony for containing inconsistencies or lacking detail, nor did he make any findings regarding Petitioner's demeanor. Rather, the IJ's adverse credibility finding was based solely on his personal conclusion that Respondent's account of persecution was implausible.

An IJ's finding that an applicant's testimony is implausible may not be based upon speculation, conjecture, or unsupported personal opinion. *See Wiransane v. Ashcroft*, 366 F.3d 889, 898 (10th Cir. 2004) ("Adverse credibility determinations based on speculation or conjecture are reversible.") (quotation and alterations omitted); *see also Vera-Villegas v. INS*, 330 F.3d 1222, 1231 (9th Cir. 2003) ("[C]onjecture is not a substitute for substantial evidence.") (quotation omitted); *El Moraghy v. Ashcroft*, 331 F.3d 195, 205 (1st Cir. 2003) ("While we defer to the IJ on credibility questions, that deference is expressly conditioned on support in the record."). Under such circumstances, it would be error for the IJ to fail to explain the basis in evidence for his or her credibility finding. *See El Moraghy*, 331 F.3d at 205 (quoted with approval in *Wiransane*, 366 F.3d at 898).

In other words, the IJ may not rest an adverse credibility determination on "his own unsupported opinion as to how an authoritarian government operates." *Gao v. Ashcroft*, 299 F.3d 266, 278 (3d Cir. 2002); *see also Cordero-Trejo v. INS*, 40 F.3d 482, 490 (1st Cir. 1994) (implausibility finding may not be "based upon 'expectations' without support in the record"); *Abdulrahman v. Ashcroft*, 330 F.3d 587, 598 (3d Cir. 2003) ("[T]he IJ fell well short of what we are entitled to expect from judicial officers her commentary was not confined to the evidence in the record and smacked of impermissible conjecture"); *Mosa v. Rogers*, 89 F.3d 601, 604-05 (9th Cir. 1996) (holding that the IJ improperly surmised, without record support, that the Afghan army would not be so desperate as to parachute a suspected mujahidin sympathizer into mujahidin territory after only one week of training) (superceded by statute on other grounds).

Although the DHS argues in its opposition motion identifies 3 parts of the Petitioner's testimony that he found implausible, the IJ failed to substantiate his skepticism with any record support. The DHS notes, (1) that the IJ found it impossible to believe that the Respondent was required to live underground while at the same time he ran his own business, worked for a company, received two degrees, had a visible public position in an agricultural association, and appeared on television; (2) that the Respondent did not leave the country for two years after receiving his passport; (3) that the incident involving the abduction of his father was inconsistent with the Respondent's overall allegations of persecution. The IJ did not explain by reference to anything in the record how these aspects of Petitioner's story were implausible, rather on the IJ's own expectations as to how an individual who is "in-hiding" and in fear of the government should act. The Immigration Judge must make a finding that the Respondent's behavior was implausible not because of his own personal opinions but in light of prevailing country conditions.

The Fourth Circuit upheld a finding of a frivolous application when the Respondent had "gone back and forth with the facts and misrepresented his case several times." *Efe v. Ashcroft*, 293 F.3d 899, 908 (4th Cir. 2002). In this case, the Respondent has maintained an internally consistent story. The IJ denied his asylum claim based on his opinion that the respondent could not be "living underground" while otherwise running a business, working for a company, educating himself and appearing on television. However, this does not amount to fabrication of his claim, nor is this sufficient for a finding that the application was frivolous. The mere fact that the Respondent attempted to maintain some sense of normalcy in his life does not in any way hamper his claim that he was persecuted or afraid in his country. Here, the Respondents testimony may not comport with the Immigration Judge's own personal opinion as to whether the Respondent was subject to persecution, but mere conjecture and speculation does not make for a negative credibility finding.

The IJ also found that the failure of the Respondent to leave his country for two years after receiving his passport was implausible. This cannot form the basis for a finding of fabrication. Since this constitutes a failure to act as opposed to affirmative statement, it cannot constitute fabrication or fraud. *Matter of G-G-*, 7 I&N Dec. 161. *See also* 9 FAM 40.63 N4.2. (Requiring in the context of visa eligibility that silence or the failure to volunteer information does not in itself constitute a misrepresentation).

V. The Findings of the Immigration Judge Do Not Preclude Consideration of the Application for Adjustment of Status Under *Velarde*

While the findings of the judge in this case may have been enough to deny asylum as a matter of discretion, the findings of the judge are not enough to constitute deliberate fabrication of a material element constituting a frivolous application pursuant to 8 C.F.R. §208.20, §1208.20. Respondent maintains that although the IJ denied asylum, he did not explicitly find the Respondent submitted a frivolous application, and if he did explicitly make such a finding it was clear error. 8 C.F.R. §208.20, §1208.20.

An alien is subject to ineligibility for adjustment of status under 208(d)(6) "only if a final order by an immigration judge or the Board of Immigration Appeals specifically finds that the alien knowingly filed a frivolous asylum application." 8 C.F.R. §208.20, §1208.20. The IJ found that "he did not believe the Respondent has been giving a true story of his life," and that the Respondent is not a "credible witness in his asylum case." The DHS extrapolates from these statements that the Respondent made a material fabrication, however looking at the entirety of the IJ's decision, he bases his holding largely on speculation and personal conjecture.

The IJ found the Respondent incredible. An adverse credibility determination is based upon inconsistencies, contradictions, and inherently improbable testimony. *Matter of S-M-J-*, 21 I&N Dec. 722, 746 (BIA 1997). An adverse credibility finding therefore does not constitute fraud because the standard fraud elements are not required for an adverse credibility finding. *Matter of G-G-*, 7 I&N Dec. 161. There is a difference between fraud and misrepresentation. Although certain parts of the Respondent's testimony may be unbelievable, this does not constitute a material misrepresentation needed for fraud. Accordingly, insufficient evidence exists to support a finding of a "frivolous asylum application" under section 208(d)(6) of the Act. As such, the BIA should have found that the opposition of the DHS to remand in this case was not founded and could not support a finding that the Respondent is otherwise ineligible for remand under *Matter of Velarde.*

VI. The BIA Holding that There Was Not an Immediately Available Visa Is Error

The BIA independently denies the Motion to Remand in this case finding that the Respondent is ineligible for adjustment of status. The BIA states, "Respondent's motion fails to establish that an immigrant visa petition filed on his behalf has been approved. Therefore, the respondent's motion does not establish that the respondent has an immigrant visa immediately available to him. Thus, the motion to remand does not establish the respondent's prima facie eligibility for adjustment of status under section 245(a)(3) of the Act." This holding has absolutely no basis in the law.

Matter of Velarde, 23 I&N Dec. 253 (BIA 2002) specifically holds that "a motion to reopen for adjustment of status based on a marriage entered into after the commencement of proceedings may be granted *notwithstanding the pendency of a visa petition filed on the alien's behalf,* where (1) the motion is timely filed; (2) the motion is not numerically barred by the regulations; (3) the motion is not barred by *Matter of Shaar,* 21 I&N Dec. 541 (BIA 1996), or on any other procedural grounds; (4) the motion presents clear and convincing evidence indicating a strong likelihood that the respondent's marriage is bona-fide; and (5) the Service either does not oppose the motion or bases its opposition solely on *Matter of Arthur.*" *Id.* at 256 (emphasis added).

The plain language of the BIA decision makes clear that there is no requirement that the I-130 be adjudicated at the time the Respondent seeks to reopen or remand the case. In fact, the plain language of the decision allows for the motion to be granted "notwithstanding the pendency of a visa petition filed on the alien's behalf." *Id.* In this case, Respondent is married to a United States citizen. As such, he is an immediate relative as defined in INA §201(b)(2)(A)(i). As an immediate relative, he is not subject to the numerical quota system for family-based immigration, and the visa is immediately available on the approval of the I-130 by U.S. Citizenship and Immigration Services, and upon approval, he becomes simultaneously eligible for adjustment of status under INA section 245(a)(3). In fact, Respondent, having legally entered the United States, could have, had he not been in removal proceedings, filed the I-485 simultaneously with the I-130 and the approval of both applications could have been done together by USCIS through the one-step procedure.

This holding was clearly error as a matter of law.

WHEREFORE, Respondent respectfully requests that the BIA reconsider its decision dated August 3, 2004, and remand the case back to the Immigration Judge for consideration of the Respondent's eligibility to adjust status as the spouse of a United States Citizen.

Respectfully submitted and dated this ___ day of __________, 20__.

[Attorney]

[ADD CERTIFICATE OF SERVICE]

CHAPTER 5
DISTRICT COURT PLEADINGS AND MEMORANDA

Doc. No. *Page No.*

CONTENTS

DISTRICT COURT PLEADINGS AND MEMORANDA

Form No. | | Page

Habeas Relief

Mandamus and Declaratory Judgment Relief

Rules and [illegible] Relief

EAJA Relief

[Document Nos. 501–06]

PETITION FOR WRIT OF HABEAS CORPUS AND COMPLAINT FOR DECLARATORY AND INJUNCTIVE RELIEF, INCLUDING MEMORANDUM OF LAW IN SUPPORT THEREOF

Description: The following are three petitions for a writ of habeas corpus and complaints for declaratory and injunctive relief with legal argument in support thereof. These habeas actions challenge the constitutionality and application of 8 CFR §1003.19(i)(2) (formerly, 8 CFR §3.19(i)(2)), a regulation allowing the ICE Office of Chief Counsel to automatically stay the custody/bond determination of an immigration judge in connection with a DHS appeal of said determination to the Board of Immigration Appeals. The regulation was published as an Interim Rule on October 31, 2001, ostensibly to be used by legacy INS/ICE in sensitive cases involving terror suspects. Today, the automatic stay authority is used by trial attorneys in many sorts of nonterror cases.

These cases arise out of nonmandatory detention under INA §236(a), not mandatory detention under INA §236(c). Federal district courts appear to retain jurisdiction over this type of habeas—which challenges unlawful detention by ICE—notwithstanding the REAL ID Act.

The following *Zavala* pleadings (Doc. Nos. 503–05) include not only the petition and complaint, but also points and authorities for legal argument, and a traverse (reply) filed by the petitioner in response to the government's opposition.

Advantages: These petitions for habeas corpus would be used when the IJ grants respondent release on bond, but the trial attorney invokes the automatic stay provision of 8 CFR §1003.19(i)(2) and respondent remains detained notwithstanding the IJ's order. The few federal courts to deal with this issue have widely found the automatic stay provision to be unconstitutional (which was the holding in the *Zavala* case). The legal arguments are strong, and a well-written habeas is likely to be a winner—potentially assisting many practitioners and non–American citizens alike with good case law. There is nothing much to lose in filing because the client is already detained pending adjudication of the BIA appeal. Further, filing this petition may result in settlement by the U.S. attorney to avoid a possible finding by the U.S. district court that the regulation is unconstitutional.

Limitations: In the post–*Demore v. Kim* era, contesting the automatic stay on constitutional grounds in nonmandatory detention cases is a new and important area of jurisprudence; that said, bad case law will affect the community. Take the case on intending to be thorough, do well, and prevail.

Notes: Ask for an emergency hearing and/or temporary restraining order. Remember, the client is detained and the Rules of Civil Procedure allow the court to move slowly unless the matter is framed as emergent.

Do not forget to ask for the EAJA fees.

Citations: 8 CFR §1003.19(i)(2); INA §236(a).

UNITED STATES DISTRICT COURT
SOUTHERN DISTRICT OF FLORIDA

IN THE MATTER OF : LUIS DOE, Petitioner / Plaintiff vs. MICHAEL CHERTOFF, as Secretary of the Department of Homeland Security; MARION DILLIS, Officer In Charge, Krome Detention Service Processing Center (SPC); Immigration and Customs Enforcement (ICE); United States Department of Security; MICHAEL ROZOS, Field Office Director, Miami ICE Detention and Removal Office, United States Department of Homeland Security, Respondents / Defendants. ______________________________/	)	CIVIL ACTION NO.

PETITION FOR WRIT OF HABEAS CORPUS PURSUANT TO 28 U.S.C. §2241 AND COMPLAINT FOR DECLARATORY AND INJUNCTIVE RELIEF

Petitioner, Luis Doe, (hereinafter, "Mr. Doe" or "Doe"), by and through his undersigned counsel, respectfully petitions this Honorable Court to enter an order dissolving the automatic stay invoked by ICE Counsel; said action would thereby grant him temporary release from custody during the pendency of his removal proceedings as originally ordered by the Immigration Judge (upon posting of a $30,000 bond). In support of this Petition and action for declaratory and injunctive relief, Petitioner alleges as follows:

PRELIMINARY STATEMENT

1. This Petition calls into question the constitutionality of 8 C.F.R. §1003.19(i)(2) on four independent grounds. 8 C.F.R. §1003.19(i)(2) is an automatic stay provision utilized in bond proceedings before the Executive Office for Immigration Review ("EOIR"). As a regulatory mechanism, it allows the Office of Chief Counsel of ICE to stay an Immigration Judge's decision to release an alien in removal proceedings on bond during the pendency of an appeal of the bond determination with the Board of Immigration Appeals ("BIA"). The auto-

matic stay may be invoked notwithstanding the fact that a full and fair evidentiary bond hearing has been conducted on the issue of release. The stay provision does not require any specific criteria as legal justification; the Office of Chief Counsel of ICE may invoke the stay without presenting any legal justification for doing so. The automatic stay provision contains no time frame for processing of the bond appeal; without a time frame for processing the underlying appeal, the automatic stay provision renders the bond hearing meaningless and obviates due process. The automatic stay provision is *ultra vires* in that it far exceeds the statutory authority granted ICE for detention of aliens; indeed, use of the stay provision in non-mandatory detention cases defies the intention of Congress at 8 USC §1236. Finally, this subparagraph of the regulation was inserted in contravention of the rulemaking procedure required by the Administrative Procedures Act ("APA").

Mr. Doe has no criminal record and is not charged in removal proceedings under a criminal-alien provision. Rather, Mr. Doe is charged with overstaying the time allotted on his visitors visa. 8 U.S.C. §1227(a)(1)(C). He is an applicant for political asylum because he fears persecution in his native country of Doeland.

Although this Petition calls into question the legality of the automatic stay provision at 8 C.F.R. §1003.19(i)(2), some very brief background may be of assistance to the Court.

[brief facts here]

Immigration Judge Hurewitz conducted a full bond hearing in two separate settings at the Krome Detention Center. Judge Hurewitz considered the evidence and listened to arguments from both parties. Weighing Doe's liberty interests with the concerns of the government, the Judge set a cash bond of $30,000. The Office of Chief Counsel for ICE, however, filed an automatic stay and effectively blocked Mr. Doe's release. ICE followed the stay with a bond appeal. The bond appeal has been pending with the Board of Immigration Appeals for three months, and Mr. Doe remains detained at Krome.

The uncontested facts are that Mr. Doe is not a danger to the United States community. This is not a case involving drugs, violence, or other heinous activity. ICE contends he is a flight risk because he is afraid to return to Doeland. (Under this criteria, all asylum seekers are flight risks and should be detained without bond.) On the other hand, Mr. Doe contends that—though certainly afraid of persecution in Doeland—he is in the end a law-abiding individual that will comply with the EOIR's orders; what's more, the $30,000 bond is sufficient to ensure his appearance at immigration hearings and appointments. Further safeguards, such as electronic monitoring and daily supervision, are at ICE' disposal and may also be utilized in this case.

The automatic stay is in violation of substantive and procedural due process as guaranteed by the Fifth Amendment to the United States Constitution. It is ultra vires because it exceeds the authority granted ICE by Congress at 8 USC §1226(a) and (c). It was inserted into the regulations in contravention of the APA. For these reasons, this Honorable Court should dissolve the stay and order Mr. Doe released as ordered by the Immigration Judge.

JURISDICTION

2. This action arises under the Constitution of the United States, the Immigration and Nationality Act of 1952, as amended ("INA"), 8 USC §1101 *et seq.*, and the Administrative Procedure Act ("APA"), 5 USC §701 *et seq.*

3. This Court has habeas corpus jurisdiction pursuant to 28 USC §2241, and Art. I, §9 C. 2 of the United States Constitution (the "Suspension Clause"), as Petitioner is presently subject to immediate detention and custody under color of the authority of the United States Government, and said custody is in violation of the Constitution, laws or treaties of the United States. This Court may also exercise jurisdiction pursuant to 28 USC §1331 (federal question jurisdiction) and may grant relief pursuant to the Declaratory Judgment Act, 28 USC §2201 *et seq.*, and the All Writs Act, 28 USC §1651.

VENUE

4. Venue lies in the United States District Court, Southern District of Florida, the judicial district where the Petitioner resides, is detained, and where the Immigration Judge issued an order granting release on bond. 28 USC §1391.

PARTIES

5. Petitioner / Plaintiff Luis Doe is a native and citizen of Doeland who entered the United States lawfully on a nonimmigrant visa.

6. The Respondent / Defendant MICHAEL CHERTOFF is the Secretary of the United States Department of Homeland Security ("DHS"). Mr. Chertoff is ultimately responsible for the administration of the DHS and the immigration laws, including enforcement and detention functions. Mr. Chertoff oversees "ICE" (Immigration and Customs Enforcement), the agency responsible for Mr. Doe's arrest and detention. This includes the Office of Chief Counsel for ICE, which invoked the stay provision and instructed the Detention Office at Krome to deny release.

7. The Respondent / Defendant MARION DILLIS, Officer in Charge, Krome Service Processing Center (SPC), Immigration and Customs Enforcement ("ICE"), United States Department of Homeland Security. Ms. Dillis is essentially the warden of Krome, and as such is the immediate custodian of Mr. Doe for purposes of the habeas corpus statute at 28 U.S.C. §2241.

8. The Respondent / Defendant MICHAEL ROZOS, Field Director, Miami ICE Detention and Removal Office, United States Department of Homeland Security, is the supervisor of Ms. Dillis and oversees the detention facilities in the Florida Region. As such, he has ultimate responsibility for the continued detention of Mr. Doe.

FACTUAL AND PROCEDURAL BACKGROUND

9. Luis Doe is an attorney educated and licensed in Doeland.

[additional brief facts, as appropriate, here]

10. On or about November 10, 2004, ICE agents entered Mr. Doe's home in the early morning hours and arrested him, transporting him to Krome.

11. Mr. Doe, through counsel, moved for a bond hearing. The bond hearing was conducted over two sessions. Evidence was presented and argument heard from both parties. Counsel for ICE presented an Interpol letter indicating that Mr. Doe was charged with **(deleted to protect confidentiality)** in connection with **(deleted).** The Intepol letter also indicated that Mr. Doe would be extradited. For his part, Mr. Doe presented a police clearance letter indicating no criminal arrests or criminal activity in Doeland, as well as evidence that the charge involved the **(deleted)** (i.e., that no fraud, theft, or unjust enrichment was alleged). In addition, Mr. Doe presented documentary proof that Doeland was not requesting extradition. This fact has proven to be true: Doeland has not requested extradition.

15. On December 2, 2004, Immigration Judge Kenneth Hurewitz ordered Mr. Doe released upon posting of a $30,000 cash bond. (exhibit 2) ICE Counsel verbally reserved appeal and on or about December 3, 2004, filed form EOIR-43. (exhibit 3) On or about December 10, 2004, Assistant Chief Counsel for ICE filed form EOIR-26 notice of appeal of the bond decision with the Board of Immigration Appeals. Pursuant to 8 CFR §1003.19(i)(2), these two steps effectively stayed the Immigration Judge's custody determination and Mr. Doe remained incarcerated.

16. The parties filed briefs with the BIA in mid-January, 2005. The bond appeal remains pending.

17. On January 20, 2005, Field Officer for Detention and Removal (and a defendant herein), Michael Rozos ordered Mr. Doe's release on the condition of posting a bond, wearing an electronic bracelot, and reporting under ICE' intensive supervision program (a daily reporting and monitoring program, including curfews and home visits). (exhibit 4) Assistant Chief Counsel assigned to the case, however, objected to release under these conditions. Based on government counsel's protests, the order of release was rescinded at a higher level. The significance of this interchange is two-fold. First, the Field Director deemed Mr. Doe a candidate for release on bond coupled with supervision. Second, ICE does have the ability to tether Mr. Doe to an electronic monitoring device and monitor his daily movements in conjunction with the $30,000. bond. (exhibit 5) Mr. Doe has agreed to these conditions and continues to agree today.

18. During the pendency of the bond appeal, the removal case has moved forward. Detained at Krome, where attorney visitation is conducted in a cramped, dirty cubicle through a plexi-glass window, Mr. Doe was unable to meaningfully assist his counsel in preparing the complicated asylum case. An asylum hearing was held on February ___, 2005. Mr. Doe presented two witnesses on his behalf, and presented over thirty-five documents as evidence in support of the claim.

19. In a decision dated February ___, 2005, the Immigration Judge denied asylum. The Judge's decision contains many factual and legal errors and is not supported by the weight of the evidence. Notably, the Judge's decision fails to cite to <u>any</u> of the documents submitted into evidence in support of the claim, including telling United States' State Department documents attesting to political corruption in Doeland's Attorney General's Office and the Supreme Court.

20. However, the Immigration Judge's decision is not an administratively final decision. On March ___, 2005, Mr. Doe, through counsel, filed an appeal with the BIA. In the event that the BIA does not sustain his appeal, Mr. Doe has a right to file a petition for review with the Court of Appeals for the Eleventh Judicial Circuit of the United States. 8 USC §1252(b).

21. It is noteworthy that, in the event the BIA sustains the Judge's decision and orders Mr. Doe's release on bond, ICE Counsel can seek but *another* stay. According to the regulation, if the Board dismisses the Government appeal and orders release, said order shall be automatically stayed for five business days. If the Commissioner certifies the custody order to the Attorney General, the Board's order remains stayed. Thus the prosecutor (the Office of Chief Counsel) has tremendous power to completely obviate the adversarial process and cancel out the administrative "judiciary's" determination regarding custody.

EXHAUSTION OF REMEDIES

22. Mr. Doe is not required to exhaust administrative remedies in this case. Indeed, exhaustion is not an issue, since this petition calls into question the constitutionality of the Department of Justice' own regulation, and the BIA is without authority to rule on the constitutionality of its own agency's regulation.

CUSTODY

23. Mr. Doe is in custody at the Krome Detention Center, Miami, Florida.

IRREPARABLE HARM

24. Mr. Doe suffers irreparable harm each day he is incarcerated at Krome. His removal proceedings could continue for over one year. He is unable to meaningfully assist in the presentation of his case. Mr. Doe is deprived liberty, separated from family members, is losing weight and has a persistent viral / respiratory infection. He is depressed and melancholy. Without this Honorable Court's intervention, an individual of in-

tegrity and character—no longer a young person—could remain unnecessarily detained in what is essentially a maximum security facility for many months to come.

EQUAL ACCESS TO JUSTICE ACT

25. Petitioner has retained the undersigned counsels to represent him in this matter and has agreed to pay counsels reasonable attorney fees, costs and expenses. Petitioner therefore seeks an award of his costs, attorneys' fees, and expenses, under the Equal Access to Justice Act (hereinafter, "EAJA"), 28 U.S.C. §2412, in this lawsuit.

FIRST CLAIM FOR RELIEF

(The automatic stay regulation, causing prolonged detention, violates substantive due process under the Fifth Amendment)

26. Petitioner incorporates by reference paragraphs 1 through 24, above, as if set forth in full and at length herein.

27. The Fifth Amendment guarantees that no person shall be deprived of liberty without due process of law. Freedom from imprisonment—government custody, detention, or other forms of physical restraint—lies at the heart of the Due Process Clause. *Zadvydas v. Davis*, 121 S. Ct. 2491, 2499 (2001). Government detention violates the Due Process Clause unless restraint is ordered in a criminal proceeding with adequate procedural safeguards, or in certain special and non-punitive circumstances where special justification outweighs the individual's constitutionally protected interest in avoiding physical restraint. *Zavala v. Ridge*, 310 F. Supp 2d 1071 (N.D. Calif. 2004). Substantive due process applies to aliens regardless of their residency status. *Zadvydas*, 533 U.S. at 693. See also: *Mathews v. Diaz*, 426 U.S. 67, 77 (1976). There is no special justification for a regulation which allows unilateral prosecutorial action following (and notwithstanding) a complete evidentiary bond hearing. The non-criminal alien's interest in liberty outweighs this unfettered exercise of prosecutorial power.

SECOND CLAIM FOR RELIEF

(The automatic stay provision violates procedural due process under the Fifth Amendment Due Process Clause)

28. Petitioner incorporates by reference as if set forth in full and at length herein paragraphs 1 through 23, *supra*.

29. The Supreme Court has articulated a three-part test to determine whether government conduct violates procedural due process. Accordingly, this Honorable Court must consider three factors: (1) the nature of the private interest affected by the government action; (2) the risk of an erroneous deprivation of the interest as a result of the procedures used; and (3) the government's interest in using its own procedures and the fiscal and administrative burdens caused by additional or substitute safeguards. *Mathews v. Eldridge*, 424 U.S. 319, 335 (1976).

29 – A. In this case, the private interest is fundamental liberty. The automatic stay results in indefinite deprivation of liberty during the removal process because no time frames are provided in the regulation.

29 – B. The risk of erroneous deprivation is enormous; the automatic stay provision <u>invites</u> (indeed, demands) arbitrary and capricious government action. ICE Counsel argues that Mr. Doe must be detained because he is afraid to return to Ecuador and thus may abscond within the U.S. Every asylum seeker is afraid to return to the native country; arguably, every asylum seeker is a flight risk and should be indefinitely detained *vis a vis* the automatic stay provision. Of course, ICE Counsel does not invoke the stay in every asylum case and the vast majority of asylum seekers who have been lawfully admitted are *not* detained. Mr. Doe case thus

presents a perfect example of the inherent arbitrary and capricious nature of the automatic stay procedure. Under the stay process, the hearing before an immigration judge is not much more than a charade; it is the prosecutor who has the inherent powers of the adjudicator and can pick and choose a few select cases (based on unidentified criteria) for the automatic stay.

29 – C. Finally, ICE's interest in utilizing the unilateral automatic stay provision is minimal. Title 8 C.F.R. §1003.19(i)(1) already allows ICE to seek a temporary stay from the BIA when it disagrees with the decision of the immigration judge. The difference between the two provisions is that, under the first subsection, ICE Counsel must present argument and justification for an automatic stay and an independent arbiter decides.

THIRD CLAIM FOR RELIEF

(The automatic stay provision was added to regulations in violation of the Administrative Procedures Act, 5 U.S.C. §551 et seq., 5 U.S.C. §701)

30. Title 8 C.F.R. §1003.19(i)(2) was implemented on an emergency basis and without public comment in October of 2001. Substantive amendments to agency regulations must be published in the Federal Register and the public must be given the opportunity to comment. 5 U.S.C. §553(b). The automatic stay provision was added to the regulation without publication or the opportunity for public comment, yet it radically alters detention and custody procedures.

FOURTH CLAIM FOR RELIEF

(8 C.F.R. §1003.19(i)(2) is ultra vires in that it exceeds the detention authority, power, and intent described by Congress at 8 U.S.C. §1236(a) and (c)).

31. In 1996, Congress authorized dramatic changes to the Immigration and Nationality Act, including in the area of detention of aliens during the pendency of removal proceedings. 8 U.S.C. §1226(c) requires the mandatory detention of most aliens who are in removal proceedings on the basis of a criminal record. Such individuals, even lawful permanent residents, are not entitled to release on bond. On the other hand, 8 U.S.C. §1226(a) addresses aliens in removal proceedings who are not removable for crime. Under subsection (a), the Attorney General may (1) continue to detain the alien, or (2) release the alien on a bond of at least $1,500. and other conditions prescribed by the Attorney General or a conditional parole. There is case law which addresses when an alien should be detained or released under 8 U.S.C. §1226(a). An alien must establish that he is not likely to abscond; is not a threat to the community; and is not a threat to national security. *Matter of Adjeni*, 22 I & N Dec. 1102 (BIA 1999); *Matter of Drysdale*, 20 I & N Dec. 815 (BIA 1994), citing: *Matter of Andrade*, 19 I & N Dec. 488 (BIA 1987); *Matter of Patel*, 15 I & N Dec. 666 (BIA 1976). The analysis set forth in these precedent cases must be considered by an independent immigration judge in determining whether to release an alien on bond under subsection (a). However, the automatic stay procedure allows an ICE prosecutor to usurp the power granted by Congress to the E.O.I.R. and trump the thoughtful analysis of an independent arbiter. Had Congress wanted to give ICE the authority to detain without bond non-criminal aliens, it could have done so. Instead, Congress provided for a system of mandatory detention only where the alien is removable for crime. In all other cases, the statute invites a thoughtful analysis of the facts and circumstances of the individual case. By exceeding the detention authority vested in ICE by Congress, 8 C.F.R. §1003.19(2)(i) is an *ultra vires* agency action in violation of 5 U.S.C. §706(2)(A) – (C).

PRAYER FOR RELIEF

WHEREFORE, Petitioner, Luis Doe, by and through his undersigned counsel, prays that this Honorable Court grant the following relief:

(1) Accept jurisdiction over this action;

(2) Grant the writ of habeas corpus;

(3) Dissolve the automatic stay which prevents Petitioner Doe's release on the $30,000. bond ordered by the Immigration Judge on December 2, 2005;

(4) Order Petitioner's release on bond and any other conditions the Honorable Court deems appropriate, including intensive supervision;

(5) Enjoin the Respondents from taking any action to prevent Petitioner Doe's release on bond;

(6) Declare the automatic stay provision at 8 C.F.R. §1003.19(i)(2) unconstitutional on its face as a violation of the Fifth Amendment Due Process Clause and as an *ultra vires* exercise of agency authority in violation of the APA's rulemaking requirements;

(7) Award to Petitioner reasonable costs and attorneys' fees; and,

(8) Grant any other relief that this Honorable Court deems appropriate.

[Dated:]

RESPECTFULLY SUBMITTED:

[Attorney]

[ADD CERTIFICATE OF SERVICE]

UNITED STATES DISTRICT COURT
SOUTHERN DISTRICT OF FLORIDA

IN THE MATTER OF :)
)
LUIS DOE) CIVIL CASE NO.
)
Petitioner/ Plaintiff)
vs.)
)
MICHAEL CHERTOFF)
SECRETARY OF THE)
DEPARTMENT OF HOMELAND)
SECURITY, *et. al*)
)
Respondents / Defendants)
_______________________________/

PETITIONER'S MEMORANDUM OF LAW IN SUPPORT OF PETITION FOR WRIT OF HABEAS CORPUS

INTRODUCTORY STATEMENT

Petitioner Luis Doe has been detained at the Krome Detention Center in Miami, Florida, for approximately four months, notwithstanding an immigration judge's order that he be released on bond. The reason that Mr. Doe remains detained is that government counsel for Immigration and Customs Enforcement ("ICE") invoked an automatic stay of the judge's order in conjunction with an appeal of the bond determination. The automatic stay is authorized not by statute, but by the following regulation:

> **8 C.F.R. §1003.19(i)(2)** Automatic stay in certain cases.
>
> In any case in which the district director has determined that an alien should not be released or has set a bond of $10,000 or more, any order of the immigration judge authorizing release (on bond or otherwise) shall be stayed upon the Service's filing of a Notice of Service Intent to Appeal Custody Redetermination (Form EOIR-43) with the immigration court within one business day of the issuance of the order, and shall remain in abeyance pending decision of the appeal by the Board of Immigration Appeals. The stay shall lapse if the Service fails to file a notice of appeal with the Board in accordance with Sec. 1003.38 within ten business days of the issuance of the order of the immigration judge. If the Board authorizes release (on bond or otherwise), that order shall be automatically stayed for five business days. If, within that five-day period, the Commissioner certifies the Board's custody order to the Attorney General pursuant to Sec. 1003.1(h)(1) of this chapter, the Board's order shall continue to be stayed pending the decision of the Attorney General.

This subparagraph was inserted in the regulations on October 31, 2001. It was implemented on an emergency basis without public comment. 66 FR 54909 (10-31-01). Petitioner Doe now seeks a writ of habeas corpus from the Court on the basis that this provision is unconstitutional.

As background, in October of 2001, the Immigration and Naturalization Service ("INS") and the Executive Office for Immigration Review ("EOIR") were both under the Department of Justice. The Attorney General spoke for both agencies. At the present time, the EOIR (which encompasses both the immigration courts and the Board of Immigration Appeals) remains under the Attorney General and the Department of Justice; however, the former INS has been broken into three components and falls under the Department of Homeland Security. Responsibility for arrest, detention, and removal proceedings falls under the agency referred to as ICE, and this includes the Office of Chief Counsel, which prosecutes removal proceedings before the immigration court. In light of these agency changes, references at 8 CFR §1003.19(i)(2) to "district director" and "Service" are references to ICE. This particular regulation falls under Part 1001 of Title Eight of the Code of Federal Regulations, which is the chapter containing EOIR regulations. Thus, the Court is considering a regulation which belongs to, for lack of a better word, the EOIR and the Attorney General. It is utilized, however, by ICE counsel.

As additional background, it is notable that prior to subparagraph (2)'s insertion at 8 C.F.R. §1003.19(i), there was a mechanism already in place that allowed the prosecutor to stay an immigration judge's order to release on bond. It is still in place. 8 C.F.R. §1003.19(i)(1) allows for an emergency stay of an immigration judge's determination of custody where ICE disagrees with the immigration court's decision. However, subparagraph (1) contrasts with its twin (subparagraph 2) in that under the former subsection the ICE prosecutor must *seek* a stay and argue legal justification for it:

> **8 C.F.R. §1003.19(i)(1)** General emergency stay authority.
>
> The Board of Immigration Appeals (Board) has the authority to stay the order of an immigration judge redetermining the conditions of custody of an alien when the Service appeals the custody decision. The Service is entitled to seek an emergency stay from the Board in connection with such an appeal at any time.

Under subparagraph (1), an independent arbiter, the BIA, determines whether an emergency stay of the judge's release order is justified. Under subparagraph (2), it is the ICE prosecutor that determines a stay is justified and unilaterally achieves it by filing a skeletal form (EOIR-43) (attached as exhibit 3 to the Petition).

Doe's Petition for Writ of Habeas Corpus asks the Court to join other federal district courts that have declared the automatic stay provision unconstitutional because it violates the Fifth Amendment. Specifically, use of the automatic stay (certainly in Doe's case) contravenes substantive and procedural due process, and is *ultra vires* to the detention authority provided by Congress in the Immigration and Nationality Act ("INA").

Certainly the Fall of 2001 was an anxious time for this nation; nevertheless, in good times and bad, the Administrative Procedures Act requires proposed regulations to be promulgated pursuant to a procedure that allows for proper notice and public comment. The promulgation procedure was not followed in the case of the automatic stay provision at 8 C.F.R. §1003.19(i)(2). Mr. Doe's Petition thus asks this Honorable Court to dissolve the stay in his case and declare the regulation unconstitutional, thereby releasing Mr. Doe upon posting of the cash bond previously set by an independent immigration judge, as well as other conditions deemed appropriate—such as an electronic bracelet and intensive supervision. The writ of habeas corpus is justified based on the reasons discussed below.

A. This Court Has Jurisdiction to Review the Constitutionality of the Regulation

Federal courts have jurisdiction over habeas corpus petitions pursuant to 28 U.S.C. §2241. This statute allows habeas petitions by anyone claiming that they are being held in violation of the United States Constitution; this includes non–American citizens within the immigration context. *Zadvydas v. Davis*, 533 U.S. 678, 687 (2001). Although 1996 legislation limited federal judicial review over certain immigration decisions by the EOIR and Department of Homeland Security, constitutional challenges to the statute or regulations remain within the courts' habeas jurisdiction. *Demore v. Kim*, 538 U.S. 510 (2003), *INS v. St. Cyr*, 533 U.S. 289 (2001).

Moreover, exhaustion of remedies within the agencies (the immigration court and the BIA) is not required where a constitutional challenge is raised. The instant Petition does not call into question a judge's discretionary determination on an application for relief; rather, the Petition challenges the constitutional viability of a regulatory mechanism that has caused indefinite detention of an asylum seeker. The immigration judge and BIA adjudicate cases but cannot and do not rule on constitutional issues—much less the constitutionality of their own regulation. Because this Petition raises an issue outside of the EOIR's jurisdiction, which will therefore not be addressed by the BIA, exhaustion is not a requirement. *Haitian Refugee Center v. Nelson*, 872 F.2d 1555, 1561 (11th Cir. 1992).

B. Eight C.F.R. §1003.19(i)(2) Violates Substantive Due Process

The core concept of substantive due process is that an individual's fundamental interest in liberty cannot be violated unless there is a compelling government interest narrowly tailored to obtain the objective. "Freedom from imprisonment—from government custody, detention, or other forms of physical restraint—lies at the heart of the liberty that Clause protects." *Zadvydas v. Davis*, 533 U.S. 678, 690 (2001).

In *Demore v. Kim*, 538 U.S. 510 (2003) the Supreme Court ruled that 8 U.S.C. §1226(c) (the statutory provision calling for mandatory detention of certain aliens removable for crime) is constitutional as applied to lawful permanent residents. The *Kim* decision is relevant to the Doe Petition because the Supreme Court found that, first, habeas jurisdiction survives as a means of judicial review of constitutional issues in immigration proceedings and, second, that non–American citizens are entitled to substantive due process.

However, the *Kim* case is otherwise different from the case at bar. In *Kim*, the underlying issue was the constitutionality of a statutory provision which calls for the detention of lawful permanent residents removable for recent criminal convictions for which they had served time in a penal institution. Individuals subject to mandatory detention have extremely limited defenses to deportation available (for example, they are not eligible to seek asylum) and may be said categorically to pose a risk to society because of their recent crimes. Moreover, *Kim* did not address the agency's regulation at 8 C.F.R. § 1003.19(i)(2), but rather, Congress' statute at 8 U.S.C. § 1226(c). The Supreme Court found that 8 U.S.C. § 1226(c), calling for the mandatory detention of certain criminal aliens, is constitutional because of a demonstrated compelling need (to detain and remove aliens convicted of serious crime) and because of expedited processing times (these individuals are generally not eligible for relief from removal, thus the removal processing time is several months only).[1]

Although research does not reveal a case within the Eleventh Judicial Circuit, several district courts across the country have discussed the constitutional viability of 8 C.F.R. § 1003.19(i)(2).[2] In addition, and as a factual matter, research suggests that ICE Counsel invokes the stay in cases where an individual has been convicted of a serious crime and is deportable for that crime, or in matters implicating national security. Its use in an individual asylum case involving no criminal conviction is unprecedented.

In *Zavala v. Ridge*, 310 F. Supp. 2d 1071 (N.D. Cal. 2004), the petitioner was a lawful permanent resident deportable for lewd act on a child. This offense occurred in 1994, hence Zavala was not subject to statu-

---

[1] As an editorial aside, undersigned counsels do not agree—based on their experience—with the processing times for removal cases relied upon by the Supreme Court in *Kim, supra*. The Court was given the impression that these removal proceedings are concluded within three to six months.

[2] It is recommended to avoid confusion that only post-*Kim* cases addressing the regulation be reviewed in this case. Prior to *Kim*, ICE utilized the stay provision to keep detained those individuals it believed were subject to mandatory detention for crime. The decision is an important line of demarcation for the instant analysis because post-*Kim* cases addressing 8 C.F.R. § 1003.19(i)(2) involve non-American citizens, like Mr. Doe, who are <u>not</u> mandatory detention and are therefore <u>not</u> subject to 8 U.S.C.§ 1226(c), but rather, § 1226(a). The latter statutory section deals with the detention of non–American citizens during the removal process who—though they may be deportable for crime—are not subject to <u>mandatory</u> detention because they were released from penal custody prior to October 8, 1998 (or, are not deportable for a criminal conviction). It is this latter section, 8 U.S.C. § 1226(a), that applies to Mr. Doe's case (he is not deportable for crime, but charged only as a visa "overstay"). Pre-*Kim* the cases involve individuals who are mandatory detention, and thus muddle the issue at hand.

tory mandatory detention (which applies to individuals released from penal custody after October 8, 1998). An immigration judge conducted a bond hearing and found that the petitioner was not a danger to the community or a significant flight risk, and ordered his release on $5,000 bond. ICE filed an automatic stay, preventing Zavala's release, and he filed a petition for writ of habeas corpus. The California court found that the automatic stay invoked notwithstanding a judge's determination that he should be released on bond pending removal proceedings to be violative of substantive due process because the government failed to show any "special justification" or compelling government interest for an automatic unilateral stay of indefinite duration. The court noted that 8 C.F.R. §1003.19(i) already provided the government with a mechanism to stay release upon a showing of special justification.

Similarly, in *Ashley v. Ridge*, 288 F. Supp. 2d 662 (D.N.J. 2003), a New Jersey District Court held the automatic stay provision to be unconstitutional because it was excessive in relation to Congress' regulatory goal. In this case, the petitioner had a 1995 conviction for endangering the welfare of a child. Nevertheless, an independent immigration judge considered issues including rehabilitation and ordered his release on a $5,000 bond. The New Jersey court noted that the automatic stay provision renders the immigration judge's bail determination an "empty gesture" and found no "special justification" which outweighs the individual's constitutional liberties. 288 F. Supp. 662 at 668.

In *Uritsky v. Ridge*, 286 F. Supp. 2d 842 (E.D. Mich 2003), the petitioner had pled guilty to third degree criminal sexual conduct, but argued that his sentencing as a juvenile did not result in a "conviction" for immigration purposes. The government argued his conviction was indeed an "aggravated felony" under the immigration law. The immigration judge ordered his release on a $5,000 bond. The government filed an appeal and automatic stay. Tellingly, the federal court in Michigan found that, because an immigration judge had already conducted an individualized determination that detention was not necessary, there was no longer a "sufficiently compelling government need." 286 F. Supp. 2d at 847.

In some cases, district courts have found the stay provision constitutional or at least dismissed the habeas petition without prejudice. These cases are distinguishable from the case at bar.

In *Ali v. Achim*, 342 F. Supp. 2d 769 (N.D. Ill 2004), the federal court in Illinois dismissed the habeas without prejudice because, although the petitioner had been granted a bond by the immigration judge, the BIA subsequently denied bond.[3] In this case, the alien had been convicted in Wisconsin of Substantial Battery—Intended Substantial Harm."

In *Piscotta v. Ashcroft*, 311 F. Supp. 2d 445 (N.J. 2004), a district court in New Jersey considered the automatic stay provision in the case of an alien who had been convicted twice of robbery and had pending first degree attempted rape charges.[4] The immigration court had ordered the alien removed for these crimes, and though initially bond was set at $12,000, the BIA had remanded this determination for further consideration. The district court did not specifically address the issue of substantive due process, and it is not known whether this issue was argued before the court. The court found that because the BIA considers detained cases on an "expedited basis", the ongoing detention is constitutionally permissible under notions of procedural due process. The court's decision makes references to "expedited" processing, and quotes a regulation which sets as a management goal that the case-in-chief be resolved "as soon as practicable."[5] The court effectively side-stepped the issue of prolonged detention by reasoning that custody would not be indefinite because it would not be longer than the removal case-in-chief. 311 F. Supp. at 445. Clearly, this conclusion

---

[3] Significantly, the court found that there was no exhaustion requirement and that *Kim* did not apply to the case because the alien's detention fell under the parameters of 8 U.S.C. § 1226(a).

[4] At the outset, this court found that (1) there was no exhaustion requirement and (2) it had habeas jurisdiction to consider the claim.

[5] 8 C.F.R. § 1003.1(e)(8) refers to processing of the case-in-chief (the removal case). It is not legally enforceable, but is described in the regulation as an internal goal or "management directive." It also allows for various exceptions and postponements of the management goal. According to 8 C.F.R. § 1003.1(8)(vi), the provisions of sub (e)(8) (the provision cited by the *Piscotta* court) do not create <u>any</u> procedural or substantive right enforceable before any immigration judge, the Board, or in any court of law or equity.

misses the point.[6] The issue is not the length of removal proceedings, but the right to liberty during the pendency of removal proceedings. More importantly, the issue is whether a government prosecutor's ability to defy an independent judge's determination and unilaterally impose indefinite detention within the overall context of removal proceedings is constitutional. Were this Court to adopt the reasoning of the *Piscotta* court, it would effectively emasculate the bond procedure Congress has adopted for individuals who are not mandatory detention, but instead fall under 8 U.S.C. §1226(a).

In the case before this Honorable Court, Mr. Doe has no criminal record. Although he is accused of a white-collar crime in Doeland,

(portion deleted for confidentiality)

Doeland is not requesting extradition. It is remarkable that ICE counsel has chosen to invoke an automatic stay at all in this case; this is certainly not in keeping with the fact patterns of other published cases, wherein—as the Court can see—the petitioners had all been convicted of serious, violent crimes. That being said, the primary issue in the context of substantive due process is whether ICE has a compelling government interest in keeping Mr. Doe detained during the duration of his asylum case—a procedure which could easily span the next twelve months. And what's more, whether the regulation is narrowly tailored to meet that need.

In this case, the answer to both questions is "no." First, the facts on their face do not rise to the level of a "compelling governmental interest." Although Mr. Doe's case is important to him, his family, and his counsels, it is in the end an ordinary asylum case like the thousands of other cases pending in the United States at this time. Second, he does not have a criminal record or pose a danger to the safety or security of the United States. Third, the compelling government interest is tempered by the judge's significant cash bond and ICE's own ability (and the Field Director's willingness) to place Mr. Doe on an electronic monitoring device and impose intensive supervision. Fourth, the regulation is not narrowly tailored because it requires no stated criteria or justification for invoking the stay and does not carry with it special processing times for the bond appeal. Eight C.F.R. §1003.19(i)(1) already provides an effective mechanism to request a stay with the BIA where the facts are unusual enough to merit special consideration.

Clearly, 8 C.F.R. §1003.19(i)(2) is violative of substantive due process.

C. Eight C.F.R. §1003.19(i)(2) Violates Procedural Due Process

Even if this Court finds that the regulation survives the test of substantive due process, its application in Mr. Doe's case must still survive procedural due process scrutiny. This Honorable Court may decline to rule on the overall constitutionality of the regulatory provision, but still find that the automatic stay's implementation in this case is not fair and results in erroneous deprivation of liberty to Mr. Doe.

In *Zavala v. Ridge*, 310 F. Supp. 2d 1071 (N.D. Cal. 2004), the district court in California, relying on Supreme Court precedent, set forth a three-part test: (1) the nature of the private interest affected by the government action; (2) the risk of an erroneous deprivation of the interest as a result of the procedures used and the probable value of additional or substitute safeguards; and (3) the government's interest in using its own procedures and the fiscal and administrative burdens by additional or substitute safeguards. 310 F. Supp. 2d at 1077-1078, citing, *Mathews v. Eldridge,* 424 U.S. 319, 335 (1976).

Applying the three factors to Mr. Doe's case, the Court will find of course that his own interest is the interest in liberty while pursuing a valid asylum claim. This fundamental liberty interest is compared with the government's interest in keeping him detained. It is not clear that the government's interest in detention is

[6] This conclusion is also erroneous. It is not atypical for the BIA to issue a decision in the bond matter months after the case-in-chief has been decided and the individual has already been granted relief or been deported.

justified. There is nothing in the record which renders Mr. Doe a danger to the United States community or the nation's security. Moreover, he is no more a flight risk than the thousands of other asylum seekers who flee detention, persecution, prosecution, and other harm in their home countries and are not detained by ICE.

Second, the risk of erroneous deprivation of liberty is substantial. Both the immigration judge and the Field Director for Detention and Removal believed Mr. Doe should be released on a combination of intensive supervision and a bond. As the California court noted in *Zavala*, the risk for error is high because it "conflates the functions of adjudicator and prosecutor." 310 F. Supp. 2d at 1078, citing, *Marcello v. Bonds*, 349 U.S. 302 305-306 (1955).

Third and lastly, the record reflects that there are adequate, alternative safeguards in place to address government concerns. Most strikingly, the Congress of the United States has already, via statute, ensured that non–American citizens in removal proceedings for recent criminal conduct will be mandatorily detained. 8 U.S.C. §1226(c). Second, the system has in place an independent bond hearing, an appeal of the bond hearing, and the opportunity to request an automatic stay to the BIA in unusual cases. 8 C.F.R. §1003.10(i)(1). Florida ICE is fortunate in that it can impose intensive supervision, which Mr. Doe accepts in this case. In sum, the statutory, regulatory, and policy framework is in place in South Florida to more than adequately address ICE's concern that Mr. Doe may flee.

It bears repeating that the risk of arbitrary and capricious usage of the automatic stay provision is well illustrated in Mr. Doe's case. As this Court researches treatment of the automatic stay provision, it will find that its use has been limited to criminal aliens, or matters involving a mass influx of refugees (raising a national security concern). Why Mr. Doe? The Court cannot ascertain the government's concern precisely because the five-minute EOIR-43 form requires no explanation, no justification. One prosecutor yields incredible power; and in this case, the power has been abused. If for no other reason, 8 C.F.R. §1003.19(i)(2) should be struck down by the Court because it ensures the arbitrary and capricious use of power by ICE counsel in determining when and where to utilize the stay.

D. The Automatic Stay Provision Is *Ultra Vires* Because it Exceeds the Detention Authority Granted by Congress

Title 8 U.S.C. §1226(a) and (c) have been mentioned countless times in the discussion, above. Title 8 U.S.C. §1226(a) is the provision which applies to this case, and it reads (in pertinent part):

> (a) Arrest, Detention, and Release.—On a warrant issued by the Attorney General, an alien may be arrested and detained pending a decision on whether the alien is to be removed from the United States. Except as provided in subsection (c) and pending such decision, the Attorney General—
> (1) may continue to detain the arrested alien; and
> (2) may release the alien on—
> (A) bond of at least $1,500 with security approved by, and containing conditions prescribed by, the Attorney General, or
> (B) conditional parole . . . .

Title 8 U.S.C. §1226(c) is the mandatory detention section, and it reads as follows (in pertinent part):

> (c) Detention of Criminal Aliens.—
> (1) Custody.—The Attorney General shall take into custody any alien who—
> (A)is inadmissible by reason of having committed any offense covered in section 212(a)(2),
> (B) is deportable by reason of having committed any offense covered in section 237(a)(2)(A)(ii), (A)(iii), (B),(C), or (D),
> (C) is deportable under section 237(a)(2)(A)(i) on the basis of an offense for which the alien has been sentenced to a term of imprisonment of at least 1 year, or

> (D) is inadmissible under section 212(a)(3)(B) or deportable under section 237(a)(4)(B),
>
> when the alien is release, without regard to whether the alien is released on parole, supervised release, or probation, and without regard to whether the alien may be arrested or imprisoned again for the same offense.

As stated above and in the Petition, Mr. Doe falls under the first section, because he is not removable for a crime. He is charged only as a visa overstay. Indeed, he filed affirmatively for asylum while in status; his visa time ran out during the pendency of the asylum application.

Thus while 8 U.S.C. §1226(c) dictates detention of certain individuals without discretion in bond-setting by an immigration judge, 8 U.S.C. §1226(a) invites thought and consideration by the Attorney General (i.e., the immigation judge) on a case-by-case basis in consideration of precedent case law criteria. Had Congress wanted all removable aliens to be detained during removal proceedings, it certainly could have said so at 8 U.S.C. §1226. It did not.

Similarly, had Congress wanted to give ICE the ability to trump the immigration judge, it could have said so at 8 U.S.C. §1226. Yet the section does not mention automatic stay authority. Indeed, even at 8 C.F.R. §236.1 there is no mention of an automatic stay procedure. This provision is entitled Apprehension and Detention of Inadmissible and Deportable Aliens and is one of legacy INS' (now ICE's) portions of the regulation. This portion was drafted and revised in 1997 in response to the 1996 legislation which introduced mandatory detention. 8 C.F.R. §236.1(d) sets forth the procedure for requesting a bond before an immigration judge, and spells out the appeal procedure available to both parties. It does not include a prosecutorial stay mechanism.

E. Eight C.F.R. §1003.19(i)(2) Was Inserted in Violation of the APA.

The Administrative Procedures Act sets forth a procedure for agency rulemaking. 5 U.S.C. §553(b) states as follows:

> (b) General notice of proposed rule making shall be published in the Federal Register, unless persons subject thereto are named and either personally served or otherwise have actual notice thereof in accordance with law. The notice shall include—
> (1) a statement of the time, place, and nature of public rule making proceedings:
> (2) reference to the legal authority under which the rule is proposed; and
> (3) either the terms or substance of the proposed rule or a description of the subjects and issues involved.
>
> Except when notice or hearing is required by statute, this subsection does not apply—
>
> (A) to interpretative rules, general statements of policy, or rules of agency organization, procedure, or practice, or
>
> (B) when the agency for good cause finds (and incorporates the finding and a brief statement of reasons therefore in the rules issued) that notice and public procedure thereon are impracticable, unnecessary, or contrary to the public interest.
>
> (c) After notice required by this section, the agency shall give interested persons an opportunity to participate in the rule making through submission of written data, views, or arguments with or without opportunity for oral presentation. After consideration of the relevant matter presented, the agency shall incorporate in the rules adopted a concise general statement of their basis and purpose. When rules are required by statute to be made on the record after opportunity for an agency hearing, sections 556 and 567 of this title apply instead.
> (d) The required publication of service of a substantive rule shall be made not less than 30 days before its effective date, except—
> (1) a substantive rule which grants or recognizes an exemption or relieves a restriction;
> (2) interpretative rules and statements of policy; or

(3) as otherwise provided by the agency for good cause found and published with the rule.

The automatic stay provision at 8 C.F.R. §1003.19(i)(2) was added to the regulation without adhering to any of the above procedures: no publication, no notice, no discussion. Quite a fiat. Even Congress must debate publicly on C-span and explain their votes to a constituency. Yet the Attorney General inserted an emergency stay provision which potentially affects the liberty of thousands of non–American citizens and did not have to answer to anyone.[7] According to the Federal Register announcement at 66 FR 54909, the interim rule became effective immediately on the day of publication: October 31, 2001. "The Department's immediate implementation of this interim rule, with provision for post-promulgation public comment, is based upon findings of good cause pursuant to 5 U.S.C. 553(b)(3)(B)." The comments, which are attached to this Memorandum for the Court's convenience, go on to discuss national security concerns and the threat of terrorism: "The immediate implementation of this interim rule without prior public comment is necessary to prevent the re-release of aliens who may pose a threat the national security . . . ." 66 FR 54910. The commentary discusses exclusively the issue of national security and public safety threat, including the "current investigation in connection with recent terrorist activities [which] has resulted in the detention of a large number of individuals." *Id.* The "risk of flight" (the justification in Mr. Doe's case for invoking the stay) is not mentioned in the commentary.

The commentary to the rule make clear that the automatic stay was intended as a discretionary tool in the fight against terrorism. Mr. Doe does not fit the bill. Moreover, adoption of the automatic stay in contravention of the section does not meet the requirements for the exception. Title 8 C.F.R. §1009.13(i)(2) does not simply interpret existing policy; it creates a radically different procedure to keep non–American citizens in detention. Moreover, it was not and never has been established that scores of terrorists were in I.N.S. custody facing removal proceedings. Hindsight is twenty-twenty. Promulgation of such a radical procedural mechanism without notice, comment, and discussion did not qualify for an exception. In any event, Mr. Doe's case clearly does not meet the stated purpose of the automatic stay provision: he is not a terrorist or a threat to national security. There was no compelling need for an emergency stay, and no impediment to ICE counsel filing for a "regular" stay with the BIA if deemed appropriate.

In reviewing the Federal Register announcement, this Court may arrive at one of two conclusions, or both. As a broad legal matter, 8 C.F.R. §1003.19(i)(2) is an illegal regulation because it was inserted into the regulations in violation of the APA without meeting one of the stated exceptions to public rulemaking. Or, on narrower terms, the Court may find that the invocation of the stay in Mr. Doe's case far exceeds the rule's intended application, which confirms the violation of his due process rights.

CONCLUSION

It is respectfully prayed that the Court grant the Petition and issue a Writ of Habeas Corpus, thereby ending the illegal and unconstitutional detention of Petitioner Luis Doe.

[Dated:]

RESPECTFULLY SUBMITTED:

[Attorney]

[ADD CERTIFICATE OF SERVICE]

[7] The national security threat potentially implicated by terrorists in our midst is not to be made light of. However, a narrowly tailored regulation that specified, for example, "only in instances of national security or in the case of alleged terrorist activity" would cause less constitutional concern.

UNITED STATES DISTRICT COURT FOR THE NORTHERN DISTRICT OF CALIFORNIA

ZAVALA, Javier Petitioner, v. Tom RIDGE, in his Official Capacity, Secretary Department of Homeland Security, John ASHCROFT, in his Official Capacity, Attorney General Department of Justice Respondents.	)	INS No. A 90-809-446 **PETITION FOR WRIT OF HABEAS CORPUS AND COMPLAINT FOR DECLARATORY AND INJUNCTIVE RELIEF**

PETITION FOR WRIT OF HABEAS CORPUS AND COMPLAINT FOR DECLARATORY AND INJUNCTIVE RELIEF

INTRODUCTION

1. Petitioner Javier ZAVALA ("Petitioner"), by and through his undersigned counsel, hereby petitions this Court for a writ of habeas corpus to review the lawfulness of his detention by the Department of Homeland Security. Petitioner also files this action for declaratory and injunctive relief, requesting that the Court find that the regulation at 8 C.F.R. §1003.19(i)(2), the basis for his custody, is unconstitutional. Three other published federal court decisions have reached the same conclusion. See Ashley v. Ridge, __ F. Supp. 2d __ 2003 U.S. Dist. LEXIS 19335 *15 (D. N. J. Oct. 29, 2003); Uritsky v. Ridge, __ F. Supp. 2d __ 2003 U.S. Dist. LEXIS 17698 *15 (E.D. Mich. Sept. 29, 2003); Bezmen v. Ashcroft, 245 F. Supp. 2d 446, 450 (D. Conn. 2003). Therefore, this Court should order Petitioner's immediate release from custody, upon the posting of the $5,000 bond already set by the Immigration Judge.

JURISDICTION

2. This action arises under the Constitution, the Immigration & Nationality Act of 1952, as amended (the "INA"), 8 U.S.C. §§1101 et seq., and the Administrative Procedure Act (the "APA"), 5 U.S.C. §§701 et seq. This Court has habeas corpus jurisdiction pursuant to 28 U.S.C. §2241 et seq.; Art. I, §9, Cl. 2 of the United States Constitution (the "Suspension Clause"); and the common law. This Court may also exercise jurisdiction pursuant to 28 U.S.C. §1331, and may grant relief pursuant to the Declaratory Judgment Act, 28 U.S.C. §2201 et seq., and the All Writs Act, 28 U.S.C. §1651.

VENUE

3. Venue is properly with this Court pursuant to 18 U.S.C. §1391(e) because the Defendants are employees or officers of the United States, acting in their official capacity, and an agency of the United States; because a sub-

stantial part of the events or omissions giving rise to the claim occurred in the Northern District of California; because the decision to hold Petitioner in custody is under the jurisdiction of the Northern District of California office of Respondents; and because Petitioner resides in the Northern District and there is no real property involved in this action. Venue is additionally proper in this Court pursuant to the Supreme Court's decision in Braden v. 30th Judicial Circuit Court of Kentucky, 410 U.S. 484, 493-94 (1973) (noting that "traditional venue considerations" for the purposes of a habeas petition under 28 U.S.C. §2241 include (1) the location where material events took place, where records and pertinent witness are likely to be found, (2) the convenience of the forum for respondent and petitioner; and (3) the familiarity of the court with the applicable laws).

INTRADISTRICT ASSIGNMENT

4. The decision to hold Petitioner in custody is under control of the San Francisco office of Respondents. Therefore, assignment to the San Francisco or Oakland Division of this Court is proper under N.D. Rule 3-2(d).

PARTIES

5. Petitioner is a native of Mexico. He is a lawful permanent resident of the United States, a status he has had since 1986. He is currently in custody in Oakland, California. On November 21, 2003 Petitioner was ordered released from custody by a United States Immigration Judge ("IJ") on a $5,000 bond.

6. Respondent Tom RIDGE is sued in his official capacity as the Secretary of the Department of Homeland Security. In this capacity he has responsibility for the administration and enforcement of the immigration laws pursuant to section 402 of the Homeland Security Act of 2002, 107 Pub. L. 296, 116 Stat. 2135 (Nov. 25, 2002). See also Armentero v. INS, 340 F.3d 1058 (9th Cir. 2003).

7. Respondent John ASHCROFT is sued in his official capacity as the Attorney General of the United States. He has responsibility for the administration and enforcement of the immigration laws pursuant to 8 U.S.C. §1103, Immigration and Nationality Act ("INA") §103. As the Immigration and Nationality Act has not been amended to reflect the designation of the Secretary of the Department of Homeland Security as the administrator and enforcer of immigration laws, Respondent ASHCROFT is sued in his official capacity to the extent that 8 U.S.C. §1102 gives him the authority to detain Petitioner. Armentero v. INS, 340 F.3d 1058 (9th Cir. 2003).

FACTS

8. Petitioner is a native and citizen of Mexico. He has lived in the United States since 1980, and has been a lawful permanent resident since 1986. His wife, Lucia Zavala, is also a lawful permanent resident. They live in Santa Cruz, California.

9. On January 19, 1994, Petitioner was convicted in the Superior Court of Sonoma County of a misdemeanor violation of one count of oral copulation with a minor, under §288a(b)(1) of the California Penal Code. He was sentenced to six months in the county jail, and probation of two years. He has successfully completed probation, and has no other arrests or convictions.

10. On February 8, 2003, Petitioner made a brief trip to Mexico. Upon his return he was questioned at the San Jose, California, airport regarding his prior criminal conviction. Petitioner honestly answered the questions, and was "paroled" into the United States while the Department of Homeland Security investigated Petitioner's admissibility to the United States. Petitioner was initially scheduled to appear at the Deferred Inspections office of the Department of Homeland Security on March 11, 2003. That appointment was then rescheduled to March 25, 2003.

11. On March 25, 2003, Petitioner appeared for the appointment with counsel. Petitioner, through counsel, explained that he was not inadmissible as a matter of law. The Deferred Inspections officer was not prepared

to make a decision, and rescheduled the appointment to April 24, 2003. On that date, Petitioner again appeared with counsel at the Deferred Inspections office, and the officer issued a Notice to Appear to Petitioner, charging him with inadmissibility due to his 1994 conviction, under 8 U.S.C. §1182(a)(2)(A)(i)(I), INA §212(a)(2)(A)(i)(I). The Notice to Appear was then filed with the Immigration Court, thereby initiating removal proceedings. Petitioner's initial master calendar hearing was scheduled initially for February 4, 2004, and then rescheduled to October 15, 2003.

12. On September 29, 2003, Petitioner, through counsel, filed a motion to terminate the removal proceedings, based on the fact that Petitioner's conviction falls under an exception to inadmissibility (known as the "petty offense exception") found in 8 U.S.C. §1182(a)(2)(A)(ii)(II), INA §212(a)(2)(A)(ii)(II), because he was convicted of a single misdemeanor and was not sentenced to over six months.

13. At the Master Calendar Hearing on October 15, 2003, counsel for the Bureau of Immigration and Customs Enforcement ("BICE") indicated that the Bureau was not opposed to the motion to terminate, as Petitioner was not inadmissable. Immigration Judge Beverly M. Phillips then terminated the removal proceedings.

14. Petitioner soon thereafter received notice that he was to appear at another appointment at the Deferred Inspections office in San Francisco, California, on November 12, 2003. Petitioner appeared as requested on that date, and was admitted into the United States, and then was taken into custody by a deportation officer. He was served with a new Notice to Appear ("NTA"), charging him with being removable under 8 U.S.C. §1227(a)(2)(A)(iii), INA §237(a)(2)(A)(iii), for having been convicted of an aggravated felony under 8 U.S.C. §1101(a)(43)(A) (sexual abuse of a minor).

15. Initially, the deportation officer in San Francisco, California, set a bond of $25,000. However, Petitioner was then immediately transferred from San Francisco, to Arizona (first to Eloy, Arizona, and then to Florence, Arizona). While Petitioner was in transit, his family was informed that it was not possible the $25,000 bond to be posted, as no officers had access to Petitioner's A-file. By the time Petitioner arrived in Florence, Arizona, on November 14, 2003, the deportation officer there changed the bond determination, revoking the $25,000 bond.

16. On November 14, 2003, Petitioner filed a request for bond redetermination, and his bond hearing was scheduled for, and held on November 21, 2003, before Immigration Judge Freerks, in Florence, Arizona. The Immigration Judge, upon consideration of written documentation filed before the hearing, documentation presented by the BICE at the hearing, and testimony given by Petitioner at the hearing, set a bond of $5,000 (Exh. A). The BICE reserved the right to appeal the immigration judge's decision to the Board of Immigration Appeals ("BIA").

17. On November 21, 2003, the BICE filed Form EOIR-43, Notice of Intent to Appeal Custody Determination, which under the applicable regulations, automatically stays Petitioner's release from custody until the BIA rules on the government's appeal. <u>See</u> 8 C.F.R. §1003.19(i)(2); (Exh. B). On December 5, 2003, the BICE filed a Notice of Appeal of the immigration judge's decision with the BIA.

18. Petitioner remains in BICE custody. On December 9, 2003, at the Master Calendar removal hearing, Petitioner requested a change of venue to San Francisco. The Immigration Judge granted that change of venue.

19. On December 10, 2003, the request for change of venue was granted. Petitioner was subsequently transferred from Florence, Arizona to Oakland, California. He is scheduled for a master calendar hearing in San Francisco Immigration Court on February 9, 2004.

CAUSES OF ACTION
COUNT ONE (SUBSTANTIVE DUE PROCESS)

20. The allegations contained in paragraphs 1 through 19 above are repeated and realleged as though fully set forth herein.

21. All persons residing in the United States, and in particular, lawful permanent residents, are protected by the Due Process Clause of the Fifth Amendment. See Zadvydas v. Davis, 121 S. Ct. 2491, 2500–01 (2001); Plyler v. Doe, 457 U.S. 202, 210 (1987); Mathews v. Diaz, 426 U.S. 67 (1976); Yamataya v. Fisher, 189 U.S. 86 (1903).

22. The Due Process Clause of the Fifth Amendment provides that "[n]o person shall be . . . deprived of life, liberty, or property, without due process of law." U.S. CONST. amend. V. "Freedom from bodily restraint has always been at the core of the liberty protected by the Due Process Clause from arbitrary governmental action." Foucha v. Louisiana, 504 U.S. 71, 80 (1992). This vital liberty interest is at stake when an individual is subject to detention by the former INS, now BICE. See Zadvydas, 121 S. Ct. at 2498 ("A statute permitting indefinite detention of an alien would raise a serious constitutional problem"); Kiareldeen v. Reno, 71 F. Supp. 2d 402, 409–10 (D.N.J. 1999) (in analyzing due process in the immigration context, that the first factor in the procedural due process analysis, "the petitioner's private interest in his physical liberty, must be accorded the utmost weight").

23. The substantive Due Process requirement of the Fifth Amendment prohibits "the government from infringing on certain fundamental rights at all . . . unless narrowly tailored to serve a compelling government interest." See Reno v. Flores, 507 U.S. 292, 302, 113 S.Ct. 1439 (1993); Collins v. Harker Heights, 503 U.S. 115, 125 (1992). There is no question that freedom from physical restraint is a fundamental liberty interest. See Reno v. Flores, 507 U.S. at 302. Because a fundamental right is implicated, the government must prove that the provision at issue is narrowly tailored to meet a compelling governmental interest. Reno v. Flores, 507 U.S. at 301–02.

24. The regulation at 8 C.F.R. §1003.19(i)(2) is not narrowly tailored to a compelling governmental interest. The regulation is unlawful, because the immigration judge found that Petitioner was not a danger to the community nor such a sufficient flight risk that a bond could not guard against. Despite the fact that Petitioner is not subject to mandatory detention under INA §236(c), 8 U.S.C. §1226(c), and an immigration judge has found that Petitioner should be released on bond, the regulations permit the BICE to override that decision pending its appeal without consideration of the individual facts by any independent arbiter. But for intervention by this Court, Petitioner has no means of release pending the BICE appeal. Thus, continued detention at this point under the regulation violates Petitioner's due process rights. See also Ashley v. Ridge, __ F. Supp. 2d __ 2003 U.S. Dist. LEXIS 19335 *15 (D. N. J. Oct. 29, 2003); Uritsky v. Ridge, __ F. Supp. 2d __ 2003 U.S. Dist. LEXIS 17698 *15 (E.D. Mich. Sept. 29, 2003); Bezmen v. Ashcroft, 245 F. Supp. 2d 446, 450 (D. Conn. 2003).

25. The provision is also not narrowly tailored because an alternative provision exists if the BICE disagrees with the immigration judge's assessment, enabling the BICE to seek a stay of the release order. The emergency stay provision at 8 C.F.R. §1003.19(i)(1) provides the government with the opportunity to obtain a stay of a release order on an individualized basis on the merits of the case by filing an emergency request for a stay of release with the Board of Immigration Appeals ("BIA"). Like in any stay request, the BIA makes a determination on whether the government has shown (1) a probability of success on the merits and the possibility of irreparable harm, or (2) that serious legal questions are raised and the balance of hardships tips sharply in its favor. Andreiu v. Ashcroft, 253 F.3d 477 (9th Cir. 2001).

COUNT TWO (PROCEDURAL DUE PROCESS)

26. The allegations contained in paragraphs 1 through 25 above are repeated and realleged as though fully set forth herein.

27. The procedural Due Process requirement of the Fifth Amendment entitles a person to be heard at a meaningful time and in a meaningful manner before a deprivation of liberty occurs. Mathews v. Eldridge, 424 U.S. 319, 334 (1976). The process that is due depends upon the private interest affected by the official action, the risk of erroneous deprivation of the interest, the value (if any) of additional or substitute procedural safeguards, and the government's interest, including fiscal and administrative burdens that additional or substi-

tute procedural requirements would impose. Mathews, 424 U.S. at 335; cf. Kiareldeen, 71 F. Supp. 2d at 413–14 (discussing use of secret evidence in immigration bond proceedings).

28. Procedural due process here requires a custody hearing before an independent and impartial adjudicator, not just a BICE employee. See Marcello v. Bonds; 39 U.S. 302, 307, 75 S.Ct. 757 (1955); Morrisey v. Brewer, 408 U.S. 471, 486-7, 92 S. Ct. 2593 (1972); United States v. Garcia-Martinez, 228 F.3d 956, 961 (9th Cir. 2000); Castro-Cortez v. INS, 239 F.3d 1037 (9th Cir. 2001); Cabreja-Rojas v. Reno, 999 F. Supp. 493, 496–97 (S.D.N.Y. 1998); St. John v. McElroy, 917 F. Supp. at 249–51; Ekekhor v. Aljets, 979 F.Supp. 640 (N.D. Ill. 1997); cf. Kiareldeen, 71 F. Supp. 2d at 418–19 ("access to a neutral judge [is] one of the 'most basic of due process protections'") (quoting Marincas v. Lewis, 92 F.3d 195, 203 (3d Cir. 1996)).

29. Here, the private interest affected by the statute is of the highest importance, namely, a fundamental liberty interest in being free from physical restraint. Second, the risk of erroneous deprivation of liberty is great in light of the fact that Petitioner is not subject to mandatory detention under INA §236(c), 8 U.S.C. §1226(c), and an immigration judge has held a full hearing and has determined that Petitioner should be released on bond.

COUNT THREE (REGULATION IS ULTRA VIRES)

30. The allegations contained in paragraphs 1 through 29 above are repeated and realleged as though fully set forth herein.

31. The regulation at 8 C.F.R. §1003.19(i)(2) exceeds the authority given to the agency by Congress. The statute at 8 U.S.C. §1226(a), INA §236(a) authorizes the discretionary release of an alien. Congress has not authorized the BICE to automatically stay Petitioner's release after it has been granted by an immigration judge.

PRAYER FOR RELIEF

WHEREFORE, Petitioner prays that this Court grant the following relief:

(1) issue an Order declaring that Petitioner's detention by Respondents is contrary to law and unconstitutional; and

(2) issuc an Ordcr that the BICE release Petitioner pursuant to the terms set forth by the Immigration Judge in his decision;

(3) issue an Order that the automatic stay provision of 8 C.F.R. §1003.19(i)(2) violates due process; and

(4) issue an Order that the automatic stay provisions of 8 C.F.R. §1003.19(i)(2) is ultra vires to 8 U.S.C. §1226(a), INA §236(a).

(5) award Petitioner his reasonable costs and fees.

(6) Grant any other and further relief that this Court may deem fit and proper.

[Dated:]

Respectfully submitted,

[Attorney for Plaintiff]

[ADD CERTIFICATE OF SERVICE]

DECLARATION OF [ATTORNEY]

I, [Attorney], do hereby declare:

I have personal knowledge of each matter stated herein for the following reasons:

1. I am attorney of record for Petitioner Javier Zavala in his immigration case. I obtained copies of the documents related to Petitioner's bond hearing from attorney Anthony Pelino, Law Offices of Pelino & Ternieden, P.O. Box 1909, Florence, Arizona, 85232, who appeared on behalf of Petitioner at his bond hearing in Florence, Arizona.

2. Mr. Pelino submitted to my office a copy of the Immigration Judge's decision ordering Petitioner's release from custody dated November 21, 2003. To the best of my knowledge, this document was obtained in the courtroom of Immigration Judge Lamonte S. Freerks on November 21, 2003. A copy of that document is attached hereto as Exhibit A.

3. Mr. Pelino submitted to my office a copy of Form EOIR-43 "Notice of INS Intent to Appeal Custody Redetermination" dated November 21, 2003. To the best of my knowledge, this document was obtained from the Department of Homeland Security in Florence, Arizona. A copy of that document is attached hereto as Exhibit B.

I declare under penalty of perjury that the foregoing is true and correct. Executed on this ____ day of

____, 2004 in **[City, State]**.

[Attorney]

[Attorneys]
[Address]
[City, State, and Zip Code]
[Telephone]
[Facsimile]

Attorneys for Petitioner

Javier ZAVALA

UNITED STATES DISTRICT COURT FOR THE NORTHERN DISTRICT OF CALIFORNIA

ZAVALA, Javier Petitioner, v. Tom RIDGE, in his Official Capacity, Secretary Department of Homeland Security, John ASHCROFT, in his Official Capacity, Attorney General Department of Justice Respondents.	)	Case No. C 04-00253 JSW **POINTS AND AUTHORITIES IN SUPPORT OF PETITION FOR WRIT OF HABEAS CORPUS AND COMPLAINT FOR DECLARATORY AND INJUNCTIVE RELIEF** Date of Hearing: Feb. 27, 2004 Time of Hearing: 9:00 a.m.

TABLE OF CONTENTS

TABLE OF AUTHORITIES

FEDERAL CASES

Andreiu v. Ashcroft, 253 F.3d 477 (9th Cir. 2001)

Armstrong v. Manzo, 380 U.S. 545 (1965)

Ashley v. Ridge, 288 F. Supp. 2d 662 (D. N. J. 2003)

Bezmen v. Ashcroft, 245 F. Supp. 2d 446 (D. Conn. 2003)

Castro-Cortez v. INS, 239 F.3d 1037 (9th Cir. 2001)

Collins v. Harker Heights, 503 U.S. 115 (1992)

Consumer Product Safety Commission v. GTE Sylvania, Inc., 447 U.S. 102 (1980)

Cordero v. United States, 992 F.2d 985 (9th Cir. 1993)

Estate of Cowart v. Nicholas Drilling Co., 205 U.S. 469 (1992)

Demore v. Kim, 538 U.S. 510 (2003)

Foucha v. Louisiana, 504 U.S. 71 (1992)

Getachew v. INS, 25 F.3d 841 (9th Cir. 1994)

Hilton v. Braunskill, 481 U.S. 770 (1987)

INS v. Cardoza-Fonseca, 480 U.S. 421 (1987)

INS v. St. Cyr, 533 U.S. 289 (2001)

Kansas v. Hendricks, 521 U.S. 346 (1997)

Kim v. Ziglar, 276 F.3d 523 (9th Cir. 2002) rev'd on other grounds Demore v. Kim, 538 U.S. 510 (2003)

Landon v. Plasencia, 459 U.S. 21, 103 S. Ct. 321 (1982)

Lindh v. Murphy, 521 U.S. 320 (1997)

Marcello v. Bonds, 39 U.S. 302 (1955)

Marincas v. Lewis, 92 F.3d 195 (3d Cir. 1996)

Marshall v. Jerrico, Inc., 446 U.S. 238 (1980)

Mathews v. Eldridge, 424 U.S. 319 (1976)

Morrisey v. Brewer, 408 U.S. 471 (1972)

Nunez by Nunez v. City of San Diego, 114 F.3d 935 (9th Cir. 1997)

Reno v. Flores, 507 U.S. 292 (1993)

Reyes-Melendez v. INS, 342 F.3d 1001 (9th Cir. 2003)

Richardson v. City and County of Honolulu, 124 F.3d 1150 (9th Cir. 1997)

Robinson v. Shell Oil, 519 U.S. 337 (1997)

Romero v. INS, 39 F.3d 977 (9th Cir. 1994)

Sanchez-Cruz v. INS, 255 F.3d 775 (9th Cir. 2001)

Solid Waste Agency v. United States Army Corps of Eng'rs, 531 U.S. 159 (2001)

Uritsky v. Ridge, 286 F. Supp. 2d 842 (E.D. Mich. 2003)

Zadvydas v. Davis, 533 U.S. 678 (2001)

AGENCY DECISIONS

Matter of Adeniji, 22 I. & N. Dec. 1102 (BIA 1999)

Matter of Rainford, 20 I. & N. Dec. 598 (BIA 1992)

FEDERAL STATUTES

Illegal Immigration Reform and Immigrant Responsibility Act of 1996 ("IIRIRA") Pub. L. 104-208, 110 Stat. 3009 (Sept. 30, 1996)

IIRIRA § 303(b)

8 U.S.C. § 1226(c), INA § 236(c)

8 U.S.C. § 1101(a)(43)(A), INA § 101(a)(43)(A)

8 U.S.C. § 1182(a)(2)(A)(ii)(II), INA § 212(a)(2)(A)(ii)(II)

8 U.S.C. § 1182(c), INA § 212(c)

8 U.S.C. § 1226(a), INA § 236(a)

8 U.S.C. § 1226(c), INA § 236(c)

8 U.S.C. §1227(a)(2)(A)(iii), INA § 237(a)(2)(A)(iii)

FEDERAL REGULATIONS

8 C.F.R. § 1003.1(d)(2)(i)(D)

8 C.F.R. § 1003.3(a)(1)

8 C.F.R. § 1003.19(i)(1)

8 C.F.R. § 1003.19(i)(2)

Executive Office for Immigration Review; Review of Custody Determinations, Review of Custody Determinations," 66 Fed. Reg. 54909 (Oct. 31, 2001)

STATE STATUTES

Cal. Penal § 288a(b)(1)

SUMMARY OF ARGUMENT

Petitioner challenges his continued custody by the Department of Homeland Security ("DHS"). The Immigration Judge ("IJ") ordered Petitioner released on a $5,000 bond. He remains in custody because the DHS has invoked an "automatic stay" of that decision under 8 C.F.R. § 1003.19(i)(2). The automatic stay allows DHS to circumvent an individualized finding that a non-citizen is neither a danger to the community nor a flight risk. When DHS invokes the regulatory stay, a non-citizen can remain detained for many months or more during the pendency of his case before the Board of Immigration Appeals ("BIA" or "Board"), and then on certification to the Attorney General. At least three district courts, in published decisions have found that this regulation violates due process. Ashley v. Ridge, 288 F. Supp. 2d 662 (D. N. J. 2003); Uritsky v. Ridge, 286 F. Supp. 2d 842 (E.D. Mich. 2003); Bezmen v. Ashcroft, 245 F. Supp. 2d 446 (D. Conn. 2003). The automatic stay provision facially violates substantive due process as it implicates the fundamental right to be free from physical restraint, but is not narrowly tailored to meet the compelling governmental interest of protecting public safety. See e.g. Reno v. Flores, 507 U.S. 292, 302, 113 S.Ct. 1439 (1993). The IJ, having considered the danger to the community and flight risk, has already set an appropriate bond. The "emergency stay" procedure at 8 C.F.R. § 1003.19(i)(1) presents a valid alternative means of staying an IJ's decision, while still giving the Board the opportunity to make an individualized determination regarding whether the non-citizen should be released from custody pending appeal.

The regulation also violates procedural due process because it permits DHS to ignore the decision of a neutral arbiter (the IJ), and thereby conflates the prosecutorial and adjudicative functions and, thus, the effective adjudicator (DHS) is inherently biased. See Marcello v. Bonds, 39 U.S. 302, 307, 75 S.Ct. 757 (1955). The automatic stay provision is also unconstitutional as applied to Petitioner, a long-term lawful permanent resident with a single ten year old misdemeanor offense. See, e.g., Landon v. Plasencia, 459 U.S. 21, 33 103 S. Ct. 321, 330 (1982). The regulation also is ultra vires to 8 U.S.C. § 1226(a), INA § 236(a), as it transforms a discretionary determination by the IJ into mandatory detention imposed by DHS. It therefore exceeds the statutory authority afforded to the agency by Congress and is unlawful.

I. STATEMENT OF FACTS AND CASE

Petitioner is a native and citizen of Mexico. He has lived in the United States since 1980, and has been a lawful permanent resident since 1986. His wife, Lucia Zavala, is also a lawful permanent resident. They live in Santa Cruz, California.

On January 19, 1994, Petitioner was convicted in the Superior Court of Sonoma County of a misdemeanor violation of § 288a(b)(1) California Penal Code. He was sentenced to six months in the county jail, and probation of two years. He successfully completed probation, and has no other arrests or convictions.

Petitioner was placed into removal proceedings in 2003 after his return to the United States from a trip abroad. He was charged with being removable under 8 U.S.C. § 1227(a)(2)(A)(iii), INA § 237(a)(2)(A)(iii), for having been convicted of an aggravated felony under 8 U.S.C. § 1101(a)(43)(A) (sexual abuse of a minor). Petitioner was taken into custody by the Bureau of Immigration and Customs Enforcement (BICE) in San Francisco. Initially, the deportation officer in San Francisco, California, set a bond of $25,000. ZN Dec. at Exh. D. However, Petitioner was then immediately transferred from San Francisco, to Florence, Arizona. While Petitioner was in transit, his family was informed that it was not possible to post the bond, as no officers had access to Petitioner's "A-file" (BICE's file on Petitioner). By the time Petitioner arrived in Florence, Arizona, on November 14, 2003, the deportation unit there changed the bond determination, revoking the $25,000 bond and making a "no bond" determination. ZN Dec. at Exh. F page 2.

On November 14, 2003, Petitioner filed a request for bond redetermination with the Immigration Judge pursuant to 8 C.F.R. § 1003.19, and his bond hearing was held on November 21, 2003, before Immigration

Judge LaMonte S. Freerks, in Florence, Arizona. Dec. of ZN at Exh. F. The Immigration Judge, upon consideration of written documentation filed before the hearing, documentation presented by the BICE at the hearing, and testimony at the hearing, set a bond of $5,000. Dec. of ZN at Exh. A, F.

On November 21, 2003, the BICE filed Form EOIR-43, Notice of Intent to Appeal Custody Determination, which under the applicable regulations, automatically stays Petitioner's release from custody until the BIA rules on the government's appeal. See 8 C.F.R. § 1003.19(i)(2); Dec. of ZN at Exh. B. On December 5, 2003, the BICE "filed" a Notice of Appeal of the Immigration Judge's decision with the BIA.[1] Dec. of ZN at Exh. D.

Petitioner remains in BICE custody and in removal proceedings. On December 9, 2003, at the Master Calendar removal hearing, Petitioner requested a change of venue to San Francisco. Petitioner was subsequently transferred from Florence, Arizona to Oakland, California.

I. ARGUMENT

a) The Automatic Stay Regulation at 8 C.F.R. § 1003.19(i)(2) Violates Substantive Due Process and Is Therefore Facially Unconstitutional

Standard principles of constitutional law establish that substantive due process "forbids the government from infringing on certain fundamental rights at all . . . unless narrowly tailored to serve a compelling government interest." See Reno v. Flores, 507 U.S. 292, 302, 113 S.Ct. 1439 (1993); see also Collins v. Harker Heights, 503 U.S. 115, 125 (1992); Nunez by Nunez v. City of San Diego, 114 F.3d 935, 952 (9th Cir. 1997); Ashley v. Ridge, 288 F. Supp. 2d at 668. Even if a right is not considered to be fundamental in nature, the government interference will violate substantive due process rights when it is shown that the action is not "rationally related to a legitimate governmental purpose." Richardson v. City and County of Honolulu, 124 F.3d 1150, 1162 (9th Cir. 1997).[2] Unquestionably, freedom from physical restraint is a fundamental liberty interest. See Reno v. Flores, 507 U.S. at 302[3]; Foucha v. Louisiana, 504 U.S. 71, 86, 112 S.Ct. 1780 (1992); see also Zadvydas v. Davis, 533 U.S. 678, 690, 121 S.Ct. 2491 (2001) ("Freedom from imprisonment -- from government custody, detention, or other forms of physical restraint -- lies at the heart of the liberty that [the Due Process] Clause protects."). Petitioner is physically detained in Oakland, California by Department of Homeland Security. In fact, the very nature of the automatic stay regulation requires that all individuals against whom it is applied are in custody with the BICE. They are all individuals who have been ordered re-

[1] The notice of appeal was never properly filed with the Board because the government did not properly serve Petitioner's counsel. The regulations at 8 C.F.R. § 1003.3(a)(1) require that a notice of appeal be served on the opposing party. The notice of appeal submitted by the government contained the wrong address on the proof of service. Dec. ZN at Exh. E. The "mailing address" in box number 11 is correctly listed as "680 S. Park St." but the proof of service in box number 12 lists the address as "686 S. Park St.". Id. The notice of appeal was not received by Petitioner's counsel until January 29, 2004. Id. In order for the automatic stay to remain in effect, the government must file a Notice of Appeal within 10 business days of the Immigration Judge's decision. See 8 C.F.R. § 1003.19(i)(2). Because the notice of appeal was not properly filed, since it was not served on Petitioner's counsel, then the automatic stay should no longer apply to Petitioner's case.

[2] Even if this Court finds that a fundamental liberty interest is not implicated, the regulation is not rationally related to a legitimate governmental interest because an Immigration Judge has already made a determination that the individual is not a flight risk nor a danger to others, and the government can seek to obtain an individualized stay on an emergency basis under 8 C.F.R. § 1003.19(i)(1) if it disagrees with the Immigration Judge's decision.

[3] Reno v. Flores involved a challenge to the INS' regulations that limited the release of juveniles in custody to only a parent or lawful guardian. 507 U.S. at 296. The Supreme Court found that the right implicated there was not fundamental in nature because it did not involve the right to be free from physical restraint but, rather, the "alleged right of a child who has no available parent, close relative, or legal guardian, and for whom the government is responsible, to be placed in the custody of a willing-and-able private custodian rather than of a government-operated or government-selected child-care institution." Id. at 302. Because a fundamental right was not implicated there, the only inquiry was whether the regulation was rationally related to a legitimate governmental purpose. Id. at 306.

leased by an Immigration Judge, but the government has stayed that release pursuant to 8 C.F.R. § 1003.19(i)(2). Thus, for every individual subject to the automatic stay provision, the fundamental right to be free from physical restraint is implicated.

Because a fundamental right is implicated, the government must prove that the provision at issue is narrowly tailored to meet a compelling governmental interest. For all cases falling under the automatic stay regulation, a neutral Immigration Judge has already rendered a determination that the alien is not a danger to others, nor such a flight risk that no bond amount could address any flight concerns, or else release would have been denied by the Immigration Judge in the first instance. Though it is reasonable for the government to have the opportunity to disagree with this assessment and to seek a stay of the release order, the emergency stay provision at 8 C.F.R. § 1003.19(i)(1) provides just that. See Bezmen v. Ashcroft, 245 F. Supp. 2d at 451 ("the emergency stay provision is appropriate as it presents a narrowly tailored, less restrictive means whereby the government's interest in seeking a stay of the custody redetermination may be protected without unduly infringing upon [petitioner's] liberty interest."); Ashley v. Ridge, 288 F.Supp. 2d at 675 (Id.).[4] With the emergency stay provision, the government is provided with the opportunity to obtain a stay of a release order on an individualized basis on the merits of the case. Like in any stay request, the BIA makes a determination on whether the government has shown (1) a probability of success on the merits and the possibility of irreparable harm, or (2) that serious legal questions are raised and the balance of hardships tips sharply in its favor. Andreiu v. Ashcroft, 253 F.3d 477 (9th Cir. 2001).

The regulation, however, allows the government to detain the alien – notwithstanding the Immigration Judge's order of release -- without making any showing to any court.[5] As the regulation stands, DHS is able to obtain a stay even if an appeal is frivolous and without any merit at all. For instance, the DHS could appeal a decision of the Immigration Judge granting bond, and then the BIA could dismiss that appeal if it finds that the "appeal is filed for an improper purpose, such as to cause unnecessary delay, or that the appeal lacks an arguable basis in fact or in law unless the Board determines that it is supported by a good faith argument for extension, modification, or reversal of existing law." 8 C.F.R. § 1003.1(d)(2)(i)(D). But regardless of whether the appeal was frivolous or made in bad faith, the alien remains detained during the duration of the appeal–and beyond, if the government asks the Attorney General to take the case on certification. Id.

Alternatively, there is already a procedure in place that allows the government to easily apply to the Board of Immigration Appeals at any time for an emergency stay of the Immigration Judge's order pursuant to 8 C.F.R. § 1003.19(i)(1). In any situation in which the DHS continues to disagree with the Immigration Judge and continues to believe the alien to be a genuine danger to the community, the DHS can easily apply to the Board of Immigration Appeals at any time for an emergency stay of the Immigration Judge's order. The emergency stay allows the BIA to consider the individual merits of an alien's release.[6]

---

[4] Every court that has considered the matter has found the regulation unconstitutional. In addition to the three published cases (Ashley v. Ridge, 288 F. Supp. 2d 662 (D. N. J. 2003); Uritsky v. Ridge, 286 F. Supp. 2d 842 (E.D. Mich. 2003); Bezmen v. Ashcroft, 245 F. Supp. 2d 446 (D. Conn. 2003)), Petitioner is aware of at least three other decisions from district courts finding that the provision is unconstitutional and is aware of no decisions to the contrary.

[5] Furthermore, the detention is potentially indefinite. See Ashley v. Ridge, 288 F. Supp. 2d at 669; Bezmen v. Ashcroft, 245 F. Supp. 2d at 449. There is no definitive time period by which the Board of Immigration Appeals must adjudicate DHS' appeal of the Immigration Judge's custody determination and, thus, no basis for determining when any individual will be released.

[6] The federal courts have similar individualized requirements for stays on appeal. In immigration habeas cases, if the district court has ordered petitioner deported, petitioner can seek to stay that order by moving the district court or, if moving the district court is impracticable or the motion has been denied, the Court of Appeals. Fed. Rule. App. Proc. 8. A petitioner on direct review to the Court of Appeals must also move for a stay of deportation. Andreiu v. Ashcroft, 253 F.3d 477 (9th Cir. 2001).

In criminal habeas cases, while a decision ordering the release of a prisoner is under review, the prisoner *must* be released (with or without surety) unless the district court, court of appeals, or Supreme Court orders otherwise. Fed. Rule. App. Proc. 23(c). In fact, there is a *presumption favoring release* of a successful habeas petitioner pending appeal. Hilton v. Braunskill, 481 U.S. 770, 774, (1987).

continued

Both Zadvydas v. Davis, 533 U.S. 678, 121 S. Ct. 2491 (2001), and Demore v. Kim, 538 U.S. 510, 123 S.Ct. 1708 (2003), also support Petitioner's position that the automatic stay regulation is not narrowly tailored. The Zadvydas decision acknowledges that freedom from imprisonment is a fundamental right. 533 U.S. at 690.[7] The decision also states that, in the detention context, due process is violated unless a special justification outweighs the "individual's constitutionally protected interest in avoiding physical restraint." Id. citing Kansas v. Hendricks, 521 U.S. 346, 356, 117 S.Ct. 2072 (1997); see also Ashley v. Ridge, 288 F. Supp. 2d at 669 ("[i]n the case at bar, the Government has not shown that any 'special justification' exists which outweighs Petitioner's constitutional liberties as to justify his continued detention without bail."). This "special justification" requirement is a "strict scrutiny" analysis. See Kansas v. Hendricks, 521 U.S. at 356 (finding that involuntary civil confinement to a limited subclass of individuals who have "been convicted of or charged with a sexually violent offense," and suffer from "a mental abnormality or personality disorder which makes the person likely to engage in the predatory acts of sexual violence" does not offend due process).[8]

In Demore v. Kim, the Supreme Court found that the mandatory detention provisions of 8 U.S.C. § 1226(c), INA § 236(c) did not offend due process because Congress had identified a narrow group of individuals who were deemed by Congress, because they were removable for criminal convictions, to pose dangers to others and to be flight risks. The Kim court relied on its earlier decision in Zadvydas to find that in the context of mandatory detention under INA § 236(c), "such detention necessarily serves the purpose of preventing deportable criminal aliens from fleeing prior to or during their removal proceedings, thus increasing the chance that, if ordered removed, the aliens will be successfully removed." Kim, 123 S.Ct at 1720.[9] The Kim court analyzed the purpose of INA § 236(c), and found that it "necessarily served the purpose" of ensuring that criminal aliens, who were preliminarily found to be removable by an Immigration Judge for criminal violations, appeared at their removal hearings. Thus, there was a "special circumstance" for the continued detention, and the statute was narrowly tailored to only apply to the group of aliens which Congress designated as threats to the larger public.

Here, however, like in Zadvydas, the automatic stay regulation does not apply only to aliens allegedly subject to mandatory detention but applies to all aliens for whom the government initially denied bond or set a bond of over $10,000. 8 C.F.R. § 1003.19(i)(2). Zadvydas v. Davis, 533 U.S. at 697. Moreover, the determination is made by low ranking immigration officials, not Congress. The stated purpose of the regulation is to "ensur[e] removal by preventing the alien from fleeing, and protect[] the public from potential harm." See "Executive Office for Immigration Review; Review of Custody Determinations," 66 Fed. Reg. 54909, 54909 (Oct. 31, 2001). However, the regulation only applies to those situations where the Immigration Judge has ordered an alien's release on bond and, hence, has already made a determination that the person is not a dan-

---

Similarly, in non-habeas criminal cases, if the district court orders the release of a criminal defendant and the government seeks to stay that order pending appeal, the government must affirmatively move to stay the order. If the defendant is ordered released before conviction, the government must seek a stay from the Court of Appeals. If the defendant is ordered released after conviction, the government must seek a stay from the district court or, if a notice of appeal from the judgment of conviction has already been filed, the Court of Appeals. See Fed. Rule App. Proc. 9(a)&(b); see generally Cordero v. United States, 992 F.2d 985 (9th Cir. 1993).

[7] In Zadvydas v. Davis, the Supreme Court addressed the issue of whether non-citizens with final orders of removal could be held in detention indefinitely. 533 U.S. at 678. The Court found that indefinite detention would be unconstitutional and read the Immigration and Nationality Act to permit post-final order detention for only a reasonable time, to give the government the opportunity to seek removal from the U.S. However, the Court found that detention after the six-month period, and when removal is not reasonably foreseeable, would violate substantive due process. 533 U.S. at 699-700.

[8] In Kansas v. Hendricks, the Supreme Court found that Kansas' statute requiring involuntary commitment was not unconstitutional because it was narrowly tailored to meet the compelling interest of protecting public safety. 521 U.S. at 364 ("The numerous procedural and evidentiary protections afforded here demonstrate that the Kansas Legislature has taken great care to confine only a narrow class of particularly dangerous individuals, and then only after meeting the strictest procedural standards.").

[9] The court relied on studies which showed that "after criminal aliens were identified as deportable, 77 % were arrested at least once more and 45 % -- nearly half -- were arrested multiple times before their deportation proceedings even began."123 S.Ct. at 1715.

ger to the public, and addressed any flight risk concerns by requiring a monetary bond. If the government disagrees with that decision, the appropriate remedy is to appeal and request a stay of the judge's order pursuant to 8 C.F.R. § 1003.19(i)(1). This procedure is "narrowly tailored" to meet the government's interest of protecting the public and ensuring removal.

b) The Automatic Stay Regulation Violates Procedural Due Process

The automatic stay regulation also violates procedural due process. The Due Process Clause protects against government violations of procedural, as well as substantive, due process. "The fundamental requirement of due process is the opportunity to be heard 'at a meaningful time and in a meaningful manner.'" Mathews v. Eldridge, 424 U.S. 319, 333 (1976) (quoting Armstrong v. Manzo, 380 U.S. 545, 552 (1965)). Due process requires a right to a full and fair hearing. Getachew v. INS, 25 F.3d 841, 845 (9th Cir. 1994); 239 F.3d 1037, 1052 (9th Cir. 2001) Castro-Cortez v. INS, 239 F.3d 1037, 1049 (9th Cir. 2001); Marincas v. Lewis, 92 F.3d 195, 203 (3d Cir. 1996). Furthermore, a neutral judge is one of the most basic due process protections. Marshall v. Jerrico, Inc., 446 U.S. 238, 243 (1980); Reyes-Melendez v. INS, 342 F.3d 1001, 1006 (9th Cir. 2003); Sanchez-Cruz v. INS, 255 F.3d 775, 779 (9th Cir. 2001); Castro-Cortez v. INS, 239 F.3d at 1049.

The determination of whether government conduct violates procedural due process requires consideration of three factors: (1) the nature of the private interest affected; (2) the risk of an erroneous deprivation of the interest as a result of the procedures used and the probable value of additional or substitute safeguards; and (3) the government's interest in using its own procedures and the fiscal and administrative burdens entailed by additional or substitute safeguards. Mathews, 424 U.S. at 335.

i) Petitioner Has Substantial Interests in Liberty and Family Unity The private interest affected by detention is among the most fundamental and valued in our society—liberty. See ' II.A; see also Zadvydas, 533 U.S. at 690 ("Freedom from imprisonment–from government custody, detention, or other forms of physical restraint–lies at the heart of the liberty that Clause protects."); Foucha, 504 U.S. at 80 ("[f]reedom from bodily restraint 'has always been at the core of the liberty protected by the Due Process Clause from arbitrary governmental action' "); Ashley, 288 F. Supp. 2d at 668; Bezman, 245 F. Supp. 2d. at 449 (same). Petitioner also has an extremely strong liberty interest in being united with his wife and family. Thus, Petitioner's private interests of liberty and family unity are extremely high.

ii) The Automatic Stay Regulation Subjects Petitioner to an Extremely High Risk of Erroneous Deprivation of His Liberty Interests.

The risk of erroneous deprivation of that interest is extremely high because Congress, in enacting the statutory detention provisions, intended for Petitioner to be eligible for release from custody, and an Immigration Judge, in ordering bond following a hearing, determined that Petitioner merits release from custody. See also Ashlcy v. Ridge, 288 F. Supp. 2d at 670.

Due process cannot be satisfied where, as here, the individualized determination provided by the Immigration Judge is rendered merely a charade. Petitioner was given a full due process hearing before the Immigration Judge. He presented witnesses and documentary evidence and both sides had the opportunity for cross-examination of witnesses. Based on the evidence, the Immigration Judge ordered Petitioner's release on bond. Yet this order has been rendered completely meaningless by the use of the automatic stay at 8 C.F.R. § 1003.19(i)(2). By invoking the automatic stay, the government has rendered the Immigration Judge's decision a nullity.

By permitting a government attorney to stay the Immigration Judge's decision ordering Petitioner's release by simply appealing, the regulation vests more control over Petitioner's custody status in the government attorney than in the Immigration Judge. Marincas, 92 F.3d at 203 (finding that a neutral judge is one of "the most basic of due process protections"); Castro-Cortez, 239 F.3d at 1049 (expressing "serious doubt" that the use of Immigration Officers to determine whether to reinstate removal orders comports with due process). The regulation simply casts aside the Immigration Judge's decision and keeps the alien detained until the BIA, or the Attorney General, has made a decision on appeal. See 66 Fed. Reg. at 54910 ("The purpose of the automatic stay is to allow the Service to maintain the status quo during such time as is necessary for the Service to take a prompt appeal to the Board.").[10]

Such a procedure raises serious due process concerns because of the inherent bias present in the decision maker. The prosecutor in the case who argued to the IJ that Petitioner should not be released (here BICE attorney Amy Martin) is the exact same individual who ultimately determined that Petitioner should (and would) continue to be detained by the usage of the automatic stay provision–despite the fact that the IJ rejected her argument in court. See ZN Dec. at Exh. B, D. This unquestionably raises due process concerns because it impermissibly mixes the prosecutorial and adjudicative functions and, thus, the ultimate adjudicator is inherently biased. See Marcello v. Bonds, 39 U.S. 302, 307, 75 S.Ct. 757 (1955) (noting that the special inquiry officer adjudicating over an immigration case cannot also undertake the functions of prosecutor); Morrisey v. Brewer, 408 U.S. 471, 486-7, 92 S. Ct. 2593 (1972) (a parole officer directly involved in decisions has a inherent bias, and thus due process requires that an objective and neutral evaluator make decisions regarding parole revocation).

iii. Review of the Government's Decision to Stay Release by the Board of Immigration Appeals Through the Procedure in 8 C.F.R. § 1003.19(i)(1) Would Greatly Reduce the Risk of Erroneous Deprivation of Petitioner's Liberty Interest with Minimal Burden to the Government.

The burden to the government of permitting the Board of Immigration Appeals to determine whether release should be stayed under 8 C.F.R. § 1003.19(i)(1) pales in comparison to the disastrous effect of permitting Petitioner to remain in detention despite the Immigration Judge's order of release. This is especially true given that no new administrative framework need be created. Permitting the Board of Immigration Appeals to determine whether a stay of release is in fact warranted in this case – as required under 8 C.F.R. § 1003.19(i)(1) -- would reduce the risk with minimal burden to DHS. Due process requires such a determination.

c) Alternatively, the Automatic Stay Regulation Is Unconstitutional as Applied to Petitioner

Even if this Court finds that the regulation at 8 C.F.R. § 1003.19(i)(2) does not violate due process on its face, the regulation is still unconstitutional as applied to Petitioner, a long-term lawful permanent resident, whose ten year old misdemeanor conviction does not bar him from remaining in the United States as a lawful permanent resident.

i) Petitioner is a Lawful Permanent Resident Who Has Resided in the U.S. For 18 Years

Courts have long recognized the preferential treatment that lawful permanent residents ("LPRs") are afforded under the immigration laws. See Landon v. Plasencia, 459 U.S. 21, 33 103 S. Ct. 321, 330 (1982) ("once an alien gains admission to our country and begins to develop the ties that go with permanent residence, his constitutional status changes accordingly"); Kim v. Ziglar, 276 F.3d 523, 528 (9th Cir. 2002) rev'd on other grounds Demore v. Kim, 538 U.S. 510, 123 S.Ct. 1708 (2003) ("Lawful permanent resident aliens are the most favored category of aliens admitted to the United States. They have the most ties to the United States of any category of aliens."). Thus, Petitioner's status as a long-term lawful permanent resident affords

[10] The regulation is even more problematic because it expressly states that the categorical designation of cases subject to the automatic stay is to "avoid the necessity for a case-by case determination of whether a stay should be granted in particular cases." 66 Fed. Reg. at 54910. Thus, even though the Immigration Judge has made an individualized determination, thereby reducing the risk of erroneous deprivation, the regulation's intent is to avoid any individualized case determination. In effect, the former Immigration and Naturalization Service (now DHS) has promulgated a regulation eliminating the authority of the Executive Office for Immigration Review ("EOIR") (which encompasses the nation's immigration courts) without any input from EOIR even though it is EOIR's authority (to order an individual released from custody) and an EOIR procedure for carrying out that authority already exists through an appeal and emergency stay request to the Board. See 66 Fed. Reg. at 54909; 8 C.F.R. § 1003.19(i)(1).

increased due process rights. The automatic stay regulation, however, applies to both non-permanent residents and LPRs. Thus, to the extent that the Court feels that the regulation may be constitutional as applied to non-permanent residents (although Petitioner does not believe that to be the case), the regulation is still unconstitutional as applied to LPRs who by their nature have established ties to the United States and, thus, increased due process rights.

ii) Petitioner's Offense was a Misdemeanor and Thus Protection of Public Safety Does Not Justify His Detention

Petitioner was convicted of a misdemeanor offense ten years ago under Cal. Penal § 288a(b)(1) and was sentenced to sixth months for that offense. ZN Dec. at Exh. C. That is his only conviction.[11] Petitioner is eligible for relief from removal pursuant to 8 U.S.C. § 1182(c), INA § 212(c) (1995). See INS v. St. Cyr, 533 U.S. 289, 121 S. Ct. 2271 (2001). Petitioner also would not be barred from adjustment of status for this conviction because it constitutes a "petty offense," and therefore it is not a ground of inadmissibility. See 8 U.S.C. § 1182(a)(2)(A)(ii)(II), INA § 212(a)(2)(A)(ii)(II); see also Matter of Rainford, 20 I. & N. Dec. 598 (BIA 1992) (aliens who are deportable for criminal convictions are able to obtain relief from deportation by re-adjusting their status to that of a lawful permanent resident).[12] Thus, this offense was not an offense that Congress found to be egregious enough to warrant permanent banishment from the United States.[13] Therefore, because Petitioner's offense was only a misdemeanor from ten years ago, and he has had no other convictions before or since, there is no basis for finding that he should be detained to protect the "public from potential harm." See "Executive Office for Immigration Review; Review of Custody Determinations," 66 Fed. Reg. at 54909.

d) The Automatic Stay Regulation Is Ultra Vires and Contrary to the Statute as Authorized by Congress

It is a well-accepted cannon of statutory construction that a Court faced with the task of interpreting a statute must first look to the language of the statute itself for evidence of its meaning. Estate of Cowart v. Nicholas Drilling Co., 205 U.S. 469, 474 (1992); Robinson v. Shell Oil, 519 U.S. 337, 340 (1997). If the statutory language is clear and unambiguous, the Court must cease its analysis and give effect to the "plain meaning" of the words. Robinson, 519 U.S. at 340; Consumer Product Safety Commission v. GTE Sylvania, Inc., 447 U.S. 102, 108 (1980). Furthermore, to the extent that the regulation goes beyond the authority of the statute by effectively eliminating the discretionary authority of Immigration Judges to determine whether an individual may be released, the regulation is ultra vires to INA § 236(a) and is, therefore, invalid. See Romero v. INS, 39 F.3d 977, 980 (9th Cir. 1994); Solid Waste Agency v. United States Army Corps of Eng'rs, 531 U.S. 159, 170-174 (2001).

Under the plain language of 8 U.S.C. § 1226(a), INA § 236(a) whether an individual should be detained during removal proceedings is a discretionary determination. Under § 236(a), the Attorney General – which refers to both DHS and the immigration courts – "may," in the exercise of discretion, decide to continue an

[11] The Immigration Court has not ruled on the question of whether Petitioner is even removable for his conviction, as Petitioner believes that the offense is sufficiently minor to not properly be categorized as an aggravated felony. This question was not at issue in the bond determination, however, as Petitioner was unquestionably eligible for bond.

[12] In addition, Petitioner is not subject to mandatory detention for this offense. See 8 U.S.C. § 1226(c), INA § 236(c). He was released from custody prior to October 9, 1998, the effective date of the mandatory detention provisions. See Matter of Adeniji, 22 I. & N. Dec. 1102 (BIA 1999) (the general provisions of INA § 236(c) does not apply if a respondent was released from criminal custody prior to the expiration of the Transition Period Custody Rules); IIRIRA § 303(b). The government does not claim in its appeal of the judge's bond determination that the judge erred on a question of statutory eligibility for release. Nor could the government do so in good faith. The use of the automatic stay provision to undermine a purely discretionary issue by the Immigration Judge is thus even more unjustified than it would be if statutory eligibility were at issue.

[13] Even the DHS had initially ordered release on bond for $25,000. Dec. of ZN at Exh. D. That order was later cancelled when Petitioner was moved to Arizona.

individual's detention or "may," in the exercise of discretion, decide to release the individual. Accordingly, the plain language of INA § 236(a) clearly states that detention under this provision is discretionary. Ashley v. Ridge, 288 F. Supp. 2d at 665; Bezmen v. Ashcroft, 245 F. Supp. 2d. at 448.

The automatic stay regulation eliminates the discretionary nature of the Immigration Judge's determination (and the authority to order release) and, on its face, is tantamount to a mandatory detention rule. The regulation provides for detention without bond (via the stay of any bond ordered by an Immigration Judge) irrespective of an Immigration Judge's individualized determination that the alien poses neither a danger to the community nor a sufficient flight risk that a bond could not guard against. Pursuant to the regulation, the Immigration Judge's ruling "shall be stayed upon the Service's filing of a Notice of Service's Intent to Appeal Custody Redetermination." 8 C.F.R. § 1003.19(i)(2) (emphasis added). As a result, this regulation gives DHS the unfettered authority to prevent the ordered release of an alien and, therefore, eliminates the effect of any individualized determination by an impartial adjudicator on that issue. See Ashley, 288 F. Supp. 2d 673; Bezmen, 245 F. Supp. 2d at 450.

The regulation, as applied here, has the effect of mandatory detention, even though Congress has specified that individuals, such as Petitioner, are not subject to mandatory detention because they were released from custody prior to October 9, 1998, the expiration date of the Transition Period Custody Rules. See Matter of Adeniji, 22 I. & N. Dec. 1102 (BIA 1999). However, the government's ability to impose mandatory detention on the individual is predetermined because the regulation authorizes such mandatory detention only in cases where DHS has initially decided not to release the individual or has set a bond of $10,000 or more. Bezmen, 245 F. Supp. 2d. at 450 ("Because the INS makes the initial custody and bond determination, the agency effectively predetermines in each individual case its ability to stay any bond ordered by an IJ by making a no release determination or setting bond at $ 10,000 or more.") But in § 236(c), Congress specifically provided for mandatory detention during removal proceedings of noncitizens with certain criminal convictions. Congress specifically exempted noncitizens without those specific criminal convictions from mandatory detention, and specifically created the transition rules for previous convictions. Had Congress intended the phrase "may" in § 236(a) to be construed as providing for mandatory detention, § 236(c) would be redundant. See INS v. Cardoza-Fonseca, 480 U.S. 421, 430-31 (1987) (addressing the proper construction of Congress' use of different language in different sections of the same Act); Lindh v. Murphy, 521 U.S. 320, 329 (1997) ("Nothing. . .but a different intent explains the different treatment [of two chapters of the same Act].").

Thus, as the Ashley Court found, Congress wished to make detention during removal proceedings mandatory only for those individuals subject to subsection (c) (which Petitioner is not):

> Such an application of § 3.19(i)(2) [to make detention mandatory] seems to fly in the face of congressional intent. If Congress wanted to make detention mandatory for all aliens who have committed crimes, it would not have devised the present bifurcated system in which mandatory detention is imposed only on a limited class of aliens, presumably those considered most dangerous. As Congress specifically exempted aliens like Petitioner from the mandatory detention of § 1226(c), it is unlikely that it would have condoned this back-end approach to detaining aliens like Petitioner through the combined use of § 1226(a) and § 3.19(i)(2). Moreover, this "conversion" to mandatory detention is not done through any process resembling a hearing that provides safeguards to ensure its fairness, accuracy and consistency with the Constitution, nor through any required showing of future dangerousness or likelihood of escape, but through the mere filing of a notice of appeal.

Ashley, 288 F. Supp. 2d at 673. Thus, there is no statutory basis that permits DHS to detain individuals, like Petitioner, after an Immigration Judge has conducted an individualized determination and ordered release. As set forth above, the regulation flouts the express language of INA § 236(a) by transforming a discretionary determination by the Immigration Judge into mandatory detention imposed by DHS, and is therefore ultra vires to the statute.

II. CONCLUSION

For all the above reasons, this Court should find that 8 C.F.R. § 1003.19(i)(2) is unlawful and order Petitioner's release from custody.

[Dated:]

Respectfully submitted,

[Attorney for Petitioner]

[ADD CERTIFICATE OF SERVICE]

DECLARATION OF [ATTORNEY]

I, **[Attorney]**, do hereby declare:

1. I am attorney of record for Petitioner Javier Zavala in his immigration case. I have personal knowledge of each matter stated herein. I obtained copies of the documents related to Petitioner's bond hearing (Exhibits A and B) in Arizona from attorney Anthony Pelino, Law Offices of Pelino & Ternieden, P.O. Box 1909, Florence, Arizona, 85232, who appeared on behalf of Petitioner at his bond hearing in Florence, Arizona.

2. Mr. Pelino submitted to my office a copy of the Immigration Judge's decision ordering

Petitioner's release from custody, dated November 21, 2003. To the best of my knowledge, this document was obtained in the courtroom of Immigration Judge Lamonte S. Freerks on November 21, 2003. A copy of that document is attached hereto as Exhibit A.

3. Mr. Pelino submitted to my office a copy of Form EOIR-43 "Notice of INS Intent to Appeal Custody Redetermination" dated November 21, 2003. To the best of my knowledge, this document was obtained from the Department of Homeland Security in Florence, Arizona. A copy of that document is attached hereto as Exhibit B.

4. I received a copy of the Notice to Appear instituting removal proceedings in Petitioner's case. A copy of that notice is attached as Exhibit C.

5. I obtained by facsimile from the Department of Homeland Security a copy of the Department of Homeland Security's order to release Petitioner on a bond of $25,000, dated November 11, 2003, which was issued in San Francisco, California. A copy of that order is attached as Exhibit D.

6. On January 29, 2004, I received from the Department of Homland Security, Office of Chief Counsel, a facsimile of the government's EOIR-26 Notice of Appeal to the Board of Immigration Appeals, Dated December 21, 2003. This was the first time I had seen the notice of appeal in Petitioner's case. Anthony Pelino, Petitioner's counsel in Arizona, informed me that he had never received the E-26 Notice of Appeal. A copy of that notice is attached as Exhibit E.

7. I received from the Immigration Court via regular mail a copy of the Immigration Judge's written decision setting forth the reasons for his November 21, 2003 decision ordering Petitioner's release from custody dated January 14, 2004. A copy of that document is attached hereto as Exhibit F.

I declare under penalty of perjury that the foregoing is true and correct. Executed on this _____ day of _____, 2004 in **[City, State]**.

[Attorney]

[Attorneys]
[Address]
[City, State, and Zip Code]
[Telephone]
[Facsimile]

Attorneys for Petitioner
Javier ZAVALA

UNITED STATES DISTRICT COURT FOR THE NORTHERN DISTRICT OF CALIFORNIA

ZAVALA, Javier Petitioner, v. Tom RIDGE, in his Official Capacity, Secretary Department of Homeland Security, John ASHCROFT, in his Official Capacity, Attorney General Department of Justice Respondents.	)	Case No. C 04-00253 JSW **PETITIONER'S TRAVERSE IN SUPPORT OF PETITION FOR WRIT OF HABEAS CORPUS AND COMPLAINT FOR DECLARATORY AND INJUNCTIVE RELIEF** Date of Hearing: Feb. 27, 2004 Time of Hearing: 9:00 a.m.

TABLE OF CONTENTS

TABLE OF AUTHORITIES
FEDERAL CASES

AGENCY DECISIONS

FEDERAL STATUTES

FEDERAL REGULATIONS

SUMMARY OF ARGUMENT

Petitioner challenges his continued custody by the Department of Homeland Security ("DHS"). Respondents' opposition fails to refute Petitioner's assertion that, under the clear precedent of the Supreme Court and the Ninth Circuit, the "automatic stay" regulation at 8 C.F.R § 1003.19(i)(2) violates both substantive and procedural due process. The automatic stay regulation allows the government to entirely ignore an immigration judge's decision to release an alien on bond by simply filing an appeal to the Board of Immigration Appeals ("BIA"). This regulation implicates a fundamental right and is not narrowly tailored to meet any compelling governmental interest of protecting public safety, because an immigration judge has already rendered a determination that the alien is neither a danger to others nor a flight risk. This regulation therefore violates substantive due process. Moreover, the government does have an option of filing for an emergency stay with the BIA which allows the government to seek—and requires the BIA to consider -- on an individual basis, a stay of an immigration judge's decision granting release from custody. As all the published decisions to consider the question have found, due process requires such an individualized determination. Ashley v. Ridge, 288 F. Supp. 2d 662 (D. N. J. 2003); Uritsky v. Ridge, 286 F. Supp. 2d 842 (E.D. Mich. 2003); Bezmen v. Ashcroft, 245 F. Supp. 2d 446 (D. Conn. 2003). The regulation also violates procedural due process because it permits the government to ignore the decision of a neutral arbiter (the immigration judge), allowing the prosecutory side to unilaterally detain aliens who have been determined not to be flight risks or dangers to the community.

None of Respondents' arguments justify this procedure. The regulation is unconstitutional as applied to all aliens because it prohibits their release from custody while, and even before, an appeal is pending, without affording them an opportunity to defend, on an individualized basis, the immigration judge's determination that they are not dangers to others nor flight risks. For that reason, the regulation is unconstitutional on its face. And Respondents have no response at all to address Petitioner's argument that the regulation is unconstitutional as applied to him because Petitioner is a long-term lawful permanent resident with a single ten year old misdemeanor offense. See, e.g., Landon v. Plasencia, 459 U.S. 21, 33 103 S. Ct. 321, 330 (1982).

I. ARGUMENT

a) Respondents' Attempt to Rebut Petitioner's Argument that the Automatic Stay Regulation, on Its Face, Violates Due Process Is Without Merit

i) Respondents Fail to Apply the Correct Standard in a Substantive Due Process Analysis

Respondents mischaracterize Petitioner's facial due process challenge to the automatic stay regulation by asserting that the challenge is solely based on the amount of time Petitioner has been in custody. As Petitioner stated in his points and authorities in support of his petition, the regulation itself violates due process because it is not narrowly tailored to meet a compelling governmental interest. This is true regardless of how long Petitioner, or any other individual is in custody under the regulation. Because a fundamental liberty interest is at issue, Respondent must demonstrate that the procedure is narrowly tailored to meet a compelling governmental interest. See Reno v. Flores, 507 U.S. 292, 302, 113 S.Ct. 1439 (1993).

Petitioner does not dispute that the government has a compelling governmental interest in protecting public safety and securing removal. As Respondents note, in Zadvydas v. Davis, 533 U.S. 678, 690, 121 S.Ct. 2491 (2001), the Supreme Court did consider whether "special circumstances" existed to keep individuals detained. Res. at 11. However, the Supreme Court did not announce a separate standard for immigration cases that departs from the "strict scrutiny" analysis articulated in Reno v. Flores, 507 U.S. at 302. Rather, the Zadvydas decision follows the traditional "strict scrutiny" analysis that permits governmental infringement on fundamental rights when a special justification outweighs the "individual's constitutionally protected interest in avoiding physical restraint." Zadvydas v. Davis, 533 U.S. at 690 citing Kansas v. Hendricks, 521 U.S. 346, 356, 117 S.Ct. 2072 (1997).

In Kansas v. Hendricks, the Supreme Court found that Kansas' statute requiring involuntary commitment was not unconstitutional because it was narrowly tailored to meet the compelling interest of protecting public safety. 521 U.S. at 364 ("The numerous procedural and evidentiary protections afforded here demonstrate that the Kansas Legislature has taken great care to confine only a narrow class of particularly dangerous individuals, and then only after meeting the strictest procedural standards."). The court found that involuntary civil commitment was constitutional because its purpose was to "hold the person until his mental abnormality no longer causes him to be a threat to others." Id. at 364. The state provision was not even utilized unless there was "proof of more than a mere predisposition to violence; rather, it requires evidence of past sexually violent behavior and a present mental condition that creates a likelihood of such conduct in the future if the person is not incapacitated." Id. at 357. Thus, while the court recognized that there was a fundamental right to be free from physical restraint, there were certain instances when custody is warranted, and an individualized finding of "future dangerousness" was sufficient to meet this exception. Id. at 358.

In Zadvydas v. Davis, 533 U.S. 678, 700, 121 S. Ct. 2491 (2001), the Supreme Court considered a reasonable time period to hold aliens with final orders of removal who were awaiting the execution of their removal orders. The Supreme Court found that indefinite detention, when there was no forseeability that an individual would be removed from the United States, would violate substantive due process. There was "special justification" in detaining individuals with final orders of removal in order to effectuate that removal order. Thus, the court created the six-month requirement so that the government had sufficient time to secure removal, and if more than six months elapsed without a "likelihood of removal in the foreseeable future," then due process required release from custody. Id. After the six-month removal period there was no longer a "special justification" to hold these individuals because there was little to no likelihood of removal. 533 U.S. at 690.

In DeMore v. Kim, 538 U.S. 510, 123 S. Ct. 1708, 1712-13 (2003), the basis for the Supreme Court's finding that mandatory detention at 8 U.S.C. § 1226(c), Immigration and Nationality Act (INA) § 1226(c) was not unconstitutional hinged on the fact that all individuals found to be subject to mandatory detention are preliminary found to be deportable for criminal offenses. Citing the Board's decision in Matter of Joseph, 22 I. & N. Dec. 799 (BIA 1999), the court noted that "[a]t the hearing, the detainee may avoid mandatory detention by demonstrating that he is not an alien, was not convicted of the predicate crime, or that the INS is otherwise substantially unlikely to establish that he is in fact subject to mandatory detention." 538 U.S. at 1713 n.3. Thus, there is an individualized determination that a non-citizen is removable for a criminal conviction.[1] The basis for the Kim decision was the determination that aliens removable or deportable for criminal convictions are more likely to re-offend and are less likely to appear for removal. 538 U.S. at 1715. In contrast, there is no preliminary assessment of removability in cases where the automatic stay is invoked. Nor is there any dangerousness finding that is at least arguably present for one deportable for a criminal offense. Thus, the rationale behind the Kim decision does not apply to these cases because there is no assessment of removability, and no presumption that they are more likely to re-offend or fail to appear for removal. See e.g. Matter of Patel, 15 I. & N. Dec. 666 (BIA 1976).

The Kim decision applied only to individuals removable for criminal convictions. Thus, the Supreme Court determined that Congress had a basis for finding that this limited group of individuals was a danger to the community and a flight risk because they were removable for criminal convictions. Demore v. Kim, 538 U.S. at 1715 (noting that Congress adopted INA § 236(c) because "deportable criminal aliens who remained in the United States often committed more crimes before being removed" and that "more than 20% of deportable criminal aliens failed to appear for their removal hearings."). Conversely, the automatic stay regulation at 8 C.F.R. § 1003.19(i)(2) is not limited to any group that categorically can be defined as a danger to others

[1] In Kim's case, he conceded removability. 538 U.S. at 1713 n.3.

or a flight risk. Rather, it applies to any individual for whom the government has initially denied bond, or set a bond of more than $10,000. There is no support for the proposition that this class of individuals is more likely to commit criminal offenses, or that the individuals are not likely to appear for removal, the issues that the Supreme Court considered justified detention, without an individualized bond hearing, in Kim. And in fact the opposite is true. For every person the DHS subjects to the automatic stay regulation, an immigration judge has already determined that the person is neither a flight risk nor a danger to the community. The automatic stay regulation, however, permits the government to detain an individual throughout the pendency of his immigration proceeding without having to provide any justification for the detention, and in fact permits the government to file frivolous appeals as a procedural mechanism for obtaining ongoing detention. The Constitution simply does not permit such detention.

Applying Kansas v. Hendricks, Zadvydas v. Davis, and DeMore v. Kim to the automatic stay regulation at 8 C.F.R. § 1003.19(i)(2), there is no "special justification" to outweigh the infringement on the fundamental liberty interest of freedom from restraint. There is no doubt that the government has the authority to detain individuals who are dangers to others or flight risks. However, all of the individuals subject to the automatic stay regulation have been found to be neither flight risks nor dangers to others because an immigration judge has ordered their release on bond. The fact that the government disagrees with this assessment does not constitute a "special circumstance" justifying detention, especially when there is already a mechanism in place for the government to stay the IJ's order, the emergency stay at 8 C.F.R. § 1003.19(i)(1).

ii) There is No "Reasonable" Amount of Time for Which Continued Custody May Be Constitutionally Enforced Once There Has Been an Individualized Determination that an Individual is Neither a Flight Risk Nor a Danger to Others

Respondents assert that because Petitioner has "only" been in custody under the automatic stay provision since November 21, 2003, his constitutional rights have not been violated by the regulation. The fact that Petitioner will have been detained for over three months by the time of the hearing in this case, while the petitioners in Bezmen v. Ashcroft, 245 F. Supp. 2d 446 (D. Conn. 2003)) and Ashley v. Ridge, 288 F. Supp.2d 662 (D. N. J. 2003)[2] had been detained for varying amounts of time, is irrelevant to Petitioner's challenge here.[3] The regulation violates due process because it allows the government to continue to detain an alien by ignoring a decision from a neutral immigration judge finding that the individual is not a danger to others nor a flight risk, without it having to obtain an individualized assessment from the BIA on the merits of its appeal. Continued detention under the regulation for even one day violates due process because all individuals subject to this regulation have already been ordered released by an immigration judge, yet they are required to stay in custody during the pendency of the government's appeal to the BIA, and possibly to the Attorney General, without any individualized assessment of the merits of the appeal, or any showing of hardship the government would face if the individual were released from custody.

The six-month "reasonableness" benchmark, articulated in Zadvydas has no applicability here whatsoever. 533 U.S. at 701. In Zadvydas, the court created this six-month period in order to limit indefinite detention for individuals with final orders of removal who could not be removed to other countries. The purpose of this six-month period was to allow the government "a period reasonably necessary to secure removal." Id. at 699. Here, the asserted purpose of the regulation is to protect the public and to prevent an alien from fleeing. However, the regulation only applies to those individuals for whom the immigration judge has ordered an alien's release on bond and, hence, has already made a determination that he or she is not a danger to the public, and has addressed any flight risk concerns by requiring a monetary bond, if appropriate. For that rea-

[2] Respondents also cite Almonte-Vargas v. Elwood, 2002 WL 145155 (E.D. Pa.2002), an unpublished decision cited in the Ashley v. Ridge, 288 F.Supp. 2d. at 674; Res. at 12. Petitioner notes that Local Rule 3-6(e) prohibits the citation of unpublished opinions.

[3] In fact, the petitioner in Ashley had been detained for two months when the court granted his petition for writ of habeas corpus. 288 F.Supp. 2d. at 664. Petitioner has now been detained for over that period.

son, continued detention pursuant to 8 C.F.R. § 1003.19(i)(2) no longer "bears [a] reasonable relation to the purpose for which the individual [was] committed." See e.g. Zadvydas, 533 U.S. at 690. The government cannot unilaterally keep individuals in custody once there has been a finding that they are not dangers to the community or flight risks simply because the government argued for a different outcome and lost. If the government believes the Immigration Judge erred, it has the option of doing what is done in every other legal setting in which a party wishes to appeal a ruling: it can make its pitch to the BIA and request an emergency stay pursuant to 8 C.F.R. § 1003.19(i)(1).

iii) Although the Amount of Time in Custody is Not Determinative of Whether the Automatic Stay Regulation Comports With Due Process, The Fact that the Automatic Stay Regulation Leaves an Individual in Custody Indefinitely Supports Petitioner's Assertion That The Regulation is Not Narrowly Tailored to Meet a Compelling Interest

While one day in detention without individualized review of the government's appeal is too many, contrary to the government's assertions, there is also no finite period of time in which an appeal must be adjudicated, allowing the government to potentially detain all aliens who fall under 8 C.F.R. § 1003.19(i)(2) indefinitely.[4] Respondents assert that, by regulation, an alien is only in custody for a short duration. However, there is no regulation that requires that the alien be released within any definite amount of time.

Citing 8 C.F.R. § 1003.1(e)(8)(i), Respondents state "all appeals assigned to a single judge of the BIA shall be disposed of within 90 days of completion of the record on appeal and all appeals assigned to a three-judge panel of the BIA shall be disposed of within 180 days, 'with a priority for cases or custody appeals involving detained aliens." Res. at 10. Thus, the fact that "the ICE filed a prompt appeal from the IJ's custody decision on December 5, 2003, and the BIA has set a briefing schedule directing the parties to file simultaneous briefs" (Res. at 10), makes Petitioner's case no different from any other alien's because all detained cases are supposed to be expedited, but many sit for months. See e.g. Uritsky v. Ridge, 286 F. Supp. 2d at 843 (petitioner detained on automatic stay for over five months); Bezmen v. Ashcroft, 245 F. Supp. 2d. at 448 (petitioner detained for over six months).[5]

Regardless of Petitioner's individual circumstances, there simply is no assurance that the appeal will be adjudicated in a finite period. The regulation at 8 C.F.R. § 1003.1(e)(8)(i) does not even apply until 90 days after "completion of the record on appeal," and whether this time starts after or before the briefs have been filed is entirely unclear. 8 C.F.R. § 1003.1(e)(8)(i). The same is true for the 180-day period "after an appeal is assigned to a three-member panel." Id. Moreover, the regulations do not make clear when a three-member panel would be assigned. In addition, if there is an "impending decision by the United States Supreme Court or a United States Court of Appeals, or impending Department regulatory amendments, or an impending *en banc* Board decision may substantially determine the outcome of a case or a group of cases pending before the Board," a decision may be stayed indefinitely. 8 C.F.R. § 1003.1(e)(8)(iii). Furthermore, if the government loses at the Board, it can ask for review by the Attorney General ("AG") and the stay is continued indefinitely without any time frame for a decision by the AG. See 8 C.F.R. § 1003.19(i)(2). Lastly, the BIA itself acknowledges that these time restrictions are no more than "internal management directives" that do not create any procedural or substantive rights enforceable in any court of law. 8 C.F.R. § 1003.1(e)(8)(vi).

Thus, there is absolutely no support for Respondents' contention that the amount of time in custody under the automatic stay is unquestionably of limited duration.

---

[4] Respondents also assert that the detention decision is entirely within the alien's control and that Petitioner could avoid detention by simply leaving. Res. at 10. The assertion is absurd. Petitioner cannot be forced to choose between his statutory right to pursue his legal remedies in court and his right to be free from arbitrary detention.

[5] Furthermore, Respondents cannot claim that the ICE's appeal of the IJ's bond determination is "fast-tracked" when the ICE requested a 21-day extension of time to file its brief, and the Board approved this extension even when the motion for extension of time was opposed by Petitioner's counsel. See Supplemental Declaration of **[Attorney]** ("ZN Supp. Dec.") at Exhs. B and C.

iv) This Court Does Not Defer to the Agency When Considering Procedural Challenges

Respondents next argue that this Court should defer to the Attorney General's rationale in exercising his authority over "custody matters." Res. at 9. However, the concept of deference does not apply to non-substantive immigration laws. Zadvydas, 533 U.S. at 695 (stating that the concept of plenary power is "subject to important constitutional limitations"); Detroit Free Press v. Ashcroft, 303 F.3d 681, 685 (6th Cir. 2002) (finding that the categorical closure of immigration hearings to the public violates the first amendment and due process). Respondents cite the Supreme Court's decision in INS v. Aguirre-Aguirre, 526 U.S. 415, 119 S. Ct. 1439 (1999) for authority that deference should apply. Res. at 9. However, Aguirre involved an interpretation of substantive law -- the "interpretation of the serious nonpolitical crime exception adopted by the Attorney General and BIA." 526 U.S. at 423. In this case, Petitioner challenges the constitutionality of a regulation and, therefore, deference does not apply. Zadvydas, 533 U.S. at 695; Ma v. Ashcroft, 257 F.3d 1095,1105 n. 15 (9th Cir. 2001).[6]

b) The Regulation at 8 C.F.R. § 1003.19(i)(2) Is Unconstitutional as Applied to Petitioner

Respondent does not even attempt to refute Petitioner's argument that the regulation is unconstitutional as applied to him because he is a lawful permanent resident and because his misdemeanor offense does not justify his detention. See Pet. Points & Authorities § II.C. In addition, Petitioner also has not conceded removability in his case. See ZN Supp. Dec. at Exh. A. There has also been no preliminary finding of removability in his case. See § I.A.1, supra. Thus, the regulation is unconstitutional as applied to Petitioner because his due process rights as a lawful permanent resident with only a misdemeanor conviction who is eligible for relief from removal, even if found removable, clearly outweigh the government's interests in keeping him detained.

c) The Automatic Stay Regulation Violates Procedural Due Process

Respondents also assert that the automatic stay regulation does not violate procedural due process because 8 C.F.R. § 1003.1(e)(8)(i) imposes time restrictions on the BIA and, thus, to the extent that the regulation renders the immigration judge's decision a "nullity or empty gesture," it does so only "for the brief period necessary for the ICE to appeal the immigration judge's decision to the BIA." Res. at 13.

First, the assertion is inaccurate. The stay applies not until the ICE appeals the immigration judge's decision to the BIA, but until the BIA renders a decision, and possibly until the Attorney General renders a decision. As stated above, this period is indefinite because a case could be submitted to a three-member panel, held in abeyance, extended as a matter of discretion, or certified to the Attorney General. There is simply no assurance that the decision will be rendered in the "brief period" set forth by Respondents.

Next, the assertion—even if true—does nothing to refute Petitioner's arguments that Mathews v. Eldridge, 424 U.S. 319, 335 (1976), requires a finding that the automatic stay regulation violates due process.[7] There is a substantial risk of erroneous deprivation -- here an erroneous finding by the prosecutor who has already lost her argument before the immigration judge that Petitioner is a flight risk and danger to the community and therefore

[6] In addition, Petitioner raises a statutory challenge to the 8 C.F.R. § 1003.19(i)(2) because it conflicts with 8 U.S.C. § 1226(a), INA § 236(a). See § I.D. This Court should not defer to Respondents' interpretation of INA § 236(a) because Congress did not leave a gap for the agency to fill, and the statute is not ambiguous or uncertain. See Castro-Cortez v. INS, 239 F.3d 1037, 1052 (9th Cir. 2001) citing Chevron, U.S.A., Inc. v. Natural Resources Defense Council, 467 U.S. 837, 843-44, 104 S. Ct. 2778 (1984). As stated in § I.D, Congress was clear that mandatory detention applies only under the terms set forth in 8 U.S.C. § 1226(c), INA § 236(c) and, therefore, did not leave the agency the authority to create another class of aliens subject to mandatory detention.

[7] The Mathews v. Eldridge test balances (1) the nature of the private interest affected; (2) the risk of an erroneous deprivation of the interest as a result of the procedures used and the probable value of additional or substitute safeguards; and (3) the government's interest in using its own procedures and the fiscal and administrative burdens entailed by additional or substitute safeguards. 424 U.S. at 335.

should be denied release from custody. The regulation simply casts aside the immigration judge's decision and keeps the alien detained until the BIA, or the Attorney General, has made a decision on appeal. See "Executive Office for Immigration Review; Review of Custody Determinations, Review of Custody Determinations," 66 Fed. Reg. 54909, 54910 (Oct. 31, 2001) ("The purpose of the automatic stay is to allow the Service to maintain the status quo during such time as is necessary for the Service to take a prompt appeal to the Board.").[8]

Such a procedure raises serious due process concerns because of the inherent bias present in the decision maker. The prosecutor in the case who argued to the IJ that Petitioner should not be released (here BICE attorney Amy Martin) is the exact same individual who made the determination that Petitioner should continue to be detained under the automatic stay provision—despite the fact that the IJ rejected her argument in court. See ZN Dec. at Exhs. B and D. This unquestionably raises due process concerns because it impermissibly mixes the prosecutorial and adjudicative functions and, thus, the adjudicator is inherently biased. See Marcello v. Bonds, 349 U.S. 302, 307, 75 S.Ct. 757 (1955) (noting that the special inquiry officer adjudicating over an immigration case cannot also undertake the functions of prosecutor);[9] Morrisey v. Brewer, 408 U.S. 471, 486-7, 92 S. Ct. 2593 (1972) (a parole officer directly involved in decisions has an inherent bias and, thus, due process requires that an objective and neutral evaluator make decisions regarding parole revocation).

Finally, Respondents do not address the fact that the emergency stay procedure at 8 C.F.R. § 1003.19(i)(1) provides for additional safeguards without fiscal and administrative burdens and, thus, is a feasible procedure that meets due process requirements. Mathews v. Eldridge, 424 U.S. at 335. This is the same procedure that aliens must pursue in order to obtain a stay of removal. See 8 C.F.R. § 1003.2(f). The fact that it "takes time to draft the filings" for an emergency stay and "transmit them to the Board in Falls Church, Virginia" simply does not justify automatic mandatory custody for an indefinite time simply because the government disagrees with Immigration Judge's decision regarding custody. See Res. at 8 citing 66 Fed. Reg. at 54910. The BIA has provided for an individual emergency stay, which it adjudicates on an emergency basis that allows the government to make its arguments regarding why an individual should not be released from custody. The Department of Homeland Security, like the government in a criminal case and an alien seeking a stay of deportation, must affirmatively request a stay, and an impartial adjudicator must make an independent evaluation of the government's (1) a probability of success on the merits and the possibility of irreparable harm, or (2) that serious legal questions are raised and the balance of hardships tips sharply in his favor. Andreiu v. Ashcroft, 253 F.3d 477 (9th Cir. 2001). This emergency stay still protects the government's interests, but recognizes an alien's right to an individual determination of his case before he is once again detained.[10]

---

[8] The regulation is even more problematic because is expressly states that the categorical designation of cases subject to the automatic stay is to "avoid the necessity for a case-by case determination of whether a stay should be granted in particular cases." 66 Fed. Reg. at 54910. Thus, even though the immigration judge has made an individualized determination, thereby reducing the risk of erroneous deprivation, the regulation's intent is to avoid any individualized case determination. In effect, the former Immigration and Naturalization Service (now DHS) has promulgated a regulation eliminating the authority of the Executive Office of Immigration Review ("EOIR") (which encompasses the nation's immigration courts) without any input from EOIR even though it is EOIR's authority (to order an individual released from custody) and an EOIR procedure for carrying out that authority already exists through an appeal and emergency stay request to the Board. See 66 Fed. Reg. 54909 (October 31, 2001); 8 C.F.R. § 1003.19(i)(1).

[9] Respondents misstate the Supreme Court's ruling in Marcello v. Bonds. See Res. at 5. Nowhere does the Court state that a single officer may serve both an adjudicative and prosecutorial function. Rather, the decision is premised on the requirement that "the presiding officer did not undertake the functions of prosecutor." 349 U.S. at 306.

[10] Respondents also claim that the regulation ensures a "fair opportunity" to challenge the Immigration Judge's release decision "without the potential danger of releasing an alien who is a threat to national security or the public." DHS, however, already had a "fair opportunity" to prove Petitioner a threat. DHS failed. The Immigration Judge determined that Petitioner is not a threat to national security or the public. The DHS, or any agency for that matter, may not override and ignore courts' orders whenever they disagree with them. Yet, under the automatic stay regulation, that is exactly what DHS has authorized itself to do.

d) The Automatic Stay Regulation Is Contrary to the Statute as Authorized by Congress

The automatic stay provision violates the plain language of 8 U.S.C. § 1226, INA § 236 and defies Congressional intent. INA § 236(a) authorizes the discretionary detention of individuals who are not otherwise subject to mandatory detention under INA § 236(c). As set forth in Pet. Hab. P&A § II.D, however, the automatic stay regulation implicitly creates a second category of individuals subject to mandatory detention. Ironically, unlike the individuals subject to mandatory detention under INA § 236(c) who are potentially dangerous due to their criminal convictions, individuals subject to detention under 8 C.F.R. § 1003.19(i)(2) have been found by an Immigration Judge not to be dangerous. If Congress intended detention under INA § 236(a) to be mandatory, the mandatory detention provision of INA § 236(c) would be redundant. Not surprisingly, Respondents have not—and cannot—offer any response to this argument.

Respondents claim that 8 C.F.R. § 1003.19(i)(2) is rationally related to the detention during removal proceedings under INA § 236(c) that was upheld in Demore v. Kim, supra. But Petitioner's detention pursuant to a regulation is not premised on any statutory authority as it was in Kim. That it is not unconstitutional for Congress to authorize mandatory detention of criminal aliens is separate and distinct from the inquiry here, i.e. whether the Constitution and the INA authorize an agency to impose mandatory detention where Congress has spoken on the issue and has not chosen to designate this class of persons for mandatory detention. Thus, there is no rationale for, as Respondents suggest, presumptively extending the Supreme Court's interpretation of the mandatory detention provision in INA § 236(c) to encompass a discretionary detention provision.[11]

II. CONCLUSION

For all the above reasons, this Court should find that 8 C.F.R. § 1003.19(i)(2) is unlawful and order Petitioner's release from custody.

[Dated:]

Respectfully submitted,

[Attorney for Petitioner]

[ADD CERTIFICATE OF SERVICE]

[11] The regulation is therefore "arbitrary, capricious, and manifestly contrary to the statute" because Congress has directly addressed the issue of what class of people shall be subject to mandatory detention. Romero v. INS, 39 F.3d 977, 980 (9th Cir. 1994).

UNITED STATES DISTRICT COURT
FOR THE DISTRICT OF COLORADO

John SMITH	)	
Petitioner	)	**Civ. No._____________**
	)	
	)	**Agency No. 25 074 582**
	)	
v.	)	**PETITION FOR WRIT**
	)	**OF HABEAS CORPUS**
	)	
Douglas MAURER, Field Director, Bureau	)	
of Immigration and Customs Enforcement	)	
("ICE") Denver District; Michael	)	
CHERTOFF, Secretary of the Department	)	
of Homeland Security (DHS); and Michael	)	
J. GARCIA, Assistant Secretary,	)	
Department Of Homeland Security (ICE);	)	
Alberto GONZALES, Attorney General,	)	
United States of America[1]	)	
	)	
Respondents	)	
	)	

PETITION FOR WRIT OF HABEAS CORPUS AND COMPLAINT FOR DECLARATORY AND INJUNCTIVE RELIEF

Petitioner, John Smith (hereinafter, "Petitioner" or "Mr. Smith"), by and through undersigned counsel, hereby respectfully moves this Honorable Court for a writ of habeas corpus and Declaratory and Injunctive Order ordering Immigration and Customs Enforcement (hereinafter, "ICE") to order his immediate release from custody pursuant to the Immigration Judge's bond order issued on October 31, 2003, setting bond in the amount of $5,000.00 and declaring the provisions of 8 C.F.R. §1003.19(i)(2) unconstitutional as applied to the Petitioner and John Ashcroft's Operation Predator directive regarding automatic stays of bond decisions to be unconstitutional as applied to Petitioner.

CUSTODY

1. Mr. Smith is in the physical custody of U.S. Immigration and Customs Enforcement, (hereinafter, "ICE"). His immediate custodian is Douglas Maurer, Field Director of the Detention and Removal Section of ICE for the Denver District. Mr. Smith is detained at the Wackenhutt/ICE Detention Facility, Aurora, Colorado, at 11901

[1] Alberto Gonzales is listed as the current Attorney General, however, John Ashcroft was the Attorney General during the implementation of "Operation Predator." As a result, Mr. Ashcroft is referenced in the Petition.

East 30th Street, Aurora, CO. ICE has contracted with the detention facility to house immigration detainees such as Mr. Smith. He is under the direct control of Respondent Maurer and his agents. When originally detained, Mr. Maurer issued a "no-bond" hold on Mr. Smith, pursuant to Attorney General John Ashcroft's mandate in the "Operation Predator" directives. (See Exhibit 1, Press Release on Operation Predator from the ICE website at *www.ice.gov*; see also attached memo from the American Immigration Lawyers Association Website confirming the memo, available at *www.aila.org*) (Exhibit 2, Bond Order from ICE). His case was flagged as an Operation Predator case. Subsequently, at a bond redetermination hearing on October 31, 2003, the Immigration Judge redetermined the bond and set bond in the amount of $5,000.00. (Exhibit 3, Order of the Immigration Judge). ICE filed form EOIR-43 with the Immigration Judge the same day and requested that the immigration judge stay the custody redetermination pending an appeal of such redetermination to the Board of Immigration Appeals. (Exhibit 4, Form EOIR 43). The form cites former section 242(a)(2) of the Immigration Nationality Act, 8 U.S.C. §1252(a)(2)(as in effect prior to April 1, 1997), Section 303(b)(3)(A) of Div. C. of Pub. L. No. 104-208 (referring to the Transitional Period Custody Rules in place between April 1, 1997 and October 9, 1998), and Section 236(c)(1) of the current Immigration and Nationality Act, 8 U.S.C. §1226(c)(1) (in place for those released from custody after October 9, 1998), as authority for ICE to stay the judge's decision. (Exhibit 4, Form EOIR-43). The form also cites DHS regulations at 8 C.F.R. §1003.19(i)(2). (Exhibit 4, Form EOIR-43). None of these statutory or regulatory sections apply to the Petitioner as Petitioner was released from custodial confinement in 1992 and was not placed into proceedings until October of 2003. *Matter of Adeniji*, 22 I&N Dec. 1102 (BIA 1999) ("Respondent is not subject to mandatory detention under section 236(c) of the Act because he was released from his non-Service custodial setting (i.e. from criminal custody) prior to the expiration of the Transition Rules.") (Exhibit 15 *Matter of Adeniji*).

JURISDICTION AND VENUE

2. This action arises under the Constitution of the United States, the Immigration and Nationality Act ("INA"), 8 U.S.C. §1101 et seq., and the Administrative Procedures Act ("APA"), 5 U.S.C. §701 et. seq. This Court has jurisdiction under 28 U.S.C. §2241 (c)(1) and (3), Article 1, Section 9, Clause 2 of the United States Constitution, 28 U.S.C. §1651 (relating to necessary Writs), §2201 (relating to Courts' ability to fashion appropriate remedies), and §2202 (relating to Courts' ability to fashion appropriate remedies). Mr. Smith is presently in custody under color of the authority of the United States, and such custody is in violation of the Constitution, laws, or treaties of the United States. Because Mr. Smith also seeks declaratory and injunctive relief, Petitioners also rely on F.R. Civ. P. 57.

3. Mr. Smith is "in custody" for purposes of habeas corpus under 28 U.S.C. §2241. Habeas corpus review remains despite the jurisdiction-stripping provisions of the Illegal Immigration Reform and Immigrant Responsibility Act of 1996, Pub. L. No. 104-208, 110 Stat. 3009. *See, e.g., INS v. St. Cyr*, 533 U.S. 289 (2001), *Zadvydas v. Davis*, 533 U.S. 678 (2001); *Calcano-Martinez v. INS*, 533 U.S. 348 (2001); *Riley v. INS*, 310 F.3d 1253, 1257 (10th Cir. 2002); *Jurado-Gutierrez v. Greene*, 190 F.3d 1135 (10th Cir. 1999). Habeas remains for detention challenges despite the jurisdiction stripping provisions of REAL ID, Pub. L. No. 109-13. This Court may grant relief pursuant to 28 U.S.C. §2241, the APA, the Declaratory Judgment Act, 28 U.S.C. §2201 et. seq., and the All Writs Act, 28 U.S.C. §1651, as well as 28 U.S.C. §1350 and F.R. Civ. P. 57.

4. Courts have also held that they have the jurisdiction to determine if they have jurisdiction. *Singh v. Reno*, 182 F.3d 504, 509 (7th Cir. 1999).

5. This Petition is also not precluded by Section 1226(e) which states that the "Attorney General's discretionary judgment regarding the application of this section shall not be subject to review." Just because ICE disagrees with the Immigration Judge's bond decision does not render the application of the stay an exercise of discretion. ICE cannot equate the Attorney General's discretion with the District Director of ICE's discretion. The two are not interchangeable. Although the District Director of ICE is a subordinate agent of the Attorney General, so is the Immigration Judge. In that capacity, the Immigration Judges also have discre-

tion to make determinations as to bond as delegates of the Attorney General. 8 C.F.R. §1003.19(a). *Almonte-Vargas v. Elwood*, 2002 U.S. Dist. LEXIS 12387 at 12-13 n.8.

6. In addition, this petition does not challenge the review of the ICE exercise of discretion, but rather the unconstitutional procedures for the stay which subject an individual to automatic detention, mandated without statutory authority and therefore are *ultra vires*, and not subject to appeal. Here the Habeas petition challenges the applicability and constitutionality of the ICE detention regulations at 8 C.F.R. 1003.19 as well as Ashcroft's detention mandates under "Operation Predator" to detain individuals without bond and seek automatic stays and appeals on all cases regardless of the merits of such appeals or stays.

7. While the decision to file a stay of a bond order may be construed as a discretionary determination, the Attorney General's implementation of "Operation Predator" mandates that anyone arrested under "Operation Predator" is to be held without bond, and that if the Immigration Judge redetermines such bond, that the ICE trial attorney is to automatically appeal such determination and request an immediate stay. Because the policy is a mandate from the Attorney General, there is no discretion involved, and no ability on the part of the detainee to prove that he is not a flight risk or danger. As such the issue is not one that involves discretion. *See, e.g., Zadvydas v. Davis*, 533 U.S. 678, 689 (2001) ("Were the INS, in an arbitrary or categorical manner, to deny an alien access to the administrative processes in place to review continued detention, habeas jurisdiction would lie to redress the due process violation caused by the denial of the mandated procedures under 8 CFR §241.4 (2001)"); *Dhangu v. INS*, 812 F.2d 455, 457-459 (9th Cir. 1987).

8. Venue for the purposes of habeas corpus lies in the United States District Court for the District of Colorado, the judicial district in which Mr. Doug Maurer, Field Director for Detention and Removal, Immigration and Customs Enforcement, resides. 28 U.S.C. §1391(e).

9. It is also the jurisdiction where petitioner is in custody, and where ICE ordered petitioner to appear before an immigration judge and all substantial events in this litigation occurred.

PARTIES AND PROCEDURAL POSTURE

10. Mr. Smith is a 48-year-old longtime lawful permanent resident of the United States. He was born in Vientiane, Laos, on February 2, 1955, the second of 13 children. His father was a captain in the army and when the Communist Party took over Laos, his father went "underground" to fight the communist occupation. Mr. Smith was accused by the communist government of communicating with his father and was threatened to be "locked up forever." As a result, he left his family and went into the forest. His wife was four months pregnant when he left. He spent 3 months in the forests of Laos with his father then spent 3 days and 3 nights to escape Laos and cross a river to a refugee camp in Thailand. His father was captured and beaten to death when he went back to Laos to bring over the rest of the family. It was one full year before his wife, mother and siblings were able to escape and join him at the refugee camp. The family waited an additional three years before obtaining official permission to enter the United States as refugees. He and the rest of his family were admitted to the United States as lawful permanent residents on September 8, 1980 as lawful permanent residents. (Exhibit 5, Notice to Appear at allegation 3). Since that time he has never left the United States.

11. He has one United States Citizen son and one lawful permanent resident son, ages 21 and 25. (Exhibit 6, Birth Certificate of Lona Smith and Social Security Card and Resident Alien Card for Nola Smith). His youngest son is a soldier serving the United States in the Iraq War. (Exhibit 7, Letter of Support from Lona Smith). He owns his own home, (Exhibit 8, Home Loan Statement) has been working for the same employer since 1995, (Exhibit 9, Employer letter), and has a retirement savings account in the amount of $22,000.00. (Exhibit 10, Retirement account). His 70-year-old mother who came to the United States with him as a refugee is now a United States Citizen and she lives with Mr. Smith. He is responsible for her financial and medical care and drives her to all of her medical appointments. (Exhibit 11, Letter of Support from brother Boupone Smith).

12. He married his current wife while still in Laos in 1977. At the time of the marriage, his wife was 15 years old. This was acceptable in the Laotian culture. He remains married to the same wife today.

13. On May 20, 1992, Mr. Smith was convicted in the District Court of the Fourth Judicial District of the State of Idaho for the offense of Statutory Rape in violation of Idaho Code section 18-6101(1). (Exhibit 12, Court Print out of Conviction Record). The court retained jurisdiction on sentencing and on November 15, 1992, the court accepted the recommendations of the Department of Corrections that he be placed on supervised probation for a period of five years. (Exhibit 12, Court Print out of Conviction Record). Because of compliance with probation, his probation was changed to unsupervised probation on August 28, 1995. (Exhibit 13, Order for Change in Probation Status).

14. On October 15, 2003, over 11 years from the date of conviction for this offense, Mr. Smith was arrested by ICE agents pursuant to "Operation Predator" and was forcibly transferred from Idaho to Denver for detention pending removal proceedings. On October 15, 2003, he was issued a Notice to Appear in removal proceedings which charges him as an aggravated felon under INA section 101(a)(43)(F), 8 U.S.C. §1101(a)(43)(F) for a crime of violence for which the sentence served was at least one year. (Exhibit 5, NTA). ICE set his bond at "no bond."

15. On October 31, 2003, Mr. Smith, through counsel submitted a Motion for Bond Redetermination with supporting documents requesting that the bond be lowered. (Exhibit 14, Bond Motion and Supporting Documents). The Immigration Judge subsequently re-determined bond and set a bond in the amount of $5,000.00. (Exhibit 3, Judge's Bond Order).

16. The same day, the trial attorney for ICE filed form EOIR-43 with the Executive Office for Immigration Review seeking an "automatic" stay of the Immigration Judge's custody decision. The form states, "The Immigration and Naturalization Service asserts that the respondent is subject to section 242(a)(2) of the Immigration and Nationality Act (INA) (as in effect prior to April 1, 1997), section 303(b)(3)(A) of Div. C. of Public Law 104-208, or section 236(c)(1) of the INA. (Exhibit 4, Form EOIR-43).

17. Mr. Smith is not subject to any of these provisions of law. Section 242(a)(2) was repealed by the Illegal Immigration Reform and Immigrant Responsibility Act of 1996 ("IIRIRA") and would only apply to those individuals who were in removal proceedings prior to the effective date of IIRIRA. *See* §303(b)(1) of IIRIRA, Pub. L. No. 104-208, 110 Stat. 3009. Section 303(b)(3)(A), the Transitional Period Custody Rules, do not apply because the section states that the Transitional rules "shall be in effect for a 1-year period beginning on the date of such notification, instead of such section or such amendments... After the end of such 1-year or 2-year periods, the provisions of such section 236(c) shall apply to individuals released after such periods." Thus, the Transitional Period Custody Rules were in effect for those in custody during the one year period between October 9, 1997 and October 9, 1998. After October 9, 1998, 1226(c) came into effect. Nevertheless, 1226(c) does not apply to the Petitioner since 1226(c) only applies to those individuals "released" from physical custody after the Transitional Period Custody Rules expired (October 9, 1998). *Matter of Adeniji*, 22 I&N Dec. 1102 (BIA 1999) (attached at exhibit 15); *Velasquez v. Reno*, 37 F. Supp. 2d 663, 670 (D.N.J. 1999); *Alwaday v. Beebe*, 43 F. Supp. 2d 1130 (D.C. Or. 1999); *Kiareldeen v. Reno*, 71 F. Supp. 2d 402 (D.N.J. 1999). Mr. Smith was released from physical custody in May of 1992 and was released from probation in 1997, well before the effective date of 236(c).

18. In cases not subject to 8 U.S.C. §1226(c) in which the defendant is released from custody prior to the expiration of the Transitional Period Custody Rules at §303(b)(1) of IIRIRA, the Immigration Court should apply the general custody provisions at 8 U.S.C. §1226(a). *Matter of Adeniji*, 22 I&N Dec. 1102 (BIA 1999). The judge correctly applied 8 U.S.C. §1226(a) in this matter and redetermined bond to the amount of $5,000.00.

19. To the extent that ICE is relying on the regulations at 8 C.F.R. §3.19(i)(2) to enforce the automatic stay in this case, such authority is *ultra vires* there being no statutory authority for the stay regulation or the directive from Operation Predator.

EXHAUSTION OF REMEDIES

20. Mr. Smith has exhausted his administrative remedies to the extent required by law, and his only remedy is by way of judicial action.

21. There is no statutory exhaustion requirement for judicial challenges to INS custody. *Tam v. INS*, 14 F. Supp. 2d 1184, 1189 (E.D. Cal. 1998)("Congress has not specifically mandated exhaustion before judicial review of [INS] custody determination").

22. *McCarthy v. Madigan* specifically provides that where Congress has not clearly required exhaustion, "sound judicial discretion governs." *McCarthy v. Madigan*, 503 U.S. 140, 144 (1992). It is within the sound judicial discretion of this Honorable Court to entertain Mr. Smith's Writ and Petition.

23. Exhaustion is not required where (1) available remedies provide no genuine opportunity for adequate relief; (2) irreparable injury may occur without immediate judicial relief; (3) administrative appeal would be futile; and (4) in certain instances a plaintiff has raised a substantial constitutional question," *Howell v. INS*, 72 F.3d 288, 291 (2d Cir. 1995). All four circumstances are present in this case.

24. Exhaustion may be excused if "the interest of the individual in retaining prompt access to a federal judicial forum [outweighs] countervailing institutional interests favoring exhaustion." *McCarthy*, 503 U.S. at 146.

25. There are no available remedies which provide adequate relief. First, there is no statutory authority for an automatic stay. As such, there is no statutory provision for appealing such a stay. Second, although there is regulatory authority for ICE to seek a stay, there is no regulatory provision for appealing such a decision. In fact, if ICE is overturned on appeal, the regulations provide that ICE may seek further review by having the stay decision certified directly to the Attorney General for further review. 8 C.F.R. §1003.19(i)(2). There is no available challenge to such unbridled power.

26. The Petitioner does not have alternative or fully adequate remedies, judicial or administrative, available to him. He has exhausted all possible remedies and he is not entitled to maintain a suit or appeal on these issues in any other forum.

27. Petitioner has made prior application for bond to the Immigration Court. The judge redetermined bond and set such bond at $5000.00.

28. While the Petitioner does not contest ICE's authority to appeal such determination to the Board of Immigration Appeals, Petitioner contends that the automatic stay pending such an appeal is a violation of his procedural and substantive due process and without any statutory authority. Such an appeal will take an indefinite amount of time and removal proceedings in this case will proceed during that time while Petitioner remains in custody. Even if the BIA overturns the stay, ICE can request that the stay decision be certified to the Attorney General for further review thus impeding the Petitioner's release for yet additional indeterminate time.

29. Furthermore, this petition presents compelling constitutional arguments that are not even addressable by the BIA. "Where the administrative forum would provide no real opportunity to present the constitutional issues . . . requiring exhaustion makes little sense." *Legalization Assistance Project v. INS*, 976 F.2d 1198, 1203 (9th Cir. 1992). Appeal to the BIA will provide no real opportunity to present the constitutional issues of due process, *ultra vires* agency action, and abuse of discretion. The BIA cannot rule on constitutional issues. Justice requires that the habeas petition with respect to the detention and due process issues be heard now.

30. At least one other district court has found that a constitutional challenge to the automatic stay provision is exactly the kind of challenge that the BIA cannot resolve. *Ashley v. Ridge*, Civ. Act. No. 03-4078 (JLL), 2003 U.S. Dist. LEXIS 19335 (D.N.J. Oct. 29, 2003) ("Petitioner is challenging . . . the automatic stay provision itself . . . The constitutionality of this regulation will not (and in fact cannot) be resolved on administrative appeal to the BIA. Therefore, Petitioner will find no recourse on this particular constitutional claim through administrative mechanisms.").

31. Mr. Smith has exhausted his administrative remedies on the detention issues to the extent required by law, and his only remedy is by way of judicial action.

32. Mr. Smith suffers irreparable injury every day in the form of his loss of liberty. He has been separated from his family in a scheme that spurns the human discipline of individualized custody hearings, and penalizes him for pursuing claims against deportation. Mandatory detention does cause irreparable injury by making Mr. Smith face the indefinite loss of income which is necessary to help support his family. His wife and daughter are deprived of his financial and physical support. He also suffers irreparable injury by missing out on unquantifiable but grievous harms such as missing family events, birthdays, and possibly deaths.

33. This court should find that Mr. Smith has exhausted all possible administrative remedies, and that further exhaustion would be futile as there are no adequate and available remedies at the administrative level, that irreparable injury will occur if not addressed by the court, and that this case presents substantial constitutional questions not addressable through normal administrative channels.

LEGAL BACKGROUND

I. ICE's use of the "automatic stay" pursuant to "Operation Predator" and Petitioner's continued detention pending appeal of the bond decision in this matter is illegal, without statutory authority and unconstitutional

34. Mr. Smith realleges and incorporates by reference each and every allegation in paragraphs 1 through 33 as if incorporated fully herein.

35. Mr. Smith has been provided an individualized hearing before an immigration judge on whether or not Mr. Smith is a flight risk or a danger to the community as required by long standing Board of Immigration Appeals precedent as well as the statute at §1226(a). *Carlson v. Landon*, 243 U.S. 524 (1952); *Matter of Patel,* 15 I&N Dec. 666 (BIA 1976); *Matter of Moise*, 12 I&N Dec. 102 (BIA 1967); *Matter of S-Y-L*, 9 I&N Dec. 575 (BIA 1962).

36. After assessing the positive and negative equities in the case, the Immigration Judge properly determined that bond should be redetermined to $5,000.00. As the trier of fact, the Immigration Judge is in the best position to determine the flight risk and danger potential of the applicant and set bond, and such determination should not be unilaterally thwarted by ICE through an *ultra vires* regulation without statutory authority.

37. The government's principle justifications for the automatic stay are ensuring the presence of criminal aliens at their removal proceedings and protecting the public from dangerous criminal aliens.

38. Mr. Smith is not a flight risk, nor is he a hazard to the public. He entered the United States at the age of 25 and is a long time lawful permanent resident, with a lawful permanent resident wife and two U.S. citizen children. He has resided in the same state for most of his time in the United States. Many of his siblings are either citizens, or legal permanent residents. He has an employer who is awaiting his return to work. Although he has been convicted of a serious offense, he contends that the relationship between him and the victim was consensual. His probation was terminated early, and he has had no other contact with law enforcement since. Mr. Smith has completed all the requirements of his probation.

The Supreme Court strongly disfavors mandatory detention.

> A statute permitting indefinite detention of an alien would raise a serious constitutional problem The Fifth Amendment's Due Process Clause forbids the Government to "deprive" any "person...of...liberty...without due process of law." Freedom from imprisonment -- from government custody, detention, or other forms of physical restraint – lies at the heart of the liberty that Clause protects.

39. *Zadvydas v. Davis,* 533 U.S. 678, 690 (2001). *See also Foucha v. Louisiana,* 504 U.S. 71, 80 (1992).

40. Although the Supreme Court determined in *Demore v. Kim,* 123 S.Ct. 1708 (2003) that mandatory detention during removal proceedings is constitutionally permissible, Id. at 1721-22, the Court was interpreting the provisions of 236(c); 8 U.S.C. §1226(c), which authorize mandatory detention for those released from custody after the expiration of the Transitional Period Custody Rules, (October 9, 1998). Because Mr. Smith was released from custody well before the effective date of 1226(c), the Court's decision in *Demore* is inapplicable. Mr. Smith is not subject to the provisions of 1226(c). Rather, his detention is governed by 1226(a). *Matter of Adeniji,* 22 I&N Dec. 1102 (BIA 1999).

41. As a result, Mr. Smith's mandatory detention in this matter is not mandated by any statute. Rather, his detention stems from a field memo from the Attorney General to field agents instructing them to file automatic stays in all cases in which a judge has determined that an individual is not subject to 1226(c), and is, in fact entitled to bond. Further, his mandatory detention is a creature of the ICE's exercise of the automatic stay provisions at 8 C.F.R. §`003.19(i)(2) which effectively allows ICE to bypass 1226(a) which authorizes release and to secure the mandatory detention of anyone regardless of whether they are subject to 1226(c). *Almonte-Vargas v. Elwood,* Civ. Act. No. 02-CV-2666, 2002 U.S. Dist. LEXIS 12387 (E.D. Pa. June 28, 2002) ("It is the operation of the appeal and automatic stay, and not §1226(c) that is technically responsible for her continued detention.").

42. The Ashcroft Operation and the automatic stay provisions essentially make the statute at 8 U.S.C. §1226(a) and the individualized bond procedure meaningless. The automatic stay applies in any case in which the original bond set by ICE is $10,000.00 or higher. 8 C.F.R. §1003.19(i)(2). If the Immigration Judge through an individualized bond hearing later sets the bond at less than the original amount, ICE can enjoin the ability to post the bond by filing an appeal and automatic stay.

43. Through a field directive, Attorney General Ashcroft has mandated that all individuals arrested under Operation Predator be held without bond. Further, he has mandated that if the immigration judge redetermines bond that ICE is required to appeal and stay all decisions. Because ICE has the original ability to set bond in the first instance, ICE ultimately has the power to trump any individualized bond determination simply by setting the bond higher than $10,000 in the first instance. Attorney General Ashcroft has effectively predetermined the mandatory detention of each individual case by mandating that the bond be set higher than $10,000.00 in the first instance. *Bezman v. Ashcroft,* 245 F. Supp. 2d 446, 450 (D. Ct. 2003). This has the effect of mooting any bond determination since ICE then has the ability to stay the bond decision by seeking a stay. "Due process is not satisfied where the individualized custody determination afforded to Petitioner was effectively a charade." *Almonte-Vargas v. Elwood,* 2002 U.S. Dist. LEXIS 123897, at 5. "In effect, the automatic stay provision renders the Immigration Judge's bail determination an empty gesture." *Ashley v. Ridge,* 2003 U.S. Dist. LEXIS 19335, at 16.

44. In addition, there is no definite termination point during which an individual can continue to be detained while the BIA and Attorney General decide the appeal. The regulation at 8 C.F.R. §1003.19(i)(2) contains definite time requirements for the filing of the stay and appeal, but contains no time limits with regard to when the BIA or Attorney General must render a decision on the stay or appeal. This distinguishes the case from the Supreme Court decision in *Demore v. Kim*. Even in *Demore v. Kim*, the Supreme Court stated that there were certain circumstances under which mandatory detention pending removal would become constitutionally impermissible.

45. First, the Court in *Kim* discussed the availability of a *Matter of Joseph* hearing in which the detainee was entitled to demonstrate that he is not subject to mandatory detention under section 1226(c). *Kim,* 123 S.Ct. at 1713 n. 2. The Respondent in *Kim* had specifically foregone this process. However, in the present case, Petitioner actually requested and received a hearing to discuss his release that was later nullified by the automatic stay provision. Ashley v. Ridge, 2003 U.S. Dist. LEXIS at 28-29. It is not clear that *Kim* would have been decided the same way had the issue been the section 3.19(i)(2) stay provision under which even if an Immigration Judge finds that an individual is entitled to be released, ICE stays that decision unilaterally. *Id.* at 29.

46. The Court in *Kim* also expressed serious concerns regarding the time limitations in detention schemes. The Court stated, "Congress . . . may require that persons . . . be detained for the brief period necessary for their removal proceedings." *Kim*, 123 S.Ct. at 1712. The time limitation has been a consistent concern of the Court in addressing detention without bond. *Zadvydas v. Davis*, 533 U.S. at 690 ("a statute permitting indefinite detention would raise a serious constitutional problem"); *Reno v. Flores*, 507 U.S. 292 , 314 (1993) (noting that juveniles would remain in custody only an average of 30 days, and that individual abuses would be remedied through habeas). In the present case, there is no statute even authorizing the automatic stay. It is authorized by ICE regulation and by Ashcroft directives. Significantly, there is absolutely no time limitation to the amount of time the BIA and Attorney General may take in deciding the appeal and stay.

47. The cases addressing the automatic stay confirm that the period can be as much as or more than six months. Ashley v. Ridge, 2003 U.S. Dist. LEXIS 19335 (August 19, 2003 to October 29, 2003 when the Court vacated the stay); *Bezman v. Ashcroft*, 245 F. Supp. 2d 446 (July 31, 2002 to February 21, 2003 when the Court vacated the stay); *Uritsky v. Ridge*, 2003 U.S. Dist. LEXIS 17698 (April 3, 2003 to September 29, 2003 when the Court vacated the stay); *Almonte-Vargas v. Elwood*, 2002 U.S. Dist. LEXIS 12387 (February 27, 2002 to June 28, 2002 when the Court vacated the stay); *Grant v. Zemski*, 54 F. Supp. 2d 437, 439 (E.D. Pa. 1999) (noting that BIA appeals of detention decisions can take three to six months).

48. As a lawful permanent resident of the United States, Mr. Smith is protected by every clause of the United States Constitution that is not expressly reserved to its citizens. This protection includes the Due Process Clause of the Fifth Amendment, which provides that "[n]o person shall be . . . deprived of life, liberty, or property, without due process of law," U.S. Const. amend. V. *e.g., Plyler v. Doe*, 457 U.S. 202, 210 (1987); *Mathews v. Diaz*, 426 U.S. 67 (1976); *Yamataya v. Fisher*, 189 U.S. 86 (1903).

49. "Freedom from bodily restraint has always been at the core of the liberty protected by the Due Process Clause from arbitrary governmental action." *Foucha v. Louisiana*, 504 U.S. 71, 80 (1992). This vital liberty interest is at stake when an individual is subject to detention by ICE. *St. John v. McElroy*, 917 F. Supp. 243, 250 (S.D.N.Y. 1996) ("[T]he private interest affected is St. John's liberty interest, which is of the highest constitutional import."); *Leader v. Blackman*, 744 F. Supp. 500, 509 (S.D.N.Y. 1990); see also *Doherty v. Thornburgh*, 943 F.2d 204, 208 (2d Cir. 1991) (finding that even aliens unlawfully present in the U.S. have a "substantive Due Process right to liberty during deportation proceedings"), cert. dismissed, *Doherty v. Barr*, 503 U.S. 901 (1992).

50. Substantive Due Process requires that detention authorized for non-punitive purposes not be "excessive in relation to the regulatory goal Congress sought to achieve." *United States v. Salerno*, 481 U.S. 739, 747 (1987). "Governmental detention in civil proceedings is only permissible in 'certain special and narrow non-punitive circumstances . . . where a special justification, such as harm-threatening mental illness, outweighs the individual's constitutionally protected interest in avoiding physical restraint.'" *Bezmen v. Ashcroft*, No. 3:02cv1389 (JBA), 254 F. Supp. 2d 446, 449 (D. Ct. 2003) citing *Zadvydas v. Davis*, 533 U.S. at 693.

51. An alien generally is not and should not be detained or required to post bond except on a finding that he is a threat to the national security, *Carlson v. Landon*, 243 U.S. 524, (1952), or that he is a poor bail risk, *Matter of Moise*, 12 I&N Dec.102 (BIA 1967); *Matter of S-Y-L*, 9 I&N Dec.575 (BIA 1962).

52. This denial of the ability to post the bond is a due process violation that has destroyed the fundamental fairness of the proceedings because the Petitioner has been denied his right to be free from custody pending his application for 212(c) relief and has been subject to mandatory detention with no statutory authority. His detention pending removal separates him from his family and his job and impedes his full ability to prepare his case by being outside detention to gather evidence and prepare a full defense to removability. His detention also impedes his access to counsel.

53. "[E]ven a short period of parole before final resolution of his removal proceeding would be significant, because even a short-term separation from family members is a deprivation which the Supreme Court has re-

peatedly ranked high among the interests of the individual." *Koifman v. Zemski*, 2001 U.S. Dist. LEXIS 15742 (E.D. Pa. 2001).

54. In *Bridges v. Wixon*, the Supreme Court emphasized the importance of strictly protecting the alien's right to procedural due process:

> Here the liberty interest of an individual is at stake . . . We are dealing here with procedural requirements prescribed for the protection of the alien. Thought deportation is not technically a criminal proceeding, it visits a great hardship on the individual and deprives him of the right to stay and live and work in this land of freedom. That deportation is a penalty—at times a most serious one—cannot be doubted. Meticulous care must be exercised lest the procedure by which he is deprived of that liberty not meet the essential standards of fairness.

Bridges v. Wixon, 326 U.S. 135, 154 (1945). Aliens have a statutory right to full access and representation by counsel, at their own expense in deportation proceedings. INA §292; 8 U.S.C. §1326 (2001). That right is an integral part of the procedural due process to which an alien is entitled. *Saakian v. INS*, 252 F.3d 21, 24-25 (1st Cir 2001), *citing Batanic v. INS*, 12 F.3d 662, 667 (7th Cir. 1993).

55. This Court has held that a due process violation occurs if the alien can demonstrate prejudice which implicates the fundamental fairness of the proceeding. *Michelson v. INS,* 897 F.2d 465, 468; *See also Lozada v. INS*, 857 F.2d 10, 13-14 (1st Cir. 1988); *Castillo-Perez v. INS*, 212 F.3d 518, 526-27 (9th Cir. 2000); *Lu v. Ashcroft*, 259 F.3d 127, 131 (3d Cir. 2001); *Huicochea-Gomez v. INS*, 237 F.3d 696, 699 (6th Cir. 2001). It is generally also expected that the alien show at least a reasonable probability of prejudice. *Michelson v. INS*, 897 F.2d 465, 468.

56. Prejudice in this case is clear given the fact that Mr. Smith is being subject to mandatory detention despite a judge's order that he be released on bond and such mandatory stay is without any statutory authority.

FIRST CLAIM FOR RELIEF (STATUTORY CLAIM)

57. Mr. Smith realleges and incorporates by reference each and every allegation contained in paragraphs 1 through 56 as if set forth fully herein.

58. ICE is acting without statutory authority in requesting an automatic stay in this matter as the Immigration and Nationality Act provides no provisions for an automatic stay in this case. Such action by regulation and by the directives of the Attorney General in "Operation Predator" is *ultra vires* and must be struck down and statutorily impermissible.

SECOND CLAIM FOR RELIEF (DUE PROCESS VIOLATION)

59. Mr. Smith realleges and incorporates by reference each and every allegation contained in paragraphs 1 through 58 as if set forth fully herein.

60. To ignore the order of the Immigration Judge ordering Mr. Smith released on a $5000.00 bond and file an automatic stay which purports to keep him in indefinite custody during the pendency of any appeal to the BIA and certification to the Attorney General is a violation of Mr. Smith's fundamental right to freedom from bodily restraint, and violates his right to substantive and procedural due process.

THIRD CLAIM FOR RELIEF (EX POST FACTO CLAUSE VIOLATION)

61. To retroactively stay provisions to conduct which occurred 11 years ago is a violation of the prohibition on the retroactive application of statutes and regulations under the Ex Post Facto clause of the United States Constitution.

62. To retroactively apply 8 C.F.R. §1003.19(i) to Mr. Smith's conviction in this case, so as to hold that he is subject to the automatic stay provisions is a violation of the prohibition on the retroactive application of statutes under the Ex Post Facto clause of the United States Constitution.

FOURTH CLAIM FOR RELIEF (BIVENS CLAIM)

63. The Petitioner is entitled to compensatory and punitive damages for injuries he has suffered as a result of the objective non-discretionary violation of his clearly established Fifth Amendment rights and as a result of a violation of his statutory right to a bond hearing pending removal since he is clearly not covered by mandatory detention. *Bivens v. Six Unknown Named Agents*, 403 U.S. 388 (1971).

CERTIFICATE OF COMPLIANCE WITH LOCAL RULE 7.1

64. Pursuant to Local Rule 7.1 of the United States District Court for the District of Colorado, counsel for Petitioner states that he has been in contact with the United States Attorney and has been unable to resolve this matter prior to filing this motion. Counsel will continue to attempt resolution pending a decision on this Motion.

PRAYER FOR RELIEF

WHEREFORE, Petitioner prays that this Honorable Court grant the following relief:

1. Grant the writ of habeas corpus;
2. Issue a permanent order ordering Respondents to withdraw the automatic stay;
3. Issue a permanent order ordering Respondents to release the Petitioner on the $5000.00 bond originally set in this matter so that he may return to his home in Idaho and prepare his 212(c) application for relief from removal;
4. Declare Mr. Smith a prevailing party and award to Mr. Smith attorney's fees and costs and EAJA fees as the position of the United States in this litigation is not substantially justified;
5. Award to Mr. Smith compensatory and punitive damages under *Bivens v. Six Unknown Named Agents*, 403 U.S. 388 (1971) for the Fifth Amendment violations;
6. And award any other relief that this court deems reasonable and proper.
7. Counsel requests that Mr. Smith be present for all court appearances, and that the court issue a writ of Habeas Corpus ad Testificandum ordering ICE to cause him to be present to the federal court for such appearances.

[Dated:]

Respectfully Submitted,

[Attorney]

[ADD CERTIFICATE OF SERVICE]

[Document Nos. 507–10]

PETITION FOR WRIT OF HABEAS CORPUS AND COMPLAINT FOR DECLARATORY AND INJUNCTIVE RELIEF; EMERGENCY MOTION FOR TRO INCLUDING MEMORANDUM OF LAW IN SUPPORT THEREOF; AND PROPOSED ORDER

Description:

The following petition for writ of habeas corpus and complaint for declaratory and injunctive relief and emergency motion for TRO and/or preliminary injunctive relief are brought on the basis that the decision of the immigration judge to deny bond violates the equal protection guarantees of the Due Process Clause of the Fifth Amendment, substantive and procedural guarantees of the Due Process Clause, the INA, and Department of Justice regulations. The action therefore arises under the U.S. Constitution, INA, and Administrative Procedure Act (APA), 5 USC §701 *et seq.* Jurisdiction is based on 28 USC §2241(c)(1) and (3); Article 1, §9, Clause 2 of the U.S. Constitution (Suspension Clause); and 28 USC §1331. A memorandum of law and proposed order regarding the emergency motion for TRO also are included. This habeas action challenges the detention without bond of a Mexican national who entered lawfully, overstayed his nonimmigrant status, and has no history of criminal arrest or conviction. The respondent wishes to remain in the United States free from detention only long enough to request voluntary departure in removal proceedings.

Advantages:

This petition for habeas corpus would be used when the IJ unconstitutionally denies bond on any condition to a detained alien who is not subject to mandatory detention under INA §236(c). This action requests release of the petitioner "on any reasonable conditions of bond that would ensure his appearance at any future immigration hearings."

Limitations:

In the post–*Demore v. Kim* era, contesting detention on constitutional grounds in nonmandatory detention cases is a new and important area of jurisprudence; that said, bad case law will affect the community. Take the case on intending to be thorough, do well, and prevail. (*Demore v. Kim*, 538 U.S. 510 (2003), held that INA §236(e) does not bar habeas jurisdiction in the absence of a specific provision barring habeas and because petitioner lodged a constitutional challenge to legislation.)

UNITED STATES DISTRICT COURT
SOUTHERN DISTRICT OF FLORIDA

[ALIEN] Petitioner/Plaintiff, vs. ALBERTO GONZALES, as Attorney General of the United States; MICHAEL CHERTOFF, as Secretary of the U.S. Department of Homeland Security; MARION DILLIS, Officer in Charge, Krome Service Processing Center (SPC), Immigration and Customs Enforcement (ICE), United States Department of Homeland Security; MICHAEL ROZOS, Field Office Director, Miami ICE Detention and Removal Office, United States Department of Homeland Security, Respondents/Defendants.	)	CIVIL ACTION NO.

PETITION FOR WRIT OF HABEAS CORPUS PURSUANT TO 28 U.S.C. §2241 AND COMPLAINT FOR DECLARATORY AND INJUNCTIVE RELIEF

Petitioner **[Alien]** (hereafter "**[First Name of Alien]**" or "Mr." **[Alien's Last Name]**), by and through his undersigned counsel, respectfully petitions this Honorable Court to enter an order granting him a temporary release from custody under all appropriate conditions pending a final determination in his removal proceedings where his sole request is to voluntarily depart the United States. In support of this Petition and action for declaratory and injunctive relief, Petitioner alleges as follows:

PRELIMINARY STATEMENT

1. This case raises the fundamental question whether an immigration judge may rely on a person's national origin as a basis to incarcerate him without bond. The Petitioner, **[Alien]**, remains incarcerated under a "no bond" decision of an immigration judge at the Krome Detention Facility because he is a citizen of Mexico. The immigration judge, in violation of the Equal Protection guarantees of the Fifth Amendment, as incorporated by the Due Process Clause, determined that no conditions of bond would satisfy the release of Mr. **[Alien]** while his immigration case was proceeding. Mr. **[Alien]** is charged solely as a person who has overstayed his time in the United States due to his being laid off by his employer. He has never been charged, nor committed any crime, in the United States and his overstay is due solely to misadvise by his previous immi-

gration counsel. In determining that he was not eligible for any bond or any *conditions* that would ensure his appearance, the immigration judge relied on his speculative belief that as a Mexican citizen Mr. **[Alien]** could obtain a Mexican birth certificate and simply cross the border to Mexico. Under this speculative scenario, no Mexican citizen would *ever be eligible for a bond* pending a final determination in his removal proceeding. The immigration judge's determination, therefore, flies in the face of the Equal Protection guarantees of the Fifth Amendment and must be reversed. Mr. **[Alien]**, who stated his willingness to accept *any conditions of bond imposed upon him*, should be released pending what will be a protracted removal hearing.

The immigration judge also violated substantive and procedural due process on its face and as applied to Mr. **[Alien]** by stating that no conditions of bond would ensure his appearance when he has never been charged with a crime in the United States, never knowingly violated any immigration laws, and never been convicted of any crime in any country. The immigration judge, by determining that he would not consider any conditions of bond, other than financial conditions, and by then determining that financial conditions alone were insufficient to ensure that Mr. **[Alien]** would not be a flight risk because, as a Mexican citizen, he could simply cross the border with his birth certificate, deprived Mr. **[Alien]** of procedural and substantive due process. The immigration judge's action, in refusing to allow Mr. **[Alien]** an opportunity to present any other conditions for bond, such as electronic monitoring, house arrest, frequent inspections or withholding passports, also violated immigration statutes and regulations.

JURISDICTION

2. This action arises under the Constitution of the United States, the Immigration & Nationality Act of 1952, as amended ("INA"), 8 USC § 1101 *et seq*., and the Administrative Procedure Act ("APA"), 5 USC § 701 *et seq.*

3. This Court has habeas corpus jurisdiction pursuant to 28 USC § 2241, and Art. 1, § 9, Cl. 2 of the United States Constitution (the "Suspension Clause"), as Petitioner is presently subject to immediate detention and custody under color of the authority of the United States, and such custody is in violation of the Constitution, laws or treaties of the United States. This Court may also exercise jurisdiction pursuant to 28 USC § 1331 (federal question jurisdiction) and may grant relief pursuant to the Declaratory Judgment Act, 28 USC § 2201 *et seq*., and the All Writs Act, 28 USC § 1651.

VENUE

4. Venue lies in the United States District Court, Southern District of Florida, the judicial district where the Petitioner resides and where the IJ issued an order of custody. 28 USC § 1391.

PARTIES

5. Petitioner/Plaintiff, **[Alien]** is a native and citizen of Mexico.

6. The Respondent/Defendant ALBERTO GONZALES is the Attorney General of the United States and heads the United States Department of Justice. Mr. Gonzales is responsible for the administration of the Executive Office of Immigration Review under which the immigration judge conducts his daily functions.

7. The Respondent/Defendant MICHAEL CHERTOFF is the Secretary of the United States Department of Homeland Security ("DHS"). Mr. Chertoff is responsible for the administration of the DHS and the implementation and enforcement of the immigration laws of the United States. In that capacity, he oversees the Immigration and Customs Enforcement ("ICE") which is responsible for the detention and removal of Mr. **[Alien]**.

8. The Respondent/Defendant MARION DILLIS, Officer in Charge, Krome Service Processing Center (SPC), Immigration and Customs Enforcement (ICE), United States Department of Homeland Security. As

the Officer in Charge at the Krome Service Processing, Ms. Dillis is the immediate custodian of Mr. **[Alien]** for purposes of the Habeas Corpus statute, 28 U.S.C. §2241.

9. The Respondent/Defendant MICHAEL ROZOS, Field Office Director, Miami ICE Detention and Removal Office, United States Department of Homeland Security, is the chief detention officer in this district and as such has direct oversight responsibility for the continued detention of Mr. **[Alien]**.

FACTUAL AND PROCEDURAL BACKGROUND

10. **[Alien]** is a university trained banker and financial consultant who has been in the United States since 1999 on a temporary visa for professionals known as an H-1B visa. Declaration of Petitioner **[Alien]** attached hereto and marked as Exhibit 8. During that time period, Mr. **[Alien]** has raised his family in Florida including two United States citizen children. He has been very active in his church and his community. *See* letters from church members and neighbors attached hereto as Exhibit 1.One of his United States citizen sons, **[Son]**, is five years old and was born out-of-wedlock. In state court proceedings, the Honorable Judge **[Judge]**, awarded Mr. **[Alien]** extensive visitation rights with his child while only allowing the mother limited supervised visitation. *See* Motion and Order Granting Extensive Supervision to Mr. **[Alien]** marked herein as Exhibit 2. In addition to these extensive ties, Mr. **[Alien]** has all his immediate relatives in the United States. His brother **[Brother]** is a lawful permanent resident. His other brothers, sister, and parents are all in the United States on lawful visas for professionals.

11. Notwithstanding all of these factors, Mr. **[Alien]** was arrested by Immigration and Customs Enforcement (ICE) on November 17, 2004, charged solely with overstaying the period granted to him in the United States by immigration authorities, and incarcerated at the Krome Detention Facility **without *any* bond**, where he remains today. *See* ICE Notice to Appear and Warrant of Arrest against Mr. **[Alien]** marked herein as Exhibit 3.

12. On August 31, 2004, Mr. **[Alien]** was laid off from his professional position. At that time, he was informed by his then immigration attorney that he had six months to depart the United States. After August 31, 2004 Mr. **[Alien]** made plans to depart the United States unaware that he was required to depart immediately. Mr. **[Alien]** had never previously violated the immigration laws of the United States and has never knowingly violated or been *accused* of violating any other laws of the United States, immigration or criminal, before his arrest and incarceration without bond.

13. His incarceration without bond simply because he inadvertently overstayed the time period given to him as a professional in the United States is extraordinary. He has asked the immigration judge to allow him pre-hearing voluntary departure under Immigration and Nationality Act ("INA") §240B(a) (1), 8 U.S.C. §1229c(a)(1), so that he may simply depart the United States and be with his family abroad. As a Mexican (as well as an Ecuadorian and Spanish) citizen he has expressed an interest to voluntarily depart to Mexico or another country of his choice. Because ICE is fighting his request for pre-hearing voluntary departure, Mr. **[Alien]** has asked for a temporary bond *under any conditions the government wishes to set*, while he defends his request for voluntary departure from the United States.

14. ICE bases their "no bond" decision on the fact that there are pending criminal charges against Mr. **[Alien]** in Ecuador. These charges were brought to ICE's attention through the mother of Mr. **[Alien]**' son who was not awarded custody of her child. She is a close relative of high government officials in Ecuador. She contacted those officials who in turn contacted the United States government. Although there are no extradition proceedings even pending in Ecuador against Mr. **[Alien]**, *See* Notice for the Supreme Court of Ecuador marked herein as Exhibit 4, the decision to call US officials regarding the criminal charges, and the subsequent arrest of Mr. **[Alien]**, has had the predictable effect of terminating his extensive visitation rights with his child and giving custody of the child to the mother.

15. Although ICE claims that Mr. **[Alien]** is a "fugitive from justice" in Ecuador, the charges arose *one and two years after Mr. [Alien] left Ecuador. See* Official Departure and Arrival Records from Immigration in Ecuador marked herein as Exhibit 5; *See* **[Alien]** Affidavit at Exhibit 8. As soon as Mr. **[Alien]** learned of the pending criminal charges, he hired counsel in Ecuador who is vigorously challenging the basis of those charge which are for improper bookkeeping and embezzlement. Ecuadorian law presumes innocence; there is no final decision on the criminal charges in Ecuador, there is no reason to believe Mr. **[Alien]** will be convicted in Ecuador, and as stated previously there are no extradition proceedings pending against him.

16. During the course of Mr. **[Alien]**'s detention, the government of Ecuador has taken radical action to undermine the rule of law in the country by removing 26 of the 31 justices of the Supreme Court of Ecuador from their positions. The actions were illegal and unconstitutional under Ecuadorian law. Expert Affidavit of **[Expert 1]** attached herein and marked as Exhibit 6.

17. On December 21, 2004, a hearing on Mr. **[Alien]**'s request to leave the United States voluntarily and at no cost to the government was held before Immigration Judge **[Immigration Judge]** at the Krome Detention Center. This hearing followed the immigration judge's first continuance for two weeks to give the government an opportunity to present their case. At the hearing on December 21, 2004, the immigration judge further continued the hearing until January 18, 2005, with the understanding that the continued hearing may be further postponed after January 18, 2005. Even if the immigration judge renders a decision in favor of Mr. **[Alien]** in January or February, 2005, ICE counsel has the right to appeal that decision to the Board of Immigration Appeals thereby ensuring Mr. **[Alien]**'s detentions for months if not years.

18. As a result of the prospect of long term detention, notwithstanding Mr. **[Alien]** simple request to voluntarily leave the country, he asked for a bond re-determination hearing from **[Immigration Judge]** pursuant to INA §236(a)(2), 8 U.S.C. §1226(a)(2) so that he may be reunited with his family while his case proceeds.

19. The immigration judge then proceeded to hold a perfunctory bond hearing. Mr. **[Alien]** stated that he would accept *any conditions for bond*, including electronic monitoring, daily reporting, the government holding all his passports and a financial bond, to ensure his appearance at his next hearing. *See* **[Alien]** Affidavit at Exhibit 8.

20. The immigration judge ruled that "no bond" should be given to Mr. **[Alien]**. His decision rested on two impermissible legal grounds—one constitutional and one statutory. His constitutional ruling rested on the theory that Mr. **[Alien]** was a flight risk because he was a Mexican citizen. As a Mexican citizen, even with all the above mentioned conditions, the immigration judge reasoned that "he could get a Mexican birth certificate and cross the border." Although no transcript or recording is maintained of an immigration bond hearing, this reasoning is reflected in the immigration judge's written bond decision which *in toto* states: "Respondent held w/o bond. Flight risk. It appears can leave at anytime to Mexico." *See* Immigration Judge's Decision on Bond incorporated herein as Exhibit 7. Under this theory, no Mexican citizen would be eligible for a bond because he or she could "get a birth certificate" and "cross the border."

21. The immigration judge also impermissibly concluded that he had no statutory authority to impose any conditions of bond, other than financial conditions, that would ensure Mr. **[Alien]**'s appearance. Ignoring all the other conditions suggested by Mr. **[Alien]**, the immigration judge reasoned that financial conditions would not ensure Mr. **[Alien]**'s appearance, because as a Mexican citizen he could obtain a birth certificate and cross the border. The immigration judge's claim that he could not impose any other conditions, such as electronic monitoring, extensive reporting, or ordering Mr. **[Alien]** to provide his passports to ICE, and therefore could not guarantee his appearance, is in clear contravention of INA §236(a)((2)(A), 8 U.S.C. §1226(a)(2)(A). Under that section, the Attorney General (and his designate the immigration judge) "may release the alien on—(A) bond of at least $1,500, with security approved by, and *containing conditions prescribed by, the Attorney General....* (emphasis added). The statutory scheme only prohibits the immigration judge from granting work authorization

to Mr. **[Alien]** as a condition of release. INA §236(a)(3). Nor do the regulations of the Department of Justice prohibit the immigration judge from setting other conditions of bond. 8 C.F.R. §1003.19 (2004).

EXHAUSTION OF REMEDIES

22. Petitioner is not required to exhaust his administrative remedies given his constitutional claims and his unconstitutional and illegal incarceration.

CUSTODY

23. Petitioner is in custody for purposes of habeas corpus relief.

IRREPARABLE HARM

24. Petitioner is irreparably harmed each day he is incarcerated because of his nationality and without the right to satisfy any conditions of bond. Absent this Court's intervention, irreparable harm to the Petitioner will continue because his removal proceeding will continue for many months if not years.

EQUAL ACCESS TO JUSTICE ACT

25. Petitioner has retained the undersigned counsel to represent him in this matter and has agreed to pay counsel a reasonable attorney's fee plus costs and expenses. Petitioner therefore seeks an award of his costs attorney's fees, and expenses under The Equal Access to Justice Act (hereafter "EAJA"), 28 U.S.C. § 2412, in this lawsuit.

FIRST CLAIM FOR RELIEF

(Unconstitutional Incarceration In Violation of the Equal Protection Guarantees of the Fifth Amendment to the United States Constitution)

26. Petitioner incorporates by reference as if set forth in full and at length herein paragraphs 1 to 23 *supra*.

27. "Freedom from imprisonment---from government custody, detention or other forms of physical restraint---lies at the heart of the liberty that [the Due Process] Clause protects." *Zadvydas v. Davis*, 121 S.Ct. 2491, 2499 (2001). In this case, the immigration judge's decision to use Mr. **[Alien]**'s Mexican citizenship as a basis to determine that *no conditions* of bond would satisfy his appearance in a removal proceeding because "he could obtain a Mexican birth certificate and cross the border" is a violation of the Equal Protection guarantees of the Due Process Clause of the Fifth Amendment. Under the immigration judge's speculative scenario, no Mexican citizen in a removal proceeding in the Untied States could be granted "freedom from imprisonment" because he would always be considered a flight risk, as he could flee the country by using his Mexican "birth certificate" to "cross the border."

SECOND CLAIM FOR RELIEF

(Violation of the Immigration and Nationality Act, DOJ Regulations and the Due Process Clause of the Fifth Amendment)

28. Petitioner incorporates by reference as if set forth in full and at length herein paragraphs 1 to 23 *supra*.

29. The Petitioner Mr. **[Alien]** offered the immigration court *any conditions of bond*, including electronic monitoring, retention of passports, daily reporting and a monetary bond as a condition or conditions to ensure his appearance at his removal proceedings.

30. The immigration judge, in violation of INA §236(a)(2)(A), 8 U.S.C. §1226(a)(2)(A) and Department of Justice regulations at 8 C.F.R. §1003.19, determined that he could not consider *any* conditions of bond other than a monetary bond and that a monetary bond would be insufficient because as a Mexican citizen Mr. **[Alien]** could cross the border with his birth certificate. By determining that he could not set any conditions, and then determining that Mr. **[Alien]** was a flight risk because he could impose no conditions other than a financial bond which would be insufficient to ensure a Mexican citizen's appearance, the immigration judge violated the INA, DOJ regulations, and the Due Process Clause. By illegally refusing to impose conditions that would ensure Mr. **[Alien]**'s appearance and then using the lack of such conditions as a basis to grant *any* bond, the immigration judge established unconstitutional conditions for bond in violation of the Due Process Clause of the Fifth Amendment.

THIRD CLAIM FOR RELIEF

(Violation of Procedural and Substantive Due Process)

31. Petitioner incorporates by reference as if set forth in full and at length herein paragraphs 1 to 23 *supra*.

32. The immigration judge refused to allow Mr. **[Alien]** to establish that he was not a flight risk by refusing to allow him to present conditions that would ensure his appearance at all future hearing. The immigration judge, by unlawfully assuming the position that he could not consider any conditions of bond except financial ones and by then saying the financial conditions were insufficient to prevent a Mexican citizen from fleeing because he could simply get his birth certificate and cross the border, deprived Mr. **[Alien]** of procedural and substantive due process. The immigration judge's actions are also a violation of substantive and procedural due process as applied to someone, such as Mr. **[Alien]**, who has never committed a crime in the United States, never knowingly violated immigration laws and never convicted of a crime outside the United States, but is now detained without any bond or possibility to prove that there are conditions that would ensure his appearance for a hearing.

PRAYER FOR RELIEF

WHEREFORE, Petitioner, **[Alien],** by and through his undersigned counsel, prays that this Honorable Court grant the following relief:

1. Accept jurisdiction over this action;
2. Grant the writ of habeas corpus;
3. Order the release of Petitioner on any reasonable conditions that would ensure his appearance at his continued removal proceedings;
4. Issue an injunction enjoining Respondents from preventing Petitioner's release on reasonable conditions of bond;
5. Declare that the actions and/or decisions of immigration judge **[Immigration Judge]** are: (a) in violation of the Equal Protection guarantees of the Due Process Clause of the Fifth Amendment by utilizing the impermissible criteria of national origin as a basis to deny bond; (b) in violation of the Due Process Clause of the Fifth Amendment by determining that no conditions of bond could be set and therefore no conditions of bond could satisfy release; (c) in violation of substantive and procedural Due Process as applied to Mr. **[Alien]**; and (d) in violation of the INA and DOJ regulations because an immigration judge does have the authority to set conditions of bond in a removal proceeding.

6. Award to Petitioner reasonable costs and attorneys' fees; and,
7. Grant any other and further relief that this Honorable Court deems just and proper.

Respectfully submitted,

[Dated:]

[Attorney]

[ADD CERTIFICATE OF SERVICE]

UNITED STATES DISTRICT COURT
SOUTHERN DISTRICT OF FLORIDA

[Alien],	)	CIVIL ACTION NO.
	)	
Petitioner/Plaintiff,	)	
	)	
vs.	)	
	)	
ALBERTO GONZALES, as Attorney General of the United States; MICHAEL CHERTOFF, as Secretary of the U.S. Department of Homeland Security; MARION DILLIS, Officer in Charge, Krome Service Processing Center (SPC), Immigration and Customs Enforcement (ICE), United States Department of Homeland Security; MICHAEL ROZOS, Field Office Director, Miami ICE Detention and Removal Office, United States Department of Homeland Security,	)	
	)	
Respondents/Defendants.	)	
______________________________________/		

PETITIONER/PLAINTIFF'S EMERGENCY MOTION FOR A TEMPORARY RESTRAINING ORDER AND/OR PRELIMINARY INJUNCTIVE RELIEF

The Petitioner/Plaintiff (hereinafter "Petitioner"), **[Alien]**, by and through his undersigned counsel, respectfully requests this Honorable Court to enter an emergency temporary restraining order and/or a preliminary injunction from this Honorable Court enjoining Respondents from preventing Petitioner's release on bond; releasing Petitioner from physical custody pending the outcome of the instant action on any reasonable conditions on bond that would ensure his appearance at any future immigration hearings; and declaring that the actions and/or decisions of Immigration Judge (IJ) **[Immigration Judge]** were (a) in violation of the Equal Protection guarantees of the Due Process Clause of the Fifth Amendment by utilizing the impermissible criteria of national origin as a basis to deny bond; (b) in violation of the Due Process Clause of the Fifth Amendment by determining that no conditions of bond could be set and therefore no conditions of bond could satisfy release; and (c) in violation of the INA and DOJ regulations because an immigration judge does have the authority to set conditions of bond in a removal proceeding.

In support of this request, the Petitioner states as follows:

1. **[Alien]** is a native and citizen of Mexico, and also a citizen of Ecuador and Spain. *See* Affidavit of Petitioner, attached as Exh. 7 to the Petition for Writ of Habeas Corpus pursuant to 28 U.S.C. § 2241 and Complaint for Declaratory and Injunctive Relief (hereinafter "Habeas Petition"). (All documents referenced herein are attached as exhibits to **[Alien]**'s Habeas Petition.)

2. **[Alien]** is a university trained banker and financial consultant who has been in the United States since 1999 on a temporary visa for professionals known as an H-1B visa. During that time period, **[Alien]** has raised his family in Florida including two United States citizen children. He has been very active in his church and his community. *See* letters from church members and neighbors attached hereto as Exhibit 1. One of his United States citizen sons, **[Son]**, is five years old and was born out-of-wedlock. In state court proceedings, the Honorable Judge **[Judge]**, awarded **[Alien]** extensive visitation rights with his child while only allowing the mother limited supervised visitation. *See* Motion and Order Granting Extensive Supervision to **[Alien]** marked herein as Exhibit 2. In addition to these extensive ties, **[Alien]** has all his immediate relatives in the United States. His brother, **[Brother],** is a lawful permanent resident. His other brothers, sister, and parents are all in the United States on lawful visas for professionals.

3. Notwithstanding all of these factors, **[Alien]** was arrested by Immigration and Customs Enforcement (ICE) on November 17, 2004, charged solely with overstaying the period granted to him in the United States by immigration authorities, and incarcerated at the Krome Detention Facility **without *any* bond**, where he remains today. *See* ICE Notice to Appear and Warrant of Arrest against **[Alien]** marked herein as Exhibit 3.

4. On August 31, 2004, **[Alien]** was laid off from his professional position. At that time, he was informed by his then immigration attorney that he had six months to depart the United States. After August 31, 2004, **[Alien]** made plans to depart the United States unaware that he was required to depart immediately. **[Alien]** had never previously violated the immigration laws of the United States and has never knowingly violated or been *accused* of violating any other laws of the United States, immigration or criminal, before his arrest and incarceration without bond.

5. His incarceration without bond simply because he inadvertently overstayed the time period given to him as a professional in the United States is extraordinary. He has asked the immigration judge to allow him pre-hearing voluntary departure under Immigration and Nationality Act ("INA") §240B(a)(1), 8 U.S.C. §1229c(a)(1), so that he may simply depart the United States and be with his family abroad. As a Mexican (as well as an Ecuadorian and Spanish) citizen he has expressed an interest to voluntarily depart to Mexico or another country of his choice. Because ICE is fighting his request for pre-hearing voluntary departure, **[Alien]** has asked for a temporary bond *under any conditions the government wishes to set*, while he defends his request for voluntary departure from the United States.

6. ICE bases their "no bond" decision on the fact that there are pending criminal charges against **[Alien]** in Ecuador. These charges were brought to ICE's attention through the mother of **[Alien]**'s son who was not awarded custody of her child. She is a close relative of high government officials in Ecuador. She contacted those officials who in turn contacted the United States government. Although there are no extradition proceedings even pending in Ecuador against **[Alien]**, *See* Notice for the Supreme Court of Ecuador marked herein as Exhibit 4, the decision to call US officials regarding the criminal charges, and the subsequent arrest of **[Alien]**, has had the predictable effect of terminating his extensive visitation rights with his child and giving custody of the child to the mother.

7. Although ICE claims that **[Alien]** is a "fugitive from justice" in Ecuador, the charges arose *two years after [Alien] left Ecuador*. *See* Official Departure and Arrival Records from Immigration in Ecuador marked herein as Exhibit 5. As soon as **[Alien]** learned of the pending criminal charges, he hired counsel in Ecuador who is vigorously challenging the basis of those charge which are for improper bookkeeping and embezzlement. Ecuadorian law presumes innocence, there is no final decision on the criminal charges in Ecuador, there is no reason to believe **[Alien]** will be convicted in Ecuador, and as stated previously there are no extradition proceedings pending against him.

8. During the course of **[Alien]**'s detention, the government of Ecuador has taken radical action to undermine the rule of law in the country by removing 26 of the 31 justices of the Supreme Court of Ecuador

from their positions. The actions were illegal and unconstitutional under Ecuadorian law. Expert Affidavit of **[Expert 1]** attached herein and marked as Exhibit 6.

9. On December 21, 2004, a hearing on **[Alien]**'s request to leave the United States voluntarily and at no cost to the government was held before Immigration Judge **[Immigration Judge]** at the Krome Detention Center. This hearing followed the immigration judge's first continuance for two weeks to give the government an opportunity to present their case. At the hearing on December 21, 2004, the immigration judge further continued the hearing until January 18, 2004, with the understanding that the continued hearing may be further postponed after January 18, 2004. Even if the immigration judge renders a decision in favor of **[Alien]** in January or February, 2004, ICE counsel has the right to appeal that decision to the Board of Immigration Appeals thereby ensuring **[Alien]**'s detentions for months if not years.

10. As a result of the prospect of long term detention, notwithstanding **[Alien]** simple request to voluntarily leave the country, he asked for a bond re-determination hearing from **[Immigration Judge]** pursuant to INA §236(a)(2), 8 U.S.C. §1226(a)(2) so that he may be reunited with his family while his case proceeds.

11. The immigration judge then proceeded to hold a perfunctory bond hearing. **[Alien]** stated that he would accept *any conditions for bond*, including electronic monitoring, daily reporting, the government holding all his passports and a financial bond, to ensure his appearance at his next hearing.

12. The immigration judge ruled that "no bond" should be given to **[Alien]**. His decision rested on two impermissible legal grounds—one constitutional and one statutory. His constitutional ruling rested on the theory that **[Alien]** was a flight risk because he was a Mexican citizen. As a Mexican citizen, even with all the above mentioned conditions, the immigration judge reasoned that "he could get a Mexican birth certificate and cross the border." Although no transcript or recording is maintained of an immigration bond hearing, this reasoning is reflected in the immigration judge's written bond decision which *in toto* states: "Respondent held w/o bond. Flight risk. It appears can leave at anytime to Mexico." *See* Immigration Judge's Decision on Bond incorporated herein as Exhibit 7. Under this theory, no Mexican citizen would be eligible for a bond because he or she could "get a birth certificate" and "cross the border."

13. The immigration judge also impermissibly concluded that he had no statutory authority to impose any conditions of bond, other than financial conditions, that would ensure **[Alien]**'s appearance. Ignoring all the other conditions suggested by **[Alien]**, the immigration judge reasoned that financial conditions would not ensure **[Alien]**'s appearance, because as a Mexican citizen he could obtain a birth certificate and cross the border. The immigration judge's claim that he could not impose any other conditions, such as electronic monitoring, extensive reporting, or ordering **[Alien]** to provide his passports to ICE, and therefore could not guarantee his appearance, is in clear contravention of INA §236(a)((2)(A), 8 U.S.C. §1226(a)(2)(A). Under that section, the Attorney General (and his designate the immigration judge) "may release the alien on—(A) bond of at least $1,500, with security approved by, and *containing conditions prescribed by, the Attorney General*.... (emphasis added). The statutory scheme only prohibits the immigration judge from granting work authorization to **[Alien]** as a condition of release. INA §236(a)(3). Nor do the regulations of the Department of Justice prohibit the immigration judge from setting other conditions of bond. 8 C.F.R. §1003.19 (2004).

A. There Is a Substantial Likelihood that the Petitioner Will Prevail on the Merits

14. As discussed in the accompanying memorandum of law, based on an erroneous interpretation and construction of federal statutes and regulations, and in violation of the equal protection and procedural and substantive due process guarantees of the Fifth Amendment, the IJ found that Petitioner was found ineligible for release on bond. This ruling was based impermissibly on protected suspect classification, namely, **[Alien]**'s Mexican citizenship. The IJ further erred in his finding that his authority as a judge did not allow him to place any conditions on bond, thus pretermitting any discussion by Petitioner of the appropriateness of such conditions. Because such rulings were violative of Petitioner's Constitutional rights under the Fifth

Amendment and based on a fundamental error in statutory construction, there exists a substantial likelihood Petitioner will prevail on the merits.

B. The Petitioner Will Suffer Irreparable and Immediate Injury Unless the Injunction Is Issued.

15. If Petitioner is denied release on bond with reasonable conditions, he will suffer irreparable injury in that he will be separated from his two U.S. citizen children who are extremely close to him. *See United States v. Wharton*, 514 F.2d 406, 408, 412 (9th Cir. 1975) ("Governmental conduct would work a serious injustice if this family were divested of the home in which they have invested so much of themselves"); *Tefel v. Reno*, 972 F. Supp. 608, 619-620 (S.D. Fla 1997) (failure to issue temporary restraining order would result in irreparable injury including family separation), *rev'd on other grounds* 180 F.3d 1286 (11th Cir. 1999).

16. Based on the letters submitted by Petitioner and his immediate family members, it is evident that his continued detention will cause them extreme emotional harm and break up their tight-knit and loving family. *See* Habeas Petition Exh. 1 (indicating that he will suffer extreme emotional harm by being separated from his family). In a physician's letter dated December 20, 2004, the doctor reports that **[Alien]**'s two children "suffer severe cases of asthma." *Id.*

17. Lastly, the fact that **[Alien]** will remain incarcerated unlawfully itself represents a continuing irreparable injury to Petitioner. *Dash v. Mitchell*, 356 F. Supp. 1292, 1309 (D.C.D.C. 1972); *Grodzki v. Reno*, 950 F. Supp. 339, 342 (N.D.Ga. 1996); *U.S. v. Montalvo-Murillo*, 495 U.S. 711 (1990).

C. The Petitioner's Injuries Overwhelmingly Outweigh Any Potential Harm to the Respondents

18. The injury to the Petitioner far outweighs the potential harm to the Respondents by permitting him to be released on conditions of bond while awaiting conclusion of his removal proceedings. As discussed *supra*, Petitioner will suffer various forms of irreparable harm if he remains in detention. On the other hand, the Respondents will suffer no harm if the Petitioner is permitted to be released on bond and remains in the United States pending his removal proceedings. He poses no risk to United States security or to his community nor is he a flight risk. To the contrary, as indicated in numerous support letters, he is man of great character and who has generously helped and positively influenced numerous individuals. *See* Exh. 1. Although the IJ found that Petitioner is a flight risk, as discussed *supra*, that finding has no support in law or in fact. Petitioner has no history of immigration law violations, prior to the NTA issued in November, nor has he ever failed to appear before the IJ when he was required to do so. The IJ failed to consider these factors that clearly establish that Petitioner does not pose any flight risk. Instead, the IJ found Petitioner to be a flight risk solely based on the judge's conjecture that "[Petitioner] could get a Mexican birth certificate and cross the border." Such a finding is based on mere speculation, and if upheld, will render bond hearings meaningless for all Mexican citizens because no Mexican citizen would ever be eligible for a bond because he or she could "get a birth certificate" and "cross the border." Because Petitioner does not pose any danger to the community or flight risk, there would be no harm to the Respondent by releasing the Petitioner.

D. The Issuance of the Injunction Is Not Adverse to the Public Interest

19. The issuance of the injunction in this case is not adverse to the public interest. In fact, the issuance of an injunction strongly favors the public interest here. It is clearly against public policy and the public's interest to separate members of an immediate family. Indeed, one of the purposes behind our immigration law is to preserve family unity. *See, e.g., INS v. Errico*, 385 U.S. 214 (1966). Furthermore, the invidious racial and national origin classification at the base of the Immigration Judge's ruling, if allowed to stand, would represent a judicial imprimatur of impermissible race and national origin discrimination. Such a ruling is not only

unfounded legally, but adverse to the public interest in protecting minorities from arbitrary, capricious and unconstitutional governmental action.

CONCLUSION

WHEREFORE, the Petitioner respectfully requests that this Honorable Court enter a Temporary Restraining Order and/or preliminary injunction enjoining Respondents from preventing Petitioner's release on bond; releasing Petitioner from physical custody pending the outcome of the instant action on any reasonable conditions on bond that would ensure his appearance at any future immigration hearings; and declaring that the actions and/or decisions of Immigration Judge **[Immigration Judge]** were (a) in violation of the Equal Protection guarantees of the Due Process Clause of the Fifth Amendment by utilizing the impermissible criteria of national origin as a basis to deny bond; (b) in violation of the Due Process Clause of the Fifth Amendment by determining that no conditions of bond could be set and therefore no conditions of bond could satisfy release; and (c) in violation of the INA and DOJ regulations because an immigration judge does have the authority to set conditions of bond in a removal proceeding.

[Dated:]

Respectfully submitted,

[Attorney]

[ADD CERTIFICATE OF SERVICE]

UNITED STATES DISTRICT COURT
SOUTHERN DISTRICT OF FLORIDA

[ALIEN] Petitioner/Plaintiff, vs. ALBERTO GONZALES, as Attorney General of the United States; MICHAEL CHERTOFF, as Secretary of the U.S. Department of Homeland Security; MARION DILLIS, Officer in Charge, Krome Service Processing Center (SPC), Immigration and Customs Enforcement (ICE), United States Department of Homeland Security; MICHAEL ROZOS, Field Office Director, Miami ICE Detention and Removal Office, United States Department of Homeland Security, Respondents/Defendants.	)	CIVIL ACTION NO.

MEMORANDUM OF LAW IN SUPPORT OF THE PETITIONER/PLAINTIFF'S EMERGENCY MOTION FOR A TEMPORARY RESTRAINING ORDER (TRO) AND/OR PRELIMINARY INJUNCTIVE RELIEF

The Petitioner/Plaintiff (hereinafter "Petitioner"), **[Alien]**, by and through his undersigned counsel, hereby submits this memorandum of law in support of his emergency motion for temporary restraining order and/or a preliminary injunction seeking an order from this Honorable Court enjoining Respondents from preventing Petitioner's release on bond; releasing Petitioner from physical custody pending the outcome of the instant action on any reasonable conditions on bond that would ensure his appearance at any future immigration hearings; and declaring that the actions and/or decisions of Immigration Judge (IJ) **[Immigration Judge]** were (a) in violation of the Equal Protection guarantees of the Due Process Clause of the Fifth Amendment by utilizing the impermissible criteria of national origin as a basis to deny bond; (b) in violation of the substantive and procedural guarantees of the Due Process Clause of the Fifth Amendment by determining that no conditions of bond, except financial conditions, could be set and therefore no conditions of bond could satisfy release; and (c) in violation of the Immigration and Nationality Act (INA) and U.S. Department of Justice (DOJ) regulations because an IJ does have the authority to set non-monetary conditions of bond in a removal proceeding. To avoid redundancy, Petitioner hereby incorporates the factual background and the procedural history of his case as set forth in the instant motion and makes reference to the supporting exhibits attached to the Petition for Writ of Habeas Corpus Pursuant to 28 U.S.C. § 2241 and Complaint for Declaratory and Injunctive Relief (hereinafter "Habeas Petition").

ARGUMENT

I. JURISDICTION

A. Subject Matter Jurisdiction

This Court has subject-matter jurisdiction over the instant petition and action under 28 U.S.C. § 2241(c)(1) and (3), Art. I, § 9, C1. 2 of the United States Constitution ("Suspension Clause"), and 28 U.S.C. § 1331, as Petitioner is in the custody of the United States Department of Homeland Security ("DHS"), acting under the color of authority, by Respondents, agents of the United States.

Despite the provisions of INA § 236(e), codified at 8 U.S.C. § 1226(e), which bar federal courts from reviewing discretionary decisions regarding parole and bond "under this section," it is well-settled that INA § 236(e) does not serve to bar federal courts from reviewing questions of statutory construction or Constitutional claims such as mandatory detention under the statutory writ of habeas corpus, 28 U.S.C. §2241. *See Demore v. Kim*, 123 S.Ct. 1708, 1713-14 (2003) (INA §236(e) does not bar habeas jurisdiction in absence of specific provision barring habeas and because petitioner lodged a constitutional challenge to legislation); *Zadvydas v. Davis*, 533 U.S. 678, 686-89, 121 S.Ct. 2491, 2497-98 (2001) (INA 236(e), 242(a)(2)(B)(ii), 242(a)(2)(C), 242(g) did not bar habeas jurisdiction for challenge to post-removal detention); *Haitian Refugee Ctr., Inc. v. Nelson*, 872 F.2d 1555, 1560 n. 9 (11th Cir. 1989) (holding that federal courts also have jurisdiction to review allegations that agency officials have acted outside their statutory authority); *Gonzalez v. O'Connell*, 355 F.3d 1010, 1014-15 (7th Cir. 2004) (Habeas jurisdiction to challenge mandatory detention even where the predicate issue to the constitutional claim was a statutory claim); *Aguilar v. Lewis*, 50 F. Supp. 2d 539, 542-43 (E.D. Va. 1999) (INA §236(e) bars discretionary decisions not statutory interpretation); *Velasquez v. Reno*, 37 F. Supp. 2d 663, 667-70 (D.N.J. 1999) (INA §236(e) barring review of detention decisions does not foreclose habeas challenge to application of statute). Moreover, INA §242(g) does not bar review of detention decisions; nor does INA §242(b)(9) or INA §242(a)(2)(B)(ii). *Zhislin v. Reno,* 195 F.3d 810 (6th Cir. 1999) (INA § 242(g) as interpreted by *Reno v. American- Arab Anti-Discrimination Comm.*, 119 S.Ct. 936, 943 (1999) does not bar review of challenge to indefinite detention); *Parra v. Perryman*, 172 F.3d 954 (7th Cir. 1999) (In light of *American Arab* INA §242(g) does not bar habeas to review detention issue); *Sillah v. Davis*, 252 F. Supp. 2d 589, 593-97 (W.D. Tenn. 2003) (INA §242(a)(2)(B)(ii) does not preclude habeas jurisdiction to challenge revocation of parole); *Bouayad v. Holmes*, 74 F. Supp. 2d 471, 473-74 (E.D. Pa. 1999) (Government conceded that habeas jurisdiction existed to challenge mandatory detention and the court determined that neither INA § 236(e) nor INA § 242(b)(9) preclude jurisdiction over detention); *Kiareldeen v. Reno*, 71 F. Supp. 2d 402, 405-07 (D. N.J. 1999) (Neither INA § 236(e) nor § 242(g) bars habeas jurisdiction to review detention based upon secret evidence); *Alikhani v. Fasano*, 70 F. Supp. 2d 1124, 1126-30 (S.D. Cal. 1999) (INA §§242(g), 242(b)(9) and 236(e) do not bar challenge to statutory and constitutional challenge to mandatory detention).

In *INS v. St. Cyr*, 533 U.S. 289, 302 (2001), the Supreme Court held that habeas is still available to challenge the legality of the Service's deportation and removal orders because the Constitution requires habeas review to extend to claims of erroneous application or interpretation of statutes. *See Calcano-Martinez v. I.N.S.*, 533 U.S. 338 (2001) (holding that aliens may bring their statutory and constitutional claims in district court by filing a habeas petition although such claims brought in petitions for review with courts of appeals would be dismissed for lack of jurisdiction); *Bejacmar v. Ashcroft*, 291 F.3d 735, 736 (11th Cir. 2002) (abandoning its reasoning in *Richardson v. Reno*, 180 F.3d 1311 (11th Cir. 1998), *cert. denied*, 120 S.Ct. 1529 (2000), and finding that "*St. Cyr* removes the last statutory pillar supporting our circuit's earlier conclusion that IIRIRA repealed district court jurisdiction in habeas cases")

Similarly, in *Zadvydas v. Davis*, 533 U.S. 678, 694-97, 121 S.Ct. 2491 2501-02 (2001), resident aliens who had been ordered removed brought habeas petitions challenging their detention during a period of custody beyond the 90-day removal period. In that case, the Supreme Court stated as follows regarding habeas jurisdiction: "We note at the outset that the primary federal habeas corpus statute, 28 U.S.C. § 2241, confers jurisdiction upon the federal courts to hear these cases." *Id.* at 687 (citing Section 2241(c)(3), authorizing any person to claim in federal court that he or she is being held "in custody in violation of the Constitution or laws. . .of the United States"). With respect to the alien's important Constitutional claims, the Court found that

> [a] statute permitting indefinite detention of an alien would raise a serious constitutional problem. The Fifth Amendment's Due Process Clause forbids the Government to "depriv[e]" any person . . . of . . . liberty . . . without due process of law." Freedom from imprisonment--from government custody, detention, or other forms of physical restraint--lies at the heart of the liberty that Clause protects. *See Foucha v. Louisiana*, 504 U.S. 71, 80, 112 S.Ct. 1780, 118 L.Ed.2d 437 (1992). And this Court has said that government detention violates that clause unless the detention is ordered in a criminal proceeding with adequate procedural protections, *see United States v. Salerno*, 481 U.S. 739, 746, 107 S.Ct. 2095, 95 L.Ed.2d 697 (1987), or, in certain special and "narrow" nonpunitive "circumstances," *Foucha*, 504 U.S. at 80, 112 S.Ct. 1780, where a special justification, such as harm-threatening mental illness, outweighs the "individual's constitutionally protected interest in avoiding physical restraint." *Kansas v. Hendricks*, 521 U.S. 346, 356, 117 S.Ct. 2072, 138 L.Ed.2d 501 (1997). The proceedings at issue here are civil, not criminal, and we assume that they are nonpunitive in purpose and effect. There is no sufficiently strong special justification here for indefinite civil detention--at least as administered under this statute.

Id. at 690 (emphasis added).

Here, Petitioner challenges: (1) the use of Petitioner's Mexican nationality as a basis to deny his liberty in violation of the equal protection guarantees of the Due Process Clause of the Fifth Amendment; and (2) the IJ's erroneous application and misinterpretation of the Immigration and Nationality Act ("INA"), Section 236(a), codified at 8 U.S.C. §1226(a), as well as implementing federal regulations, *viz.*, 8 C.F.R. §1003.19, 8 C.F.R. § 1236.1(d), which resulted in the IJ's denial of Petitioner's request for release on bond. The IJ's order denying release on bond subjected the Petitioner to detention pending the actual execution of his removal, based solely on his national origin and despite the fact that Petitioner has absolutely no criminal record in the United States, and in fact has never committed nor ever been accused of any criminal acts in this country. The only charge in his Notice to Appear (NTA) issued November 19, 2004, the charging document issued by the U.S. Department of Homeland Security, agents of Respondents, concerned Petitioner's inadvertent overstay of his H1-B status. *See* Habeas Petition, ¶ 11; *see also* Exh. 3 attached to Habeas Petition. Moreover, as will be discussed, **[Alien]** is not required to exhaust his administrative remedies in this case. Therefore, this Court has subject matter jurisdiction over Petitioner's habeas claims which are now ripe for review.

B. Exhaustion of Administrative Remedies Is Not Required in This Case

"Of 'paramount importance' to any exhaustion inquiry is congressional intent. Where Congress specifically mandates, exhaustion is required. But where Congress has not clearly required exhaustion, sound judicial discretion governs." *McCarthy v. Madigan*, 503 U.S. 140, 144, 112 S.Ct. 1081 (1992); *Haitian Refugee Ctr., Inc. v. Nelson*, 872 F.2d 1555, 1561 (11th Cir. 1989) ("We note at the outset that the application of the judicial exhaustion doctrine is subject to the discretion of the trial court.") (citing *Panola Land Buyers Ass'n v. Shuman*, 762 F.2d 1550, 1556-57 (11th Cir. 1985); *Haitian Refugee Center v. Smith*, 676 F.2d 1023, 1034 (5th Cir. 1982) ("the exhaustion requirement is not a jurisdictional prerequisite but a matter committed to the sound discretion of the trial court"). Here, Congress has not specifically mandated exhaustion before judicial review of custody determinations. Because exhaustion is not required by statute, sound judicial discretion must govern this Court's decision of whether to exercise jurisdiction absent exhaustion. *See McCarthy*, 503 U.S. at 144. Exercise of such sound judicial discretion is warranted here because there is an abundant body of law that supports this Court's jurisdiction over this case absent exhaustion.

First, exhaustion does not apply where, as here, a petition challenges only the agency action collateral to removal proceedings, such as bond. *Welch v. Reno*, 101 F. Supp. 2d 347, 351 (D. Md. 2000) (Statutory exhaustion only for review of final orders of removal); *Aguilar v. Lewis*, 50 F. Supp. 2d 539, 541 (E.D. Va. 1999) (No federal statute imposes an exhaustion requirement concerning bond); *Rowe v. INS*, 45 F. Supp. 2d 144, 145-46 (D. Mass. 1999) (and cases cited therein); *Pastor-Camarena v. Smith*, 977 F. Supp. 1415, 1417 (W.D. Wash. 1997) (and cases cited therein); *Montero v. Cobb*, 937 F. Supp. 88, 90-91 (D. Mass. 1976). *Alikhani v. Fasano*, 70 F. Supp. 2d 1124, 1129- 30 (S.D. Cal. 1999). The instant petition only seeks review of the IJ's bond determination, and not of a final order of removal.

In addition, exhaustion is not required "where [, as here,] an agency's exercise of authority is clearly at odds with the specific language of the statute." *McClendon v. Jackson Television Inc.*, 603 F.2d 1174, 1177 (5th Cir. 1979). As discussed infra, the IJ's exercise of authority to deny Petitioner release on bond solely on the ground that the IJ has no statutory authority to impose bond conditions other than monetary conditions directly contravenes the specific language of § 236(a), which confers the IJ such authority.

Moreover, exhaustion is also not required where a review procedure exists but it is not mandated by statute or agency regulations. *Darby v. Cisneros*, 113 S.Ct. 2539 (1993) (Where regulation provided that ALJ's determination shall be final unless the Sec. of HUD, in his discretion, decides to review the decision after request of a party, such regulation does not provide for mandatory review and plaintiff could file suit without making request to Sec.); *Noriega-Lopez v. Ashcroft*, 335 F.3d 874, 880-82 (9th Cir. 2003) (Failure to file a motion to reconsider BIA decision is neither statutorily required under INA §242(d)(1) nor prudentially required); *Chang v. U.S.*, 327 F.3d 911, 922- 24 (9th Cir. 2003) (Where investor was not required to seek a removal proceeding to review denied petition and where IJ in removal could not address APA, estoppel and constitutional claims and where statutes now limit the scope of removal proceedings, plaintiffs did not have to exhaust removal proceeding). Here, although Petitioner may appeal the IJ's decision to the BIA, such appeal is not mandated by statute or agency regulations. See 8 C.F.R. § 1003.19(f) ("An appeal from the determination by an Immigration Judge may be taken to the Board of Immigration Appeals pursuant to § 1003.38") (emphasis added).

Finally, exhaustion of administrative remedies would be futile in this case because the BIA has no jurisdiction to adjudicate constitutional issues raised here.[1] *See Mathews v. Eldridge*, 424 U.S. 319, 328-30 (1976) (A constitutional challenge to administrative action does not require exhaustion.); *Jean v. Nelson*, 727 F.2d 957, 981 (11th Cir. 1984) (en banc), aff'd, 472 U.S. 846, 105 S.Ct. 2992 (1985) (allowing exception to exhaustion requirement where remaining administrative remedies could not cure alleged defect in agency procedures); *Ramirez-Osorio v. INS*, 745 F.2d 937, 939 (5th Cir. 1984) (holding that "exhaustion is not required when administrative remedies are inadequate"); *Haitian Refugee Center v. Smith*, 676 F.2d 1023, 1033-36 (5th Cir. 1982) (same). Some courts have held that, notwithstanding the constitutional claims, exhaustion is still required if the claims involve a procedural error that is correctable by the administrative tribunal. *Vargas v. INS*, 831 F.2d 906, 908 (9th Cir. 1987); *Dhangu v. INS*, 812 F.2d 455, 460 (9th Cir.1987). Nonetheless, exhaustion is not required here since the BIA has no expertise to adjudicate the equal protection claim raised in the instant case. *See Gar-*

[1] It should be noted that the instant case is <u>distinguishable</u> from *Boz v. United States*, 248 F.3d 1299 (11th Cir. 2001), wherein the Eleventh Circuit affirmed the district court's dismissal of a habeas petition for lack of jurisdiction on the ground that the petitioner failed to exhausted the administrative remedies available to him. However, *Boz* does not apply here because that case involved the post-removal mandatory detention of <u>criminal</u> aliens under INA § 236(c) and § 241, where administrative remedies were available to the petitioner, 90-days after issuance of his final order of removal. To the contrary, the instant case involves pre-removal non-mandatory detention of a <u>non-criminal</u> alien under <u>INA § 236(a)</u>. Here, the Petitioner "need not exhaust his administrative remedies" because the only available administrative remedy, appeal to the BIA, would be futile as it "will not provide relief commensurate with the claim" raised in the instant case. *Haitian Refugee Ctr., Inc. v. Nelson*, 872 F.2d 1555, 1561 (11th Cir. 1989). In addition, the continuing validity of *Boz* is in doubt in light of *Zadvydas v. Davis*, 533 U.S. 678, 701, 121 S.Ct. 2491 (2001). Subsequent to *Boz*, the Supreme Court in *Zadvydas* held that detention of permanent resident aliens beyond six months following issuance of an alien's final order of removal is <u>presumptively</u> unreasonable. *Zadvydas*, 533 U.S at 701-02. In *Boz*, the petitioner had been held in post-removal detention for approximately three (3) years. *Boz*, 248 F.3d at 1300.

berding v. INS, 30 F.3d 1187, 1188 n.1 (9th Cir. 1994) (Although a party may be required to exhaust a procedural due process claim that could be remedied by the IJ, an equal protection claim that the IJ/BIA cannot decide does not require exhaustion); *Jankowski v. INS*, 138 F. Supp. 2d 269, 273-76 (D. Conn. 2001) *rev'd on other grounds* 291 F.3d 172 (2d Cir. 2002) (Equal protection challenge does not require exhaustion).

C. This Court's Authority to Grant the Instant Motion

This Court has the discretion to enter a temporary restraining order and a preliminary injunction. *See Haitian Refugee Center v. Nelson*, 872 F.2d 1555, 1561-1562 (11th Cir. 1989). In order for preliminary relief to issue, the movant must establish the following: (1) a substantial likelihood that the movants will ultimately prevail on the merits; (2) that he will suffer irreparable injury if the injunction is not issued; (3) that the threatened injury to the movant outweighs the potential harm to the opposing party; and (4) that the injunction, if issued, would not be adverse to the public interest. *Id.* As discussed below, all of these factors heavily weigh in the Petitioner's favor in the instant case.

II. SUBSTANTIAL LIKELIHOOD THAT THE PETITIONER WILL PREVAIL ON THE MERITS OF HIS CLAIMS

A. Statutory Violation of INA § 236(a)

1. Standard of Statutory Construction

When reviewing an agency's interpretation of a statute, the Court must apply established canons of statutory construction. *I.N.S. v. Cardoza-Fonseca,* 480 U.S. 421, 431, 107 S.Ct. 1207, 94 L.Ed.2d 434 (1987). The words used are to be given their ordinary meaning, *Chevron v. Natural Resources Defense Council, Inc.*, 467 U.S. 837, 104 S.Ct. 2778 (1984), and the language in question is to be construed in harmony with related provisions and the statute as a whole. *K Mart Corp. v. Cartier Inc.*, 486 U.S. 281, 291, 108 S.Ct. 1811, 100 L.Ed.2d 313 (1988). Furthermore, the language should not be construed in a way that renders a term surplusage. *United States v. Menasche*, 348 U.S. 528, 75 S.Ct. 513, 99 L.Ed. 615 (1955). If the language regarding intent is ambiguous, the Court must defer to the agency's reasonable interpretation of the statute. *Chevron,* 467 U.S. at 843. If the language of the statute is not ambiguous, the intent of Congress must be given effect. *Hughes Aircraft Co. v. Jacobson*, 525 U.S. 432, 438, 119 S.Ct. 755, 142 L.Ed.2d 881 (1999); *Chevron, U.S.A.,* 467 U.S. 837 at 842-43, 104 S.Ct. 2778, 81 L.Ed.2d 694. An agency's interpretation may be overturned only if it is arbitrary, capricious, or manifestly contrary to law. *Chevron, U.S.A.*, 467 U.S. at 842-43, 104 S.Ct. 2778. However, the federal courts should defer to an agency decision only when the statute, "applying the normal 'tools of statutory construction,' [is] ambiguous." *INS v. St. Cyr*, 533 U.S. 289, 320 n. 45, 121 S.Ct. 2271 (internal citations omitted).

2. Section 236(a) clearly authorizes the IJ to "prescribe" and impose bond conditions he deems appropriate

Applying these standards, it is clear that § 236(a) authorizes the IJ to "prescribe" and impose bond conditions he deems appropriate. Under § 236(a)(2), the Attorney General (and his designate the immigration judge) "may release the alien on—(A) bond of at least $1,500, with security approved by, and *containing conditions prescribed by, the Attorney General* . . . (emphasis added). The plain language of the statute, therefore, authorizes the IJ to "prescribe" and impose conditions for bond. Under the statute, the only limit imposed on the IJ's authority is granting work authorization to **[Alien]** as a condition of release. INA §236(a)(3). Therefore, giving the words of the statute their ordinary meaning, as required, *Chevron,* 467 U.S. 837, § 236(a) authorizes the IJ to impose bond conditions he deems appropriate. Federal case law interpreting

§ 236(a) in the context of the IJ's authority to impose bond conditions also supports Petitioner's construction of the statute. Petitioner's research reveals only three federal district court cases that interpreted § 236(a) in that context. All of these cases clearly indicate that, when determining release on bond under § 236(a), the IJ has statutory authority to impose any conditions he/she deems appropriate. *Quezada-Bucio v. Ridge*, 317 F.Supp.2d 1221 (W.D. Wash. 2004) ("The IJ would then determine, based on the standard set forth in INA § 236(a), whether, and *under what conditions*, petitioner may be released from custody pending the resolution of his appeal before the BIA") (emphasis added). *Alwaday v. Beebe*, 43 F.Supp.2d 1130 (D. Or. 1999) (same); *Pastor-Camarena v. Smith,* 977 F. Supp. 1415, 1418 (W.D. Wash. 1997) (same).

3. Companion Regulations to § 236(a) also Authorize the IJ to Impose Bond Conditions He Deems Appropriate

Nor do the regulations of the Department of Justice prohibit the IJ from setting other conditions of bond. 8 C.F.R. §1003.19 (2004); 8 C.F.R. § 1236.1(d). In fact, 8 C.F.R. § 1236.1(d) provides that the IJ may impose conditions other than monetary condition. This regulatory provision provides that:

> After an initial custody determination by the district director, including the setting of a bond, the respondent may, at any time before an order under 8 CFR part 1240 becomes final, request *amelioration of the conditions under which he or she may be released.* (emphasis added). Prior to such final order . . . the immigration judge is authorized to exercise the authority in section 236 of the Act . . . to detain the alien in custody, release the alien, and determine the amount of bond, if any, under which the respondent may be released, as provided in § 1003.19 of this chapter. If the alien has been released from custody, an application for amelioration of the terms of release must be filed within 7 days of release.

This regulatory provision provides that an alien in removal proceedings may seek reconsideration of the Service's initial custody determination before an IJ at any time before a final order of removal is issued against him, including amelioration of conditions of his release. It further provides that such alien may seek amelioration of the terms of release even after he is released. This by implication means that the IJ has authority to impose various conditions of his release before a final order of removal is issued.

In addition, the regulatory provision provides that the IJ has authority under INA § 236 to release the alien, and determine the amount of bond, if any, under which the respondent may be released, as provided in § 1003.19 of this chapter. As indicated previously, § 236 only prohibits the IJ from granting work authorization to **[Alien]** as a condition of release, and authorizes the IJ to "prescribe" and impose conditions for bond. INA §236(a)(2)(A). Nor does 8 C.F.R. §1003.19 prohibit the IJ from setting other conditions of bond. Therefore, reading "in harmony" these "related" statutory and regulatory provisions "as a whole," as required, *K Mart*, 486 U.S. at 291, the only logical conclusion that can be drawn is that the IJ has authority under INA §236(a) to "prescribe and impose" any conditions for bond he deems necessary. Reading the statute otherwise would render the terms of the statute surplusage, *see Menasche, supra*, contravening the intent of Congress in enacting the statute.

4. The IJ's Decision Directly Contravenes § 236(a) and its Companion Regulations

The IJ's bond determination in the instant case was arbitrary, capricious, and manifestly contrary to law, because it directly contradicts the plain meaning of § 236(a) and companion regulations, which authorize him to consider conditions other than monetary condition for bond. *Chevron, U.S.A.*, 467 U.S. at 842-43, 104 S.Ct. 2778 (An agency's interpretation may be overturned only if it is arbitrary, capricious, or manifestly contrary to law.). The IJ impermissibly concluded that he had no statutory authority to impose any conditions of bond, other than financial conditions, that would ensure **[Alien]**'s appearance. Ignoring all the other conditions suggested by **[Alien]**, the IJ reasoned that financial conditions would not ensure **[Alien]**'s appearance, because as a Mexican citizen he could obtain a birth certificate and cross the border. *See* Habeas Petition, ¶ 20; *see also* Declaration Under Penalty of Perjury of **[Alien]**, attached as Exh. 8 to Habeas Petition (hereinafter refferred to as "**[Alien]** Decl."), ¶¶ 10-11. As discussed, *supra*, the IJ's claim that he could not impose any other conditions, such as electronic monitoring, extensive reporting, or ordering **[Alien]** to provide his passports to ICE, and therefore could not guarantee his appearance, is in clear contravention of INA §236(a)(2)(A), 8 U.S.C. §1226(a)(2)(A), and its companion regulations.

B. The IJ Violated Petitioner's Equal Protection Rights Under the Fifth Amendment to the United States Constitution

At the hearing, the IJ denied Petitioner's release on bond, specifically on the basis of his Mexican citizenship. According to the IJ, because Petitioner is a citizen of Mexico he may not be released on bond because he "could use his Mexican birth certificate to cross the border into Mexico" and, therefore, again according to the IJ, this makes Petitioner a "flight risk" and not eligible for release. However on the basis of this faulty and speculative reasoning, any alien of Mexican nationality before any immigration judge in the future could be disabled from being released on bond, merely on the basis of his Mexican national origin. Such a result is discriminatory and plainly unconstitutional, as will be discussed. It is clear that the IJ's decision to deny release on bond on such a basis was in contravention of equal protection and due process clause contained in the Fifth Amendment to the United States Constitution.

It is well-settled that equal protection applies to aliens who are physically present in, and admitted to, the United States to the same scope and extent as United States citizens. *Yick Wo v. Hopkins*, 118 U.S. 356, 369 (1886) (holding that the protections of the Constitution "are universal in their application to all persons within the territorial jurisdiction, without regard to any differences of race, of color or of nationality"); *Plyler v. Doe*, 457 U.S. 202, 211-12, 102 S.Ct. 2382, 2391-92, (1982) (the Fifth, Sixth, and Fourteenth Amendments apply to all persons within the United States, including excludable aliens); *Korematsu v. U.S.*, 323 U.S. 214, 216 (1944) (applying strict scrutiny to incarceration of Japanese in United States during World War II); *Bolling v. Sharpe*, 347 U.S. 497 (1954) (applying strict scrutiny to race discrimination in schools in Washington, D.C.); *Castaneda v. Partida*, 430 U.S. 482 (1977); *Hernandez v. Texas*, 347 U.S. 475 (1954) (holding that national origin discrimination against Hispanics in grand jury selection impermissible); *Oyama v. California*, 332 U.S. 633, 644-47 (1948) (holding that restriction on transfer of agricultural property of Japanese lawful permanent resident is a violation of equal protection).

The Supreme Court in *Zadvydas v. Davis, discussed supra*, underscored in that decision the importance of constitutional rights attaching to aliens within the borders of the United States. As the Court clearly stated, "[t]he distinction between an alien who has effected an entry into the United States and one who has never entered runs throughout immigration law. . . It is well established that certain constitutional protections available to persons inside the United States are unavailable to aliens outside of our geographic borders. *Zadvydas*, 533 U.S. at 693 (citing *United States v. Verdugo-Urquidez*, 494 U.S. 259, 269, 110 S.Ct. 1056, 108 L.Ed.2d 222 (1990) (Fifth Amendment's protections do not extend to aliens outside the territorial boundaries); *Johnson v. Eisentrager*, 339 U.S. 763, 784, 70 S.Ct. 936, 94 L.Ed. 1255 (1950) (same). The Court made clear however that "once an alien enters the country, the legal circumstance changes, for the Due Process Clause applies to all "persons" within the United States, including aliens, whether their presence here is lawful, unlawful, temporary, or permanent. *Id.* (citing *Plyler v. Doe*, 457 U.S. 202, 210, 102 S.Ct. 2382 (1982); *Mathews v. Diaz*, 426 U.S. 67, 77, 96 S.Ct. 1883 (1976); *Kwong Hai Chew v. Colding*, 344 U.S. 590, 596-598, and n. 5, 73 S.Ct. 472, 97 L.Ed. 576 (1953); *Yick Wo v. Hopkins*, 118 U.S. 356, (1886)).

Petitioner has been admitted to the United States since 1999, and therefore unquestionably enjoys the full protection of the Equal Protection Clause under the case law cited above. *See* Habeas Petition, ¶ 10; Decl. ¶ 1. **[Alien]**'s only charge of removal appearing in his Notice of Removal, issued November 19, 2004, is that he failed to maintain or comply with the conditions of his change of status, in violation of INA § 237(a)(1)(C)(i). *See* Habeas Petition, Exh. 3. The reason for his overstay was inadvertent, *see* Habeas Petition, ¶ 12; Decl. ¶ 4, as **[Alien]** was laid-off from his professional position and was given faulty advice by prior counsel that he had six months to depart the United States after his lay-off. *Id.* **[Alien]** had never previously violated any immigration laws of the United States and has never knowingly violated or even been *accused* of violating any other laws of the United States, immigration or criminal, before his arrest and incarceration without bond. *Id.*

Because the IJ's decision rested on a "suspect classification," namely Petitioner's national origin as a Mexican citizen, it is well-settled that there must be some compelling governmental interest for the imposition of such classification for it to be permissible under the United States Constitution. As the Supreme Court noted in *Demore v. Hyung Joon Kim*, 538 U.S. 510, 123 S.Ct. 1708 (2003), there is an "uncontroversial requirement that detention serve a compelling governmental interest and that detainees be afforded adequate procedures ensuring against erroneous confinement." *Id.* at 566 n. 22 (citing *Zadvydas v. Davis*, 533 U.S. 678, 721 (2001) (Kennedy, J., dissenting) (stating that due process requires "adequate procedures" permitting detained aliens to show that "they no longer present special risks or danger" warranting confinement)). Moreover, any action by the government based on an individual's national origin must be "narrowly tailored" to effectuate the asserted compelling governmental interest. *See Adarand Constructors, Inc. v. Pena*, 515 U.S. 200, 115 S.Ct. 2097 (1995) (holding that all racial classifications, imposed by whatever federal, state, or local governmental actor, must be analyzed by reviewing court under strict scrutiny; in other words, such classifications are constitutional only if they are narrowly tailored measures that further compelling governmental interest); *see also City of Richmond v. J.A. Croson Co.*, 488 U.S. 469, 109 S.Ct. 706 (1989).

In the case at bar, there is no question Petitioner's continued detention solely based on the mere fact of his Mexican national origin was arbitrary, capricious and not narrowly tailored in any way to the effectuation of any compelling governmental interest. The lack of "narrow tailoring" is especially apparent due to the fact that undersigned counsel for Petitioner had agreed to the imposition of "any conditions" to the release of Petitioner that the government may have been inclined to require or the IJ inclined to impose. For example, the Petitioner could have been released into a program of home detention, which requires the wearing of an ankle bracelet to closely monitor his whereabouts. In the alternative (or additionally) the IJ could have imposed a requirement that Petitioner report to the Service or any appropriate agency on a daily or weekly basis. These options would have allowed the governmental interests in monitoring and assuring the Petitioner's continued presence to be met while also allowing Petitioner to be released from incarceration.[2]

C. The IJ Also Violated Petitioner's Due Process Rights Under the Fifth Amendment to the United States Constitution

In addition to violating Petitioner's equal protection rights, the IJ additionally violated **[Alien]**'s substantive and procedural due process rights because the IJ determined (erroneously) that he had no power to set any conditions of bond, and that, therefore and *a fortiori*, no conditions of bond could possibly satisfy the government's concerns that Petitioner might constitute a "flight risk." This failure to impose any conditions

[2] The government will allege that the compelling governmental interest is premised on **[Alien]**'s alleged status as a "fugitive." However, there is simply no evidence that Petitioner has engaged in any crime, nor has he ever fled any jurisdiction to evade criminal prosecution while any charges were pending. To the contrary, the evidence will show that **[Alien]** left Ecuador in 1999, and charges were not brought against him until one (1) and two (2) years following his departure. *See* Habeas Petition, ¶ 15 and Exh. 5; Decl. ¶ 8. As soon as charges were brought against him, he retained counsel in Ecuador who is currently vigorously fighting those charges. Ecuadorian law contains a presumption of innocence and there is no convicton against **[Alien]**. Indeed, there is absolutely no evidence that Ecuador is particularly concerned about **[Alien]** as the Ecuadorian courts have not initiated any extradition proceedings against him. *See* Habeas Petition, Exh. 4; Decl. ¶ 7. No extradition proceedings are currently pending. *Id.* Moreover, **[Alien]** has remained in the United States for over five years without any indication that he would hide his presence or flee the country. *See e.g.* Exhibit 1. Finally, the recent interest in **[Alien]** is tied directly to the mother of his child who has used Ecuadorian authorities as a means to snatch custody of their child from him and to thwart the decision of Florida state court custody proceedings. Exh. 2.

on Petitioner's release on bond, including, as discussed, electronic monitoring, as well as retention of passports, daily reporting and a monetary bond, was an impermissible basis to deny release on bond. In addition, by refusing to impose *any* conditions, the IJ thereby pretermitted any meaningful opportunity for **[Alien]** to be heard on the issue of whether he could be released on bond. Had the IJ exercised his clear statutory authority to set conditions on bond, then **[Alien]** would certainly have argued that such conditions adequately ensure his presence at future hearings, and assuage the government's concerns about his risk of flight.

As the Supreme Court has stated, "[a]n essential principle of due process is that a deprivation of life, liberty, or property be preceded by notice and opportunity for hearing appropriate to the nature of the case." *Hamdi v. Rumsfeld*, -- U.S. --, 124 S.Ct. 2633, 2648 (2004) (quoting *Mullane v. Central Hanover Bank & Trust Co.*, 339 U.S. 306, 313, 70 S.Ct. 652, 94 L.Ed. 865 (1950)); *Concrete Pipe & Products of Cal., Inc. v. Construction Laborers Pension Trust for Southern Cal.*, 508 U.S. 602, 617, 113 S.Ct. 2264 (1993) ("due process requires a 'neutral and detached judge in the first instance'") (quoting *Ward v. Monroeville*, 409 U.S. 57, 61-62, 93 S.Ct. 80 (1972)). The Court also reiterated that "[f]or more than a century the central meaning of procedural due process has been clear: 'Parties whose rights are to be affected are entitled to be heard; and in order that they may enjoy that right they must first be notified.' It is equally fundamental that the right to notice and an opportunity to be heard 'must be granted at a meaningful time and in a meaningful manner.'" *Id.* at 2648-49 (emphasis added) (citing *Fuentes v. Shevin*, 407 U.S. 67, 80, 92 S.Ct. 1983, 32 L.Ed.2d 556 (1972) (quoting *Baldwin v. Hale*, 1 Wall. 223, 233, 17 L.Ed. 531 (1864); *Armstrong v. Manzo*, 380 U.S. 545, 552, 85 S.Ct. 1187, 14 L.Ed.2d 62 (1965) (other citations omitted)). "These essential constitutional promises may not be eroded." *Id.*

In the instant case, Petitioner's substantive due process rights were violated by the IJ's application of a clearly incorrect legal principle, namely that he is prohibited under legal authority from setting any conditions on bond other than monetary conditions. *See* 8 C.F.R. §§ 1236.1 and 1003.19. Such a blatant and fundamental legal error meets the test for a substantive due process violation. As the stated by the court in *Amsden v. Moran*, 904 F.2d 748 (1st Cir. 1990), "a substantive due process claim implicates the essence of state action rather than its modalities; such a claim rests not on perceived procedural deficiencies but on the idea that the government's conduct, regardless of procedural swaddling, was in itself impermissible. . . .It has been said, for instance, that substantive due process protects individuals against state actions which are 'arbitrary and capricious,' . . . or those which run counter to 'the concept of ordered liberty'" *Id.* at 754. The IJ's conduct in holding that he was without authority to impose conditions when he actually had such authority was "stunning, evidencing more than humdrum legal error," as is required to meet the test for a substantive due process violation. *Id.* at 754 n. 5.

Moreover, Petitioner's procedural due process rights were also violated because he was pretermitted from engaging in any discussion of the appropriateness of any conditions on bond due to the IJ's erroneous impression that the judge lacked any authority to impose such conditions. As discussed above, the IJ does possess such authority. *See Quezada-Bucio v. Ridge*, 317 F. Supp. 2d 1221 (W.D. Wash. 2004); *Alwaday v. Beebe*, 43 F. Supp. 2d 1130 (D. Or. 1999); *Pastor-Camarena v. Smith,* 977 F. Supp. 1415, 1418 (W.D. Wa.1997). Such an error worked a violation of Petitioner's right to be heard and to meaningfully present his claims in such an important matter such that **[Alien]** was prevented from protecting his liberty interest to be free from continued detention.

III. THE PETITIONER WILL SUFFER IRREPARABLE INJURY IF THE INJUNCTION IS NOT ISSUED

1. Continued Detention Itself Represents a Continuing Irreparable Injury to Petitioner

The fact that **[Alien]** will remain incarcerated unlawfully represents in and of itself a continuing irreparable injury to Petitioner. *United States v. Montalvo-Murillo*, 495 U.S. 711 (1990) ("[I]t is well to remember the magnitude of the injury that pretrial detention inflicts and the departure that it marks from ordinary forms of constitutional governance"); *Grodzki v. Reno*, 950 F. Supp. 339, 342 (N.D. Ga. 1996) ("The court . . .finds that the continued detention of [the petitioner], a permanent resident alien, without affording him an individualized bond determination hearing, constitutes irreparable injury and that emergency relief is necessary to prevent this injury"); *Dash v. Mitchell*, 356 F. Supp. 1292, 1309 (D. D.C. 1972) ("Pretrial detention inflicts irreparable injury on persons detained by subjecting them to incarceration without any compensation, even if the detention is subsequently held to have been wrongfully imposed").

2. Petitioner's Continued Detention Will Separate Him from His Family

Furthermore, if Petitioner is denied release on bond with reasonable conditions, he will suffer irreparable injury in that he will be separated from his wife and two U.S. citizen children who are extremely close to him. *See United States v. Wharton*, 514 F.2d 406, 408, 412 (9th Cir. 1975) ("Governmental conduct would work a serious injustice if this family were divested of the home in which they have invested so much of themselves"); *Tefel v. Reno*, 972 F. Supp. 608, 619-620 (S.D. Fla. 1997) (failure to issue temporary restraining order would result in irreparable injury including family separation), *rev'd on other grounds* 180 F.3d 1286 (11th Cir. 1999).

Based on the letters submitted by Petitioner and his immediate family members, it is evident that his continued detention will cause them extreme emotional harm and break up their tight-knit and loving family. *See* Habeas Petition, Exh. 1 (indicating that he will suffer extreme emotional harm by being separated from his family). In a physician's letter dated December 20, 2004, the doctor reports that **[Alien]**'s two children "suffer severe cases of asthma."*Id.*

IV. THE PETITIONER'S INJURIES OVERWHELMINGLY OUTWEIGH ANY POTENTIAL HARM TO THE RESPONDENTS

The injury to the Petitioner far outweighs the potential harm to the Respondents by permitting him to be released on conditions of bond while awaiting conclusion of his removal proceedings. As discussed *supra*, Petitioner will suffer various forms of irreparable harm if he remains in detention. On the other hand, the Respondents will suffer no harm if the Petitioner is permitted to be released on bond and remains in the United States pending his removal proceedings. He poses no risk to United States security or to his community nor is he a flight risk. To the contrary, as indicated in numerous support letters, he is man of great character and who has generously helped and positively influenced numerous individuals. *See* Exh. 1. Although the IJ found that Petitioner is a flight risk, as discussed *supra*, that finding has no support in law or in fact. Petitioner has no history of immigration law violations, prior to the NTA issued in November, nor has he ever failed to appear before the IJ when he was required to do so. The IJ failed to consider these factors that clearly establish that Petitioner does not pose any flight risk. Instead, the IJ found Petitioner to be a flight risk solely based on his speculation that "he could get a Mexican birth certificate and cross the border." Such a finding is based on mere speculation, and if upheld, will render bond hearings meaningless for all Mexican citizens because no Mexican citizen would ever be eligible for a bond because he or she could "get a birth certificate" and "cross the border." Because Petitioner does not pose any danger to the community or flight risk, there would be no harm to the Respondent by releasing the Petitioner.

V. THE ISSUANCE OF THE INJUNCTION IS NOT ADVERSE TO THE PUBLIC INTEREST

The issuance of the injunction in this case is not adverse to the public interest. In fact, the issuance of an injunction strongly favors the public interest here. It is clearly against public policy and the public's interest to separate members of an immediate family. Indeed, one of the purposes behind our immigration law is to preserve family unity. *See, e.g., INS v. Errico*, 385 U.S. 214 (1966). Furthermore, the invidious racial and national origin classification at the base of the IJ's ruling, if allowed to stand, would represent a judicial imprimatur of impermissible racial and national origin discrimination. Such a ruling is not only unsupported legally, but also adverse to the public interest in protecting minorities from arbitrary, capricious and unconstitutional governmental actions.

CONCLUSION

WHEREFORE, the Petitioner respectfully requests that this Honorable Court enter an order enjoining Respondents, and their agents, from preventing Petitioner's release on bond; releasing Petitioner from physical custody pending the outcome of the instant action on any reasonable conditions on bond that would ensure his appearance at any future immigration proceedings; and declaring that the actions and/or decisions of **[Immigration Judge]** were (a) in violation of the Equal Protection guarantees of the Due Process Clause of the Fifth Amendment by utilizing the impermissible criteria of national origin as a basis to deny bond; (b) in violation of the Due Process Clause of the Fifth Amendment by determining that no conditions of bond could be set and therefore no conditions of bond could satisfy release; and (c) in violation of the INA and DOJ regulations because an immigration judge does have the authority to set conditions of bond in a removal proceeding.

[Dated:]

Respectfully submitted,

[Attorney]

[ADD CERTIFICATE OF SERVICE]

UNITED STATES DISTRICT COURT
SOUTHERN DISTRICT OF FLORIDA

[Alien]	)	CIVIL ACTION NO.
	)	
Petitioner/Plaintiff,	)	
	)	
vs.	)	
	)	
ALBERTO GONZALES, as Attorney General of the United States; MICHAEL CHERTOFF, as Secretary of the U.S. Department of Homeland Security; MARION DILLIS, Officer in Charge, Krome Service Processing Center (SPC), Immigration and Customs Enforcement (ICE), United States Department of Homeland Security; MICHAEL ROZOS, Field Office Director, Miami ICE Detention and Removal Office, United States Department of Homeland Security,	)	
	)	
Respondents/Defendants.	)	

______________________________________/

ORDER GRANTING PETITIONER'S/PLAINTIFF'S MOTION FOR A TEMPORARY RESTRAINING ORDER

THIS CAUSE came before this Court at _____ a.m./p.m., on December _____, 2004, upon Petitioner/Plaintiff **[Alien]**'s Motion for a Temporary Restraining Order (TRO). Upon review of the pleadings and after hearing oral argument, being otherwise fully advised in the underlying premises, it is hereby ordered and adjudged that:

1. Petitioner/Plaintiff's Motion for a Temporary Restraining Order is granted until January, ____, 2005;

2. The Respondents, their agents, officers and employees are enjoined and restrained from preventing Petitioner's release on bond; and

3. The Respondents, through their agents, officers or employees, are directed to immediately release Petitioner **[Alien]** from physical custody pending the outcome of the instant action on any reasonable conditions on bond that would ensure his appearance at any future immigration hearings.

4. Absent a change in circumstances, this Order shall be automatically renewed for an additional ten (10) days from the date this Order expires;

5. Absent agreement between the parties, a preliminary injunction hearing will be held before this Court on January ____, 2005.

DONE and ORDERED on this ____ day of December, 2004, in chambers at Miami, Country of Miami-Dade, Florida.

[United States District Judge]

cc: All counsel of record

[Document No. 511]

EMERGENCY PETITION FOR WRIT OF HABEAS CORPUS TO PREVENT UNLAWFUL REMOVAL

Description: This petition for writ of habeas corpus is filed on an "emergency" basis seeking to stop ICE from removing a person from the United States. This particular type of writ would be appropriate in the limited circumstances of DHS failing to follow constitutional processes in obtaining and effectuating the order or removal. This petition for a writ of habeas corpus was filed with the U.S. district court before the REAL ID Act was enacted, and it still should be viable after the Act's passage. Moreover, the federal district courts appear to retain jurisdiction over this type of habeas—which challenges unconstitutional removal by ICE—notwithstanding the REAL ID Act. The habeas petition calls into question the constitutionality of this particular removal process.

Advantages: Use of this petition for habeas corpus may force ICE to stop a foreign national's physical removal from the United States, which may be necessary to ensure that the foreign national has been permitted to seek relief to which he or she is entitled. The legal arguments are strong, and the well-written habeas is likely to be a winner. There is nothing much to lose because the client is already detained pending removal.

Limitations: Frankly, while the contributor and editors are confident this type of habeas would survive the REAL ID Act, no guarantees are given until that statute has undergone several years of judicial review. The worst case scenario would be to file this habeas in the circuit court instead.

Final Tips: Ask for an emergency hearing and/or TRO. Remember, the client is detained and the Rules of Civil Procedure allow the court to move slowly unless counsel frames the matter as emergent. Do not forget to ask for the EAJA fees.

UNITED STATES DISTRICT COURT
FOR THE DISTRICT OF COLORADO

[Alien]	)	
	)	
Petitioner-Plaintiff	)	Civ. No.____________
	)	
v.	)	
	)	
DOUGLAS MAURER,	)	
Field Director, Immigration & Customs	)	
Enforcement, DHS	)	
	)	
DEPARTMENT OF HOMELAND SECURITY	)	
	)	
Respondent- Defendant.	)	
____________________________________	)	

EMERGENCY PETITION FOR WRIT OF HABEAS CORPUS AND COMPLAINT FOR DECLARATORY AND INJUNCTIVE RELIEF

Petitioner, **[Alien]**, by and through his undersigned counsel, hereby respectfully petitions this Honorable Court for a writ of habeas corpus to prevent her unlawful removal, to provide an opportunity for her to have meaningful review of the Respondent's failure to provide her with a meaningful review of her immigration case and to enjoin Respondents from removing Petitioner, finding her ineligible for relief, and/or subject to detention and removal from the United States.

In support of this petition and complaint for declaratory and injunctive relief, Petitioner alleges as follows:

CUSTODY

1. Respondent previously detained **[Alien]** at the DHS detention facility at 11901 E. 30th Avenue, Aurora, Colorado. On Monday, March 7, without prior notice to counsel, Respondents delivered **[Alien]** into the custody of at least one unidentified agent, and began the process of effecting her removal from the United States to Israel with an itinerary having a brief layover in Newark, New Jersey.

2. Pursuant to preliminary negotiations with Respondent (as well as due to the possibility that **[Alien]** might be of interest to the US government as a material witness in an unrelated criminal matter), Respondents agreed to refrain from placing **[Alien]** on the connecting flight from Newark to Israel pending resolution of her value as a witness.

3. During her time in New Jersey, **[Alien]** has been temporarily housed at the ICE detention facility in Elizabeth, New Jersey; however, despite numerous attempts by counsel to confirm not only **[Alien]**'s actual whereabouts but also to have direct communications with her, agents of Respondent indicated that control

over the case rested with Denver ICE, as both the custodian effecting the removal, as well as the office undertaking execution of the actual order of removal.

4. Counsel has been informed that Respondents intend to place **[Alien]** on the continuing leg of her flight from Newark to Israel ***this evening*** at approximately 10:00 pm EST.

5. Petitioner remains under the direct and constructive control of Respondents and their agents.

JURISDICTION AND VENUE

6. This action arises under the Constitution of the United States, the Immigration and Nationality Act ("INA"), 8 U.S.C. § 1101 *et seq.,* and the Administrative Procedure Act ("APA"), 5 U.S.C. § 701 *et seq.* This Court has jurisdiction under 28 U.S.C. § 2241(c)(1) & (3), art I. § 9, cl. 2 of the United States Constitution ("Suspension Clause"), and 28 U.S.C. § 1331, as Petitioner subject to imminent custody under color of the authority of the United States, and such custody is in violation of the Constitution, laws, or treaties of the United States. This Court may grant relief pursuant to 28 U.S.C. § 2241, the APA, the Declaratory Judgment Act, 28 U.S.C. § 2201 *et seq.*, and the All Writs Act, 28 U.S.C. § 1651.

7. Venue lies in the United States District Court for Colorado, the judicial district in which Respondents routinely conduct business and Petitioner resides. 28 U.S.C. § 1391(e).

PARTIES

8. Petitioner is a native of Uzbekistan, and citizen of Israel. Her two sons and daughter are naturalized U.S. citizens; her husband is a legal permanent resident or "green card" holder. Petitioner resides in Denver, Colorado.

9. Defendant Maurer is the Interim Field Director, Immigration & Customs Enforcement, a subdivision of the Department of Homeland Security, for the Denver District. Respondent Maurer has direct and continuing control over Petitioner, have ordered and authorized her detention in Aurora, Colorado, as well as her imminent removal to Israel.

10. Defendant, Department of Homeland Security ("DHS"), has responsibility for the administration of the immigration laws pursuant to 8 U.S.C. § 1103, routinely does and transacts business in Colorado, has responsibility for any determination on voluntary departure and is responsible for Petitioner's arrest, detention and current attempted deportation.

11. Defendant-Respondent DHS is made a party/defendant for purposes of obtaining declaratory and injunctive relief pursuant to the APA and the Declaratory Judgment Act. DHS, through USICE exercise power and authority over aliens on a nationwide basis and are sued in their capacities as a legal custodians of Petitioner-Plaintiff.

EXHAUSTION OF REMEDIES

12. Petitioner's request to DHS to refrain from removing her at this time has been denied. A Motion to Reopen, based on the numerous legal and constitutional deficiencies, is being filed with the Board of Immigration Appeals, however no decision on this Motion will be forthcoming in advance of Petitioner's scheduled removal. Thus, Petitioner has exhausted her administrative remedies to the extent required by law, and her only remedy is by way of this judicial action.

STATEMENT OF FACTS

13. Petitioner is a native of Uzbekistan and citizen of Israel, who entered the United States lawfully in early 1988 as a B-2 visitor. She has neither a criminal record nor record of any immigration violations, but for her overstay of her authorized period of stay.

14. Petitioner is the beneficiary of an approved I-130 Immigrant Relative petition filed by her US citizen daughter, which provides her with an immediately available immigrant visa.

15. Petitioner initially retained an attorney, **[Attorney 1]**, to help her regularize her status. The attorney did not speak Russian or Hebrew; Petitioner's primary languages are Russian and Hebrew. Petitioner had little or no experience with English at the time of her entry, and at the time she undertook her efforts to regularize her status spoke and understood little or no English. Petitioner relied on her daughter to translate in some cases, but essentially trusted counsel's recommendations.

16. Petitioner was referred to immigration court for a deportation hearing in approximately the middle of 1994. Although the attorney who had previously represented her appeared at the initial hearing, he apparently either failed to enter an appearance or withdrew. Petitioner's daughter was present, and served as an informal reference for her mother, letting her know that (1) the judge was recommending that they return for a continued hearing to allow her to retain a new attorney; and (2) their attorney indicated would referred the case to a "colleague."

17. Petitioner was referred to **[Individual]**, who appeared with Petitioner at a deportation hearing. **[Individual]** represented himself to Petitioner as an attorney; however, the record reflects that he was merely an immigration "consultant." **[Individual]** did not speak Russian or Hebrew, and was unable to communicate with Petitioner at the hearing.

18. No translator was provided to Petitioner at the time of either hearing. Petitioner did not understand the proceedings because they were conducted entirely in English. Any advisals, including required advisals related to her rights to continue with her asylum application, availability of other relief, appeal rights or even the basic information about voluntary departure and consequences for failure to timely depart, were never communicated to Petitioner. The Immigration Judge apparently ordered voluntary departure.

19. It is unclear if an appeal of the order was waived or reserved, however, even if "waived" through **[Individual]**, such a waiver would not have been effective because it could not have been made knowingly or willingly, given that there was no way to communicate with Petitioner due to the language barrier.

20. On the basis of his representations following the hearing, Petitioner retained **[Individual]** to file an appeal in her case, paying approximately $4,000 to continue her pursuit of lawful status. Petitioner believed that the appeal—like many filed in immigration cases—was simply pending for several years. Unfortunately, the record reflects that no appeal of the initial order was ever perfected.

21. When Petitioner's daughter naturalized, becoming a US citizen, Petitioner became eligible for sponsorship as an immediate relative, providing her with an immediately available visa.

22. Petitioner applied for permanent residence on the basis of that filing, and although eligible to adjust and otherwise admissible, she was informed that she was ineligible to receive status at that time, because of the prior deportation hearing.

23. Respondents, through Denver USCIS, informed Petitioner that she should file a Motion to Reopen her case, which would allow her to proceed with finalizing her residency application.

24. Petitioner, with the assistance of her daughter, filed a pro se Motion to Reopen the matter with USCIS. USCIS denied the Motion to Reopen, stating (correctly) that the office did not have jurisdiction over the matter.

25. In March 2002, Petitioner, again pro se, refilled the Motion with the Immigration Court in New York, stating clearly the errors committed by **[Individual]** and explaining that she was otherwise eligible to proceed with the application for residence but for the prior immigration proceedings.

26. The Immigration Judge denied the Motion, citing only that it was out of time (beyond the 90 day filing requirements). In a footnote, the Immigration Judge noted that the matter appeared to be related to ineffective assistance of counsel, providing an exception to the filing deadline, however, Petitioner's pro se Motion allegedly failed to comply with requirements under *Matter of Lozada*, 19 I& N Dec. 637 (BIA 1988).

27. The denial for failure to show compliance with *Lozada* was unwarranted as **[Individual]** was not an attorney. See *Rabiu v. INS*, 41 F.3d 879, 882. Petitioner hired counsel, **[Attorney 2]**, who timely appealed the Immigration Judge's denial to the Board of Immigration Appeals.

28. While **[Attorney 2]** did bring to the Board's attention the fact that strict construction of *Lozada* was unnecessary, he failed to inform the Board of the egregious lack of basic procedural due process provided Petitioner when she appeared before the immigration court, including the failure to provide Petitioner with a reading of her rights, an explanation of the available avenues of relief, an explanation of voluntary departure, the ability to extend it through a request to the INS District Director or the consequences of failing to timely depart, or even a translator so that she could understand the proceedings at all. By doing so, **[Attorney 2]** also failed to provide the Board with an explanation of the prejudice she suffered in the prior proceedings.

29. Further, **[Attorney 2]** failed to indicate the relief Petitioner was now eligible to pursue (at a minimum, adjustment of status based on her daughter's approved petition) or to even provide proof of Petitioner's eligibility as required.

30. The Board was forced to deny the appeal, finding that **[Attorney 2]** had not even presented an approved visa petition or application for adjustment of status (the residency application) as part of the filing. Both the approved visa petition and properly completed application for adjustment of status were in **[Attorney 2]**'s possession at the time the appeal was filed; his failure to include them or provide the information to the Board regarding the lack of a translator, advisals and prejudice is inexplicable.

31. Petitioner is fully eligible to apply for permanent residence by way of moving the Board of Immigration Appeals to reopen the proceedings expressly for that purpose. DHS agents are required to join in that effort where such application is not barred by statutory ineligibility or otherwise not merited in the exercise of discretion. *Matter of Velarde-Pacheco*, 23 I&N Dec. 253 (BIA 2002*); see also* General Counsel Memo, "Motions to Reopen for Consideration of Adjustment of Status," May 17, 2001.

32. Based on the failure of the immigration court to provide Petitioner with the minimum due process, the actual prejudice to Petitioner from this error. Based on the procedural deficiencies in the underlying matter, Petitioner's overstay of voluntary departure would not render her statutorily ineligible for adjustment of status. *Matter of Shaar*, Int. Dec. 3290 (BIA 1996). Further, because more than five years have elapsed since the entry of the order of voluntary departure, Petitioner is not now barred from applying for relief.

33. As a person residing in the United States, Petitioner is protected by every clause of the United States Constitution that is not expressly reserved to its citizens. This protection includes the Due Process Clause of the Fifth Amendment, which provides that "[n]o person shall be . . . deprived of life, liberty, or property, without due process of law," U.S. CONST. amend. V. *e.g., Plyler v. Doe*, 457 U.S. 202, 210 (1987); *Mathews v. Diaz*, 426 U.S. 67 (1976); *Yamataya v. Fisher*, 189 U.S. 86 (1903); *see also Doherty v. Thornburgh*, 943 F. 2d 204, 208 (2d Cir. 1991) (finding that even aliens unlawfully present in the U.S. have a "substantive due process right to liberty during deportation proceedings"), *cert. dismissed, Doherty v. Barr*, 503 U.S. 901 (1992).

34. The Fifth Amendment also creates a procedural due process right to be heard at a meaningful time and in a meaningful manner. *Mathews v. Eldridge*, 424 U.S. 319, 334 (1976).

CLAIM FOR RELIEF

35. Petitioner realleges and incorporates by reference each and every allegation contained in the paragraphs 1 through 34 as if set forth fully herein.

36. Respondents' intended deportation of Petitioner is in violation of law and violates Petitioner's right to substantive and procedural due process by depriving her of the ability to proceed with her application for adjustment of status to permanent residence, attached as part of her Motion to Reopen, now pending before the Board of Immigration Appeals. The denial further subjects Petitioner to a ten-year bar to re-entry without review and would separate her from her husband, and three children, all whom are legally resident or citizens of the United States.

GROUNDS FOR RELIEF

1. Due Process Right to Legal Representation

Petitioner is entitled to Due Process of law under the Fifth Amendment to the Constitution of the United States. A long line of cases, including Supreme Court precedents, have established that deportable non-citizens—even those who are unlawfully present in the United States, are protected by the Constitution. *See Yamataya v. Fisher*, 189 U.S. 86 (1903); *Plyler v Doe*, 457 U.S. 202 (1982); *Mathews v. Diaz*, 426 U.S. 67 (1976). The *Plyler* Court explicitly stated that "the Fifth Amendment protects aliens whose presence in this country is unlawful." 457 U.S. at 210. Under the Due Process Clause there is no question that a "vital liberty interest" is at stake when an individual is subject to detention and deportation by legacy INS/DHS. Freedom from custody is a fundamental interest that may not be denied without some individualized determination that the individual poses a safety or flight risk. *Leader v. Blackman*, 744 F. Supp. 500, 509 (S.D. N.Y. 1990); *Caballero v. Caplinger*, No. 95-3129 (E.D. La. Feb. 6, 1996).

Although non-citizens do not possess a Sixth Amendment right to assistance of counsel at government expense in immigration proceedings, they do have a right to competent representation at their own expense. *See* INA §§ 242(b)(2) & 292, 8 U.S.C. §§ 1252(b)(2) & 1362; 8 C.F.R. §§ 3.1(b) & 242.10; *See also Olvera v. INS*, 504 F.2d 1372 (5th Cir. 1974). This fundamental right is considered a part of the Due Process guarantees under the Fifth Amendment to the Constitution. *See Orantes-Hernandez v. Thornburgh*, 919 F.2d 549, 554 (9th Cir. 1990).

In the instant case, **[Alien]** appeared before the Immigration Court with an individual who held himself out to her (and apparently, the Court) as an attorney. Subsequent investigations have revealed, however, that this individual was not duly licensed.

In circumstances such as the instant case where a non-citizen has been the victim of not only ineffective assistance of counsel but outright fraudulent representation, courts have granted relief even absent a showing of prejudice. *See, e.g., Waldron v. INS*, 17 F.3d 511, 518 (2d Cir. 1994).

In the instant case, prejudice is clearly present. Petitioner would have been eligible for relief through an application for suspension of deportation under then-section 244 of the INA within a matter of months. Had she sought to prosecute such an application and schedule a merits hearing, it is extremely likely that the Court would not have been able to find a date prior to which she would become eligible.[1] Although suspension of deportation has been eliminated as a form of relief from deportation and its replacement, cancellation of removal, includes a "stop-time" rule which cuts off accrual of residency upon service of a charging document, at the time of her hearing, it was common practice to continue cases for a few months until an applicant

[1] In most jurisdictions, merits hearings are scheduled at least six months from the date of a calendar due to the volume of cases on an individual Judge's docket.

could meet the seven year requirement. Even if the Judge had refused to continue the matter for such relief, a timely prosecuted appeal would have provided the extra time necessary to qualify and would have justified a motion to remand for consideration of her application. Based on the substantial equities in her case and the extensive family ties she has in the U.S., **[Alien]** would have presented a quite compelling case.

2. Due Process Right to a Fundamentally Fair Hearing

Both statutes and regulations require that individuals placed in immigration proceedings be informed of their right to counsel, their right to examine the evidence against them, their right to present testimony on their own behalf, and their right to appeal the Immigration Judge's decision (among other rights). *See* 8 C.F.R. § 1240.10 (current regulations governing advisals which are essentially identical to those in effect at the time of **[Alien]**'s hearing).

Whether the Judge attempted to inform **[Alien]** of any of these rights (as required) is difficult to determine because a transcript of the proceeding was never ordered. Fortunately, in the instant case, no transcript is necessary because whatever attempts the Judge may have made would have been entirely futile without an interpreter. To this day **[Alien]**'s English skills are fairly limited. At the time she appeared before the Court, her skills were practically non-existent. She first appeared before the Immigration Court, with her prior attorney, who apparently withdrew and referred her to a "colleague," who turned out to be only a consultant. No translator was present (only her daughter—whose English was also fairly limited at the time—was present); the attorney did not speak either Russian or Hebrew. **[Alien]** was able to seek a continuance in order to obtain legal representation.

When she appeared at the next court proceeding, with new "counsel," **[Individual]**, neither she, **[Individual]**, nor the court, could communicate or interpret the proceedings.[2] In and of itself, the failure to provide an interpreter constitutes a denial of due process. *See, e.g., He v. Ashcroft*, 328 F.3d 593, 598 (9th Cir. 2003) ("Due process requires that an applicant be given competent translation services."); *Amadou v. INS*, 226 F.3d 724 (6th Cir. 2000) (finding denial of due process for incompetent interpretation); *see also Matter of Exilus*, 18 I & N Dec. 276 (BIA 1982) (holding that although due process does not require translation of an entire administrative hearing, certain portions of the hearing must be translated in order for the proceeding to be fair). But, equally important, any advisals which might have been provided by the Court would have been totally ineffectual and she was denied an explanation of any of the rights to which she was entitled. *See Accardi v. Shaughnessy*, 347 U.S. 260 (1954) (holding that compliance with its own regulations is an essential safeguard of an alien's right to due process).

In a similar vein, any waiver of rights which may have been asserted by **[Alien]** could not have been considered either knowing or intelligent. She had absolutely no idea of whether she eligible for any relief, whether she could ask for more time, or whether she could appeal the Judge's decision. *See U.S. v. Ahumada-Aguilar*, 295 F.3d 943 (9th Cir. 2002) (finding prejudice where an alien had not been advised of right to appeal the Judge's decision in order to gain sufficient time to qualify for alternative relief); *U.S. v. Arrieta*, 224 F.3d 1076, 1079 (9th Cir. 2000) (holding that pro se alien's waiver of the right to appeal his deportation order was invalid where the IJ failed to inform him about his eligibility for relief from deportation).

Under ordinary circumstances, an individual is bound by the representations of their chosen counsel. In the instant case, however, where counsel (if that term can even be used) was so clearly ineffective any representations which may have been made should be given no effect.

Apart from the lack of an interpreter and the ineffective assistance of counsel, the hearing which ultimately determined her fate suffered from another significant flaw: she was never advised of her right to prosecute the application for asylum which had prompted her referral to immigration proceedings in the first place. While

[2] Her "attorney" did not speak either Russian or Hebrew, the languages in which **[Alien]** is fluent. They had communicated at his office through an interpreter.

Immigration Judges are not required to advise every respondent before them of their eligibility to file for asylum, they are required to explain such rights in cases where an individual has either expressed a fear or otherwise manifested an intent to seek asylum. *Opoku v. INS*, 1989 U.S. Dist. LEXIS 7011 (S.D. N.Y. 1989).

In the instant case, the file in front of the Immigration Judge undoubtedly included a completed Form I-589 application for asylum. If such a form did not manifest her intent to seek asylum, it would be hard to contemplate a more effective means of conveying such a desire. Nevertheless, she was not advised of her eligibility to "renew" the application and have the Judge consider it on the merits.[3]

Finally, in cases where pro se respondents appear to be eligible for forms of discretionary relief from deportation, the Immigration Courts do have an obligation to determine whether the respondents are aware of their eligibility and wish to prosecute an application. Former 8 C.F.R. § 242.17 (1997) (in effect at the time of **[Alien]**'s hearing); *Matter of Cordova*, 22 I & N Dec. 966 (BIA 1999) (noting Immigration Judge's "duty to inform aliens of potential forms of relief for which they are apparently eligible"); *Bui v. INS*, 76 F.3d 268 (9th Cir. 1996) (immigration judge must inform an alien in a deportation hearing of an alien's 'apparent eligibility' to seek relief). There is no indication in the (limited) record (or recollection of **[Alien]**) that the Court ever informed her that she would be eligible for suspension of deportation within a few months.

Between the ineffective assistance of counsel, the lack of interpreter, and the failure to be advised of her rights (to seek relief and appeal), it could hardly be any clearer that **[Alien]**'s rights to a fundamentally fair hearing were denied. But for the infringement of these rights, she would have had an opportunity to present a compelling case for suspension of deportation.

Further, the failure of **[Attorney 2]** to properly prosecute the appeal of the later-filed pro se Motion to Reopen was also woefully inadequate, and Petitioner should be allowed the opportunity to pursue the matter being filed with the Board of Immigration Appeals.

PRAYER FOR RELIEF

WHEREFORE, Petitioner prays that this Honorable Court grant the following relief:

1. Grant the writ of habeas corpus;
2. Enjoin Respondents from effecting the deportation of Petitioner;
3. Order that Respondents join in Petitioner's efforts to reopen the removal proceedings on the basis of her application for adjustment of status to permanent residence as authorized and directed;
4. Award Petitioner's reasonable costs and attorneys' fees; and
5. Grant any other and further relief which this Honorable Court deems just and proper.

[Dated:]

Respectfully Submitted,

[Attorney]

[ADD CERTIFICATE OF SERVICE]

[3] It should be noted that **[Alien]** is not asserting that she presented a claim which would have entitled her to asylum. She is simply asserting, however, that had she been informed of her right to a hearing on the application, she would have had sufficient time to qualify for alternative relief—suspension of deportation.

MANDAMUS ACTIONS: AVOIDING DISMISSAL AND PROVING THE CASE

by AILF's Legal Action Center[*]

This advisory provides basic information about filing an immigration-related mandamus action in federal district court. It discusses the required elements of a successful mandamus action as well as the jurisdictional concerns that sometimes arise. The information in this document is accurate and authoritative as of August 15, 2005, but does not substitute for individual legal advice supplied by a lawyer familiar with a client's case.

Mandamus can be a relatively simple and quick remedy in situations where the government has failed to act when it has a duty to do so. However, there are a number of adverse published decisions, some of which are discussed in this advisory. Although it is helpful to understand these cases—and to identify the weaknesses in the courts' analyses—potential plaintiffs should not be discouraged. Most successful mandamus actions are unreported and/or do not result in written decisions. In fact, often, the filing of a mandamus action prompts the government to take whatever action is requested and the case ultimately is dismissed.

INTRODUCTION

Mandamus can be used to compel administrative agencies to act. The Mandamus Act, codified at 28 USC §1361 says, in its entirety:

> *Action to compel an officer of the United States to perform his duty.* The district courts shall have original jurisdiction of any action in the nature of mandamus to compel an officer or employee of the United States or any agency thereof to perform a duty owed to the plaintiff.

The Mandamus Act authorizes the court to order a remedy. It does not provide independent, substantive grounds for a suit. A mandamus plaintiff must demonstrate that: (1) he or she has a clear right to the relief requested; (2) the defendant has a clear duty to perform the act in question; and (3) no other adequate remedy is available. *Iddir v. INS*, 301 F.3d 492, 499 (7th Cir. 2002). Under the Mandamus Act, the court may compel the government to take action, but the court cannot compel the agency to exercise its discretion in a particular manner, nor can it grant the relief the plaintiff seeks from the agency.

JURISDICTION AND CAUSE OF ACTION

Plaintiffs in a mandamus action may allege subject matter jurisdiction under both the mandamus statute, 28 USC §1361, and the federal question statute, 28 USC §1331.[1] Generally, it is better to allege both grounds, in part because some courts have confused the issue of subject matter jurisdiction under §1361, *see, e.g.*, footnote 1, and in part because the same complaint may seek mandamus relief and other forms of relief as well.

The Administrative Procedures Act (APA), 5 USC §551 *et seq.* does not provide an independent basis for subject matter jurisdiction. *See Califano v. Sanders*, 430 U.S. 99, 105 (1977). However, the APA provides a basis for the suit when the government unreasonably delays action or fails to act. *See* 5 USC §§555(b) and 706(1). Thus, the plaintiff may allege the APA as a cause of action. *Id.*

ELEMENTS OF A SUCCESSFUL MANDAMUS ACTION

A mandamus plaintiff must establish that

- he or she has a clear right to the relief requested;

[*] **The Legal Action Center** (LAC) is the litigation arm of the American Immigration Law Foundation.

[1] The court's subject matter jurisdiction is a separate issue from the court's authority to grant mandamus relief. *Ahmed v. DHS*, 328 F.3d 383, 386–87 (7th Cir. 2003). Subject matter jurisdiction is a threshold question that determines whether the court has the power to think about the case in the first place. *Id.* at 387. After the court has determined that the petitioner's "claim is plausible enough to engage the court's jurisdiction," the court turns to the question of whether it has authority to grant the particular relief. *Id.*

The Seventh Circuit decision *Ahmed v. DHS* provides a good discussion of these two issues. Furthermore, *Ahmed* cites several cases where the courts have tended to collapse the question of subject matter jurisdiction into the analysis of the merits of the case. *See Ahmed*, 328 F.3d at 386; *see also Davis Associates v. Sec. of Dept. of Housing and Urban Dev.*, 498 F.2d 385, 388–89 (1st Cir. 1974).

- the defendant has a clear duty to perform the act in question; and
- no other adequate remedy is available.

Not all courts analyze these issues the same way, or even consistently. Often, the courts mesh these issues or frame them differently. However, for clarity and completeness, this advisory addresses these issues individually.

Does the Plaintiff Have a Clear Right?

A mandamus plaintiff must show that he or she has a clear right to the relief requested. Sometimes, the courts say that a person has a clear right when they fall within the "zone of interests" of a particular statute. This means that the interests the plaintiff seeks "to be protected are within those 'zone of interests' to be protected or regulated by the statute . . . in question."[2]

In immigration-related mandamus actions, plaintiffs generally will identify a specific provision of the INA that creates a clear right to relief. The courts will look to the purpose of the statute—both the specific statutory provision in question, as well as the general purpose of the INA—to determine whether the mandamus plaintiff is an intended beneficiary of the statute. Said another way, the statute should indicate that the government owes a duty *to the plaintiff*.

Numerous courts have found that the INA establishes a clear right to relief for adjustment of status applicants. For example, diversity lottery applicants have established that the INA confers a right to have their applications adjudicated. *See Iddir*, 301 F.3d at 500 (affirmed in *Ahmed v. DHS*, 328 F.3d 383 (7th Cir. 2003));[3] *Paunescu v. INS*, 76 F. Supp. 2d 896, 901 (N.D. Ill. 1999). Likewise, in *Yu v. Brown*, 36 F. Supp. 2d 922, 932 (D.N.M. 1999), the court said that applicants under the special immigrant juvenile program "fell within the zone of interest of the INA provisions for SIJ and LPR status."

In contrast, several courts have said that the INA does not create a clear right to have deportation proceedings initiated. *See Campos v. INS*, 62 F.3d 311, 314 (9th Cir. 1995); *Hernandez-Avalos v. INS*, 50 F.3d 842, 847–48 (10th Cir. 1995); *Giddings v. Chandler*, 979 F.2d 1104, 1109–10 (5th Cir. 1992); *Gonzalez v. INS*, 867 F.2d 1108, 1109–10 (8th Cir. 1989). In these cases, the plaintiffs—immigrants who were serving criminal sentences—argued that former INA § 242(i) created a clear right to an immediate deportation hearing. Former §242(i) said that the Attorney General shall initiate deportation proceedings "as expeditiously as possible after the date of conviction." The courts concluded that this provision was enacted not to benefit the noncitizens, but instead, to address prison overcrowding and avoid the costs of detaining noncitizens; thus, the detainees themselves are outside of the "zone of interest" of the statute.[4]

Is There a Mandatory Duty?

In addition to having a clear right to relief, the plaintiff must show that *the defendant owes* him or her a duty.[5] The courts have said that this duty must be mandatory or ministerial, but mandamus actions can be used to compel the government to exercise its discretion in a case where the government has failed to take any action.[6] Courts distinguish between the govern-

---

[2] *See Association of Data Processing Service Organizations, Inc. v. Camp*, 397 U.S. 150, 150 (1970). The zone of interests test was first articulated by the Supreme Court in *Data Processing*. Although this case addressed the issue of standing, the zone of interests test was later used by some courts as a way to determine if the plaintiff has a clear right to relief for purposes of mandamus.

[3] In both *Iddir* and *Ahmed*, the court denied the mandamus relief on other grounds, *i.e.*, that the government did not have a duty to the plaintiffs.

[4] The Ninth Circuit initially found that detained immigrants were within the zone of interests protected by former INA §242(i). *Garcia v. Taylor*, 40 F.3d 299 (9th Cir. 1994); *Silveyra v. Mozhcorak*, 989 F.2d 1012 (9th Cir. 1993). In *Campos*, however, the court held that a subsequent amendment to the INA, which provided that §245(i) "shall not be construed to create any substantive or procedural right or benefit," overrules its prior rulings in *Garcia* and *Silveyra*. *Campos*, 62 F.3d at 314 (citing §225 of the Immigration and Nationality Technical Corrections Act of 1994). *See also Hernandez-Avalos*, 50 F.3d at 848 (citing §225 as barring detainees' standing).

[5] *See, e.g., Naporano Metal & Iron Co. v. Sec'y of Labor*, 529 F.2d 537 (3d Cir. 1976) (duty to issue labor certification); *Harriott v. Ashcroft*, 277 F. Supp. 2d 538, 545 (E.D.P.A. 2003) (ministerial duty to issue derivative citizenship); *Rios v. Aguirre*, 276 F. Supp. 2d 1195, 1199–1200 (D. Kan. 2003) (no duty to entertain motion to reconsider).

[6] For example, the court may order the defendant to adjudicate an application or petition. *See, e.g., Iddir v. INS*, 301 F.3d 492, 500 (7th Cir. 2002) (duty to adjudicate applications under the diversity lottery program); *Patel v. Reno*, 134 F.3d 929, 933 (9th Cir. 1997) (duty to adjudicate visa application); *Yu v. Brown*, 36 F. Supp. 2d 922, 932 (D.N.M. 1999) (duty to process SIJ application in a reasonable amount of time).

ment's duty to take *some* discretionary action and the actual discretionary decision that the government makes. A court generally will not order the defendant to exercise its discretion in any particular manner. *See Silveyra v. Moschorak*, 989 F.2d 1012, 1015 (9th Cir. 1993). ("Mandamus may not be used to instruct an official how to exercise discretion unless that official has ignored or violated 'statutory or regulatory standards delimiting the scope or manner in which such discretion can be exercised.'") Rather, the court will order the government to take *some* action. As a result, be aware that filing a mandamus action may result in a prompt denial of the application.

The question of the defendant's mandatory duty is closely related to the question of the plaintiff's clear right to relief, and in many cases, the answer to these questions will be same. However, just because there is a clear right to relief does not mean that the government has an affirmative duty and vice versa. For example, in *Iddir v. INS*, the plaintiffs had a clear right to have their adjustment applications adjudicated, but the defendants did not have a duty to adjudicate them because the fiscal year statutory deadline had passed. 301 F.3d 492, 500–01 (7th Cir. 2002).[7] Alternatively, in *Giddings v. INS*, the court held that although the INA imposes "a duty on the Attorney General to deport criminal aliens, we stop short of concluding that this created a duty *owed to the alien*." 979 F.2d 1104, 1110 (5th Cir. 1992). In doing so, the court noted the distinction between "imposing a duty on a government official and vesting a right in a particular individual." *Id.* (citing *Gonzalez v. INS*, 867 F.2d 1108, 1109 (8th Cir. 1989)).

Even if the government has a nondiscretionary duty to adjudicate an application, mandamus is appropriate only if the government fails to act within a reasonable amount of time. *See Kim v. Ashcroft*, 340 F. Supp. 2d 384 (S.D.N.Y. 2004) (noting that §555(b) of the APA requires the government to act within a reasonable amount of time); *Yu*, 301 F.3d at 930 (same). Where there is no statutory deadline for adjudicating an application, what is "reasonable" will depend on the circumstances of the case. The courts have found government delays unreasonable when the passage of time causes a plaintiff to become ineligible for the relief sought. *See, e.g., Harriott v. Ashcroft*, 277 F. Supp. 2d 538 (E.D. Pa. 2003) (granting mandamus where INS unreasonably delayed issuing derivative citizenship); *Yu v. Brown*, 36 F. Supp. 2d 922 (D.N.M. 1999) (granting mandamus where INS delayed adjustment under special immigration juvenile status); *but c.f. Ahmed*, 328 F.3d at 287 (finding no right to relief because delay resulted in plaintiff becoming ineligible for relief, but noting that the result may have been different if case filed while government still had authority to act).

A mandamus plaintiff may look to regulations or internal operating procedures to find out if the agency itself has set guidelines.[8] Plaintiffs also may look to what the agency's average adjudication period is; however, just because a delay is "not unusual" does not make it reasonable. *See Jefrey v. INS*, 710 F. Supp. 486 (S.D.N.Y. 1989).

The following issues provide guidance on what is reasonable:

(1) the time agencies take to make decisions must be governed by a "rule of reason";

(2) where Congress has provided a timetable or other indication of the speed with which it expects the agency to proceed in the enabling statute, that statutory scheme may supply content for this rule of reason;

(3) delays that might be reasonable in the sphere of economic regulation are less tolerable when human health and welfare are at stake;

(4) the court should consider the effect of expediting delayed action on agency activities of a higher or competing priority;

(5) the court should also take into account the nature and extent of the interests prejudiced by delay;

[7] Note, however, that the Eleventh Circuit did not reach the issue of whether the government had a duty to adjudicate the petitioner's adjustment of status application under the diversity visa program. *Nyaga v. Ashcroft*, 323 F.3d 906 (11th Cir. 2003). Rather, in *Nyaga*, the court dismissed the case as moot because the fiscal year had ended.

In two district court cases where the plaintiffs filed mandamus complaints prior to the end of the fiscal year, relief was granted even though the visa was not issued prior to the end of the fiscal year. *See Przhebelskaya v. USCIS*, 338 F. Supp. 2d 399 (E.D.N.Y. 2004); *Paunescu v. INS*, 76 F. Supp. 2d 896 (N.D. Ill. 1999).

[8] However, the agency's delay may be unreasonable even if it adjudicates an application within the agency-specified timeframe. *See Singh v. Ilchert*, 784 F. Supp. 759, 764 (N.D. Cal. 1992) (finding that "the mere fact that the INS promulgates a regulation establishing a time period in which applications must be adjudicated does not, in and of itself, mean that an adjudication within the time period cannot constitute unreasonable delay").

(6) the court need not "find any impropriety lurking behind agency lassitude in order to hold that agency action is 'unreasonably delayed.' "

TRAC v. FCC, 750 F.2d 70, 80 (D.C. Cir. 1984) (quoted in *Yu v. Brown*, 36 F. Supp. 2d 922, 934 D.N.M. 1999)).

Is There Another Remedy Available?

The courts will not grant mandamus relief if the plaintiff has an alternative, fully adequate remedy available. This means that plaintiffs must exhaust their administrative remedies. *See, e.g.*, *Cheknan v. McElroy*, 313 F. Supp. 2d 270, 274 (S.D.N.Y. 2004); *Henriquez v. Ashcroft*, 269 F. Supp. 2d 106, 108 (E.D.N.Y. 2003). Failure to exhaust may be excused, however, when one of the exceptions are established.[9]

Furthermore, courts generally will not grant relief if the plaintiff has a judicial alternative available. For example, in *Bhatt v. Board of Immigration Appeals*, the plaintiff asked the court to compel the BIA to adjudicate his motion to reconsider. 328 F. 3d 912 (7th Cir. 2003). The court held that to the extent that the plaintiff can challenge the BIA's inaction, it must do so as part of a petition for review in the court of appeals. *Id.* at 915 n.3 (citing INA §242(b)(9)). Similarly, in *Kulle v. Springer*, the court dismissed a mandamus action that sought to compel discovery in an immigration court proceeding. 566 F. Supp. 279 (N.D. Ill. 1983). The court said that the determinations involving discovery fall within the scope of the judicial review provisions of the INA (former §106(a)). *Id.* at 280.

In several cases, the government has argued that applicants for adjustment of status are precluded from mandamus when the government has not initiated removal proceedings against them. The government has reasoned that: (1) adjustment applicants have not exhausted remedies because they have not re-adjudicated their applications before the immigration court and the Board of Immigration Appeals in removal proceedings; and/or (2) there is (or will be) an alternative judicial forum available after removal proceedings conclude (*i.e.*, petition for review under INA §242). Although some courts have agreed with the government, *see, e.g.*, *Sadowski v. INS*, 107 F. Supp. 2d 451 (S.D.N.Y. 2000), most courts have implicitly rejected this reasoning, and a few courts have rejected it explicitly. In *Iddir*, the court said that even though INS may initiate removal proceedings in the future, administrative exhaustion is excused because this situation constitutes an "'indefinite timeframe for administrative action.'"[10] 301 F.3d at 498–99 (quoting *McCarthy v. Madigan*, 503 U.S. 140, 147 (1992)).

OTHER THRESHOLD ISSUES

The following are some jurisdictional and other threshold issues that often arise in immigration mandamus actions.

Mootness

The courts will dismiss a civil action where the plaintiff's claim is moot. Some courts have found that when an agency fails to adjudicate an application, and, as result of the passage of time, the applicant becomes ineligible for the benefit requested, the issue is moot.

For example, in *Nyaga v. Ashcroft*, 323 F.3d 906 (11th Cir. 2003), the plaintiff asked the court to compel the government to adjudicate his adjustment application under the diversity visa program. The court found that the plaintiff was no longer eligible to receive a diversity visa because the fiscal year during which the visa was available had ended. *Nyaga*, 323 F.3d at 915–16.[11] As a result, his claim was moot.[12]

---

[9] Failure to exhaust may be excused if: (1) requiring exhaustion of administrative remedies causes prejudice, due to unreasonable delay or an "indefinite time frame for administrative action"; (2) the agency lacks the ability or competence to resolve the issue or grant the relief requested; (3) appealing through the administrative process would be futile because the agency is biased or has predetermined the issue; or (4) substantial constitutional questions are raised. *See Iddir v. INS*, 301 F.3d at 498 (citations omitted).

[10] The court also found that two other exhaustion exceptions applied: (1) the agency lacks the ability to grant the relief requested; and (2) exhausting the administrative process would be futile.

[11] The plaintiff filed the complaint after the expiration of the fiscal year for which he had won the diversity visa lottery. Thus the court may have reached a different result if the complaint had been filed before the end of the year. *See Nyaga*, 323 F.3d at 915 n.7 (plaintiff's case arguably distinguishable from a case where complaint filed before end of year); *Paunescu v. INS*, 76 F. Supp. 2d 896, 898 (N.D. Ill. 1999) (mandamus issued where complaint filed before end of fiscal year); *see also Przhebelskaya v. USCIS*, 338 F. Supp. 2d 399, 405 (E.D.N.Y. 2004) (motion to compel granted where mandamus issued prior to end of fiscal year).

[12] Note that in *Iddir*, the Seventh Circuit reached the same result, but did not rely on mootness. Rather, the court found that the government did not have a duty to adjudicate the

continued

Id. at 916. Likewise, in *Sadowski v. INS*, the court found that the plaintiff's claim was moot because he no longer was eligible for derivative beneficiary status, having turned 21. 107 F. Supp. 2d 451, 454 (S.D.N.Y. 2000). *But see Harriott v. Ashcroft*, 277 F. Supp. 2d 538, 545 (E.D.P.A. 2003) (court ordered government to issue derivative citizenship *nunc pro tunc* where plaintiff alleged very compelling factors and government acted unreasonably).

Statutory Bars to Review under INA §242, Including Amendments by the REAL ID Act

Section 242 of the INA bars jurisdiction over a variety of different issues in immigration cases. The REAL ID Act of 2005[13] amended INA §242 to include specific bars to judicial review by mandamus action. It is not clear what, if any, impact these purported bars will actually have. The majority of the amendments to provisions of INA §242 pertain to judicial review of orders of removal or removal proceedings.[14] Courts generally do not review removal orders or removal proceedings by means of mandamus actions. In fact, in one case in which this was tried in the past, the court found that INA §242(g) barred jurisdiction in mandamus cases. The Second Circuit said that the court lacked jurisdiction to compel the government to execute a final order of deportation. *Duamutef v. INS*, 386 F.3d 172, 180–81 (2d Cir. 2004). Likewise, two courts have held that §242(g) bars a plaintiff from seeking to have removal proceedings commenced. *Chapinksi v. Ziglar*, 278 F.3d 718, 721 (7th Cir. 2002); *Alvidres-Reyes v. Reno*, 180 F.3d 199, 205 (5th Cir. 1999).

The government also frequently argues that INA §242(a)(2)(B)(i) (bar over certain discretionary decisions) bars review in mandamus actions. The REAL ID Act amended this section to specifically bar mandamus review of discretionary decisions that are covered by INA §242(a)(2)(B)(i). *See* REAL ID Act §106(a)(1)(A)(ii). Additionally, the REAL ID Act amended this section so that it now applies to both removal and non-removal immigration cases. *See* REAL ID §101(f)(2).

application because the plaintiff was no longer eligible for a diversity visa. *Iddir*, 301 F.3d at 501.

[13] Pub. L. No. 109-13, 119 Stat. 231 (May 11, 2005).

[14] *See* amended INA §§242(a)(2)(A), (B) and (C); new §242(a)(4); new §242(a)(5); amended §242(b)(9); and amended §242(g).

Notwithstanding the REAL ID Act's amendment to INA §242(a)(2)(B)(i), this section generally will not apply in mandamus actions. Through mandamus, the plaintiff seeks an order compelling the government to take action; the court will not compel the government to grant or deny an application. Thus, because the plaintiff is not challenging a decision to deny relief, the relief sought is not discretionary and in fact, is by definition a mandatory duty. *See Iddir*, 301 F.3d at 497–98.

Additional information regarding the REAL ID Act can be found at AILF's REAL ID Act resource page, *www.ailf.org/lac/lac_realidresources.htm.*

Consular Nonreviewability

If a person is seeking to compel a consular officer to process an application or petition abroad, the government likely will claim that such a claim is barred under the doctrine of consular nonreviewability. The courts generally have held that they lack authority to review consular decisions. *See, e.g., Saavedra Bruno v. Albright*, 197 F.3d 1153, 1159–60 (D.C. Cir. 1999).

However, the law is not firmly settled regarding the applicability of the consular nonreviewability doctrine to mandamus cases. *See Ahmed v. DHS*, 328 F.3d 383, 388 (7th Cir. 2003). And, in fact, the Ninth Circuit has found that it has authority to grant mandamus relief to compel a consular officer to act on a visa petition. In *Patel v. Reno*, 134 F.3d 929 (9th Cir. 1997), the court ordered the U.S. Consulate in Bombay, India to act on the plaintiff's visa petition. Although the court acknowledged that "[n]ormally, a consular official's discretionary decision to grant or deny a visa petition is not subject to review," the court found mandamus jurisdiction when the consul "fail[s] to take an action." *Id.* at 931–32.

PROCEDURES

Mandamus is a civil action, and therefore, the Federal Rules of Civil Procedure and the district court's local rules apply. The local rules are available on the courts' websites.

Whom to Sue and Serve: Because mandamus actions seek to force an officer or employee of the government of the United States to take an action, the named defendant depends on the type of action the suit seeks to compel. For example, a mandamus action to compel U.S. Citizenship and Immigration Services (USCIS) to adjudicate an application may name the USCIS District Director, USCIS Director, and the Secretary of the Department of Homeland Security (DHS) as defendants. It is better to be over-inclusive in naming defendants, and if it is unclear which officer had the duty to act, name the agency/department or even the United States.[15]

If the defendant is DHS (or a department or officer within DHS), by regulation[16] the complaint must be served to:

Office of the General Counsel
United States Department of Homeland Security
Washington, DC 20528

For more information about identifying the defendants and about service, please see AILF's Practice Advisory, "Whom to Sue and Whom to Serve in Immigration-Related District Court Litigation" (Amended Aug. 19, 2004).

Venue: Venue for the mandamus action, unless otherwise specified in some other statute, can be in any judicial district in which the defendant "resides;" in which a substantial part of the events or omissions giving rise to the claim occurred; or in which the plaintiff resides. 28 USC §1391(e).

Fee: Parties instituting a civil action in district court are required to pay a filing fee pursuant to 28 USC §1914. The current fee is $150. Complaints may be accompanied by an application to proceed in *forma pauperis*, if the plaintiff is unable to pay the filing fee.

Injunctive/Declaratory Relief: A mandamus suit is an action for affirmative relief, as compared to injunctive relief, which typically seeks to prohibit improper action. Although 28 USC §1361 does not authorize injunctive relief, mandamus jurisdiction permits a flexible remedy. Furthermore, the same complaint may request declaratory, injunctive, and mandamus relief. For example, the court could declare a policy or regulation illegal, enjoin its enforcement, and order affirmative relief all at the same time.

[15] If the complaint turns out to be overinclusive, the court may dismiss the complaint against the improperly named defendants and continue with the proper defendants. *See Patel v. Reno*, 134 F.3d 929, 933 (9th Cir. 1997) (granting defendant's summary judgment in part, and denying in part).

[16] Service of Summonses and Complaints, 6 CFR §5.42 (2004). The regulations list the zip code for DHS as 20258. The postal service indicates that no such zip code exists, however, and thus, this appears to be a typographical error. The USCIS website lists the zip code noted above: 20528.

CIRCUMVENTING NATURALIZATION DELAYS: HOW TO GET JUDICIAL RELIEF UNDER 8 USC §1447(b) FOR A STALLED NATURALIZATION APPLICATION

*by Linda Rose and Mary Kenney**

BACKGROUND

Your client filed an application, and finally, after a two-year wait, U.S. Citizenship and Immigration Services (USCIS) interviews your client. All goes well. The examiner tells you that your client will be scheduled for a swearing-in date in due time. More time goes by . . . three months . . . four months . . . six months. . . . Your client is becoming increasing anxious and impatient. And to top it off, the prolonged delay makes it look like you're not doing a good job.

Of course you've made all the phone calls, faxes, and e-mails you could to USCIS and AILA liaison. And the Congressional Aide knows nothing more than you, namely, the case remains pending.

Your initial inclination might be to file a *Mandamus Complaint*. But in this particular scenario, where the interview has already taken place, you can do something better—file a *Petition for Hearing on Naturalization Application* in the U.S. District Court.

THE APPLICABLE LAW

INA §336(b), 8 USC §1447(b), specifically provides for judicial review for a stalled naturalization petition in these circumstances. It states as follows:

> If there is a failure to make a determination under [INA] §335 [8 USC §1446] before the end of the 120-day period after the date on which the examination is conducted under such section, the applicant may apply to the United States District Court for the District in which the applicant resides for a hearing on the matter. Such court has jurisdiction over the matter and may either determine the matter or remand the matter, with appropriate instructions to the Service to determine the matter.

In short, the statute says that if more than 120 days have passed since the naturalization interview, the applicant can seek judicial relief. The judicial relief can come in two forms:

(1) An adjudication of the naturalization application in court and by the court; or

(2) A remand to USCIS for immediate adjudication.

Which form of relief you choose to seek is a strategy decision that will depend on a number of factors, such as the merits of the case, the attitude of the local office, and the federal judge hearing the case. In many cases, however, you will likely want to ask the court to decide the application, rather than submit to the delays associated with further agency proceedings.

WHEN CAN THE FEDERAL COURT INTERVENE?

The statute is very specific in identifying precisely when a naturalization applicant can ask the district court to intervene and decide the case due to agency delay: when the agency fails to make a decision on the application within 120 days after the examination. 8 USC §1447(b). The examination referred to is the initial interview scheduled under 8 USC §1446(a). *See also* 8 CFR §335.2.

In some offices, examiners may ask—or sometimes pressure—the applicant to sign a waiver of the 120-day decision deadline. An applicant is not required to sign such a waiver. It is wise to consider your response to this possibility in advance, and to prepare your client. In limited circumstances, it may be to your client's benefit to sign the waiver—such as when he or she needs additional time to prepare for the civics test.

In many cases, USCIS continues the initial examination on the naturalization applicant and instructs the applicant to submit additional evidence. USCIS will then schedule a *re-examination* of the

* **Linda Rose** is the managing partner at the Rose Immigration Law Firm in Nashville. **Mary Kenney** is a staff attorney at the Legal Action Center (LAC) of the American Immigration Law Foundation. This was published as an LAC Practice Advisory (amended May 25, 2004).

applicant. *See* 8 CFR §335.3(b). Even when this happens, however, USCIS still must make its decision within 120 days of the *initial* examination. The government might claim that this is not correct, and instead argue that the 120-day period does not begin to run until after the re-examination. For example, in a case in which the initial examination has been continued, if a §1447(b) suit is filed 140 days after the initial examination, but prior to the re-examination being scheduled, the government may claim that the suit is premature. Neither the statute nor the regulations support this position, however. In fact, the regulations specifically differentiate between an "initial" examination and a "reexamination" following a continuance. 8 CFR §335.3(b) ("[T]he reexamination on the continued case shall be scheduled within 120 days of the initial examination.") The regulations then reiterate that the decision must be made within 120 days of the "first" examination. *See* 8 CFR §336.1(a).

Obviously, the period between the initial examination and USCIS's initial decision is not the only period of delay in naturalization cases. USCIS often delays in scheduling the initial examination and also delays in holding a hearing and making a decision after an administrative appeal. However, by its terms, 8 USC §1447(b) is not available to redress these delays. *See, e.g., Langer v. McElroy*, No. 00-2741, 2002 U.S. Dist. LEXIS 123847 (S.D.N.Y. Dec. 16, 2002) (no jurisdiction under §1447(b) where agency delays in acting on the administrative appeal) (unpublished decision). Where extensive delays occur at these other stages of the agency's adjudication, a mandamus action in district court might be appropriate. In a mandamus action, however, the sole relief available would be for the court to order USCIS to act on the application. Unlike §1447(b), mandamus does not give the court the jurisdiction to actually decide the application. For more on mandamus actions, see AILF's practice advisory entitled, "Mandamus Actions: 'How To' and Summary of Relevant Case Law," at *www.ailf.org/lac/lac_pa_071803.asp.*

NUTS AND BOLTS

Notifying the Government of Your Intention to File

As a practical matter, you should request cooperation by USCIS before filing the petition. In many cases, you will already have sent status inquiries and might have used your congressional liaison. Also, as a strategic matter, you should send a copy of the "draft" petition to USCIS and to the U.S. Attorney and indicate a deadline when you intend to file the petition. This will give the U.S. Attorney an opportunity to put some pressure on USCIS to adjudicate the application and to avoid the time and expense of litigation. It might also save your client a major expense. *If USCIS does not respond by your stated deadline, do not hesitate to file the petition. Otherwise, you will have damaged your credibility in the future.* Do not threaten to file the petition unless you absolutely intend to do so.

Filing the Petition

As the statute directs, you must file the case in the district court for the district in which your client resides. The statute does not specify exactly how to "apply" to the court for a hearing. But what seems to satisfy the judicial process is a document entitled "Petition for Hearing on Naturalization Application." This pleading is not much more complicated than a Petition for Review. Every district court has local rules, so be sure to consult the local rules regarding filing the petition.

In the pleading, you need to set out the court's jurisdiction, provide the pertinent dates, recite the procedural history of the naturalization application, and request the statutory relief. Since the statute provides the court with two options, you need to specify what it is you want the court to do. You can also ask for the other form of relief in the alternative. Be certain that at least 120 days have passed since the initial interview. Refer to the interview as the "examination" since this is the language used in the statute.

Additionally, where you are asking the court to decide the naturalization application, you can include in the petition allegations that your client satisfies all of the requirements for naturalization. You can also attach the naturalization application and other documents as exhibits to your petition.

Naming and Serving Defendants/Respondents

You must name as defendants/respondents the officers with responsibility over the processing of the naturalization application. Thus, the defendants/respondents will include the Attorney General; Secretary of the Department of Homeland Security (DHS); Director of the U.S. Citizenship and Immigration Services (USCIS); and the Director of the local USCIS office that is handling your client's naturalization application. You can also name the agency itself—USCIS.

Rule 4(i) of the Federal Rules of Civil Procedure (FRCP) governs service of the summons in suits against the United States or its agencies, officers, or employees. Additionally, regulations for DHS instruct that service of the summons and complaint in suits against DHS or its officers and employees is to be sent to the Office of General Counsel, United States Department of Homeland Security, Washington, DC, 20528. *See* 6 CFR §5.42(a).

After the summons and complaints have been served on all defendants/respondents, you will need to file proof of service with the court. *See* FRCP 4(l). Courts may have different procedures for doing this, so check your local rules and do not hesitate to place a call to the clerk. Court clerks are there to help and in most instances they are very helpful.

For a complete discussion of naming and serving defendants in immigration-related suits such as this, see AILF's Practice Advisory, "Whom to Sue and Whom to Serve in Immigration-Related District Court Litigation," at *www.ailf.org/lac/lac_pa_111203.asp*.

Settlement, Discovery, Case Management Conference, and Hearing

Following service of the complaint and summons, the defendants/respondents will have 60 days to answer. FRCP Rule 12(a)(3). After the defendants/respondents file an answer, the parties will be required to engage in an initial exchange of information. *See, e.g.*, FRCP 16, 26. The attorney for petitioner must contact the U.S. Attorney to attempt settlement and discuss discovery. *Id.* Thereafter, the court will issue a scheduling order and may set a scheduling conference. *Id.* Among other things, the scheduling order will set the time for amending the pleadings, completing discovery, and filing motions. FRCP 16(b).

You should always be sure to check the local rules of the court as they may contain additional requirements or explain local practice. For example, some courts might classify this action as one involving admission to citizenship, which under local rules may render the action exempt from a case management conference (although not from the initial meeting of the parties and the scheduling order, outlined in FRCP 16 and 26). If the court does not schedule a conference, or if your local rules exclude this from a case management conference, you may nevertheless file a motion to request one.

Some judges hold the case management conference in chambers, while others do so in the formal courtroom. In either case, your goal in this meeting or hearing will be to outline the issues in the case and the relief you seek. You can use this opportunity to make apparent to the judge the government's unnecessary and prolonged delay, and the court's authority to step in and adjudicate the naturalization application. Case management conferences are usually short and to-the-point, so keep your statements simple and clear. Most judges will simply want to know what the case is about, why the clients are entitled to a hearing, and why the government has delayed. Beware of the U.S. Attorney's tendency to take control of the hearing. Do not hesitate to jump in and make your case.

Bear in mind that many federal judges will have never heard this type of case before, so the judge may be intrigued and inclined to set the matter for a hearing. Judges frequently are sympathetic to the individual who has been subjected to the government's inexcusable delay. Following the case management conference, the court will issue a scheduling order with mandatory deadlines for each step of the case. FRCP 16(b).

You will be able to engage in discovery. *See* FRCP 26, *et seq.* Among other things, you can ask for a copy of the entire USCIS file on your client, if you do not already have it. *See* FRCP 34. You may also wish to direct interrogatories to defendants/respondents (FRCP 33) or to seek admissions from them. FRCP 36.

If there are any purely legal issues not involving disputed facts, the court may be willing to resolve them pursuant to a motion for summary judgment or for partial summary judgment. *See* FRCP 56. If there are factual disputes, you will be able to present evidence at a hearing. The court will not be restricted to reviewing only evidence that is already before the agency, but can consider additional evidence that you present. The court's review of your client's naturalization application will be *de novo*. *See United States v. Hovsepian*, 359 F.3d 1144 (9th Cir. 2004) (*en banc*) (comparing judicial review under §1447(b) to judicial review of a final denial of a naturalization application under 8 USC §1421(c)).

District Court vs. Agency Jurisdiction

Frequently, after suit is filed under 8 USC §1447(b), USCIS will quickly adjudicate the naturalization application and file a motion to dismiss the district court proceedings as moot. The agency has historically taken the position that it retains concurrent jurisdiction with the district court after a suit under §1447(b) is filed, and thus argues that it has the authority to continue to process the application. Moreover, where the application is denied by USCIS, USCIS takes the position that the individual must exhaust the administrative appeal required by statute before he or she will be able to go back into district court. *See* 8 USC §1421(c) (judicial review over a final denial of a naturalization application); 8 USC §1447 (setting forth the administrative appeal process); 8 CFR §336.9(d); *cf. Chavez v. INS*, 844 F.Supp. 1224 (N.D. Ill. 1993) (no jurisdiction to reinstate §1447(b) suit where agency denied application following remand; applicant had to exhaust administrative remedies before seeking judicial review under 8 USC §1421(c)).

Recently, the Ninth Circuit Court of Appeals rejected the argument that USCIS retains concurrent jurisdiction over the application. The court held that, once suit was filed under 8 USC §1447(b), the district court assumed *exclusive* jurisdiction over the naturalization application, and USCIS lost the authority to decide the case. *United States v. Hovsepian*, 359 F.3d 1144 (9th Cir. 2004) (*en banc*). In *Hovsepian*, the applicant filed for judicial review under 8 USC §1447(b) after legacy INS failed to decide his application within 120 days of the initial examination. While the case was pending at the district court, legacy INS denied the naturalization application. The district court determined that legacy INS no longer had jurisdiction over the case, and the court thus disregarded legacy INS's decision and instead proceeded to approve the naturalization application. On appeal by legacy INS, the Ninth Circuit found that the district court was correct in asserting exclusive jurisdiction. In reaching this conclusion, the court considered the plain language of §1447(b), the larger statutory context, and Congress's policy objectives.

Thus, it is now clear that in cases arising in states within the Ninth Circuit, USCIS will lose jurisdiction over a case as soon as the applicant files for judicial review under 8 USC §1447(b). In these states, USCIS will not be able to deprive the court of jurisdiction by attempting to moot the federal court case by denying the naturalization application. Because *Hovsepian* is the only published decision that addresses this issue, however, it remains an open question in other circuits. In these other circuits, should USCIS deny your client's application after you have filed for district court review of the case under 8 USC §1447(b), you can rely on *Hovsepian* to argue that the district court should disregard USCIS's decision and instead independently adjudicate the application.

If USCIS conditionally approves the naturalization application, however, you will not need to raise the jurisdiction issue with the court, since your client will have prevailed on his or her naturalization application. Instead, you should request an immediate scheduling for swearing-in your client. You can immediately ask the district court to hold the case in abeyance until your client is actually sworn-in. Do not withdraw the complaint on the basis that the application was "approved" and do not submit to the U.S. Attorney's attempt to moot the issue. The naturalization application is not fully adjudicated until your client is sworn-in, and therefore, your need for federal court relief still exists up until that point.

Equal Access to Justice Fees (EAJA)

If the court approves your client's naturalization application, do not forget to file a timely application for attorney fees under the Equal Access to Justice Act (EAJA). 28 USC §2412. To be timely, the application must be filed within 30 days of the "final judgment." Additionally, if USCIS adjudicates the naturalization application as the result of your suit—whether favorably or unfavorably—you may also be entitled to attorney's fees under EAJA. There are several legal issues you will need to address, particularly the "prevailing party" issue. For starters, *see Buckhannon Board & Care Home, Inc. v. W. Virginia Dept. of Health & Human Services.*, 532 U.S. 598, 625 (2001).

EAJA fees are beyond the scope of this practice advisory, so for now, hit the keyboard and get that Petition for Hearing on Naturalization Application on file.

Good luck, and "see you in court!"

[Document No. 512]
COMPLAINT FOR WRIT OF MANDAMUS (NATURALIZATION)

Description: This mandamus complaint seeks to compel the Department of Homeland Security (DHS) to complete the naturalization process. It asks for this relief under both the general mandamus grounds, and also under the specific grounds of INA §336(b), which requires USCIS to adjudicate the naturalization application within 120 days of the interview.

Advantages: This complaint seeks a writ of mandamus to compel the naturalization of a lawful permanent resident for whom there is no reason not to grant such status. It seeks to compel DHS to perform its adjudicatory function in this regard so that the newly-minted United States citizen can file the I-130 petition for the spouse as an immediate relative and preclude the spouse's removal from the United States. This action demonstrates the power of a mandamus not only to seek an adjudication that has been unjustifiably delayed, but also as a tool in deportation and removal cases. By invoking the terms of INA §336(b), 8 USC §1447(b), the judge also may naturalize the client.

Limitations: As with any mandamus action, there is always a possibility that DHS will act promptly, but not in the alien's favor. To the extent that naturalization applications are discretionary (*e.g.*, an old criminal matter), DHS may act promptly and exercise its discretion negatively toward the alien. The mandamus only requires that DHS act—not act in a way that necessarily benefits the alien.

Citations: INA §§336(b); 28 USC §§1331, 1361, 2201 *et seq.*, §1391; 5 USC §701.

UNITED STATES DISTRICT COURT
NORTHERN DISTRICT OF GEORGIA
ATLANTA DIVISION

[Alien and A Number],	)	
Plaintiff,	)	
	)	
v.	)	
	)	Civil Action No. __________
ALBERTO GONZALES, Attorney General of the United States;	)	
MICHAEL CHERTOFF, Secretary, Department of Homeland Security;	)	
ROSEMARY MELVILLE, Director, Atlanta Office, U.S. Citizenship and Immigration Services;	)	
ROBERT DIVINE, Acting Director, U.S. Citizenship and Immigration Services	)	
Defendants.	)	
________________________________	)	

COMPLAINT FOR WRIT OF MANDAMUS

To the Honorable Judges of Said Court:

Plaintiff, **[Alien]**, through undersigned counsel, alleges as follows:

INTRODUCTION

1. This is a civil action brought pursuant to 8 U.S.C. § 1447, 28 U.S.C. §1331 and 1361, 5 U.S.C. § 701 and 28 U.S.C. §2201 *et. seq*. to redress the deprivation of rights, privileges and immunities secured to Plaintiff to compel Defendants to perform a duty Defendants owe to Plaintiff. Jurisdiction is also conferred by 5 U.S.C. §704.

2. This action is brought to compel Defendants and those acting under them to take action on a Form N-400, Application for Naturalization, (hereafter "the Application") in order for Plaintiff to become a Naturalized Citizen of the United States. The Application was filed with the former Immigration and Naturalization Service's Atlanta District Office on or about June 2000 by **[Alien]**. **[Alien]** was interviewed by Immigration Officer **[Name]** on December 18, 2000 and successfully passed the English language and history and government tests. (See Ex. 1, Form N-652, Naturalization Interview, for proof of successful passage of both tests). To this day, over four years after the interview, **[Alien]** still awaits the decision. Certainly more than 120 days have passed since the interview in this matter, thus vesting jurisdiction with this court under 8 U.S.C. § 1447.

3. Plaintiff is eligible to have his Application adjudicated.

4. Defendants, the Department of Homeland Security and U.S. Citizenship and Immigration Services (USCIS), are charged by law with the statutory obligation to adjudicate this Application.

5. Venue is proper under 28 USC §1391(e) because the Plaintiff resides in this district and no real property is involved in this action.

FACTS

6. **[Alien]** is a native and citizen of Ghana. **[Alien]** received his Permanent Resident status as a result of a Diversity Visa Lottery. (<u>See</u> Ex. 2, copy of **[Alien's]** Resident Alien Card, front and back.)

7. **[Alien's]** Permanent Resident Status was granted on June 29, 1995 (<u>See</u> Ex. 2), and he became statutorily eligible to file a Form N-400, Application for Naturalization, on March 29, 2000, four years and nine months after to grant of Permanent Resident Status.

8. **[Alien]** filed his Form N-400, Application for Naturalization, with the former Immigration and Naturalization Service's Atlanta District Office on or about June 2000.

9. **[Alien]** was interviewed by Immigration Officer **[Name]** on December 18, 2000 and successfully passed the English language and history and government tests. (<u>See</u> Ex. 1, Form N-652, Naturalization Interview, for proof of successful passage of both tests). To this day, over four years after the interview, **[Alien]** still awaits the decision.

10. Atlanta District office of the Citizenship & Immigration Services is currently processing Forms N-400 filed on January 4, 2004. **[Alien's]** application was filed in June 2000 and, therefore, its processing is significantly overdue. (<u>See</u> Ex. 3, Atlanta district office processing time report).

10. **[Alien]** has inquired about his Application a number of times, but the Service has neither provided a reason for the delay, nor adjudicated the Application. (<u>See</u> Ex. 4, Status Inquiry Form dated December 30, 2002, a copy of the letter dated February 4, 2004, from the law offices of **[Firm]** inquiring about the status of **[Alien's]** Application, and a copy of the standard response to the inquiry, dated March 11, 2004, stating that **[Alien]** will be "notified by mail when further action has been taken" in his case).

11. In October 2003, after **[Alien]** inquired yet again about the status of his case, USCIS instructed him to get fingerprinted again, because the previously done fingerprints expired. **[Alien]** had his fingerprints taken by the Immigration Service on October 18, 2003. (<u>See</u> Ex. 5, a copy of the DBI Tenprinter Applicant Information Worksheet stamped by the Atlanta Application Support Center). Under DHS policy, the fingerprints are only valid for fifteen months. If an application requiring fingerprints is not adjudicated within the fifteen-month time frame, the fingerprints expire and must be taken again. More than fifteen months have passed since the date when **[Alien]** was last fingerprinted, and USCIS's failure to adjudicate his Application in a timely manner will result in the need to schedule a new fingerprint appointment, further delaying the processing of the Application.

CLAIMS

17. Defendants have willfully and unreasonably have delayed in and have refused to adjudicate the Application, thereby depriving the Plaintiff of the benefit of becoming a Naturalized U.S. Citizen.

18. Defendants owe Plaintiff a duty to adjudicate the Petition and have unreasonably failed to perform that duty.

19. Plaintiff has exhausted any administrative remedies that may exist.

WHEREFORE, Plaintiff prays that the Court:

1. Assume jurisdiction over the case and naturalize the Plaintiff under the terms of 8 USC 1447(b); or
2. Compel Defendants and those acting under them to perform their duty to adjudicate the Petition; and
3. Grant such other and further relief as this Court deems proper under the circumstances; and
4. Grant Attorney's fees and costs of Court to Plaintiff under the Equal Access to Justice Act.

Respectfully submitted this ___ day of __________, 20__.

[Attorney]

[ADD CERTIFICATE OF SERVICE]

[Document No. 513–14]

COMPLAINT FOR WRIT OF MANDAMUS (ADJUSTMENT OF STATUS)

Description: These are sample writs of mandamus to compel the Department of Homeland Security (DHS) to act on a pending adjustment of status application.

Advantages: The first complaint sets forth the basic requirements that DHS act on a pending application. It seeks to have DHS exercise its adjudicatory function where there has been an unreasonable and unjustified delay. This action is for employment-based adjustment along with the derivative spouse.

The second complaint seeks to compel action on a petition for nonimmigrant worker filed with DHS by an employer on behalf of the alien, and applications for lawful permanent resident status properly filed by the alien and his spouse.

Limitations: These are complaints for a writ of mandamus against DHS and the district director where the application for the benefit was filed. Regarding the first complaint, since many employment-based adjustment of status applications are being filed with the service center, there may be no proper venue against the district director in the area where the alien resides. The remoting of applications to service centers may "defeat" more localized venue in federal court. Review the venue issues with the district court before filing.

Notes: A writ of mandamus is a useful tool. Frequently, the threat of filing one or merely filing it achieves the desired goal of having DHS take the necessary action. However, one should be careful in pursuing a writ of mandamus in circumstances where there are significant questions regarding the alien's entitlement to the benefit. Remember, the writ of mandamus, if granted, only requires DHS to take an action, not necessarily to rule in the alien's favor.

Citations: 28 USC §§1331, 1361, 2201, *et seq.*, 1391; and 5 USC §701.

UNITED STATES DISTRICT COURT
NORTHERN DISTRICT OF GEORGIA
ATLANTA DIVISION

[Aliens and A Numbers], Plaintiffs,	)	
v.	)	
ALBERTO GONZALES, Attorney General of the United States; MICHAEL CHERTOFF, Secretary, Department of Homeland Security; ROSEMARY MELVILLE, Director, Atlanta Office, U.S. Citizenship and Immigration Services; ROBERT DIVINE, Acting Director, U.S. Citizenship and Immigration Services Defendants.	)	Civil Action No. __________

COMPLAINT FOR WRIT OF MANDAMUS

To the Honorable Judges of Said Court:

Plaintiffs, **[Aliens]**, through undersigned counsel, allege as follows:

INTRODUCTION

1. This is a civil action brought pursuant to 28 U.S.C. §1331, and 28 U.S.C. §1361, to redress the deprivation of rights, privileges and immunities secured to Plaintiffs to compel Defendants to perform a duty Defendants owe to Plaintiffs. Jurisdiction is also conferred by 5 U.S.C. §701.

2. This action is brought to compel Defendants and those acting under them to take action on the Applications to Adjust Status, Form I-485, in order for Plaintiffs, to become Permanent Residents the United States.

3. Plaintiffs are eligible to have their Applications adjudicated.

4. Defendants, the Department of Homeland Security and U.S. Citizenship and Immigration Services, are charged by law with the statutory obligation to adjudicate these Applications to Adjust Status, Form I-485.

5. Venue is proper under 28 USC §1391(e) because the Plaintiffs reside in this district and no real property is involved in this action.

FACTS

6. Plaintiffs are citizens of Malaysia. **[Alien]** is the beneficiary of a Petition for Alien Worker, Form I-140, which was approved on July 13, 2001. *See* Exhibit 1 (copy of Form I-140 Approval Notice).

7. Based upon **[Alien's]** approved I-140, on September 28, 2001 Plaintiffs. **[Aliens]** applied to adjust their status to that of Permanent Resident Aliens by submitting Forms I-485. *See* Exhibit 2 (copy of **[Aliens']** I-485 applications).

8. On August 24, 2004 Plaintiffs appeared and were interviewed by Officer **[Name]** of the U.S. Citizenship and Immigration Services, in Atlanta, Georgia, pursuant to the adjustment of status process. *See* Exhibit 3 (copy of Interview Notices).

9. At the end of the interview, Officer **[Name]** informed **[Alien]** that he had two "A" files, and that only one was in Atlanta.

10. Officer **[Name]** further informed **[Alien]** that she would order his other A file, and approve their applications upon its arrival.

11. It has now been nine months since Plaintiffs were interviewed by Officer **[Name]**, and their Applications to Adjust Status, Form I-485, have now been pending for over three years. Plaintiffs have made several requests to determine the status of their applications and the delays associated with their approval, but have yet to receive any response from any governmental agency.

CLAIMS

1. Defendants have willfully and unreasonably delayed in, and have refused to, adjudicate Plaintiffs' Applications to Adjust Status, Form I-485, thereby depriving the Plaintiffs of the benefit of becoming Permanent Residents of the United States, and the peace of mind they are entitled to;
2. Defendants owe Plaintiffs a duty to adjudicate their Applications, and have unreasonably failed to perform that duty;
3. Plaintiffs have exhausted any administrative remedies that may exist.

WHEREFORE, Plaintiffs prays that the Court:

1. Compel Defendants and those acting under them to perform their duty to adjudicate Plaintiffs' Applications;
2. Grant such other and further relief as this Court deems proper under the circumstances; and
3. Grant Attorney's fees and costs of Court to Plaintiffs under the Equal Access to Justice Act.

Respectfully submitted this ___ day of______, 20__.

[Attorney]

[ADD CERTIFICATE OF SERVICE]

UNITED STATES DISTRICT COURT
SOUTHERN DISTRICT OF OHIO
EASTERN DIVISION

[Aliens and A Numbers]	:	
Plaintiffs,	:	
v.	:	
MICHAEL CHERTOFF, Secretary of Homeland Security; TERRY WAY, Director, U.S. Citizenship and Immigration Services; ROBERT DIVINE, Acting Director, U.S. Citizenship and Immigration Services; and MARK HANSEN, District Director, U.S. Citizenship and Immigration Services, Cleveland, Ohio,	:	Case No. ____________ Judge ____________ **PLAINTIFFS' COMPLAINT FOR WRIT OF MANDAMUS**
Defendants.	:	

COME NOW **[First and Last Name]** ("Mr. **[Alien]**") and **[First and Last Name]** ("Ms. **[Alien]**"), husband and wife, and **[Employer]**. Plaintiffs in the above-styled and numbered case, and for their cause of action would show the Court the following:

1. This action is brought against the Defendants to compel action on a Petition for Nonimmigrant Worker filed with the Defendants by **[Employer]** on behalf of Mr. **[Alien]** and applications for lawful permanent resident status properly filed by Mr. **[Alien]** and Ms. **[Alien]**. The Petition for a Nonimmigrant Worker and the applications to adjust status were filed and remain within the jurisdiction of the Defendants, who have improperly withheld action on said petition and applications to Plaintiffs' detriment.

PARTIES

2. Mr. **[Alien]** is a 49 year old native of Sudan and citizen of Canada. He was last admitted to the United States on January 2, 1999, in H-1B nonimmigrant status under the Immigration & Nationality Act (INA), §101(a)(15)(H)(i)(B), Title 8 U.S.C. § 1101(a)(15)(H)(i)(B). Since his last admission in 1999, Mr. **[Alien]** has been lawfully employed by **[Employer]** at its Columbus, Ohio home office. He was initially authorized for employment under the terms of a grant of Optional Practical Training by the Immigration & Naturalization Service (INS), predecessor to the Department of Homeland Security, U.S. Citizenship & Immigration Services (USCIS), and later upon the approval of H-1B nonimmigrant visa status which was valid from February 11, 1998 through December 1, 2000. On February 15, 2001, INS approved an extension of Mr. **[Alien]**'s H-1B status from December 2, 2000 until September 30, 2003 based upon the petition filed by **[Employer]**.

3. Ms. **[Alien]** is a 34 year old native and citizen of Sudan and the wife of Mr. **[Alien]** and is therefore entitled to seek lawful permanent resident status as "accompanying" her husband pursuant to INA § 203(d), 8 U.S.C. § 1153(d).

4. Ms. **[Alien]** was admitted to the United States in derivative H-4 status as the spouse of Mr. **[Alien]** and was later granted Temporary Protected Status (TPS) from June 6, 2000 until November 2, 2000. The Immigration & Naturalization Service has determined that TPS is a lawful nonimmigrant status. Ms. **[Alien]** remained eligible to adjust status when the application was filed on April 20, 2001, as described more fully below. INA § 245(k); 8 U.S.C. § 1255(k).

5. Plaintiff **[Employer]** is a **[Business Type]** incorporated in the State of Ohio, with its principal place of business in Columbus, Ohio. **[Employer]** has over 33,000 employees in multiple subsidiaries, affiliates and related business operations, including Mr. **[Alien]**. Mr. **[Alien]** has been employed by **[Employer]** at its Columbus headquarters as a computer programmer since November 1997. His current title is **[Title]**, and his responsibilities and job duties remain functionally equivalent to the job duties when he was hired in November 1997.

6. Defendant Michael Chertoff is the Secretary of the Department of Homeland Security of the United States (the "Secretary"), and this action is brought against him in his official capacity. He is generally charged with enforcement of the INA, and is further authorized to delegate such powers and authority to subordinate employees of the Department of Homeland Security. INA § 103(a); 8 U.S.C. § 1103(a). More specifically, the Secretary is responsible for the adjudication of applications for adjustment of status filed pursuant to INA § 245, 8 U.S.C. § 1255. The USCIS is an agency within the Department of Homeland Security to whom the Secretary's authority has in part been delegated, and is subject to the Secretary's supervision.

7. Defendant Robert Divine, is the Acting Director of the USCIS, and is generally charged with the administration of the benefits governed by the INA. INA § 103(c); 8 U.S.C. § 1103(c).

8. Defendant Terry Way is an official of the USCIS generally charged with supervisory authority over all operations of the Nebraska Service Center. Defendant Terry Way is the official with whom the Plaintiffs' applications for lawful permanent resident status and **[Employer]**'s Petition for a Nonimmigrant Worker were properly filed.

9. Defendant Mark Hansen is the District Director for the USCIS generally charged with supervisory authority over all operations of the Cleveland, Ohio District Office and the satellite office in Columbus, Ohio. Defendant Mark Hansen is the official with whom the individual Plaintiffs' applications for lawful permanent resident status are currently pending.

JURISDICTION

10. Jurisdiction in this case is proper under 28 U.S.C. §§ 1331 and 1361, 5 U.S.C. § 701 *et seq.*, and 28 U.S.C. § 2201 *et seq*. Relief is requested pursuant to said statutes.

VENUE

11. Venue is proper in this court pursuant to 28 USC § 1391(e), in that this is an action against officers and agencies of the United States in their official capacities, brought in the District where a Defendant resides and where a substantial part of the events or omissions giving rise to Plaintiffs' claims occurred. More specifically, the individual Plaintiffs' applications for lawful permanent resident status were properly filed with the Nebraska Service Center and have been transferred to the Columbus office of the USCIS and, to Plaintiffs' knowledge, remain pending with that office. The Petition for a Nonimmigrant Worker, filed by **[Employer]**, was properly filed and remains pending with the Nebraska Service Center.

EXHAUSTION OF REMEDIES

12. Plaintiffs have exhausted their administrative remedies. Plaintiffs have, through their attorney, made numerous inquiries concerning the status of the applications to no avail. Plaintiffs have promptly and com-

pletely responded to all of Defendants' requests for additional evidence, purportedly to complete adjudication of their applications.

FIRST CAUSE OF ACTION

13. After Mr. **[Alien]**'s last admission as a nonimmigrant worker, on December 27, 1999, **[Employer]** applied for Alien Labor Certification with the Department of Labor. This application was approved by the Regional Certifying Officer on June 14, 2000. Thereafter, on January 3, 2001, **[Employer]** filed an Immigrant Petition for Alien Worker on behalf of Mr. **[Alien]**, which was approved by the INS on January 22, 2001 pursuant to INA § 203(b)(3)(A), 8 U.S.C. § 1153(b)(3)(A). A true and authentic copy of the Approval Notice is attached hereto as Exhibit A. Approval of this petition was a prerequisite to Mr. **[Alien]** applying for adjustment of status to lawful permanent resident pursuant to INA § 245, 8 U.S.C. §1255.

14. All legal prerequisites having been satisfied, Mr. **[Alien]** and Ms. **[Alien]** both applied for adjustment of status to become lawful permanent residents with the Nebraska Service Center on April 20, 2001. The INS issued receipts for each application, expressly stating that "it usually takes between 370 to 400 days from the date of this receipt to process this type of application." True and authentic copies of the INS receipts are attached hereto as Exhibits B and D. It has been approximately 1117 days since the date of the receipt, more than 3 years. Defendants have failed and refused to adjudicate the applications.

15. On March 13, 2002, Defendant Terry Way issued a Request for Evidence with regard to Ms. **[Alien]**'s application to adjust status. Counsel for Ms. **[Alien]** responded with the requested evidence on April 1, 2002. It has been over two years since the requested evidence was submitted. A true and authentic copy of the USCIS website documenting the status of Ms. **[Alien]**'s application is attached hereto as Exhibit E.

16. On October 7, 2003, the Nebraska Service Center transferred Mr. **[Alien]**'s case to the Cleveland, Ohio District Office for adjudication. A true and authentic copy of the USCIS website documenting the status of Mr. **[Alien]**'s application is attached hereto as Exhibit C. The Cleveland office of the USCIS has assigned the case to the adjudications section of the satellite office in Columbus, Ohio, where it remains pending.

17. Mr. **[Alien]** and Ms. **[Alien]** provided fingerprints in response to a request from the INS on June 19, 2001. Upon information and belief, it was the INS policy, and is now the policy of the USCIS, that fingerprints are valid for 15 months, after which time they "expire" and must be retaken. The fingerprints for both individual Plaintiffs were provided to the USCIS again, upon request, on February 26, 2004.

18. At an interview on February 26, 2004, Defendant Mark Hansen, through the Adjudications Officer in Columbus, requested additional information and records from Mr. **[Alien]**. The additional information and records were provided to the Defendants on February 27, 2004.

19. Defendants have sufficient information to determine Plaintiffs' eligibility pursuant to applicable requirements. To date, said applications have not been adjudicated. The status of pending applications is available to the public on the USCIS web site together with the anticipated processing times for each application, true and authentic copies of which are attached hereto as Exhibits H and I.

20. The USCIS web site reports on Mr. **[Alien]**'s application that the case was transferred to Cleveland for adjudication on October 7, 2003. Exhibit C. The web site reports that employment-based adjustment applications at the Nebraska Service Center filed on "December 15, 2001" are currently being processed. Exhibit H. The web site reports that applications to adjust status filed in Columbus, Ohio on "August 3, 2003" are currently being processed. Exhibit I. By the internal standards set for normal processing times at both the Nebraska Service Center and the USCIS office in Columbus, Ohio, Mr. **[Alien]**'s application has now been pending either several months or several years beyond the expected normal and reasonable processing times. As noted, Mr. **[Alien]**'s application was filed on April 20, 2001, making its adjudication inexplicably late, even by USCIS standards.

21. Defendants' refusal to act in this case is arbitrary and not in accordance with the law. Defendants willfully, and unreasonably, have delayed in and have refused to, adjudicate Plaintiffs' applications for over three years, thereby depriving them of the right to a decision on their status to which Plaintiffs are entitled.

22. Mr. **[Alien]** can lawfully remain employment by any of three occurrences: (a) upon approval of his adjustment application for permanent resident status; (b) upon approval of his H-1B extension petition; or (c) upon approval of an Employment Authorization Document (EAD) during the pendency of his adjustment application, pursuant to 8 C.F.R. § 274a.12(c)(9).

23. In response to past EAD applications by Mr. **[Alien]**, Defendants have arbitrarily limited him to 30-day increments at a time and have required him to appear at Defendant's offices to request a new EAD for an additional 30-day period each month. This process consumes several hours each month, during which time Mr. **[Alien]** is unable to work. A true and authentic copy of the most recent Employment Authorization Document issued to Mr. **[Alien]** by USCIS on May 4, 2004, including its arbitrary designation of 30-day validity, is attached hereto as Exhibit J. On information and belief, for other applicants Defendants routinely approve EAD applications for one year increments.

24. Because he is being singled out for delay and limitations on the duration of his EAD applications, Mr. **[Alien]** must spend one day per month just to secure an EAD to continue his employment.

25. Mr. **[Alien]** has been damaged in that the validity of his pending application to adjust status depends upon his continued employment with the petitioning employer, or in a same or similar occupation, INA § 204(j); 8 U.S.C. § 1154(j), leaving him no choice but to apply for a renewed EAD on a monthly basis. This additional and unreasonable burden on Mr. **[Alien]** is unnecessary and furthers no legitimate governmental interest.

26. Mr. **[Alien]** and Ms. **[Alien]** have further been damaged by being deprived of the status of lawful permanent residents during the interminable pendency of their various applications. Mr. **[Alien]** and Ms. **[Alien]** seek to integrate fully into American life, society and culture. Naturalization as an American citizen, with the rights and privileges inherent therein, depends upon prior permanent resident status for at least 5 years. INA §316(a); 8 U.S.C. § 1427(a)(1). Plaintiffs are therefore being deprived of the right to accumulate the requisite time as permanent residents before they are eligible to apply for naturalization, as a direct result of Defendants' failure to timely adjudicate their applications to adjust status.

27. Defendants, in violation of the Administrative Procedures Act, 5 U.S.C. §§ 555(b), 701 *et seq.*, are unlawfully withholding or unreasonably delaying action on Plaintiffs' applications and have failed to carry out the adjudicative functions delegated to them by law with regard to Plaintiffs' case.

28. Plaintiffs have made numerous inquiries in an attempt to secure adjudication of their applications, all to no avail. Accordingly, Plaintiffs have been forced to retain the services of an attorney to pursue the instant action.

SECOND CAUSE OF ACTION

29. Plaintiffs restate the allegations of paragraphs 1 through 28 as though fully rewritten herein.

30. Plaintiff **[Employer]** filed the Petition for Nonimmigrant Worker to extend Plaintiff **[Alien]**'s H-1B status on October 1, 2003. Defendants issued a receipt for this petition, expressly stating that processing the case "usually takes between 30 to 120 days from the date of this receipt." It has been approximately 223 days from the date of the receipt, but Defendants have nevertheless failed and refused to adjudicate the petition.

31. The applicable regulation, 8 C.F.R. § 274.12(b)(20), provides that permission for continued authorization for employment continues for 240 days while the petition is pending with the USCIS. This provision provides adequate time for Defendants to adjudicate the petition. The USCIS reports on its web site that as of May 6, 2004, the Nebraska Service Center is currently adjudicating petitions filed on "March 16, 2004." Exhibit H. Within the next 17 days, unless the Nebraska Service Center adjudicates the petition, Mr. **[Alien]**

will lose his ability to remain employed by the passage of time, as a direct result of Defendants' failure and refusal to properly adjudicate **[Employer]**'s petition.

32. Mr. **[Alien]** is therefore forced to appear at Defendants' offices and request an EAD every 30 days because Defendants have continuously failed and refused to adjudicate either Mr. **[Alien]**'s application for permanent resident status or **[Employer]**'s petition for an extension of the H-1B status.

33. Defendants have sufficient information to determine Plaintiffs' eligibility for an extension of H-1B status pursuant to applicable requirements. Nevertheless, the petition has not been adjudicated.

34. Defendants' refusal to act in this case is arbitrary and not in accordance with the law. Defendants willfully, and unreasonably, have delayed in and have refused to adjudicate Plaintiffs' applications for over three years, thereby depriving them of the right to a decision on their status and the peace of mind to which Plaintiffs are entitled.

35. Plaintiffs have been damaged by the failure of Defendants to act in accordance with their duties under the law.

36. Defendants, in violation of the Administrative Procedures Act, 5 U.S.C. §§ 555(b), 701 *et seq.*, are unlawfully withholding or unreasonably delaying action on **[Employer]**'s application and have failed to carry out the adjudicative functions delegated to them by law with regard to Plaintiffs' case.

PRAYER

37. WHEREFORE, in view of the arguments and authorities noted herein, Plaintiffs respectfully pray that Court enter an order:

(a) Requiring Defendants to adjudicate Plaintiff **[Employer]**'s petition for a nonimmigrant worker and Mr. **[Alien]**'s and Ms. **[Alien]**'s applications for adjustment of status;

(b) Awarding Plaintiffs their reasonable attorney's fees;

(c) Granting a preliminary injunction to maintain the status quo until the lawsuit can be determined on its merits; and

(d) Granting such other relief at law and in equity as justice may require.

Respectfully submitted,

[Attorney]

[ADD CERTIFICATE OF SERVICE]

LIST OF ATTACHMENTS

Exhibit

A INS Visa Petition Approval Notice, dated January 22, 2001

B Receipt for Application to Adjust Status filed by Plaintiff **[Employer]** showing Defendants' acceptance of the application on April 20, 2001.

C Printout of Case Status Search from USCIS web site explaining the status or Mr. **[Alien]**'s application as of April 27, 2004.

D Receipt for Application to Adjust Status filed by Plaintiff **[Employer]** showing Defendants' acceptance of the application on April 20, 2001.

E Printout of Case Status Search from USCIS web site explaining the status or Ms. **[Alien]**'s application as of April 27, 2004.

F Receipt for Petition for Nonimmigrant Worker filed by **[Employer]** showing Defendant's acceptance of the petition on October 1, 2003.

G Printout of Case Status Search from USCIS web site explaining the status of **[Employer]**'s petition as of April 27, 2004.

H Printout of the Nebraska Service Center Processing Dates posted on the USCIS web site on April 22, 2004.

I Printout of the USCIS office in Columbus, Ohio Processing Dates posted on the USCIS web site on April 22, 2004.

J Copy of the Employment Authorization Document issued by USCIS on November 3, 2003 valid for 30 days.

[Document No. 515]

COMPLAINT FOR WRIT OF MANDAMUS (DIVERSITY LOTTERY)

Description: This pleading is brought in U.S. district court to force the Department of Homeland Security (DHS) to take action on an application for adjustment of status based on a selection under that year's diversity lottery.

Advantages: This complaint sets forth the jurisdiction of the court to compel DHS to take action on a delayed application where such delay will seriously prejudice the applicant. It calls for the courts to order DHS to complete its work, not necessarily to produce the desired response. This can be particularly useful in DV lottery situations such as the subject of this complaint, given the need to adjudicate the application in a given fiscal year.

Limitations: This action could be denied by the court if the court finds that DHS has no mandatory, regulatory timeframe for making that particular decision. Also, while mandamus will help an individual client, it does not solve the backlog issue generally.

Citations: 28 USC §§1331, 1361, 2201 *et seq.*; and 5 USC §701.

UNITED STATES DISTRICT COURT
NORTHERN DISTRICT OF GEORGIA
ATLANTA DIVISION

[Alien and A Number], Plaintiff, v. ALBERTO GONZALES, Attorney General of the United States; MICHAEL CHERTOFF, Secretary, Department of Homeland Security; ROSEMARY MELVILLE, Director, Atlanta Office, U.S. Citizenship and Immigration Services; ROBERT DIVINE, Acting Director, U.S. Citizenship and Immigration Services Defendants.	)	Civil Action No. __________

COMPLAINT FOR WRIT OF MANDAMUS

To the Honorable Judges of Said Court:

Plaintiff, **[Alien]**, through undersigned counsel, alleges as follows:

INTRODUCTION

1. This is a civil action brought pursuant to 28 U.S.C. §1331 and 28 U.S.C. §1361 to redress the deprivation of rights, privileges and immunities secured to Plaintiff, by which jurisdiction is conferred, to compel Defendants to perform a duty Defendants owe to Plaintiffs. Jurisdiction is also conferred by 5 U.S.C. §701.

2. This action is brought to compel Defendants and those acting under them to rule upon the application duly filed with the former INS on March 20, 1998, by Plaintiffs.

3. Plaintiff **[Alien and A Number]**, is an applicant for adjustment of status to lawful permanent residence, residing in Atlanta, Georgia. Plaintiff is eligible for adjustment as the derivative beneficiary of her husband, who won the 1998 Diversity Immigrant Lottery (DV-1998), and who has already adjusted status.

4. Defendants are charged by law with the statutory obligation to adjudicate Applications to Adjust Status to Lawful Permanent Residence (Form I-485).

FACTS

1. On March 20, 1998, Plaintiff filed with the former Immigration and Naturalization Service an Application to Adjust Status to Lawful Permanent Resident Status (Form I- 485), pursuant to 8 U.S.C. §1255, INA §245, based upon an approved 1998 Diversity Lottery Application, to obtain permanent residency as the statute provides. This application was filed by her prior counsel.

2. Upon information and belief, the INS only has until September 30, 1998, to adjust Plaintiff's status under the 1998 Diversity Lottery. All of the information required by the Service to adjust **[Alien's]** status is in the possession of the Service. In addition, **[Alien]** even obtained an additional set of fingerprints for FBI approval on September 23, 1998. These prints were supposed to have been expeditiously processed.

CLAIMS

3. Defendants have willfully, and unreasonably have delayed in and have refused to adjudicate the Application to Adjust to Permanent Resident Status of Plaintiff thereby depriving her of the right to permanent residency and to allow the peace of mind to which Plaintiff is entitled under the Immigration and Nationality Act.

4. Defendants owe Plaintiff the duty to act upon her Application to Adjust Status to Lawful Permanent Residence and have unreasonably failed to perform that duty.

5. Plaintiff has exhausted any administrative remedies that may exist.

WHEREFORE, Plaintiff prays that the Court:

1. Compel Defendants and those acting under them to perform their duty to rule upon the Application to Adjust Status to Lawful Permanent Residence (Form I- 485 of Plaintiff).

2. Grant such other and further relief as to this Court seems proper under the circumstances; and

3. Grant Attorney's fees and costs of Court to Plaintiff under the Equal Access to Justice Act.

Respectfully submitted this ____ day of _________, 20__.

[Attorney]

[ADD CERTIFICATE OF SERVICE]

[Document No. 516]

PLAINTIFF'S OPPOSITION TO MOTION TO DISMISS COMPLAINT FOR WRIT OF MANDAMUS (ADJUSTMENT OF STATUS)

Description: Defendant Department of Homeland Security (DHS) has filed a motion to dismiss plaintiff's mandamus action in U.S. district court against DHS for failure to adjudicate delayed applications for permanent resident status. This response covers jurisdictional matters and entitlement to relief.

Advantages: This brief contains a thorough discussion of the differences between removal and adjustment issues that DHS tries to claim can be used interchangeably to support its position that the court had no jurisdiction to hear this mandamus action.

Limitations: This type of grasping at straws by DHS should encourage others to take on cases in federal court.

Citations: INA §242(g); 28 USC §1331.

UNITED STATES DISTRICT COURT
NORTHERN DISTRICT OF GEORGIA
ATLANTA DIVISION

[Alien and Entity], Plaintiffs,	)	
v.	)	Civil Action No.
MICHAEL CHERTOFF, Secretary, Department of Homeland Security; ROBERT DIVINE, as Acting Director of the Citizenship And Immigration Services, and ROSEMARY MELVILLE, as Director of the Atlanta Office of the of Citizenship and Immigration Services,	)	Agency No. **[A Number]**
Defendants.	)	

PETITIONER'S BRIEF IN OPPOSITION TO MOTION TO DISMISS

Plaintiffs **[Alien]** and **[Entity]**, submit this brief in opposition to Defendants' Motion to Dismiss because jurisdiction is proper in this Court. Plaintiffs seek a Writ of Mandamus to order Defendants to perform a duty they owe to Plaintiffs, namely to adjudicate their Petition for Alien Worker and Application for Adjustment of Status (hereafter "the Petitions"). Plaintiffs seek this writ because Defendants have unreasonable delayed in processing the Petitions. Defendants assert in their Motion to Dismiss that this court does not have jurisdiction because the purpose of the Petitions is to prevent removal. Defendants mischaracterize the Petitions and misunderstand the applicable law. Because Defendant's Motion to Dismiss is without merit, it should be denied.

INTRODUCTION

I. Subject Matter Jurisdiction is Proper Under INA §242

When Congress promulgated the Illegal Immigration Reform and Immigrant Responsibility Act ("IIRIRA") in 1996, it limited the federal court's authority to review decisions by the Immigration Courts pertaining to removal. 8 U.S.C. §1252(g). Immigrants may no longer challenge the Attorney General's "decision or action" to "commence proceedings, adjudicate cases or execute removal orders." Reno v. American-Arab Anti-discrimination Committee, 525 U.S. 471, 481 (1999). Plaintiffs and Defendants do not dispute this. They do dispute, however, the nature of Plaintiff's request. Defendants erroneously assert that Plaintiffs' Petitions at issue in this lawsuit are intended to prevent their deportations. Defendants agree that if they were seeking relief from removal, this court would not have jurisdiction. However they are not seeking such relief. Plaintiffs are simply asking that Defendants do their job by adjudicating the Petition. They are not challenging any government action concerning removal proceedings, cases or orders. Plaintiff **[Alien]** has not been served with a Notice to Appear and to her knowledge there are no removal proceedings pending against her. (Affidavit of **[Alien]**.) 8 U.S.C. §1252(g) has absolutely nothing to do with this case because the case does not concern proceedings, cases or removal orders.

Defendants admit that Plaintiffs "do not directly seek to compel the Attorney General to initiate proceedings or adjudicate their deportability." Defendants assert, however, that Plaintiffs' purpose in filing this lawsuit is to "prevent their deportation." Defendants claim that **[Alien]** "seeks to challenge the Attorney General's exercise of discretion related to whether and when to prosecute or adjudicate removal proceedings." This belies logic. To **[Alien]**'s knowledge, DHS[1] has not reviewed her file to determine if she may be removable. She has not been served with a Notice to Appear and has not been notified of any court hearings. **[Alien]** is very pleased with ICE's decision not to commence removal proceedings against her, and has no desire to "challenge" anyone's exercise of discretion not to prosecute her. [2] ICE's authority to commence removal proceedings against Plaintiff would not be altered by the issuance of a Writ. If ICE has probable cause to issue a Notice to Appear and commence removal proceedings, it can do so before or after this court decides this case.

Even if **[Alien]** were challenging ICE's discretion to commence removal proceedings, **[Entity]** clearly is not. **[Entity]** is a corporation, not an alien, and cannot be removed. Plaintiff **[Entity]**'s sole purpose in filing this mandamus action is to have USCIS make a decision to approve or deny the Petitions. This court therefore has jurisdiction to hear Plaintiffs' claims.

Furthermore, Defendants Rosemary Melville and Robert Divine, as employees of U.S. Citizenship and Immigration Services, do not have the authority to "commence proceedings, adjudicate cases or execute removal orders." Reno v. American-Arab Anti-Discrimination Committee, 525 U.S. 471, 481 (1999). When the INS was dissolved and the Department of Homeland Security was created, these functions were delegated to the Immigration and Customs Enforcement (ICE). ICE is not a defendant in this lawsuit. Although Michael Chertoff, as Secretary of the Department of Homeland Security, has supervisory authority over ICE, nothing in Plaintiffs' Petition for Writ of Mandamus mentions ICE, its actions or its responsibilities, or Secretary Chertoff's relationship to that organization. Neither the Interim Director of the Atlanta office of ICE, Mike Rozos, nor Michael Garcia, the Assistant Secretary of ICE, are named as Defendants.

Defendants' reliance on Cardoso v. Reno, 216 F. 3d 512 (2000) is misplaced. In Cardoso, INS had adjudicated and denied the adjustment of status applications of each of the three Plaintiffs. The Cardoso Plaintiffs asked the court to "require the Attorney General to '(a) allow them to remain in the United States, (b) issue work authorization and, when a visa is available to them (c) allow them to adjust status in the United States.'" Id. at 514 (2000). In fact, they were asking the Attorney General to change INS's previous decisions and approve the adjustment of status applications. Unlike the Petitioners in Cardoso, Plaintiffs are not asking this court to order Defendants to change a decision. They are simply asking that the Defendants make a decision. This court clearly has such authority.

II. The Administrative Procedures Act Applies to Mandamus Actions

The Administrative Procedures Act in conjunction with 28 U.S.C. §1331 provides subject matter jurisdiction for cases in which courts are asked to review agency actions. Califano v. Sanders, 430 U.S. 99, 107 (1977) ("The obvious effect of this modification [of section 1331], subject only to preclusion-of-review statutes created or retained by Congress, is to confer jurisdiction on federal courts to review agency action, regardless of

[1] The Department of Homeland Security assumed the responsibility of prosecuting and adjudicating removal proceedings from the Attorney General when it was created.

[2] **[Alien]** makes no claims in this action as to her removability.

whether the APA of its own force may serve as a jurisdictional predicate." In Nyaga v. Ashcroft, 186 F. Supp. 1244 (N.D. Ga. 2002), where Plaintiff's were seeking an order to compel USCIS to adjudicate an application, this court did not reach the issue of jurisdiction under the APA because it found mandamus jurisdiction to be proper. However, where courts have reached the issue, they have found jurisdiction. Zemin Hu, 2000 U.S. Dist. LEXIS 5030, 2000 WL 425174 (N.D. Tx 2000) (finding that the APA and 28 U.S.C. §1331 together vest court with authority to order agencies to act); JianJun Fu v. Reno, 2000 U.S. Dist. LEXIS 16110 (N.D. Tx. 2000) ("the APA in conjunction with section 1331 does provide [subject-matter] jurisdiction").

Case law relied on by Defendants to support this argument is not relevant to this lawsuit. In each of the cases relied on by Defendants, Afsharzadehyadzi v. Perryman, 214 F. Supp. 2d 884 (N.D. Ill 2002), Holasek v. United States Department of Justice, 124 F. Supp. 2d 1126 (N.D. Ill 2000), and Diallo v. Reno, 61 F. Supp. 2d 1361 (N.D. Ga. 1999), the INS had already decided and denied Plaintiffs' applications for adjustment of status, and Plaintiffs were seeking to have that decision reversed. As explained above, USCIS has not denied **[Alien]** and the**[Entity]** Petitions, and they are not seeking to have the court order Defendants to change a decision. They are simply seeking to have the government make a decision.

Plaintiffs' case is identical to other cases in which parties have brought suit to compel the government to act on a pending application. In those cases the courts have consistently ruled that they have jurisdiction to hear such claims. Although Defendants cite Iddir v. Immigration and Naturalization, 166 F. Supp. 2d 1250 (N.D. Ill 2001) in their discussion on the Administrative Procedures Act, the court in Iddir does not discuss jurisdiction under the APA, but rather finds jurisdiction under the Madamus Act, as will be discussed below.

Defendants also argue that the APA does not apply because Plaintiffs have not exhausted their administrative remedies. Defendants are putting the cart before the horse. Once Defendants make a decision on the Petitions, and if that decision is a denial, then the Plaintiffs will have a decision on which to exhaust remedies. Until Defendants make that decision, however, there is nothing to be appealed.

III. Plaintiffs have a Right to a Writ of Mandamus Under 28 U.S.C. §1361.

The Court has authority to issue a Writ of Mandamus when Plaintiffs show they have a clear right to relief, the Defendants have a clear non-discretionary duty to act, and no other adequate remedy is available. Nyaga v. Ashcroft, 186 F. Supp. 2d 1244, 1252 (2002) *rev'd on other grounds*, 323 F. 3d 906 (11th Cir. 2003), citing Heckler v. Ringer, 466 U.S. 602 (1984); District Lodge No. 166, Intern. Ass'n of Machinists and Aerospace Workers, AFL-CIO v. TWA Services, Inc., 731 F. 2d 711, 717 (11th Cir. 1984).

The Mandamus Act grants district courts the power to compel a government agency or employee to discharge a duty. It grants jurisdiction over "any action in the nature of mandamus to compel an officer or employee of the United States or any agency thereof to perform a duty owned to the plaintiff." 28 U.S.C. §1361. The Act requires Plaintiffs to show that "(1) they have a clear right to have their applications adjudicated; (2) that defendants have a nondiscretionary duty to rule on the applications; and (3) that they have no other adequate remedy." Zemin Hu v. Reno, 2000 U.S. Dist. Lexis 5030 (N.D. Tx. 2000) (court has mandamus authority to order INS to adjudicate a pending adjustment of status application); Nyaga v. Ashcroft, 186 F. Supp. 2d 1244, 1252 (N.D. Ga 2002) 323 F.3d 906 (11th Cir. 2003) *reversed on other grounds* (defendants were ordered to adjudicate pending adjustment of status application under court's mandamus authority); Iddir v. Immigration and Naturalization, 166 F. Supp. 2d 1250 (N.D. Ill 2001) (Court has mandamus jurisdiction pursuant to 28 U.S.C. §1361 to order the adjudication of an application for adjustment of status.)

The Court may not use mandamus to compel the government to perform a discretionary action. Heckler v. Ringer, 466 U.S. 602 (1984). It may, however, "compel the Government to exercise its discretion without actually interfering with that exercise." Nyaga v. Ashcroft, 186 F. Supp. 2d 1244, 1253 (2002). Federal Courts have reviewed this issue in the context of immigration petitions, and repeatedly held that Mandamus is an appropriate vehicle for compelling the government to adjudicate petitions.

In Nyaga v. Ashcroft, 186 F. Supp. 2d 1244, 1253 (2002), Plaintiffs had filed a petition for adjustment of status under the visa lottery program. Because Defendants had not adjudicated their application in what Plaintiffs deemed to be a reasonable time, they filed a petition for writ of mandamus with this court. This court held that it had mandamus jurisdiction over the case. It further found that the government had a non-discretionary duty to "make diligent efforts" to adjudicate the visa lottery applications. The court recognizes that it cannot compel a particular outcome, but it can compel the government to adjudicate the petition.

> Where, as here, the evidence shows that the Government failed to act to process Plaintiff Nyaga's application, the court may order Defendants to exercise their discretion by ordering them to adjudicate the application thoroughly and make a decision one way or another… What this court may not do is mandate a certain outcome in that adjudication, as the final decision is the discretionary act.

Nyaga at 1253. This is exactly what Plaintiffs in this case are seeking – a court order to Defendants to adjudicate the Petitions. See also Jianjun Fu v. Reno, 2000 U.S. Dist Lexis 16110 (N.D. Tx 2000) (District Court has authority to order Defendant to adjudicate pending adjustment of status application).

The case at bar is identical. Plaintiffs have filed an application, the Defendants failed to adjudicate the application within a reasonable period of time.

IV. DHS Does Not Have a First-In First-Out Policy of Adjudicating Petitions

Contrary to the statements of Mr. Paul S. Sturgeon contained in the affidavit submitted with the Defendant's Motion, Texas Service Center (TSC) does not always adjudicate applications and petitions in the order they are received. In fact, TSC has approved Form I-140's, Immigrant Petition for Alien Workers, which were filed after the Plaintiffs filed their Petition. Plaintiffs do not have access to statistical data or USCIS records of filing and adjudication dates of all of the Petitions filed with TSC. But even from the small number of clients of Plaintiff's counsel who have filed their Petitions after Plaintiffs, four have already had their petitions adjudicated by TSC.

Plaintiffs filed their Immigrant Petition on March 13, 2003. One of Plaintiff's client's other clients, **[Client]**, filed her Immigrant Petition after Plaintiffs, on April 3, 2003, and it was approved on January 21, 2004. Similarly, **[Client]** filed his Petition on May 30, 2003 and it was approved less than three weeks later, on June 17, 2003. **[Client]** filed his Immigrant Petition on August 13, 2003, and it was approved on November 24, 2003. **[Client]** filed his Immigrant Petition on August 4, 2003, five months after Plaintiffs filed theirs, and it was approved on January 26, 2004. **[Client]**'s petition was approved in only four months. He filed it on August 7, 2003, (in Vermont) and it was approved on December 11, 2003. Plaintiffs, however, are still waiting for their Petition to be adjudicated.

V. It Is USCIS's Policy to Expedite Applications Where There Are Dependent Removal Proceedings.

The American Immigration Lawyers Association asked Defendant USCIS to expedite petitions for beneficiaries in removal proceedings. In the AILA/USCIS benefits liaison meeting on October 1, 2003, USCIS indicated that it would adjudicate a visa petition when failing to do so could effect the outcome of a removal hearing.

> CIS recognizes the considerable equities favoring expedited processing of a pending petition in this type of situation. CIS is developing policy guidance on this issue. Until that policy is finalized CIS will work with AILA to identify a process that promotes identification well before the hearing to permit CIS offices an opportunity to adjudicate the visa petition.

See AILA/USCIS Benefits Liaison Meeting Minutes, October 1, 2003. In this case, however, Defendants violated their own policy and failed to assist in adjudicating the Plaintiffs' petition. Plaintiffs' attorney mailed and faxed a letter to USCIS Atlanta's chief counsel, **[Individual]**, on November 5, 2003, asking that **[Alien]**'s case be adjudicated. Defendants did not follow USCIS procedure and adjudicate Plaintiffs' petitions, however. It never responded to Plaintiff's request.

CONCLUSION

For the above-stated reasons, Plaintiffs ask that Defendants' Motion to Dismiss be denied.

Respectfully submitted this ___ day of __________, 20__.

[Attorney]

[ADD CERTIFICATE OF SERVICE]

[Document No. 517]

PLAINTIFFS' OPPOSITION TO DEFENDANTS' MOTION TO DISMISS ACTION FOR MANDAMUS (NATURALIZATION)

Description: Defendant Department of Homeland Security (DHS) has moved to dismiss a class action in federal district court based on failure to state a claim on which relief can be granted. Plaintiffs' response outlines the standard in the Eleventh Circuit for the court's decision, reviews the mandatory nature of the regulations applicable to naturalization adjudications as well as the failure of DHS to follow its own regulations, and outlines the lack of other appropriate relief.

Advantages: A thorough review of applicable law when DHS fails to follow its own rules.

Limitations: Case law is appropriate to the Eleventh Circuit and must be adapted.

Citations: INA §336(b).

UNITED STATES DISTRICT COURT
FOR THE SOUTHERN DISTRICT OF FLORIDA

[Aliens], et al., on behalf of themselves and all others similarly situated	)	
Plaintiffs,	)	Case No.
v.	)	MAGISTRATE JUDGE **[NAME]**
ALBERTO GONZALES, et al.	)	
Defendants.	)	

PLAINTIFFS' OPPOSITION TO DEFENDANTS' MOTION TO DISMISS

INTRODUCTION

Defendants' Motion to Dismiss argues that Plaintiffs fail to state a claim on which relief can be granted. The arguments raised by Defendants in their Motion to Dismiss are substantially the same as those raised in Defendants' Opposition to Plaintiffs' Motion for Preliminary Injunction. Plaintiffs responded to those arguments in Plaintiffs' Reply in Support of Plaintiffs' Motion for Preliminary Injunction filed on **[date]**. For the convenience of the Court relevant sections of those arguments are incorporated herein at Sections II and IV.

I. DEFENDANTS' MOTION TO DISMISS MUST BE EVALUATED UNDER A VERY HIGH STANDARD

The Eleventh Circuit has repeatedly emphasized the appropriate standard by which to decide a motion to dismiss for failure to state a claim:

> Over and over againCbut apparently not enoughCthis Court has stated, explained, reiterated, stressed, rephrased, and emphasized a simple long established, well publicized Rule of Federal Procedure: A motion to dismiss for failure to state a claim should not be granted unless it *appears to a certainty* that Plaintiff would not be entitled to recover under any set of facts which could be proved in support of his claim.

Jackman v. Hospital Corp. of America Mideast Ltd., 800 F.2d 1577, 1581 (11th Cir. 1986) (quoting *Cook & Nichols, Inc. v. Plimsoll Club*, 451 F.2d 505, 506 (5th Cir. 1971)) (emphasis added). As more recently stated by this court in *Klaskala v. U.S. Dept. of Health and Human Services*, 889 F. Supp. 480, 483 (S.D.Fla. 1995):

> Motions to dismiss for failure to state a claim are generally viewed with disfavor and rarely granted. *Eaton v. Coal Par of West Virginia, Inc.*, 580 F. Supp. 572, 576 (S.D.Fla. 1984). It is well settled that a "complaint should not be dismissed for failure to state a claim unless it appears beyond doubt that the plaintiff can prove no set of facts which would entitle him to

relief." *Conley v. Gibson*, 355 U.S. 41, 45-46, 78 S.Ct. 99, 102, 2 L.Ed.2d 80 (1957). In ruling on a motion to dismiss, a federal court must view the complaint in the light most favorable to the plaintiff and take its allegations as true. *Hishon v. King & Spaulding*, 467 U.S. 69, 73, 104 S.Ct. 2229, 2232, 81 L.Ed.2d 59 (1984).

II. THE APPLICABLE REGULATIONS IMPOSE A MANDATORY, NONDISCRETIONARY DUTY ON DEFENDANTS TO DECIDE APPLICATIONS FOR NATURALIZATION WITHIN 120 DAYS OF THE EXAMINATION

Defendants argue at length in their Motion to Dismiss that Plaintiffs' interpretation of 8 USC §1447(b) is not compelled by the language of the statute. However, their own regulations and explanations of those regulations, far more powerfully than any argument of plaintiffs, have consistently adopted plaintiffs' interpretation of the statute. For example, 8 CFR §312.5, first issued as an interim rule in October, 1991, contains a clear explanation of defendants' prelitigation interpretation of 8 USC §1447(b) when it describes "the *requirement* under *section 336 of the Act* [8 USC §1447] that the Service *must* render a determination on the application within 120 days from the initial interview." In their initial explanation of that interim rule, the Justice Department repeatedly reiterated this interpretation of the statute:

> IMMACT [Immigration Act] now requires the INS officer who initially examines the applicant to make a formal determination to grant or deny the application within 120 days after the date of first examination.

56 FR 50475, *50475, available in 1991 WL 198206.

> The most significant changes resulting from the passage of IMMACT arise from the authority now conferred upon the Attorney General to make final determinations on applications for naturalization...The statute mandates that the INS examiner assigned to the initial examination of the applicant *must* make a decision to either grant or deny the application within a 120 day period from the date of that examination.....Each application must be decided on its merits as either a grant or denial within the statutorily mandated time frame...

Id. at *50476. (Emphasis added.) And, in the same interim rule explanation, the Justice Department explained why the naturalization administrative appeal process was not subject to the 120 day limit by stating:

> Because the administrative review process contained in section 336 of the Act is separate and distinct from the initial examination procedure under section 335 of the Act [8 USC §1447], it is not subject to the 120 day rule.

Id. at *50476. Again, in the same interim rule explanation, the Department describes 8 CFR Part 335, which contains 8 CFR §335.3, "[a] decision to grant or deny the application shall be made at the time of initial examination of the applicant or within 120 days after...the examination", as being "draw[n] directly from the statute." *Id.* at *50477.

It is these contemporaneous interpretations that courts examine to determine an agency's true interpretation of a statute, not attorney-prepared explanations designed to protect the agency's litigation position. *Securities Industry Association v. Bd. of Governors*, 468 U.S. 137, 82 L.Ed.2d 107, 104 S.Ct. 2979 (1984) (post litigation statutory interpretations by agency counsel not entitled to deference.)

More importantly, however, defendants also ignore Plaintiffs' claims which are based independently upon the clear language of the regulations. (Complaint ¶¶ 20 - 21.) Defendants are as legally bound to follow the mandates of their own properly issued regulations as they are those of a statute. As early as 1923 Mr. Justice Brandeis held that the INS (now USCIS) must follow its own regulations: "It may be assumed that one under investigation with a view to deportation is legally entitled to insist upon observance of rules promulgated by the Secretary pursuant to law." *Bilokumsky v. Tod*, 263 U.S. 149, 155 (1923). In <u>United States v.</u>

Shaughnessy, 374 U.S. 260, 265 (1953), the Court again held that validly issued INS regulations had "the force and effect of law". *See also Bridges v. Wixon*, 326 U.S. 135, 153 (1945). In *Service v. Dulles*, 354 U.S. 363, 388 (1957), the Court, citing *Shaughnessy*, found that where the regulations imposed obligations in excess of those required by statute the agency "could not, so long as the regulations remained unchanged, proceed without regard to them". More recently, in *Nixon v. U.S.*, 418 U.S. 683 (1974), the Court held the Attorney General bound by his own regulations:

> So long as this regulation is extant it has the force of law...[I]t is theoretically possible for the Attorney General to amend or revoke the regulation defining the Special Prosecutor's authority. But he has not done so. So long as this regulation remains in force the Executive Branch is bound by it, and indeed the United States as the sovereign composed of the three branches is bound to respect and to enforce it.

Id. at 696. As recently as last week the Ninth Circuit reaffirmed these cases in *Sameena v. U.S. Air Force*, WL 354 213, (9th Cir. 7/6/98) stating:

> The Supreme Court has long recognized that a federal agency is obliged to abide by the regulations it promulgates. *See Vitarelli v. Seaton*, 359 U.S. 535, 545 (1959); *Service v. Dulles*, 354 U.S. 363, 372 (1957); *Accardi v. Shaughnessy*, 347 U.S. 260, 267 (1954)...Where a prescribed procedure is intended to protect the interests of a party before the agency, "even though generous beyond the requirements that bind such agency, the procedure must be scrupulously observed." *Vitarelli*, 359 U.S. 547 (Frankfurter, J. concurring).

Id. (Slip Opinion, p.6). *See also Doe v. U.S. Department of Justice*, 753 F.2d 1092, 1098 (D.C. Cir. 1985), ("Courts, of course, have long required agencies to abide by internal, procedural regulations...even when those regulations provide more protection than the Constitution or relevant civil service laws.")

American Farm Lines v. Black Ball Freight Service, et al., 397 U.S. 532 (1970), relied upon by defendants, actually supports the plaintiffs' position. In *American Farm Lines*, the Court found that violations of rules could be overlooked *only* where the rules were not created for the benefit of the complaining party and the complaining party was not substantially prejudiced. This has been the consistent interpretation of *American Farm Lines* by other courts. For example, in *Doe v. U.S. Department of Justice*, *supra*, the court held that the rule of *American Farm Lines* was limited to those "rules not intended primarily to confer important procedural benefits upon individuals in the face of otherwise unfettered discretion." *Id.* at 1098. In *Sun Oil Co. v. Federal Power Commission*, 256 F.2d 233 (5th Cir. 1958), relied upon by defendants, the court considers the lack of harm to be crucial in its decision to permit the changed rule:

> No injury to Sun has been shown...None is threatened so far as appears. There is no need to anticipate an injury not presently threatened and not shown to be something likely to arise in the future...

Id. at 239. *Amcor, Inc. v. Brock*, 780 F.2d 897 (11th Cir. 1986), cited by defendants in their Opposition to Plaintiffs' Motion for a Preliminary Injunction, similarly cites *American Farm Lines* for the narrow proposition that an agency may waive a procedural regulation only when "such a waiver will not prejudice the other party." *Id.* at 899.[1] More recently, in *Port of Jacksonville v. U.S. Coast Guard*, 788 F.2d 705 (11th Cir. 1986), the Eleventh Circuit affirmed an even narrower reading for this Circuit in which there is no need to even show prejudice in cases involving rules which confer a procedural benefit:

---

[1] *United States v. Caceres*, 440 U.S. 742 (1978), also cited by defendants in their Opposition to Plaintiffs' Motion for Preliminary Injunction, is simply inapposite as it involves the constitutional question as to whether an administrative exclusionary rule should be created to bar evidence obtained in violation of an administrative regulation.

> A framework governing review of an agency's deviation from its own regulations is given in *American Farm Lines*, 397 U.S. at 538-39, 90 S.Ct. at 1292-93: determine whether the regulation was intended 1) to require the agency to exercise its independent discretion or 2) to confer a procedural benefit to a class to which complainant belongs, or 3) to be a "mere aid" to guide the exercise of agency discretion. If the first or second, [citations omitted] invalidate the action; if the third, a further determination must be made whether the complainant has been substantially prejudiced. If he has, invalidate the action; if not, affirm. [citations omitted]

Id. at 708. That narrower reading has also been adopted by the Second Circuit in *Montilla v. INS*, 926 F.2d 162, 163 (2d Cir. 1991) ("The INS may not fairly administer the immigration laws on the notion that on some occasions its rules are made to be broken.")

Manhattan-Bronx Postal Union v. Gronouski, 350 F.2d 451 (1965), also cited by defendants in their Opposition to Plaintiffs' Motion for Preliminary Injunction, is inapposite as it does not involve the enforcement of a validly issued regulation but rather an Executive Order. (Accord, *Chasse v. Chasen*, 595 F.2d 59, 62 (1st Cir. 1979).

Obviously, the regulations at issue here are intended for the express benefit of the Plaintiffs, and their violation has significantly prejudiced the Plaintiffs. The language of the regulations themselves specifically bestow important procedural rights on the applicants.[2] For example, 8 CFR §312.5(b) requires a *written waiver of the right to a determination within 120 days by the applicant* even when the applicant requests the continuance. Only important procedural rights require a written waiver.[3] Moreover, the "prejudice" resulting from defendants' practice could not be more demonstratively presented than by the allegations of the Complaint (Complaint ¶¶ 28-41, 48). Plaintiffs, many elderly or disabled, who have waited for years for some word on their applications, whose hardships are so cavalierly dismissed by defendants, have been severely prejudiced by the delay. As catalogued in the Complaint, they suffered the loss of:

> [the] protection of the laws of the United States equal to that granted to citizens; political rights, including the right to vote; the right to enter and remain in the United States; freedom of movement and travel; the right to obtain a United States passport; the protection of the United States government when outside the country; and the right to transmit citizenship to children born abroad. They have also been subjected to the fear, despair and uncertainty engendered by the inability to obtain citizenship; the inability to travel and carry out necessary activities, including medical treatment, out of concern they may miss a long-delayed swearing-in ceremony; the inability to file petitions for immediate relatives as a United States citizen; as well as the loss, or threatened loss, of life sustaining benefits.

Complaint, ¶48. These are precisely the sorts of injuries that administrative naturalization was designed to prevent. As Rep. Morrison explained,

> All of us have had the experience of being contacted as elections approach or as other opportunities which citizenship would provide occur in the lives of individuals, and we find ourselves unable to move the process forward because of the backlog resulting from the current system...and this legislation is directed to change that process and to create a one-step option which will allow citizenship to be more expeditiously provided to those who qualify.
>
> Administrative naturalization will restore the most vital elements of our system by which applicants receive naturalization: Employment opportunities, immigration petition rights with respect to relatives, travel opportunities, and most critically, the right to vote.

---

[2] Defendants' completely unsupported statement that the regulation is not for the predominant benefit of plaintiffs has no basis in the statutory or regulatory history nor have defendants attempted to demonstrate any.

[3] Defendants argue that because the right can be waived it must not be statutorily based. However, all rights, even constitutional rights, are waivable. *Garnet v. U.S.*, 424 U.S. 648 (1976).

135 Cong. Rec. H4539-02, *H4542 (July 31, 1989), *available in* 1989 WL 182156.

Given the Eleventh Circuit rule, as stated in *Port of Jacksonville v. U.S. Coast Guard*, *supra*, and the Complaint's allegations of severe prejudice, Defendants' argument that they can ignore with impunity the regulatorily and statutorily mandated 120 day time limit violates both the express terms of the Administrative Procedures Act and its fundamental policies. These regulations were first promulgated in October, 1991 as interim rules. They were subject to comment and there was in fact substantial comment. In 1993, the agency discussed and responded to the comments and modified the regulations in response. After that significant public process spanning several years, the Defendants, without any attempt at public input or reasoned discourse, are attempting to totally ignore the entire process, stating, as their explanation, only that they do not wish to be a "slave to [their] own rules." (Motion to Dismiss, p.11.)

III. THE COMPLAINT CONTAINS NO BASIS FOR EXCUSING DEFENDANTS' POLICY OF IGNORING THEIR OWN REGULATIONS

In evaluating a Motion to Dismiss the court may not consider factual allegations outside of the Complaint. When the Defendant attempts to introduce evidence to support explanations or allegations which conflict with those in the Complaint, they may not be considered in determining the motion to dismiss. *Sanner v. Board of Trade of City of Chicago*, 62 F.3d 918 (7th Cir. 1995). Thus, this court must ignore defendants' references to "Congress continuing concern" and "recent efforts to enhance the quality and accountability of administrative decisions" as evidence of the "reasonableness" of Defendants' current practice. As this Court is aware, Defendants have cited a litany of these factors, including virtually every recent occurrence in the naturalization arena, as excuses for their failure to obey the mandated time limits within their regulations. In Defendants' filings in Opposition to Plaintiffs' Motion for Preliminary Injunction they have quoted extensively from newspapers, press releases and Congressional testimony in support of these allegations. None of these allegations are relevant to this court's determination of the Motion to Dismiss.

The allegations of the Complaint are clear and the court is limited to these allegations for purposes of this Motion. Defendants are mandated by the applicable statutes and regulations to provide plaintiffs with a decision on their naturalization application within 120 days of the examination and, if they are approved, to provide them with a timely swearing in. (Complaint ¶24.) Defendants have a policy and practice of refusing to obey their own statutory and regulatory requirements and of denying plaintiffs the rights secured under those statutes and regulations. (Complaint ¶¶ 25 - 27.) Plaintiffs have been grievously and irreparably injured by Defendants' practice. (Complaint ¶¶ 1, 28-40, 41.)

IV. THE STATUTORY REMEDY PROVIDED BY 8 USC §1447(b) DOES NOT DEFEAT PLAINTIFFS' CLAIMS FOR RELIEF

(a) 8 USC §1447(b), as interpreted by defendants, does not provide an adequate alternative remedy.

Defendants argue that 8 USC §1447(b) provides an adequate alternative basis for granting plaintiffs' relief, thereby precluding relief pursuant to mandamus, 28 USC §1361, or the Administrative Procedures Act, 5 USC §701 *et seq*. However, defendants then argue that 8 USC §1447(b) bars exactly the type of relief plaintiffs are requesting and permits only "individualized consideration of these cases rather than class consideration."

Assuming, arguendo, that defendant' interpretation of 8 USC §1447(b) is correct,[4] their argument proves

[4] As plaintiffs demonstrate in their Reply in Support of Motion for Class Certification filed July 15, 1998, Plaintiffs believe that class wide injunctive relief is available pursuant to 8 USC §1447(b). *Califano v. Yamasaki*, 442 U.S. 682, 61 L.Ed.2d 176, 99 S.Ct. 2545 (1979). If this is true then Defendants' argument here is academic since the court will be able to grant full relief under mandamus, the APA or 8 USC §1447(b).

too much. Plaintiffs brought this action for the sole purpose of enjoining Defendants' illegal practice of failing and refusing to determine class members' applications for naturalization within 120 days of their examination as required by 8 CFR §§335.3(a) and 312.5(b). Plaintiffs specifically prayed for class wide injunctions compelling Defendants' future compliance with the obligations imposed by those sections. Complaint pp. 27-28. Defendants cannot have it both ways. If, as defendants argue, 8 USC §1447(b) prohibits such relief, then it cannot be considered an "adequate" alternative remedy sufficient to prohibit mandamus jurisdiction or APA review.

In *Bowen v. Massachusetts*, 487 U.S. 879, 108 S.Ct. 2722, 101 L.Ed.2d 749 (1988), the Court discusses the evaluation of the "adequacy" of an alternative court remedy in the context of the Administrative Procedures Act. In *Bowen* the State of Massachusetts filed an action for declaratory and injunctive relief against the Secretary of Health and Human Services, challenging the Secretary's policy of refusing federal reimbursement for certain State Medicaid expenses. The complaint, *inter alia*, requested prospective relief enjoining future enforcement of the policy. Similar to the Defendants' position in the present case, the Secretary in *Bowen* challenged the jurisdiction of the federal court under the APA, arguing that the plaintiff had an adequate alternative remedy for money damages in the Court of Claims under the Tucker Act. The Court categorically rejected that argument. The Court stated that the APA was to be interpreted to provide as broad a review as possible. *Bowen*, at 904. The Court then went on to demonstrate that the Tucker Act remedy was inadequate precisely because the Court of Claims could not offer all of the relief requested by the plaintiff.

> The Claims Court does not have the general equitable powers of a district court to grant prospective relief. Indeed, we have stated categorically that "the Court of Claims has no power to grant equitable relief." [citations omitted]. As the facts of this case illustrate, the interaction between the State's administration of its responsibilities under an approved Medicaid plan and the Secretary's interpretation of his regulations may make it appropriate for judicial review to culminate in the entry of declaratory or injunctive relief that requires the Secretary to modify future practices. We are not willing to assume that a naked money judgment will always be an adequate substitute for prospective relief...

Id. at 905. In the present case, as in *Bowen*, the Plaintiffs seek classwide mandamus and declaratory and injunctive relief. Defendants clearly argue that 8 USC §1447(b), as they interpret it, does not permit the court to grant the classwide prospective relief requested. As they read it, the statute can only serve as a basis for an individual *de novo* determination of each class member's claim. This relief is obviously insufficient to prospectively address the illegal policy identified by the plaintiffs. It fails even to directly affect defendants or their illegal policy. Rather it merely burdens federal district courts with thousands of individual actions, permitting defendants to continue to conduct the processing of those applications in violation of their own regulations and federal law.

(b) 8 USC §1447(b) was never intended to, nor does it, preclude relief pursuant to Mandamus or the Administrative Procedure Act

Alternatively, Defendants argue that Congress expressly intended that the limited individual review which Defendants read into 8 USC §1447(b) is the exclusive means of relief for naturalization applicants complaining about the systematic refusal to decide their naturalization applications. Nowhere do Defendants cite a shred of evidence for this position. Moreover, any analysis of the language of the statute or the legislative history supports a contrary reading - that 8 USC §1447(b) could only have been intended to provide an additional avenue of review and certainly not to have limited the ability of injured applicants to enjoin a systematic and illegal refusal to process their applications.

Initially, statutory analysis should begin with the language of the statute itself. *Chevron U.S.A. v. Natural Res. Def. Council*, 467 U.S. 837 (1984). Unlike other statutes which have been held to preclude other means of review, 8 USC §1447(b) makes no mention of any such intent. *See, e.g.*, 5 USC §701(a); 12 USC §1735b(c). Congress obviously knows how to limit or preclude review when it desires to do so but it declined to do so in this case. The language of 8 USC §1447(b) is similar to the Medicaid statute discussed by the Supreme Court in *Bowen v. Michigan Academy of Family Physicians*, 476 U.S. 667, 90 L.Ed.2d 623, 106 S.Ct. 2133 (1986) in which the court found that the statute did not preclude alternative means of review:

> Section 1395ff on its face is an explicit authorization of judicial review, not a bar. As a general matter, "the mere fact that some acts are made reviewable should not suffice to support an implication of exclusion as to others. The right to review is too important to be excluded on such slender and indeterminate evidence of legislative intent." [citations omitted]

Id. at 674.

Interpreting 8 USC §1447(b) as merely providing an additional means of providing review is the only interpretation consistent with the intent of the Immigration Act of 1990, which was to streamline and speed up naturalization processing. *See infra* at pp.4B5. It would be totally inconsistent with such an intent to create a judicial review procedure which insulated from review *systematic, illegal* administrative policies and instead required literally thousands of individual applicants to seek individual review in federal court.

Moreover, Courts have consistently guaranteed administrative review to enjoin systematic illegal policies even though statutes could be narrowly read to limit or preclude review. For example, in *Accardi v. Shaughnessy* 347 U.S. 260, 74 S.Ct. 499, 98 L.Ed. 681 (1954), an alien challenged an illegal practice of the Attorney General in instructing the Board of Immigration Appeals as to how to decide certain cases. The Court, acknowledging that it could not review the Board's exercise of discretion, held that it did have jurisdiction to enjoin a *policy* clearly in violation of the applicable regulations. Again in *Bowen v. Michigan Academy of Family Physicians, supra*, at 675, the court permitted a challenge to the Medicare payment schedule, stating that the statute did not limit "challenges mounted against the *method* by which such amounts are to be determined rather than the *determinations* themselves." [Emphasis in original.] Similarly, in *Graham v. Caston*, 568 F.2d 1092 (5th Cir. 1978), the court found jurisdiction to require the defendant U.S. Department of Housing and Urban Development officials to review homeowners' claims despite a statute which specifically precluded judicial review of the Department's determinations, stating:

> If an administrative official clearly departs from statutory authority, the administrative action is subject to judicial review even though a jurisdictional withdrawal statute is otherwise applicable. [citations omitted]. Likewise, judicial review is available where the administrative agency fails to follow procedures adopted by the administrative agency. *Accardi v. Shaughnessy*, 347 U.S. 260, 74 S.Ct. 499, 98 L.Ed. 681 (1954).

Id. at 1097. Consistent with this principal, the Eleventh Circuit has, on numerous occasions, found jurisdiction in the district court to review policies and practices of INS which violate the rights of immigrants despite statutes limiting judicial review. In *Haitian Refugee Center v. Smith*, 676 F.2d 1023 (5th Cir. Unit B 1982), the plaintiffs challenged in District Court an INS policy which systematically denied Haitians their rights in deportation and asylum hearings. The Department argued that, by statute, jurisdiction was limited to the Court of Appeals, 8 USC §1105a(a). The Court of Appeals rejected that argument and affirmed the District Court's jurisdiction stating:

> Although a court of appeals may have sole jurisdiction to review alleged procedural irregularities in an individual deportation hearing to the extent these irregularities may provide a basis for reversing an individual deportation order, that is not to say that a program, pattern or scheme by immigration officials to violate the constitutional rights is not a separate matter subject to examination by a district court and to the entry of at least declaratory and injunctive relief. The distinction we draw is one between the authority of a court of appeals to pass upon the merits of an individual deportation order and any action in the deportation proceeding to the extent it may affect the merits determination, on the one hand, and, on the other, the authority of a district court to wield its equitable power when a wholesale, carefully orchestrated, program of constitutional violations is alleged.

Id. at 1033. Similarly in *Jean v. Nelson*, 727 F.2d 957, 980 (11th Cir. 1984), (in banc), aff'd, 472 U.S. 846, 105 S.Ct. 2992, 86 L.Ed.2d 664 (1985), the court affirmed district court jurisdiction over a challenge to the wholesale, systematic violation by INS employees of the statutory and regulatory rights of the plaintiff class. Again in *Haitian Refugee Center, Inc. v. Nelson*, 872 F.2d 1555 (11th Cir. 1989), aff'd, 498 U.S. 479 (1991) the court reaffirmed the same principle:

> In *Jean v. Nelson*, 727 F.2d 957, 980 (11th Cir. 1984), (in banc) aff'd, 472 U.S. 846, 105 S.Ct. 2992, 86 L.Ed.2d 664 (1985), we reaffirmed that section 106 of the INA...does not deprive district courts of jurisdiction to review allegations of systematic abuses by INS officials...We explained that to postpone "judicial resolution of a disputed issue that affects an entire class of aliens until an individual petitioner has an opportunity to litigate it on habeus corpus would foster the very delay and procedural redundancy that Congress sought to eliminate..."

Id. at 1560.

CONCLUSION

For the reasons discussed herein, plaintiffs respectfully request this court to deny Defendants' Motion to Dismiss.

[Attorney]

[ADD CERTIFICATEOF SERVICE]

[Document Nos. 518–20]

COMPLAINT FOR DECLARATORY AND INJUNCTIVE RELIEF

Description: These complaints challenge the legacy Immigration and Naturalization Service's/Department of Homeland Security's (DHS) decision to deny an H-1B extension of status based on its misinterpretation of the six-year stay limit on H-1B visas, and on DHS's decision to deny H-1B classification to a foreign national, arguing that the action were arbitrary and capricious, and inconsistent with regulatory guidance.

Advantages: Sometimes, DHS/USCIS makes mistakes. While the typical place to seek relief and exhaust administrative remedies would be the Administrative Appeals Office (AAO) for USCIS issues, there may be no relief available there. To correct *legal* errors of USCIS, the declaratory and injunctive relief pleadings are essential.

Limitations: Counsel will likely have to convince a federal court that it has jurisdiction under INA §242 to hear these cases, as the DHS counsel will certainly argue against jurisdiction, as a matter of routine. However, it appears clear that this type of complaint survives the REAL ID Act of 2005.

UNITED STATES DISTRICT COURT
EASTERN DISTRICT OF LOUISIANA

The Louisiana Philharmonic Orchestra Plaintiff, v. United States Immigration and Naturalization Service Defendants.	)))))))))	Civ. Action 98-2855 "L" (1)

FIRST AMENDED COMPLAINT FOR JUDICIAL REVIEW OF DENIAL OF A PETITION FOR A NONIMMIGRANT WORKER

The Louisiana Philharmonic Orchestra (the "Orchestra"), plaintiff, complains against the United States Immigration and Naturalization Service (the "INS"), defendant, as follows:

1. This is an action for judicial review of (a) the August 28, 1998 decision of the Immigration and Naturalization Service ("INS"), LIN 96-045-51375, which denied a petition by the Orchestra to employ a nonimmigrant, Ying Liang Zhao, in category H-1B, and (b) the May 3, 1999 decision of the INS, which reaffirmed its August 28, 1998 decision, following the April 5, 1999 Order and Reasons and the April 6, 1999 Judgment in this action.

JURISDICTION

2. The United States District Court has jurisdiction of this action under 28 USC § 1331.

THE PARTIES

3. The Louisiana Philharmonic Orchestra is a Louisiana nonprofit membership corporation. It has its principal place of business and registered office in New Orleans, Louisiana, within the Eastern District of Louisiana. The Orchestra's orchestra is the only full-time, full-size professional symphonic orchestra located between Houston and Atlanta. The members of the corporation are the musicians who comprise the orchestra.

4. The United States Immigration and Naturalization Service is part of the United States Department of Justice. The INS administers the Immigration and Nationality Act pursuant to 8 USC § 1103 and 8 CFR § 2.1.

VENUE

5. The Eastern District of Louisiana is a proper venue for this action under 28 USC § 1391(e), because the plaintiff resides in the district and no real property is involved in the action.

PROCEEDINGS BEFORE THE I.N.S.

6. On November 22, 1995, the Orchestra filed its petition for nonimmigrant worker for Ying Liang Zhao in categories H-1B and O-1. The record of proceedings before the INS through August 28, 1998 (the "Administrative Record") was filed in Civil Action 98-2855.

7. Categories H-1B and O-1 are named for INA § 101 (a)(15)(H)(i)(b) and (a)(15)(O)(i), 8 USC § 1101 (a)(15)(H)(i)(b) and (a)(15)(O)(i), which provide in part:

> (15) The term "immigrant" means every alien except an alien who is within one of the following classes of nonimmigrant aliens—
>
> . . .
>
> (H) an alien (i) . . . (b) subject to section 212(j)(2),[1] who is coming temporarily to the United States to perform services (. . . other than services described . . . in subparagraph (O) or (P)) in a *specialty occupation* described in section 214(i)(1). . .
>
> . . .
>
> (O) an alien who:
>
> (i) has extraordinary ability in the sciences, arts, education, business, or athletics which has been demonstrated by sustained national or international acclaim, . . . and seeks to enter the United States to continue work in the area of extraordinary ability or. . .

(Emphasis added.) INA § 214 (i)(1), 8 USC § 1184(i)(1), supplies the following definition of the phrase "specialty occupation", which defines the H-1B category:

> (1) For purposes of section 101(a)(15)(H)(i)(b) and paragraph (2), the term "specialty occupation" means an occupation that requires--
>
> (A) theoretical and practical application of a body of highly specialized knowledge, and
>
> (B) attainment of a bachelor's or higher degree in the specific specialty (or its equivalent) as a minimum for entry into the occupation in the United States.

See also 8 CFR § 214.2 (h)(4)(ii) and (iii).

8. On May 6, 1996, the INS denied the petition. A copy of the decision of the Director of the Northern Service Center is attached hereto as appendix 1. (Ad. Rec. 119). The Director said:

> As the petitioner has not established that the position offered meets one of the above criteria as enumerated in 8 CFR 214.2(h)(4)(iii)(A), supra, it cannot be concluded that the position qualifies as a specialty occupation.

(Ad. Rec. 123). The Orchestra offered evidence to establish that the job offered satisfied the requirements of 8 CFR § 214.2 (h)(4)(iii)(A)(4):

> (A) Standards for specialty occupation position. To qualify as a specialty occupation, the position must meet one of the following criteria:
>
> . . .
>
> (4) The nature of the specific duties are so specialized and complex that knowledge required to perform the duties is usually associated with the attainment of a baccalaureate or higher degree.

Such evidence appears at Ad. Rec. 24-30, 79, 85-87 and 149-50.

---

[1] 8 USC § 1182(j)(2) provides for immigration of foreign medical graduates, and is not at issue in this action.

9. On May 16, 1996, the Orchestra filed a Notice of Appeal to the Administrative Appeals Unit of the INS. (Ad. Rec. 125).

10. On August 28, 1998, the Administrative Appeals Unit dismissed the Orchestra's appeal. A copy of the decision of the Associate Commissioner, Examinations is attached hereto as appendix 2. (Ad. Rec. 166)

11. The Orchestra sought judicial review of the Associate Commissioner's Decision in this action. A copy of the Court's Reasons and Order dated April 5, 1999 is attached hereto as appendix 3.

12. Following the judgment in the prior action, the INS rendered its Decision dated May 3, 1999, which again dismissed the Orchestra's appeal from the denial of its petition. A copy of said Decision is attached hereto as appendix 4.

GROUNDS FOR RELIEF

13. The August 28, 1998 and May 3, 1999 Decisions of the INS are "arbitrary, capricious, an abuse of discretion or otherwise not in accordance with law." 5 USC § 706 (2)(A).

14. The Decisions of the INS are "arbitrary, capricious, an abuse of discretion or otherwise not in accordance with law", because the LPO, on any fair reading of the record, met its burden of proof that "The nature of the specific duties are so specialized and complex that knowledge required to perform the duties is usually associated with the attainment of a baccalaureate or higher degree." 8 CFR § 214.2 (h)(4)(iii)(A)(4). The record on this issue consists of the statements of numerous persons who have knowledge of the attainments of professional symphonic orchestra musicians and of the hiring practices of professional symphonic orchestras. These statements indicate the basis of their makers' knowledge; are addressed to the applicable legal standard, as interpreted by the INS regulation; indicate the facts which underlie the conclusion which they state; and are not contradicted.

15. The Decisions of the INS are "arbitary, capricious, an abuse of discretion or otherwise not in accordance with law", because the Decisions are silent with respect to the evidence and authorities submitted by the Orchestra. *Abdel-Masieh v. INS*, 73 F3rd 579, 585 nn. 7-8 (5th Cir. 1996), citing precedents.

16. The Decisions of the INS are "arbitrary, capricious, an abuse of discretion or otherwise not in accordance with law", because the Decisions rest on a description of the "occupation" in which employment is offered, which is not supported by substantial evidence in the record, and which is contradicted by the weight of the evidence in the record. A finding by the INS which is not supported by substantial evidence is "arbitrary, capricious, an abuse of discretion or otherwise not in accordance with law". *Abdel-Masieh v. INS*, 73 F3rd 579, 586 n. 10 (5th Cir. 1996); *Immediate Business Systems v. Richard*, 645 F. Supp. 355, 359 (N.D. Ga. 1986); *Mars Jewelers, Inc. v. I.N.S.*, 702 F. Supp. 1570, 1575-76 nn. 4-5 (N.D. Ga. 1988).

17. The Decisions of the INS are "arbitrary, capricious, an abuse of discretion or otherwise not in accordance with law", because the Decisions are inconsistent with prior decisions of the INS and of the courts which have interpreted and applied the statute at issue in this action and the similar provisions of prior law.

18. The Decisions of the INS are "arbitrary, capricious, an abuse of discretion or otherwise not in accordance with law", because the Decisions are inconsistent with prior decisions of the INS involving musicians employed to play in full-time, professional symphony orchestras. (Ad. Rec. 20 and 81). *Omni Packaging, Inc. v. U.S. I.N.S.*, 733 F. Supp. 500, 504 nn. 9 (D. P.R. 1990); *Mars Jewelers, Inc. v. I.N.S.*, 702 F. Supp. 1570, 1575-76 (N.D. Ga. 1988); *Safer, Inc. v. United States Immigration and Naturalization Service*, CA no. 3-87-2761-R (USDC N.D. Tex. 1989), 1989 U.S. Dist. LEXIS 6514; cf. *Wellington v. I.N.S.*, 108 F3d 631, 637 n. 16 (5th Cir. 1997). The INS has previously denied an H-1B petition by the Orchestra, see *The Louisiana Philharmonic Orchestra v. United States Immigration and Naturalization Service*, Civ. no. 94-2874, United States District Court, Eastern District of Louisiana.

WHEREFORE, The Louisiana Philharmonic Orchestra prays for judgment against the United States Immigration and Naturalization Service and prays that the court shall

a) compel the agency action unlawfully withheld and remand the case for approval of the Orchestra's petition for nonimmigrant worker;

b) hold unlawful and set aside the decisions of August 28, 1998 and May 3, 1999; and

c) grant judgment in favor of the Orchestra and against the INS for costs and all other relief to which the Orchestra may be entitled under the law and the evidence.

[Attorney]

[ADD CERTIFICATE OF SERVICE]

IN THE
UNITED STATES DISTRICT COURT
CENTRAL DISTRICT OF CALIFORNIA
SAN DIEGO, CA

[Aliens],
Plaintiffs,

v.

Case No. ________

Christine Poulos, Acting Center Director, California Service Center of the Immigration and Naturalization Service, and James Ziglar, Commissioner of the Immigration and Naturalization Service

Defendants.

COMPLAINT FOR DECLARATORY, MANDAMUS, AND INJUNCTIVE RELIEF

Plaintiffs, by their Attorney, complaining of Defendants, allege as follows:

1. Plaintiffs, **[Aliens]**, are individuals, residents of the City of Irvine, California, and natives and citizens of Mexico, who claim a right to reside, on a temporary basis, within the United States pursuant to 8 U.S.C. §1101(a)(15)(H)(b)(i), Section 101(a)(15)(H)(b)(i) of the Immigration and Nationality Act as amended, or commonly known as an "H-1B1" visa and the H-4 dependent visa for Plaintiff, Gabriela Salas. Plaintiffs sue Defendants for a refusal to comply with their federally mandated duties under the Immigration and Nationality Act (8 U.S.C. §1101 et seq.) and the Code of Federal Regulations, 8 C.F.R.§214.2(h) *et seq.*
2. James Ziglar is the Commissioner of the Immigration and Naturalization Service and is sued in his official capacity. Commissioner Ziglar is the head of the Immigration and Naturalization Service and is charged with the execution and enforcement of the immigration laws of this country.
3. Christine Poulos is the Acting Director of the California Service Center of the Immigration and Naturalization Service and is sued in her official capacity. Acting Director Poulos is charged with the management of the California Service Center which is responsible for the adjudication of various applications and petitions seeking benefits under the immigration laws of this country.
4. This Court has subject matter jurisdiction over this action pursuant to 28 U.S.C. §1331 (Federal Question) because Plaintiffs' claims arise under the federal laws of the United States, specifically the Immigration and Nationality Act, 8 U.S.C.§1101 *et seq.* This Court may grant relief in this action under 28 U.S.C. §1361 (Mandamus Act), 28 U.S.C.§1651 (All Writs Act), 28 U.S.C.§2201 (Declaratory Judgment Act) and under 5 U.S.C.§701 *et seq.* (Administrative Procedures Act or the "APA").
5. Venue is proper in this Court because the Defendants Ziglar and Poulos are officers of the United States acting in their official capacity and the Immigration and Naturalization Service is an agency of the United

States and because the Plaintiffs reside within this District and a substantial part of the events, acts or omissions which give rise to this action took place and occurred within the jurisdiction of this District Court.

6. On or about June 13, 2001 Plaintiff, **[Alien]**, and his employer filed a petition to extend the temporary stay of Plaintiff, **[Alien]**, under the H-1B1 visa classification and Plaintiff, **[Alien]**, filed an application to extend her H-4 visa status with Defendant Poulos. This petition and application sought extensions of stay for the remaining period of the legally permissible time in the United States until October 30, 2002, pursuant to 8 C.F.R.§214.2(h)(13)(iii).

7. On September 27, 2001, Defendants issued a Request for Evidence (Exhibit A). Plaintiff, **[Alien]**'s, employer filed a timely response to Defendants' Request for Evidence on October 5, 2001 (Exhibit B). On January 2, 2002, Defendants "denied" Plaintiffs' extensions (Exhibit C). Plaintiffs' employer submitted a timely Motion to Reconsider the denial of their petition on January 24, 2002, pursuant to 8 C.F.R. §103.3(a)(2) (Exhibit D). The Defendants received the Motion to Reconsider by February 5, 2002, and must decide within forty-five days whether or not favorable action is warranted. 8 C.F.R. §103.3(a)(2)(iii). To date, no response from the Defendants has been received. Plaintiffs have no further remedy under the law since there is no appellate review of the denial of an extension of stay of nonimmigrant status. 8 C.F.R. §103.1(f)(3)(iii).

8. Plaintiffs have exhausted all available administrative remedies.

9. Defendants' actions in refusing to grant an extension of Plaintiffs' stay until October 30, 2002, is a violation of law and regulation. No facts are in dispute. Plaintiffs have not been in the United States for six years in H-1B1 or H-4 status.

10. Defendants are not complying with their mandatory duties. As a direct consequence of Defendants' actions, Plaintiffs are facing the risk of being deported from the United States, and may be accruing time in "unlawful presence" pursuant to 8 U.S.C.§1182(a)(9), Plaintiff, **[Alien]**, has lost employment eligibility and both are suffering other substantial harm and injuries.

11. Defendants have been unwilling to ameliorate their harm to Plaintiffs.

12. Defendants' stated legal position is that the limitations under 8 U.S.C.§214(g)(4) include time the Plaintiffs spent outside the United States when they were not admitted to this country in H-1B1 and H-4 status, and that such time spent outside the United States during the six-year period commencing with Plaintiffs' first arrival in the United States may not be recovered and added back to complete a full six year period.

13. Defendants' legal position is arbitrary, capricious and contrary to the plain and unambiguous language of the law and regulations and is *ultra vires.* It changes the plain language of the law as enacted and is inconsistent with Defendants' past practice of many years in granting such extensions to recover time spent outside this country. Furthermore, the Defendants' basis for the denial of Plaintiffs' extension of stay is entirely false. Defendants claim that *Sandeep Nair and Asha Nair vs. Dona Coultice, et al.*, 162 F. Supp. 2d 1209 (August 10, 2001), a recent Southern District Court Decision on this same issue is not binding on the Defendants because it is not a published decision. However, this decision is not only published, but the District Court awarded attorney fees in the amount of $6,138.75 and costs in the amount of $303.00 because the Court held that the Defendants' position was not "substantially justified." 28 U.S.C. §2412(d)(1)(A) (Exhibit E). *Sandeep Nair and Asha Nair vs. Dona Coultice, et al.*, 162 F.Supp. 2d 1209 (August 10, 2001).

14. On October 17, 2000, President Clinton signed into law, P.L. 106-313 which, but for the Defendants' illegal actions, would now provide eligibility to Plaintiffs to seek further extensions of stay in H-1B1 and H-4 status pursuant to Section 104 (c) of that new law. Plaintiffs are ineligible for the benefits of P.L. 106-313 since they are not in legal H-1B1 and H-4 status.

Wherefore, Plaintiffs respectfully prays for:

1. An order from this Court declaring that Defendants' legal position in refusing to permit Plaintiffs a full six years in H-1B1 and H-4 status in the United States is an error of law, arbitrary and capricious;
2. A order in the form of a writ of mandamus compelling the Defendants to grant, *nunc pro tunc*, an extension of stay and eligibility for employment as an H-1B1 temporary worker to Plaintiff, **[Alien]**, and an extension of stay in H-4 status to Plaintiff, **[Alien]**, to October 30, 2002;
3. An injunction barring Defendants from enforcing any provision of 8 U.S.C. §1182(a)(9) against Plaintiffs;
4. An award of attorney fees as may be appropriate; and
5. Any other relief which may be appropriate and which will remedy and repair the harm caused to Plaintiffs by Defendants.

[Dated:]

Respectfully submitted:

[Attorney]

[ADD CERTIFICATE OF SERVICE]

IN THE
UNITED STATES DISTRICT COURT
CENTRAL DISTRICT OF CALIFORNIA

[Aliens],	)	
	)	
Plaintiffs,	)	
	)	
v.	)	
	)	Case No. __________
Christine Poulos, Acting Center Director,	)	
et al.,	)	
	)	
Defendants.	)	

NOTICE OF MOTION FOR SUMMARY JUDGMENT

TO DEFENDANTS AND THEIR ATTORNEYS OF RECORD

PLEASE TAKE NOTICE that on **[date]** or as soon thereafter as the matter may be heard by the above-entitled Court, located at **[court address]**, Plaintiffs, **[Aliens]**, will move the Court for summary judgment on the merits of the complaint filed in this matter.

This motion is based on the this Notice of Motion, Plaintiffs' Points and Authorities filed herewith and the pleadings and papers on file herein, and upon such other matters as may be presented to the Court at the time of the hearing.

[Dated:]

Respectfully submitted:

[Attorney]

[ADD CERTIFICATE OF SERVICE]

[Document No. 521]

MEMORANDUM OF LAW IN SUPPORT OF MOTION FOR TEMPORARY RESTRAINING ORDER

Description: The attached pleading can be used in cases involving extraordinary relief where the government has failed to provide an adequate explanation for its actions.

Advantages: The pleading details the failure of the government to provide any rational explanation for its decision to deny benefits. This is a particularly valuable pleading in situations where the government is either silent as to the reasons for denial and/or where the government appears to be using a secret agenda for adjudication of an application. In this instance, the government has been denying medical waiver exemptions to N–400 applications without explanation.

Limitations: In situations where the government appears to be acting on the basis of a "secret agenda," it is imperative to force DHS to make that agenda public. This is required by the APA and general due process notions of the government operating "in the sunshine." This pleading also comes within the ambit of filings challenging government use of boilerplate language in its decisions. In this instance, the government denies the requested benefit without any meaningful explanation of its decision.

Citations: 8 CFR §312.

UNITED STATES DISTRICT COURT
FOR THE SOUTHERN DISTRICT OF FLORIDA
MIAMI DIVISION

[Aliens] on behalf of themselves and all others similarly situated,	)	
	)	Case No.
Plaintiffs,	)	
vs.	)	**PLAINTIFFS' MEMORANDUM OF LAW IN SUPPORT OF PLAINTIFFS' EMERGENCY MOTION FOR A TEMPORARY RESTRAINING ORDER AND/OR PRELIMINARY INJUNCTION**
U.S. Citizenship and Immigration Services	)	
Defendants.	)	

INTRODUCTORY STATEMENT

Plaintiffs, who are poor, disabled legal permanent residents attempting to become naturalized U.S. citizens, seek temporary injunctive relief and/or a preliminary injunction as to two of the named plaintiffs, **[Alien 1]** and **[Alien 2]**, "to preserve the status quo during the course of litigation in order to prevent irreparable injury to the moving party and in order to preserve the ability of the court to render complete relief," *Federal Leasing, Inc. v. Underwriters at Lloyds*, 487 F. Supp. 1248, 1259 (D. Md. 1980), *aff'd*, 650 F.2d 495 (4th Cir. 1981). Defendants' final naturalization examination and interview of these two plaintiffs is presently scheduled for September 25 and September 28, respectively. Plaintiffs seek to stop those two examinations and interviews from going forward until this Court has an opportunity to rule on their request for preliminary injunctive relief.

THE NATURALIZATION PROCESS

The naturalization process is generally divided into four stages. First, a naturalization applicant must complete and submit an N-400 citizenship application to U.S. Citizenship and Immigration Services (USCIS). 8 USC §1445(a); 8 CFR §334.2. Second, USCIS conducts a background investigation of the applicant, including review of all pertinent records, police department checks, and, unless waived by the Attorney General, a neighborhood investigation. 8 USC §1446(a); 8 CFR §335.1. Third, the applicant is interviewed and examined by a USCIS officer. As part of that examination process Congress has required that, unless waived, an applicant for naturalization must demonstrate "an understanding of the English language, including an ability to read, write and speak words in ordinary usage...", 8 USC §1423(a)(1), and a "knowledge and understanding of the fundamentals of the history, and of the principles and form of government of the United States" 8 USC §1423(a)(2). In order to lessen the impact of these requirements on otherwise qualified, deserving immigrants, Congress also provided that the "English language" and "history and civics" requirements "shall not apply to any person who is unable because of physical or developmental disability or mental impairment to comply therewith." 8 USC §1423(b)(1). This exemption from the "English language" and "history and civics" requirements is termed the "medical waiver exemption". Fourth, the last stage of processing is the scheduling of an applicant for the oath ceremony. 8 USC §§1421, 1448; 8 CFR Parts 310, 337, 1337.

THE MEDICAL WAIVER EXEMPTION PROCESS

Defendants have established a comprehensive scheme of "medical waiver exemption" regulations, 8 CFR §312 et seq., and interpretive policies. The fundamental concern of these regulations and policies is that the medical determination as to the applicants' ability to comply with the "English language" and "history and civics" requirements be made by a qualified medical professional. Pursuant to those regulations and interpretive policies, "it is the responsibility of the medical professional to make the medical determination." Supplemental Policy Guidance 3/12/97, p. 7. (A copy of the Supplemental Policy Guidance is attached hereto as Appendix I.) "These medical professionals shall be experienced in diagnosing those with physical or mental medically determinable impairments" and shall also be able to "attest to the origin, nature and extent of the medical condition as it relates to the disability exceptions". 8 CFR §312.2(b)(2). The medical professional's determination is communicated to defendants by means of an N-648 form, which serves as both an application for a medical waiver exemption and an attestation by the medical professional to USCIS as to the origin, nature and extent of the medical condition.

USCIS officers reviewing the medical waiver requests are reminded by the policy that they "are not medical professionals, advocates, or social workers and should not place themselves in the position of attempting to second guess the medical evaluation of the qualified medical professional certifying a disability exception on the N-648. Nor should the officers place themselves in the position of being a medical professional and thereby denying the existence of a disability." Supplemental Policy Guidance 3/12/97, p. 7.

The regulations further provide that "the Service also reserves the right to refer the applicant to another authorized medical source for a supplemental disability examination. This option should be invoked when the Service has credible doubts about the veracity of a medical certification that has been presented by an applicant". 8 CFR §312.2(b)(2).

The instructions then set forth a detailed procedure which must be followed prior to requesting a second medical certification from an applicant. Finally, the guidelines caution against requesting a second medical certification unless absolutely necessary because of the inconvenience it causes the applicant:

> Officers are instructed to use *extreme restraint* in exercising these options and should only do so when doubts remain after the steps outlined...have been completed...*Officers should always remember that they are responsible for determining the eligibility for naturalization not for making or rendering a medical determination*.

Supplemental Policy Guidance 3/12/97.

THE STATEMENT OF EMERGENT NEED

September 25 and 28 are imminent. Should plaintiffs **[Alien 1]** and **[Alien 2]** be denied citizenship on those dates, no remedy at law can adequately compensate them for this loss. Reapplication and appeal are not meaningful options. Plaintiffs will lose the opportunity to vote and otherwise fully participate in life as U.S. citizens. Due to their age and poor health, any denial of citizenship at this time may remain in affect for the remainder of these plaintiffs' lives.

THE ORDERS REQUESTED

Plaintiffs **[Alien 1]** and **[Alien 2]** concede that they are unable to demonstrate an understanding of the English language or a knowledge and understanding of the fundamentals of the history, and of the principles and form of government of the United States sufficient to pass the naturalization exam. Since their requests for a medical waiver of those requirements have been rejected and they have no new medical information to present, they believe that defendants will formally deny their naturalization applications if they are required to proceed with their final naturalization interviews on September 25 and 28, 1998. They therefore request this Court to enjoin the defendants from denying their naturalization applications and from conducting any further naturalization interviews or examinations in their cases (other than renewing expired fingerprint clearances) pending this Court's disposition of plaintiffs' request for a preliminary injunction and the final disposition of this case.

THE LEGAL STANDARD

To obtain a temporary restraining order and/or a preliminary injunction, the plaintiffs must establish: (1) a substantial likelihood that they will prevail on the merits; (2) a substantial threat of irreparable injury if the injunction is not granted; (3) greater injustice to plaintiffs if the injunction is denied than harm caused by granting the injunction; and (4) no substantial disservice to the public interest. *Tepper v. Miller*, 82 F.3d 989, 992-93 n.3 (11th Cir. 1996); *Levi Strauss & Co. v. Sunrise Int'l Trading, Inc.*, 51 F.3d 982 (11th Cir. 1995); *Shatel Corp. v. Maota Lumber and Yacht Corp.*, 697 F.2d 1352, 1354-1355 (11th Cir. 1983); *Canal Authority v. Callaway*, 489 F.2d 567 (5th Cir. 1974).

This standard is not rigidly applied by assigning a fixed quantitative value to each of the four factors. Rather, a flexible scale–which balances each consideration and arrives at the most equitable result, given the particular circumstances of each case–is used. *Texas v. Seatrain International, S.A.*, 518 F.2d 175, 180 (5th Cir. 1975). "It is the threat of harm that cannot be undone which authorizes exercise of this equitable power to enjoin before the merits are fully determined." *Parks v. Dunlop*, 517 F.2d 785, 787 (5th Cir. 1975).

An injunction is especially appropriate when, as here, it would preserve the status quo ante. *Northeastern Florida Chapter of Assoc. of Gen. Contractors v. City of Jacksonville*, 896 F.2d 1283, 1284 (11th Cir. 1990) ("The chief function of a preliminary injunction is to preserve the status quo until the merits of the controversy can be fully and fairly adjudicated.").

A. Substantial Likelihood Exists That Plaintiffs Will Prevail on the Merits

1. Defendants Fail to Process Plaintiffs' Requests for Medical Waiver in Conformance with Their Own Regulation

A fundamental principle of federal law is that a federal agency must follow its own rules. *Morton v. Ruiz*, 415 U.S. 199, 233-235 (1974) ("[W]here the rights of individuals are affected, it is incumbent upon agencies to follow their own procedures.") Likewise in *Simmons v Block*, 782 F.2d 1545 (11th Cir. 1986), in rejecting the FMHA's reliance on an internal policy, which conflicted with its published regulations, the court found that:

> The failure of an agency to follow its own regulations constitutes arbitrary and capricious conduct. *Boyd v. Secretary of Agriculture*, 459 F. Supp. 418 (D.S.C.1978). The courts must overturn agency actions which do not scrupulously follow the regulations and procedures promulgated by the agency itself. *U.S. v Heffner*, 420 F.2d 809, (4th Cir. 1969)...

Id. at 1550. Moreover, courts have continuously held that these principles apply to USCIS as much as any other agency. "[I]t is clear...that agency deviation from its own regulations and procedures may justify judicial relief... [citations omitted]", *Haitian Refugee Center v. Smith*, 676 F.2d 1023, 1041 (5th Cir. Unit B 1982). *See also Jean v. Nelson*, 727 F.2d 957 (11th Cir. 1984), *aff'd* 472 U.S. 846, 105 S.Ct. 846, 86 L.Ed.2d 664 (1985); *Nicholas v. INS*, 590 F.2d 802, 809, (9th Cir. 1979), (court held that INS violated its own regulation regarding the processing of a noncitizen's request for immigration records); *Louis v. Nelson*, 544 F. Supp. 973 (S.D.Fl. 1982); *Tefel v. Reno*, 972 F. Supp. 608 (S.D.Fl. 1997).

The defendants' medical waiver regulations, as interpreted by the defendants, incorporate two fundamental requirements. First, assuming a completed N-648 certification, the defendants and their officers *must accept* the certification of the medical professional unless there is cause to doubt its veracity. Second, absent fraud, if there is cause to doubt the veracity of the medical professional, the only options available to the examining officer are to attempt to resolve the doubts in favor of the applicant or to request a second certification. The defendants' interpretation of the regulation detailing both of these requirements has been explicitly set forth in an extensive policy guidance, Supplemental Policy Guidance, 3/12/97. The defendants' interpretation of its own regulations as set forth in this policy guidance is entitled to great deference and absent clear conflict should be accepted by the court. *Wells v. F.A.A.*, 755 F.2d 804 (11th Cir. 1985); *Booth v. United States*, 956 F.2d 1171 (11th Cir. 1993).

The March 12, 1997 interpretations repeatedly emphasize the need to accept the medical judgment of the medical practitioner absent fraud or some other extraneous factor affecting veracity. The interpretations state that reviewing officers "should not place themselves in the position of attempting to second guess the medical evaluation of the qualified medical professional certifying a disability exception on the N-648" and further that "Officers should always remember that they are responsible for determining the eligibility for naturalization not for making or rendering a medical determination." Similarly, the interpretations understand the regulations to require that the reviewing officer exhaust any reasonable means of resolving doubts in favor of the applicant and only after such efforts are fruitless should the applicant be referred for a second certification by a *different* medical professional.

In the present case, the defendants and their officers have failed to follow the regulations, as interpreted by defendants, in every respect. As is shown by the Declaration of **[Individual]**, there has been no attempt to contact the medical professional to discuss concerns nor has there been any attempt to solicit specific additional documentation from the medical professional. There has been no attempt to speak with other governmental agencies that have found the applicant disabled. Finally, the applicant was never referred for a second certification by a different medical professional. As a matter of practice the defendants' officers in the Miami District Office do none of this. The medical waiver is simply rejected, without accommodation, advice, referral or reason.

2. The Defendants' Violation of Their Own Regulations and Congressional Statutes Is also a Violation of the Administrative Procedures Act 5 USC §701 *et seq.*

Courts have consistently held that policies or practices of legacy INS/USCIS which fail to follow the statutory or regulatory law violate the Administrative Procedures Act (APA), 5 USC §701 *et seq.*, *Jean v. Nelson, supra.; Haitian Centers Council, Inc. v. Sale*, 823 F. Supp. 1028 (E.D.N.Y. 1993). The current policy and practice of the defendants violates the APA, 5 USC §701 *et seq.*, in that it constitutes an agency action which is "arbitrary, capricious, an abuse of discretion, or otherwise not in accordance with law" and "in excess of statutory jurisdiction, authority, or limitations, or short of statutory right", 5 USC §706(2)(A). Specifically, the current policy and practice violates the APA in that it is in violation of each of the following statutes and regulations.

i. Violation of 8 CFR §312.1 and 312.2

As stated in Section A(1.) above, the current practice of the Miami District office violates the defendants' own regulations 8 CFR §§312.1 and 312.2, as they have interpreted them. A violation by an agency of its own regulations also constitutes a violation of the Administrative Procedures Act in that the agency's action is "arbitrary, capricious, an abuse of discretion, or otherwise not in accordance with law". 5 USC §706(2)(A). As stated in *Raymond Proffit Foundation v. U.S. Environmental Protection Agency*, 930 F. Supp. 1088, (E.D. Pa. 1996),

> Where judicial review includes actions taken pursuant to agency regulations, validly promulgated regulations have the force of law. *Frisby v. United States Dep't of Hous. & Urban Dev.*, 755 F.2d 1052, 1055 (3d Cir. 1985). When an agency fails to act in compliance with its own regulations, such actions are "not in accordance with law." *Id.* at 1055-56 (citations and quotations omitted).

Id. at 1104.

ii. Violation of 5 USC §552

The most serious harm occasioned by defendants" practices is the inability of the applicants to fathom what standards are actually being used to deny them. Applicants, such as **[Alien 1]** and **[Alien 2]**, and the other plaintiffs, without question, have obvious disabilities which prevent them from learning English and basic Civics. They could probably conform to any set of medical waiver evaluation standards, even "arbitrary and capricious" standards, if they could just determine what they were. Yet, to the applicants' consternation and that of their medical professionals, their applications for a medical waiver are consistently rejected without the applicant or the medical professional ever knowing what the standards are.[1] It is precisely to prevent this type of secret evaluation that the Freedom of Information Act, 5 USC §552, prevents an agency from utilizing any rules, statements of policy, interpretations, etc. which have not been either published or indexed and made available to the public.

A final order, opinion, statement of policy, interpretation, or staff manual or instruction that affects a member of the public may be relied on, used or cited as precedent by an agency against a party other than an agency only if—

(i) it has been indexed and either made available or published as provided by this paragraph; or

(ii) the party has actual and timely notice of the terms thereof.

5 USC §552(a)(2). In *Smith v. National Transportation Safety Board*, 981 F.2d 1326 (D.C. Cir. 1993), the court overturned a sanction decision in which the Agency had relied upon an internal administrative directive which had not been made available to the public. The court stated the purpose of the statute: "The purpose of the APA availability requirement is obviously to give the public notice of what the law is so that each individual can act accordingly." *Id.* at 1328. *See also Firestone Tire & Rubber v. Coleman*, 432 F. Supp. 1359 (N.D. Ohio 1976).

This is all that is requested in the present case. It is obvious and virtually beyond dispute that many applicants, who are disabled by any reasonable meaning of the regulations, are being denied simply because they, and their medical professionals, are unable to conform to evaluation standards which have never been disclosed. Plaintiffs demand that those standards be disclosed, so that plaintiffs, as well as other members of the plaintiff class, will be able to request that their medical professionals redo their attestations in conformity with them. However, lacking that knowledge, the plaintiffs and their medical professionals have little ability, other than mere chance, to conform to a set of essentially secret standards.

iii. Violation of 5 USC §553

Again, as stated in Section A(1.) above, defendants' current practice with respect to the evaluation of medical waiver requests cannot under any construct be held to reasonably conform to their own regulations. Yet defendants refuse to disclose what additional standards they are employing. Not only is such a failure to disclose a violation of the Freedom of Information Act, 5 USC §552, but any policy or criteria which substantially affects the agency's ultimate decision making is a "rule" and must be subject to the notice and comment provisions of the Administrative Procedures Act, 5 USC §553.

While it is obviously difficult to discuss the contents of defendants' internal decision making policy while it remains secret, it is possible to determine certain attributes solely by examining the results in individual determinations. First, the internal policy appears to substantially determine the medical waiver decision. Second, the internal policy is substantially different than the current regulation, as interpreted by defendants, in that none of the policies and procedures dictated by that regulation are followed. Both of these attributes have been consistently held to demand that such secret rules be subject to the notice and comment

[1] It is obvious from the decisions that there are standards or "rules of thumb" being employed in addition to the regulations, as interpreted by defendants. Indeed, defendants' supervisors have mentioned the existence of such standards.

of the Administrative Procedures Act. In *McClouth Steel Products Corp. v. Thomas*, 838 F.2d 1317 (D.C. Cir 1988), the court held that a standard being used by the defendant agency to determine if certain wastes were "hazardous" was a "substantive rule" and thus subject to the APA procedures. The court quoted *Pickus v. U.S. Board of Parole*, 507 F.2d 1107, 1112-13 (D.C.Cir.1974):

> legislative rules "narrow [the decisionmaker's] field of vision" and are of a kind calculated to have a substantial effect on the ultimate [agency] decisions and *Guardian Federal Savings & Loan Ass'n v. FSLIC*, 589 F.2d 658, 666-67 (D.C. Cir. 1978):

> If it appears that a so-called policy statement is in purpose or likely effect one that narrowly limits administrative discretion, it will be taken for what it is--a binding rule of substantive interpretation to determine the type of rule which must be published.

In the present case, there can be no doubt that the defendants' undisclosed standard fulfills these criteria as it is profoundly affecting the ultimate agency decisions.

In addition to the foregoing, the defendants' undisclosed policy adds requirements to a published rule which itself was subject to notice and comment. 5 USC §553(b). As stated in *American Mining Congress v. MSHA*, 995 F.2d 1106 (D.C. Cir. 1993):

> If a second rule repudiates or is irreconcilable with [a prior legislative rule], the second rule must be an amendment of the first; and, of course, an amendment to a legislative rule must itself be legislative. *National Family Planning & Reproductive Health Association v. Sullivan*, 979 F.2d 227, 235 (D.C. Cir. 1992)

Id. at 1109. In *United States v. Picciotto*, 875 F.2d 345 (D.C. Cir. 1989), the Park Service *published* a substantive rule which expressly permitted them to add "reasonable conditions" to individual permits for demonstrations. Then the Park Service, *without publication*, added a set of uniform conditions for all demonstrations occurring in one specific park. The court invalidated the uniform conditions as an amendment to the published rule, holding that any amendment to a published rule must itself be published.

In the present case, defendants appear to be utilizing a separate and additional set of standards for evaluating medical waivers in the Miami District Office. Thus these additional standards, whatever they are, must be subjected to the same notice and comment procedures as the original regulations.

iv. Violation of 5 USC §555(e)

As is stated above, many of the plaintiffs' most serious concerns could be obviated by simply disclosing and regularizing the standards being employed against them. Since they are disabled under any reasonable standard, they merely need to know the standard in order to conform. As is also argued above, the Administrative Procedures Act and the Freedom of Information Act are largely designed to guarantee that individuals in the administrative process are provided with that knowledge. The Administrative Procedures Act, 5 USC §555(e), also attempts to further that identical protection by requiring that any notice of denial "shall be accompanied by a brief statement of the grounds for denial." As is clearly demonstrated by the Declaration of Ms. **[Individual]**, as well as the allegations of the other plaintiffs, no meaningful notice is provided to the denied applicants for medical waivers. As is demonstrated in the statement of facts, Ms. **[Individual]**'s first statement of denial was worse than meaningless, bordering on the insulting. It marked every box on the form. It stated, for example, that the application did not state her name or the qualifications of her doctor, when such was obviously not the case.[2] When Ms. **[Individual]** attempted to remedy the initial denial and submit an amended form she was denied again, this second time without *any* attempt at explanation. While the practice of denying without *any* notice clearly violates 5 USC §555(e), the practice of providing a meaningless

[2] It is not even clear which medical attestation form the denial notice was discussing since Ms. **[Individual]** had submitted three separate attestations, two typed and one handwritten.

notice has also been condemned by the courts. In *Washington v. Office of Comptroller of the Currency*, 856 F.2d 1507 (11th Cir. 1988), the defendant similarly attempted to fulfill the requirements of 5 USC §555(e) by providing a supposed "statement of reasons" which did nothing to assist the applicant in understanding the basis for the denial. In *Washington*, the Comptroller of the Currency denied a request for a hearing to a group opposing a bank merger. The notice of denial stated the reason as:

> In light of the nature of the issues and facts to be presented...the parties will not be significantly prejudiced by presenting their cases in written form...and an oral presentation would not be beneficial to the decision making process...the substantial expense and inconvenience...is not warranted.

Id. at 1512. The court correctly dismissed the notice as violative of 5 USC §555(e) in that it provided no basis for actually understanding the "determinative reason" for the action of the agency.

> No such explanation was contained in the notice of rejection of the request for a hearing in this case. In effect, the OCC response to the request for a hearing was simply that "no hearing is needed." The statement that "the substantial expense and inconvenience...is not warranted," obviously added nothing to the statement. This was not "a brief statement of the grounds for denial" as required under Section 555(e).

Id. at 1513. Similarly, in the present case, the Declaration of Ms. **[Individual]**, as confirmed by the allegations of the other plaintiffs, demonstrates that the practice of the defendants is to provide no explanation of the reasons for the denial, again frustrating plaintiffs' ability to conform their requests to the standards being utilized by the defendants.

3. The Defendants' Failure to Provide the Plaintiffs With Any Meaningful Notice Is also a Violation of Their Rights Under the Due Process Clause of the Fifth Amendment to the United States Constitution

Not only does the failure to provide meaningful notice violate the Administrative Procedures Act, 5 USC §555(e), it also deprives the plaintiffs of their procedural due process rights as guaranteed to them under the Fifth Amendment to the United States Constitution. It is axiomatic that the most minimal "fair procedures" required by due process include a meaningful notice. As stated in *Mathews v. Eldridge*, 424 U.S. 319, 47 L.Ed.2d 18, 96 S.Ct. 893 (1976):

> The essence of due process is the requirement that "a person in jeopardy of serious loss [be given] notice of the case against him and an opportunity to meet it." *Joint Anti-Fascist Comm. v. McGrath*, 341 US, at 171-172, 95 L Ed 817, 71 S Ct 624 (Frankfurter, J., concurring).

Id., 424 U.S. at 348. Moreover, as the current case amply demonstrates, without adequate notice all other procedures become meaningless. As stated in *Gray Panthers v. Schweiker*, 652 F.2d 146 (D.C. Cir. 1980):

> It is universally agreed that adequate notice lies at the heart of due process. Unless a person is adequately informed of the reasons for denial of a legal interest, a hearing serves no purpose B and resembles more a scene from Kafka than a constitutional process.

Id. at 168. In *Cosby v. Ward*, 843 F.2d 967 (7th Cir. 1988), the plaintiffs faced an administrative nightmare not unlike the situation here. In *Cosby* the plaintiffs were unemployed workers seeking unemployment benefits. Not only were they were being denied by secret "rules of thumb" utilized by the defendants but the notices of denial failed to even mention the utilization of the "rules of thumb" in the determination. The court found that the notices of denial violated the plaintiffs' due process rights. *Cosby*, 843 F.2d at 982. However, the court also found that it was an even more fundamental violation of due process to not inform the plaintiffs of the standards *prior* to their application.

> This requirement [i.e., notice of the "rule of thumb" in the reasons for denial] will be of little help to the plaintiffs, however, unless they are also informed of [defendants'] rules of thumb at the outset of their work searches. *See Carey v. Quern*, 588 F.2d 230, 232 (7th Cir. 1978).

Id. at 984. The court then continued by finding that prior notice must be more than vague general brochures.

> The [district] court found that the notices told claimants what they needed to know "without a level of detail that might have made the forms even more difficult to comprehend than they are." [625 F. Supp.] at 639. To the contrary, the notices only hinted at the requirements imposed by the five rules of thumb. It would have been no more difficult for [the defendants] to set out a checklist of the rules of thumb than it was for the state merely to allude to the requirements and trust the claimants to infer from the notices' general language five specific rules.

Id. at 985. Similarly, in the present case plaintiffs are being asked to conform their applications for medical waiver to a standard that is never given in the notices of denial and perhaps more importantly is never made public at all.

B. Plaintiffs Face Irreparable Injury If Injunctive Relief Is Not Granted

As described in Plaintiffs' Motion and accompanying declarations, plaintiffs **[Alien 1]** and **[Alien 2]**will be irreparably injured by the September 25 and 28 denials of their application for United States citizenship. They will lose the opportunity to vote and otherwise fully participate in our democracy as United States citizens. The law is clearly established that denial of the opportunity to vote is irreparable injury per se. *E.g.*, *NAACP v. Alabama*, 357 U.S. 449 (1958); *Reynolds v. Sims*, 377 U.S. 533 (1964); *Lubin v. Panish*, 415 U.S. 709 (1974); *Anderson v. Celebrezze*, 460 U.S. 780 (1983); *Williams v. Salerno*, 792 F.2d 323 (2d Cir. 1986).

Furthermore, no meaningful appeal or reapplication process is available to plaintiffs since all decisions on their appeals or reapplications will ultimately be made by the same USCIS staff in the Miami District office who have already denied their requests for a medical waiver, under the same unlawful practices, policies and procedures utilized in defendants' Miami District office. Indeed, no appeal or reapplication process is available at all to plaintiffs **[Alien 1]** and **[Alien 2]** since they are indigent and both the appeal process and the reapplication process require fees that are beyond their extremely limited means.

C. Plaintiffs Will Suffer Greater Injustice If Injunctive Relief Is Denied than Any Harm Caused by Granting Such Relief

The irreparable harm that plaintiffs **[Alien 1]** and **[Alien 2]** will suffer if an injunction does not issue is well-documented above and in Plaintiffs' Motion and Exhibits. Defendants will suffer little or no harm if the injunction sought by plaintiffs is granted since they will merely be prevented from immediately proceeding with denials of applications for naturalization.

In determining whether to issue an injunction, the Court should balance the plaintiffs' likelihood of success with the relative threatened hardship. *Florida Medical Assoc. v. U.S. Dept. of Health, Education and Welfare*, 601 F.2d 199 (5th Cir. 1979); *Louis v.* ____________, 530 F. Supp. 924 (S.D.Fla. 1981).

> It is not necessary that plaintiffs be able in an abbreviated proceeding, to prove with certainty eventual success....[T]he importance and nature of the [likelihood of success] requirement can vary significantly, depending upon the magnitude of the injury which would be suffered by the movant in the absence of interlocutory relief and the relative balance of the threatened hardship. *State of Texas v. Seatrain International*, 518 F.2d 175, 180 (5th Cir. 1975) (citing *Canal Auth. of State of Florida v. Callaway*, 489 F.2d 567 (5th Cir. 1974)).

Here, the balance of hardships tips sharply in favor of the plaintiffs. Absent an injunction, plaintiffs **[Alien 1]** and **[Alien 2]** will suffer real, immediate, and lasting harm.

D. Granting Plaintiffs Injunctive Relief Will Not Disserve the Public Interest

The public interest in enforcing federal law, the balance of equities in this case, and the fact that plaintiffs **[Alien 1]** and **[Alien 2]** will be irreparably injured in the event that injunctive relief is denied, all show that granting plaintiffs' Motion here will not disserve the public interest. Moreover, plaintiffs have requested that they not be required to post any cash bond. In spite of the literal language of Rule 65(c) of the Federal Rules of Civil Procedure, this Court clearly has the discretion to issue a preliminary injunction without requiring plaintiffs to give security. *See, e.g., Caterpillar, Inc. v. Nationwide Equipment*, 877 F. Supp. 611, 617 (M.D.Fla. 1994); *Baldree v. Cargill, Inc.*, 758 F. Supp. 704 (M.D.Fla. 1990), *aff'd*, 925 F.2d 1474 (11th Cir. 1991).

Because plaintiffs in the instant case are indigent and disabled and seek only to vindicate their federal statutory and constitutional rights, this case implicates the public interest and the balance of hardships tips sharply in favor of plaintiffs. Therefore this Court should not require plaintiffs to give security. *See Pharmaceutical Soc'y of N.Y. v. Dep't of Soc. Serv.*, 50 F.3d 1168, 1174 (2d Cir. 1995); *Crowley v. Local 82 Furniture and Piano Moving, Furniture Store Drivers, Helpers, Warehouseman and Packers*, 679 F.2d 978, 999 (1st Cir. 1982), *rev'd on other grounds*, 467 U.S. 526 (1984).

Respectfully submitted,

[Attorney]

[ADD CERTIFICATE OF SERVICE]

[Document Nos. 522–27]

BIVENS ACTIONS AND ACTIONS UNDER THE FEDERAL TORT CLAIMS ACT

Description: The foundation of *Bivens* actions was established in the landmark Supreme Court case, *Bivens v. Six Unknown Named Agents of Federal Bureau of Narcotics*, 403 U.S. 388 (1971); the Federal Tort Claims Act (FTCA) is found at 28 USC §2671, *et seq*. Both actions permit the recovery of money damages.

The first complaint herein is fairly simple and straightforward, combining FTCA and *Bivens* claims to challenge false imprisonment and allege unconstitutional torts against the plaintiff, seek money damages, and demand a jury trial.

Next are three documents chosen—again for illustration—from a set of pleadings from a Ninth Circuit district court action, *Sissoko v. Rocha*, No. 03-55667, CV-98-07010-ABC (CD Cal. June 13, 2005), challenging the plaintiff's detention as unconstitutional under *Bivens*. Also included is a summary of the Ninth Circuit decision, holding that Mr. Sissoko's Fourth Amendment right to be free from unlawful detention was violated.

The third set of documents are administrative and district court complaints from *Araujo v. U.S.*, an FTCA case in which a district court found that collateral estoppel precluded the government from arguing that the plaintiff's arrest and deportation were lawful. The court held that because the court of appeals had concluded in a challenge to the removal order that the petitioner had been unlawfully removed (*Castro-Cortez v. INS*), the agency was estopped from arguing that it had not engaged in an unlawful arrest and detention.

Advantages: *Bivens* and FTCA claims are federal court actions for money damages. Limited attorneys' fees may be awarded under the FTCA (but FTCA does not permit the award of punitive damages or a jury trial), and the FTCA waives sovereign immunity against the United States for certain torts committed by federal employees. *Bivens* actions may be brought directly against a federal employee for violating the plaintiff's constitutional rights.

Notes: The FTCA and precedent cases regarding *Bivens* actions must be consulted to determine whether either or both of these actions are advisable in light of the particular facts of the case.

Caveat: Guidance on *Bivens* and FTCA actions is traditionally beyond the scope of immigration law publications or CLE. Still, it is important to know that these options exist. Attorneys unfamiliar with this area of law should first thoroughly research the basis and procedures for filing these actions, including a familiarity with the Federal Rules of Civil Procedure and local federal court rules.

IN THE UNITED STATES DISTRICT COURT
FOR THE WESTERN DISTRICT OF TEXAS
EL PASO DIVISION

ANTONIO GARZA,	)	
	)	
Plaintiff,	)	
	)	
vs.	)	**NO. EP-03-CA-0071-KC**
	)	
SEAN MUNLEY and UNITED STATES OF AMERICA,	)	
	)	
Defendants	)	**JURY TRIAL DEMAND**

PLAINTIFF'S FIRST AMENDED COMPLAINT

INTRODUCTION

Plaintiff Antonio Garza files this lawsuit against Border Patrol Agent Sean Munley and the United States alleging violations of his civil rights and requesting relief under the United States Constitution and the Federal Tort Claims Act.

On or about March 6, 2002, Plaintiff Garza was detained and falsely arrested by Agent Munley in El Paso, Texas. That day, Plaintiff Garza was walking in his neighborhood. He did not appear suspicious and nothing in his conduct indicated that he was breaking the law. Nevertheless, Agent Munley stopped Mr. Garza, frisked him, took away his cell phone and driver's license, and brusquely forced Mr. Garza into the Border Patrol vehicle. Agent Munley knew that Mr. Garza was a U.S. citizen but nevertheless stopped him continued to detain him. Agent Munley also denied Mr. Garza's request for an attorney. Plaintiff Garza was not free to leave the encounter and was detained in the vehicle for more than one hour.

Plaintiff brings this action to challenge his unlawful arrest and detention. Plaintiff Garza seeks monetary relief against Sean Munley and the Defendant United States of America pursuant to <u>Bivens v. Six Unknown Named Agents of the Federal Bureau of Narcotics (Bivens)</u>, 403 U.S. 388 (1971), the Federal Tort Claims Act, 28 U.S.C. § 2671, et seq., and the laws of Texas.

JURISDICTION AND VENUE

1. Jurisdiction over Plaintiff's <u>Bivens</u> and Federal Tort Claims action is provided by 28 U.S.C. §§ 1331 and 1346(b).

2. Venue is proper in the Western District of Texas under 28 U.S.C. § 1402(b) because the events giving rise to these claims occurred in this judicial district.

3. Plaintiff Garza filed a timely administrative complaint with the former Immigration and Naturalization Service ("INS"). The INS denied Plaintiff Garza's claim on August 27, 2002. (See attached). Jurisdiction is appropriate pursuant to 28 U.S.C. § 2675 (a).

PARTIES

4. Plaintiff Garza resides at 1212 Randolph, Apt. 3, El Paso, Texas.

5. Defendant Sean Munley is a federal officer employed with the United States Border Patrol in El Paso Texas. Defendant Munley resides in El Paso, Texas.

6. Defendant United Sates of America is a sovereign nation responsible for the enforcement of the immigration laws through officers, agents and employees of the Department of Homeland Security and the U.S. Border Patrol.

STATEMENT OF FACTS

7. Mr. Garza is a United States citizen.

8. In September of 2001, Defendant Munley stopped and questioned Mr. Garza. At that time, Mr. Garza told Defendant Munley that Plaintiff was a United States citizen, and Defendant Munley released Mr. Garza after approximately 20 minutes.

9. On or about March 6, 2002, Mr. Garza was walking in his neighborhood.

10. During his walk, Mr. Garza was stopped by Defendant Munley.

11. Defendant Munley asked Mr. Garza if Plaintiff recognized Defendant Munley. Mr. Garza responded affirmatively.

12. Defendant Munley then requested to see Mr. Garza's identification. Mr. Garza cooperated fully and showed his driver's license.

13. Defendant Munley took Mr. Garza's license.

14. Defendant Munley then frisked Mr. Garza and instructed him to go inside the Border Patrol vehicle.

15. As Mr. Garza started to comply with Defendant Munley's instructions, Agent Munley pushed Mr. Garza's face and spun him around and into the Border Patrol vehicle.

16. Mr. Garza's cell phone rang and Defendant Munley took the phone away from Plaintiff.

17. Mr. Garza told Defendant Munley that Plaintiff was a United States citizen. Defendant Munley stated that he knew Mr. Garza was a United States citizen but continued to detain Mr. Garza.

18. Mr. Garza requested the assistance of an attorney but Defendant Munley ignored Mr. Garza's request.

19. Defendant Munley then told Mr. Garza that he was being taken to the "station" to be questioned by the FBI.

20. Mr. Garza was detained in the vehicle against his will. He was not free to leave during the encounter.

21. After approximately one hour, Defendant Munley released Mr. Garza and returned his cell phone and driver's license.

CAUSES OF ACTION

FEDERAL TORT CLAIMS ACT
False Imprisonment

22. Plaintiff re-alleges and incorporates by reference paragraphs 1 through 21 above.

23. Mr. Garza was willfully detained by a federal agent without Mr. Garza's consent and without authority of law.

BIVENS
Unconstitutional Torts

24. Plaintiff re-alleges and incorporates by reference paragraphs 1 through 21 above.

25. Defendant Munley violated Mr. Garza's rights under the U.S. Constitution.

DAMAGES

26. Mr. Garza seeks recovery for the emotional distress, mental anguish, humiliation, loss of dignity, and physical pain he suffered as a result of Defendants' conduct.

27. Mr. Garza is entitled to actual, compensatory, and punitive damages.

JURY TRIAL DEMAND

28. Mr. Garza demands a trial by jury for his Bivens claim.

PRAYER FOR RELIEF

WHEREFORE, PREMISES CONSIDERED, Plaintiff prays that this Court provide the following relief:

1. Award Plaintiff Garza actual and compensatory damages, in an amount to be determined at trial, against Defendant United States of America for claims arising under the Federal Tort Claims Act;

2. Award Plaintiff Garza actual, compensatory and punitive damages, in an amount to be determined at trial, against Defendant Sean Munley for violating the U.S. Constitution;

3. Award Plaintiff Garza any other relief that this Court deems just and proper at law and in equity.

Respectfully submitted,

[Attorneys for Plaintiff]

[ADD CERTIFICATE OF SERVICE]

UNITED STATES DISTRICT COURT
CENTRAL DISTRICT OF CALIFORNIA
WESTERN DIVISION

OUMAR SISSOKO, and individual and JULIE SISSOKO an individual, Plaintiffs, v. UNITED STATES, LOYDA R. ROCHA, etc., et al. Defendants	CASE NO. CV 98-7010-ABC(SHx) Consolidated with No. CV 99-8762-ABC(SHx) **FIRST AMENDED CONSOLIDATED COMPLAINT AND DEMAND FOR JURY TRIAL** Trial Date ....June 4, 2002

Plaintiffs, OUMAR SISSOKO, and JULIE SISSOKO, complaining against UNITED STATES, LOYDA R. ROCHA, Immigration Inspector, United States Immigration and Naturalization Service, FOUR UNKNOWN NAMED OFFICERS of the United States Immigration and Naturalization Service, JOSEPH CHEN, M.D., and UNKNOWN NAMED EMPLOYEES of the United States Public Health Service, allege as follows:

I. INTRODUCTION

1. This is an action arising out of a series of occurrences and transactions which commenced between May 14, 1997 and November 17, 1997, and which took place at a number of United States facilities and civilian facilities including the United States Immigration and Naturalization Service Offices located at 300 Los Angeles Street, Los Angeles, California, the Processing Center of the United States Immigration and Naturalization Service located at 2000 Seaside Avenue, Terminal Island, San Pedro, California, the Processing Center of the United States Immigration and Naturalization Service located at in 1115 North Imperial Avenue, El Centro California, St. Mary's Hospital, located at 1050 Linden Avenue, Long Beach, California and Long Beach Memorial Medical Center Hospital, located at 1720 Termino Avenue, Long Beach, California.

2. The Plaintiffs sue to secure redress for the violation of their rights by Defendants, individually and collectively, between the May 14, 1997, and November 17, 1997.

3. The Plaintiffs seek damages for the intentional and negligent tortuous actions by the Defendants and the violations of their civil and constitutional rights as otherwise guaranteed under the laws and constitutions of the United States and the State of California.

II. JURISDICTION AND VENUE

4. Plaintiffs bring this action for damages and attorneys fees pursuant to 28 U.S.C. §§1331, 1343(a)(3),1346(b),1367 and 2671 et. seq. because this action arises not only under the Federal Tort Claims Act against the United States, but as well under the Constitution of the United States against the individuals, whether named or having names unknown to Plaintiffs at this time, for illegal, improper, wrongful and unconstitutional actions, omissions, and conduct practiced and taken against the Plaintiffs between May 14, 1997 and November 17, 1997, while said named and unknown Defendants were performing duties and functions as officers of the United States Immigration and Naturalization Service or as health care professionals and health care providers of the United States Public Health Service and in all such circumstances as employees of the United States of America.

5. Venue of this action is proper under 28 U.S.C. § 1391(b) and 1391(e).

6. Plaintiffs have complied with all conditions precedent to the bringing the causes of action set forth herein, including the filing of administrative claims under the Federal Tort Claims Act, which claims have been denied by operation of law.

III. PARTIES

7. Plaintiff, OUMAR SISSOKO, (hereinafter sometimes "SISSOKO") is over the age of 18, an applicant for permanent residence in the United States, residing in the County of Los Angeles, State of California.

8. Plaintiff, JULIE SISSOKO, is a resident of the County of Los Angeles, State of California, a United States Citizen, and the wife of Plaintiff, OUMAR SISSOKO.

9. At all times herein mentioned, the UNITED STATES IMMIGRATION AND NATURALIZATION SERVICE (hereinafter "INS"), was and is a federal agency as defined in 28 U.S.C. § 2671.

10. At all times herein mentioned, the UNITED STATES PUBLIC HEALTH SERVICE (hereinafter "PHS"), was and is a federal agency as defined in 28 U.S.C. § 2671.

11. At all times herein mentioned, the INS, maintained a detention facility pursuant to federal law, the Immigration and Naturalization Act and other applicable acts of Congress, located at 2000 Seaside Avenue, Terminal Island, San Pedro, California (hereinafter "TI").

12. At all times herein mentioned, the INS, maintained a detention facility pursuant to federal law, the Immigration and Naturalization Act and other applicable acts of Congress, at 300 Los Angeles Street, Los Angeles, California (hereinafter "LA").

13. At all times herein mentioned, the INS, maintained a detention facility pursuant to federal law, the Immigration and Naturalization Act and other applicable acts of Congress, located at 1115 North Imperial Avenue, El Centro, California, (hereinafter "EC").

14. At all times herein mentioned, the PHS, maintained a medical facility and provided medical and health care services to detainees pursuant to federal law, the Immigration and Naturalization Act and other applicable acts of Congress at LA, TI and EC.

15. At all times herein mentioned, the INS, maintained at LA, TI and EC, a force of security, detention and administrative officers pursuant to federal law, the Immigration and Naturalization Act and other applicable acts of Congress.

16. At all times hereinafter mentioned, the PHS, maintained at LA, TI and EC, a staff of medical and health care service professionals and providers, including but not limited to doctors, nurses and orderlies, pursuant to federal law, the Immigration and Naturalization Act and other applicable acts of Congress.

17. At all times relevant hereto, Defendants, FOUR UNKNOWN NAMED OFFICERS of the United States Immigration and Naturalization Service (hereinafter individually "UNKNOWN INS OFFICER" and collectively including, LOYDA R. ROCHA, "INS OFFICERS") and Defendant, INS inspector, LOYDA R. ROCHA (hereinafter "ROCHA"), were federal officers of the Immigration and Naturalization Service engaged in that employment at LA, TI and EC and elsewhere in the County of Los Angeles, State of California, and at all times mentioned, were acting in such capacity as the agents, servants, and employees of the INS. They are sued herein individually and in their official capacities.

18. At all times relevant hereto, Defendants, UNKNOWN NAMED EMPLOYEES of the United States Public Health Service (hereinafter individually "UNNAMED PHS EMPLOYEE" and collectively including JOSEPH CHEN, M.D. "PHS EMPLOYEES") and Defendant, JOSEPH CHEN, M.D. (hereinafter "CHEN") were agents and employees of the United States of America and performing duties and functions, as either doctors, nurses, agents, employees and in particular as medical and health care professionals and providers of the PHS, and performed their duties, agencies and employment at LA, TI, EC and elsewhere within the County of Los Angeles, State of California.

19. Intentionally left blank to maintain numbering continuity with Plaintiffs' First Amended Complaint herein.

20. Intentionally left blank to maintain numbering continuity with Plaintiffs' First Amended Complaint herein.

21. Intentionally left blank to maintain numbering continuity with Plaintiffs' First Amended Complaint herein.

22. At all times relevant and material to this complaint, all of the individually named defendants and the UNKNOWN INS OFFICERS and UNNAMED PHS EMPLOYEES were acting under the color of federal law and pursuant to written policies of the INS.

23. From May 14 through May 16, 1997, and from August 26, 1997, through November 17, 1997, Plaintiff SISSOKO was detained, incarcerated and imprisoned in a number of institutions, including but not limited to LA, TI, ST. MARY'S HOSPITAL, LONG BEACH MEMORIAL MEDICAL CENTER HOSPITAL and EC at all times under the supervision, care, custody and control of the INS, the PHS and each and all of the Defendants.

IV. GENERAL FACTUAL ALLEGATIONS

24. On and before March 3, 1997, SISSOKO had two pending applications on file with the INS requesting permanent resident status in the United States. At all times relevant hereto, SISSOKO has desired to become a naturalized citizen of the United States and has employed and continues to employ legal counsel to assist him in that endeavor.

25. At all times relevant hereto, SISSOKO has committed no crimes of any kind, nature or severity.

26. On March 3, 1997, Plaintiff, OUMAR SISSOKO, lawfully applied to the INS for an "Advance Parole" to leave the United States for a brief period of time to attend his father's funeral in Senegal.

27. On March 3, 1997, SISSOKO's application for an Advance Parole Visa was granted by RICHARD K. ROGERS, Regional Director of the INS, for a period commencing on that date and ending on April 2, 1997. At that time and place the INS advised SISSOKO in writing that:

> "The above-captioned alien [SISSOKO] has established a prima facie case for eligibility under Section 245A of the Immigration and Nationality Act. Subject is to be paroled into the United States, provided no other excludabilities exist, to Indefinitely."

28. On March 19, 1997, SISSOKO tried to reenter the United States at Washington D.C. under said valid Advance Parole Visa and was denied entry. Instead he was placed on "deferred inspection" without any reason or justification (i.e. SISSOKO was not paroled into the United States per the aforesaid document from the INS). Thereafter, Plaintiff SISSOKO was ordered to appear at the INS offices as and when requested.

29. On April 5, 1997, SISSOKO underwent emergency abdominal surgery in which a section of his large intestines were removed and he was placed on a strict dietary regimen.

30. On May 14, 1997, Plaintiff SISSOKO reported on time for a scheduled appointment with INS OFFICERS. On that date ROCHA admitted to SISSOKO that she had only one of two files concerning SISSOKO which she knew were in existence. On that date and time, Defendant INS Inspector, LOYDA R. ROCHA, knew that Plaintiff SISSOKO had one or more viable applications for permanent residence on file with the INS, and that SISSOKO had been found by the INS to be prima facie eligible for permanent resident status, and therefore, entitled to reenter the United States forthwith in accordance with the terms and conditions provided in the aforesaid Advance Parole.

31. Nevertheless, on said date, Defendant, LOYDA R. ROCHA, detained Plaintiff, SISSOKO, and caused him to be placed in physical restraints including handcuffs and shackles, and caused him to be touched, and manhandled without his consent, and caused him to be searched and placed in a cell where he was imprisoned.

32. Plaintiff, SISSOKO, who had the absolute right to be informed as to why he was being detained, requested an explanation from Defendant, ROCHA. He was told by her that both of his applications for permanent residence had been denied. At that time, Defendant, ROCHA knew that neither of SISSOKO's applications had been denied and that her statement to the contrary was untrue. Said Defendant also told SISSOKO that she had had an all day briefing on the new law (which went into effect on April 1, 1997), and that she was now empowered to have him deported without due process.

33. After being taken into custody, on May 14, 1997, Plaintiff SISSOKO notified Defendant, ROCHA and UNNAMED PHS EMPLOYEES that he was recovering from abdominal surgery, and needed to conform to a stringent diet until completely recovered, and that while putting on his socks earlier in the day, he had heard a sound emanating from his back.

34. Shortly after said notification, while searching SISSOKO, an UNNAMED INS OFFICER, flexed SISSOKO's back in such a manner as to cause SISSOKO to exclaim, "be careful of my back". Shortly after the incident, SISSOKO began to experience severe pain in his back and legs.

35. Between fifteen and twenty minutes after the aforesaid search, SISSOKO notified INS Officers of the pain he was experiencing in his back and legs and requested medical attention.

36. Thereafter SISSOKO was examined by UNNAMED PHS EMPLOYEES and his back was x-rayed. Based upon the physical and radiological examination, Plaintiff SISSOKO was given pain medication, a back brace to wear and wheelchair to use, but was not released from custody nor retained in an infirmary or another medical facility.

37. On May 15, 1997, the INS Officers were aware of the Plaintiff, SISSOKO's special post surgery dietary needs, but gave him food contraindicated by his diet, which caused him severe stomach cramps.

38. During the aforesaid detention, SISSOKO was approached by Defendant, ROCHA and told that unless he filled out and signed a Request for Asylum Form, which was proffered, he most likely would be put on a plane and deported forthwith. Confronted in this fashion, Plaintiff, SISSOKO filled out, signed and returned the Request for Asylum. At no time prior to August 27, 1997, was SISSOKO interviewed in connection with that "Request" notwithstanding the obligation of the INS to conduct such interview to ascertain the merit of the applicant's claim.

39. On May 16, 1997, Plaintiff, SISSOKO was released from custody. SISSOKO's understanding of the reason for his release was that ROCHA's supervisor allegedly found a second viable application for permanent residence had been found by the INS Officers. Upon his release from custody, SISSOKO stayed at his brother and sister-in-law's home. Plaintiff was nearly immobile from the back pain and slept on the floor in an effort to find some relief from his symptoms. During this period, SISSOKO consulted an orthopedic surgeon who obtained empirical evidence that SISSOKO was suffering from an 8 mm disc bulge between his fourth and fifth lumbar vertebrae. Plaintiff, SISSOKO was advised that surgery was one of the options that he should consider.

40. On August 21, 1997, Plaintiff, SISSOKO, married his white American girlfriend, Julie Strommen, in a civil ceremony. In a separate Muslim ceremony conducted on August 24, 1997, OUMAR and JULIE SISSOKO were married with family and friends attending.

41. On the morning of August 26, 1997, a Marriage Petition was filed by SISSOKO with the INS, shortly after a scheduled amnesty interview. At the time and place of said filing and interview, SISSOKO's attorney DAN AGYEMAN was present.

42. On the morning of August 26, 1997, neither SISSOKO nor Attorney AGYEMAN had received written notice of the status of either of SISSOKO's amnesty applications. In addition, at that time, the status of SISSOKO's Request for Asylum, (given to Defendant, ROCHA by SISSOKO for processing during his May, 1997, imprisonment) was also unknown to them.

43. On August 26, 1997, after filing his Marriage Petition at LA, SISSOKO with attorney, DAN AGYEMAN met with Defendant, ROCHA at approximately 12:15 pm in the same building. At that time, Defendant, ROCHA, told SISSOKO and AGYEMAN to return at 1:15 p.m. for the scheduled interview. Also at that time and place, DAN AGYEMAN inquired of Defendant, ROCHA whether or not anything of significance to SISSOKO was intended by her at the 1:15 p.m. meeting. He went on to advise her he had a matter in the same building with another client that he needed to attend to at 1:15 p.m. In response to his inquiry, ROCHA, assured attorney AGYEMAN that there was no reason why he should be present when she met with SISSOKO, and he should feel free to attend his other business.

44. At 1:15 p.m. without Attorney, AGYEMAN with him, Plaintiff, SISSOKO arrived for his meeting with Defendant, ROCHA. At the time he noted that ROCHA had called an UNKNOWN INS OFFICER to stand by her office.

45. Upon the commencement of the meeting Defendant, ROCHA told SISSOKO that both of his Amnesty Applications had been denied. She said nothing about his Request for Asylum. She then said "You're going down!"; clearly insinuating that he was again going to be incarcerated. In response, SISSOKO showed said Defendant a copy of his Marriage Petition which had already been filed..

46. Upon seeing the Marriage Petition, ROCHA became extremely agitated and angry and said to SISSOKO, referring to the Petition, "Its meaningless, its not going to help you at all." She then accused SISSOKO of not telling her previously that he was married. ROCHA then asked him whether or not Plaintiff, JULIE SISSOKO had a criminal re-

cord; to which he responded in the negative. Then ROCHA asked where Plaintiff, JULIE SISSOKO worked, and he responded that JULIE SISSOKO was a radiology technician at U.C.L.A. Medical Center.

47. Without further inquiry, explanation or conversation, ROCHA called in the UNKNOWN INS OFFICER standing by her office and had SISSOKO handcuffed and taken into custody.

48. Upon being taken into custody the UNKNOWN INS OFFICER who had been charged by ROCHA to take SISSOKO into custody, conducted a search of his person during and after which Plaintiff, SISSOKO experienced the onset of severe pain and numbness in his back and legs similar to that he had first felt when he was imprisoned in May, 1997 by the INS.

49. Some thirty minutes after he was put in a cell, Defendant ROCHA came to the cell and threatened SISSOKO that he would be deported no matter what "your black Ghanaian lawyer does" (apparently referring to SISSOKO's then current immigration case counsel DAN AGYEMAN). She also said "Your lawyer doesn't know anything about the new law." In the same conversation she also remarked, "Do you Africans think you can just come over here and settle that easy?" After being so threatened, and harassed, SISSOKO called his brother and asked that he relate this incident to Attorney AGYEMAN.

50. On the same day but after the aforesaid confrontation by Defendant ROCHA, SISSOKO immediately notified INS personnel of the symptoms he was experiencing, and shortly thereafter began exhibiting classic, easily identifiable and visible manifestations of a severe back injury. Amongst other things, when he walked he assumed a stooped over posture and would appear to drag his leg rather than lift it. He also advised the same personnel or the dietary restrictions he needed to follow as a result of his abdominal surgery earlier in the year.

51. On August 26, 1997, at LA, Commander MARILYN A. HILLS, RN, of the PHS, who had seen SISSOKO during his May imprisonment, examined SISSOKO.

52. On August 27, 1997, Defendant ROCHA removed SISSOKO from his cell and sat him down in front of a team of INS security guards. She said that AGYEMAN had gone to her supervisor and accused her of abusing SISSOKO. She then threatened SISSOKO by telling him that he would remain in custody until he changed his mind about being abused.

53. On August 27, 1997, Commander MARILYN A. HILLS, RN, of the PHS, issued a "Medical Alert" which Plaintiff, SISSOKO, is informed and believes and thereon alleges was published by her to the INS OFFICERS at TI and which provided in pertinent part that:

> "MEDICAL/PSYCHIATRIC ALERT"
>
> "Remarks: This detainee has a disk problem which he says requires surgery. It is important that he isn't injured while in custody. It is difficult for him to sit for any length of time. He consistently complains and docs have a valid reason. Please see that his time in custody is minimal."

54. On every day of his incarceration (except during periods of outside hospitalization as described below), SISSOKO was approached by UNNAMED PHS EMPLOYEES who inquired about the state of his health. On each such occasion Plaintiff, SISSOKO, earnestly complained about the pain he was suffering. He also complained that because of the bowel surgery performed on him in April, 1997, he still needed multiple small meals per day consisting of special foods without which he experienced regular and severe cramps.

55. Plaintiff, SISSOKO was not on any such occasion subjected to x-ray or magnetic resonant imaging examination to ascertain whether he exhibited certain objective manifestations which would account for the pain he was experiencing. Plaintiff, SISSOKO is informed and believes and on such information and belief alleges that neither the INS nor the PHS had SISSOKO's prior medical records and reports to assist in their assessment of his condition.

56. Notwithstanding SISSOKO's complaints and Defendants daily examination of him, no physical appliances (such as a back brace or wheel chair) were provided as was the case during his May, 1997 imprisonment. Between August 26, 1997 and August 30, 1997 no physical therapy was administered to SISSOKO, nor was a special dietary regimen prescribed or offered. No prescription to restrict his movement or accommodation for his physical limitations and severe pain were provided by any INS or PHS employees.

57. Each morning between August 26, 1997, and August 30, 1997, at TI while PHS employee, JOSEPH CHEN, M.D., examined SISSOKO, he continually berated Plaintiff, SISSOKO, by accusing him of being a shirker, and malingerer and ascribing to Plaintiff, SISSOKO humiliating attributes and propensities based on his race and country of origin.

58. Between August 26, 1997 and August 29, 1997, Plaintiff, SISSOKO repeatedly complained to INS OFFICERS of the pain and numbness he was experiencing, and on each occasion requested that he be given treatment and that he be provided with an alternate form of sleeping arrangement to reduce the pain he felt while in the bed provided. No treatment was given, and no accommodation was made during that period of time, and SISSOKO was retained in the general detention population and not removed to the PHS facility at TI or to any other medical facility. SISSOKO is informed and believes and thereon alleges that on no occasion before August 30, 1997, did an INS officer request an employee of PHS to attend to SISSOKO's physical complaints. Plaintiff further alleges on information and belief that no employee of PHS did in fact see him except as described in Paragraphs Numbered 51 thorough 56 herein above.

59. On August 29, 1997, Plaintiff SISSOKO, was called to the visiting area of TI to see members of his family. As he arrived in the visiting area, SISSOKO's family noticed that he was dragging his left leg, exhibiting obvious signs that he was having severe physical problems. At that time and place, SISSOKO told his family members that his leg was numb and that he was experiencing severe pain in his back. He begged them to get him medical help. He told them to contact the INS and request that he be provided treatment. Immediately and repeatedly after their visit with Plaintiff SISSOKO, members of his family tried to persuade INS OFFICERS to give SISSOKO medical attention.

60. On August 29, 1997, after begging for an accommodation for his sensitive back, SISSOKO was taken out of the general detention population and, instead of being put in the infirmary, was put in isolation with two other detainees.

61. At all times from and after August 30, 1997, each and every one of the INS OFFICERS knew or should have known with the exercise or ordinary care and prudence and in particular because of the published "MEDICAL/PSYCHIATRIC ALERT" that SISSOKO had a severe medical condition related to his back.

62. On the morning of August 30, 1997, at approximately 8:30 a.m. an UNNAMED INS OFFICER asked SISSOKO and the other detainees in his cell whether they wanted showers. SISSOKO responded in the affirmative, whereupon said UNNAMED INS OFFICER ordered Plaintiff, SISSOKO to place his hands and wrists through a low opening in the cell's steel door (the slot used to pass food through the door) so he could be handcuffed in anticipation of being taken to the showers. Plaintiff, SISSOKO is approximately six feet seven inches tall and the opening in cell door is, based on SISSOKO's information and belief, approximately three feet from the floor.

63. Notwithstanding the additional pain it caused him, Plaintiff, SISSOKO complied with the request of the aforesaid UNNAMED INS OFFICER and placed has hands and wrists through the opening in the cell door, whereupon said UNNAMED INS OFFICER yanked SISSOKO's hands further through the opening in the door, cuffed him and told him to move away from the door. At that moment in time, SISSOKO responded that he could no longer move because of his back. Notwithstanding that statement, the UNNAMED INS OFFICER responded by saying "Move away from the door, Nigger!", and pushed SISSOKO backwards.

64. Having totally lost the ability to move his lower body to avoid or protect himself from a fall, SISSOKO fell onto his cell mates and then onto the floor where he lay immobile and paralyzed from the waist down. At the same time his bladder failed and his clothing became urine soaked. SISSOKO believes this personally embarrassing event to have been a direct consequence of a coincident injury to his spine.

65. For approximately three hours after he was shoved by the UNNAMED INS OFFICER until he was removed from TI by ambulance, Plaintiff SISSOKO was allowed to remain lying in his urine on the floor of his cell.

66. During the three hour period, an unknown employee of PHS offered SISSOKO pain medication but he was unable to lift himself far enough off the floor to swallow the proffered pill.

67. Upon his removal from TI, SISSOKO was first transported to Saint Mary's Hospital and was, hours later, transported to Long Beach Memorial Hospital.

68. On the evening of August 30, 1997, at Long Beach Memorial Hospital, without being allowed to contact his family to inform them of his plight and avail himself of their opinion as to whether or not he should consent to surgery, and without the opportunity to obtain a second opinion or have a surgeon of his own choosing perform the proposed operation, SISSOKO was subjected to a three hour laminectomy at the site of his fourth and fifth lumbar interspace.

69. On August 30, 1997 following the aforesaid surgery, an UNKNOWN NAMED INS OFFICER shackled plaintiff SISSOKO to the Gurney until an irate nurse at that facility interceded and caused the UNKNOWN NAMED INS OFFICER to remove the shackles. Following the surgery mentioned hereinabove, on September 12, 1997, SISSOKO was transported from Long Beach Memorial Medical Center Hospital to St. Mary's Hospital where he was provided with post surgery care and treatment.

70. While recovering at St. Mary's Hospital, SISSOKO was under 24 hour INS guard. Notwithstanding his need for rest to recover from his back injury, and surgery therefore, INS guards watched television in his room all day and night so Plaintiff could not sleep. On complaining to a head nurse about this activity, an INS Security Officer exclaimed in SISSOKO's and the nurse's presence "I wish [hope] he [meaning SISSOKO] dies". Not long thereafter, SISSOKO was admitted to the cardiac unit of the hospital suffering from tachycardia.

71. On October 3, 1997, Plaintiff SISSOKO was returned to detention; however, instead of being returned to TI, he was transported to EC some four hours in driving time away from his family and attorney in Los Angeles.

72. Except for an initial examination on October 3, 1997, at EC, between said date and November 17, 1997, the Defendant UKNOWN PHS EMPLOYEE physician charged with the responsibility of SISSOKO's post surgery care failed to examine, diagnose, treat medicate or administer any medical attention or care to SISSOKO whatsoever.

73. On the occasion of the single examination by the aforementioned Defendant UNKNOWN PHS EMPLOYEE physician, said to SISSOKO "Prepare to be in here [imprisoned at EC] for the next four years."

74. From October 3, 1997, to his release on November 17, 1997, the INS and PHS, and each of them, failed and refused to provide Plaintiff SISSOKO with any physical therapy, exercise or any treatment to assist him in recovering from back surgery. Plaintiff was in fact left in PHS' infirmary for the balance of his imprisonment. He was not given an exercise program, nor was he given physical therapy, adequate surgical wound treatment or any other post surgery treatment other than pain medication.

75. On November 17, 1997, Plaintiff SISSOKO was released from custody on bond, not on his own recognizance.

76. In February, 1998, in a courtroom proceeding, SISSOKO, through his counsel, was, for the first time provided with the denials of his Amnesty Applications. They were both dated August 26, 1997.

V. ALLEGATIONS AGAINST THE UNITED STATES ARISING UNDER THE FEDERAL TORT CLAIMS ACT

AS AND FOR A FIRST CAUSE OF ACTION AGAINST THE UNITED STATES OF AMERICA AND UNITED STATES IMMIGRATION AND NATURALIZATION SERVICE AND THE UNITED STATES PUBLIC HEALTH SERVICE, ON BEHALF OF PLAINTIFF OUMAR SISSOKO

77. Plaintiff, SISSOKO realleges Paragraphs Numbered 1 through 77 of this Complaint as though again set forth in their entirety herein.

78. Plaintiff, SISSOKO, asserts a claim of battery and assault against United States Defendants under the Federal Tort Claims Act.

79. Although Plaintiff, SISSOKO, was imprisoned at LA, TI, EC and civilian medical facilities, the INS OFFICERS and PHS EMPLOYEES, agents, servants or employees unlawfully placed various restraints on Plaintiff SISSOKO, including but not limited to handcuffs and leg restraints and on one occasion applied leg restraints to plaintiff to prohibit him from leaving a hospital Gurney immediately following emergency back surgery.

80. While Plaintiff, SISSOKO, was imprisoned at LA, TI, EC and elsewhere, the Defendant, INS OFFICERS and PHS EMPLOYEES using their hands, limbs, bodies, handcuffs, shackles, needles, syringes, surgical instruments, improper and contraindicated medications and other devices and modalities, pulled, pushed, shoved, punctured, incised, injected and touched SISSOKO's person without cause, justification, permission, excuse or consent thereby committing assaults and batteries upon Plaintiff, SISSOKO, all the while threatening him with serious bodily injury and deportation.

81. As a direct and proximate result of the aforesaid provocations and harmful touching the Plaintiff, SISSOKO, was caused great physical pain, fear of bodily contact and humiliation, as well as physical, emotional, and psychological injuries.

82. By reason of the foregoing, the Plaintiff, SISSOKO, has been required, and will be required in the future to employ the services of psychiatrists, physicians, surgeons, physical therapists, other health care professionals, providers and facilities including but not limited to hospitals, clinics, and physical therapy centers, as well as being required to purchase drugs and medicines and undergo continuing psychiatric counseling for an indeterminate time in the future.

83. From and after the intentional, malicious and tortious conduct of the Defendants, and each of them, Plaintiff, SISSOKO, has suffered as a direct consequence and proximate result thereof, injuries, and damages to his physical and mental health of such moment, gravity and severity as to cause him to become and remain unable to engage in his regular and customary activities, employment, education or enjoyment of his life and consortium with his wife Plaintiff, JULIE SISSOKO.

84. As a direct and proximate result of the aforesaid acts and/or omissions of the Defendants, and each of them, Plaintiff, SISSOKO, seeks compensatory damages in the sum of Ten Million Dollars ($10,000,000).

AS AND FOR A SECOND CAUSE OF ACTION AGAINST THE UNITED STATES OF AMERICA AND UNITED STATES IMMIGRATION AND NATURALIZATION SERVICE AND THE UNITED STATES PUBLIC HEALTH SERVICE, ON BEHALF OF PLAINTIFFS OUMAR SISSOKO AND JULIE SISSOKO

85. Plaintiffs reallege Paragraphs Numbered 1 through 77 of this Complaint as though again set forth in their entirety herein.

86. Plaintiff, SISSOKO, asserts a claim of intentional and reckless infliction of emotional distress against United States Defendants under the Federal Tort Claims Act.

87. Between May 14, 1997 and May 16, 1997, and August 26, 1997, and November 17, 1997, Defendants regularly threatened Plaintiff, SISSOKO with deportation or indefinite incarceration and carried on each and all of their activities with such careless disregard for Plaintiff SISSOKO's physical well being so as to cause said Plaintiff to fear for his life.

88. The acts of the Defendants INS and PHS its officers, agents, servants and employees were done willfully wantonly, maliciously, outrageously, deliberately and purposely with the intention to inflict emotional distress upon the Plaintiff, SISSOKO, and/or were done with reckless disregard of the probability of causing said Plaintiff emotional distress, and these acts did in fact result in severe and extreme emotional distress for said Plaintiff.

89. By virtue of the foregoing, extreme mental distress was inflicted upon SISSOKO when the INS and PHS and their constituted officers, agents, servants and/or employees, all acting in the performance of their employment and within the scope of their authority, manifested extreme and outrageous conduct during the performance of their duties, responsibilities, and/or assignments in intentionally, recklessly, and/or maliciously causing extreme emotional distress to Plaintiff, SISSOKO..

90. Such outrageous conduct was without excuse, privilege or other legal reason.

91. As a direct and proximate result of the aforesaid extreme and outrageous conduct engaged in by each and all of the Defendants herein, Plaintiff, SISSOKO, sustained extreme emotional and mental pain, suffering and distress, including but not limited to severe depression, paranoia, insomnia and claustrophobia.

92. From and after the intentional, malicious and tortious conduct of the Defendants, and each of them, Plaintiff, SISSOKO, has suffered as a direct consequence and proximate result thereof, severe and irreparable injury to his mental and emotional health and well being in a manner and to an extent of such moment, gravity and severity as to cause him to become and remain unable to engage in his regular and customary activities, employment, education or enjoyment of his life and consortium with his wife Plaintiff, JULIE SISSOKO.

93. By reason of the foregoing, the Plaintiff, SISSOKO, has been and will be required to employ the services of psychiatrists, physicians, hospitals, physical therapists and related professionals, as well as purchase drugs and medicines and undergo continuing psychiatric counseling for an indeterminate time in the future.

94. As a direct and proximate result of the foregoing acts and/or omissions of the Defendants, Plaintiff, SISSOKO, seeks compensatory damages in the sum of Ten Million Dollars ($10,000,000.00).

95. As a further direct and proximate consequence of the aforesaid intentional, unlawful, and negligent treatment described herein above, Plaintiff, JULIE SISSOKO, has for the period of August 26, 1997 through November 17, 1997, suffered the loss of consortium with her husband Plaintiff, OUMAR SISSOKO.

96. As a further direct and proximate consequence of the aforesaid intentional, unlawful, and negligent treatment described herein above, Plaintiff, JULIE SISSOKO, is informed and believes and thereon alleges that from and after August 26, 1997, for an indeterminate period in the future, her consortium with Plaintiff, OUMAR SISSOKO will be severely impaired.

97. As a direct and proximate result of the foregoing acts and/or omissions of the Defendants, Plaintiff JULIE SISSOKO, seeks compensatory damages in the sum of Five Million Dollars ($5,000,000.00)

AS AND FOR A THIRD CAUSE OF ACTION AGAINST THE UNITED STATES OF AMERICA AND UNITED STATES IMMIGRATION AND NATURALIZATION SERVICE AND THE UNITED STATES PUBLIC HEALTH SERVICE, ON BEHALF OF PLAINTIFF OUMAR SISSOKO

98. Plaintiff SISSOKO realleges Paragraphs Numbered 1 through 77 of this Complaint as though again set forth in their entirety herein.

99. Plaintiff, SISSOKO, asserts against United States Defendants the claim of racial discrimination and alien discrimination under 42 U.S.C. §§ 1981, 1982, 1985 and 1986 in that he was subjected to same by officers, agents, representatives and employees of the INS and PHS while he was imprisoned at LA, TI and EC.

100. On more than one occasion during his detention Plaintiff, SISSOKO, was told by INS officers that neither he nor his black Ghanaian lawyer would save him from being deported, thereby intimating that neither SISSOKO nor his attorney had the intellect, experience knowledge, or capacity to accomplish that which those of the different races and nationalities could accomplish.

101. On a number of occasions on and after October 3, 1997, PHS EMPLOYEES ascribed certain humiliating, degrading and reprehensible attributes to Plaintiff, SISSOKO, as a member of the class of aliens whose origin was Africa.

102. That the foregoing acts of INS and PHS officers caused Plaintiff, SISSOKO, severe personal injuries, social stigma, damage to his reputation, mental anguish and distress, including depression, paranoia, insomnia and claustrophobia, all as a direct and proximate result of the aforesaid outrageous conduct.

103. As a direct and proximate result of the aforesaid acts and/or omissions of the INS and PHS, Plaintiff SISSOKO seeks compensatory damages in the sum of Ten Million Dollars ($10,000,000).

AS AND FOR A FOURTH CAUSE OF ACTION AGAINST THE UNITED STATES OF AMERICA AND UNITED STATES IMMIGRATION AND NATURALIZATION SERVICE AND THE UNITED STATES PUBLIC HEALTH SERVICE, ON BEHALF OF PLAINTIFFS OUMAR SISSOKO AND JULIE SISSOKO

104. Plaintiff SISSOKO realleges Paragraphs Numbered 1 through 77 of this Complaint as though again set forth in their entirety herein.

105. Plaintiff, SISSOKO asserts a claim of negligence and gross negligence against the United States Defendants Under the Federal Tort Claims Act for negligent hiring and negligent supervision of its employees.

106. The INS and PHS were, at all times relevant herein, the employers of the INS OFFICERS and PHS EMPLOYEES respectively at LA, TI and EC and elsewhere in medical institutions wherein SISSOKO was confined.

107. The INS and PHS so negligently, carelessly, recklessly and unlawfully hired, trained, controlled, supervised and employed its INS OFFICERS and PHS EMPLOYEES as to condone, ratify, exonerate, allow and permit said INS OFFICERS and PHS EMPLOYEES to unlawfully, unreasonably and without justification restrict Plaintiff SISSOKO's freedom, placing various restraints on said Plaintiff, including but not limited to handcuffs and leg restraints; allowing said INS OFFICERS and PHS EMPLOYEES to commit batteries upon SISSOKO by unlawfully and intentionally yanking said Plaintiff's wrists and shoving said Plaintiff; by performing surgery on his back and otherwise touching him without cause, justification, permission, excuse or consent including; and allowing, permitting and ratifying, the use by said INS OFFICERS and PHS EMPLOYEES of their fists, limbs, body upon the arms, hands, wrists, legs and body of the Plaintiff,

SISSOKO, and by allowing, condoning, and permitting said INS OFFICERS and PHS EMPLOYEES to threaten Plaintiff SISSOKO with deportation thereby putting Plaintiff, SISSOKO in fear of bodily contact and physical, emotional, and psychological injuries.

108. During the term of the Plaintiff SISSOKO's detention, the INS and PHS inadequate supervision of its INS OFFICERS, and PHS EMPLOYEES resulted in the false imprisonment of SISSOKO, assault and battery upon SISSOKO, inflicting of physical and emotional injury to Plaintiff, SISSOKO all of which willful, wanton and reckless conduct has caused and will continue to cause severe physical and emotional damages to said Plaintiff in amounts and to an extent which remain to be ascertained.

109. During the term of SISSOKO's detention, inadequate supervision by the PHS of its PHS EMPLOYEES at LA, TI and EC resulted in inadequate and inappropriate treatment being given to SISSOKO prior to August 30, 1997, when treatment and care were indicated and thereafter from October 3, 1997 to November 17, 1997, inadequate, inappropriate and insufficient post operative care, as direct and proximate result of which Plaintiff SISSOKO has sustained permanent injury to his physical, emotional and psychological well being.

110. The INS and PHS have, at all times mentioned herein, owed a duty of reasonable care to SISSOKO to hire competent, qualified and sensible employees.

111. The INS and PHS breached their duty of reasonable care by hiring employees who were incompetent, unfit and dangerous.

112. Upon information and belief, the INS and PHS knew or should have known about the misconduct of the INS OFFICERS and misconduct of the PHS EMPLOYEES attended to the imprisonment and health and medical needs of Plaintiff, SISSOKO.

113. Pursuant to other practices and procedures in full force and effect at the time that the Plaintiff, SISSOKO was a detainee at LA, TI and EC the INS and PHS had a duty to supervise their agents, employees, servants, detention and INS officers and the staff of PHS EMPLOYEE medical and health care professionals and providers when making contact with a detainee. Specifically, the INS and PHS had a duty to Plaintiff, SISSOKO to supervise their agents, employees, servants, detention and INS officers and staff of medical and health care service professionals and providers to insure the safety of detainees such as said Plaintiff, in particular, from the acts, assault, battery, intentional infliction of emotional distress, misfeasances, malfeasances and omissions committed upon Plaintiff SISSOKO as described above.

114. The INS and PHS breached their duty of supervision over their agents, employees, servants, detention and INS officers as well as the staff of medical and health care service professionals and providers by not supervising them adequately as and when they interacted with Plaintiff SISSOKO.

115. The injuries sustained by SISSOKO were as a direct and proximate result of and due to negligence and/or gross negligence and recklessness of the INS and PHS in, among other things, the hiring disciplining, investigation, training, instruction, supervision, and/or direction of its officers, staff of medical and health care service provider, personnel, agents, servants and employees, and in the performance of medical, custodial, correctional, legal, clerical and/or INS officers' duties, and in the establishment of procedures, rules and/or regulations for said INS officers, staff of medical and mental health care service providers agents, servants, personnel, and employees.

116. By reason of the foregoing misfeasances, malfeasances and nonfeasances of INS and PHS, Plaintiff, SISSOKO, has been, and will be required to employee the services of the psychiatrists, physicians, surgeons, physical therapists, other health care professionals, providers and facilities including but not limited to hospitals, clinics, and physical therapy centers, as well as being required to purchase drugs and medicines and undergo continuing psychiatric counseling for an indeterminate time in the future.

117. From and after the intentional, malicious and tortious conduct of the Defendants, and each of them, Plaintiff, SISSOKO, has suffered as a direct consequence and proximate result thereof, injuries, and damages to his physical and mental health of such moment, gravity and severity as to cause him to become and remain unable to engage in his regular and customary activities, employment, education or enjoyment of his life and consortium with his wife Plaintiff, JULIE SISSOKO.

118. As a further direct and proximate consequence of the aforesaid intentional, unlawful, and negligent treatment described herein above, Plaintiff, JULIE SISSOKO, has for the period of August 26, 1997 through November 17, 1997, suffered the loss of consortium with her husband Plaintiff, OUMAR SISSOKO.

119. As a further direct and proximate consequence of the aforesaid intentional, unlawful, and negligent treatment described herein above, Plaintiff, JULIE SISSOKO, is informed and believes and thereon alleges that from and after August 26, 1997, for an indeterminate period in the future, her consortium with Plaintiff, OUMAR SISSOKO will be severely impaired.

120. As a direct and proximate result of the aforesaid misfeasances, malfeasances and nonfeasances of the INS and PHS, the Plaintiff, SISSOKO, seeks compensatory damages from said Defendants in the sum of Ten Million Dollars ($10,000,000.00).

121. As a direct and proximate result of the aforesaid acts and/or omissions of Defendants, INS OFFICERS, Plaintiff, JULIE SISSOKO, seeks compensatory damages in the amount of Five Million Dollars ($5,000,000.00).

AS AND FOR A FIFTH CAUSE OF ACTION AGAINST THE UNITED STATES OF AMERICA, UNITED STATES IMMIGRATION AND NATURALIZATION SERVICE, AND UNITED STATES PUBLIC HEALTH SERVICE, ON BEHALF OF PLAINTIFFS OUMAR SISSOKO AND JULIE SISSOKO

122. Plaintiff SISSOKO realleges paragraphs 1 through 77 of this Complaint as though again set forth in their entirety herein.

123. Plaintiff, SISSOKO asserts a claim of medical negligence and gross negligence against the United States under the Federal Tort Claims Act.

124. At all times relevant hereto, and, in particular, during the term of Plaintiff, SISSOKO's imprisonment by the INS, the INS and PHS had an absolute an irrevocable duty and obligation to provide medical services, doctors, nurses, medicines and psychiatric care and assistance to detainees at LA, TI and EC at least commensurate with that afforded to the citizen residing in the community in which said governmental detention facilities were operated.

125. At all times relevant hereto, it was the duty of INS and PHS to have a sufficient number of qualified personnel to monitor the Plaintiff, SISSOKO's medical condition and conduct and exercise adequate supervision, care and control over the Plaintiff SISSOKO to prevent harm to said Plaintiff.

126. The INS and PHS, failed to exercise reasonable and ordinary care, skill and diligence, and departed from the generally accepted and recognized standard of care or skill in the control, care, and supervision of Plaintiff, SISSOKO, so as to protect said Plaintiff from harm by, failing to treat SISSOKO; failing to provide said Plaintiff with adequate medical care; failing to provide Plaintiff SISSOKO with adequate psychiatric care; failing to provide said Plaintiff with access to psychiatric care; failing to take a complete and accurate medical and/or psychiatric history from SISSOKO before commencing treatment of him; failing to obtain said Plaintiff's medical records and failure to study said records before commencement and during the treatment of Plaintiff SISSOKO; and ignoring of the said Plaintiff's medically determined and prescribed treatment protocols; prescribing contra indicated post surgery exercise regimen; failing to diagnose at all or correctly diagnose the Plaintiff medical and mental condition; unlawfully, unreasonably, without justification and for an unreasonable length of time, leaving SISSOKO in the general detention population without medical access, leaving SISSOKO immobile paralyzed and in pain while in immediate need of medical attention; applying leg restraints to prohibit him from leaving a Gurney; conducting surgical operations without first obtaining a knowing consent from SISSOKO, and as a result causing said Plaintiff great pain, fear of bodily contact and physical, emotional, and psychological injuries.

127. As a direct and proximate result of the foregoing misfeasances, malfeasances and nonfeasances of Defendants, and each of them, Plaintiff, SISSOKO has been required in the past, and will be required in the future, to employ the services of physicians, surgeons, psychiatrists, chiropractors, physical therapists and related health care professionals and providers; and has and will in the future be required to undergo surgeries, physical therapy, post surgical treatment, continuing psychiatric counseling and has and will in the future be required engage facilities where the aforesaid procedures and treatments have and will be performed; and has and will in the future be required to purchase prescription and non-prescription medications all to said Plaintiff's damage in amounts which Plaintiff will prove at time of trial.

128. From and after the intentional, malicious and tortious conduct of the Defendants, and each of them, Plaintiff, SISSOKO, has suffered as a direct consequence and proximate result thereof, injuries, and damages to his physical and mental health of such moment, gravity and severity as to cause him to become and remain unable to engage in his regular and customary activities, employment, education or enjoyment of his life and consortium with his wife Plaintiff, JULIE SISSOKO.

129. As a further direct and proximate consequence of the aforesaid intentional, unlawful, and negligent treatment described herein above, Plaintiff, JULIE SISSOKO, has for the period of August 26, 1997 through November 17, 1997, suffered the loss of consortium with her husband Plaintiff, OUMAR SISSOKO.

130. As a further direct and proximate consequence of the aforesaid intentional, unlawful, and negligent treatment described herein above, Plaintiff, JULIE SISSOKO, is informed and believes and thereon alleges that from and after August 26, 1997, for an indeterminate period in the future, her consortium with Plaintiff, OUMAR SISSOKO will be severely impaired.

131. As a direct and proximate result of the aforesaid acts and/or omissions of the Defendants the plaintiff, SISSOKO seeks compensatory damages in the sum of Ten Million Dollars ($10,000,000).

132. As a direct and proximate result of the aforesaid acts and/or omissions of Defendants, INS OFFICERS, Plaintiff, JULIE SISSOKO, seeks compensatory damages in the amount of Five Million Dollars ($5,000,000.00).

VI. ALLEGATIONS AGAINST INDIVIDUAL DEFENDANTS ARISING UNDER THE CIVIL RIGHTS ACT AND THE CONSTITUTION

AS AND FOR A SIXTH CAUSE OF ACTION AGAINST LOYDA R. ROCHA, AND UNNAMED INS OFFICERS ON BEHALF OF PLAINTIFF OUMAR SISSOKO AND JULIE SISSOKO

133. Plaintiffs OUMAR SISSOKO and JULIE SISSOKO reallege Paragraphs Numbered 1 through 77 of this Complaint as though again set forth in their entirety herein.

134. Pursuant to *Bivens v. Six Unknown Named Agents of Federal Bureau of Narcotics*, 403 U.S. 388 (1971), the Plaintiff, SISSOKO, asserts a claim that his civil rights were violated, as said rights are secured by the United States Constitution, against LOYDA R. ROCHA, an Inspector employed by the INS and INS Officers whose names are unknown to plaintiff at this time. This action is against the INS OFFICER (as defined in Paragraph Number 17 herein above) in their individual, and not their official capacity.

135. At all times herein mentioned, INS officer LOYDA R. ROCHA knew on August 26, 1997, that neither of Plaintiff SISSOKO's applications had been denied and there was no reasonable, rational or procedural basis to take him into custody. On the same day and at the same time, said Defendant knew that Plaintiff SISSOKO had filed for a marital adjustment based on his marriage to Plaintiff, JULIE SISSOKO.

136. On August 26, 1997, and thereafter until November 17, 1997, Defendant LOYDA R. ROCHA, knew that Plaintiff, SISSOKO, was not an alien subject to exclusion under the laws of the United States in that he had the right on said date and on all days prior and subsequent thereto to be paroled into the United States and neither detained or imprisoned in its detention facilities.

137. Knowing as she did on August 26, 1997, that detaining the Plaintiff, SISSOKO, in light of the circumstances set forth in Paragraph Numbered 24, 25 and 27 would be unlawful and a clear and wanton disregard of the rules, procedures and regulation promulgated by the INS, when Defendant, LOYDA R. ROCHA, took Plaintiff, SISSOKO, into custody by so imprisoning him, she thereby acted with deliberate malice and with the purpose of punishing Plaintiff SISSOKO and with a conscious disregard of having deprived him of his freedom and liberty.

138. Each and all of the Defendants herein ratified the aforesaid conduct of said Defendant LOYDA R. ROCHA.

139. The acts of individual Defendants and each of them as herein alleged were willful, wanton, malicious, and oppressive, and justify the awarding of punitive damages in an amount to be ascertained at time of trial.

140. By the actions described above, and the official customs, policies and practices alleged hereafter, Defendants, LOYDA R. ROCHA and the INS OFFICERS, by their acts in furtherance of the official policies and/or customs of the INS, deprived the Plaintiff, SISSOKO, of the following clearly established and well-settled constitutional rights:

1. Freedom from the use of excessive an unreasonable force, said rights being secured by the Fourth Amendment of United States Constitution,

2. Freedom from the deprivation of liberty and summary punishment without due process of the law, as said rights are secured by the Fifth, Eighth, and Fourteenth Amendments of United States Constitution;

3. Freedom from unreasonable searches and seizure of the plaintiff's person and property, as said rights are secured by the Fourth and Fourteenth Amendments of United States Constitution;

4. Freedom to enjoy equal protection of the laws under the Fourteenth Amendment of United States Constitution.

141. The INS OFFICERS committed the foregoing acts or omissions without just and legal cause, thereby violating the rights of Plaintiff, SISSOKO, under the laws and Constitution of United States, in particular the First, Fourth, Fifth, Eighth and Fourteenth Amendments.

142. In committing the aforesaid acts and omissions, the INS OFFICERS acted illegally and directly violated the rules and regulations of the INS and failed to enforce the aforesaid rules and regulations, in particular those rules and regulations requiring all detention and INS officers to conform their conduct to the laws of the Federal Government and the State of California and to not use their public employment in the furtherance of illegal or tortious ends and the other appropriate rules and regulations governing Defendants that were applicable in the circumstances.

143. The INS OFFICERS acted pursuant to and in furtherance of, an official policy or custom of the INS, or such acts or omissions were performed by such persons whose activities themselves constitute official customs and practices of the INS.

144. The INS OFFICERS were not privileged or justified in any manner, in their tortuous conduct toward Plaintiff, nor was said conduct in any way consented to by Plaintiff, SISSOKO.

145. By their unlawful, willful, wanton and reckless conduct said INS OFFICERS directly and proximately caused the Plaintiff, SISSOKO, severe personal injuries, social stigma, damage to his reputation, and mental anguish and distress.

146. As a direct and proximate result of the intentionally tortious conduct of the Defendants, INS OFFICERS, and each of them, Plaintiff, SISSOKO, sustained and will continue to experience extreme emotional and mental pain, trauma and distress, including depression, paranoia, persistent nightmares, insomnia and claustrophobia.

147. As a direct and proximate result of the above described violations of Plaintiff, SISSOKO's constitutional and statutory rights, SISSOKO suffered grievous bodily harm and emotional injury, all of which were in violation of his rights under the laws and Constitution of the United States, in the First, Fourth, Fifth, Eighth, and Fourteenth Amendments.

148. As a direct and proximate result of the foregoing misfeasances, malfeasances and nonfeasances of the individual Defendants, and each of them, Plaintiff, SISSOKO has been required in the past, and will be required in the future, to employ the services of physicians, surgeons, psychiatrists, chiropractors, physical therapists and related health care professionals and providers; and has and will in the future be required to undergo surgeries, physical therapy, post surgical treatment, continuing psychiatric counseling and has and will in the future be required engage facilities where the aforesaid procedures and treatments have and will be performed; and has and will in the future be required to purchase prescription and non-prescription medications all to said Plaintiff's damage in amounts which Plaintiff will prove at time of trial..

149. From and after the aforesaid intentional, unlawful, reckless and malicious conduct of the Defendants INS OFFICERS, and each of them, Plaintiff, SISSOKO, has suffered as a direct consequence and proximate result thereof, injuries, and damages to his physical and mental health of such moment, gravity and severity as to cause him to become and remain unable to engage in his regular and customary activities, employment, education or enjoyment of his life and consortium with his wife Plaintiff, JULIE SISSOKO.

150. As a further direct and proximate consequence of the aforesaid intentional, unlawful, reckless and malicious conduct of said Defendant, INS OFFICERS and each of them against Plaintiff, SISSOKO, Plaintiff, JULIE SISSOKO, has for the period of August 26, 1997 through November 17, 1997, suffered the loss of consortium with her husband Plaintiff, OUMAR SISSOKO.

151. As a further direct and proximate consequence of the aforesaid intentional, unlawful, reckless and malicious conduct of said Defendant, INS OFFICERS and each of them against Plaintiff, SISSOKO, Plaintiff, JULIE SISSOKO, is informed and believes and thereon alleges that from and after August 26, 1997, for an indeterminate period in the future, her consortium with Plaintiff, OUMAR SISSOKO will be severely impaired.

152. As a direct and proximate result of the aforesaid acts and/or omissions of Defendants, INS OFFICERS, Plaintiff, SISSOKO, seeks compensatory damages in the amount of Ten Million Dollars ($10,000,000.00).

153. As a direct and proximate result of the aforesaid acts and/or omissions of Defendants, INS OFFICERS, Plaintiff, JULIE SISSOKO, seeks compensatory damages in the amount of Five Million Dollars ($5,000,000.00).

154. The Plaintiffs have no effective means other than the judiciary to enforce these rights. No Congressional declaration denies recovery, nor do special factors counsel hesitation.

AS AND FOR A SEVENTH CAUSE OF ACTION AGAINST LOYDA R. ROCHA, AND UNNAMED INS OFFICERS ON BEHALF OF PLAINTIFFS OUMAR SISSOKO AND JULIE SISSOKO

155. Plaintiffs OUMAR SISSOKO and JULIE SISSOKO reallege Paragraphs Numbered 1 through 77 of this Complaint as though again set forth in their entirety herein.

156. Pursuant to *Bivens v. Six Unknown Named Agents of Federal Bureau of Narcotics*, 403 U.S. 388 (1971), the Plaintiff, SISSOKO, asserts a claim that his civil rights were violated, as said rights are secured by the United States Constitution, in that he was falsely imprisoned by the INS OFFICERS, for an inordinately long period. This cause of action is against the INS OFFICERS (as defined in Paragraph Number 17 herein above) in their individual, and not in their official capacity.

157. At all times commencing on August 27, 1997, the INS OFFICERS knew as a result of the "MEDICAL/PSYCHIATRIC ALERT" issued by the PHS that Plaintiff, SISSOKO, physical condition was such that the physical rigors of incarceration would more likely that not injure Plaintiff, SISSOKO.

158. On and after August 27, 1997, the INS OFFICERS, had been advised by PHS to:

"Please see that his [SISSOKO's] time in custody is minimal." [*See* Paragraph 53 for additional text]

159. At all times on and after August 26, 1997, the INS OFFICERS, knew that on March 19, 1997, when Plaintiff, SISSOKO, returned from his father's funeral in Senegal, he should have been paroled into the United States, and as of August 26, 1997, he should not have been on deferred inspection but rather should have been awaiting a marital adjustment based on his petition therefore and the underlying basis therefor, his marriage to Plaintiff JULIE SISSOKO.

160. On and after August 26, 1997, Defendants INS OFFICERS knew that any incarceration for more than a few days would be unlawful and without rational basis. Nevertheless, Defendants INS OFFICERS and each of them elected to falsely imprison Plaintiff, SISSOKO, from August 26, 1997 through November 17, 1997, beyond all bounds and reason and in violation of the rules, procedures and regulations promulgated by the INS for the benefit of detainees such as Plaintiff herein. Said continued imprisonment of Plaintiff, SISSOKO, by said INS OFFICERS, and each of them was deliberate, malicious and done with the purpose of punishing Plaintiff SISSOKO and with a conscious disregard of having wrongfully and unlawfully deprived him of his freedom and liberty.

161. Each and all of the Defendants herein ratified the aforesaid conduct of said Defendant LOYDA R. ROCHA and the INS OFFICERS.

162. The acts of Defendants and each of them as herein alleged were willful, wanton, malicious, and oppressive, and justify the awarding of punitive damages in an amount to be ascertained at time of trial.

163. By the actions described above, and the official customs, policies and practices alleged hereafter, Defendants, LOYDA R. ROCHA and the INS OFFICERS, by their acts in furtherance of the official policies and/or customs of the INS, deprived the Plaintiff, SISSOKO, of the following clearly established and well-settled constitutional rights:

1. Freedom from the use of excessive an unreasonable force, said rights being secured by the Fourth Amendment of United States Constitution,

2. Freedom from the deprivation of liberty and summary punishment without due process of the law, as said rights are secured by the Fifth, Eighth, and Fourteenth Amendments of United States Constitution;

3. Freedom from unreasonable searches and seizure of the plaintiff's person and property, as said rights are secured by the Fourth and Fourteenth Amendments of United States Constitution;

4. Freedom to enjoy equal protection of the laws under the Fourteenth Amendment of United States Constitution.

164. The INS OFFICERS committed the foregoing acts or omissions without just and legal cause, thereby violating the rights of Plaintiff, SISSOKO, under the laws and Constitution of United States, in particular the First, Fourth, Fifth, Eighth and Fourteenth Amendments.

165. In committing the aforesaid acts and omissions, the INS OFFICERS acted illegally and directly violated the rules and regulations of the INS and failed to enforce the aforesaid rules and regulations, in particular those rules and regulations requiring all detention and INS officers to conform their conduct the laws of the Federal Government and the State of California and to not use their public employment in the furtherance of illegal or tortious ends and the other appropriate rules and regulations governing Defendants that were applicable in the circumstances.

166. The INS OFFICERS acted pursuant to and in furtherance of, an official policy or custom of the INS, or such acts or omissions were performed by such persons whose activities themselves constitute official customs and practices of the INS.

167. The INS OFFICERS were not privileged or justified in any manner, in their tortuous conduct toward Plaintiff, nor was said conduct in any way consented to by Plaintiff, SISSOKO.

168. By their unlawful, willful, wanton and reckless conduct said INS OFFICERS directly and proximately caused the Plaintiff, SISSOKO, severe personal injuries, social stigma, damage to his reputation, and mental anguish and distress.

169. As a direct and proximate result of the intentionally tortious conduct of the Defendants, INS OFFICERS, and each of them, Plaintiff, SISSOKO, sustained and will continue to experience extreme emotional and mental pain, trauma and distress, including depression, paranoia, persistent nightmares, insomnia and claustrophobia.

170. As a direct and proximate result of the above described violations of Plaintiff, SISSOKO's constitutional and statutory rights, SISSOKO suffered grievous bodily harm and emotional injury, all of which were in violation of his rights under the laws and Constitution of the United States, in the First, Fourth, Fifth, Eighth, and fourteenth Amendments.

171. As a direct and proximate result of the foregoing misfeasances, malfeasances and nonfeasances of LOYDA R. ROCHA, the INS OFFICERS, and each of them, Plaintiff, SISSOKO has been required in the past, and will be required in the future, to employ the services of physicians, surgeons, psychiatrists, chiropractors, physical therapists and related health care professionals and providers; and has and will in the future be required to undergo surgeries, physical therapy, post surgical treatment, continuing psychiatric counseling and has and will in the future be required engage facilities where the aforesaid procedures and treatments have and will be performed; and has and will in the future be required to purchase prescription and non-prescription medications all to said Plaintiff's damage in amounts which Plaintiff will prove at time of trial.

172. From and after the aforesaid intentional, unlawful, reckless and malicious conduct of the Defendants INS OFFICERS, and each of them, Plaintiff, SISSOKO, has suffered as a direct consequence and proximate result thereof, injuries, and damages to his physical and mental health of such moment, gravity and severity as to cause him to become and remain unable to engage in his regular and customary activities, employment, education or enjoyment of his life and consortium with his wife Plaintiff, JULIE SISSOKO.

173. As a further direct and proximate consequence of the aforesaid intentional, unlawful, reckless and malicious conduct of said Defendant, INS OFFICERS and each of them against Plaintiff, SISSOKO, Plaintiff, JULIE SISSOKO, has for the period of August 26, 1997 through November 17, 1997, suffered the loss of consortium with her husband Plaintiff, OUMAR SISSOKO.

174. As a further direct and proximate consequence of the aforesaid intentional, unlawful, reckless and malicious conduct of said Defendant, INS OFFICERS and each of them against Plaintiff, SISSOKO, Plaintiff, JULIE SISSOKO, is informed and believes and thereon alleges that from and after August 26, 1997, for an indeterminate period in the future, her consortium with Plaintiff, OUMAR SISSOKO will be severely impaired.

175. As a direct and proximate result of the aforesaid acts and/or omissions of Defendants, INS OFFICERS, Plaintiff, SISSOKO, seeks compensatory damages in the amount of Ten Million Dollars ($10,000,000.00).

176. As a direct and proximate result of the aforesaid acts and/or omissions of Defendants, INS OFFICERS, Plaintiff, JULIE SISSOKO, seeks compensatory damages in the amount of Five Million Dollars ($5,000,000.00).

177. The Plaintiffs have no effective means other than the judiciary to enforce these rights. No Congressional declaration denies recovery, nor do special factors counsel hesitation.

AS AND FOR A EIGHTH CAUSE OF ACTION AGAINST AN UNNAMED INS OFFICER ON BEHALF OF PLAINTIFFS OUMAR SISSOKO AND JULIE SISSOKO

178. Plaintiffs OUMAR SISSOKO and JULIE SISSOKO reallege Paragraphs Numbered 1 through 77 of this Complaint as though again set forth in their entirety herein.

179. Pursuant to *Bivens v. Six Unknown Named Agents of Federal Bureau of Narcotics,* 403 U.S. 388 (1971), the Plaintiff, SISSOKO, asserts a claim that his civil rights were violated, as said rights are secured by the United States Constitution, in that he was assaulted and battered by an UNNAMED INS OFFICER as more particularly set forth in Paragraph Number 13 hereinabove. This cause of action is against an UNNAMED INS OFFICER (as defined in Paragraph Number 17 hereinabove) in his individual, and not in his official capacity.

180. At all times commencing on August 27, 1997, the UNNAMED INS OFFICER knew or should have known with the exercise of reasonable care, as a result of the "MEDICAL/PSYCHIATRIC ALERT" issued by the PHS that Plaintiff, SISSOKO's, had a severe back injury which necessitated said UNNAMED INS OFFICER's exercise of extreme care when coming in contact with said detainee.

181. On the morning of August 30, 1997, at approximately 8:30 a.m. an UNNAMED INS OFFICER caused SISSOKO to seriously exacerbate the damage to his back by bending his knees and back so as to be able to comply with said UNNAMED INS OFFICER's demand that he put his wrists through a low opening in a cell door so he could be handcuffed.

182. Once Plaintiff, SISSOKO, had placed his wrists through the opening, Defendant UNNAMED INS OFFICER, with complete and utter disregard for the Plaintiff's medical condition, unjustifiably and maliciously yanked Plaintiff, SISSOKO's wrists further through the opening, thereby committing a battery upon the person of the Plaintiff, SISSOKO.

183. Almost immediately thereafter, while invoking a racial epithet, said Defendant, UNNAMED INS OFFICER, pushed Plaintiff, SISSOKO, thereby committing a second battery upon the said Plaintiff.

184. As a direct and proximate result of the batteries committed upon the person of the Plaintiff, SISSOKO, by said Defendant, UNNAMED INS OFFICER, said Plaintiff was severely, and irreparably injured in his health, strength and vitality.

185. Each and all of the Defendants herein ratified the aforesaid conduct of said Defendant, UNNAMED INS OFFICER.

186. The acts of individual Defendants and each of them as herein alleged were willful, wanton, malicious, and oppressive, and justify the awarding of punitive damages in an amount to be ascertained at time of trial.

187. By the actions described above, and the official customs, policies and practices alleged hereafter, Defendants, UNNAMED INS OFFICER and the INS OFFICERS, by their acts in furtherance of the official policies and/or customs of the INS, deprived the Plaintiff, SISSOKO, of the following clearly established and well-settled constitutional rights:

1. Freedom from the use of excessive an unreasonable force, said rights being secured by the Fourth Amendment of United States Constitution,

2. Freedom from the deprivation of liberty and summary punishment without due process of the law, as said rights are secured by the Fifth, Eighth, and Fourteenth Amendments of United States Constitution;

3. Freedom from unreasonable searches and seizure of the plaintiff's person and property, as said rights are secured by the Fourth and Fourteenth Amendments of United States Constitution;

4. Freedom to enjoy equal protection of the laws under the Fourteenth Amendment of United States Constitution.

188. The INS OFFICERS committed the foregoing acts or omissions without just and legal cause, thereby violating the rights of Plaintiff, SISSOKO, under the laws and Constitution of United States, in particular the First, Fourth, Fifth, Eighth and Fourteenth Amendments.

189. In committing the aforesaid acts and omissions, the INS OFFICERS acted illegally and directly violated the rules and regulations of the INS and failed to enforce the aforesaid rules and regulations, in particular those rules and regulations requiring all detention and INS officers to conform their conduct the laws of the Federal Government and the State of California and to not use their public employment in the furtherance of illegal or tortious ends and the other appropriate rules and regulations governing Defendants that were applicable in the circumstances.

190. The INS OFFICERS acted pursuant to and in furtherance of, an official policy or custom of the INS, or such acts or omissions were performed by such persons whose activities themselves constitute official customs and practices of the INS.

191. The INS OFFICERS were not privileged or justified in any manner, in their tortuous conduct toward Plaintiff, nor was said conduct in any way consented to by Plaintiff, SISSOKO.

192. By their unlawful, willful, wanton and reckless conduct said INS OFFICERS directly and proximately caused the Plaintiff, SISSOKO, severe personal injuries, social stigma, damage to his reputation, and mental anguish and distress.

193. As a direct and proximate result of the intentionally tortious conduct of the Defendants, INS OFFICERS, and each of them, Plaintiff, SISSOKO, sustained and will continue to experience extreme emotional and mental pain, trauma and distress, including depression, paranoia, persistent nightmares, insomnia and claustrophobia.

194. As a direct and proximate result of the above described violations of Plaintiff, SISSOKO's constitutional and statutory rights, SISSOKO suffered grievous bodily harm and emotional injury, all of which were in violation of his rights under the laws and Constitution of the United States, in the First, Fourth, Fifth, Eighth, and fourteenth Amendments.

195. As a direct and proximate result of the foregoing misfeasances, malfeasances and nonfeasances of Defendants INS OFFICERS, and each of them, Plaintiff, SISSOKO has been required in the past, and will be required in the future, to employ the services of physicians, surgeons, psychiatrists, chiropractors, physical therapists and related health care professionals and providers; and has and will in the future be required to undergo surgeries, physical therapy, post surgical treatment, continuing psychiatric counseling and has and will in the future be required engage facilities where the aforesaid procedures and treatments have and will be performed; and has and will in the future be required to purchase prescription and non-prescription medications all to said Plaintiff's damage in amounts which Plaintiff will prove at time of trial.

196. From and after the aforesaid intentional, unlawful, reckless and malicious conduct of the Defendants INS OFFICERS, and each of them, Plaintiff, SISSOKO, has suffered as a direct consequence and proximate result thereof, injuries, and damages to his physical and mental health of such moment, gravity and severity as to cause him to become and remain unable to engage in his regular and customary activities, employment, education or enjoyment of his life and consortium with his wife Plaintiff, JULIE SISSOKO.

197. As a further direct and proximate consequence of the aforesaid intentional, unlawful, reckless and malicious conduct of said Defendant, INS OFFICERS and each of them against Plaintiff, SISSOKO, Plaintiff, JULIE SISSOKO, has for the period of August 26, 1997 through November 17, 1997, suffered the loss of consortium with her husband Plaintiff, OUMAR SISSOKO.

198. As a further direct and proximate consequence of the aforesaid intentional, unlawful, reckless and malicious conduct of said Defendant, INS OFFICERS and each of them against Plaintiff, SISSOKO, Plaintiff, JULIE SISSOKO, is informed and believes and thereon alleges that from and after August 26, 1997, for an indeterminate period in the future, her consortium with Plaintiff, OUMAR SISSOKO will be severely impaired.

199. As a direct and proximate result of the aforesaid acts and/or omissions of Defendants, INS OFFICERS, Plaintiff, SISSOKO, seeks compensatory damages in the amount of Ten Million Dollars ($10,000,000.00).

200. As a direct and proximate result of the aforesaid acts and/or omissions of Defendants, INS OFFICERS, Plaintiff, JULIE SISSOKO, seeks compensatory damages in the amount of Five Million Dollars ($5,000,000.00).

201. The Plaintiffs have no effective means other than the judiciary to enforce these rights. No Congressional declaration denies recovery, nor do special factors counsel hesitation.

AS AND FOR A NINTH CAUSE OF ACTION AGAINST JOSEPH CHEN, AND UNNAMED EMPLOYEES OF PHS ON BEHALF OF PLAINTIFFS OUMAR SISSOKO AND JULIE SISSOKO

202. Plaintiffs OUMAR SISSOKO and JULIE SISSOKO reallege Paragraphs Numbered 1 through 77 of this Complaint as though again set forth in their entirety herein.

203. Pursuant to *Bivens v. Six Unknown Named Agents of Federal Bureau of Narcotics,* 403 U.S. 388 (1971), the Plaintiff, SISSOKO, asserts a claim that his civil rights were violated, as said rights are secured by the United States Constitution, in that from and after August 26, 1997 through and including August 30, 1997, Defendant JOSEPH CHEN, M.D., acting as Plaintiff, SISSOKO's primary care physician at TI had an absolute and irrevocable duty and obligation to provide appropriate medical care and treatment to the detainees at TI including Plaintiff, SISSOKO. Said irrevocable obligations included, but were not limited to the obligation to examine visually, and with the aid of appropriate diagnostic equipment and testing procedures and protocols the physical and mental health of SISSOKO, and thereafter upon diagnosing a physical ailment, injury, disease or malady, to conduct himself or supervise the dispensing of the medically appropriate treatment modalities for each and all of ailments, injuries, diseases and maladies diagnosed.

204. From August 26, 1997, through and including August 30, 1997, the Defendant JOSEPH CHEN, M.D., breached his duty of due care to Plaintiff SISSOKO by failing to take a complete and accurate medical and psychiatric history from SISSOKO ; by failing to properly examine him; by failing to employ the customary and appropriate diagnostic procedures and protocols while examining the person of Plaintiff SISSOKO; by failing to properly diagnose said Plaintiff's physical and mental condition; by failing to conduct or order and supervise the medically appropriate care and treatment for SISSOKO's physical and mental conditions; by generally failing to exercise reasonable, prudent and ordinary care, skill and diligence in his medical care of SISSOKO; and by departing from the generally accepted and recognized standards of care established for the use medical professionals such as Defendant, CHEN; and by ignoring previously prescribed treatment modalities prescribed in connection with said Plaintiff's post abdominal surgery recovery; and by failing to admit Plaintiff into TI's infirmary, and by failing to administer any medical treatment after Plaintiff SISSOKO was injured by the UNNAMED INS OFFICER.

205. The acts and omissions of Defendant JOSEPH CHEN, M.D. were beyond all bounds and reason and in violation the rules, procedures and regulations promulgated by the INS and PHS for the benefit of detainees such as Plaintiff SISSOKO. The misfeasances, malfeasances and nonfeasances of Defendant CHEN were deliberate, malicious and done with the purpose of physically punishing Plaintiff SISSOKO and thereby directly and proximately depriving him of the following clearly established and well-settled constitutional rights:

1. Freedom from the use of excessive an unreasonable force, said rights being secured by the Fourth Amendment of United States Constitution, which guarantees that Plaintiff, SISSOKO,
2. Freedom from the deprivation of liberty and summary punishment without due process of the law, as said rights are secured by the Fifth, Eighth, and Fourteenth Amendments of United States Constitution;
3. Freedom from unreasonable searches and seizure of the plaintiff's person and property, as said rights are secured by the Fourth and Fourteenth Amendments of United States Constitution;
4. Freedom to enjoy equal protection of the laws under the Fourteenth Amendment of United States Constitution.

206. Defendant, JOSEPH CHEN, M.D., committed the foregoing misfeasances, malfeasances and nonfeasances without just and legal cause, thereby violating the rights of Plaintiff, SISSOKO, under the laws and Constitution of United States, in particular the First, Fourth, Fifth, Eighth and Fourteenth Amendments.

207. In committing the aforesaid acts and omissions, Defendant, JOSEPH CHEN, M.D., acted illegally and directly violated the rules and regulations of the INS and PHS and failed to enforce the aforesaid rules and regulations, in particular those rules and regulations requiring all PHS employees to conform their conduct the laws of the Federal Government and the State of California and to not use their public employment in the furtherance of illegal or tortious ends and the other appropriate rules and regulations governing such Defendants that were applicable in the circumstances.

208. Defendant, JOSEPH CHEN, M.D. acted pursuant to and in furtherance of, an official policy or custom of the INS, and the Defendant PHS, or caused his misfeasances, malfeasances and nonfeasances to become and constitute the customs and practices of the INS and PHS.

209. Defendant, JOSEPH CHEN, M.D. was not privileged or justified in any manner, in his conduct towards Plaintiff, SISSOKO and said Plaintiff in no manner or fashion consented to the same.

210. By reason of the aforesaid negligent, careless, reckless and unlawful conduct of Defendant, JOSEPH CHEN, M.D., Plaintiff, SISSOKO has been required in the past, and will be required in the future, to employ the services of physicians, surgeons, psychiatrists, chiropractors, physical therapists and related health care professionals and providers; and has and will in the future be required to undergo surgeries, physical therapy, post surgical treatment, continuing psychiatric counseling and has and will in the future be required engage facilities where the aforesaid procedures and treatments have and will be performed; and has and will in the future be required to purchase prescription and non-prescription medications all to said Plaintiff's damage in amounts which Plaintiff will prove at time of trial.

211. By reason of the aforesaid negligent, careless, reckless and unlawful conduct of Defendant, JOSEPH CHEN, M.D., and as a direct and proximate result thereof, Plaintiff, SISSOKO, has suffered injuries, and damages to his physical and mental health of such moment, gravity and severity as to cause him to become and remain unable to engage in his regular and customary activities, employment, education or enjoyment of his life and consortium with his wife Plaintiff, JULIE SISSOKO.

212. By reason of the aforesaid negligent, careless, reckless and unlawful conduct of Defendant, JOSEPH CHEN, M.D. described hereinabove, and as a direct and proximate result thereof, Plaintiff, JULIE SISSOKO, has for the period of August 26, 1997 through November 17, 1997, suffered the loss of consortium with her husband Plaintiff, OUMAR SISSOKO.

213. As a further direct and proximate consequence of the aforesaid, negligent, careless, reckless and unlawful conduct of Defendant, JOSEPH CHEN, M.D., Plaintiff, JULIE SISSOKO, is informed and believes and thereon alleges that from and after August 26, 1997, for an indeterminate period in the future, her consortium with Plaintiff, OUMAR SISSOKO will be severely impaired.

214. As a direct and proximate result of the aforesaid acts and/or omissions of the Defendant, JOSEPH CHEN, M.D., the Plaintiff, SISSOKO seeks compensatory damages in the sum of Ten Million Dollars ($10,000,000).

215. As a direct and proximate result of the aforesaid acts and/or omissions of Defendants, INS OFFICERS, Plaintiff, JULIE SISSOKO, seeks compensatory damages in the amount of Five Million Dollars ($5,000,000.00).

216. The acts of the Defendant JOSEPH CHEN were done willfully, wantonly, maliciously, outrageously, deliberately and purposely with the intention to inflict injury and emotional distress upon the Plaintiff, SISSOKO, and were done with a conscious and reckless disregard of the probability of causing said Plaintiff physical injury and emotional distress and therefore justify the awarding of exemplary and punitive damages against said Defendant.

217. The Plaintiffs have no effective means other than the judiciary to enforce these rights. No Congressional declaration denies recovery, nor do special factors counsel hesitation.

AS AND FOR A TENTH CAUSE OF ACTION AGAINST AN UNNAMED PHS EMPLOYEE, ON BEHALF OF PLAINTIFFS OUMAR SISSOKO AND JULIE SISSOKO

218. Plaintiffs OUMAR SISSOKO and JULIE SISSOKO reallege Paragraphs Numbered 1 through 77 of this Complaint as though again set forth in their entirety herein.

219. Pursuant to *Bivens v. Six Unknown Named Agents of Federal Bureau of Narcotics,* 403 U.S. 388 (1971), the Plaintiff, SISSOKO, asserts a claim that his civil rights were violated, as said rights are secured by the United States Constitution, in that from and after October 3, 1997 through and including November 17, 1997, Defendant UNNAMED PHS EMPLOYEE, acting as Plaintiff, SISSOKO's primary care physician at EC had an absolute and irrevocable duty and obligation to provide appropriate medical care and treatment to the detainees at EC including Plaintiff, SISSOKO. Said irrevocable obligations included, but were not limited to the obligation to examine visually, and with the aid of appropriate diagnostic equipment and testing procedures and protocols the physical and mental health of SISSOKO, and thereafter upon diagnosing a physical ailment, injury, disease or malady, to conduct himself or supervise the dispensing of the medically appropriate treatment modalities for each and all of ailments, injuries, diseases and maladies diagnosed.

220. From October 3, 1997, through and including November 17, 1997, the Defendant UNNAMED PHS EMPLOYEE, breached his duty of due care to Plaintiff SISSOKO by failing to take a complete and accurate medical and psychiatric history from SISSOKO ; by failing to properly examine him; by failing to employ the customary and appropriate diagnostic procedures and protocols while examining the person of Plaintiff SISSOKO; by failing to properly diagnose said Plaintiff's physical and mental condition; by failing to conduct or order and supervise the medically appropriate care and treatment for SISSOKO's physical and mental conditions; by generally failing to exercise reasonable, prudent and ordinary care, skill and diligence in his medical care of SISSOKO; and by departing from the generally accepted and recognized standards of care established for the use medical professionals such as Defendant, UNNAMED PHS EMPLOYEE; and by ignoring previously prescribed treatment modalities prescribed in connection with said Plaintiff's post abdominal surgery recovery and post spinal surgery recovery; and by failing after a single examination of Plaintiff SISSOKO on October 4, 1997, to ever again examine him or even speak to said Plaintiff to inquire as to his health or physical condition.

221. The acts and omissions of Defendant UNNAMED PHS EMPLOYEE were beyond all bounds and reason and in violation the rules, procedures and regulations promulgated by the INS and PHS for the benefit of detainees such as Plaintiff SISSOKO. The misfeasances, malfeasances and nonfeasances of Defendant UNNAMED PHS EMPLOYEE were deliberate, malicious and done with the purpose of physically punishing Plaintiff SISSOKO and thereby directly and proximately depriving him of the following clearly established and well-settled constitutional rights:

1. Freedom from the use of excessive an unreasonable force, said rights being secured by the Fourth Amendment of United States Constitution, which guarantees that Plaintiff, SISSOKO,

2. Freedom from the deprivation of liberty and summary punishment without due process of the law, as said rights are secured by the Fifth, Eighth, and Fourteenth Amendments of United States Constitution;

3. Freedom from unreasonable searches and seizure of the plaintiff's person and property, as said rights are secured by the Fourth and Fourteenth Amendments of United States Constitution;

4. Freedom to enjoy equal protection of the laws under the Fourteenth Amendment of United States Constitution.

222. Defendant, UNNAMED PHS EMPLOYEE, committed the foregoing misfeasances, malfeasances and nonfeasances without just and legal cause, thereby violating the rights of Plaintiff, SISSOKO, under the laws and Constitution of United States, in particular the First, Fourth, Fifth, Eighth and Fourteenth Amendments.

223. In committing the aforesaid acts and omissions, Defendant, UNNAMED PHS EMPLOYEE, M.D., acted illegally and directly violated the rules and regulations of the INS and PHS and failed to enforce the aforesaid rules and regulations, in particular those rules and regulations requiring all PHS employees to conform their conduct the laws of the Federal Government and the State of California and to not use their public employment in the furtherance of illegal or tortious ends and the other appropriate rules and regulations governing such Defendants that were applicable in the circumstances.

224. Defendant, UNNAMED PHS EMPLOYEE acted pursuant to and in furtherance of, an official policy or custom of the INS, and the Defendant PHS, or caused his misfeasances, malfeasances and nonfeasances to become and constitute the customs and practices of the INS and PHS.

225. Defendant, UNNAMED PHS EMPLOYEE was not privileged or justified in any manner, in his conduct towards Plaintiff, SISSOKO and said Plaintiff in no manner or fashion consented to the same.

226. By reason of the aforesaid negligent, careless, reckless and unlawful conduct of Defendant, UNNAMED PHS EMPLOYEE, and as a direct and proximate result thereof, the Plaintiff, SISSOKO, has been required and will be required in the future to employee the services of physicians, surgeons, psychiatrists, physical therapists and related health care professionals and providers; and has been and will be required in the future to be admitted or attend hospitals, clinics, physical therapy centers and doctors offices, and has been and will be required in the future to purchase drugs, prescription medications and has been and will be required in the future to undergo surgeries and post surgery care and physical therapy and continuing psychiatric counseling all for a period in the future which is unknown to Plaintiff SISSOKO at this time.

227. By reason of the aforesaid negligent, careless, reckless and unlawful conduct of Defendant, UNNAMED PHS EMPLOYEE, and as a direct and proximate result thereof, Plaintiff, SISSOKO, has suffered injuries, and damages to

his physical and mental health of such moment, gravity and severity as to cause him to become and remain unable to engage in his regular and customary activities, employment, education or enjoyment of his life and consortium with his wife Plaintiff, JULIE SISSOKO.

228. By reason of the aforesaid negligent, careless, reckless and unlawful conduct of Defendant, UNNAMED PHS EMPLOYEE described hereinabove, and as a direct and proximate result thereof, Plaintiff, JULIE SISSOKO, has for the period of October 3, 1997 through November 17, 1997, suffered the loss of consortium with her husband Plaintiff, OUMAR SISSOKO.

229. As a further direct and proximate consequence of the aforesaid, negligent, careless, reckless and unlawful conduct of Defendant, UNNAMED PHS EMPLOYEE, Plaintiff, JULIE SISSOKO, is informed and believes and thereon alleges that from and after August 26, 1997, for an indeterminate period in the future, her consortium with Plaintiff, OUMAR SISSOKO will be severely impaired.

230. As a direct and proximate result of the aforesaid acts and/or omissions of the Defendant, UNNAMED PHS EMPLOYEE, the Plaintiff, SISSOKO seeks compensatory damages in the sum of Ten Million Dollars ($10,000,000).

231. As a direct and proximate result of the aforesaid acts and/or omissions of Defendants, UNNAMED PHS EMPLOYEE, Plaintiff, JULIE SISSOKO, seeks compensatory damages in the amount of Five Million Dollars ($5,000,000.00).

232. The acts of the Defendant UNNAMED PHS EMPLOYEE were done willfully, wantonly, maliciously, outrageously, deliberately and purposely with the intention to inflict injury and emotional distress upon the Plaintiff, SISSOKO, and were done with a conscious and reckless disregard of the probability of causing said Plaintiff physical injury and emotional distress and therefore justify the awarding of exemplary and punitive damages against said Defendant.

233. The Plaintiffs have no effective means other than the judiciary to enforce these rights. No Congressional declaration denies recovery, nor do special factors counsel hesitation.

AS AND FOR A ELEVENTH CAUSE OF ACTION AGAINST AN UNNAMED PHS EMPLOYEE, ON BEHALF OF PLAINTIFF JULIE SISSOKO

234. Plaintiffs JULIE SISSOKO reallege Paragraphs Numbered 1 through 77 of this Complaint as though again set forth in their entirety herein.

235. Pursuant to *Bivens v. Six Unknown Named Agents of Federal Bureau of Narcotics,* 403 U.S. 388 (1971), the Plaintiff, JULIE SISSOKO, asserts a claim that her civil rights were violated, as said rights are secured by the United States Constitution, in that as the direct and proximate result of the misfeasance, malfeasance and nonfeasance of each of the Defendants herein, her rights to consortium with her husband OUMAR SISSOKO have been lost, curtailed diminished and impaired.

236. At all times from and after August 21, 1997, Plaintiff, OUMAR SISSOKO and Plaintiff, JULIE SISSOKO were, husband and wife.

237. As alleged in Paragraphs 1 through 234, inclusive, which are incorporated herein by reference as though fully set forth, Defendants and each of them are liable in tort for the injuries and damages sustained by Plaintiff SISSOKO.

238. Prior to the injuries suffered by OUMAR SISSOKO as set forth hereinabove, he was able to and did perform his duties as spouse of Plaintiff JULIE SISSOKO. From and after the intentional, negligent, careless, reckless and unlawful conduct of Defendants, as each of them, complained of by Plaintiff, OUMAR SISSOKO hereinabove, and as a direct and proximate result of the injuries he sustained thereby, he has been unable to perform the work and services usually and customarily performed by him in the care, maintenance, and management of the family home, and his ability, facility and capability to provide the personal care, affection, conjugal fellowship, sexual relations, love, companionship, society and solace to Plaintiff, JULIE SISSOKO as her spouse has been lost, curtailed diminished and impaired all to Plaintiff, JULIE SISSOKO damage.

239. Plaintiff JULIE SISSOKO's is informed and believes and thereon alleges that as a direct and proximate result of the intentional, negligent, careless, reckless and unlawful conduct of Defendants, as each of them, complained of by Plaintiff, OUMAR SISSOKO hereinabove, and as a direct and proximate result of the injuries he sustained thereby, he will, for an indeterminate period in the future be unable to perform the work and services usually and customarily performed by him in

the care, maintenance, and management of the family home, and his ability, facility and capability to provide the personal care, affection, conjugal fellowship, sexual relations, love, companionship, society and solace to Plaintiff, JULIE SISSOKO as her spouse will remain lost, curtailed diminished and impaired all to Plaintiff, JULIE SISSOKO damage.

240. As a direct and proximate result of the aforesaid acts and omissions of Defendants, and each of them, Plaintiff, JULIE SISSOKO, seeks compensatory damages in the amount of Five Million Dollars ($5,000,000.00).

DEMAND FOR JURY TRIAL

Plaintiffs, OUMAR SISSOKO and JULIE SISSOKO hereby demand a jury trial with respect to all causes of action with respect to which Plaintiffs are entitled to a jury trial.

WHEREFORE, Plaintiffs pray judgment against Defendants, and each of them as follows:

AS TO PLAINTIFFS' FIRST CAUSE OF ACTION

1. As to OUMAR SISSOKO, the sum of $10,000,000.00 in general damages,
2. As to JULIE SISSOKO, the sum of $5,000.000.00 in general damages,
3. All actual, consequential, and incidental damages, including without limitation, general damages for emotional and mental distress in an amount to be proven at trial;

AS TO PLAINTIFFS' SECOND CAUSE OF ACTION

1. As to OUMAR SISSOKO, the sum of $10,000,000.00 in general damages,
2. As to JULIE SISSOKO, the sum of $5,000.000.00 in general damages,
3. All actual, consequential, and incidental damages, including without limitation, general damages for emotional and mental distress in an amount to be proven at trial;

AS TO PLAINTIFFS' THIRD CAUSE OF ACTION

1. As to OUMAR SISSOKO, the sum of $10,000,000.00 in general damages,
2. As to JULIE SISSOKO, the sum of $5,000.000.00 in general damages,
3. All actual, consequential, and incidental damages, including without limitation, general damages for emotional and mental distress in an amount to be proven at trial;

AS TO PLAINTIFFS' FOURTH CAUSE OF ACTION

1. As to OUMAR SISSOKO, the sum of $10,000,000.00 in general damages,
2. As to JULIE SISSOKO, the sum of $5,000.000.00 in general damages,
3. All actual, consequential, and incidental damages, including without limitation, general damages for emotional and mental distress in an amount to be proven at trial;

AS TO PLAINTIFFS' FIFTH CAUSE OF ACTION

1. As to OUMAR SISSOKO, the sum of $10,000,000.00 in general damages,
2. As to JULIE SISSOKO, the sum of $5,000.000.00 in general damages,
3. All actual, consequential, and incidental damages, including without limitation, general damages for emotional and mental distress in an amount to be proven at trial;

AS TO PLAINTIFFS' SIXTH CAUSE OF ACTION

1. As to OUMAR SISSOKO, the sum of $10,000,000.00 in general damages,
2. As to JULIE SISSOKO, the sum of $5,000.000.00 in general damages,
3. All actual, consequential, and incidental damages, including without limitation, general damages for emotional and mental distress in an amount to be proven at trial,
4. For exemplary and punitive damages in an amount to be determined at trial;

AS TO PLAINTIFFS' SEVENTH CAUSE OF ACTION

1. As to OUMAR SISSOKO, the sum of $10,000,000.00 in general damages,
2. As to JULIE SISSOKO, the sum of $5,000.000.00 in general damages,
3. All actual, consequential, and incidental damages, including without limitation, general damages for emotional and mental distress in an amount to be proven at trial,
4. For exemplary and punitive damages in an amount to be determined at trial;

AS TO PLAINTIFFS' EIGHT CAUSE OF ACTION

1. As to OUMAR SISSOKO, the sum of $10,000,000.00 in general damages,
2. As to JULIE SISSOKO, the sum of $5,000.000.00 in general damages,
3. All actual, consequential, and incidental damages, including without limitation, general damages for emotional and mental distress in an amount to be proven at trial,
4. For exemplary and punitive damages in an amount to be determined at trial;

AS TO PLAINTIFFS' NINTH CAUSE OF ACTION

1. As to OUMAR SISSOKO, the sum of $10,000,000.00 in general damages,
2. As to JULIE SISSOKO, the sum of $5,000.000.00 in general damages,
3. All actual, consequential, and incidental damages, including without limitation, general damages for emotional and mental distress in an amount to be proven at trial,
4. For exemplary and punitive damages in an amount to be determined at trial;

AS TO PLAINTIFFS' TENTH CAUSE OF ACTION

1. As to OUMAR SISSOKO, the sum of $10,000,000.00 in general damages,
2. As to JULIE SISSOKO, the sum of $5,000.000.00 in general damages,
3. All actual, consequential, and incidental damages, including without limitation, general damages for emotional and mental distress in an amount to be proven at trial,
4. For exemplary and punitive damages in an amount to be determined at trial;

AS TO PLAINTIFFS' ELEVENTH CAUSE OF ACTION

1. As to OUMAR SISSOKO, the sum of $10,000,000.00 in general damages,
2. As to JULIE SISSOKO, the sum of $5,000.000.00 in general damages,

3. All actual, consequential, and incidental damages, including without limitation, general damages for emotional and mental distress in an amount to be proven at trial,
4. For exemplary and punitive damages in an amount to be determined at trial;

AS TO ALL CAUSES OF ACTION

1. For attorneys' fees incurred in this action as permitted by applicable law;
2. For costs of suit herein incurred; and
3. For such other and further relief as the court in its discretion may deem just in the premises.

Dated: March 14, 2000

[Attorney]

[ADD CERTIFICATE OF SERVICE]

[Attorney]
[Firm]
[Address]
[Phone]
[Facsimile]

Attorneys For: OUMAR SISSOKO

UNITED STATES DISTRICT COURT
CENTRAL DISTRICT OF CALIFORNIA
WESTERN DIVISION

OUMAR SISSOKO, and individual and JULIE SISSOKO an individual, Plaintiffs, v. UNITED STATES, LOYDA R. ROCHA, etc., et al. Defendants	CASE NO. CV 98-7010-ABC(SHx) Consolidated with No. CV 99-8762-ABC(SHx) **REVISED MEMORANDUM OF POINTS AND AUTHORITIES IN SUPPORT OF MOTION FOR SUMMARY ADJUDICATION OF ISSUES RELATED TO THE LAWFULNESS OF PLACING PLAINTIFF, OUMAR SISSOKO, IN DETENTION ON AUGUST 26, 1997**

Date of Hearing .... April 1, 2002
Time .... 8:30 AM
Courtroom .... 550 Roybal

TABLE OF CONTENTS

TABLE OF AUTHORITIES

INTRODUCTION

Plaintiff is a native and citizen of Senegal who entered the United States on a visitor visa and remained in the United States after the expiration of that visa. Upon the expiration of his visa, his Immigration and Naturalization Service status was that of a "B-2 overstay" [*See* Exhibit "A" at page 4 Opinion and Order In Removal Proceedings].

Plaintiff contends and the INS does not dispute, that on January 14, 1991, Plaintiff applied for legalization under section 245A of the Immigration and Nationality Act, 8 U.S.C. § 1255a (1998 & Supp. III 1991) and was assigned alien file "A93 094 512" [*See* Exhibit "B" Memorandum from Office of District Director Los Angeles District to Carolyn Muzyka Acting Deputy Regional Director Western Region dated September 18, 1997, Page 1 Paragraph 2].

Although the period for filing amnesty applications ended on May 4, 1988 [*See* 8 C.F.R. § 245a.2(a)] Sissoko's late application was accepted for adjudication on the grounds that he was presumptively a member of a class of late filing applicants covered by the rulings and orders in *Catholic Social Services v. Thornburgh,* 956 F.2d 914 (9th Cir. 1992) and its progeny (the "CSS" cases).

Sissoko filed a separate application for legalization under Section 245A on May 5, 1992. After filing that application, the INS opened new file number "A93 262 083" in connection with his claim for benefits under the act. Because of his late filing, the INS was required to and did find Mr. Sissoko preliminarily satisfied the criteria established for CSS class membership and his designation as such was recorded as a "CS1" in the "Central Index System of the Immigration and Naturalization Service."[1]

On March 2, 1997, shortly after learning that his father had passed away in Senegal, he applied as a 245A legalization applicant under 8 C.F.R. § 245a.2(m)(1) (1991)[2] for "advance parole" to attend his father's funeral. The advance parole applied for was issued by the INS with an expiration date of April 2, 1997. The advance parole visa ("APV" Exhibit "C") a United States Department of Justice Form I-512 (Rev. 6-15-79) provided in part:

> Presentation of original of this document prior to 04/02/97 will authorize an Immigration Officer at a port of entry in the United States to permit the named bearer, whose photograph appears hereon, to enter the United States. {XX} as an alien paroled pursuant to Section 212(d)(5)[3] of the Immigration and Nationality Act. (Class 3).

In a separate section delimited by a block outline for emphasis, the APV provided:

> The above-captioned alien has established a prima facie case for eligibility under Section 245A of the Immigration and Nationality Act. Subject is to be paroled into the United States, provided no other excludabilities exist to indefinite. . . .

There is no use of the words or reference of any sort on the face of the APV to "Deportation", "Exclusion", "Removal" or "Expedited Removal" or any other consequences attendant the application for and issuance of the APV.

It is not disputed that Oumar Sissoko departed the United States in March of 1997 as a CSS class member having the status of a B-2 overstay with a pending application for Adjustment of Status under Section 245A [*See* Exhibit "A" at page 4 Opinion and Order In Removal Proceedings at Page 4].

---

[1] 70 *Interpreter Releases, No. 22*, June 7, 1993 at 744, the INS specifically explained that the status of an alien seeking admission as a CSS class member may be checked through its Central Indexing System ("CIS"), and "is indicated by the class of admission CS1" *See also* Exhibit "D" CIS printout on March 16, 1997 showing Sissoko to be a CS1 class member under his A93 262 083 file.

[2] 8 C.F.R. § 245a.2(m)(1) states: "During the period from the date that an alien's application establishing prima facie eligibility for temporary resident status is reviewed at a Service Legalization Office and the date status as a temporary resident is granted, the alien applicant can only be *readmitted* to the United States provided his or her departure was authorized under the Service's advance parole provisions contained in 212.5(e) of this chapter." [Emphasis added]

[3] Sec. 212 [8 U.S.C. 1182] (d)(5)(A): The Attorney General may, except as provided in subparagraph (B) or in section 214(f), in his discretion parole into the United States temporarily under such conditions as he may prescribe only on a case-by-case basis for urgent humanitarian reasons or significant public benefit any alien applying for admission to the United States, but such parole of such alien shall not be regarded as an admission of the alien and when the purposes of such parole shall, in the opinion of the Attorney General, have been served the alien shall forthwith return or be returned to the custody from which he was paroled and thereafter his case shall continue to be dealt with in the same manner as that of any other applicant for admission to the United States.

Following his father's funeral, Plaintiff flew back to the United States arriving at the United States Port of Entry at Washington D.C. on March 16, 1997. At that time he presented to INS inspectors his passport and APV. Aside from interrogating Mr. Sissoko, the INS officers queried the "CIS" Index ("Immigration Service Central Index") and obtained a printout of Oumar Sissoko's "immigration status" (Exhibit "D"). The printout showed that Mr. Sissoko had two "A" files and that his immigration status on file a 93 262 083 was listed as "CS1". Notwithstanding the status designation in the INS computer, Mr. Sissoko was deferred to Los Angeles for completion of inspection on March 31, 1997 on the grounds that he was a:

> "☒ Non-bona fide Nonimmigrant" (Exhibit E— Order to Appear at Deferred Inspection)
>
> because when questioned:
>
> ". . . Subject has no credible story of his purported arrival by ship, nor does he have any accurate account of subsequent 16+ years. Deferred for review of A-file & supporting doc's + exclusion if appropriate. Also subject appears to have 2 A files (CIS indexed)". (Exhibit E— Order to Appear at Deferred Inspection).

"At the port March 16, 1997 Sissoko attempted entry at WAS in possession of Form I-512; deferred to LOS to March 31, 1997." [*See* Exhibit B, Memorandum from Office of District Director Los Angeles District to Carolyn Muzyka Acting Deputy Regional Director Western Region, dated September 18, 1997, Page 1 Paragraph 5].

On March 31, 1997, Sissoko went to the deferred inspection office and reported to Defendant Immigration and Naturalization Service Inspector Loyda Rocha of the INS deferred inspection unit who was empowered by the United State Immigration and Naturalization Service to arrest persons for violation of federal laws.

At the time of his appearance before Inspector Rocha, on March 31, 1997, Mr. Sissoko was neither interviewed nor inspected but was "re-deferred to May 15, 1997 to determine legalization status" and "was released on his own recognizance". [*See* Exhibit B, Memorandum from Office of District Director Los Angeles District to Carolyn Muzyka, Acting Deputy Regional Director Western Region, dated September 18, 1997, Page 1 Paragraph 6].

On May 15, 1997, when Mr. Sissoko appeared at the INS deferred inspection unit in Los Angeles, INS Inspector Loyda Rocha prepared and signed a "Withdrawal of Application for Admission/Consular Notification" [Form I- 275, Exhibit F] on which she marked the box, "Ordered removed (inadmissible) by INS—Section 235(b)(1)[4] (order attached). At that time, she placed him in Expedited Removal Proceedings and took him into custody. She also took his "Work Authorization" which has never been returned to him.

In justification for this decision, Ms. Rocha, in the box provided on the form for "Reasons (Include pertinent facts concerning denial of application for admission, including use of altered, counterfeit or fraudulent document)," wrote that:

> A CALLED [SIC] WAS PLACED TO EAST L.A. LEGALIZATION TO CONFIRM THE SUBJECT [SIC] PENDING STATUS. ACCORDING TO LETI AT THE EAST L.A. LEGALIZATION UNIT THE SUBJECT HAD BEEN DENIED ON BOTH CASES. AFTER CONFIRMING THIS INFORMATION, THE SUBJECT WAS DETAINED PENDING REMOVAL FROM THE UNITED STATES . . .

In her deposition, Ms. Leti Leyva of East L.A. Legalization denied having such a conversation with Ms. Rocha and stated that it was her practice not to release such information even if it were true. [Deposition Transcript of Ms. Leti Leyva Page 105:20 – 107:4].

"Q. Okay.

"Without the file, was there any way of ascertaining whether or not the applicant was a C.S.-1 or a C.S.-2?"

"MR. BUCK: Objection; ambiguous."

---

[4] 8 C.F.R. § 235(b)(1) "[Inspection by immigration officers; expedited removal of inadmissible arriving aliens; referral for hearing] (b) Inspection of applicants for admission. (1) Inspection of aliens arriving in the United States and certain other aliens who have not been admitted or paroled. (A) Screening. (i) In general. If an immigration officer determines that an alien . . . who is arriving in the United States or is described in clause (iii) is inadmissible under section 212(a)(6)(C) or 212(a)(7) [8 USC § 1182(a)(6)(C) or 1182(a)(7)], the officer shall order the alien removed from the United States without further hearing or review unless the alien indicates either an intention to apply for asylum under section 208 [8 USC § 1158] or a fear of persecution. [Emphasis added]

"Q. You can answer."

"A. Let me say this: Revocations were done only with the file present. Revocations."

[Leticia Leyva Deposition, March 23, 2001, 84:1-9]

ON MAY 15, 1997, WHEN MR. SISSOKO WAS PLACED IN EXPEDITED REMOVAL AND TAKEN INTO CUSTODY UNTIL MAY 19, 1997, NEITHER OF HIS APPLICATIONS HAD BEEN DENIED AND HIS STATUS WAS STILL THAT OF A CSS CLASS MEMBER.

Ms. Rocha's handwritten notes to the file on May 15, 1997, the day she took Mr. Sissoko into custody, which notes have been identified as hers in the deposition of Michael A. Cochran [Deposition Transcript of Michael Alexander Cochran 59:3-59:7], [Exhibit G, Notes in INS File A93 262 083] state:

> 5/15/97 spoke to LETI at E.L.A. Legalization subject needs to be interview [SIC] for revocation of CS-1 status.

At the time of being taken into custody, Ms. Rocha took Mr. Sissoko's work permit issued pursuant to CSS court orders under his A93 262 083 file and retained it throughout the period relevant to this case [*See* Exhibit K—"August 26, 1997 . . . the I-688A (work authorization) is with officer Loyda Rocha (Deferred)"].

Mr. Sissoko's A93 262 083 file included an unsigned copy of a letter on May 15, 1997 addressed to Mr. Oumar Sissoko by the U.S. Department of Justice Immigration and Naturalization Service that stated in pertinent part:

> On March 16, 1997 you were paroled into the United States for a Deferred Inspection. You also obtained an Advance Parole Form I-512 on March 03, 1997. Such parole was pursuant to Section 212(d)(5) of the Immigration and Nationality Act of 1952, as amended.
>
> In accordance with Title 8, Code of Federal Regulations, Section 212.5(d)(2)(i), you are hereby informed that your parole is revoked. It is revoked concurrent with your placement into Expedited Removal proceedings.
>
> During the pendency of your removal you will be in the custody of this Service." [Exhibit H]

Mr. Sissoko's A93 262 083 file also included a Form entitled "Supervisory Checklist" [Exhibit I]. At the top of that form in the box identified as "Charges," a regulation citation appears as follows: "212(a)(5)(7)". The section provides in pertinent part:

8 C.F.R. § 212 [8 U.S.C. 1182] (a) Classes of Aliens Ineligible for Visas or Admission. Except as otherwise provided in this Act, aliens who are inadmissible under the following paragraphs are ineligible to receive visas and ineligible to be admitted to the United States:

> (5) Labor certification and qualifications for certain immigrants.
>
> (7) Documentation requirements.—
>
> (A) Immigrants.—
>
> (i) In general. Except as otherwise specifically provided in this Act, any immigrant at the time of application for admission—
>
> (I)Who is not in possession of a valid unexpired immigrant visa, reentry permit, border crossing identification card, or other valid entry document required by this Act, and a valid unexpired passport, or other suitable travel document, or document of identity and nationality if such document is required under the regulations issued by the Attorney General under section 211(a).

Mr. Sissoko was never charged under 8 C.F.R. § 212(a)(5)(6)(C) having to do with "Misrepresentation and fraud". This fact is relevant with respect to Mr. Sissoko's rights under the CSS cases.

On May 19, 1997, Mr. Sissoko was "released from custody pending status determination on second file (A93 262 083 512) had not been reviewed. Second file may contain an additional application. Deferred status continued." [Exhibit B, Memorandum from Office of District Director Los Angeles District to Carolyn Muzyka, Acting Deputy Regional Director Western Region, dated September 18, 1997, Page 1 Paragraph 8]

On June 30, 1997, the INS issued "Policy Concerning Pre-April 1, 1997 Parolees" [Exhibit J [*See also* 74 *Interpreter Releases* 1258, August 18, 1997] directed to Regional Directors, District Directors, Border Patrol Sector Chiefs, Officers in Charge (Including SPCs), Asylum Office Directors, Regional counsel and District Counsel, which provides in pertinent part:

> This memorandum provides instruction and guidance on a new policy concerning aliens who were paroled into the United States before April 1, 1997 under INA §. 212(d)(5). Under this new policy, such persons are not subject to the expedited removal process. As of the date of this memorandum, any pre-April 1, 1997 parolee whose parole is terminated, when appropriate, should be placed in regular Section 240, not expedited removal proceedings.
>
> . . . The new 8 CFR 1.1(q) will exclude from the arriving aliens definition, only for the purposes of expedited removal, aliens who were paroled before April 1, 1997.
>
> If a pre-April 1, 1997 parolee has been issued an expedited removal order and the order has not yet been executed, or the parolee was placed in expedited removal proceedings and has been determined not to have a credible fear of persecution, the parolee will have been issued a form I-860, Notice and Order of Expedited Removal. The INS District Office should cancel the Notice and Order and issue a form I-862, Notice to Appear placing the alien in proceedings under section 240 of the Act. An appropriate additional charge should be added to the Notice to Appear in such cases. . . .

On August 23, 1997, Mr. Sissoko married Julie Stormmen, a U.S. citizen. [*See* Exhibit B, Memorandum from Office of District Director Los Angeles District to Carolyn Muzyka, Acting Deputy Regional Director Western Region, dated September 18, 1997, Page 1 Paragraph 9].

On August 26, 1997, Mrs. Julie Sissoko, a U.S. citizen filed I-130, I-485 and I-765 marital petitions on behalf of her husband Oumar Sissoko. [Exhibit B, Memorandum from Office of District Director Los Angeles District to Carolyn Muzyka, Acting Deputy Regional Director Western Region, dated September 18, 1997, Page 1 Paragraph 8].

Also on August 26, 1997, Mr. Sissoko presented himself for a class membership revocation interview before Ms. Pacita Pabilla. Ms. Pabilla, according to her deposition testimony on February 13, 2002 [which will be supplied to the Court as soon as available, in the interim please see the declaration of Martin Simone filed herewith] interviewed Mr. Sissoko with respect to both of his "A Files". On the processing sheet, she prepared [Exhibit K] she notes in the top right corner both of Mr. Sissoko's "A File" numbers. However, in her testimony, she admitted that she only had one file and that she had never seen the other file.

Following his interview Mr. Sissoko was told by Ms. Pabilla that his eligibility for CSS class membership had been revoked, and he was given a Form I-72 filled in handwriting by Ms. Pabilla [Exhibit L, Form I-72], stating that he had failed to establish class membership and that he was not prima facie eligible under IRCA because he did not establish that he had been in the United Stated in an illegal status prior to January 1, 1982.

On August 26, 1997, the injunction in *Catholic Social Services, Inc. v. Richard Thornburgh* as implemented by the INS required with respect to CSS class member revocations that:

> . . . All legalization litigation cases in which service intent is to revoke status, must be processed according to the following instructions:
>
> "1. Two elements must still be present: Fraud and <u>some kind of aggravating circumstance</u>. The sting cases qualify for this."
>
> "2. Headquarters adjudications must still be contacted with the circumstances and for authorization. Contact M. Moglia or P. Chang at (202) 514-5014."
>
> "3. If applicable, a sworn statement should be taken."
>
> "4. A written notice of the reason for revocation must be given to the alien at the time the I-688A, Employment Authorization card, is lifted. A sample notice was sent to all offices under separate cover."

> "5. The I-688A is to be lifted, notice given and the alien given an opportunity to respond in 15 days with additional evidence as to why revocation should not become final."
>
> "6. Offices are to hold cases separately for 15 days from date of issuing notice to allow aliens to rebut the revocation notice"
>
> "7. If 15 days elapse with no rebuttal, the revocation is automatically permanent, the file marked according to previous instructions. . . ."[Exhibit M]

Although Mr. Sissoko was given the Notice in Exhibit L, he was never given notice of his right to rebut the determination as provided under the CSS rulings and his *revocation of status on August 26, 1997 was not final and would not become final for 15 days following August 26, 1997.*

On August 26, 1997, following his interview with Ms. Pabilla, Mr. Sissoko had a pre-arranged inspection with Ms. Loyda Rocha. Mr. Sissoko presented proof of his wife's marital petition having been filed.

Ms. Rocha nevertheless placed Mr. Sissoko in "Expedited Removal Proceedings" and took him into custody where he remained for 77 days until the INS withdrew their Expedited Removal Order," thereby allowing Mr. Sissoko to be placed in normal removal proceedings under Section 240 of the Act as set forth in the June 30, 1997 policy statement, [*see* Exhibit J], and he bonded out of custody.

Again, she filled out and signed a "Withdrawal of Application for Admission/Consular Notification [Exhibit N] indicating not only that Mr. Sissoko was ordered removed under Section 235(b)(1) [FN 4], but that "☒ Application for Admission Withdrawn". In addition, Ms. Rocha stated in the reasons section of the form the identical reasons for her determination in May, 1997, when she incarcerated Mr. Sissoko for the first time, even including that she had confirmed with "Leti" not "Ms. Pabilla" who had conducted the interview that he had been "denied on both cases". Ms. Rocha also stated "THE SUBJECT IS NOT MARRIED NOR HAS ANY CHILDREN", and "THE SUBJECT LEGALIZATION CASES HAVE BEEN DENIED".

Neither Leti nor Ms. Pabilla admits having provided any information about Mr. Sissoko's status to Ms. Rocha. Pursuant to the rulings in the CSS case as implemented by the INS the revocation of Mr. Sissoko's case would not become permanent for 15 days after he had received notice, including notice of his rights to rebut the revocation.

1. A PLAINTIFF MAY SEEK SUMMARY ADJUDICATION OF A CLAIM

A party seeking to recover upon a claim, counterclaim, or cross-claim or to obtain a declaratory judgment may, at any time after the expiration of 20 days from the commencement of the action or after service of a motion for summary judgment by the adverse party, move with or without supporting affidavits for a summary judgment in the party's favor upon all or any part thereof. [F.R.C.P. § 56(a)]. Plaintiff seeks an adjudication of his first, fourth, sixth, and seventh causes of action under his First Amended Consolidate Complaint with respect to the illegality of Plaintiff, Oumar Sissoko's detention.

2. ON MAY 15, 1997, NEITHER LOYDA ROCHA NOR THE INS HAD A FACTUAL OR LEGAL BASIS UPON WHICH TO DETAIN PLAINTIFF OR PLACE HIM IN EXPEDITED REMOVAL PROCEEDINGS

Notwithstanding Ms. Rocha's statement in Exhibit F, supplying the basis for her placing him in Expedited Removal and taking him into custody, that both of Mr. Sissoko's applications had been denied, all of the defendants knew the statement to be untrue and Ms. Rocha by her notes on Exhibit G acknowledge both Mr. Sissoko's unrevoked CS-1 status and that rulings in the CSS case (per LETI) demanded a failed interview by Mr. Sissoko before CS-1 status could be revoked:

> 5/15/97 spoke to LETI at E.L.A. Legalization subject needs to be interview [SIC] for revocation of CS-1 status. [*See* Exhibit G].

Absent any other excuse than was provided by Ms. Rocha on Exhibit F, there was no factual or legal basis for Mr. Sissoko being placed in Expedited Removal and incarcerated on May 15, 1997 for five days.

3. MR. SISSOKO WAS NOT AN "ARRIVING ALIEN" AND THEREFORE SHOULD NOT HAVE BEEN PLACED IN EXPEDITED REMOVAL PROCEEDINGS OR DETAINED

The Immigration and Naturalization Service rely for support of their having placed Mr. Sissoko in Expedited Removal Proceedings and incarcerating him on the following provisions of the Immigration and Nationality Act.

(a) Pursuant to § 235(a)(1) [8 U.S.C. 1255] of the Immigration and Nationality Act (INA), "*An alien . . . who arrives in the United States . . . shall be deemed for purposes of this Act an applicant for admission.*"

(b) Pursuant to § 235(b)(1)(A)(i) of INA [8 U.S.C. 1255], "*If an immigration officer determines that an alien . . .who is arriving in the United States . . .is inadmissable under § 212(a)(6)(C)(i) or 212(a)(A)(7)(i)(I), the officer shall order the alien removed from the U.S. without further hearing or review. . . .*"

(c) Pursuant to § 212 (a)(6)(C)(i), "*Any alien who, by fraud or wilfully misrepresenting a material fact, seeks to procure (or has sought to procure or has procured) a visa, other document or admission into the U.S. or other benefit provided under the Act is inadmissible*" and pursuant to § 212(a)(7)(A)(i)(I), "*. . . any immigrant at the time of application of admission who is not in possession of a valid unexpired immigrant visa, re-entry permit . . . or other valid entry document required by this Act . . . is excludable.*"

On August 26, 1997, Loyda Rocha, caused Mr. Sissoko to be placed in Expedited Removal Proceedings pursuant to § 235(b)(1)(A)(i) and §212(a)(7)(A)(i)(I). It should be noted here that the repeated contention on the part of Defendants has been that he was guilty of fraud and had made misrepresentations on his applications. However, in every document requiring a statement of charges against him the Service only cites that he was not in possession of the necessary documents § 212(a)(7)(A)(i)(I).

Pursuant to § 235(A)(1), when Mr. Sissoko presented himself to INS Inspectors at Washington D.C. on March 16, 1997, he, according to the INS, became an applicant for admission. At this time Mr. Sissoko was in possession of a valid and unexpired APV entitling him to "readmission".

On December 19, 2001, Joseph R. Greene, Acting Deputy Executive Associate Commissioner for Field Operations at the INS testified before the House Judiciary Committee's subcommittee on Immigration and Claims regarding INS detention and release policies. As reported in I*nterpreter Releases* Report and analysis of immigration and nationality law:

> Mr. Greene outlined the INS's current detention policies for the subcommittee. Those policies classify aliens according to four categories: *Category I—mandatory detention (primarily aliens subject to expedited removal under INA § 235* or mandatory detention under INA § 236(c)); Category II—high priority detention (aliens who have committed security and related crimes, other criminals not subject to mandatory detention, aliens deemed to be a danger to the community or a flight risk and alien smugglers); Category III—medium priority detention (inadmissible non-criminal aliens not in expedited removal proceedings, aliens who committed fraud or were smuggled into the U.S., and those apprehended at worksites); and *Category IV—lower priority detention (non-criminal aliens apprehended at the border, other aliens not subject to mandatory detention, and aliens placed in expedited removal who are referred for removal under INA §240).*" [Emphasis added—79 *Interpreter Releases* 34-35 (January 7, 2002)].

What is apparent from a reading of these policies is that the INS mandates that an alien, such as Sissoko, who has rightfully or wrongfully been placed in expedited removal proceedings under Section 235 of the Immigration and Nationality Act must be detained as was Mr. Sissoko; while an alien is not required to be placed in detention who has been placed in expedited removal proceedings under Section 240 of the Immigration and Nationality Act.

Further, there is *no* requirement at all that an alien in removal proceedings (Sissoko's situation upon his release from custody in November, 1997), rather than *expedited* removal under Section 240 of the INA be detained at all.

Section 212(a)(A)(7)(i)(I) only permits the placing into Expedited Removal Proceedings persons who are not in possession of a valid unexpired entry document at the time of application for admission, and since Mr. Sissoko was in possession of the APV on March 16, 1997, and further, for purposes of INA, he became an applicant for admission on March 16, 1997 [§235(A)(1)]). Furthermore, pursuant to the orders in the CSS case as set forth in Exhibit M, until 15 days after notice of revocation of his applications, on August 26, 1997, he was only presumptively no longer a member of the CSS class, pending his production of additional evidence to rebut the incipient revocation.

Ms. Rocha and the INS unlawfully placed Mr. Sissoko in Expedited Removal. Plaintiffs contend that had Mr. Sissoko been placed in Removal Proceedings, he would have been afforded the right to seek his release on bond, which we contend he would have promptly accomplished, thereby gaining his quick release from custody.

Moreover, had he not been placed in Expedited Removal Proceedings Ms. Rocha and the INS would have been required to assess whether, in their discretion, it would have been appropriate for them not to take Mr. Sissoko into custody pending Removal Proceedings. Factors which they would have been required to consider, pursuant to their own guidelines, including whether he had previously presented himself to the INS as instructed by them, (which he had), had substantial ties to the community, (which he had), was married to a U.S. Citizen, (which he was), and other factors relating to the likelihood that he would appear at matters scheduled in connection with the Removal Proceedings.

4. PURSUANT TO INS POLICY OF JUNE 30, 1997, MR. SISSOKO ONCE REVOCATION OF PERMANENT (IF ACCOMPLISHED) SHOULD HAVE BEEN PLACED IN REMOVAL PROCEEDINGS UNDER § 240 OF THE ACT

Pursuant to the Immigration and Naturalization Service's own policy, Mr. Sissoko should not have been placed in expedited removal proceedings.

In a memo from Brian Perryman, Executive Associate Commissioner, dated June 30, 1997, (Exhibit "9"), it is directed that aliens who were paroled into the United States before April 1, 1997 under INA § 212(d)(5) are not subject to Expedited Removal Proceedings. Said memo was addressed to Regional Directors, District Directors, Border Patrol Senior Chiefs, Officers in Charge (including SPCs), Asylum Office Directors, Regional Counsel and District Counsel.

The memo states that a ". . . decision has now been made to exempt from expedited removal proceedings aliens who were paroled into the United States before April 1, 1997." The memo further states that "The new 8 CFR 1.1(q) will exclude from the arriving aliens definition, only for expedited removal, aliens who were paroled before April 1, 1997." Despite this memo, Mr. Sissoko, who was paroled on March 16, 1997 pursuant to INA § 212(d)(5), was taken into custody on August 26, 1997 and placed into Expedited Removal Proceedings by Officer Rocha.

The new 8 CFR § 1.1(q) reads as follows:

> *(q) The term arriving alien means an applicant for admission coming or attempting to come into the United States at a port-of-entry, or an alien seeking transit through the United States at a port-of-entry, or an alien interdicted in international or United States waters and brought into the United States by any means, whether or not to a designated port-of-entry, and regardless of the means of transport. An arriving alien remains such even if paroled pursuant to section 212(d)(5) of the Act,* ***except that an alien who was paroled before April 1, 1997, or an alien who was granted advance parole which the alien applied for and obtained in the United States prior to the alien's departure from and return to the United States, shall not be considered an arriving alien for purposes of section 235(b)(1)(A)(I) of the Act.*** (Emphasis added)

Plaintiff contends that it was therefore unlawful for Mr. Sissoko to be placed in Expedited Removal Proceedings and detained by the INS. Rather, upon a finding 15 days after his interview with Ms. Padilla (presuming also that she had both "A" files to review) that he had not presented rebuttal evidence, an opportunity which he hand not been notified of or allowed to pursue because of this incarceration from August 26, 1997, he should have been placed in removal proceedings wherein he may also have had make the same contentions here with regard to the causal effects of the defendants' conduct as were made in connection with Argument 1.

5. READMISSION NOT ADMISSION

As an applicant for legalization under Section 245A of the Act, who left the U.S. for a brief, casual and innocent absence, after securing an Advance Parole Visa, Mr. Sissoko is not considered an arriving alien seeking admission and therefore was wrongfully placed in Expedited Removal Proceedings.

Pursuant to 8 C.F.R. § 245a.2(m)(1), "During the time period from the date that an alien's application establishing prima facie eligibility for temporary resident status is reviewed at a Service Legalization Office and the date status as a temporary resident is granted, the alien applicant can only be readmitted to the United States provided his or her departure was authorized under the under the Service's advance parole provisions contained in 212.5(e)." The term "readmitted" as used in the above cited regulation is a term of art used to convey what was originally Congressional Intent, and later INS intent. That "intent" was the intent to protect the original status of a traveler if that traveler complied with the requirements of applying for legalization, asking INS for permission to travel and then return within 30 days. Mr. Sissoko was not seeking admission to the United States; he was seeking to be "readmitted." Neither the Act, nor implementing regulation transmute his status upon his return to the United States on March 16, 1997 to that of a mere parolee/arriving alien [*See* Exhibit A]. As such, Mr. Sissoko should have been "readmitted" to the United States and should not have been placed in either "Expedited Removal Proceedings" or "Removal Proceedings".

This mandate is further expressed in 8 C.F.R. § 245a.2(1)(2) in which it is stated: "A brief, casual and innocent absence means a departure authorized by the Service (advance parole) subsequent to May 1, 1987 for not more than thirty (30) days for legitimate emergency or humanitarian purposes unless a further period of authorized departure has been granted in the discretion of the district director or a departure was beyond the alien's control."

Under section 245A(a)(3)(B) of the Act, ". . . An alien shall not be considered to have failed to maintained continuous physical presence in the United States for purposes of subparagraph (A) by virtue of brief, casual and innocent absences from the United States." In other words, a brief, innocent and casual departure is not considered a departure at all and as such, it was improper for the Service to place Mr. Sissoko in either Expedited Removal Proceedings or Removal Proceedings.

CONCLUSION

For all of the reasons set forth above, Plaintiff respectfully requests that the Court grant Plaintiffs' Motion herein for summary adjudication of Plaintiff's first, fourth, sixth and seventh causes of action under his First Amended Consolidated Complaint.

[Dated:]

[Attorney]

[ADD CERTIFICATE OF SERVICE]

[Attorneys]
[Firm]
[Address]
[Phone]
[Facsimile]

Attorneys for: OUMAR SISSOKO

UNITED STATES DISTRICT COURT
CENTRAL DISTRICT OF CALIFORNIA
WESTERN DIVISION

OUMAR SISSOKO, and individual and JULIE SISSOKO an individual, Plaintiffs, v. UNITED STATES, LOYDA R. ROCHA, etc., et al., Defendants.	CASE NO. CV 98-7010-ABC(SHx) Consolidated with No. CV 99-8762-ABC(SHx) **PLAINTIFFS' OPPOSITION TO DEFENDANTS' MOTION to Alter or Amend Judgment Re Claim 6**

TABLE OF CONTENTS

TABLE OF AUTHORITIES

Cases

Statutes

Other Authorities

Rules

Treatises

Regulations & INA

I. INTRODUCTION

This matter is before the Court on Defendant, Loyda Rocha's, "Motion to Alter or Amend Judgment Re Claim 6". Plaintiff Oumar Sissoko filed suit against the United States and Immigration and Naturalization Service ("INS") Senior Inspector, Loyda Rocha, for intentional torts and violation of his Fourth Amendment rights pursuant to the Federal Tort Claims Act, stemming from his arrest and detention by Immigration and Naturalization Service agents of which Defendant Rocha was one. In her Motion to Alter or Amend Judgment Re Claim 6, Ms. Rocha claims this Court lacks subject matter jurisdiction. The issue presented is whether Section 242(g) of the Immigration and Naturalization Act, as amended by the Illegal Immigration Reform and Immigrant Responsibility Act of 1996, Pub. L. No. 104-208, 110 Stat. 3009 (codified as 8 U.S.C. § 1252(g)), deprives the Court of jurisdiction over Plaintiff Sissoko's action against the Immigration and Naturalization Service under the Federal Tort Claims Act and against Loyda Rocha under the rule in *Bivens v. Six Unknown Named Agents of Federal Bureau of Narcotics,* 403 U.S. 388, 91 S.Ct. 1999, 29 L.Ed.2d 619 (1971). For the reasons stated below, the Court should hold that Section 1252(g) does not divest the Court of jurisdiction over Plaintiff's claims. And for those same reasons Plaintiffs' urge this Court to deny Defendant's Motion to Alter or Amend Judgment Re Claim 6.

II. BACKGROUND

In lieu of setting out again the detailed factual setting in this case, Plaintiffs adopt the Court's recital of background facts as they appear in the Court's "Order Re: Cross-Motions for Summary Judgment". Plaintiffs wish to emphasis that those facts amply satisfy the conclusion by this court that "Defendant Rocha's proffered reasons for arresting Plaintiff are unsupportable; no reasonable INS officer would have detained Mr. Sissoko on those grounds" [*See* Order Re: Cross-Motions for Summary Judgment 20:12-14] and that Ms. Rocha is not entitled to qualified immunity from *Bivens*, *id.* liability under the criteria enunciated in *Ramirez v. U.S.* (2000), 81 F. Supp. 2d. 53 and other cases. Nevertheless, Defendant Rocha, contrary to the permitted basis for reconsideration by this Court, and without offering a new or unexposed statutory, regulatory or evidentiary justification persists in her argument that she was entitled to detain Mr. Sissoko on August 26, 1997.

Plaintiff was detained and placed in "expedited removal proceedings" by Defendant Rocha on the patently false grounds that Plaintiff was, on August 26, 1997, an undocumented [8 C.F.R. § 212(a)(5)(7)(A)(i)(I)] arriving alien [8 C.F.R. § 235(b)(1)]. In fact Plaintiff, Oumar Sissoko, on that date remained a class action plaintiff in *Catholic Social Services v. Thornburgh*, 956 F.2d 914 (9th Cir. 1992), with a pending application for legalization under 8 U.S.C. § 1255a (Section 245a of the INA) and was the beneficiary of a filed marital petition under Section 201(b) of the Act. In addition, on that same date, Mr. Sissoko, was not to be considered an arriving alien for purposes of section 235(b)(1)(A)(I) of the Act[1], and was not to be placed in expedited removal proceedings pursuant to that certain INS order effective June 30, 1997.[2]

Plaintiff's expedited removal proceedings were terminated on December 5, 2000 by order of Immigration Judge Ira Banks [*See* Exhibit 1 to Plaintiffs' Motion for Summary Adjudication].

---

[1] 8 C.F.R. 1.1 § (q): "(q) The term arriving alien means an applicant for admission coming or attempting to come into the United States at a port-of-entry, or an alien seeking transit through the United States at a port-of-entry, or an alien interdicted in international or United States waters and brought into the United States by any means, whether or not to a designated port-of-entry, and regardless of the means of transport. An arriving alien remains such even if paroled pursuant to section 212(d)(5) of the Act, *except that an <u>alien who was paroled before April 1, 1997</u>, or an alien who was granted advance parole which the alien applied for and obtained in the United States prior to the alien's departure from and return to the United States, <u>shall not be considered an arriving alien for purposes of section 235(b)(1)(A)(I) of the Act</u>*" (Emphasis added).

[2] Memorandum of INS dated June 30, 1997 [Exhibit J to Plaintiffs' Motion for Summary Adjudication]. "This memorandum provides instruction and guidance on a new policy <u>concerning aliens who were paroled into the United States before April 1, 1997 under INA §. 212(d)(5).</u> *Under this new policy, such persons <u>are not subject to the expedited removal process</u>.* As of the date of this memorandum, any pre-April 1, 1997 parolee whose parole is terminated, when appropriate, *should be placed in regular Section 240, <u>not expedited removal proceedings</u>.*

> "...The new 8 CFR 1.1(q) will exclude from the arriving aliens definition, only for the purposes of expedited removal, aliens who were paroled before April 1, 1997."

[Emphasis Added—Exhibit J to Plaintiffs' Motion for Summary Adjudication]

Plaintiff filed an administrative claim under the Federal Tort Claims Act with the INS. After Plaintiff's administrative claim was denied, he filed the present Complaint, alleging amongst other causes of action, assault and battery, false arrest, false imprisonment, intentional or negligent infliction of emotional distress, and the *Bivens* claims against Defendant Loyda Rocha discussed herein.

III. STANDARD OF REVIEW

Pursuant to Federal Rule of Civil Procedure 12(b)(1), a claim may be dismissed for lack of subject matter jurisdiction. Where subject matter jurisdiction is challenged, the burden of proving such is on the plaintiff. *See Richmond, Fredericksburg & Potomac R. Co. v. United States*, 945 F.2d 765, 768 (4th Cir.1991). The court may look beyond the jurisdictional allegations of the complaint and consider whatever evidence has been submitted on the issue to determine whether subject matter jurisdiction exists. *See Evans v. B.F. Perkins Co.*, 166 F.3d 642, 647 (4th Cir.1999).

IV. THE FEDERAL TORT CLAIMS ACT AND SUBJECT MATTER JURISDICTION

Absent a waiver, sovereign immunity shields the federal government and its agencies from suit. *See FDIC v. Meyer*, 510 U.S. 471, 475, 114 S.Ct. 996, 127 L.Ed.2d 308 (1994). In 1946, Congress passed the Federal Tort Claims Act ("FTCA"), which waived the sovereign immunity of the United States for certain torts committed by federal employees. See 28 U.S.C.A. §§ 1346(b) (West Supp.1999); *id.* §§ 2671-2680 (West 1994). Specifically, Section 1346(b) provides that the United States government can be sued for the negligent or wrongful act or omission of any employee of the Government while acting within the scope of his office or employment, under circumstances where the United States, if a private person, would be liable to the claimant in accordance with the law of the place where the act or omission occurred.

Congress excepted from the waiver of sovereign immunity any claims arising out of an intentional tort, including assault, battery, false imprisonment, and false arrest. *See* 28 U.S.C.A. § 2680(h); *see also Thigpen v. United States*, 800 F.2d 393, 394 (4th Cir.1986). The FTCA also bars claims which depend on the assault and battery by a government employee. *See Thigpen*, 800 F.2d at 395. However, Congress also limited this exception by exempting investigative and law enforcement officials who commit an intentional tort. *See* 28 U.S.C.A. § 2680(h). Thus, this section of the FTCA serves as an exception to the exception. The federal government waives sovereign immunity for the acts of investigative and law enforcement officials who commit an intentional tort against an individual.[3]

INS agents constitute investigative and law enforcement officers for purposes of the FTCA. *See Caban v. United States*, 671 F.2d 1230, 1234 n. 4 (2d Cir.1982) (holding that the alleged actions of the INS in detaining the plaintiff were not protected by the discretionary function exception of the FTCA); *Ramirez v. United States,* 998 F. Supp. 425, 433 (D.N.J.1998) (holding that the United States was not immune from an FTCA claim which alleged wrongful conduct by INS agents who were law enforcement officers). Pursuant to 8 U.S.C. §§ 1225(a) and 1357, INS agents are federal officers who have the power to search, seize, and arrest. *See* 8 U.S.C.A. §§ 1225(a), and 1357 (West 1999). The FTCA waives sovereign immunity for liability of certain intentional torts committed by INS agents. In this case Defendant Rocha seized and arrested Mr. Sissoko following his interview with legalization officer Pacita Pabilla and committed intentional torts against him. Thus, the FTCA waives the government's sovereign immunity as it relates to the agents' seizure and arrest of Mr. Sissoko.

In its Motion to Alter or Amend Judgment Re Claim 6, Defendant Rocha contends that the 1996 amendment to the Immigration and Naturalization Act repealed an individual's right to bring a civil action for intentional torts under the FTCA against INS agents. Therefore, the issue before the Court is whether its jurisdiction to hear Mr. Sissoko's claims was subsequently repealed by the Immigration and Naturalization Act, as amended by the Illegal Immigration Reform and Immigrant Responsibility Act of 1996.

[3] While the FTCA waives the government's sovereign immunity for intentional torts committed by federal employees, it does not waive sovereign immunity for constitutional torts that may be committed. *See* 28 U.S.C.A. § 2679(b)(1)-(2). In this case Plaintiffs must rely on the holding in *Bivens v. Six Unknown Agents of Federal Bureau of Narcotics,* 403 U.S. 388, 395-97, 91 S.Ct. 1999, 29 L.Ed.2d 619 (1971) to support their claims against Defendant Rocha.

V. JURISDICTIONAL LIMITATIONS AND THE ILLEGAL IMMIGRATION REFORM AND IMMIGRANTRESPONSIBILITY ACT OF 1996

Judicial review of immigration decisions to admit or exclude aliens is generally governed by the Immigration and Naturalization Act ("INA"). In 1996, the INA was amended by two statutes: the Antiterrorism and Effective Death Penalty Act ("AEDPA"), Pub. L. 104-132, 110 Stat. 1214 (April 24, 1996), and the Illegal Immigration Reform and Immigrant Responsibility Act ("IIRIRA"), Pub. L. No. 104-208, 110 Stat. 3009 (September 30, 1996). Both of these statutes significantly restricted the availability of judicial review of immigration decisions to admit or exclude aliens under the INA.[4] However, the IIRIRA went further than the AEDPA and restructured the scope of judicial review of immigration decisions.[5] As related to this motion, Section 242(g) of the INA, as amended under the IIRIRA, and codified as 8 U.S.C. § 1252(g) (hereinafter "§ 1252(g)"), is entitled "Exclusive Jurisdiction" and provides:

> Except as provided in this section and notwithstanding any other provision of law, no court shall have jurisdiction to hear any cause or claim by or on behalf of any alien arising from the decision or action by the Attorney General to commence proceedings, adjudicate cases, or execute removal orders against any alien under this chapter.

8 U.S.C.A. § 1252(g) (West 1999). The parties dispute whether § 1252(g) divests the Court of subject matter jurisdiction to hear Plaintiff's FTCA claims against the INS.

Relying on segments of the statute, Defendant Rocha contends that this action is barred by § 1252(g) of the IIRIRA. Defendant specifically relies on the portion which states "notwithstanding any other provision of law" no court shall have jurisdiction to hear any claim arising out of the decision of the Attorney General to "commence proceedings, adjudicate cases, or execute removal orders against any alien under this Act." *Id.* § 1252(g). Defendant submits that this section grants the INS exclusive jurisdiction over certain removal actions taken by the Attorney General. *See* 8 U.S.C.A. § 1252(g); *see also Reno v. American-Arab Anti-Discrimination Committee*, 525 U.S. 471, 119 S.Ct. 936, 142 L.Ed.2d 940 (1999) [hereinafter "*AADC*"]; *Stewart v. USINS*, 181 F.3d 587 (4th Cir.1999); *Humphries v. Various Federal USINS Employees*, 164 F.3d 936 (5th Cir.1999). Defendant contends that Congress explicitly withdrew any basis for jurisdiction, under the FTCA or any other provision of law, for a court to evaluate Plaintiff's specified claims.

Defendant Rocha submits that Plaintiff's Complaint is premised upon his claim that INS wrongfully initiated removal proceedings against him. Following Defendant's argument, if Plaintiff was assaulted by INS agents executing an INS warrant, then he has no right to access the courts under the FTCA because there is a clear causal link between the Attorney General's decision and the INS's actions in taking Plaintiff into custody. *See Humphries*, 164 F.3d at 943 (dismissing an alien's claim that he was excluded in retaliation for exercise of his First Amendment rights because the Attorney General's decision to place the plaintiff in exclusion fell under § 1252(g)). In essence, Defendant, Rocha alleges that Congress silently repealed the FTCA for intentional tort claims against the government for acts of INS agents.

In opposition, Plaintiff Sissoko argues that Congress did not intend to affect or revoke that jurisdiction of the federal courts to adjudicate FTCA actions in the aforementioned statutory amendment, but only to restructure the scope of judicial review of immigration decisions and to streamline the judicial process in removal decisions. Despite Defendant Rocha's reliance on the *AADC* case, Plaintiffs' contend that *AADC*'s holding is inapplicable to the present case involving an FTCA claim for money damages. Plaintiffs submit that in *AADC* the justices construed § 1252(g)'s jurisdictional limitations within the limited context of avoiding the "deconstruction, fragmentation, and hence prolongation of removal proceedings." *Ibid.* 525 U.S. at 486-87, 119 S.Ct. 936. Plaintiffs argue that where Congress intends to preclude judicial review of constitutional claims its intent to do so must be clear. *See Webster v. Doe*, 486 U.S. 592, 603, 108 S.Ct. 2047, 100 L.Ed.2d 632 (1988). Furthermore, Plaintiffs submit that since there is no ongoing deportation proceeding and since Plaintiff Oumar

---

[4] The AEDPA began the process of streamlining the procedures to expedite judicial review of immigration decisions. It eliminated the judicial review process of deportation and exclusion orders for noncitizens convicted of "aggravated felonies" and eliminated the INA's statutory basis for habeas corpus relief. INA § 106(a)(10)(amending 8 U.S.C. § 1105a(a)(10)(1970)). Prior to the amendment, Section 1105a(a)(10) provided that "[A]ny alien held in custody pursuant to an order of deportation may obtain judicial review thereof by habeas corpus proceedings."8 U.S.C. § 1105a(a)(10)(repealed 1996).

[5] The IIRIRA largely eliminated the distinction between exclusion and deportation proceedings from the past, replacing it with a single removal proceeding. It continued the distinction for the "criminal aliens." However, IIRIRA § 306 repealed INA § 106 in its entirety and replaced it with revised INA § 242, codified at 8 U.S.C. § 1252.

Sissoko has successfully avoided entry of a removal order, the FTCA is Plaintiff's only avenue to vindicate his rights. Plaintiff, Oumar Sissoko, does not seek to review or modify the INS decision in his immigration matter; rather Plaintiffs seek monetary damages for alleged violation of his constitutional rights and for civil wrongs.

The United States Supreme Court has held that "where Congress intends to preclude judicial review of constitutional claims its intent to do so must be clear." *Webster v. Doe,* 486 U.S. 592, 603, 108 S.Ct. 2047, 100 L.Ed.2d 632 (1988) (citing *Johnson v. Robison,* 415 U.S. 361, 373-74, 94 S.Ct. 1160, 39 L.Ed.2d 389 (1974)). In *Johnson,* the Court stated that it required "'clear and convincing' evidence of congressional intent . . . before a statute will be construed to restrict access to judicial review." 415 U.S. at 373-74, 94 S.Ct. 1160. The Court noted that it requires this "heightened showing in part to avoid the 'serious constitutional question' that would arise if a federal statute were construed to deny any judicial forum for a colorable constitutional claim." *See Webster*, 486 U.S. at 603, 108 S.Ct. 2047 (citing *Bowen v. Michigan Academy of Family Physicians*, 476 U.S. 667, 106 S.Ct. 2133, 90 L.Ed.2d 623 (1986)).

In general, repeals of statutes by implication are particularly disfavored. *See Traynor v. Turnage*, 485 U.S. 535, 548, 108 S.Ct. 1372, 99 L.Ed.2d 618 (1988); *Bowrin v. USINS*, 194 F.3d 483, 489 (4th Cir.1999). In fact, under principles of statutory construction, the courts must apply a presumption against the implied repeal of prior law.[6] *See Patten v. United States*, 116 F.3d 1029, 1034 (4th Cir.1997); *Ely v. Velde*, 451 F.2d 1130, 1134 (4th Cir.1971). However, the presumption against repeal by implication can be overcome by showing that there was clear legislative intent. *See Patten*, 116 F.3d at 1034. Congressional intent can be shown when: (1) the two acts are in irreconcilable conflict; or (2) the later act covers the whole subject of the earlier one and is clearly intended as a substitute. *See id.* (citing *United States v. Mitchell*, 39 F.3d 465, 472 (4th Cir.1994)).

In this case, IIRIRA does not explicitly divest the district court of jurisdiction to hear Mr. Sissoko's FTCA claims. Furthermore, Defendant Rocha fails to overcome the presumption against implied repeal. In order to effect a repeal, Congress should have stated that it intended to repeal the FTCA as it related to aliens. As it stands, the statute as well as the legislative history is devoid of such a statement that repeals subject matter jurisdiction for FTCA claims. *See* Report of the Committee on the Judiciary, House of Representatives on H.R. 2202, Rept. 104-469 (1996). Furthermore, the IIRIRA and the FTCA are not in conflict. Mr. Sissoko's claims do not serve to challenge his removal, but serve to assert his rights for civil torts and to compensate him for alleged violation of his liberty and constitutional rights.

This is not the first time that the United States has advanced an expansive view of the effect of the AEDPA and the IIRIRA in a matter touching upon the right of aliens' access to our courts. The United States in its opposition to Plaintiffs' Petition for Habeas Corpus, filed in September, 1997, proposed this same jurisdictional limitation on the district court. In an analogous context, the district court's exercise of habeas corpus jurisdiction has been challenged under the INA, as amended by the AEDPA and IIRIRA. Section 2241 of Title 28 of the United States Code provides the statutory authority for the writ of habeas corpus. Specifically, the statute authorizes the court to grant writs of habeas corpus for persons "in custody under or by color of the authority of the United States." 28 U.S.C.A. § 2241(c)(1), (3) (West 1994). Neither the IIRIRA nor the AEDPA expressly amended § 2241. Yet, at times, the United States has asserted that the great writ of habeas corpus was repealed by these amendments.

The Supreme Court has held that habeas corpus jurisdiction cannot be amended or repealed absent express language. *See Felker v. Turpin*, 518 U.S. 651, 661, 116 S.Ct. 2333, 135 L.Ed.2d 827 (1996)(holding that under the "clear statement" rule, § 2241 jurisdiction cannot be repealed by implication); *see also Bowrin*, 194 F.3d at 489 (holding that neither the language of either the AEDPA nor the IIRIRA eliminated general habeas corpus review under § 2241 where there was no specific reference to the statute). While the AEDPA eliminated the writ of habeas corpus as stated in the INA, the AEDPA did not eliminate the writ of habeas corpus pursuant to 28 U.S.C. § 2241[7]. *See Henderson v. INS*, 157 F.3d 106, 117-122 (2d Cir.1998)(holding that the federal courts have jurisdiction under § 2241 to grant writs of habeas corpus to aliens when they are in custody in violation of the Constitution or law of the United States); *Goncalves v. Reno*, 144 F.3d 110, 122 (1st Cir.1998) (stating that the court's refusal to find express repeal of § 2241 in INA § 242(g) eliminates the need to address serious and complex constitutional issues); *Salazar-Haro v. INS*, 95 F.3d 309, 311 (3rd Cir.1996) ("To the extent, therefore, that constitutional rights applicable to aliens may be at stake, judicial review may not be withdrawn by statute."); *Williams v. INS*, 114 F.3d 82, 84 (5th Cir.1997) (while acknowledging that the AEDPA precluded judicial review of a final deportation order, stating that a limited opportunity to apply for a

[6] *See also* Norman J. Singer, *Sutherland Statutory Construction* § 23.10 (5th ed.)
[7] *See* discussion *supra* note 4.

writ of habeas corpus may remain); *Mansour v. INS*, 123 F.3d 423, 426 (6th Cir.1997) (finding that AEDPA's limits on review were constitutional because of the continued availability of habeas review). But *see Yang v. INS*, 109 F.3d 1185, 1195-96 (7th Cir.1997) (stating that IIRIRA as codified in § 1252(g) abolishes review under 28 U.S.C. § 2241)

Similarly, in this case, Mr. Sissoko asserts his claims pursuant to a statutory basis that is separate and distinct from the INA. Mr. Sissoko brings his suit for monetary damages under provisions of the FTCA, 28 U.S.C. § 2671, *et seq*., and 28 U.S.C. § 1346(b)(1). Nothing in the INA expressly amends or repeals the FTCA. If the IIRIRA and AEDPA cannot implicitly repeal or amend the separate statutory basis for habeas relief, then the IIRIRA cannot eliminate Mr. Sissoko's claims under the FTCA pursuant to 28 U.S.C. § 1346(b).

Only the Fifth Circuit has addressed the application of § 1252(g) in a similar context. *See Humphries v. Various Federal USINS Employees*, 164 F.3d 936 (5th Cir.1999). In that case, an alien brought civil rights and contract claims against various INS agents for monetary damages. The court stated the section's jurisdictional limitations may apply to certain monetary damage claims, but only with respect to such claims that clearly are connected directly and immediately with a decision or action by the Attorney General to commence proceedings, adjudicate cases, or execute removal orders. *See id.* at 943. The court reinstated the plaintiff's claims for involuntary servitude and mistreatment, holding that these claims did not arise from the decision of the Attorney General to commence proceedings, adjudicate cases, or execute removal orders. *See id.* at 944. The court found that § 1252(g) applied to prevent the court from hearing the plaintiff's *Bivens* claims. *See id.* at 945. However, the Court in *Medina v. United States*, 92 F. Supp. 2d 545, 554 (2000) disagreed with the majority's decision in Humphries because there is nothing in § 1252(g) which indicates that it was intended to foreclose monetary damages based on violations of federally protected rights. *See id.* at 947-951 (Dennis, J., concurring in part and dissenting in part)(stating that there was an insufficient basis for believing that Congress intended to divest the district courts of their jurisdiction under the federal question jurisdictional statute).

Defendant Rocha relied heavily on *AADC*, a Supreme Court case addressing the exclusive jurisdiction clause of the IIRIRA. 525 U.S. 471, 119 S.Ct. 936, 142 L.Ed.2d 940 (1999). In that case, a group of resident aliens filed suit claiming that they had been targeted for deportation because of their affiliation with a politically unpopular group in violation of their First Amendment rights. *See id.* at 472-73, 119 S.Ct. 936. The federal courts enjoined the INS from proceeding with the deportation hearings. *See id.* at 475, 119 S.Ct. 936. The Supreme Court held that the exclusive jurisdiction clause of the IIRIRA deprived the courts of jurisdiction over the action to enjoin INS decisions to exclude aliens. *See id.* at 478, 119 S.Ct. 936.

However, this Court should find that *AADC* is inapplicable to the present case as it involved a different set of facts and legal principles. In that case, the aliens were waging a collateral attack to enjoin INS action in a pending deportation proceedings against them. Thus, the Supreme Court focused primarily on the propriety of collateral claims for injunctive and declaratory relief of the INS decision to exclude them from the country. In Mr. Sissoko's case, he is not seeking a collateral attack of ongoing immigration proceeding. His claim is for monetary damages for alleged violations of his rights and was brought after the Immigration Judge terminated the proceedings against him.

The distinction between prohibiting judicial intervention in a pending immigration proceeding and permitting a tort claim after the termination of a proceeding is consistent with the rationale articulated by the Supreme Court. Although the Court issued four separate opinions, each states that the purpose of § 1252 was to streamline the judicial review of deportation issues in pending proceedings.[8] Writing for the majority, Justice Scalia noted that the IIRIRA was specifically directed at protecting the Executive's discretion from the courts and "the deconstruction, fragmentation, and hence prolongation of removal proceedings." 525 U.S. at 486-87, 119 S.Ct. 936. Justice Ginsberg stated that "Congress has established an integrated scheme for deportation proceedings, channeling judicial review to the final order, and deferring issues outside of the agency's authority until that point. Given Congress' strong interest in avoiding delay of deportation proceedings . . . I find the opportunity to raise a claim during the judicial review phase sufficient." *Id.* at 495, 119 S.Ct. 936 (Ginsberg, J., concurring). Justice Stevens wrote that "the meaning of 8 U.S.C. §§ 1252(b)(9) and (g)(1994 ed., Supp. III) is perfectly clear. The former postpones judicial review of removal proceedings until the entry of a final order and the latter deprives federal courts of jurisdiction over collateral challenges to ongoing administrative proceedings." *Id.* at 499, 119 S.Ct. 936 (Stevens, J., concurring) (footnotes omitted). Even in his dissent, Justice Souter explained that "The intent of this provision was presumably to preclude judicial review of nonfinal steps

[8] The majority opinion was issued by Justice Scalia, with two concurring opinions from Justice Ginsberg, who was joined by Justice Breyer as to Part I, and Justice Stevens. Justice Souter wrote a dissent.

in the removal procedure in the interim before IIRIRA's effective date of April 1, 1997." *Id.* at 504 n. 1, 119 S.Ct. 936 (Souter, J., dissenting).

The Supreme Court's analysis is consistent with Congress' intent. The Supreme Court noted that "Section 1252(g) was directed against a particular evil: attempts to impose judicial constraint upon prosecutorial discretion." *See AADC*, 525 U.S. at 485 n. 9, 119 S.Ct. 936. IIRIRA sought to "enable the prompt admission of those who are entitled to be admitted, the prompt exclusion or removal of those who are not so entitled, and [make] the clear distinction between these categories." Report of the Committee on the Judiciary, House of Representatives on H.R. 2202, Rept. 104-469, at 111 (1996). Limiting judicial review of pending immigration proceedings promotes the Executive's prompt decisions. Specifically, § 1252(g) furthers these goals by removing from judicial review claims arising from the Attorney General's commencement or prosecution of removal proceedings and execution of removal until the order has become final. *See Humphries*, 164 F.3d. at 950-51 (Dennis, J., dissenting).

Plaintiffs urge this Court not to apply an expansive reading of § 1252(g). In *AADC*, the Supreme Court interpreted § 1252(g) to mean that it does not preclude judicial review of all "decisions or actions that may be part of the deportation process." 525 U.S. at 482, 119 S.Ct. 936. The Court rejected the concept of the section applying to "the universe of deportation claims." *Id.* Instead, the Court reiterated that this provision applies to a narrow set of circumstance: three discrete actions taken by the Attorney General, commencing proceedings, adjudicating cases, or executing removal orders. *See id.* The Court went on to say that "[i]t is implausible that the mention of three discrete events along the road to deportation was a shorthand way of referring to all claims arising from deportation proceedings." *Id.*

Based on preceding discussion, it is patently clear that § 1252 does not reach Plaintiffs' right to bring a claim for money damages for intentional torts and violations of constitutional rights against the United States under the FTCA in this case where the immigration proceedings have terminated. The removal proceedings were completed on December 5, 1997—long before Mr. Sissoko instituted the present suit. However, as there was no final order of removal, Mr. Sissoko has nothing to challenge on appeal. His only recourse to bring his claim for injuries resulting from intentional torts and constitutional violations of his rights is to challenge the action pursuant to the FTCA and *Bivens* and pursue a claim for monetary relief.

VI. JURISDICTIONAL LIMITATIONS ON CLAIMS FOR VIOLATION OF CONSTITUTIONAL RIGHTS

If the Court were to adopt the Defendant Rocha's broad reading of § 1252, there would be no judicial review of a claim by an alien that stems from an arrest on an INS detention order even where there is blatantly lawless and unconstitutional conduct by the INS agents—placing their conduct beyond judicial review and creating grave constitutional issues.[9] As long as there is no removal, there is no review. Under this expansive reading, it is questionable whether the Court would be able to hear *Bivens* actions against the individual agents for constitutional violations. *See Bivens v. Six Unknown Named Agents of Federal Bureau of Narcotics*, 403 U.S. 388, 91 S.Ct. 1999, 29 L.Ed.2d 619 (1971). According to the Fifth Circuit, the court could not. *See Humphries*, 164 F.3d at 945.

In *Humphries*, the Fifth Circuit held that the district court lacked jurisdiction to hear the plaintiff's *Bivens* claim for retaliatory exclusion in violation of the First Amendment. *See id.*[10] However, *Bivens* expressly intended to provide a cause of action against federal officers, acting under the color of federal authority, for money damages resulting from constitutional violations. 403 U.S. at 395-97, 91 S.Ct. 1999. "[W]here federally protected rights have been invaded, it has been the rule from the beginning that courts will be alert to adjust their remedies so as to grant the necessary relief." *Id.* at 392, 91 S.Ct. 1999 [quoting *Bell v. Hood,* 327 U.S. 678, 684, 66 S.Ct. 773, 90 L.Ed. 939 (1946)]. As noted by the Court in *Medina v. United States* 92 F.Supp.2d 545, 554 (2000) disapproving of *Humphries*:

> "Clearly, § 1252(g) does not indicate that Congress intended to divest the court of jurisdiction over *Bivens* actions arising out of the unconstitutional conduct of federal officers. The court should not

---

[9] There is no reason to conclude that acts of INS agents are entitled to this protection, which is not afforded to those of a president, congressman, or other federal officers.

[10] The Fifth Circuit rationalized its decision by stating that an alien attempting to raise a *Bivens* claim may proceed through a petition for review or for habeas corpus. *See Humphries*, 164 F.3d at 945. However, the court recognized that if these avenues of relief were unavailable, it might find itself confronted with the precise "serious constitutional question" which would arise if a federal statute were construed to deny any judicial forum for a colorable constitutional claim. *See id.* at 945 n. 9 (citing *Webster*, 486 U.S. at 603, 108 S.Ct. 2047).

have inferred Congress' intention. For this reason, this Court is not persuaded by the United States' reliance on *Humphries*".

As expressed in Plaintiffs' Motion for Summary Adjudication, and Opposition to Defendants' Motion for Summary Judgment, Defendant Rocha's detention of Oumar Sissoko was entirely based on facts she fabricated to make it appear that that the detention of Mr. Sissoko was justifiable under INS Regulations. Without the fabricated justification, INS Inspector Rocha's arrest and detention of Mr. Sissoko constituted an unlawful and unreasonable deprivation of Mr. Sissoko's clearly established Constitutional right to be free from unlawful seizure.

VII. QUALIFIED IMMUNITY: NOT AVAILABLE WHERE CONDUCT IS UNREASONABLE

Plaintiffs' claims against Defendant Rocha are for her violation of his clearly established constitutional rights [*See Mitchell v. Forsyth*, 472 U.S. 511, 526, 105 S.Ct. 2806, 86 L.Ed.2d 411 (1985) (allowing dismissal of action against governmental official where claim was no violation of clearly established law) and because the ". . . conduct of the immigration officer[s] was so unreasonable and contrary to established law that they are not entitled to qualified immunity." *Ramirez v. United States*, 81 F. Supp. 2d 532, 536 (2000). To overcome the defense of qualified immunity, plaintiff must show: (1) that there was a violation of his clearly established constitutional rights; and (2) that the conduct of the immigration officers was so unreasonable and contrary to established law that they are not entitled to qualified immunity. *See generally Harlow v. Fitzgerald*, 457 U.S. 800, 817, 102 S.Ct. 2727, 73 L.Ed.2d 396 (1982).

Ms. Rocha points to the fact that the inspectors at the port deferred Mr. Sissoko's inspection to Los Angeles as though that act was lawful and somehow justifies her conduct thereafter [*See* "Motion to Alter or Amend Judgment Re Claim 6" 16:1-6]. The fact is that no matter what their suspicions about Mr. Sissoko's legalization case, he was entitled pursuant to his Advance Parole Document to be paroled into the United States upon that documentation's presentation at the port. His legalization was entirely up to the legalization department of the INS not the Deferred Inspection Unit which wasn't even entitled to look at Mr. Sissoko's legalization file. There was therefore, no legitimate basis to defer Mr. Sissoko's inspection at the port or thereafter from March 16, 1997 to August 26, 1997.

Mr. Sissoko's entitlement to protection under the Fourth Amendment from unlawful seizures is well established *See Landon v. Plasencia*, 459 U.S. 21, 32-34, 103 S.Ct. 321, 74 L.Ed.2d 21 (1982), "[O]nce an alien gains admission to our country and begins to develop the ties that go with permanent residence, his constitutional status changes accordingly."); *cf. Kiareldeen v. Reno*, 71 F. Supp. 2d 402, 409 (D.N.J.1999). This protection is tempered, but not eliminated, by the discretion granted to immigration inspectors under the statutes cited by defendants. Border searches and detentions of returning residents are not subject to the strict probable cause and warrant requirements usually required by the Fourth Amendment. *See United States v. Vega-Barvo*, 729 F.2d 1341, 1344 (11th Cir.1984). Rather, the INS inspectors must have acted "reasonably" in deciding to detain plaintiff. *See id.* and *generally United States v. Montoya de Hernandez*, 473 U.S. 531, 542, 105 S.Ct. 3304, 87 L.Ed.2d 381 (1985) (determining whether a traveler's border detention was reasonable under the Fourth Amendment).

Plaintiffs adopt the Court's view in *Ramirez id* at 537 where the court decided "Defendants' argument that a *Bivens* action is inappropriate because plaintiff completely lacks a constitutional right to be free of unlawful seizure and arrest fails. A *Bivens* action will lie against the INS officials if they acted "unreasonably" when they: (1) detained plaintiff; (2) did not release him for five hours; and (3) paroled him to Hudson County". Of course in the case at bar, Plaintiff was detained not for five hours but for 77 days.

VIII. QUALIFIED IMMUNITY: ACTIONS OF INS INSPECTORS

Officials are shielded from liability "as long as their actions could reasonably have been thought consistent with the rights they are alleged to have violated." *Anderson v. Creighton*, 483 U.S. 635, 638, 107 S.Ct. 3034, 97 L.Ed.2d 523 (1987) (quoting *Harlow*, 457 U.S. at 817, 102 S.Ct. 2727). *Anderson*, 483 U.S. at 638, 107 S.Ct. 3034. This rule "gives ample room for mistaken judgment by protecting 'all but the plainly incompetent or those who knowingly violate the law.'" *Hunter v. Bryant*, 502 U.S. 224, 228, 112 S.Ct. 534, 116 L.Ed.2d 589 (1991). Ms. Rocha knew on August 26, 1997, that Oumar Sissoko was married and that he had just filed for adjustment of status pursuant to an "Immediate Relative Petition" under 8 C.F.R. § 201(b). Although her supervisor was not obligated but did have the discretion to allow Mr. Sissoko to "parole to adjust" pursuant to that Immediate Relative Petition, Ms. Rocha told her supervisor and the INS by way of her official documents that:

"THE SUBJECT IS NOT MARRIED"

> [*Exhibit "N"* to Plaintiff's Motion for Summary Adjudication (Form I-275 "Withdrawal of Application for Admission/Consular Notification Signed by Loyda R. Rocha, II)],

thereby foreclosing Mr. Sissoko even from being considered by her supervisor and the INS for that discretionary benefit.

Qualified immunity will not be abridged "if the defendant acted in an objectively reasonable manner." *Malley v. Briggs*, 475 U.S. 335, 341, 106 S.Ct. 1092, 89 L.Ed.2d 271 (1986); *Capone v. Marinelli*, 868 F.2d 102, 105 (3d Cir.1989) ("Reliance on the objective reasonableness of an official's conduct, as measured by reference to clearly established law, should avoid excessive disruption of government and permit the resolution of many insubstantial claims on summary judgment."). But Ms. Rocha did not act in an objectively reasonable manner. Her conduct was not consistent with the law she violated and her lying in order to deprive Mr. Sissoko of his freedom is egregious and unconscionable and as such does not entitle her to qualified immunity.

Although Ms. Rocha claimed the opposite on her official forms, on May 15, 1997, and again on August 26, 1997, neither of Mr. Sissoko's legalization petitions had been denied and his *CSS* class membership was not finally rescinded [that could not be accomplished until the expiration of 15 days (*i.e.* September 10, 1997) after his interview by Pacita Pabilla on August 26, 1997, and then only if Plaintiff had *not* rebutted Ms. Pabilla's tentative revocation with additional evidence of his eligibility].

8 C.F.R. § 235(b)(1) is the section used by Ms. Rocha to take Mr. Sissoko into custody and place him in expedited removal proceedings (Prior to April 1, 1997, exclusion proceedings) in May, 1997 and again in August. But by August 26, 1997, not only was Ms Rocha and the INS not permitted to treat Mr. Sissoko as an "arriving alien" subject to exclusion or expedited removal, but the justification for placing him in those proceedings had been invalidated by rules promulgated by the INS itself.

> 8 C.F.R. § 235.3(b)(1) *Applicability*. The expedited removal provisions shall apply to the following classes of aliens who are determined to be inadmissible under section 212(a)(6)(C) or (7)[11] of the Act (i) Arriving aliens, as defined in § 1.1(q) of this chapter, except for citizens of Cuba arriving at a United States port-of-entry by aircraft;

Ms. Rocha placed Mr. Sissoko in custody and expedited removal proceedings on August 26, 1997 *on the grounds that under* 8 C.F.R. § 212(a)(5)(7)(A)(i)(I) [*See* Exhibit I to Plaintiffs' Motion for Summary Adjudication—"Supervisory Check List"], he was an undocumented alien. This she knew to be an absolute fabrication, because she had had no communication with the adjudication officer who had interviewed Mr. Sissoko and had no way of knowing what the outcome of that interview was until it was posted perhaps weeks later on the INS CIS computer system.

IX. CONCLUSION

In light of Ms. Rocha's unreasonable and outrageous conduct toward Mr. Sissoko, this Court must not reward her with a grant of qualified immunity, nor should this Court fail to exercise its clear grant of subject matter jurisdiction to hear Plaintiffs' claims under the FTCA and *Bivens*.

Respectfully submitted.

Dated: October 28. 2002

[Attorney]

[ADD CERTIFICATE OF SERVICE]

[11] 8 C.F.R. 212(a)(7) Documentation requirements. An applicant for admission ". . . who is not in possession of a valid unexpired immigrant visa, reentry permit, border crossing identification card, or other valid entry document required by this Act, and a valid unexpired passport, or other suitable travel document, or document of identity and nationality if such document is required under the regulations issued by the Attorney General under section 211(a)."

SUMMARY OF DECISION IN *SISSOKO v. ROCHA*

Ninth Circuit Finds Fourth Amendment Violation, Affirms District Court Jurisdiction over Bivens Suit

Sissoko v. Rocha, No. 03-55667, CV-98-07010-ABC (9th Cir. June 13, 2005), *summary and link to decision posted on* AILA InfoNet at 05072165

Mr. Sissoko, a native and citizen of Senegal, entered the United States in the early 1980s on a visitor's visa, which he overstayed. He twice applied for legalization pursuant to a relief order in *Catholic Soc. Servs., Inc. v. INS*, 232 F.3d 1139 (9th Cir. 2000) (en banc) (*CSS*), a class action lawsuit filed on behalf of certain legalization applicants. INS provisionally approved Mr. Sissoko's second application for membership in a *CSS* subclass and issued him a temporary resident card and employment authorization card. Mr. Sissoko's father died in Spring 1997, while both his legalization applications were still pending. Mr. Sissoko obtained an advanced parole document to attend the funeral. On his return, the immigration officer did not believe his account of his initial arrival in the United States and noticed that he had two alien registration numbers (one for each legalization application). Despite the advance parole authorization, the officer denied him entry and ordered him to report to the Los Angeles Deferred Inspection Unit.

When Mr. Sissoko reported to the Los Angeles Deferred Inspection Unit, he was taken into custody by Defendant Rocha, an immigration inspector, based on her conclusion that he was an "arriving alien" without proper admission documents and, thus, subject to an expedited removal order under INA §235(b). Petitioner was released after two days. Three months later he married a U.S. citizen and filed an application for adjustment of status. Five days after his marriage, Mr. Sissoko attended an interview on his legalization application. The legalization adjudicator concluded that he had not established *CSS* class membership.

Defendant Rocha took Mr. Sissoko into immigration custody on the same day of his legalization interview, again indicating that he was subject to an expedited removal order under INA §235(b). Mr. Sissoko remained in detention for nearly three months, from August 26, 1997 to November 17, 1997.

INS commenced removal proceedings against Mr. Sissoko. INS asserted he was ineligible for adjustment of status based on his marriage, because he was an "arriving alien." The immigration judge (IJ) disagreed, finding that the regulations implementing the legalization provision indicated a legalization applicant, like Mr. Sissoko, who obtained advance parole, would be "readmitted," rather than treated as a newly-arriving alien applying for admission. In addition, the IJ noted that Mr. Sissoko was not advised of the possibility that he might not be readmitted after his trip abroad. Thus, under these circumstances, the IJ permitted Mr. Sissoko to apply for adjustment of status and granted his application. INS appealed to the Board of Immigration Appeals (BIA). The BIA denied INS's appeal and affirmed the IJ's conclusions.

Prior to the BIA's decision, Mr. Sissoko and his wife (Plaintiffs) filed suit in district court alleging that Defendant Rocha falsely arrested Mr. Sissoko and wrongfully took him into custody on August 26, 1997, in violation of his Fourth Amendment rights. The foundation for such an action was established in the landmark Supreme Court case *Bivens v. Six Unknown Named Agents of Federal Bureau of Narcotics*, 403 U.S. 388 (1971), which permits the recovery of money damages.

The district court granted of summary adjudication in favor of Plaintiffs, finding that the detention was illegal and denied the government's motion for summary judgment on qualified immunity grounds. The government then filed a motion for reconsideration under Federal Rule of Civil Procedure 59(e). In the motion, the government argued—for the first time—that INA §242(g) barred the district court from reviewing the legality of Mr. Sissoko's detention claim and that a *Bivens* remedy is not available in immigration cases. The district court held that INA §242(g) did not preclude review of Mr. Sissoko's challenge to the manner in which Defendant Rocha's detention decision was carried out. As to the question whether a *Bivens* remedy is available in immigration cases, the court held that this issue was not properly raised in a motion to reconsider because it was a legal issue that could and should have been raised earlier. The government filed an interlocutory appeal pursuant to 28 U.S.C. §1292(b) and a notice of appeal from the denial of qualified immunity pursuant to 28 U.S.C. §1291. The Ninth Circuit consolidated the appeals.

On appeal, the Ninth Circuit found that the district court properly denied the Rule 59(e) motion with regard to the newly raised legal issue concerning *Bivens*. Thus, the court addressed: (1) whether the district court had subject-matter jurisdiction to consider Plaintiffs' claims; (2) whether Sissoko's constitutional rights were violated; and (3) whether on the present record Defendant Rocha is entitled to qualified immunity.

Subject Matter Jurisdiction

INA §242(g) states that "no court shall have jurisdiction to hear any cause or claim by or on behalf of any alien arising from the decision or action by the Attorney General to commence proceedings, adjudicate cases, or execute removal orders against any alien under this Act." In *Reno v. American-Arab Anti-Discrimination Committee*, 525 U.S. 471 (1999), the Supreme Court held that this provision "applies only to three discrete actions that the Attorney General may take: her 'decision or action' to 'commence proceedings, adjudicate cases, or execute removal orders." The court found that Plaintiffs' challenge to the execution of Defendant Rocha's detention decision did not fall within these three actions.

Even assuming *arguendo* that expedited removal is a "proceeding," the court said, INA §242(g) "only bars review of issues arising from decisions to *commence* such proceedings; it does not serve as an outright bar to any litigation related to such proceedings." The court further found that "a decision to detain an alien does not 'arise from' a decision to 'commence proceedings,' even expedited removal proceedings." Any other interpretation of INA §242(g), the court reasoned, would preclude all review of the constitutional claims related to Sissoko's detention, which would raised a "serious constitutional question."

The court also found that Plaintiffs' claim did not arise from the decision or action by the Attorney General to adjudicate his case because "the term 'adjudicate' in ordinary parlance refers to a formal decisional process, in this case, a process to consider whether to grant or deny specific relief requested by an alien or the INS . . . [and] does not include a purely administrative decision to detain an allegedly arriving alien, without any hearing at all." In addition, the court determined that Plaintiffs were not challenging a decision or action arising from the execution of a removal order because no removal order was ever "executed" and the action did not seek to prevent the execution of a future removal order.

The court also held that INA §242(a)(2)(A), as amended by §106(a)(1)(A) of the REAL ID Act, did not preclude review of Plaintiffs' claims. "[INA §242(a)(2)(A)] is a bar only to claims arising out of removal orders. As it turns out that there is no removal order here, [INA §242(a)(2)(A)] does not apply, and the language of [new INA §242(a)(5) ("Exclusive Means of Review")] is therefore not implicated." The court discussed at length the fact that "the order of removal itself and references to the actual existence of any order of removal are conspicuously absent from the record."

Lastly, the court held that INA §242(e), which bars review of challenges to expedited removal orders which seek "declaratory, injunctive, or other equitable relief," did not apply to damages actions such as *Bivens* suits. In addition, the court said that INA §242(e)(3) "does not cover damages claims concerning discrete actions of INS officials applying the statute and applicable regulations and policies."

Thus, the court concluded that INA §242 does not preclude jurisdiction over Plaintiffs' *Bivens* action.

Constitutional Violations, Qualified Immunity

Plaintiffs claimed that Mr. Sissoko's detention, from August to November 1997, violated his Fourth Amendment rights. Defendant Rocha asserted that she is entitled to qualified immunity from any damages liability.

Because Defendant Rocha took Mr. Sissoko into custody solely pursuant to the authority of the expedited removal statute, INA §235(b)(1), the court reasoned that "only if Sissoko was an arriving alien inadmissible under [INA §212(a)(6)(C) or INA §212(a)(7)—was the detention valid," the court explained. The court found that the governing statute and regulations, the IJ's and BIA's legal determinations, and Ninth Circuit case law (*Navarro-Alspura v. INS*, 53 F.3d 233 (9th Cir. 1995)) all evidenced that Mr. Sissoko was not an arriving alien upon his return to the United States. Thus, there was no reasonable basis for detaining Mr. Sissoko.

Defendant Rocha contended that she had determined Mr. Sissoko was subject to expedited removal because he did not possess a valid entry document as required by INA §212(a)(7). However, the court determined that the record unequivocally established the contrary; that Mr. Sissoko had a valid entry document (an advanced parole document) and that Rocha should have known about it because the interviewing officer at the airport specifically noted the existence of the document on the notice ordering Mr. Sissoko to appear at the Los Angeles Deferred Inspection Unit.

In sum, the court held that Defendant Rocha had no legal basis to identify Mr. Sissoko as subject to expedited removal and, accordingly, had no legal basis to place him in detention pursuant to the expedited removal statute. Thus, the court found that Defendant Rocha violated Mr. Sissoko's Fourth Amendment right to be free from unlawful detention.

Next, the court considered whether the possession of the proper advance parole document was sufficient to establish Mr. Sissoko's right to enter the country. In light of precedent in the administrative and Ninth Circuit case law establishing this right, the court found that Mr. Sissoko's "possession of a valid advance parole document and his temporary resident status entitled him to re-enter the United States and precluded detaining him as an inadmissible arriving alien, even once his legalization applications were denied." Accordingly, the court concluded that "it would have been clear to a reasonable immigration officer that detaining Sissoko would violate his Fourth Amendment rights" and, therefore, held that Defendant Rocha is not entitled to qualified immunity for her actions."

Thus, the court affirmed the district court's grant of summary adjudication to Plaintiffs, affirmed the denial of the government's motion for summary judgment on qualified immunity grounds, and remanded for further proceedings.

February 28, 2001

Via Overnight Mail
Office of the Regional Counsel
U.S. Immigration and Customs Enforcement
Western Regional Office
[Address]
[City, State, and Zip Code]

Office of General Counsel
U.S. Immigration and Customs Enforcement
[Address]
Washington, DC

Office of the Chief Counsel
U.S. Immigration and Customs Enforcement
[Address]
[City, State, and Zip Code]

Re: Notification of Incident and Claim for Damages Under the Federal Tort Claims Act in the Matter of Jose Luis and Maria Araujo

To Whom It May Concern:

Our office represents claimants Jose Luis Araujo and his wife, Maria Araujo, in their claim against the U.S. Immigration and Naturalization Service ("INS"). Pursuant to 28 U.S.C. §2675(a) and 28 C.F.R. §14.2(a), we hereby provide notification of an incident that occasions liability under the Federal Tort Claims Act, and present a claim for money damages in the amount of $500,000 for personal injuries resulting from agents of the INS having committed the torts of: (1) intentional infliction of extreme emotional distress; (2) negligent infliction of emotional distress; (3) assault; (4) battery; (5) false arrest; (6) false imprisonment; and (7) violation of their rights to liberty and security under Article I §§ 1, 7, and 13 of the California Constitution.

NOTICE

1. Claimants: Jose Luis Araujo resides at Rancho Puerta Grande, Municipio de Romita, Guanajuato, Mexico. Maria Araujo resides at 3562 Peralta Boulevard in Fremont, California 94536.

2. Place and Date of Incident: The incident underlying the instant claim began on Tuesday, March 2, 1999, at approximately 6:30 a.m., when four INS agents came to 3562 Peralta Boulevard in Fremont, California where Jose Luis and Maria Araujo were then residing together and where Maria Araujo still resides and arrested Mr. Araujo. He was then driven to four different stops before being transported to the Newark police station where he remained in the parking lot for approximately one hour. Afterwards, he was transferred to a van and taken to the San Francisco Office of the Immigration and Naturalization Service, located at: 630 Sansome Street in San Francisco, California where he remained until approximately 6:00 p.m. that evening, March 2, 1999. Mr. Araujo was then driven in a van to the Oakland International Airport in Oakland, California where he waited in the van for approximately one hour until the plane was ready to depart. From Oakland, Mr. Araujo was flown to Phoenix, Arizona and arrived there at approximately 2:00 a.m. on

March 3, 1999. He was then put on a bus to Nogales, Mexico, where he arrived at approximately 6:00 a.m. on March 3, 1999.

3. Background:[1] On April 20, 1996, Mr. Araujo married Mrs. Araujo, who is a United States citizen. Mr. Araujo has a nineteen year old United States citizen son, Joe Luis Araujo, born to a previous marriage. Mr. Araujo made several good faith efforts to obtain lawful permanent residency. In July 1980, his brother, Joseph Servin, filed a relative immigrant visa which was approved on September 8, 1980. On October 16, 1981, a visa petition filed on behalf of petitioner by his then U.S. citizen wife, Penny Anderson, was approved. On November 20, 1991, Mr. Araujo and Ms. Anderson divorced. On September 3, 1996, Maria. Araujo filed an immediate relative visa petition on behalf of Mr. Araujo and he simultaneously filed an application for adjustment of status. On June 3, 1997, Mr. and Mrs. Araujo appeared for a routine interview before the San Francisco INS regarding the adjustment application. Mr. Araujo's application for permanent residency remained pending when he was arrested at his home in Fremont, California in the early morning of March 2, 1999. The very next day, the INS deported petitioner to Mexico, applying §1231(a)(5) to a prior order of deportation and refusing to adjudicate his application for adjustment of status.

4. Description of Incident:[2] In mid-February 1999, Mr. Araujo was released from Washington hospital after having suffered a double stroke. His doctor recommended that he receive physical therapy and prescribed medication.

On Tuesday, March 2, 1999, at approximately 6:30 a.m., Mr. Araujo was awakened to the sound of loud banging at the front door of the house he shared with his U.S. citizen wife, Maria Araujo, at 3562 Peralta Boulevard, Fremont, California. Still half-asleep, Mr. Araujo believed that the person at the door might have been my wife, as she usually goes to church in the morning. Actually, Mrs. Araujo had not actually yet left for church. Mr. Araujo crawled to the door and opened it just a crack. Outside were three men and one woman, who proceeded to kick open the door and barged into the house. Mr. Araujo feared for his life. The individuals did not identify themselves and he had no idea who they were. One of the men asked him if his name was Jose Luis Araujo, and he answered "Yes."

In an unjustifiable exhibition of excessive force, two of the male INS agents then started pushing Mr. Araujo, put their knee in his back, pulled his hair and handcuffed him. Mr. Araujo, still in the clothes he slept in at the time, did nothing to provoke such excessive use of force. Mrs. Araujo screamed for them to stop, because of Mr. Araujo's health condition. One of the agents told Mrs. Araujo that they didn't "give a shit." An agent then pushed Mrs. Araujo into the bedroom and she fell on the floor, crying hysterically. The female agent approached one of the men and asked why he was using so much force.

The agents took Mr. Araujo outside and put him into a car without any opportunity to gather any personal belongs, identification, or money. All Mr. Araujo was wearing at the time of his arrest was a T-shirt, sweat pants and a pair of sandals. No one explained to Mr. or Mrs. Araujo where Mr. Araujo was being taken to or why he was being taken from his home.

Mrs. Araujo begged the agents to at least allow Mr. Araujo to take his medications, since he was still so fragile from his stroke and recent hospitalization. She was rudely told that he could not take anything with him. Mrs. Araujo continued screaming at the agents, imploring them to take Mr. Araujo's medications and his cane. The agents responded that they would not take them and told her to "shut up." The female agent then took the medication from Mrs. Araujo, in an almost secretive manner, as if she did not want the men she was with to know. The whole incident lasted approximately 20 minutes.

After the agents left, Mrs. Araujo called the police department in Fremont, California and asked whether they were responsible for her husband's arrest, and learned that they were not. Mrs. Araujo then

[1] All relevant documents can be found in Mr. Araujo's INS File, A24-263-643.

[2] The description of the incident is supported by claimants declarations, attached hereto as Exhibits A and B.

asked whether the police could find out what had happened and what could be done. An officer at the Fremont police department told her the matter might be immigration-related, and that he would follow up with the INS in Santa Rita and get back to her. Approximately three hours later, Mrs. Araujo received a call from the police officer informing her that her husband was in the custody of the INS in San Francisco. Mrs. Araujo then called the couple's former immigration attorney, Ms. Melba Espartero-Cawit, and spoke with her secretary, who informed her that Ms. Espartero-Cawit was not in the office.

After being taken from his home, Mr. Araujo was driven to four separate stops, and at one of the stops we made, the INS agents picked up another individual. Along with this individual, Mr. Araujo was taken to the Newark police station parking lot, where he remained for approximately one hour. He was then transferred by van to the San Francisco Immigration and Naturalization Service, located at 630 Sansome Street in San Francisco, California. At the INS office, Mr. Araujo was asked if his name was Jose Luis Araujo, and he answered "Yes."He was then told by an INS agent that he was "going straight to Mexico." Mr. Araujo asked the officers to allow him to call his wife or his attorney before his removal from the country. They responded "No!"[3] He was then placed in a holding cell with other individuals who were also being deported to Mexico that day.

With the assistance of her son, Mrs. Araujo scheduled a late-afternoon emergency appointment with undersigned counsel's office. While at his office, Mrs. Araujo learned that her husband's name and alien registration number did not appear in the Immigration Court central computer system.

Mr. Araujo remained at the San Francisco INS until approximately 6:00 p.m. that evening, March 2, 1999. At that time, he was driven by van to the Oakland International Airport where he waited for approximately one hour until the plane was ready to depart. Mr. Araujo was then put on a plane and flown to Phoenix, Arizona, where he arrived at approximately 2:00 a.m. the next day, March 3, 1999. From there, Mr. Araujo was bussed to Nogales, Mexico, where he arrived at approximately 6:00 a.m. He was then released without any identification or money.

On or about March 4, 1999, Mr. Araujo called his wife collect from Nogales, Mexico to tell her what had happened. In his weakened state from the stroke, Mr. Araujo could not remember his home telephone number and had to obtain the telephone number from his medication bottle. When Mrs. Araujo asked Mr. Araujo whether he had eaten, he said that he had not. Mr. Araujo, penniless, asked his wife to wire him some money and Mrs. Araujo wired him $100.00 that same day. Later that night, Ms. Araujo flew to Tijuana, Mexico and stayed with Mr. Araujo for two days and one night. Mr. Araujo was very weak and ill, and Mrs. Araujo's worries were even more exacerbated. She insisted that he go to the doctor in Tijuana. When he did see the doctor, he was given an injection and medication. She left him with enough money to travel to Rancho Puerta Grande, in Guanajuato, where he remains to this day.

The Araujos have only been able to maintain contact by telephone. Due to financial constraints, Mrs. Araujo cannot afford to travel to Mexico to visit her husband. Because Mrs. Araujo cannot write in Spanish and Mr. Araujo cannot read English, written communication is virtually impossible. Their forced separation and the manner in which it was brought have created a tremendous amount of emotional stress in their lives.

The stress of Mr. Araujo's deportation and the way it was carried out, has also contributed to Mrs. Araujo failing health condition. Since his departure, Mrs. Araujo has been hospitalized for a bladder condition and a stroke. Mr. Araujo's health also remains extremely precarious. He is in constant worry of suffering another stroke, and Mrs. Araujo feels helpless in this situation. In addition, Mrs. Araujo is struggling to make ends meet financially.

[3] Mr. Araujo's former attorney, Melba Espartero-Cawit, never received notice from the INS of their intention to remove Mr. Araujo from the country or the order of removal. Exhibit C.

On January 23, 2001, the United States Court of Appeals vacated Mr. Araujo's order of removal and ordered that the INS immediately admit him to the United States (to date, the INS has refused to do so) because the mandate has not issued. In Castro-Cortez v. INS, __ F.3d __, 01 C.D.O.S. 618, 2001 U.S. App. LEXIS 855 (9th Cir. January 23, 2001),[4] the Ninth Circuit held that INA §241(a)(5)— the provision on which Mr. Araujo's deportation order was based—cannot be retroactively applied to individuals who reentered the United States before April 1, 1997. 2001 U.S. App. LEXIS at *46. Although the Court also decided the case on these grounds, the Court also gave every indication that the INS' procedures for reinstating a prior order of deportation under that section violate due process,[5] including the denial of access to counsel.[6]

The INS through its agents acted with reckless and callous indifference to Mr. and Mrs. Araujo's civil and constitutional rights when they (1) forced themselves into the Araujo's home without identifying themselves; (2) used excessive force against both Mr. and Mrs. Araujo during the arrest—especially in light of Mr. Araujo's precarious condition; (3) arrested, detained and then deported Mr. Araujo without regard to his medical condition;(4) intentionally denied Mr. Araujo's former counsel notice of his arrest, detention, and deportation; (5) intentionally denied Mr. Araujo access to counsel; (6) arrested, detained and deported Mr. Araujo unlawfully. In every way, the Araujos were treated like criminals, and Mr. Araujo's rights to counsel and to communicate with his family were blatantly ignored. As a direct result of the INS' misconduct on March 2, 1999 and March 3, 1999, Mr. and Mrs. Araujo have suffered physical and mental abuse and are continuing to suffer severe emotional distress.

5. Witnesses: The following individuals are witnesses to the incident:

Jose Luis Araujo — Rancho Puerta Grande, Municipio de Romita, Guanajuato, Mexico.

Maria Araujo — 3562 Peralta Boulevard, Fremont, California 94536.

Current and/or former employees of the INS whose identities are presently unknown to Mr. and Mrs. Araujo.

6. Personal Injury: Claimants have suffered and continue to suffer severe emotional distress, as a direct and proximate result of misconduct by the INS and its agents or employees. During the incident, Mrs. Araujo suffered extreme emotional distress when she saw her husband who had just been released from the hospital after suffering a double stroke being pushed, being kneed in the back, having his hair pulled, and being handcuffed by strangers who never once identified themselves. Mrs. Araujo's reaction was to scream, imploring the agents to stop their abusive treatment of her husband. As a result, Mrs. Araujo was pushed to the ground by one of the agents. Mrs. Araujo's emotional agony continued as she worried about where Mr. Araujo was being taken in his weakened stated of health and whether he would receive proper medication and/or treat-

[4] Although Mr. Araujo's name is not in the case title, Mr. Araujo is one of five cases that the Court addressed in that decision, which is attached hereto as Exhibit D.

[5] Castro-Cortez, 2001 U.S. App. LEXIS 855 at *3 ("we seriously doubt that the government's new reinstatement procedure comports with the Due Process Clause"); at *27-*28 ("The reinstatement process raises very serious due process concerns, and is caused not by a change mandated by Congress as part of IIRIRA, but by an administrative decision to amend the regulations governing reinstatement proceedings in the wake of IIRIRA."); at *33 ("In light of Marincas, we have serious doubt whether the use of Immigration Officers to determine whether to reinstate removal orders comports with due process."); at *35 ("Nevertheless, while we have serious doubts as to the constitutionality of these procedures, we do not decide that question because we may rule in petitioners' favor on a narrower ground."). Emphasis added.

[6] The Court stated:

> Not only are aliens subject to reinstatement denied the opportunity to appear before an impartial decision-maker, but the regulations do not provide them with access to counsel. . . . Fundamental to due process is the right to counsel, and we have previously held that, in deportation hearings, aliens have the "right to obtain counsel of their choice at their own expense." Orantes-Hernandez v. Thornburgh, 919 F.2d 549, 554 (9th Cir. 1990). We see no reason why this right does not apply in the case of reinstatement proceedings.
>
> Id. at *33-f34.

ment. The emotional toll brought about by this incident has caused Mrs. Araujo to suffer nightmares and has weakened her own physical condition. Since the incident, she has been hospitalized for a bladder infection and a mild-stroke. Moreover, Mrs. Araujo continues to harbor anxiety about the manner in which the INS agents took her husband from her.

During the incident, Mr. Araujo suffered physical abuses and extreme emotional distress as well. Knowing his own fragile health condition, he was extremely distraught by the excessive force being used against him and the fact that he was virtually defenseless to the physical abuse that he was suffering at the hands of the arresting INS agents. The physical abuse that Mr. Araujo suffered by being pushed, kneed in the back and having his hair pulled by unidentified INS agents was a completely unwarranted, excessive use of force under the circumstances. Mr. Araujo continues to suffer from severe emotional distress as a result of this incident.

CLAIM FOR DAMAGES

Claimants demand damages in the amount of $500,000.

We look forward to the INS's prompt response to this demand. Please contact the undersigned should you have additional questions or require additional documentation to evaluate this claim.

Sincerely yours,

[Attorneys]
[Firm]

Enclosures

cc: Jose Luis Araujo
Maria Araujo

[Attorney]
[Firm]
[Address]
[Telephone]
[Facsimile]

Attorneys for Plaintiffs
Jose Luis ARAUJO
Maria ARAUJO

UNITED STATES DISTRICT COURT
FOR THE NORTHERN DISTRICT OF CALIFORNIA

Jose Luis ARAUJO **Maria ARAUJO,** **Plaintiffs,** **vs.** **UNITED STATES OF AMERICA,** **Defendant.**	)	**Case No. ____________** **COMPLAINT FOR DAMAGES**

JURISDICTION AND PROCEDURAL PREREQUISITES TO SUIT

1. Plaintiffs' claims are within the subject matter jurisdiction of this Court under 28 U.S.C. §1331, 28 U.S.C. §1343(a)(4), 28 U.S.C. §1346(b)(1), and 5 U.S.C.§702.

2. On March 1, 2001 Plaintiffs filed an administrative claim with the United States Immigration and Nationalization Service ("INS") pursuant to the Federal Tort Claims Act, 28 U.S.C. §2671 *et seq.* ("FTCA"). Plaintiffs' claim was denied by the INS on July 22, 2002.

VENUE

3. Venue is proper in this district under 28 U.S.C. §1391.

INTRADISTRICT ASSIGNMENT

4. Plaintiffs'claims arose in the counties of San Francisco and Alameda. Therefore, assignment to the San Francisco or Oakland Division of this Court is proper under N.D. Rule 3-2(d).

PARTIES

5. Plaintiff Jose Luis Araujo (hereafter "Mr. Araujo") is a Citizen of Mexico. He is a resident of Alameda County, California.

6. Plaintiff Maria Araujo (hereafter "Mrs. Araujo") is a United States citizen and the wife of Plaintiff Jose Luis Araujo.

7. Defendant United States of America exists under the Constitution of the United States of America and laws enacted by the United States Congress. The Immigration and Naturalization Service is, and at all times mentioned herein was, an agency of the United States Department of Justice, organized and existing under the laws of the United States. The United States is vicariously liable for the misconduct of its agents and employees and is directly liable for any policies of the United States or its agencies leading to or contributing to such misconduct, including but not limited to failure to supervise employees properly, failure to train employees properly, and failure to implement sufficient procedures to guard against the type of misconduct that occurred in this case.

FACTUAL ALLEGATIONS

8. On April 20, 1996, Mr. Araujo and Mrs. Araujo, a United States citizen, were married. On September 3, 1996, Mrs. Araujo filed an immediate relative visa petition on behalf of Mr. Araujo with the INS. As well, an application for adjustment of status to lawful permanent residency was filed by Mr. Araujo.

9. On June 3, 1997, Mr. and Mrs. Araujo appeared for a routine interview before the San Francisco INS regarding the adjustment of status application. They did not receive a decision from the INS on the application and the application remained pending.

10. In mid-February 1999, Mr. Araujo was released from Washington hospital after having suffered a double stroke. His doctor recommended that he receive physical therapy and prescribed medication.

11. On Tuesday, March 2, 1999, at approximately 6:30 a.m., Mr. Araujo was awakened by the sound of loud banging at the front door of the house he shared with his wife at 3562 Peralta Boulevard, Fremont, California. Mr. Araujo was asleep in bed at the time and still weak, as he was still recovering from the stroke which occurred only two weeks before.

12. Mr. Araujo opened the door to find three men and one woman who proceeded to kick open the door and storm into the house. Mr. Araujo feared for his life. The individuals did not identify themselves, and he had no idea who they were. One of the men asked him if his name was Jose Luis Araujo, and he answered "Yes."

13. Two of the male intruders, later determined to be INS agents, then started pushing Mr. Araujo, threw him onto the floor, put a knee in his back, pulled his hair and handcuffed him. Mr. Araujo, still in the clothes he slept in at the time, did nothing to provoke the use of force.

14. Mrs. Araujo screamed at the INS agents to stop and told them that Mr. Araujo had suffered a stroke and was still recovering. One of the agents told Mrs. Araujo that they didn't "give a shit." One of the men then pushed Mrs. Araujo against the wall and then into the bedroom where she fell on the floor, crying hysterically. From there she continued to scream for them to stop.

15. The female intruder, also later determined to be an INS agent, approached one of the men and questioned the need for so much force. The male agent did not respond.

16. The intruders took Mr. Araujo outside and put him into a car without any opportunity to gather any personal belongings, identification, or money. All Mr. Araujo was wearing at the time of his abduction was a T-shirt, sweat pants and a pair of sandals.

17. None of the intruders explained to Mr. or Mrs. Araujo where Mr. Araujo was being taken to or why he was being taken from his home.

18. Mrs. Araujo begged the intruders to at least allow Mr. Araujo to take his medications, since he was still so fragile from his stroke and recent hospitalization. However, the agents refused to allow Mr. Araujo to take his medications or other possessions with him.

19. Mrs. Araujo continued screaming at the agents, imploring them to take Mr. Araujo's medications and his cane. The male agents responded that they would not take them and told her to "shut up." The female agent finally took the medication from Mrs. Araujo, in a secretive manner, outside of the view of the male agents accompanying her.

20. This incident occurring in the Araujo household lasted approximately 20 minutes.

21. Mrs. Araujo was in complete panic after the agents left with Mr. Araujo. She had no idea what had happened and believed that he had been kidnaped.

22. After the individuals left, Mrs. Araujo called the police department in Fremont, California. Mrs. Araujo asked whether the police could find out what had happened and what could be done.

23. Only three hours later did Mrs. Araujo finally learn from a police officer through a phone call that her husband was in the custody of the INS in San Francisco.

24. After being taken from his home, Mr. Araujo was driven to four separate stops. Mr. Araujo was finally taken to the Newark, California police station parking lot, where he remained for approximately one hour.

25. He was then transferred by van to the San Francisco INS office, located at 630 Sansome Street in San Francisco, California. At the INS office, Mr. Araujo was asked if his name was Jose Luis Araujo, and he answered "Yes." He was then told by an INS agent that he was "going straight to Mexico."

26. Mr. Araujo asked the officers to allow him to call his wife or his attorney before his removal from the country. They refused to allow him to call his wife, attorney, or anyone else. He was then placed in a holding cell with other individuals who were also being deported to Mexico that day.

27. Mr. Araujo's former attorney Melba Espartero-Cawit never received any notice from the INS that it intended to remove Mr. Araujo from the U.S. pursuant to 8 U.S.C. §1231(a)(5), the reinstatement of removal statute.

28. Mr. Araujo remained at the San Francisco INS until approximately 6:00 p.m. that evening, March 2, 1999. At that time, he was driven by van to the Oakland International Airport where he waited for approximately one hour until the plane was ready to depart. Mr. Araujo was then put on a plane and flown to Phoenix, Arizona, where he arrived at approximately 2:00 a.m. the next day, March 3, 1999. From there, Mr. Araujo was bused to Nogales, Mexico, where he arrived at approximately 6:00 a.m. He was then released without any identification or money.

29. On or about March 4, 1999, Mr. Araujo called his wife collect from Nogales, Mexico to tell her what had happened. In his weakened state from the stroke, Mr. Araujo could not remember his home telephone number and had to obtain the telephone number from his medication bottle. When Mrs. Araujo asked Mr. Araujo whether he had eaten, he said that he had not. Mr. Araujo, penniless, asked his wife to wire him some money and Mrs. Araujo wired him $100.00 that same day. Later that night, Ms. Araujo flew to Tijuana, Mexico and stayed with Mr. Araujo for two days and one night. Mr. Araujo was very weak and ill, and Mrs. Araujo's worries were even more exacerbated. She insisted that he go to the doctor in Tijuana. When he did see the doctor, he was given an injection and medication. She left him with enough money to travel to Rancho Puerta Grande, in Guanajuato, Mexico where he remained for over two years.

30. While Mr. Araujo was in Guanajuato, he was taken to a hospital in nearby Leon because he was so ill. He remained in the hospital for approximately six days.

31. During Mr. Araujo's stay in Mexico, the Araujos were only able to maintain contact by telephone. Their forced separation and the manner in which it was brought created a tremendous amount of emotional stress in their lives.

32. On March 31, 1999, Mr. Araujo, through counsel, filed a petition for review of the decision of the Immigration and Naturalization Service ("INS") dated March 2, 1999 with the Ninth Circuit Court of Appeals ("Ninth Circuit"). That decision had ordered Mr. Araujo removed from the United States under the reinstatement of removal provisions at 8 U.S.C. §1231(a)(5).

33. On January 23, 2001, the United States Court of Appeals vacated Mr. Araujo's order of removal as unlawful, and ordered that the INS immediately admit him to the United States. The INS paroled Mr. Araujo into the United States on approximately April 18, 2001.

34. In its decision on Mr. Araujo's case, Castro-Cortez v. INS, 239 F.3d 1037 (9th Cir. 2001), the U.S Court of Appeals for the Ninth Circuit held that 8 U.S.C. §1231(a)(5)—the provision on which Mr. Araujo's deportation order was based—could not be retroactively applied to individuals who reentered the United States before April 1, 1997. Although the Court only decided the case on the retroactivity ground, the Court indicated that it believed that the INS' treatment of Mr. Araujo and the petitioners violated due process.

35. Upon his return, Mr. Araujo immediately saw a doctor in Fremont, California. He remains under a specialist's care and supervision, and has residual effects from the combination of the stroke and events of his deportation. His left arm is completely numb, he tires easily, he leans to his side because his equilibrium is unbalanced, and he is unable to work on a regular basis.

36. Both Mr. and Mrs. Araujo have suffered tremendously from the events of Mr. Araujo's deportation. In addition to Mr. Araujo's medical issues, Mrs. Araujo sees a licensed therapist regularly, in part due to the emotional damage she suffered as a result of the manner of her husband's removal, and his fragile physical state when this occurred.

37. As a direct and proximate result of Defendant's conduct, Mr. and Mrs. Araujo have been harmed.

38. In every way, the Araujos were treated like criminals, and Mr. Araujo's rights to counsel and to communicate with his family were blatantly ignored. As a direct result of the INS' misconduct on March 2, 1999 and March 3, 1999, Mr. and Mrs. Araujo have suffered physical and mental abuse and are continuing to suffer severe emotional distress.

FIRST CLAIM FOR RELIEF

(False Arrest and Imprisonment)
(Against Defendant United States of America)
(Federal Tort Claims Act)

39. Plaintiffs refer to and incorporate paragraphs 1 through 38 as though fully set forth herein.

40. By committing the above-described acts, Defendant United States falsely arrested and imprisoned Mr. Araujo without legal justification or privilege, causing him the harms herein alleged.

41. Plaintiffs are informed and believe that Defendant United States at all times either knew, recklessly and callously disregarded, or reasonably should have known the unlawful nature of the arrest and imprisonment.

SECOND CLAIM FOR RELIEF

(Assault)
(Against Defendant United States of America)
(Federal Tort Claims Act)

42. Plaintiffs refer to and incorporate paragraphs 1 through 41 as though fully set forth herein.

43. By committing the above-described acts, Defendant placed Mr. and Mrs. Araujo in reasonable apprehension of imminent physical harm.

THIRD CLAIM FOR RELIEF

(Battery)
(Against Defendant United States of America)
(Federal Tort Claims Act)

44. Plaintiffs refer to and incorporate paragraphs 1 through 43 as though fully set forth herein.

45. In committing the above-described acts, Defendant used an unreasonable amount of force and caused harmful and offensive contact to Mr. and Mrs. Araujo.

FOURTH CLAIM FOR RELIEF

(Intentional Infliction of Emotional Distress)
(Against Defendant United States of America)
(Federal Tort Claims Act)

46. Plaintiffs refer to and incorporate paragraphs 1 through 45 as though fully set forth herein.

47. Defendant's conduct, as alleged above, was extreme and outrageous, and Plaintiffs are informed and believe that Defendant engaged in such conduct with the intention of causing, or reckless disregard for the probability of causing, Plaintiff's severe emotional/mental distress. As a proximate result of such conduct, Mr. Araujo and Mrs. Araujo have experienced severe and lasting emotional and mental distress, fear, anxiety humiliation, and stress as more fully described above.

FIFTH CLAIM FOR RELIEF

(Negligence)
(Against Defendant United States of America)
(Federal Tort Claims Act)

48. Plaintiffs refer to and incorporate paragraphs 1 through 47 as though fully set forth herein.

49. Defendant owed a duty of care not to cause the harms alleged without legal justification. By committing the above described acts without legal justification and without having taken reasonable precautions to avoid such harms, Defendant breached its duty of care and proximately harmed Mr. Araujo, as described above. Such harm includes but is not limited to those described in paragraph 8-37 above, which Defendant United States knew or should have known would result from its conduct.

SIXTH CLAIM FOR RELIEF

(Negligent Infliction of Emotional Distress)
(Against Defendant United States of America)
(Federal Tort Claims Act)

50. Plaintiffs refer to and incorporate paragraphs 1 through 49 as though fully set forth herein.

51. Defendant owed a duty of care not to cause the harms alleged without legal justification. By committing the above-described acts, Defendant created a foreseeable risk of injury to Mr. Araujo. The harm alleged above is the proximate cause of such acts.

52. By committing the above-described acts, it was foreseeable that Mrs. Araujo would suffer emotional shock as a proximate result of such conduct, and such shock did occur, as alleged above.

PRAYER FOR RELIEF

WHEREFORE, Plaintiffs pray that:

1. Judgment be entered in favor of Plaintiffs Jose Luis and Maria Araujo on all claims for relief;

2. Plaintiffs Jose Luis and Maria Araujo be awarded actual and compensatory damages against Defendant United States of America in the amount of $ 500,000;

3. The Court award reasonable costs, attorneys' fees, and expenses herein; and

4. The Court award such other relief as it may deem just and proper.

[Dated:]

[Attorney]

[ADD CERTIFICATE OF SERVICE]

REQUESTING ATTORNEYS' FEES UNDER THE EQUAL ACCESS TO JUSTICE ACT

by Trina Realmuto and Stacy Tolchin, for AILF's Legal Action Center[*]

INTRODUCTION

The Equal Access to Justice Act (EAJA), 28 USC §2412(d) and 5 USC §504 *et seq.*, authorizes payment of attorneys' fees and costs for successful litigation against the government in the federal courts. A successful litigant who establishes eligibility under EAJA is entitled to a fee award for both litigating the case and litigating the fee request. Fees and costs under EAJA can be awarded without regard to what the client paid or did not pay, including in cases taken on a pro bono basis.

This advisory addresses the deadline for filing an EAJA fee application and discusses the statutory requirements for eligibility. In addition, the advisory addresses procedural aspects of filing an EAJA fee application, including documenting and calculating fees. Highlights of this advisory include:

Preparing for Filing an EAJA Fee Application Even Before Commencing Litigation

- Have a clear, written agreement with your client (and co-counsel, if any) at the outset of the representation regarding who is entitled to the fees in the event of a court award or settlement. Fees belong to the client absent a representation agreement to the contrary.
- Keep contemporaneous time records with descriptive billing entries on all time spent by attorneys, paralegals, and law clerks preparing for and litigating the case and an itemization and description of all costs incurred.
- Pursuant to the Supreme Court's decision in *Buckhannon Board of Care & Home Inc. v. West Virginia Dep't of Health and Human Resources*, a judicially enforceable court order or settlement agreement memorializing a federal court victory is necessary to establish prevailing party status.
- Although EAJA does not require it, it may be advisable to state in the original pleadings or brief that attorneys' fees will be requested under EAJA.

Assessing EAJA Fee Eligibility; Filing an EAJA Fee Application After Winning in Federal Court

- The fee application must be filed within 30 days of entry of final judgment in the action, *i.e.*, within 30 days after the expiration of time for filing an appeal, or, if an appeal is filed, within 30 days of entry of final judgment by the court of appeals or Supreme Court.
- The fee application must establish that the petitioning party is a prevailing party who has met the appropriate "net worth" requirements. The application also must allege that the pre-litigation and litigation position of government was not substantially justified and that there are no special circumstances that would make an award unjust.
- The fee application must include a statement of the total amount of fees and costs requested along with an itemized account of time expended and rates charged.
- If the fee application is for work performed in more than one court (*i.e.*, district court and court of appeals), check the relevant case law and local court rules to see where the application should be filed.

This advisory does not substitute for individual legal advice supplied by a lawyer familiar with a client's case. As the case law relating to EAJA is extensive and is not limited to immigration cases, attorneys are advised to research the case law in their circuits and consult local court rules.

PROCEDURAL REQUIREMENTS

Overview of Components of an EAJA Fee Application

An application for fees and costs under EAJA should include the following:

[*] **The Legal Action Center** (LAC) is the litigation arm of the American Immigration Law Foundation. **Trina Realmuto** is a European-based immigration attorney working with LAC as a consultant. **Stacy Tolchin** is an associate attorney with Van Der Hout, Brigagliano & Nightingale in San Francisco. The firm specializes in immigration law, as well as litigation under the Equal Access to Justice Act.

- A written motion explaining why your client is statutorily eligible.
- A signed affidavit executed by each named party attesting that he or she met the appropriate net worth requirements at the time the action was filed.
- Contemporaneous time records and description of costs.
- Evidence of award calculation/formula used to calculate the requested fee award.

In addition, an application may include:

- An application form, if required by local rule;
- Evidence of prevailing market rates for paralegal or law clerks in your area (surveys, declarations from other attorneys);
- Evidence of prevailing market rates for attorneys claiming enhanced rates based on specialized knowledge.

These requirements are discussed *infra*.

Before filing an EAJA fee request (if not done earlier), attorneys should have a clear, written agreement with their client (and co-counsel) regarding who is entitled to the fees in the event of a court award or settlement. Fees belong to the client absent a representation agreement to the contrary.

Documenting Fees and Costs

Compensable Work

In general, fee-shifting statutes like EAJA compensate for time that is "reasonably expended *on the litigation*." *Hensley v. Eckerhart*, 461 U.S. 424, 433 (1983) (emphasis added). In preparing the fee request, the petitioning party should exercise "billing judgment," *i.e.*, "make a good-faith effort to exclude from a fee request hours that are excessive, redundant, or otherwise unnecessary. . . ." *Hensley*, 461 U.S. at 434.

The initial work performed before the immigration service or the immigration courts is not compensable.[1] However, requesting compensation for time preparing litigation is permissible. The Supreme Court has expressly approved compensation for time spent drafting the initial pleadings and developing the theory of the case. *Webb v. Board of Education*, 471 U.S. 234, 243 (1985) (citation omitted).[2]

A petitioning party who has established eligibility for fee award is entitled to recover "fees on fees." In other words, the party is entitled to compensation for time reasonably expended on litigating the fee request. *Commissioner, INS v. Jean*, 496 U.S. 154, 163–65 (1990).

Keeping Contemporaneous and Detailed Time Records

The EAJA fee applicant bears the burden of documenting fees and costs. *Hensley v. Eckerhart*, 461 U.S. 424, 438 (1983). A fee award may be reduced for insufficient or inadequate documentation. For this reason, it is best to keep contemporaneous time records indicating: (1) the date; (2) the identity of the timekeeper; (3) a description of the specific task performed; and (4) the amount of the time spent on the task.

Include some detail when describing the specific task performed. For example, instead of "research and drafting legal brief or motion," one might write "research for opening brief" or "drafting habeas petition."[3]

Maintain a list containing the date and description of all costs stemming from the litigation, including, for example, filing fees, long-distance telephone and facsimile charges, messenger/courier fees, computer research, and expert witness fees.

Itemize the fees and costs incurred. This will assist the court in determining whether the hours and costs claimed are reasonable for the work performed. Thus, an EAJA fee application should include a tally of the total number of hours expended on the litigation by each timekeeper, the total amount of costs, and the total amount of combined fees and costs requested.

---

[1] *See Ardestani v. INS*, 502 U.S. 129, 135 (1991). *See also infra* note 9.

[2] *But see LaPointe v. Windsor Locks Bd. of Educ.*, 162 F. Supp. 2d 10, 18 (D. Conn. 2001) (reducing fee award for pre-litigation time spent in telephone conferences with client and co-counsel, drafting memos to file, drafting correspondence to her client because that court concluded, "none of these activities were actually spent 'on the litigation.'").

[3] *See Hensley v. Eckerhart*, 461 U.S. 424, 437 n.12 (1983) ("plaintiff's counsel . . . is not required to record in great detail how each minute of his time was expended. But at least counsel should identify the general subject matter of his time expenditures.").

Defending Against Allegations of Improper Time Records

Once an EAJA fee application is filed, the government's response often raises objections to billing entries that it deems to be vague, imprecise, or duplicative. The government will usually request that the court remedy the alleged impropriety by reducing any fee award in the exercise of discretion.

Case law addresses the degree of specificity required for billing records and whether the records, taken in context, are sufficient to identify the substance of the work done. In addition, presenting documentary or testimonial evidence from qualified attorneys who have reviewed the billing records and can attest that the records comport with general standards of timekeeping may rebut the government's allegations of vague or nondescriptive billing records.

The government may also contest a claimed EAJA fee based on duplication and similarly request the court to reduce the award in the exercise of discretion. At least one circuit court has held that reductions for alleged duplication, however, are appropriate "only if the attorneys are *unreasonably* doing the *same* work."[4] The burden is on government to show specific instances of unreasonable duplication.[5]

The need for multiple attorneys to prepare briefs to ensure timely filing, share information, assign responsibilities, and plan strategy is well-recognized.[6]

FILING DEADLINE

The EAJA statute requires fee applications to be filed within 30 days of "final judgment" in the action. 28 USC §2412(d)(1)(B). A "final judgment" means a judgment that is final and not appealable, and includes an order of settlement. 28 USC §2412(d)(2)(G). Thus, a motion for fees must be filed within 30 days after the expiration of time for filing an appeal. In immigration cases (where longer appeal deadlines apply because the government is always a party), the time for filing an appeal varies depending on whether the case was litigated in district or circuit court.

In district court cases, a party has 60 days after the judgment or order is entered by the district court to file an appeal. Fed. R. App. P. 4(a)(1)(B). Thus, an EAJA fee application must be filed within 30 days after the expiration of the 60-day time period for filing an appeal. If an appeal is taken, the district court's judgment is not final and therefore the 30-day period for filing an EAJA fee application does not begin to run until all the appellate proceedings are concluded. *Al-Harbi v. INS*, 284 F.3d 1080, 1084 (9th Cir. 2002) ("final judgment" is "the date on which a party's case has met its final demise, such that there is no longer any possibility that the district court's judgment is open to attack").

If the circuit court remands the case, a motion for fees must be filed within 30 days after the expiration of time for filing an appeal following the district court's entry of judgment on remand.

In circuit court cases, a party has 90 days after the judgment or order is entered by the circuit court to file a petition for certiorari to the Supreme Court. Sup. Ct. R. 13(1). Thus, an EAJA fee application must be filed within 30 days after the expiration of the 90-day time period for filing a petition for certiorari. *Al-Harbi v. INS*, 284 F.3d 1080 (9th Cir. 2002) and cases cited therein.

If a petition for rehearing is filed in the court of appeals, the 90-day period to file a petition for certiorari runs from the date of the denial of the petition for rehearing or, if the petition for rehearing is granted, the subsequent entry of judgment. Sup. Ct. R. 13(3). Moreover, if the losing party files a petition for certiorari, the circuit court's judgment is not final and therefore the 30-day period for filing an EAJA fee application would not begin to run until the Supreme Court denies the petition for certiorari. In the event that the Supreme Court grants the petition for certiorari, the 30-day period would not begin to run until the Supreme Court enters judgment or, if the case is remanded, until the circuit (or possibly the district court if the circuit court orders remand) enters judgment.

WHERE TO FILE

The EAJA statute does not specify where to file an EAJA fee request. However, logic and common practice dictate that where only one court has considered the merits of the case, that same court should consider the merits of the EAJA fee request. In a petition for

---

[4] *Johnson v. University College*, 706 F.2d 1205, 1208 (11th Cir. 1983) (emphasis in original).

[5] *McGrath v. County of Nevada*, 67 F.3d 248, 255–56 (9th Cir. 1995).

[6] *See, e.g., Berberena v. Coler*, 753 F.2d 629, 633–34 (7th Cir. 1985); *McKenzie v. Kennickell*, 645 F. Supp. 437, 450 (D.D.C. 1986).

review, an EAJA fee application is properly filed in the court of appeals that adjudicated the petition. In district court actions where neither side appealed to the court of appeals, the application is properly filed in the district court where the action was adjudicated.

In district court actions where one side appeals on the merits, the issue of where to file is more complicated as the appellate court may issue the final judgment in the case when adjudicating the appeal or may remand the case for further proceedings. When an EAJA fee request includes fees for appellate work, it is advisable to review the appropriate circuit court case law and consult the court's local rules.

Some courts have indicated a preference for district courts to adjudicate fee requests that include appellate fees.[7] Other courts have awarded fees for appellate work without remanding for the district court to award fees in the first instance.[8] Still other courts have suggested that either the district court or the court of appeals may adjudicate fee requests that include fees for work on appeal.[9] In the Second Circuit, applications for appellate fees are filed directly with the court of appeals.[10]

Some courts have separate local rules for attorneys' fees requests in general and local rules for fee requests under EAJA. Many local rules expressly provide that the court of appeals may remand fee requests filed in the courts of appeals to the district court for adjudication upon a motion or in the exercise of the court's discretion.[11]

For a discussion regarding where to file an EAJA fee application for work done before the Supreme Court, see *Dague v. Burlington*, 976 F.2d 801, 803–05 (2d Cir. 1991).

STATUTORY REQUIREMENTS

The EAJA statute, 28 USC §§2412(d)(1)(A) and (B), directs that a fee application must include:

- A showing that the petitioning party is a prevailing party;
- An allegation that the pre-litigation and litigation position of government was not substantially justified. *See also* 28 USC §2412(d)(2)(D);

---

[7] *See, e.g.*, *Foster v. Mydas Assocs., Inc.*, 943 F.2d 139, 144–45 (1st Cir. 1991) (noting that determination of fee award by appellate court in first instance would usurp trial court function); *McDonald v. Secretary of Health and Human Services*, 884 F.2d 1468, 1481 (1st Cir. 1989) ("Plaintiffs may also apply to the district court for attorneys' fees reasonably incurred in connection with the present appeal.") (footnote omitted); *Garcia v. Schweiker*, 829 F.2d 396, 398 (3d Cir. 1987) (reiterating the district court should set the fees for work in both courts when representation in each was required) (citation omitted); *Smith v. Detroit Bd. of Educ.*, 728 F.2d 359, 360 (6th Cir. 1984) (per curiam) (district court more appropriate forum to award fees incurred in appeal); *Smith v. CMTA-IAM Pension Trust*, 746 F.2d 587, 588–91 (9th Cir. 1984) (remanding to district court to reconsider award of attorney fees for appellate work); *Aspen Highlands Skiing Corp. v. Aspen Skiing Co.*, 738 F.2d 1509, 1527 (10th Cir. 1984) (antitrust action remanded to district court to award appropriate attorney fees for appellate work), *aff'd*, 472 U.S. 585 (1985). *See also Spell v. McDaniel*, 852 F.2d 762, 766 (4th Cir. 1988) (reviewing district court award of fees for appellate work under §1988). *And see Perkins v. Standard Oil Co.*, 399 U.S. 222 (1970) (stating that the amount of attorneys' fee award for appellate services under §4 of the Clayton Act "should, as a general rule, be fixed in the first instance by the District Court, after hearing evidence as to the extent and nature of the services rendered.").

[8] *See, e.g.*, *Jenkins by Jenkins v. Missouri*, 127 F.3d 709, 719 (8th Cir. 1997) and cases cited therein.

[9] *Martin v. Heckler*, 754 F.2d 1262, 1265 n. 6 (5th Cir. 1985) ("In some cases, applications for fees and expenses should be considered in the district court in the first instance. In *continued*

others, we may consider them first.") (citations omitted); *Ekanem v. Health & Hosp. Corp.*, 778 F.2d 1254, 1257 (7th Cir. 1985) ("our research reveals that a petition on entitlement to appellate attorneys fees may be filed in either the district court or the court of appeals"). *See also* 11th Circuit R. 39-2 (e) (permitting attorneys fees request to be filed in district court in lieu of court of appeals where appeal resulted in remand for further proceedings).

[10] *Smith v. Bowen*, 867 F.2d 731, 736 (2d Cir. 1989) ("applications [under the EAJA] for appellate fees in this Circuit should be filed directly with the Court of Appeals"); *McCarthy v. Bowen*, 824 F.2d 182, 183 (2d Cir. 1987) (per curiam) (directing the filing of EAJA appellate fee applications in court of appeals so that it may determine whether to enlist the aid of the district court in resolving disputed issues).

[11] *See, e.g.*, 1st Circuit R. 39(a) ("The court in its discretion may remit any such [EAJA fee] application to the district court for a determination."); 8th Circuit R. 47A ("On the Court's own motion or at the request of the prevailing party, a motion for attorneys fees may be remanded to the district court or administrative agency for appropriate hearing and determination."); 9th Circuit R. 39-1.8 ("Any party who is or may be eligible for attorneys fees on appeal to this Court may . . . file a motion to transfer consideration of attorneys fees on appeal to the district court . . . from which the appeal was taken."); 11th Circuit R. 39-2 (d) (permitting motion to transfer fee application to district court from which the appeal was taken).

- An allegation that there are no special circumstances that would make an award unjust;
- A showing that the petitioning party has met the appropriate "net worth" requirements. *See also* 28 USC §2412(d)(2)(B);
- A statement of the total amount of fees and costs sought along with an itemized account of time expended and rates charged.

Each of these statutory requirements is discussed in detail below.

Prevailing Party Status

To qualify for an EAJA award, the petitioning party has the burden of proving that he or she is a prevailing party. A "prevailing party" is one who "has been awarded some relief by a court." *Buckhannon Board of Care & Home Inc. v. West Virginia Department of Health and Human Resources*, 532 U.S. 598, 603 (2001).

Prevailing Party Status Cannot Be Based on the "Catalyst Theory"

Under the so-called "catalyst theory," a litigant was entitled to prevailing party status if the lawsuit was a catalyst that prompted the government to voluntarily alter its conduct. For example, a party could be considered a "prevailing party" under the catalyst theory if the lawsuit prompted the government to voluntarily grant the requested relief or pass legislation that mooted the federal case.

In *Buckhannon*, the Supreme Court held that the "catalyst theory" is no longer a permissible basis for an attorneys' fees award under the fee-shifting statutes at issue in that case. The "catalyst theory" "allows an award where there is no judicially sanctioned change in the legal relationship of the parties." 532 U.S. at 605. The Court held that a party can only be deemed a prevailing party, for purposes of fee-shifting statutes such as EAJA, if there has been an enforceable "alteration of the legal relationship of the parties." *Id.* at 621. Thus, under *Buckhannon*, a party whose suit prompts the precise relief sought may be a prevailing party if there is a judicially enforceable court entry memorializing the victory.

Types of Court Entries That May Prove Prevailing Party Status

Examples of court entries that may serve as the basis for an award of EAJA fees include enforceable judgments on the merits and settlement agreements that are favorable to one-side and enforceable through a consent decree. *Buckhannon*, 532 U.S. at 604–06. A consent decree is technically a judgment entered by consent of the parties whereby the government agrees to stop the alleged illegal activity without necessarily admitting guilt or wrongdoing.

Examples of court entries that may not serve as the basis for an award of attorneys' fees include judicial pronouncements that the government has violated the INA or the Constitution without any grant of judicial relief. *Id.* at 606–07. In addition, changes in the actual circumstances of the parties that are not related to the federal court case may not be used as the basis for an EAJA fee award. *Id.* For example, if the BIA grants a motion to reopen or reconsider after the filing of federal lawsuit challenging the final removal order, the petitioner in the federal lawsuit cannot be considered a prevailing party for purposes of an EAJA fee award if the federal case has been mooted out by the BIA's order.

In light of *Buckhannon*, if the government grants the relief sought before the court decides the case on the merits, memorializing the victory in a court-approved order or settlement will preserve eligibility for an award of EAJA fees. In this situation, counsel also may face tactical and ethical questions, including whether to attempt to negotiate attorneys' fees and costs in the order or settlement agreement or wait and file an EAJA fee request after the court approves the order or settlement agreement.

Court-Ordered Remand

Remand Where the Court Enters Judgment

Whether a court-ordered remand to the Board confers prevailing party status can be tricky. The primary case on this issue is *Shalala v. Schaefer*, 509 U.S. 292 (1993). In *Shalala*, the Supreme Court held that a Social Security claimant who obtained a reversal and remand of a Secretary of Health and Human Services' administrative decision pursuant to sentence four of 42 USC §405(g) was a prevailing party. 509 U.S. at 300–01. Significantly, in cases remanded under this section, the court enters judgment in the claimant's favor immediately and the litigation is terminated. In cases remanded under another Social Security provision, the court enters judgment after post-remand agency proceedings have been completed and their results are filed with the court. The Court's opinion in *Shalala* relied heavily on this distinction.

Therefore, *Shalala* supports finding prevailing party status when a court orders remand to the agency, enters a formal judgment immediately and does not retain jurisdiction over the federal court action. Arguably, the securing of the remand order is itself sufficient success on the merits to confer prevailing party status.

In *Rueda-Menicucci v. INS*, 132 F.3d 493 (9th Cir. 1997), the Ninth Circuit granted the petition for review of the denial of petitioners' asylum applications and remanded their case to the BIA for further proceedings in light of its decision. The court's order terminated the proceedings and the court did not retain jurisdiction over future appeals. Petitioners then sought attorneys' fees under EAJA. The Ninth Circuit reasoned that, since it could "perceive no difference between a 'sentence four' remand under 42 USC §405(g) [at issue in *Shalala*] and a remand to the BIA for further proceedings," petitioners who obtain such remand are prevailing parties. *Rueda-Menicucci*, 132 F.3d at 495. *See also Salem v. United States INS*, 122 F. Supp. 2d 980, 984 (C.D. Il. 2000) (finding remand to the INS conferred prevailing party status under the rationale of *Rueda-Menicucci*).

As a practical matter, because the question of whether a party has prevailed on a significant issue in litigation potentially could be equated with whether the party requested the relief obtained, it is advisable to ask the court to vacate *and/or remand* the decision of the immigration service or court when drafting a request for relief.

Remand Where Court Postpones Entering Judgment

If the court orders remand to the agency, postpones entering judgment until the completion of post-remand agency proceedings, and also retains jurisdiction over the federal court action, the petitioning party still may be eligible for prevailing party status if they are successful before the agency on remand.[12] In this situation, there is some authority—primarily in the nonimmigration context—suggesting that it *might* be possible to recover fees for administrative work on remand.

In *Ardestani v. INS*, 502 U.S. 129, 135 (1991), the Supreme Court held that EAJA fees cannot be awarded for the initial work done in administrative immigration proceedings. However, some courts have held that fees and costs for administrative work done pursuant to a remand order where the court retains jurisdiction (and postpones entering judgment until the remand proceedings are complete) are recoverable. *See Sullivan v. Hudson*, 490 U.S. 877, 889–90 (1989); *Melkonyan v. Sullivan*, 501 U.S. 89, 97 (1991); *Pollgreen v. Morris*, 911 F.2d 527, 536 (11th Cir. 1990) (INS forfeiture case); *Hafner v. Sullivan*, 972 F.2d 249, 252 (8th Cir. 1992).

Substantial Justification

An initial EAJA fee application must, at a minimum, *allege* that the position of the United States was not substantially justified. 28 USC §2412(d)(1)(B).[13] However, as the government routinely attempts to demonstrate that its position was substantially justified, it is advisable to fully brief this important issue in the initial fee application rather than waiting to brief it in the reply brief when page space is more limited.

Once the petitioning party establishes prevailing party status, the government can avoid payment of fees only if it can show that its pre-litigation conduct and litigation position were "substantially justified." In order to meet this heavy burden of proof, the government must show that its position has a reasonable basis both in law and in fact.[14] The government should meet this threshold twice—it must independently establish that the agency misconduct that gave rise to the litigation was substantially justified, and that its litigation positions were also substantially justified.[15]

---

[12] *Shalala*, 509 U.S. 299–300, discussing *Sullivan v. Hudson*, 490 U.S. 877, 892 (1989). *See also Former Emples. of Motorola Ceramic Prods. v. United States*, 336 F.3d 1360, 1361 (Fed. Cir. 2003) ("We hold that parties who secure a consent order remanding a proceeding to an administrative agency because of an alleged error on the merits (where the court also retains jurisdiction) are 'prevailing parties' under EAJA if they succeed on the merits in the remand proceeding."); *Davidson v. Veneman*, 317 F.3d 503, 505–06 (5th Cir. 2003) (where district court ordered remanded to Farm Services Agency and stayed motion for EAJA fees pending completion of remand proceedings and plaintiff was successful in remand proceedings, plaintiff was entitled to prevailing party status).

[13] In *Scarborough v. Principi*, __U.S.__, 124 S. Ct. 1856 (May 3, 2004), the Supreme Court held that a timely filed EAJA fee application may be amended after the 30-day filing period has run to cure an initial failure to allege that the government's position in the litigation lacked substantial justification.

[14] *See Pierce v. Underwood*, 487 U.S. 552, 565 (1988) (defining substantially justified as "'justified in substance or in the main'—that is, justified to a degree that could satisfy a reasonable person").

[15] 28 USC §2412(d)(2)(D); *Commissioner, INS v. Jean*, 496 U.S. 154, 158–60 (1990); *Dantran, Inc. v. United States DOL*, 246 F.3d 36, 41 (1st Cir. 2001) ("To satisfy its burden,

continued

Thus, if the court finds that the government's underlying, pre-litigation conduct lacks substantial justification, arguably the court need not consider whether its litigation positions were substantially justified.[16]

A court evaluates whether the government's position is reasonable based on several factors, including the clarity of the governing law;[17] the foreseeable length and complexity of the litigation, the consistency of the government's position, views expressed by other courts on the merits, legal merits of the government's position, and the stage at which the litigation was resolved. *See generally Jean v. Nelson*, 863 F.2d 759, 767–68 (11th Cir. 1988), *aff'd by Commissioner, INS v. Jean*, 496 U.S. 154 (1990).

In some circuits, there may be case law finding a *per se* lack of substantial justification where the government's position violates the Constitution, a statute, or its own regulations. *See, e.g., Mendenhall v. National Transp. Safety Bd.*, 92 F.3d 871, 874 (9th Cir. 1996) (citation omitted). *See also Role Models Am., Inc. v. Brownlee*, 353 F.3d 962, 967 (D.C. Cir. 2004) (concluding that "the agency's position lacked substantial justification because it was 'wholly unsupported by the text' of the applicable regulations.") (citation omitted).

Once the court determines that the government's position lacks substantial justification, the prevailing party is presumptively eligible for fees for all phases of the federal case unless the prevailing party has "unreasonably protracted" a portion of the litigation, which would warrant exempting fees for that portion of the litigation from the award.[18]

Special Circumstances

The government has the burden of proving the existence of special circumstances that would make a fee award unjust.[19] This "special circumstances" exception to awarding attorneys' fees was intended as a "safety valve" to allow the government to advance "novel but credible" legal theories and to give courts discretion to deny awards for equitable considerations. This provision of the EAJA is to be narrowly construed so as to not interfere or defeat Congress's purpose in passing the EAJA.[20]

Special circumstances include close or novel questions.[21] Equitable considerations can mean that the "prevailing party" acted in bad faith or has "unclean hands."[22]

Net Worth

If an individual plaintiff's net worth did not exceed $2 million at the time the lawsuit was filed, he or she has met the net worth requirement for EAJA fee eligibility. 28 USC §2412(d)(2)(B). A corporation must establish that it did not have more than

---

the government must justify not only its pre-litigation conduct but also its position throughout litigation."); *Kali v. Bowen*, 854 F.2d 329, 332 (9th Cir. 1988) ("The inquiry into the existence of substantial justification therefore must focus on two questions: first, whether the government was substantially justified in taking its original action; and, second, whether the government was substantially justified in defending the validity of the action in court.").

[16] *Commissioner, INS v. Jean*, 496 U.S. 154, 160 (1990) ("The single finding that the Government's position lacks substantial justification, like the determination that a claimant is a 'prevailing party,' thus operates as a one-time threshold for fee eligibility."); *Roanoke River Basin Ass'n v. Hudson*, 991 F.2d 132 , 138 (4th Cir. 1993) (". . . *Jean* instructs that a single finding of governmental misconduct compelling a party to resort to litigation or to prolong litigation can open the door to recovery under the EAJA. . . ."); *Anthony v. Sullivan*, 982 F.2d 586, 589 (D.C. Cir. 1993) (stating that "once a court determines that the government's position on the merits of the litigation is not substantially justified, it may not revisit that question as to any component of the dispute.") (citations omitted).

[17] However, the government's position is not *per se* justifiable simply because the case involves a new statute or an issue of first impression. *United States v. Real Prop.* at 2659; *Roundhill Drive*, 283 F.3d 1146, 1153 (9th Cir. 2002) (citing *Gutierrez v. Barnhart*, 274 F.3d 1255, 1261 (9th Cir. 2001)) ("There is no per se rule that EAJA fees cannot be awarded where the government's position contains an issue of first impression"). *But see Cornella v. Schweiker*, 741 F.2d 170, 172 (8th Cir. 1984) (holding government reasonable in defending a district court judgment where "all of the purely legal issues were questions of first impression").

[18] 28 USC §2412(d)(2)(D); *Commissioner, INS v. Jean*, 496 U.S. 154, 161 (1990).

[19] 28 USC §2412(d)(1)(A); *Abela v. Gustafson*, 888 F.2d 1258, 1266 (9th Cir. 1989).

[20] *Martin v. Heckler*, 773 F.2d 1145, 1149 (11th Cir. 1985).

[21] *National Truck Equip. Ass'n v. NHTSA*, 972 F.2d 669, 671 (6th Cir. 1992); *S & H Riggers & Erectors, Inc. v. OSHRC*, 672 F.2d 426, 431 (5th Cir. 1982).

[22] *Taylor v. U.S.*, 815 F.2d 249, 252–54 (3d Cir. 1987); *Midwest Research Institute v. United States*, 554 F. Supp. 1379, 1392 (W.D. Mo. 1983), *aff'd*, 744 F.2d 635 (8th Cir. 1984); *Oguachuba v. INS*, 706 F.2d 93, 98 (2d Cir. 1983).

500 employees and its net worth did not exceed $7 million at the time the lawsuit was filed. 28 USC §2412(d)(2)(B). A nonprofit entity must only show that it did not have more than 500 employees at the time the lawsuit was filed.

Net worth is calculated for each individual named party to the lawsuit. Net worth should, at a minimum, be documented by submitting a signed affidavit attesting that the petitioning party met the appropriate requirements at the time the lawsuit was filed.[23]

CALCULATING FEES, RATES, AND ADJUSTMENT FOR INFLATION

EAJA fees are based upon "prevailing market rates for the kind and quality of the services furnished, except . . . attorney fees shall not be awarded in excess of $125 per hour unless the court determines that an increase in the cost of living or a special factor, such as the limited availability of qualified attorneys for the proceedings involved, justifies a higher fee." 28 USC §2412(d)(2)(A).

Thus, the statutory hourly rate of compensation for attorneys is $125 for cases commenced on or after March 29, 1996. This amount can be "adjusted" or "enhanced" for inflation based on cost of living adjustments (COLA) or the presence of a special factor.

EAJA Statutory Rate Adjusted for Inflation

Most courts calculate the "adjustment" or "enhancement" for inflation by using the Consumer Price Index for All Urban Consumers (CPI-U).[24] The CPI-U is published by the Bureau of Labor Statistics and is updated monthly. It can be located online at *ftp://ftp.bls.gov/pub/special.requests/cpi/cpiai.txt*. The courts measure the COLA as of March 1996, when the statutory hourly rate of attorney compensation was raised from $75 per hour to $125 per hour. The March 1996 CPI-U is 155.7, and also can be located online at the link above.

One formula that is often used for calculating the cost of living adjustment is:

$$\$125 \times \frac{\text{(current CPI-U)}}{\text{(March 1996 CPI-U)}}$$

See Ramon-Sepulveda v. INS, 863 F. 2d 1458, 1463, fn. 4 (9th Cir. 1988); *Role Models Am., Inc. v. Brownlee*, 353 F.3d 962, 969 (D.C. Cir. 2004); *Edwards v. Barnhart*, 214 F. Supp. 2d 700, 702, n. 3 (W.D. Tex. 2002); *Walker v. Barnhart*, 302 F. Supp. 2d 1072, 1075 (S.D. Iowa 2002).

Case law suggests that the regional CPI-U, and not the national, is appropriate to use in computing the EAJA rate adjusted for inflation.[25] For individuals in areas with higher costs of living, the use of the regional CPI-U would mean a higher statutory rate of compensation.

Some courts have required that COLA calculation be done for the year of the fee award. In the equation set forth above, this would mean that the "current" CPI-U reflects the figure of the current year.[26] More recently, however, courts have applied a COLA adjustment for each year in which the work was performed.[27] In the equation set forth above, this means that the hourly rate for each year attorney work was performed would require a separate COLA rate calculation using a different CPI-U figure for each year.

Enhanced Rates Based on Special Factors

Attorney rates also may be increased if a special factor, such as the limited availability of qualified attorneys for the proceedings involved, justifies a higher fee. 28 USC §2412(d)(2)(A)(ii). The Supreme Court has addressed the meaning of the phrase "the limited availability of qualified attorneys for the proceedings involved" as follows:

> We think it refers to attorneys having some distinctive knowledge or specialized skill needful for the litigation in question—as opposed to an

---

[23] *United States v. Heavrin*, 330 F.3d 723, 732 (6th Cir. 2003); *Shooting Star Ranch, LLC v. United States*, 230 F.3d 1176, 1178 (10th Cir. 2000).

[24] *See, e.g., Harris v. Sullivan*, 968 F.2d 263, 264–66 (2d Cir. 1992) and cases cited therein; *Dewalt v. Sullivan*, 963 F.2d 27, 27–30 (3d Cir. 1992); *Sullivan* v. *Sullivan*, 958 F.2d 574, 578 (4th Cir. 1992); *Begley v. Secretary of HHS*, 966 F.2d 196, 199–200 (6th Cir. 1992); *Johnson v. Sullivan*, 919 F.2d 503, 504 (8th Cir. 1990); *Ramon-Sepulveda v. INS*, 863 F. 2d 1458, 1463 (9th Cir. 1988).

[25] *See Chen v. Slattery*, 842 F. Supp. 597, 600 n.2 (D.D.C. 1994); *Stanfield v. Apfel*, 985 F. Supp. 927, 931 (E.D. Mo. 1997); *Peterson v. Shalala*, 818 F. Supp. 241, 245 n. 3 (S.D. Ill. 1993).

[26] *See, e.g., Johnson v. Sullivan*, 919 F.2d 503, 504 (8th Cir. 1990); *Garcia v. Schweiker*, 829 F.2d 396, 401–02 (3d Cir. 1987).

[27] *See, e.g., Sorenson v. Mink*, 239 F.3d 1140, 1143 (9th Cir. 2001); *Wilkett v. Interstate Commerce Com.*, 857 F.2d 793, 875 (D.C. Cir. 1998); *Perales v. Casillas*, 950 F.2d 1066, 1076 (5th Cir. 1992).

> extraordinary level of general lawyerly knowledge and ability useful in litigation. An example of the former would be an identifiable practice specialty such as patent law, or knowledge of foreign law or language.

Pierce v. Underwood, 487 U.S. 552, 572 (1988).[28]

Some courts have recognized that a specialized knowledge of immigration law could warrant enhanced attorney rates.[29]

Special factors do *not* include the limited availability of qualified attorneys, litigation that involves novel and difficult issues, the undesirability of the case, expertise of counsel, or the results obtained. These factors are considered "applicable to a broad spectrum of litigation. . . ." *Pierce*, 487 U.S. at 573.

Declarations from other attorneys will help document a claim for enhanced rates based on expertise in immigration law. The declarations could explain why immigration law expertise was necessary to litigating the case and further attest that petitioner(s) would be unable to find an attorney with the requisite immigration expertise at the $125 EAJA statutory rate.

Prevailing Market Rates

Attorneys Seeking Enhanced Rates

An attorney who has demonstrated entitlement to an enhanced rate based on special factors should be compensated based on prevailing market rates, 28 USC §2412(d)(2)(A)(ii), without regard to whether the attorney is *pro bono* or retained for a fee. *Blum v. Stenson*, 465 U.S. 886, 895–96 (1984). The prevailing market rate need not reflect the rate charged to the client.

Market rate surveys are available to demonstrate prevailing rates of attorneys based on specialization, location, and years of experience. Declarations from other attorneys of similar expertise and years of experience attesting to their individual and/or firm's hourly rate can also be submitted to establish prevailing market rates. For example, an attorney in Los Angeles with eight to 10 years of immigration experience who is claiming an enhanced rate of $300 per hour could document the prevailing market rate for their services by submitting one or more declarations from other immigration lawyers in Los Angeles with eight to 10 years of similar immigration experience attesting that they routinely charge an hourly rate of $300 (or more).

Law Clerks, Paralegals, and Expert Witnesses

Law clerks, paralegals, and expert witnesses also may be compensated under EAJA at the prevailing market rate.[30] The prevailing market rate need not reflect the rate charged to the client. The statute provides that expert witnesses cannot be compensated at a "rate in excess of the highest rate of compensation for expert witnesses paid by the United States." 28 USC §2412(d)(2)(A)(i).

Market rate surveys often contain information on prevailing rates for law students and paralegals. Declarations from other attorneys attesting to the rates paid to law students and paralegals in the area also can be submitted to establish prevailing rates.

---

[28] In the Ninth Circuit, an enhanced rate may be warranted if the attorney possesses distinctive knowledge and skills developed through a practice specialty; the skills are needed in the litigation; and the skills are not available elsewhere at the statutory rate. *Love v. Reilly*, 924 F.2d 1492, 1496 (9th Cir. 1991) (citation omitted).

[29] *See, e.g.*, *Rueda-Menicucci v. INS*, 132 F.3d 493 (9th Cir. 1997) (stating "a specialty in immigration law could be a special factor warranting an enhancement of the statutory rate" if that specialty is "needful for the litigation in question"); *Pollgreen v. Morris*, 911 F. 2d 527, 537–38 (11th Cir. 1990) (recognizing that a "special factor" rate adjustment might be appropriate for attorneys who have a special expertise in immigration law); *Douglas v. Baker*, 809 F. Supp. 131, 135 (D.D.C. 1992) (awarding enhanced EAJA rate based, in part, on attorneys extensive experience in immigration law). *But see National Ass'n of Mfrs. v. United States DOL*, 962 F. Supp. 191 (D.D.C. 1997) ("Unlike patent law, no technical education is necessary to excel in either" immigration or administrative law). *See also Atlantic Fish Spotters Ass'n v. Daley*, 205 F.3d 488, 492–93 (1st Cir. 2000) (finding enhanced EAJA rate was improper because special experience in fisheries law was not required for competent representation in the case).

[30] 28 USC §2412(d)(2)(A); *Jean v. Nelson*, 863 F.2d 759, 778 (11th Cir. 1988); *Richardson v. Byrd*, 709 F.2d 1016, 1023 (5th Cir. 1983); *Jordan v. U.S. DOJ*, 691 F.2d 514, 522–24 (D.C. Cir. 1982). *See also Missouri v. Jenkins*, 491 U.S. 274, 281–89 (1989).

[Document No. 528]
MOTION FOR ATTORNEYS' FEES AND COSTS UNDER THE EQUAL ACCESS TO JUSTICE ACT

Description: This is the proscribed format for requesting attorneys' fees and costs under the Equal Access to Justice Act, after successful federal court litigation against the Department of Homeland Security (DHS) or any other federal agency.

Advantages: This petition, if successful, reimburses the client for his or her out-of-pocket costs for attorneys' fees. It is also a useful tool in deterring the government from further action in a case.

Limitations: Under the statute, the petitioner for attorneys' fees must show that he or she prevailed on the merits and that the government's position was "substantially justified." Close questions of law and disputed issues of fact typically result in a denial of the petition. Also, the hourly fee of the recovery is limited, unless petitioner can establish why a higher hourly rate is proper.

Notes: Advocates of requesting attorneys' fees from the government under EAJA typically first analyze whether the cost of seeking attorneys' fees is greater then the actual recovery of fees would be. Although entitled to fees for work done seeking EAJA fees, in some cases that cost is too great in terms of time expenditure (that time being better spent in other activities). However, in meritless actions, nothing sends a better message to DHS than an award of attorneys' fees. Remember to include the attorney affidavit on fees along with the motion. The fees must be broken down into time-measured units.

See also the preceding discussion, "Attorneys' Fees and Costs Under the Equal Access to Justice Act."

Citations: 5 USC §504 *et seq.*

UNITED STATES DISTRICT COURT
WESTERN DISTRICT OF WASHINGTON
AT SEATTLE

[Alien] *et al.*, Plaintiffs, v. UNITED STATES OF AMERICA, Defendant.	**CIVIL CASE NO:** **PLAINTIFFS' MOTION FOR COSTS, ATTORNEYS' FEES AND OTHER EXPENSES UNDER THE EQUAL ACCESS TO JUSTICE ACT AND INCORPORATED MEMORANDUM OF LAW** **ORAL ARGUMENT REQUESTED**

Eligible[1] Plaintiffs, **[Alien]**, et al., by and through their undersigned counsel, pursuant to 28 U.S.C. §2412, respectfully request this Honorable Court to grant them their costs, attorneys' fees, and expenses under Equal Access to Justice Act (EAJA), and state in support thereof as follows:

I. PLAINTIFFS ARE THE PREVAILING PARTY

Plaintiffs are the prevailing party for the purposes of being granted attorneys' fees and costs under EAJA. On November 1, 2004, this Court issued its Order and Judgment granting the Plaintiffs' Motion for Partial Summary Judgment and denying Defendant's Motion to Dismiss.

A. Prevailing Parties

A "prevailing party" is one who has been awarded some relief by the court on the merits of at least some of his claims. *Hanrahan v. Hampton*, 446 U.S. 754, 758 (1980). To obtain an award of attorneys' fees and expenses under EAJA, a plaintiff must demonstrate that he or she was the "prevailing party" within the meaning of the Act. *Buckhannon Board and Care Home, Inc. v. West Virginia Dept. of Health*, 532 U.S. 598 (2001). In designating parties eligible for an award of litigation costs, the U.S. Supreme Court has held that "Congress employed the term 'prevailing party,' a legal term of art, defined by Black's Law Dictionary, as '[a] party in whose favor a judgment is rendered, regardless of the amount of damages awarded <in certain cases, the court will award attorney's fees to the prevailing party>.--Also termed successful party.' " *Id.* at 603. As stated above, a "prevailing party" is one "who has been awarded some relief by the court." *Id.* (emphasis added). In the Ninth Circuit, *Buckhannon* has been applied and interpreted as holding that "to be considered a prevailing party, one must have obtained a 'judicial imprimatur' that alters the legal relationship of the parties, such as a judgment on

[1] As will be discussed, only <u>eligible</u> Plaintiffs may recover fees under the Equal Access to Justice Act (EAJA), codified at 28 U.S.C. § 2412. Not all Plaintiffs are eligible to receive fees. Some plaintiffs do not meet the EAJA requirement that their net worth did not exceed $2 million at the time of filing the instant action. An affidavit from **[Expert 1]** is attached which addresses this issue. *See* Exh. A.

the merits or a court-ordered consent decree . . . Judgments and consent decrees are examples of that, but they are not the only examples." *Watson v. County of Riverside*, 300 F.3d 1092 (9th Cir. 2002) (holding that plaintiffs may be "prevailing party" even where only preliminary injunction granted).

1. Chronology of Events

On October 3, 2003, subsequent to the Ninth Circuit's ruling in *Chang v. United States*, 327 F.3d 911 (9th Cir. 2003), the Plaintiffs, **[Alien]**, et. al., filed their Complaint in the instant action for injunctive and declaratory relief inter alia seeking to prohibit Defendant, the United States of America, and its agents, from retroactively applying new rules and requirements in connection with their administration of the laws permitting Plaintiffs to become lawful permanent residents through investments in the United States, 8 U.S.C. § 1153(b)(5) ("Immigrant Investor Law" or "Immigrant Investment Program" or "EB-5 Program"). See Comp at ¶ 1; *Chang*, 327 F.3d at 915-16. On June 8, 2004, Plaintiffs' filed their Motion for Partial Summary Judgment. On June 9, 2004, Plaintiff filed a motion to allow the use of prior discovery in a related case currently pending in the Central District of California, *Ahn v. United States*, which motion was granted by the Court on June 10, 2004. Shortly thereafter, on June 14, Defendant filed its Motion to Dismiss, or in the Alternative, for Judgment on the Pleadings. In its Order and Judgment issued November 1, 2004, this Court denied Defendant's Motion to Dismiss or in the alternative for judgment on the pleadings, and granted Plaintiff's Motion for Partial Summary Judgment.

2. The Nature of the Relief Granted

The Court, on November 1, 2004, granted Plaintiffs' Motion for Partial Summary Judgment, holding that the Ninth Circuit's recent decision in *Chang* "prohibits retroactive application of the precedent decisions as a basis upon which to deny I-829 petitions when the immigrant investors' I-526 petitions were approved before the precedent decisions were issued. Plaintiffs here are similarly situated as the plaintiffs in *Chang*, and therefore, the same result is warranted." See Order, p. 13. This relief shows that Defendant, by and through its agents, is prohibited from denying Plaintiffs' I-829 petitions based on the retroactive application of the *Izumii* precedent decisions.

On November 5, 2004, Plaintiffs filed with this Court a motion seeking clarification and/or reconsideration of the November 1, 2004 order and judgment, to determine inter alia whether the Court intended to grant injunctive as well as declaratory relief. The instant motion for EAJA fees, however, is not affected by the outcome of the Motion for Clarification and/or Reconsideration because, in any event, Plaintiffs are the "prevailing party" in this litigation. The relief that has been granted, even assuming arguendo it is not inclusive of injunctive relief, satisfies the test for the "prevailing party" standard. *See Buckhannon Board and Care Home*, 532 U.S. at 603 ("prevailing party" is one "who has been awarded some relief by the court"). Even though the Court granted Plaintiffs' Motion for Partial Summary Judgment, it is apparent from the November 1, 2004 Judgment itself that the Court construed its ruling as a final judgment disposing of all claims either directly or by necessary implication. In the words of the Court,

> IT IS ORDERED AND ADJUDGED: Pursuant to Rule 56, summary judgment is granted on Plaintiffs' claim for improper retroactive application of [the precedent decisions]. . . Defendant may not retroactively apply these. . .decisions as a basis upon which to deny Plaintiffs' I-829 petitions when their I-526 petitions were approved before the precedent decisions were issued. Plaintiffs' remaining claims are rendered moot by the Court's order. Therefore, entry of final judgment is appropriate.

See Nov. 1, 2004 Judgment. Accordingly, it is apparent that the November 1st Judgment was a final judgment.

II. THE GOVERNMENT'S POSITION WAS NOT SUBSTANTIALLY JUSTIFIED IN THIS CASE

The government's position in this case was not substantially justified. To demonstrate substantial justification, it is the government's burden to establish that its position was substantially justified. *Pierce v. Underwood*, 487 U.S. 552, 108 S.Ct. 2541, 101 L.Ed.2d 490 (1988). Substantial justification requires the government to demonstrate that its position in law and fact was "justified in substance or in the main -- that is justified to a degree that would satisfy a reasonable person." *Id.* at 565-66 (citing *United States v. Yoffe*, 775 F.2d 447, 449-450 (1st Cir. 1985); *Dubose v. Pierce*, 761 F.2d, at 917-918; *Citizens Council of Delaware County v. Brinegar*, 741 F.2d 584, 593 (3d Cir. 1984); Anderson v. Heckler, 756 F.2d 1011, 1013 (4th Cir. 1985); *Hanover Building Materials, Inc. v. Guiffrida*, 748 F.2d 1011, 1015 (5th Cir. 1984); *Trident Marine Construction, Inc. v. District Engineer*, 766 F.2d 974, 980 (6th Cir. 1985); *Ramos v. Haig*, 716 F.2d 471, 473 (7th Cir. 1983); *Foster v. Tourtellotte*, 704 F.2d 1109, 1112 (9th Cir. 1983) (per curiam); *United States v. 2,116 Boxes of Boned Beef*, 726 F.2d 1481, 1486-1487 (10th Cir.), cert. denied sub nom. *Jarboe-Lackey Feedlots, Inc. v. United States*, 469 U.S. 825, 105 S.Ct. 105, 83 L.Ed.2d 49 (1984); *Ashburn v. United States*, 740 F.2d 843, 850 (11th Cir. 1984). To demonstrate substantial justification, the government must make a "strong showing." *S&H Riggers and Rectors, Inc. v. Occupational Safety and Health Review Commission*, 672 F.2d 426, 430 (5th Cir. Unit B 1982). To be "substantially justified" means, "of course, more than merely undeserving of sanctions for frivolousness; that is assuredly not the standard for Government litigation of which a reasonable person would approve." *Pierce*, 487 U.S. at 566.

The government's position in this case was without substantial justification. The actions of Defendant and its agents of adjudicating Plaintiffs' I-526 application by retroactively applying *Matter of Izumii*, 22 I & N Dec. 169 (1998) and other precedent decisions was contrary to law, arbitrary, capricious and an abuse of discretion. Additionally, Defendant's position as presented in its Motion to Dismiss, among other documents, also cannot be viewed as substantially justified. Defendant maintained that the instant action was foreclosed under the law of the case doctrine and *res judicata* despite the fact, as this Court noted, that the immigrant investors in the case at hand were "not parties to the *Golden Rainbow* case." *See* Order, p. 7. This Court explicitly stated in its Order that "none of the cases cited by the government apply the law of the case doctrine to two different cases where one of the parties is different from a party in the previous case. Likewise, the Court's research revealed no such cases." *Id.* With respect to its *res judicata* argument, the government's position was equally unsupported. The government's only contention in support its position regarding the alleged identity of the plaintiffs in the present case and the prior *Golden Rainbow* litigation was that "they are really the same parties." *Id.*, p. 8. As the Court held, "merely asserting that 'they are really the same parties' and that their interests are identical is not sufficient." *Id.*

Moreover, the *Chang* case had been decided on appeal and a decision had been issued <u>on April 29, 2003</u>, well before the filing of Plaintiffs' Complaint on October 3, 2003 in the instant case. *See Chang v. United States*, 327 F.3d 911 (9th Cir. 2003). However, despite this earlier decision, as noted by this Court in its order, the holding of the Ninth Circuit in *Chang* regarding retroactivity were directly applicable in the present case. Despite this directly controlling adverse authority, the government's position failed to concede that *Chang* applied. This failure to admit that *Chang* directly applied was not substantially justified and resulted in the needless re-litigation of an issue already decided by a higher court.

Because the Defendant's position in the instant case was <u>not substantially justified</u>, Plaintiffs are entitled to attorneys' fees, expenses, and costs pursuant to the EAJA.

III. THE APPLICANT PLAINTIFFS ARE ELIGIBLE TO RECEIVE AN AWARD UNDER THE EAJA, EVEN THOUGH SOME NON-APPLICANT PLAINTIFFS EXCEED THE NET WORTH REQUIREMENT

Eligibility for an award under EAJA also is dependent upon a plaintiff's net worth, which must not have exceeded $2,000,000 "at the time the civil action was filed." 28 U.S.C. § 2412 (d)(2)(B). In the instant action, some of the Plaintiffs had more significant assets and therefore do not qualify for EAJA fees under this criterion. Nevertheless, Circuit Courts of Appeal that have considered the issue have determined that such a situation is not fatal to the granting of EAJA fees to the Plaintiffs who are eligible. *See Sierra Club v. U.S. Army Corps of Engineers*, 776 F.2d 383 (2d Cir. 1985), cert. denied sub nom. *New York State Dept. of Transp. v. Sierra Club*, 475 U.S. 1084 (1986).

In *Sierra Club*, the Second Circuit held that fees may be awarded even where there are some non-qualifying Plaintiffs. *Id.* at 393. The court reasoned as follows:

> The district court noted that the only issue is whether one plaintiff's ineligibility under the EAJA should be attributed to all plaintiffs. The statute is silent on this point and there is no case law directly on point. Appellees claim that the statute should be read so that only the status of the applicants is considered when determining eligibility for fees. The [Army Corps of Engineers], naturally, agrees with the district court's position that the court should look beyond the applicants to all of the plaintiffs and that if one plaintiff is ineligible, they are all ineligible.
>
> [A majority of the panel] Judge Oakes and Judge Kearse believe that a point midway between the two extremes advanced by the parties should be adopted. They believe that in determining eligibility, a court must look beyond the applicants to all of the plaintiffs. The court must then determine the number of eligible plaintiffs and award fees based on the ratio of eligible plaintiffs to total plaintiffs, here eleven to twelve. This result is supported by *Citizens Council of Delaware County v. Brinegar*, 741 F.2d 584 (3d Cir.1984). In *Citizens Council*, the court found that two of the four plaintiffs were ineligible for fees. Yet, that court remanded the case for a determination as to the fees the two eligible plaintiffs were entitled to recover. 741 F.2d at 598. Thus, the majority holds that the district court's conclusion that appellees are not entitled to recover under the EAJA is reversed. The case is remanded to the court for a determination of fees recoverable under the EAJA in accordance with the majority view.

Id. (emphasis added). As the above passage reveals, the correct procedure to be followed in such cases is to create a ratio of eligible to ineligible plaintiffs and apply this proportion to the total fees to be awarded. Moreover, the ineligible Plaintiffs in the instant case do not join in the instant Motion for Costs, Attorneys' Fees and Other Expenses, and therefore cannot be considered applicants for EAJA fees. *See* Affidavit of **[Expert 1]**, who reviewed financial statements of Plaintiffs indicating the ratio of eligible to ineligible Plaintiffs (Exh. A).

Since most Plaintiffs in this case are individuals whose net worth **did not** exceed two million dollars ($2,000,000) at the time the civil action was filed, they are eligible to receive attorneys' fees under the EAJA. 28 U.S.C. § 2412(d)(2)(B). Thus, fees should be awarded based upon a ratio of eligible to ineligible plaintiffs as the court in *Sierra Club v. U.S. Army Corps of Engineers*, 776 F.2d 383 (2d Cir. 1985), made clear.

IV. PLAINTIFFS' COUNSEL IS PROVIDING HEREIN AN ITEMIZED STATEMENT OF ATTORNEYS' FEES, EXPENSES AND COSTS

The United States Congress provided for the recovery of costs, fees and other expenses, including expert witness fees and reasonable attorneys' fees, under EAJA. 28 U.S.C. § 2412(d)(2)(A). Attorneys' fees are limited to a rate of one hundred twenty-five dollars ($125.00) per hour unless the Court determines that an increase in the cost of living or a special factor permits a higher fee. *Id.*

Under *Pierce*, this Court must engage in a two-step analysis. *Jean v. Nelson*, 863 F.2d 759, 773-74 (11th Cir. 1988). First, the Court must determine the prevailing market rates for the kind and quality of the services furnished by Plaintiffs' counsel. *Jean v. Nelson*, 863 F.2d at 773. Once the prevailing market rate is determined, if it is above one hundred twenty-five dollars per hour, the Court must then award, at the least, the one hundred twenty-five dollars per-hour rate. The attached expert affidavits demonstrate the market rates for the range of skill levels for all attorneys in this case. *See* Expert Affidavits of **[Expert 2]** (Exh. B) and **[Expert 3]** (Exh. C); *see also* Affidavits of **[Attorney 1]** (Exh. D), **[Attorney 2]** (Exh. E), and **[Attorney 3]** (Exh. F).

The Court may then determine that a party is entitled to more than one hundred twenty-five dollars per hour based on the cost of living or other special factors, *Jean v. Nelson*, 863 F.2d at 773-74, such as the limited availability of counsel where attorneys "have some distinctive knowledge or specialized skill needful for the litigation in question." *Pierce*, 108 S.Ct. at 2554. Immigration law is a narrow legal specialty that may be considered a special factor to raise the fee in excess of the one hundred twenty-five dollars per-hour cap. *Jean v. Nelson*, 863 F.2d at 774, n. 12. Moreover, Circuit Courts of Appeals have recognized that the judgment as to whether or not an immigration attorney or every immigration lawsuit warrants an upward adjustment of the hourly rate is "better left to the discretion of the district court as application of the phrase will necessarily depend on the complexity of the case ('the litigation in question') and on the experience ('distinctive knowledge') and acquired expertise ('specialized skill') of the particular billing attorney." *Id.*

In the present case, Plaintiffs' counsel are all experienced in matters concerning immigration and federal court litigation, and some are recognized nationally for their expertise. *See* Affidavits of Experts and of Counsel, attached hereto as Exhs. B through F. This case involved intricate issues of immigration law, involving the interpretation of statutory and INS (now CIS) regulations governing issues involving the EB-5 program and its requirements. Plaintiffs' counsel also have particular expertise in federal litigation involving immigration issues—an expertise shared by few immigration lawyers. *See* Expert Affidavits of **[Expert 1]** (Exh. B); **[Expert 2]** (Exh. C); and Affidavit of **[Attorney 1]** (Exh. D).

Included in this application are the hours expended by each attorney that were reasonably and necessarily incurred in this litigation. Each attorney has also requested an hourly fee based on the market value of their services and the above-mentioned factors. Plaintiffs' claims for attorneys' fees under the EAJA total <u>$100,564.00</u> and are as follows:

Action filed in this Court, W.D. Wash. District Court:

[Attorney 1], ESQ.

Fees: $25,095

Hours: 71.70

Rate: $350.00

[Attorney 2], ESQ.

Fees: $11,770

Hours: 42.80

Rate: $275.00

[Attorney 3], ESQ.

Fees: $60,435

Hours: 268.60

Rate: $225.00

(Paralegal Services) **[Paralegal 1]/[Paralegal 2]**

Fees: $3,263.75

Hours: 29.53

Rate: $125.00

Plaintiff has also submitted, concurrently with this application, a bill of costs pursuant to 28 U.S.C. § 1920 and § 2412 by attorneys in the total amount of $ 12,234.97 for the case filed in Federal District Court, which are attached hereto as Exh. G.

WHEREFORE, *Eligible* Plaintiffs respectfully request that this Honorable Court grant them fair and reasonable attorneys' fees, expenses and other costs in this litigation.

Dated: November 30,2004

Respectfully Submitted,
By: /s/ **[Attorney]**

LIST OF EXHIBITS

Exh A	Affidavit of **[Expert 1]**
Exh B	Expert Affidavit of **[Expert 2]**
Exh C	Expert Affidavit of **[Expert 3]**
Exh D	Affidavit of **[Attorney 1]**
Exh E	Affidavit of **[Attorney 2]**
Exh F	Affidavit of **[Attorney 3]**
Exh G	Bill of Costs

CHAPTER 6
COURT OF APPEALS PLEADINGS AND MEMORANDA

How to File a Petition for Review

by the AILF Legal Action Center[*]

HIGHLIGHTS OF THIS ADVISORY

This practice advisory addresses the current procedures[1] and general requirements for filing and litigating a petition for review. In addition, it addresses the following fundamental points of which counsel should be aware when filing a petition for review:

- Petitions for review must be filed no later than 30 days after the date of the decision of the Board of Immigration Appeals (BIA) or the U.S. Immigration and Customs Enforcement (ICE). This deadline is jurisdictional and, with limited exceptions, *cannot* be tolled. The petition for review must be received by the clerk's office on or before the 30th day and not merely mailed by that date.
- The 30-day deadline for filing a petition for review of the underlying decision is *not* extended by the filing of a motion to reopen or reconsider nor is it extended by the grant or extension of voluntary departure. To obtain review of issues arising from a BIA decision and issues arising from the denial of a motion to reopen or reconsider, separate petitions for review of each BIA decision must be filed.
- Filing a petition for review does *not* stay the individual's removal from the country.
- Filing a petition for review does *not necessarily stay the individual's voluntary departure period.*
- ICE can deport an individual *before* the 30-day deadline expires.
- If in doubt about whether the court of appeals has jurisdiction, it may be prudent to timely file the petition for review to preserve the individual's right to seek review.

Sample petitions for review are attached as Appendices A and B. A copy of IIRAIRA §309 is attached as Appendix C. A list of websites for the courts of appeals is attached as Appendix D. A list of national addresses for service of the petition is attached as Appendix E. An unofficial "redlined" version of INA §242, that is, showing the amendments made by the REAL ID Act of 2005, Pub. L. 109-13, 119 Stat. 231 (May 11, 2005) is located at *www.ailf.org/lac/lac_realidresources.htm.* The information in this document is current as the date of this advisory,[2] but does not substitute for individual legal advice supplied by a lawyer familiar with a client's case.

BACKGROUND AND INTRODUCTION

A petition for review is the document filed by, or on behalf of, an individual seeking review of an agency decision in a circuit court of appeals. In the immigration context, a petition for review is commonly filed to obtain review of a decision of deportation, exclusion, or removal issued by the BIA. In addition, a petition for review may be filed to obtain review of a removal order issued by ICE under certain provisions of the Immigration and Nationality Act (INA).

Through the enactment of Illegal Immigration Reform and Immigrant Responsibility Act of 1996 (IIRAIRA), Congress eliminated the distinction between deportation and exclusion proceedings and combined them into a single "removal" proceeding. Judicial review of final removal orders, resulting from removal proceedings commenced after IIRAIRA's effective date (Apr. 1, 1997), is governed by INA §242, 8 USC §1252. On May 11, 2005, through the enactment of the REAL ID Act of 2005, Congress amended this provision. The REAL ID Act expands the jurisdiction of the courts of appeals to consider, on petition for review, certain issues previously precluded by IIRAIRA. The courts of appeals now have jurisdiction to review all constitutional issues and questions of law related to a final order of removal, deportation, or exclusion issued before, on, or after the enactment date. The REAL ID Act also purports to eliminate all review of final orders of removal, deportation, or exclusion by habeas corpus.[3]

Prior to the enactment of the REAL ID Act, judicial review of final deportation or exclusion orders, resulting from proceedings commenced before April 1997, was generally governed by transitional rules

---

[*] **The Legal Action Center** (LAC) is the litigation arm of the American Immigration Law Foundation.

[1] Last updated May 25, 2005 (following the enactment of the REAL ID Act of 2005).

[2] See Note 1, *supra.*

[3] *See generally* INA §242 as amended by the REAL ID Act.

set forth in IIRAIRA §309. The REAL ID Act modified this rule, stating that petitions for review of orders of deportation or exclusion filed under the transitional rules "shall" be treated as if filed as a petition for review under new INA §242 (as amended by REAL ID Act §106(d)). A copy of IIRAIRA §309 is reprinted in Appendix C.

AILF has issued a practice advisory on the new judicial review provisions of the REAL ID Act.[4]

COURT OF APPEALS' JURISDICTION OVER PETITIONS FOR REVIEW

Determining whether a circuit court possesses subject matter jurisdiction to review a decision or a particular issue often requires a complicated legal analysis. Such determinations also are highly dependent on constantly evolving case law. The amendments made by the REAL ID expand the scope of petition for review jurisdiction. In time, the courts will decide the extent of that jurisdiction.

This section is meant to illustrate the types of decisions that may be reviewed through a petition for review. It is not exhaustive and should not be substituted for independent legal research regarding governing case law.

The following are examples of the types of decisions that may be reviewed through a petition for review:

A BIA decision to:

- issue a final removal order, including an affirmance without opinion;
- deny a motion to reconsider or a motion to reopen; or
- affirm an immigration judge's denial of an asylum application.

An order of removal issued by ICE under:

- INA §241(a)(5); or
- INA §238(b).

A challenge to a BIA or ICE decision may involve one or more of the following types of claims: legal, constitutional, factual, or discretionary. In general, legal claims assert that the BIA/ICE erroneously applied or interpreted the law (for example, the INA or the regulations); constitutional challenges assert that the BIA/ICE violated a constitutional right (for example, due process or equal protection); factual claims assert that certain findings of fact made by the BIA/ICE were erroneous; and discretionary claims assert the BIA/ICE reached the wrong conclusion when exercising discretion.

Whether a claim is reviewable in the court of appeals involves additional analysis. The first question to consider is whether the INA contains a bar to review related to the decision, nature of the claim, or the person bringing the challenge. For example, INA §208(a)(3), 8 USC §1158(a)(3), bars review of determinations regarding whether an asylum application was timely filed within one year of arrival; INA §242(a)(2)(A), 8 USC §1252(a)(2)(A), bars court of appeals review of expedited removal orders; INA §242(a)(2)(B), 8 USC §1252(a)(2)(B), and IIRAIRA §309(c)(4)(E) bar review of certain discretionary judgments, and INA §242(a)(2)(C), 8 USC §1252(a)(2)(C), and IIRAIRA §309(c)(4)(G) bar petitions for review filed by, or on behalf of, individuals found removable due to certain criminal offenses.

If, and only if, the INA contains a bar to review related to the decision, nature of the claim, or the person bringing the challenge, then the claim must present either a question of law or a constitutional claim for the court to have jurisdiction over the petition for review. The REAL ID Act added new INA §242(a)(2)(D), 8 USC §1252(a)(2)(D), which provides that the bars to judicial review do *not* apply if the petition for review raises a question of law or constitutional claim. Thus, under the REAL ID Act, a court of appeals has jurisdiction over a petition for review that raises constitutional issues or questions of law even in cases that otherwise would be barred.

In addition, courts should continue to retain jurisdiction to determine whether they have jurisdiction over the petition for review. AILF believes that this should be true even if the issues involve mixed questions of law and fact.

As discussed in the section on "Petition Requirements" below, until the courts address the REAL ID Act amendments, and specifically which, if any, issues remain reviewable via habeas corpus, it is advisable to *timely* file a petition for review to preserve petitioner's right to seek review.[5]

---

[4] *See* "Judicial Review Provisions of the REAL ID Act" (May 12, 2005), at *www.ailf.org/lac/lac_pa_051205.pdf.*

[5] AILF believes review of detention issues still is available in habeas corpus proceedings.

PETITION REQUIREMENTS

Filing Deadline—New Cases

A petition for review "*must be filed not later than thirty days after the date of the final order*" of removal or the final order of exclusion or deportation. *See* INA §242(b)(1), 8 USC §1252(b)(1) (removal orders); IIRAIRA §309(c)(4)(C) as amended by REAL ID §106(d) (deportation and exclusion orders) (emphasis added).

The 30-day deadline for filing a petition for review of the underlying decision is *not* extended by the filing of a motion to reopen or reconsider nor is it extended by the grant or extension of voluntary departure. To obtain review of issues arising from a BIA decision and issues arising from the denial of a motion to reopen or reconsider, separate petitions for review of each BIA decision must be filed. If separate petitions are not filed, the court's review may be limited to the issues arising from the BIA decision for which review is sought. For example, if a petition for review of the BIA's decision denying a motion to reopen or reconsider has been filed but a petition for review of the BIA decision underlying the motion has *not* been filed, issues arising from the underlying BIA decision may not be preserved for review.

The deadline for filing a petition for review is "mandatory and jurisdictional" and is "not subject to equitable tolling."[6] Because the 30-day deadline is jurisdictional, circuit courts lack authority to consider late-filed petitions for review.[7]

The 30-day time period begins running from the date of the BIA's decision affirming the immigration judge. If the BIA denied a motion to reopen or reconsider, the 30-day time period begins running from the date of the BIA decision denying the motion. In reinstatement cases under INA §241(a)(5) or administrative deportation cases under INA §238(b), the 30-day deadline begins running from the date of the final ICE order.[8] The petition for review must be received by the clerk's office on or before the thirtieth day and not merely mailed by that date.

Where the 30-day deadline has expired due to ineffective assistance of counsel, new counsel may consider filing a motion to reopen to the BIA (provided the motion is filed within the 90-day statutory time period for filing motions to reopen). Counsel may also consider filing a motion requesting that the BIA rescind and re-issue its decision to allow petitioner to seek judicial review.[9]

Filing Deadline—District Court Cases Transferred Pursuant to the REAL ID Act

The new law provides that district courts "shall" transfer habeas corpus petitions challenging a final order of removal that are pending in the district court on May 11, 2005 (the date that the REAL ID Act was enacted) to the court of appeals in which a petition for review could have been filed (*i.e.*, the circuit having jurisdiction over the place the immigration judge completed proceedings). The REAL ID Act specifies that only habeas petitions that challenge final orders of deportation, exclusion, or removal (or the part of the habeas petition challenging such an order) should be transferred.

The courts of appeals must treat the transferred case as if it was filed as a petition for review, with one exception. The one exception is that the requirement that a petition for review must be filed within 30 days of the final removal order does not apply to these transferred cases. This means that a habeas petition challenging a final order that was pending in district court on May 11, 2005, will be transferred to the court of appeals even if the habeas petition was not filed within 30 days of the final re-

---

[6] *Stone v. INS*, 514 U.S. 386, 405 (1995).

[7] There are very few situations in which a court might excuse a late-filed petition for review, for example: (1) where the court or the BIA provided misleading information as to the deadline for filing a petition for review; and (2) where the BIA failed to comply with the applicable regulations regarding mailing the decision to petitioner or petitioner's counsel. For further information on these situations and potential remedies, see AILF's practice advisory entitled "Suggested Strategies for Remedying Missed Petition for Review Deadlines or Filings in the Wrong Court" (Apr. 20, 2005), located at *www.ailf.org/lac/lac_pa_042005.pdf*.

[8] Pursuant to *Morales-Izquierdo v. Ashcroft*, 388 F.3d 1299 (9th Cir. 2004) (rehearing pending), only immigration judges may make reinstatement determinations under INA §241(a)(5). Presumably, the immigration judge's decision may be appealed to the BIA. Thus, in the Ninth Circuit, the 30-day clock should begin running from the date of the BIA's decision.

[9] For further information regarding motions to rescind and reissue, see AILF's practice advisories entitled "Suggested Strategies for Remedying Missed Petition for Review Deadlines or Filings in the Wrong Court" (Apr. 20, 2005) and "Judicial Review Provisions of the REAL ID Act: Strategies For Dealing With The Expansion Of Jurisdiction In The Court Of Appeals," (May 20, 2005) both located on AILF's website at *www.ailf.org/lac/lac_index.asp*.

moval order. However, the 30-day deadline continues to apply to all other petitions for review.

This potentially creates a serious problem for some individuals. Prior to the REAL ID Act, an individual barred from filing a petition for review might have been able to get review through a habeas corpus petition. For example, many individuals with criminal convictions were barred from filing a petition for review under INA §242(a)(2)(C). However, these individuals previously could have filed a habeas corpus petition. There is no deadline for filing a habeas petition. There will be individuals who relied on pre–REAL ID Act law and thus will not have filed a petition for review within 30 days of their final order. If they did not have a habeas petition pending on May 11, 2005, they may be unable to have their cases transferred to the court of appeals pursuant to the REAL ID Act's transfer provision. Thus, these individuals conceivably could be barred from any federal court review under the REAL ID Act: they will no longer be able to file a habeas petition and will have missed the 30-day deadline for filing a petition for review. AILF has issued a practice advisory with administrative suggestions for people in this situation.[10] AILF is also exploring federal court arguments. If you have a client in this situation, please contact *realidcourts@ailf.org*.

Attachments and Contents

Under INA §242(c), 8 USC §1252(c), a petition for review must and need only: (1) include a copy of the final administrative order; and (2) state whether any court has upheld the validity of the order, and if so, state which court, the date of the court's ruling, and the type of proceeding.

The petition should state the name of each individual petitioning for review and should not use "et al." to reference more than one petitioner.[11] For example, where a family is in immigration proceedings but the BIA decision only references the lead respondent, the petition for review should name each family member whose case was decided by that order, even if not specifically mentioned in the order.

A sample petition for review is attached as Appendix A. Although it is not necessary at this stage to discuss the jurisdictional basis or merits of the petition, a more detailed sample petition for review, containing the basis for jurisdiction and venue, is also provided as a reference and is attached as Appendix B.

STAY OF REMOVAL AND STAY OF VOLUNTARY DEPARTURE

ICE can deport petitioner *before* the 30-day deadline for filing a petition for review has run.

ICE may deport an individual as soon as the BIA issues its order. In reinstatement cases under INA §241(a)(5) and administrative removal cases under INA §238(b), deportation may occur as soon as ICE issues its removal order. In the post-AEDPA and IIRAIRA era, serving the petition for review does *not* stay deportation "unless the court orders otherwise."[12] Thus, petitioner also may want to file for a stay of the removal order pending the petition for review. The court must grant the stay request to prevent petitioner's removal from the country.

The varying circuit standards for, and strategic pros and cons of, applying for a stay of removal are discussed in greater detail in AILF's October 2004 Practice Advisory entitled, "Applying for a Stay of Removal in Federal Court Proceedings" (*www.ailf.org/lac/lac_pa_102504.pdf*).

In addition to requesting a stay of removal, the petitioner also may need to file a motion for stay of the voluntary departure period. In most circuits, the voluntary departure period begins to run from the date that the BIA issues its decision. If the petitioner remains in the United States past the departure date, he or she may lose the opportunity to depart voluntarily and may become ineligible for various forms of relief from removal for a period of 10 years.[13] A motion for a stay of the voluntary departure period may need to be filed before the voluntary departure period expires.

The law regarding how to protect voluntary departure while the petition for review is pending is unsettled in many circuits; in fact, there are many pending cases that will address this issue. Attorneys are advised to review AILF's practice advisories on this topic (*www.ailf.org/lac/lac_pa_092604.pdf*) and

---

[10] *See* "Judicial Review Provisions of the REAL ID Act: Strategies for Dealing with the Expansion of Jurisdiction in the Court of Appeals (May 20, 2005), at *www.ailf.org/lac/lac_pa_realid2_052005.pdf*.

[11] Federal Rule of Appellate Procedure (FRAP) 15(a)(2)(A).

[12] Compare former INA §1106(a)(3), 8 USC §1105a(a)(3) with INA §242(b)(3)(B), 8 USC §1252(b)(3)(B) and IIRAIRA §309(c)(4)(F).

[13] *See* INA §240B(d), 8 USC §1229c(d).

to independently confirm whether the law in their circuit has changed since the date of that advisory.

WHERE TO FILE THE PETITION FOR REVIEW

Venue is restricted to the court of appeals for the judicial circuit in which the immigration judge completed the proceedings.[14] This requirement imposes a special hardship on individuals who are ordered removed while detained at detention centers in remote locations where counsel is often limited or unavailable.

FILING FEE

The filing fee for a petition for review is usually $250, but counsel should check local court rules to verify the fee amount. A list of web addresses for the U.S. courts of appeals is attached in Appendix D and can also be located at *www.uscourts.gov*. Petitioner may request leave to proceed *in forma pauperis* by filing a motion and supporting affidavit with the court. *See* FRAP 24(b) and corresponding local circuit rules.

SERVICE ON RESPONDENT

Whom to Sue

Through the enactment of IIRAIRA §306(a)(2), Congress changed the designated respondent in a petition for review from the Immigration and Naturalization Service (INS) to the Attorney General.[15] Therefore, in *removal* cases, the respondent is the Attorney General, Alberto Gonzales.

Judicial review of *deportation and exclusion* cases is governed by IIRAIRA's transitional rules. Because the REAL ID Act provides that petitions for review in transitional rule cases shall be treated as if filed under INA §242 as amended by the new law, the Attorney General should be named as the respondent.[16] As INA §242(b)(3)(A) provides that the respondent is the Attorney General in removal cases, the provision should also apply in transitional rule cases. Thus, in deportation and removal cases, the respondent is also the Attorney General, Alberto Gonzales.

Whom to Serve

The petition must be served "on the Attorney General and on the officer or employee of the Service in charge of the Service district in which the final order of removal under section 240 was entered."[17]

Serve the Attorney General by sending a complete copy of the petition for review to the address set forth in Appendix E. Attorneys from the Office of Immigration Litigation (OIL), a division within the Civil Division of the Department of Justice, litigate on behalf of the Attorney General with one exception.[18] Thus, it is advisable to also serve a copy of the petition on OIL at the address listed in Appendix E. After receiving a copy of the petition, the OIL attorneys assigned to the case will usually enter their appearance before the court by letter and should inform petitioner's counsel.

To serve the officer in charge of the district, counsel should serve the ICE Field Office Director for Detention and Removal with jurisdiction over the district where the final administrative order was issued. Counsel may need to make inquiries to learn the name of the officer in charge of detention and removal in their area. Counsel will also need to ascertain the proper mailing address for the ICE Field Office Director in order to serve this official.

At the same time, petitioner must file a certificate of service listing the names and addresses of those served and the manner of service. Federal Rules of Appellate Procedure (FRAP) 15(c). Addresses for the Attorney General and the Office of Immigration Litigation are attached as Appendix E. Because local ICE office addresses are subject to change, there is no list of these addresses attached. Instead, counsel will need to contact the local ICE office to get the correct address. FRAP 15(c) further requires that petitioner must give "the clerk enough copies of the petition . . . to serve each respondent." Presumably, an original plus one copy of the petition must be filed where the Attorney General is the only named respondent. However, counsel should verify the number of copies required by checking local procedures or contacting the clerk's

[14] INA §242(b)(2), 8 USC §1252(b)(2); IIRAIRA §309(c)(4)(D).

[15] *Compare* former INA §106(a)(3), 8 USC §1105a(a)(3) *with* INA §242(b)(3)(A), 8 USC §1252(b)(3)(A).

[16] *See* REAL ID §106(d).

[17] INA §242(b)(3)(A), 8 USC §1252(b)(3)(A). If the order of removal was entered under another section of law, for example, INA §§238(b) or 241(a)(5), counsel presumably is still bound by the service requirements of INA §242(b)(3)(A), 8 USC §1252(b)(3)(A).

[18] In the Second Circuit, Assistant U.S. Attorneys handle petitions for review.

office. *See also* FRAP 25 (Filing and Service) and corresponding local court rules.

Service of Future Pleadings

After opposing counsel has entered their appearance, future pleadings "must be made on the party's counsel" by a prescribed method.[19] Such pleadings must be filed with either: (1) an acknowledgement of service by the person served; or (2) a statement by the person effectuating service attesting to the date and manner of service, the names of those served, and the appropriate mail, e-mail or delivery address or facsimile number, depending on the manner of service. The proof of service may appear on or be affixed to the pleading.[20] The local rules set out acceptable methods of service. A list of websites for the courts of appeals is attached as Appendix D.

LITIGATING THE PETITION IN THE COURT OF APPEALS

Admission and Entry of Appearance

Attorneys must be admitted to practice before the court of appeals in which the petition for review is filed or, in some courts, must file an application for admission either simultaneously or within a proscribed time period. Some courts allow an attorney who is not admitted to appear *pro hac vice* or, if appointed, to represent a petitioner proceeding *in forma pauperis*.

Virtually all courts of appeals require counsel to enter an appearance in each case. Entry of Appearance forms are generally available on the court's website and from the clerk's office.

For further information regarding admission and appearance requirements, counsel should consult FRAP 46 and corresponding local circuit rules. Information is also available on court websites. See Appendix D, listing websites for the courts of appeals.

Federal Rules of Appellate Procedure

The rules and procedure for litigation in the courts of appeals are governed by the Federal Rules of Appellate Procedure in conjunction with each circuit's local rules. This advisory provides a brief overview of appellate procedure related to petition for review litigation; however, it does not address all of the Federal Rules of Appellate Procedure nor does it address local circuit rules.

Once a petition for review is filed, the court generally issues an order/schedule for the parties to file the Certified Record of Proceedings (also known as the Administrative Record), Petitioner's Opening Brief (and possibly Excerpts of Record), Respondent's Answering Brief (and possibly Excerpt of Record), and Petitioner's Reply Brief (optional).

Certified Record of Proceedings

The agency is obligated to file the Certified Record of Proceeding (also called the Certified Administrative Record), within 40 days of service of the petition for review.[21] The record must include: (1) the order involved; (2) any findings or report on which it is based; and (3) pleadings, evidence, and other parts of the proceeding before the agency, including the transcripts of hearings.[22] Where the petition seeks review of a BIA order, the record is prepared by the Executive Office for Immigration Review and filed by OIL.

Supplemental Authorities—28(j) Letters

If pertinent and significant authorities come to petitioner's attention after briefing is completed or after oral argument but before the court issues a decision, counsel should advise the court of the supplemental citations pursuant to FRAP 28(j). The advisal is made by letter and copied to opposing counsel. "The letter must state the reasons for the supplemental citations, referring either to the page of the brief or to a point argued orally. The body of the letter must not exceed 350 words. Any response must be made promptly and must be similarly limited."[23]

Oral Argument

Pursuant to FRAP 34, any party may file, or a court may require by local rule, a statement explaining why an oral argument should, or need not, be permitted. Oral arguments must be permitted unless a panel of three judges decides that:

1. the appeal is frivolous;
2. the dispositive issue(s) have already been decided; or

[19] FRAP 25(b) and (c).

[20] *See* FRAP 25(d)(3).

[21] FRAP 17(a).

[22] FRAP 16(a).

[23] FRAP 28(j).

3. the facts and arguments are adequately presented in the briefs and records.

The court clerk will notify the parties of the date, time, place, and time allotted for argument if the court determines oral argument is necessary.

Judgment and Post-Judgment Review Timing

The judgment (or decision) is entered on the docket by the clerk after he or she receives the court's opinion or upon the court's instruction (where judgment is rendered without opinion).[24] A petition for rehearing or petition for rehearing *en banc* may be filed within 45 days after entry of judgment, unless otherwise specified by the court or local rule.[25] Unless the court directs otherwise, the mandate will automatically issue seven calendar days after the time to file a petition for rehearing expires, or seven calendar days after entry of an order denying a timely petition for panel rehearing, petition for rehearing *en banc*, or motion for stay of mandate, whichever is later.[26]

Briefing Schedule

INA §242(b)(3)(C), 8 USC §1252(b)(3)(C), states that petitioner must serve and file the opening brief no later than 40 days after the date on which the administrative record is available, and further states that petitioner may serve and file a reply brief within 14 days *after service* of the government's brief.[27] The statute and rule say these deadlines may only be extended by motion upon a showing of good cause.[28] Also, if the brief is not filed, INA §242(b)(3)(C) instructs courts to dismiss the appeal unless a manifest injustice would result.

Most courts do not rely on the time frame in the statute or rule, but rather issue a schedule setting out due dates for the filing of both the administrative record and the briefs. Further, it is common for counsel on either side or both sides to move to extend the briefing schedule or move to hold briefing in abeyance. Written motions are governed by FRAP 27 and corresponding local rules. Some courts also allow telephonic motions for an extension of time to file a brief.

Some confusion may arise if the government fails to timely file the administrative record, the court has not issued a new schedule reflecting a later due date for petitioner's opening brief and the brief due date is approaching. Although arguably the due date for petitioner's opening brief should automatically be postponed in this situation (by operation of INA §242(b)(3)(C) and FRAP 31(a)(a)), the courts operate under their own briefing schedules. Petitioner will be well advised to move for an extension of the briefing schedule on the basis that the administrative record has not been filed, citing the statute and the rule. The court should grant the motion and set a new briefing deadline.

However, the courts rarely but occasionally have denied such a motion and have required petitioners to file an opening brief without the administrative record. In this event, petitioner should comply with the court's order and timely file the opening brief. If counsel has all or some of the record below (perhaps as a result of prior representation or a Freedom of Information Act Request), petitioner should include an appendix with the relevant portions of the record accompanied by a motion for leave to file those portions and should cite to the improvised record in the opening brief. Counsel could object, either in the brief or in an accompanying pleading, that the court's requiring the opening brief to be filed without the administrative record infringes on petitioner's right to appeal, as counsel cannot adequately present an appeal without access to the complete record below. Counsel also might move to file a supplemental or corrected brief, if necessary, after the administrative record is filed.

In addition, the briefing schedule may be delayed or vacated if the government files a motion to dismiss for lack of subject matter jurisdiction claiming that petitioner is barred from direct review in the court of appeals (under INA §242(a)(2), 8 USC §1252(a)(2) or IIRAIRA §309(c)(4)).

When filing briefs in the circuit courts, counsel should consult FRAP 28 (Briefs), 30 (Appendix to the Briefs), 31 (Serving and Filing), and 32 (Form of Briefs, Appendices, and Other Papers), as well as all corresponding local rules. A list of websites for the courts of appeals is attached as Appendix D.

---

[24] FRAP 36 (Entry of Judgment).

[25] FRAP 35 (*En Banc* Determination) and 40 FRAP (Petition for Panel Rehearing).

[26] FRAP 41.

[27] *See also* FRAP 31(a)(1) ("The appellant must serve and file a brief within 40 days after the record is filed.").

[28] INA §242(b)(3)(C); FRAP 31(a)(1).

APPENDIX A: SAMPLE PETITION FOR REVIEW

Notes:

1. Complete *all* underlined spaces (except "Case File No.") as appropriate, depending on whether petitioner seeks review of a final order of removal, deportation, or exclusion. The Court Clerk's Office will assign a Case File Number.
2. Attach a copy of the BIA decision. If seeking review of an order of removal under INA §§241(a)(5) or 238(b), attached a copy of the ICE decision (see n.4).
3. Attach a Certificate of Service, attesting to service on: (1) the Attorney General; (2) the Office of Immigration Litigation; and (3) ICE Field Office Director for Detention and Removal.
4. Always check local circuit court rules regarding filing fee amount, pleading format, the number of copies required for submission, and rules regarding admission and entry of appearance as counsel.

UNITED STATES COURT OF APPEALS FOR THE ______ CIRCUIT

[Name of Petitioner],	)	
	)	
Petitioner,	)	**Case File No.**______________
	)	
v.	)	
	)	**Immigration File No.: [A Number]**
Alberto GONZALES,	)	
Attorney General,	)	
	)	**PETITION FOR REVIEW**
Respondent.	)	

The above-named Petitioner hereby petitions for review by this Court of the final order of removal / deportation / exclusion entered by the Board of Immigration Appeals / Immigration and Customs Enforcement (ICE) (if ordered removed under INA §241(a)(5) [see n. 4] or INA §238(b)) on date of decision. A copy of the decision is attached.

To date, no court has upheld the validity of the order. [*Note*: If the validity of the order has been upheld, state name of the court, date of court's ruling, and the kind of proceeding.]

[Date] Respectfully submitted,

[Attorney]
[Firm/Organization]
[Address]
[Telephone]
[Facsimile]
Attorney(s) for Petitioner

APPENDIX B: SAMPLE PETITION FOR REVIEW (MORE DETAILED)

Notes:

1. Complete *all* underlined spaces (except "Case File No.") as appropriate, depending on whether petitioner seeks review of a final order of removal, deportation, or exclusion. The Court Clerk's Office will assign a Case File Number.
2. Attach a copy of the BIA decision. If seeking review of an order of removal under INA §§241(a)(5) or 238(b), attached a copy of the ICE decision (see n. 4).
3. Attach a Certificate of Service, attesting to service on: (1) the Attorney General; (2) the Office of Immigration Litigation; and (3) ICE Field Office Director for Detention and Removal.
4. Always check local circuit court rules regarding filing fee amount, pleading format, the number of copies required for submission, and rules regarding admission and entry of appearance as counsel.

UNITED STATES COURT OF APPEALS FOR THE _______CIRCUIT

[Name of Petitioner],)	
)	
Petitioner,)	**Case File No.**__________
)	
v.)	
)	**Immigration File No.: [A Number]**
Alberto GONZALES,)	
Attorney General,)	
)	**PETITION FOR REVIEW**
Respondent)	

The above-named Petitioner hereby petitions for review by this Court of the final order of removal / deportation / exclusion entered by the Board of Immigration Appeals / Immigration and Customs Enforcement (ICE) (if ordered removed under INA §241(a)(5) [see n. 4] or INA §238(b)) on date of decision. A copy of the decision is attached.

To date, no court has upheld the validity of the order. [*Note*: If the validity of the order has been upheld, state name of the court, date of court's ruling, and the kind of proceeding].

Jurisdiction is asserted pursuant to 8 USC §1252(a)(1) (removal cases) / §309(c) of the Illegal Immigration Reform and Immigrant Responsibility Act of 1996 (IIRAIRA) as amended by §106 of the REAL ID Act of 2005 (deportation and exclusion cases).

Venue is asserted pursuant to 8 USC §1252(b)(2) (removal cases) / IIRAIRA §309(c)(4)(D) (deportation/exclusion cases) because the immigration judge / ICE (in cases under INA §§241(a)(5) or 238(b)) completed proceedings in **[City, State]**, within the jurisdiction of this judicial circuit.

This petition is timely filed pursuant to 8 USC §1252(b)(1) (removal) / IIRAIRA §309(c)(4)(C) (deportation / exclusion) as it is filed within 30 days of the final order of removal / deportation / exclusion.

[Date]

Respectfully submitted,

[Attorney]
[Firm/Organization]
[Address]
[Telephone]
[Facsimile]
Attorney(s) for Petitioner

Appendix C: Transitional Rules

***Note*: The transitional rules set forth in former INA §106(a)(1995) and IIRAIRA §309 (below) must be read in conjunction with §106(d) of the REAL ID Act of 2005, which provides:**

(d) Transitional Rule Cases. A petition for review filed under former INA §106 of the Immigration and Nationality Act (as in effected before its repeal by section 306(b) of the Illegal Immigration Reform and Immigrant Responsibility Act of 1996 (8 USC §1252 note) shall be treated as if filed as a petition for review under 242 of the Immigration and Nationality Act (8 USC §1252), as amended by this section. Notwithstanding any other provision of law, (statutory or nonstatutory), including section 2241 of Title 28, United States Code, or any other habeas corpus provision, and sections 1361 and 1651 of such title, such petition for review shall be the sole and exclusive means for judicial review of an order of deportation or exclusion.

IIRAIRA §309

Effective Dates; Transition.

(a) In General.—Except as provided in this section and sections 303(b)(2), 306(c), 308(d)(2)(D), or 308(d)(5) of this division, this subtitle and the amendments made by this subtitle shall take effect on the first day of the first month beginning more than 180 days after the date of the enactment of this Act (in this title referred to as the "title III-A effective date").

(b) Promulgation of Regulations.—The Attorney General shall first promulgate regulations to carry out this subtitle by not later than 30 days before the title III-A effective date.

(c) Transition for Aliens in Proceedings.—

(1) General rule that new rules do not apply.—Subject to the succeeding provisions of this subsection, in the case of an alien who is in exclusion or deportation proceedings before the title III-A effective date—

(A) the amendments made by this subtitle shall not apply, and

(B) the proceedings (including judicial review thereof) shall continue to be conducted without regard to such amendments.

(2) Attorney General option to elect to apply new procedures.—In a case described in paragraph (1) in which an evidentiary hearing under section 236 or 242 and 242B of the Immigration and Nationality Act has not commenced as of the title III-A effective date, the Attorney General may elect to proceed under chapter 4 of title II of such Act (as amended by this subtitle). The Attorney General shall provide notice of such election to the alien involved not later than 30 days before the date any evidentiary hearing is commenced. If the Attorney General makes such election, the notice of hearing provided to the alien under section 235 or 242(a) of such Act shall be valid as if provided under section 239 of such Act (as amended by this subtitle) to confer jurisdiction on the immigration judge.

(3) Attorney General option to terminate and reinitiate proceedings.—In the case described in paragraph (1), the Attorney General may elect to terminate proceedings in which there has not been a final administrative decision and to reinitiate proceedings under chapter 4 of title II the Immigration and Nationality Act (as amended by this subtitle). Any determination in the terminated proceeding shall not be binding in the reinitiated proceeding.

(4) Transitional changes in judicial review.—In the case described in paragraph (1) in which a final order of exclusion or deportation is entered more than 30 days after the date of the enactment of this Act, notwithstanding any provision of section 106 of the Immigration and Nationality Act (as in effect as of the date of the enactment of this Act) to the contrary—

(A) in the case of judicial review of a final order of exclusion, subsection (b) of such section shall not apply and the action for judicial review shall be governed by the provisions of subsections (a) and (c) of such in the same manner as they apply to judicial review of orders of deportation;

(B) a court may not order the taking of additional evidence under section 2347(c) of title 28, United States Code;

(C) the petition for judicial review must be filed not later than 30 days after the date of the final order of exclusion or deportation;

(D) the petition for review shall be filed with the court of appeals for the judicial circuit in which the administrative proceedings before the special inquiry officer or immigration judge were completed;

(E) there shall be no appeal of any discretionary decision under section 212(c), 212(h), 212(i), 244, or 245 of the Immigration and Nationality Act (as in effect as of the date of the enactment of this Act);

(F) service of the petition for review shall not stay the deportation of an alien pending the court's decision on the petition, unless the court orders otherwise; and

(G) there shall be no appeal permitted in the case of an alien who is inadmissible or deportable by reason of having committed a criminal offense covered in section 212(a)(2) or section 241(a)(2)(A)(iii), (B), (C), or (D) of the Immigration and Nationality Act (as in effect as of the date of the enactment of this Act), or any offense covered by section 241(a)(2)(A)(ii) of such Act (as in effect on such date) for which both predicate offenses are, without regard to their date of commission, otherwise covered by section 241(a)(2)(A)(i) of such Act (as so in effect).

APPENDIX D: WEBSITES FOR U.S. COURTS OF APPEALS

First Circuit: *www.ca1.uscourts.gov*

Second Circuit: *www.ca2.uscourts.gov*

Third Circuit: *www.ca3.uscourts.gov*

Fourth Circuit: *www.ca4.uscourts.gov*

Fifth Circuit: *www.ca5.uscourts.gov*

Sixth Circuit: *www.ca6.uscourts.gov*

Seventh Circuit: *www.ca7.uscourts.gov*

Eighth Circuit: *www.ca8.uscourts.gov*

Ninth Circuit: *www.ca9.uscourts.gov*

Tenth Circuit: *www.ca10.uscourts.gov*

Eleventh Circuit: *www.ca11.uscourts.gov*

DC Circuit: *www.cadc.uscourts.gov*

APPENDIX E: LIST OF ADDRESSES FOR SERVICE OF A PETITION FOR REVIEW

ATTORNEY GENERAL

Alberto Gonzales
Attorney General
U.S. Department of Justice
950 Pennsylvania Avenue, NW
Washington, DC 20530-0001

OFFICE OF IMMIGRATION LITIGATION

Thomas W. Hussey, Director
Office of Immigration Litigation
U.S. Department of Justice / Civil Division
1331 Pennsylvania Avenue, NW
Washington, DC 20004

ICE DISTRICT OFFICES

Service must also be made on the Field Office Director or, where none exists, the most senior officer in the Detention & Removal Unit. Counsel will need to contact the local ICE office to obtain the name and position title of the appropriate local officer and to obtain the mailing address for service on this individual.

[Document Nos. 601–03]

PETITION FOR REVIEW OF BIA OR DISTRICT COURT DECISION

Description: The following pleadings are used to petition the U.S. Courts of Appeals for a review of a final administrative order of the Board of Immigration Appeals (BIA) or a decision of a federal district court for an issue over which the federal district courts have jurisdiction (*e.g.*, habeas corpus cases).

Advantages: A petition for review secures independent judicial review of a final administrative order of removal of the BIA, or appellate review of a district court judgment.

Limitations: IIRAIRA declares that certain matters are not subject to judicial review. These include denials of discretionary relief, such as cancellation of removal or adjustment of status, and final orders of deportation against criminal aliens. Furthermore, IIRAIRA provides that the court of appeals shall decide the petition only on the administrative record on which the order of removal is based; that the administrative findings of fact are conclusive unless any reasonable adjudicator would be compelled to conclude to the contrary; and that the Attorney General's denial of an asylum claim is conclusive unless manifestly contrary to the law and an abuse of discretion.

Notes: Petitions for review must be filed within 30 days after the date of the final order of removal.

Citations: INA §242.

UNITED STATES COURT OF APPEALS
FOR THE TENTH CIRCUIT

Petitioners	)	
	)	
vs.	)	
	)	**PETITION FOR REVIEW**
ALBERTO R. GONZALES	)	No. ________________
U.S. ATTORNEY GENERAL,	)	BIA File No: **[A Number]**
	)	USCIS File No: **[File Number]**
Respondent.	)	
____________________________	)	

PETITION FOR REVIEW

Pursuant to Rule 15, Fed. R. App. P., Petitioners, **[Alien]** and his son, **[Alien]**, respectfully ask this Court to review the decision and order of the Board of Immigration Appeals entered on June 16, 2005 (the "Order"), dismissing Petitioners' appeal from the revocation of their petition for alien relative. A copy of the Order is attached to this petition.

Pursuant to 8 U.S.C. § 1252(a)(2)(D), this Court has jurisdiction to review final, non-discretionary, administrative actions of the Board of Immigration Appeals which raise pure questions of law.

Venue is proper in this Circuit because petitioners have, at all relevant times, resided in the State of Wyoming and the revocation which is the subject of this petition was initiated following review by the Denver District Office of U.S. Citizenship and Immigration Services.

Petitioners have not litigated any of the issues associated with this petition in any other courts. Thus, the validity of the order has not been upheld by any of the federal courts. By appealing to the Board of Immigration Appeals, Petitioners have exhausted all administrative remedies prior to commencing this appeal for review.

[Dated:]

Respectfully submitted,

[Attorney]

[ADD CERTIFICATE OF SERVICE]

UNITED STATES COURT OF APPEALS
FOR THE ELEVENTH CIRCUIT

Petitioner	)	
vs.	)	**PETITION FOR REVIEW**
ALBERTO R. GONZALES U.S. ATTORNEY GENERAL,	)	
Respondent.	)	

Petitioner, **[Alien]**, respectfully requests the Court to review the decision of the District Court (copy attached), for the reasons set forth below:

I

Petitioner seeks review of the Judgment of the District Court's dated January 8, 1998, denying the Petition for Writ of Habeas Corpus and Request for Stay of Deportation.

II

The jurisdiction of this Court is based upon 28 USC §2241.

III

Venue is properly before this Court pursuant to 28 USC §2241 because Petitioner resides in this judicial circuit, and his case was heard by the District Court in Atlanta, Georgia.

IV

Petitioner is a native of Colombia who was admitted to the United States as a lawful permanent resident on January 20, 1986. Petitioner currently resides in Tucker, Georgia.

V

Petitioner was convicted of one count of conspiracy to possess cocaine with the intent to distribute, in violation of 21 USC §846. Petitioner was served with an Order to Show Cause on October 15, 1995, was charged with being deportable under INA §241(a)(2)(B)(i) (two crimes involving moral turpitude), 241(a)(2)(B)(I) (a crime relating to a controlled substance), and 241(a)(2)(C) (firearm conviction).

VI

Mr. **[Alien]** filed an Application for Advance Permission to Return to Unrelinquished Domicile (Form I-191) on April 23, 1996. He also filed an Application for Waiver of Ground of Excludability (Form I-601) on October 28, 1996. Mr. **[Alien]** attended a Master Calendar hearing on October 29, 1996. Mr. **[Alien]** admitted the allegations of the Order to Show Cause and conceded deportability. However, he submitted to the Immigration Judge that he was eligible to apply for relief from deportation pursuant to 8 USC §1182(c) and 8 USC §1182(h). The Immigration Judge decided on October 29, 1996, that Mr. **[Alien]** was not eligible to apply for relief under 8 USC §1182(c) or under 8 USC §1182(h).

Petitioner appealed from that decision on November 25, 1996. The appeal was denied by the Board of Immigration Appeals on August 24, 1997, for the reason that the Antiterrorism and Effective Death Penalty Act of 1996, Pub. L. No. 104-132, 110 Stat. 1214 §440(d) (AEDPA) and *Matter of Soriano*, Interim Decision 3289 (A.G., Feb. 21, 1997) render Mr. **[Alien]** ineligible for relief. AEDPA violates the Equal Protection Clause of the Constitution.

WHEREFORE, Petitioner requests that:

1. This Petition for Judicial Review be granted;
2. The Order of the Immigration Judge and the Decision of the Board of Immigration Appeals in this matter be overturned and Petitioner be permitted to apply for relief pursuant to 8 USC §1182(c) and 8 USC §1182(h) before the Immigration Judge, after a finding of the unconstitutionality of the provision of AEDPA; and
3. The Court grant such other and further relief as may be appropriate.

RESPECTFULLY SUBMITTED this ____ day of_______, 20__.

[Attorney]

[ADD CERTIFICATE OF SERVICE]

UNITED STATES COURT OF APPEALS
FOR THE ELEVENTH CIRCUIT

	)	
Petitioner	)	
	)	
vs.	)	
	)	**PETITION FOR REVIEW**
ALBERTO R. GONZALES	)	
U.S. ATTORNEY GENERAL,	)	
	)	
Respondent.	)	
______________________________	)	

Petitioner, **[Alien]**, respectfully requests the Court to review the decision of the Board of Immigration Appeals of the Executive Office of Immigration Review (copy attached), for the reasons set forth below:

I

Petitioner seeks review of the Board of Immigration Appeals' decision dated **[date]**, denying the appeal of Petitioner and affirming the denial of asylum by the Immigration Judge.

II

The jurisdiction of this Court is based upon 8 USC ' 1252(a)(2)(B)(ii).

III

Venue is properly before this Court pursuant to 8 USC ' 1252(b)(2) because petitioner resides in this judicial circuit.

IV

Petitioner is a native of Cuba who applied for admission to the United States as on **[date]**. Petitioner currently resides in Dade County, Florida.

V

Petitioner's original Request for Asylum in the United States was denied by the Immigration Judge on **[date]**. Petitioner was placed in proceedings before an Immigration Judge pursuant to an Notice to Appear issued by ICE on **[date]**.

VI

Petitioner made application for relief under Section 208 of the Immigration and Nationality Act, 8 USC ' 1158. The Immigration Judge denied Petitioner's Request for Asylum. Petitioner timely appealed from that decision. The appeal was denied by the Board of Immigration Appeals on **[date]**.

WHEREFORE, Petitioner requests that:

1. This Petition for Judicial Review be granted;
2. The Order of the Immigration Judge and the Decision of the Board of Immigration Appeals in this matter be overturned and Petitioner be granted asylum in the United States.
3. The Court grant such other and further relief as may be appropriate.

RESPECTFULLY SUBMITTED this ____ day of _______, 20__.

[Attorney]

[ADD CERTIFICATE OF SERVICE]

[Document Nos. 604–05]

MOTION FOR STAY OF REMOVAL PENDING PETITION FOR REVIEW AND MEMORANDUM SUPPORTING MOTION

Description: These motions are the style of motion required to be submitted to a circuit court of appeals when seeking a stay of removal or deportation. Supporting memoranda provide examples of the structure of the request.

Advantages: The mere filing of a petition for review does not stay DHS's removal of a client. The circuit court of appeals must actually grant a stay of removal in order to ensure the client is not removed from the United States during pendency of proceedings.

Limitations: A practitioner will likely have to allege a constitutional violation or fear of return to the country of origin in order to convince a circuit court to stay the removal, and some circuits require practitioners to show that the petitioner/appellant is likely to be successful on the merits of the case.

Notes: Be factually specific as to the reasons for the stay, particularly if dealing with a novel legal issue or if the client has a fear of returning to his or her home country.

Citations: Fed. R. App. P. 18.

IN THE UNITED STATES COURT OF APPEAL
FOR THE ELEVENTH CIRCUIT

Appellant,)
)
vs.)
)
ALBERTO R. GONZALES)
U.S. ATTORNEY GENERAL,)
)
Appellee.)
______________________________)

APPELLANT'S EMERGENCY MOTION FOR STAY OF DEPORTATION PENDING RESOLUTION OF APPEAL FROM ORDER OF DISTRICT COURT AND MEMORANDUM OF LAW IN SUPPORT OF STAY OF DEPORTATION

Appellant, **[Alien]**, through undersigned counsel, hereby moves this Court for an Order staying his physical deportation from the United States until such time as this Court has issued a final decision on his appeal from the District Court Order. In support of such Motion, Appellant states through counsel as follows:

1. Appellant has filed this day an appeal to this Court from an Order of the District Court (filed on **[date]**).

2. In cases involving aggravated felons, such as this case, there is no longer an automatic stay of deportation. The Immigration Act of 1990. P.L. 101-649 (Nov. 24, 1990). Appellant is therefore subject to being physically removed and deported from the United States at any time in spite of the fact that an appeal is pending with this Court.

3. Appellant has been free on a bond the entire time he has been in deportation proceedings. This morning, **[date]**, Appellant is to appear as ordered by ICE, to the ICE office in Charlotte, North Carolina. He is subject to being detained and deported at any time by ICE. Counsel affirmatively states that he believes Mr. **[Alien]** to be subject to immediate deportation. Consequently, counsel affirmatively believes and presents to this Court that the Appellee ICE is planning to deport as soon as it is able to secure travel documents, unless the Court intervenes with a Stay of Deportation. For this reason, Appellant, through counsel, files this Emergency Motion for Stay of Deportation.

4. Mr. **[Alien]**'s case presents identical issues to a case presently set for oral argument before this court on **[date]**, *Gutierrez-Martinez v. Reno, et al.*, No., 98-8211. That case has been almost fully briefed (the Reply Brief is due shortly) (undersigned counsel also represents **[Alien]**). The resolution of that case (either way it is decided) will be dispositive of the issues in Mr. **[Alien]**'s case. The same provisions on which appeal is sought in this matter have recently been found to not be retroactive by the First Circuit Court of Appeals, contrary to the District Court's decision in *Gutierrez-Martinez v. INS*, 989 F. Supp. 1205 (N.D. GA 1998). *See Goncalves v. Reno*, 144 F.3d

110 (1st Cir. 1998) (holding that the habeas jurisdiction remains vested with the Circuit Court and that AEDPA §440(d) could not be applied retroactively).

5. Specifically, the issues presented for de novo review to this Court in *Gutierrez-Martinez* will answer the issues raised in Mr. **[Alien]**'s appeal. The affirmative answers to these questions are imperative to helping a long-time lawful permanent resident business owner, whose wife and children are U.S. Citizens. A man who made a mistake; a mistake that should not cost him a lifetime separation from his wife and children.

6. First, this Court clearly has jurisdiction under 28 USC §2241 to hear this case, but the standard under Mr. **[Alien]**'s claim must be judged is not the one proscribed by the District Court.

7. Second, The Antiterrorism and Effective Death Penalty Act of 1996 (AEDPA) §440(d) does have a retroactive effect, in that it deprives Mr. **[Alien]** of any relief from deportation—relief that was previously available to him. Eliminating 8 USC §1182(c) is not illusory, it impaired a real right and imposed new limits on individuals such as Mr. **[Alien]** (whose conviction predates the act by eight years).

8. Third, AEDPA §440(d) violates the Due Process Clause of the Constitution in that this provision prejudices Mr. **[Alien]** to such an extent that it is fundamentally unfair to deprive him of the pre-existing and vested right to seek relief under 8 USC §1182(c).

9. Appellant has a substantial liberty interest at stakeChis right to remain with his family and not be virtually exiled. *Landon v. Plasencia*, 459 U.S. 21 (1982). His has considerable equities under the immigration laws. A denial of the Stay of Deportation would allow ICE to deport him and render his appeal moot, even if the Court subsequently decides that the issues presented by Mr. **[Alien]** have been incorrectly decided by the District Court. As Appellant's appeal raises substantial and novel issues of law as to whether the District Court applied the correct legal standards to this case, a stay is warranted. *See Abassi v. INS*, No. 98-70375, 1998 U.S. App. LEXIS 8797 (9th Cir. May 1, 1998). Should Mr. **[Alien]** be denied a stay of deportation, he will be denied the opportunity to seek legal redress on serious legal questions that will shortly be decided by this Court in *Gutierrez-Martinez*.

10. Counsel for Appellees has previously opposed any request to stay Appellant's deportation. She has not indicated what the Appellees' position on this motion is at the time it was written. A complete copy of the Motion was hand-delivered to **[Attorney]** before it was filed with this Court.

11. This Court is the proper Court in which to seek this stay. Appellant, therefore, seeks the protection of this Court and asks that the Court issue an Order granting a Stay of Deportation during its consideration of the Appellant's Motion for Stay and during its consideration of the Appeal in this case (especially since this Court will fully address these exact issues in *Gutierrez-Martinez*). Further, counsel requests oral argument on the issue of the stay, should the Court believe it helpful.

Respectfully Submitted this ____ day of _______, 20__

[Attorney]

[ADD CERTIFICATE OF SERVICE]

UNITED STATES COURT OF APPEALS
FOR THE TENTH CIRCUIT

[Alien],		
Petitioner	)	Case No: 04-9581
	)	
	)	**MOTION FOR**
v.	)	**STAY OF REMOVAL**
Alberto GONZALES, Attorney	)	
General United States of	)	
America,	)	Agency Case No: [__________]
	)	**A[Number]**
Respondent.	)	

MOTION FOR STAY OF REMOVAL PENDING A DECISION ON THE INSTANT PETITION FOR REVIEW

Petitioner, **[Alien]**, through undersigned counsel respectfully requests that this Court grant a stay of Petitioner's removal pending the Court's final decision on his Petition for Review.

I. INTRODUCTION

The Petition for Review raises issues regarding clear errors of law made by the Board of Immigration Appeals (hereinafter "BIA" or "The Board") in the appeal before the administrative agency and contends that substantial evidence compels a decision to the contrary. Specifically, the Petition for Review raises the following issues:

1. Did the BIA err in concluding that the Judge's determination that the Petitioner's story was "implausible" based on personal conjecture and without specific, cogent reasons supported in the record was sufficient to support an adverse credibility determination?
2. Did the BIA abuse its discretion in concluding that the Motion to Remand the case back to the Immigration Judge should be denied based on the mere fact that the Department of Homeland Security (hereinafter, "DHS") opposed the motion without review of the adequacy or sufficiency of the DHS opposition and when the record did not support the DHS position that the Petitioner had "fabricated" his asylum claim?
3. Did the BIA err in failing to grant the Motion to Remand based on the pending application for adjustment of status which had been properly filed by his United States Citizen wife under 8 U.S.C. 1255(a)?

The Petitioner is likely to prevail on the Petition for Review and will face separation from his United States Citizen wife and severe persecution and possibly death if returned to Algeria. The government will not be disserved by the grant of the stay and the public will not be harmed if the stay is granted. *Lim v. Ashcroft,* 375 F.3d 1011, 1012 (10th Cir. 2004). Petitioner requests the option to supplement this Motion for Stay of Removal and reply to the Respondent's opposition thereto, if any.

Petitioner also requests that the filing of this Motion stay the Petitioner's removal temporarily until the Court rules on the stay motion. *DeLeon v. INS,* 115 F.3d 643, 644 (9th Cir. 1997).

II. STATEMENT OF JURISDICTION

In this immigration case, the Petitioner, a private non-citizen, is currently detained at the Immigration and Customs Enforcement (hereinafter, "ICE") detention facility in Aurora, Colorado. ICE authorities have indicated a present intention to effectuate his removal to Algeria immediately absent an order from this Court to the contrary. His photograph has been taken and his travel documents have been ordered from the Algerian Embassy.

Petitioner, through counsel, timely filed the Petition for Review in this matter on September 2, 2004, within 30 days of the BIA decision dismissing the appeal and denying the Motion to Remand. 8 U.S.C. §1252(b)(1).

This Petition for Review arises under 8 U.S.C. section 1252 (a)(1) challenging a final order of deportation entered by the BIA. This Court may review the discretionary decision of the BIA to deny relief in the form of asylum under 8 U.S.C. section 1158(a). 8 U.S.C. 1252(a)(2)(B)(ii). In addition, this Court has authority to review the denial of the Motion to Remand in consolidation with the Petition for Review. 8 U.S.C. 1252(b)(6). This Court also has jurisdiction pursuant to federal question jurisdiction of 28 U.S.C. §1331.

Jurisdiction is not precluded by the express provisions of 8 U.S.C. section 1252(a)(2) [relating to expedited removal under section 1225(b)(1), denials of discretionary relief under 8 U.S.C. section 1182(h), 1182(i), 1229a, 1229c, and 1255, or orders against criminal aliens], all of which are inapplicable to Petitioner. Although the Immigration and Nationality Act precludes judicial review of discretionary denials of relief under 8 U.S.C. §1255, this Petition for Review does not seek review of the denial of discretionary relief. Rather, it seeks review of the Petitioner's right to a consideration of his Section 1255 adjustment of status application in removal proceedings as a form of relief from removal. *Matter of Velarde,* 23 I&N Dec. 253 (BIA 2002).

Federal courts may also conduct plenary review of questions of law, including questions of statutory construction and interpretation pursuant to Section 10(c) of the Administrative Procedures Act 5 U.S.C. §706 (1976) as well as the REAL ID amendments to the Immigration and Nationality Act, Pub. L. No. 109-13 (May 5, 2005) amending INA §242(a)(2)(D).

This Court has authority to grant a stay under 8 U.S.C. §1252(b)(3)(B). *Lim v. Ashcroft,* 375 F.3d 1011, 1012 (10th Cir. 2004); Fed. R. App. P. 18, 10th Cir. R. 18.1.

III. STATEMENT OF FACTS

Petitioner, **[Alien]**, is a native and citizen of Algeria. He was born in Algiers, but raised 50 km outside of Algiers in a town called Blida. (Transcript, A.R. at 174-76). He lived with his parents, his brother, and five sisters. (A.R. at 73). Petitioner's father was politically active. (A.R. at 176-177). The Petitioner was inspired by his father's democratic ideals and followed in his father's footsteps. (A.R. at 180-184). In particular, he was a member and leader of several political and quasi-political organizations. In 1988, he joined the El-Irchad, a national charitable organization whose philosophy is based on a moderate interpretation of the Muslim faith as described in the Koran. (A.R. at 12-18, 182-184). He joined and helped found a political party related to El-Irchad called HAMAS in 1991. (A.R. at 12-18, 186-189). HAMAS later changed its name to the Society Movement of Peace (MSP). This party, which also is based on a moderate interpretation of the Muslim faith, promotes a secular democratic Algeria. (A.R. at 12-18, Tr. at 186-189). It was established as an alternative to the fundamental Islamic party, Islamic Salvation Front (FIS), which seeks to impose an Islamic government on the people. (A.R. at 189-90). As such, there was always competition and tension between FIS and MSP, and FIS perceived MSP as pro-government. (A.R. at 191, 193, 191, lines 21-23). Petitioner had a leadership position with MSP and was responsible for political party activities in the region of Zabana, which includes his hometown of Blida, Algeria. (A.R. at 191). In 1989 or 1990, while attending the University of Blida, Petitioner also became a member and leader of a student political organization called UGEL, the General Union of Free Students, which also supported a free, democratic Algeria. (A.R. at 76). FIS student members did not join UGEL, and there was tension between the two groups on campus. (A.R. at 195).

Parliamentary elections were held in December 1991, and FIS was poised to win several seats, so the government cancelled the elections in January of 1992. (A.R. at 14). As a result, since that time, FIS and its supporters have resorted to violence and terrorism in order to overthrow the government. (A.R. at 14, 16).

Petitioner had his first confrontation with FIS in approximately May of 1992, when he was a student at the University of Blida. (A.R. at 14, 198-200). FIS members had called for a strike at the campus, but the Petitioner and his organization, UGEL, were opposed to the strike. While the FIS boycott and strike were still in place, the Petitioner attempted to return to his class in protest. He was confronted by approximately five to six individuals who entered his classroom, and whom he recognized as FIS sympathizers. These individuals berated him for ignoring the strike and trying to reopen the classrooms. They also threatened him with additional problems and beat him severely all over his body. (Tr. at 199-201, 14-18). Petitioner did not report the incident to the police because he thought it would be futile. (A.R. 200-201).

Because Petitioner was dedicated to a peaceful resolution to the political situation in Algeria, he continued to be politically active and to play a leadership role in both MSP and UGEL. (A.R. 12-18). In approximately mid 1993, radical members of FIS, who believed in the use of violence to protest, formed the Armed Islamic Group (GIA). (A.R. 12-18, Tr. at 202-204). In addition to random violence, the GIA specifically has targeted prominent members of political and civic organizations, including El-Irchad, MSP and UGEL, in its attempt to disrupt the Algerian economy and society for the sake of obtaining recognition of its political group, FIS. (A.R. at 12-18, 202-04). As of February 2001, approximately 100,000 people had been killed due to the standoff between FIS/GIA supporters and the ruling government. (A.R. at 83). The government has not been able or willing to minimize these violent acts committed by this group and similar groups. (A.R. 111-12, 123-24, 126-27).

In 1993, GIA killings became severe, and people similarly situated to Petitioner, such as members of MSP and UGEL were being killed by the GIA. (A.R. 12-18, 202). As such, Petitioner no longer lived with his parents and began living with friends and family in Blida, so that the GIA would not know where he was at any given time. (A.R. 12-18, Tr. at 202-03). In addition, Petitioner was not accessible to GIA/FIS supporters at school because in 1993, he was conducting research for his thesis and no longer needed to attend classes. (Tr. at 35, ln. 17-24).

Petitioner also testified consistently that in 1994, his political activities took a more prominent role. He co-founded the National Agriculture Union (UNA), which is a professional organization involving several former members of UGEL who were interested in solving the agricultural crisis in Algeria. (A.R. 12-18, 26-39, 205). The organization was not political, but it endorsed political candidates who were anti-socialist. (A.R. 205, 207). UNA, in approximately 1995, became recognized by the government and began to participate in many nationally-televised debates concerning the land issue. (A.R. 12-18, 208-09). The Petitioner appeared in these political debates on national television on behalf of UNS, and FIS perceived his actions on behalf of UNA as anti FIS. (A.R. 12-18, 209). As a result of his appearances, Petitioner believed that he was at increased risk of being targeted by FIS/GIA. (A.R. 12-18, 77, 209-210). Despite his strong interest in promoting change to the agricultural system, Petitioner stopped appearing on television, avoided public places, and continued to move his residence around. (A.R. 12-18, 209-210).

Between 1994 and 1995, Petitioner testified that while spending the night at his sister's office, someone delivered a death shroud to the office as a threat to him. (A.R. 210-11). After this event, the Petitioner realized that the GIA knew where he was staying, so he moved to Algiers, the capital. (A.R. 213). While he was in Algiers, he also moved from place to place. (A.R. 214). While living in the capital, two GIA members kidnapped his father in 1996. Petitioner provided a detailed account of what happened to his father. (A.R. 12-18, 214-217). His father was eventually released (A.R. 215). His father reported the incident and as a result, was taken into custody by the police, although eventually released. (A.R. 216). As a result, his father moved from his hometown, to Algiers as well. (A.R. 218).

Petitioner continued to be on-alert while living in Algiers, stating that he sometimes woke up between two and three o'clock in the morning at the slightest noise, and at one point he had to leave a house by jumping through a window due to his fear of being caught by GIA. (A.R. 219). Nevertheless, Petitioner still functioned in society despite his lack of a permanent address and his fear of the GIA. The moving from place-to-place was not uncommon for political activists. (A.R. 117-18). He took a job as Delegate Sales Manager that allowed him to travel, which he thought was advantageous for avoiding the GIA. (A.R. 12-18). He also obtained a second degree in Computer Information Systems and Management during this time. (A.R. 12-18).

While in Algiers, he consistently testified that rumors circulated in neighborhoods where he was living that GIA people were asking for him, however, he qualified that he never received a direct threat until a letter was sent to the national office of agronomists. (A.R. 12-18, 219-20). The letter was sent to all members of his office, but he was one of the persons named in the letter. (A.R. 12-18, 220). The Petitioner testified at the hearing that the letter was already a *fáit accomplí* as members of this organization, including himself, already felt threatened by GIA. (A.R. 221).

In April of 1999, President Bouteflika was elected, and prior to the elections, most political parties considered this to be fairly positive. (A.R. 12-18). The new president had signed an agreement with the terrorist groups in hope that they would lay down their arms and eliminate the excessive violence and terrorism that had gripped the country for over a decade. (A.R. at 83, 12-18, 222). Initially, it seemed that the violence had subsided, but eventually, FIS/GIS decided that they would no longer honor the agreement, and violence and terrorism re-ensued. (A.R. 95, 12-18). In any event, during the initial peace, Petitioner believed that things were improving and therefore, decided to move back to Zabana, and start his own business in landscaping. (A.R. 12-18, 222). He also moved back to his family home because he thought the peace would last. (A.R. 12-18, 223). It was only after the resurgence in political killings and violent attacks, and rumors that GIA was coming to get the Petitioner that he began again to fear for his life and again moved away from his boyhood home. (A.R. 12-18, 223). Petitioner moved back to Algiers. (A.R. 225).

During this time, Petitioner also explained that he now became eligible to leave the country, and could not have fled earlier even if he wanted to because of the fact that he had not completed his military service. (A.R. 160, 237). The Algerian government restricts foreign travel and does not permit "young men who are eligible for the draft and who have not yet completed their military service to leave the country if they do not have special authorization." (A.R. at 89).

In the Spring of 2000, while Petitioner was living in Algiers, he consistently testified that two men dressed as women came to the family home and confronted his mother. Petitioner testified that the men were GIA and interrogated his mother about the Petitioner. They also searched the house and gave her a package for the Petitioner. The Petitioner's mother opened it and found another death shroud with a note addressed to the Petitioner which stated something to the effect that "This is the punishment of those who support tyrants." (A.R. at 12-18, 74, 77, 224-27).

It was after this last shroud was delivered that Petitioner's fear for his life again peaked, and he began to lose hope for any time of real legitimate change. (A.R. 227, 238). At about the same time, one of the Petitioner's sisters, who lived in the United States, attempted to encourage him to come to the U.S., and he applied for a visitor visa. (A.R. at 227-28).

In the meantime, Petitioner's mother became ill due to the stress of the shroud incident, and her health deteriorated. (A.R. 12-18, 226). Petitioner desired to leave the country, but felt very guilty about his mother's declining health. (A.R. 12-18, 227, ln. 11). In addition, it is culturally unacceptable for children to abandon their parents when they are ill. (A.R. 74). Petitioner received a visitor visa on November 6, 2000 (A.R. 160), but his mother's health worsened, and she was hospitalized in December 2000. He stayed in Algeria with his ailing mother until she died on January 3, 2001. (A.R. 12-18, 228-29). Merely twelve days later, Petitioner left for the United States. (A.R. 12-18, 228-29). Initially, Petitioner was only coming for a temporary period of time because he was depressed and, obviously, grieving over the loss of his mother. (A.R. 230). It was only after he came to the United States that he became aware of the process for applying for asylum and evaluated the danger of returning home at that time. (A.R. 230).

Petitioner entered the United States at Denver, Colorado, on January 15, 2001, on a B-2 visitor visa for a period not to exceed six months. (A.R. 22). Petitioner affirmatively filed for asylum and withholding of removal on June 13, 2001, based on past persecution and fear of future persecution on account of his political opinion by militant Islamic groups that the Algerian government could not and did not control. (A.R. 12-18).

On October 30, 2001, the INS denied his request for asylum claiming that the Petitioner had not established that he is a refugee because the problems that he faced in the past did not amount to persecution. In addition, the INS also found that the Petitioner did not establish that there was a reasonable possibility he would suffer persecution in the future. Petitioner's case was then transferred to the Denver Immigration Court where he conceded removability based on overstaying his visa, but renewed his asylum, withholding of removal and Torture Convention claims. (A.R. 167). After hearing his testimony and receiving additional corroborative evidence, the Immigration Judge, on November 19, 2002, rendered a decision denying the Petitioner's applications for asylum and withholding of removal. (A.R. 153-65)

In his decision, the IJ did not believe the Petitioner to be a credible witness, claiming that the Petitioner's testimony with regard to his necessity to move around from place to place in order to avoid contact with FIS/GIA did not make sense in his mind, in light of the fact that the Petitioner also earned two degrees, worked for a company, ran his own business, and had been on television. (A.R. 162-63). Secondly, the IJ based his decision on his determination that Petitioner's father's abduction and threats by GIA members was "concocted" based on the IJ's assumption that it would have been "relatively easy" for GIA to find and detain the Petitioner. (A.R. 164). Finally the IJ also found that the Petitioner's claim was incredible based on the fact that there was some delay in his flight from Algeria when he obtained a passport and visa. Petitioner timely appealed the decision to the Board of Immigration Appeals.

In 2002, while the appeal was pending, the Petitioner was employed at Smith and Associates where a friend and work colleague, **[Name 1]**, introduced the Petitioner to her sister-in-law, **[Name 2]**. Petitioner met Ms. **[Name 2]** in January of 2003, and they began to date each other. On June 5, 2003, Petitioner married **[Name 2]** in Denver, Colorado, in a ceremony that was celebrated by family and friends.

On July 28, 2003, Ms. **[Name 2/Spouse]** filed an I-130 relative immigration visa petition on behalf of the Petitioner with the Nebraska Service Center. (A.R. 258). On January 12, 2004, a Motion to Remand for Consideration of Adjustment of Status was filed with the BIA. (A.R. 252-357)

On January 23, 2004, the trial attorney for DHS filed a Brief in Response to the Motion to Remand lodging objections based on the statutory presumption against the bona fides of a marriage entered into while in proceedings and based on previous "fabrications" during removal proceedings. The trial attorney noted that the Petitioner had failed to seek an exemption pursuant to 8 C.F.R. 204.2(a)(1)(iii)(A). (A.R. 358-59).

On February 4, 2004, the attorney for the Petitioner filed with the Nebraska Service Center a written request that the Petitioner be considered for the bona fide marriage exemption of 8 C.F.R. 204.2(a)(I)(iii)(B) to address the DHS attorney's concerns. (A.R. 368-72).

On February 4, 2004, the attorney for the Petitioner also filed a Reply Brief to the DHS attorney's Response Brief. In the Reply Brief, the Petitioner noted that the Response Brief of the DHS was not timely filed, and that it should have been deemed unopposed. In addition, the Reply Brief argued that the inconsistencies noted by the Immigration Judge did not render the asylum application fabricated, frivolous or fraudulent. The Brief also noted that the bona fide marriage exemption was specifically requested. (A.R. 360-63).

On August 3, 2004, the BIA denied the Motion to Remand without addressing the issue of whether the Petitioner's testimony was indeed fabricated as alleged by DHS. The BIA also denied the Motion because there was not an immediately available visa since the I-130 had not yet been approved. (A.R. 1-2).

On September 2, 2004, the Petitioner filed a Petition for Review of this decision with the 10th Circuit Court of Appeals. This is currently pending.

On September 2, 2004, the Petitioner through undersigned counsel filed a Motion to Reconsider with the Board of Immigration Appeals. This is currently pending with the BIA. (A.R. 377-390, 391-92, 393-97).

On Friday November 12, 2004, the Petitioner and his United States Citizen wife were scheduled for an interview on a pending I-130 at the local Denver District Office. They appeared as scheduled and the I-130 was approved. (A.R. 397). The Petitioner, as the spouse of a United States Citizen, with an approved I-130, is the beneficiary of an immediately available visa and has the ability to now adjust his status to lawful permanent residence if the case is reopened. 8 U.S.C. §1255(a). This basis of the BIA's decision is no longer valid.

On the same date, however, the Petitioner was taken into ICE custody pursuant to the final order of removal of August 3, 2004. **Petitioner is currently in ICE custody and is being held without bond. His photo has been taken and his travel documents have been requested from the Algerian Embassy. He is in immediate danger of removal to Algeria. This will occur absent action from this Court staying his removal.**

IV. STANDARD FOR GRANTING A STAY OF REMOVAL

To obtain a stay of removal pending judicial review, the petitioner "must show (a) a likelihood of success on appeal; (b) the threat of irreparable harm if the stay or injunction is not granted; (c) the absence of harm to opposing parties if they stay or injunction is granted; and (d) any risk of harm to the public interest." *Lim v. Ashcroft,* 375 F.3d 1011, 1012 (10th Cir. 2004), *citing O Centro Espirita Beneficiente Uniao de Vegetal v. Ashcroft,* 314 F.3d 463, 465-66 (10th Cir. 2002) (quoting 10th Cir. R. 8.1 as formerly numbered); *see also* Fed. R. App. P. 18; 10th Cir. R. 18.1.

A. Likelihood of Success on Appeal

i. The BIA erred in upholding the Immigration Judge's adverse credibility finding

The IJ committed clear erroneous error in his adverse credibility finding since there were no discrepancies or omissions in the Petitioner's testimony and the IJ's determination that the story was "implausible" is not supported by substantial and probative evidence in the record. *Kapcia v. INS,* 944 F.2d 702, 705 (10th Cir. 1991). Credibility determinations are subject to the substantial evidence test. *Sheik-Elzour v. Ashcroft,* 378 F.3d 1143, 1150 (10th Cir. 2004). In order to determine whether an alien is a credible witness, the IJ must give "specific, cogent reasons" for disbelieving his testimony. *Id.* citing *Sviridov v. Ashcroft,* 358 F.3d 722, 727 (10th Cir. 2004). The Court will not blindly accept an IJ's determination that an alien seeking asylum is not credible. *Sheik-Elzour,* 378 F.3d at 1152, *quoting Aguilera-Cota v. INS,* 914 F.3d 1375, 1381 (9th Cir. 1990)("The fact that an IJ considers a petitioner not to be a credible witness constitutes the beginning not the end of our inquiry."). An IJ's adverse credibility finding may appropriately be based on such factors as inconsistencies in the witness' testimony, lack of sufficient detail, or implausibility. *Sheik-Elzour,* 378 F.3d at 1152. It may also be based on the witness' testimonial demeanor. *Id.* at 1152-53.

If, however, the IJ's finding is based on a belief that the story is implausible, such a finding may not be based on speculation, conjecture, or unsupported personal opinion. *Id.* at 1153, *citing, Wiransane v. Ashcroft,*

366 F.3d 889, 898 (10th Cir. 2004). Accordingly, when an IJ finds testimony "implausible" that finding must be supported by substantial evidence in the record. *Sheik Elzour,* 378 F.3d at 1153. Under such circumstances, it would be error for the IJ to fail to explain the basis *in evidence* for his or her credibility finding. *Id.* "In other words, the IJ may not rest an adverse credibility determination on 'his own unsupported opinion as to how an authoritarian government operates'". *Id. quoting Gao v. Ashcroft,* 299 F.3d 266, 278 (3d Cir. 2002); *Cordero-Trejo v. INS,* 40 F.3d 482, 490 (1st Cir. 1994)("Implausibility finding may not be 'based on 'expectations' without support in the record'"); *Abdulrahman v. Ashcroft,* 330 F.3d 587, 598 (3d Cir. 2003)("The IJ fell well short of what we are entitled to expect from judicial officers. Her commentary was not confined to the evidence in the record and smacked of impermissible conjecture.").

In *Sheik Elzour*, The facts of that case are nearly identical to the Petitioner's case. In *Sheik-Elzour,* the Immigration Judge had found the alien's testimony "implausible," and based on such made an adverse credibility finding. *Id.* at 1148. The IJ in that case found it implausible that (1) the Syrian government would arrest a member of the military in the manner that the alien described; (2) that Syria would be interested in the alien more than one year after the 1982 Hamah uprising; (3) that Syria would arrest the alien even though neither he, nor his brother were supporters of the Muslim Brotherhood; (4) that the alien had been detained arbitrarily for the length of time he claimed; and (5) that the alien had been compensated by the Syrian military after his first release from prison. *Id.*

Although the IJ found five different parts of the alien's testimony to be implausible, he failed to substantiate his disbelief with any support in the record. *Id.* Rather, the conclusions of the IJ were based on his own expectations of how the Syrian government would operate and how the alien should have reacted. *Id.* In remanding the case back to the BIA, the Court held, "[B]ecause of the lack of substantial evidence to support the adverse credibility determination, we will remand back in order for the agency to further explain or supplement the record." *Id.* at 1154.

Similarly, in the instant case, the IJ referred to three factual scenarios which, in his mind, made Petitioner's testimony implausible. Nevertheless, the Immigration Judge failed to articulate any specific or cogent reason based on evidence in the record as to why the Petitioner's testimony was inconsistent, vague or otherwise incredible. He merely found Petitioner's consistent and detailed testimony "implausible."

If an applicant's claim is sufficiently detailed, believable and consistent, an adverse credibility finding by an IJ will not be supported for specific and cogent reasons. *Matter of S-A-,* 22 I&N Dec. 1328 (BIA 2000). Moreover, where an applicant's testimony is sufficiently detailed, believable and consistent, an alien's testimony alone can be sufficient without corroborative evidence to provide a plausible and coherent account of the basis for his well-founded fear of persecution. *Matter of Mogharrabi,* 19 I&N Dec. 439 (BIA 1987).

The Board has warned IJs to be sure to make explicit findings on the credibility of witnesses, stating:

> It is even more important for the IJs to make comprehensive findings of fact, including explicit findings as to the credibility of witnesses, rather than just those findings pertinent to one issue that the IJ may deem dispositive of the case . . . If incomplete findings of fact are entered and the IJs decision ultimately cannot be affirmed on the basis that he or she decided the case, a remand of the case for further fact-finding may be unavoidable.

Matter of S-H-, 23 I&N Dec. 462 (BIA 2002).

In this case, the IJ first erroneously determined that the Petitioner's lack of a permanent residence in order to avoid exposure to FIS and GIA members was "implausible" considering that Petitioner had obtained two degrees, worked as a manager, started his own business and was on television. In particular the IJ stated:

> [Petitioner] stated that his first death threat was May 3, 1992, in school, and after that, he received several types of threats in person and in writing, and he claims that he was undergrounds all of this time, that he was living from place to place. Yet the facts do not bear out

> that he was someone who was in hiding during this time. He ran his own business. He worked for a company. He received two degrees. He had a high position in the agricultural association where he was often seen in public. He was on television. So I think it is quite inaccurate to say that the [Petitioner] was hiding out during that time. A person who is supposedly hiding out does not make himself so prominent in society as he did. (A.R. 162-63).

First, it should be noted that the IJ did not articulate any inconsistencies or omissions with regard to the Petitioner's testimony on these facts. *Matter of A-S-,* 21 I&N Dec. 1106 (BIA 1998). Secondly, the record shows that Petitioner provided consistent and detailed testimony, through his affidavit and testimony at hearing, as to the timing of his professional and political activities and when he began to live a transient life. *Matter of Mogharrabi,* 19 I&N Dec. 439 (BIA 1987).

Rather, the IJ over-emphasized the term "in-hiding" quite literally which, although used in Petitioner's affidavit, really is about the Petitioner's lack of a physical permanent physical residence due to his interest in avoiding becoming an easy target for the GIA. (A.R. 12-18, 203). Petitioner consistently and in detailed manner, testified to the fact that after 1993, he began moving around from place to place. Whether "hiding out" is the correct term or not, the gist of the Petitioner's claim is that he, in fact, did not live in the same place after 1993 in order to avoid becoming an easy target for the GIA or FIS.

The IJ correctly noted that the Petitioner's first death threat and altercation with FIS members came in approximately May 1992, while the Petitioner was in school. (A.R. at 199-201). However, it was not until the more extremist group, GIA, arose in 1993 and began to kill individuals similarly situated to the Petitioner that the Petitioner believed his life could be threatened and therefore that he should not remain living in his boyhood home in Blida. (A.R. 202-03). When questioned by counsel as to whether the GIA would find him at school, the Petitioner replied, "It was the end of the year at the University so I really didn't go there all the time. I was doing my thesis and research . . .so I didn't really have to go to the University every day or at a specific time." (A.R. 203). Thereafter, Petitioner consistently testified that he lived with friends and relatives and that he was sleeping on several occasions at his sister's office.

The fact that the Petitioner also became politically active during this time in the UNA and participated in television debates is not inconsistent with living from place to place. Petitioner is an activist and has revealed that he is passionate about political and economic change. So, although he was threatened by GIA, he also plausibly believed that he had been successful in avoiding the GIA due to his transient existence. Petitioner testified that becoming a more public figure did increase his problems, and that as a result, he stopped appearing on television, avoided public places, and continued to move his residence around. (A.R. 209-10). More specifically, he discussed that while sleeping in his sister's office he received a death shroud. (A.R. 210-11). Shortly after this serious threat, he moved to Algiers. (A.R. 213). His behavior is corroborated in an article discussing that to avoid death, political activists either lived an unpredictable daily routine, moved around or fled the country. In addition, the Petitioner testified, and the 2001 Department of State Country Report for Algeria corroborates that he could not even leave the country at this time due to a rule regarding military service.

The IJ failed to recognize that the Petitioner testified in his affidavit that his position as commercial delegate manager allowed him to travel and provided him with the opportunity to move around so that he could avoid the GIA. (A.R. at 12-18). Petitioner also obtained a computer degree some time in 1996, but the facts are not clear as to how he obtained the degree (i.e. through night classes, part-time, etc.) The DHS attorney and the IJ did not inquire as to how the Petitioner was able to obtain a second degree while living in different places. Therefore, it is plausible that the Petitioner could have obtained the second degree and worked, but still not have a fixed address while living in Algiers.

Finally, the IJ erroneously depicted Petitioner's establishment of a new business as inconsistent with living a life of fear of the GIA. The record shows that with the April 1999 elections were held, Petitioner's new hope regarding the political situation and more stability. (A.R. at 7, 12-18, 213). As such, Petitioner moved back to his hometown and established a business. (A.R. 12-18, 222). It was only after a few months that violence ensued again. Petitioner again felt unsafe and moved back to Algiers. (A.R. 224).

The IJ failed to see the chronology of events which led to Petitioner's decision to start a business. Therefore, Petitioner had taken the threats on his life very seriously and responded in a plausible manner.

The IJ also based his adverse credibility finding on the fact that there was a delay in time from when Petitioner was eligible to leave and when he actually left the country:

> Even after he received a visa to the United States, he waited 10 weeks. His mother was ill, but it would seem like if someone was in imminent threat of his life, he would leave the country right away. [Petitioner] received a passport on April 1, 1999. he was cleared for his military service then. He had received several death threats and yet he did not leave the country and go to a neighboring country where he could easily get a visa or to any other country. Instead, he stayed for another two years; and not only that, he started his business after that time. This shows me that either he has concocted his story or if there were these threats as he claimed, he did not really take them seriously.

(A.R. 163).

Again, Petitioner did not provide any inconsistent information either in his original application or at hearing regarding the time frame for when he was eligible to leave and left the country, and the IJ did not point out or request clarification of such inconsistencies or omissions with regard to Petitioner's delay in leaving. *See Matter of A-S-,* 21 I&N Dec. 1106 (BIA 1998). Petitioner provided specific, cogent, and detailed testimony with regard to his time frame for leaving. *Matter of Mogharabi,* 19 I&N Dec. 439 (BIA 1987). Based on his own assumptions about how people should react to particular situations, the IJ again, merely did not "buy the story." As such, this non-evidence based assumption and lack of any articulation of inconsistency or omission in the decision is clearly erroneous.

Moreover, Petitioner's consistent testimony reveals that his story regarding delay is, in fact, plausible. Petitioner was not eligible to leave the country until he first completed military service. This fact is corroborated by the 2001 Department of State County Report for Algeria which states that the government "does not permit young men who are eligible for the draft and who have not yet completed their military service to leave the country if they do not have special authorization."

Petitioner also testified that in the spring of 2000, a death shroud was delivered to his parents' place of residence by two individuals dressed as women. (A.R. 12-18, 224-27). The death threat was specifically targeted toward Petitioner, and significantly and negatively affected his mother's health. (A.R. 12-18, 226). Petitioner was very upset and depressed over this and at this time, took his sister's advice to visit the United States. He applied for a visitor visa. (A.R. 228-30). Thereafter, his mother's health deteriorated, and Petitioner felt extremely responsible for this. (A.R. 12-18, 227). His sister elaborated that it would not have been culturally acceptable for Petitioner to just leave while his mother was so ill. (A.R. 74).

Petitioner, in fact received a visitor visa in November 2000, when the health of his mother was precarious. Petitioner's mother was hospitalized in December 2000, and died on January 3, 2001. (A.R. 12-18, 228-29). A mere twelve days later, Petitioner left Algeria for the United States. (A.R. 12-18, 228-29). There was no evidence in the record as to his living arrangements at this time. Although perhaps not the choice the IJ may have made in the same situation, this so-called "delay" is very plausible and explained by evidence in the record.

Petitioner's testimony was consistent, detailed and did not show any significant omission which would cause it be incredible. *See Matter of A-S-,* 21 I&N Dec. 1106 (BIA 1998). As such, the IJ's determination that the "delay" of the Petitioner's flight suggests that he really was not threatened is clearly erroneous.

Finally, the IJ also made an adverse credibility finding based on the fact that he thought the Petitioner's testimony with regard to his father being kidnapped and abducted was implausible. Again, the IJ did not find any inconsistencies or omissions with Petitioner's affidavit and testimony regarding his father's kidnapping. *Id.*. The only reason he provided for not believing the Petitioner's story was that "it simply doesn't make sense to me that for a period of nine years, [Petitioner] was under constant death threats, he had visible positions, and yet all this group did was threaten his family, threaten his father, and send notes when one would think that it will be relatively easy to get their hands on him." (A.R. 163-64). The IJ assumes, that because the Petitioner functioned in society, he was easily accessible to the GIA and, therefore, finds it incredible that the GIA would threaten his father if, in fact, Petitioner is accessible. Since this finding is not based on facts in the record, it is clearly erroneous.

To the contrary, Petitioner's testimony as to his father's abduction, release and reporting to the police is very plausible based on the record. According to the record, Petitioner was living in Algiers at the time of his father's abduction in 1996. (A.R. 12-18, 214-17). His father was living in his hometown in the region of Zabana. (A.R. 214-17). The IJ appeared to ignore these facts, as they were not recited in his opinion and the IJ never inquired into these facts during the hearing. Prior to and during that time, Petitioner had had no direct contact or exposure to the GIA, perhaps due to his success in moving around from place to place in Algiers. As such it is very plausible that the GIA decided to target the Petitioner's family, as the record shows that the Petitioner was not accessible to the GIA contrary to the IJ's assumption.

The only reason that the IJ found the story of the father's abduction to be implausible was again based on his own western-based assumptions, not grounded in the facts, that Petitioner was somehow accessible to the GIA due to his political and professional activities.

According to the standards established in *Matter of A-S-*, 21 I&N Dec. 1106 (BIA 1998). The IJ's credibility findings are not supported by discrepancies or omissions in the Petitioner's testimony. There are no specific and cogent reasons articulated by the IJ to show why the record demonstrates that the Petitioner is incredible. Petitioner was never given any opportunity to explain and assumed discrepancies and omissions. Moreover, Petitioner's circumstances were very plausible given a careful evaluation of the record.

ii. The BIA erred in refusing to remand the case based on the pending adjustment of status application based on the mere unsupported allegations of ICE counsel that the Petitioner's asylum claim was "fabricated

In the denial of the appeal and denial of the Motion to Remand, the Board held that the Motion to Remand must be denied "because the Respondent's motion is opposed by DHS on a separate basis." (A.R. 1-2). Specifically, DHS opposed the Motion to Remand on the basis that the Petitioner is not "deserving of adjustment of status because the respondent fabricated elements of his asylum claim." (A.R. 358). There is no basis for such a finding in the record. The Immigration Judge, while finding inconsistencies in the Petitioner's testimony and making a negative credibility determination, never made a finding that the application was frivolous, fabricated or fraudulent. In addition, the Board, while agreeing with the IJ regarding discrepancies in the Petitioner's testimony, never found that the testimony was fabricated or frivolous. (A.R. 1-2).

The Board, in its decision, never addresses the references to the record made by DHS in its motion in opposition to remand, and never made any specific finding regarding whether the references to the Immigration Judge's findings constitute "fabrication." Absent such analysis by the Board, there is no means of judicial review by a Circuit Court as to what, if anything, the Board found to be fabricated elements.

A case of fabrication cannot be made just because the DHS says it is so. Furthermore, the Board cannot simply "react" to the arguments of the DHS without a reasoned analysis of the arguments presented by both sides. Individuals have a right to a reasoned, individualized and articulated opinion that clearly announces that the reviewing administrative court has reviewed the record and has adopted the decision of the immigration judge. *Turri v. INS*, 997 F.2d 1306, 1310 (10th Cir. 1993). This decision must be articulated with sufficient analysis to allow the Court of Appeals to perform judicial review. *Panrit v. INS,* 19 F.3d 544, 546 (10th Cir. 1994).

In *Panrit,* the 10th Circuit laid out the requirements that must be included in an opinion such that it is clear to the appellant that the reviewing agency has engaged in an independent analysis. Since *Panrit* was decided, eight other Circuit Courts have followed the rationale of *Panrit.* See, *Gandarillas-Zambrana v. BIA,* 44 F.3d 1251, 1255 (4th Cir. 1995); *Maashio v. INS,* 45 F.3d 1235, 1238 (8th Cir. 1995); *Alaelua v. INS*, 45 F.3d 1379, 1382-83 (9th Cir. 1995); *Urokov v. INS,* 55 F.3d 222, 227-28 (7th Cir. 1995); *Gomez-Mejia v. INS,* 56 F.3d 700, 702 (5th Cir. 1995); *Prado-Gonzalez v. INS,* 75 F.3d 631, 632 (11th Cir. 1996); *Bing Feng Chen v. INS*, 87 F.3d 5, 8 (1st Cir. 1996).

In *Panrit,* the 10th Circuit held that the Board of Immigration Appeals is not required to "write an exegesis on every contention." *Id.* at 545. However, the BIA must "consider the issues and announce its decision in terms sufficient to enable . . . a reviewing Court to perceive that it has heard and considered the arguments rather than merely reacted." *Id.* The Court also requires, at a minimum, that the decision of the Board specifically recite that it has "reviewed the record and the immigration judge's decision and that it is content to rest its decision on the immigration judge's reasoning." *Id.* at 546. But clarifying this point, the Court held that this does not grant the Board "unrestricted license to summarily adopt immigration judges' decisions without examining those decisions to ensure that all of the factors urged by the alien were in fact fully considered by the immigration judge." *Id.* Otherwise, the Board would be "effectively remove[d] . . . as a separate reviewing body." *Id.*

In this case, the Board simply relies on the statements made by DHS in their response brief and concurs with the statements made by DHS without any analysis or explanation as to why the statements made by DHS were correct as a matter of law.

Petitioner did not submit a frivolous asylum application. Applicable regulations provide that "an asylum application is frivolous if any of its material elements is deliberately fabricated." 8 C.F.R. §208.20. The IJ based his denial of asylum heavily on the fact that he found the Petitioner's certain facts of the Petitioner's story implausible as opposed to any deliberate fabrication of a material element of his asylum claim.

Although 8 C.F.R. §208.20, §1208.20 refer to a frivolous application, it is understood to refer to a fraudulent application. *Barreto-Clara v. U.S. Attorney General*, 275 F.3d 1334, 1339 (11th Cir. 2001). The Petitioner did not commit fraud in his application for asylum. The BIA has held that "fraud" should be defined "in the commonly accepted legal sense, that is, as consisting of false representations of a material fact made with knowledge of [their] falsity and with intent to deceive the other party. The representation must be believed and acted upon by the party deceived to his disadvantage." *Matter of G-G-*, 7 I&N Dec. 161, 164 (BIA 1956).

There is no hint in the IJ's decision of a frivolous application, since he makes no mention that any material elements were deliberately fabricated. The IJ also did not make an explicit finding that the Petitioner's application was frivolous as <u>specifically required</u> under 8 C.F.R. §208.20, §1208.20.

Furthermore, as argued above, an unsupported implausibility finding, in and of itself, is not necessarily grounds for a negative credibility finding, much less a finding that the asylum application was fabricated.

The Fourth Circuit upheld a finding of a frivolous application when the Respondent had "gone back and forth with the facts and misrepresented his case several times". *Efe v. Ashcroft*, 293 F.3d 899, 908 (4th Cir. 2002). In this case, the Petitioner has maintained an internally consistent story. Petitioner's testimony may not comport with the Immigration Judge's own personal opinion as to whether the Petitioner was subject to persecution, but mere conjecture and speculation does not make for a negative credibility finding, much less a story that has been fabricated.

While the findings of the judge in this case may have been enough to deny asylum as a matter of discretion, the judge never made that finding. The findings of the judge in this case, however, are not enough to constitute deliberate fabrication of a material element constituting a frivolous application pursuant to 8 C.F.R. §208.20, §1208.20. Petitioner maintains that although the IJ denied asylum, he did not explicitly find that the Petitioner submitted a frivolous application, and if he did explicitly make such a finding it was clear error. 8 C.F.R. §208.20, §1208.20.

iii. The BIA refusal to remand the case based on a properly filed application for adjustment of status under 1255(a) was clear error

The Board denied the Motion to Remand on two bases. First, the BIA denied the Motion to Remand finding that the BIA's decision in *Matter of Velarde,* 23 I&N Dec. 253 (BIA 2002) prohibits a remand for purposes of adjustment of status if the DHS opposes the motion on an independent basis. (A.R. 1-2). In this case, the DHS opposed the Motion to Remand on the basis that the Petitioner had "fabricated" his asylum claim. (A.R. 358-59). The BIA without any analysis of the legitimacy of the DHS opposition, refused to remand the case.

This was clear error. An alien is subject to ineligibility for adjustment of status under 1158(d)(6) "only if a final order by an immigration judge or the Board of Immigration Appeals specifically finds that the alien knowingly filed a frivolous asylum application". *See also,* 8 C.F.R. §208.20, §1208.20. The IJ found that "he did not believe the Respondent has been giving a true story of his life," (A.R. 162) and that the Respondent [Petitioner] is not a "credible witness in his asylum case." (A.R. 162). The DHS extrapolates from these statements that the Petitioner made a material fabrication, however, as argued above, looking at the entirety of the IJ's decision, he based his holding largely on speculation and personal conjecture.

An adverse credibility determination is based upon inconsistencies, contradictions, and inherently improbable testimony. *Matter of S-M-J-*, 21 I. & N. Dec. 722, 746 (BIA 1997). An adverse credibility finding therefore does not constitute fraud because the standard fraud elements are not required for an adverse credibility finding. *Matter of G-G-, supra.* There is a difference between fraud and misrepresentation. Although certain parts of the Petitioner's testimony may be unbelievable, this does not constitute a material misrepresentation needed for fraud. Accordingly, insufficient evidence exists to support a finding of a "frivolous asylum application" under section 1158(d)(6) of the Act. As such, the BIA should have found that the opposition of the DHS to remand in this case was not founded and could not support a finding that the Petitioner was otherwise ineligible for remand under *Matter of Velarde,* 23 I&N Dec. 253 (BIA 2002).

In addition to refusing to remand the case based on the allegations of DHS, the BIA refused to remand on the basis that an immigrant visa was not immediately available. This was also clear error. The BIA states, "Respondent's motion fails to establish that an immigrant visa petition filed on his behalf has been approved. Therefore, the respondent's motion does not establish that the respondent has an immigrant visa immediately available to him. Thus, the motion to remand does not establish the respondent's prima facie eligibility for adjustment of status under section 245(a)(3) of the Act." (A.R. 1-2). This holding has absolutely no basis in the law.

Matter of Velarde, 23 I&N Dec. 253 (BIA 2002) specifically holds that "a motion to reopen for adjustment of status based on a marriage entered into after the commencement of proceedings may be granted *notwithstanding the pendency of a visa petition filed on the alien's behalf,* where (1) the motion is timely filed; (2) the motion is not numerically barred by the regulations; (3) the motion is not barred by *Matter of Shaar,* 21 I&N Dec. 541 (BIA 1996), or on any other procedural grounds; (4) the motion presents clear and convincing evidence indicating a strong likelihood that the respondent's marriage is bona-fide; and (5) the Service either does not oppose the motion or bases its opposition solely on *Matter of Arthur.*" *Id.* at 256. (emphasis added).

The plain language of *Velarde* makes clear that there is no requirement that the I-130 be adjudicated at the time the alien seeks to reopen or remand the case. In fact, the plain language of the decision allows for the motion to be granted "notwithstanding the pendency of a visa petition filed on the alien's behalf." *Id.* In this case, **[Alien]** is married to a United States Citizen. As such, he is an immediate relative as defined in INA §1151(b)(2)(A)(i). As an immediate relative, he is not subject to the numerical quota system for family-based immigration, and the visa is immediately available on the approval of the I-130 by the Citizenship and Immigration Service, and upon approval, he became simultaneously eligible for adjustment of status under INA section 1255(a)(3). In fact, **[Alien]**, having legally entered the United States, could have, had he not been in removal proceedings, filed the I-485 simultaneously with the I-130 and the approval of both applications could have been done together by the Citizenship and Immigration Service through the one-step procedure.

Notwithstanding the erroneousness of the BIA decision, **[Alien]** and his wife appeared for an interview on the pending I-130 petition on November 12, 2004. The Petition was approved at the interview, and the visa is now immediately available. (A.R. 397). Thus, this basis of the BIA decision is no longer a concern.

B. The Threat of Irreparable Harm if the Stay Is Not Granted

Here, the likelihood of harm is great, given the Petitioner's claims for asylum, withholding of removal and relief under the United Nations Convention Against Torture. *See, e.g.*, INA §101(a)(42); 8 U.S.C. §101(a)(42); 8 C.F.R. §208.13, §1208.13. If the stay of removal is not granted before this Court may review the merits of the case, the Petitioner faces possible persecution and death on his forced return to Algeria.

In addition, the Petitioner is married to a United States Citizen. He has an approved I-130 immigrant visa petition based on that marriage. (A.R. 397). This approval provides the basis on which the Petitioner may seek to adjust his status and obtain his residency in the United States. 8 U.S.C. §1255(a). If Petitioner is removed from the country, however, under a final order of deportation, he will be barred from reentering the United States for a period of 10 years due to the Order of Deportation. 8 U.S.C. §1182(a)(9)(A)(ii)(II). In addition, having been physically present in the United States for longer than one year without lawful status, Petitioner faces inadmissibility from the United States for a period of ten years under 8 U.S.C. §1182(a)(9)(B)(i)(II). Although there are waivers available for these grounds of inadmissibility, both waivers depend on the unreviewable discretion of a singular consular officer at an overseas post in Algeria, and even if ultimately granted, the Petitioner faces separation from his United States Citizen wife for the lengthy time during which the Petition and Waivers must be processed overseas.

The combination of family separation and possible harm or death of the stay is not granted should outweigh any inconvenience the government may suffer by the denial of the stay.

C. The Absence of Harm to Opposing Parties if the Stay Is Granted

The Petitioner remains in ICE custody. As such, the Respondent would suffer little or no administrative inconvenience if the stay is granted. The Petitioner cannot be claimed to be a flight risk, nor can the government claim any burden to be had by the stay of removal since the Petitioner is currently in the ICE custody pending removal from the United States. If the Respondent is concerned about the cost of his detention during the pendency of the appeal, the Respondent possesses unilateral authority to release the Petitioner on terms and conditions which he deems appropriate including electronic ankle monitoring under the Intensive Supervised Appearance Program. ("ISAP"). The Petitioner is willing to abide by any reasonable terms and conditions for his release from custody during the pendency of the Petition for Review.

D. Harm to the Public Interest

The Petitioner has no criminal history, and no previous immigration violations. He has stable employment. There is no reason to believe that he would, in any way, be a harm to the public interest.

V. EXHAUSTION OF REMEDIES

Counsel for Appellant has contacted Counsel for Respondent, the Office of Immigration Litigation in Washington D.C. at approximately 10:00 AM on November 22, 2004. Counsel spoke with **[Attorney]**, attorney of record. **[Attorney]** indicated that her office would confer with agents of ICE and review this motion and present their position to the Petitioners as soon as possible.

Once we receive the position of the Respondent, we will notify the Court.

WHEREFORE, Petitioners pray that this Court grant the Motion for a Stay of Removal pending this Court's decision on the Petition for Review and grant a Temporary Stay of Removal pending this Court's decision on the Instant Motion for Stay of Removal.

Respectfully Submitted,

[Attorney]

[Date]

[ADD CERTIFICATE OF SERVICE]

[Document No. 606]
Motion for Extension of Time to File Reply Brief

Description: This motion requests additional time for filing a reply brief.

Advantages: The pleading sets forth reasons for requesting additional time, including a delay in receipt of the preceding brief, and includes the agreement of government's counsel to the new schedule.

Limitations: Barring exceptional circumstances, without the acquiescence of counsel for the government, the court is unlikely to grant an extension of time.

Citations: Fed. R. App. P. 31.

IN THE UNITED STATES COURT OF APPEALS
FOR THE ELEVENTH CIRCUIT

No.______)
Appellant)
vs.)
)
ALBERTO R. GONZALES)
U.S. ATTORNEY GENERAL,)
)
Appellee.)
______________________________)

MOTION FOR EXTENSION OF TIME TO FILE REPLY BRIEF

Pursuant to Fed. R. App. P. 31, 11th Cir. R. 31-1, I.O.P. 2, Appellant hereby requests an extension of time in which to file the Reply Brief in this matter. Appellant did not receive Respondent's Response brief until **[date]**, although it was dated **[date]**. Appellant has confirmed with Respondent's counsel, **[Attorney]**, that Respondent has no objection to an extension to time in which to file the Reply brief in this matter. Further, Petitioner's counsel has a hearing in U.S. Immigration Court on **[date]**, the due date of this brief. Petitioner's counsel also has a hearing in U.S. Immigration Court on **[date]**. An extension of time will allow for preparation of the Reply Brief.

Therefore, Petitioner requests a 15-day extension in which to file the Reply Brief in this matter, until **[date]**.

Respectfully submitted this ____ day of ______, 20__.

[Attorney]

[ADD CERTIFICATE OF SERVICE]

[Document No. 607]
APPELLANT'S OPENING BRIEF TO COURT OF APPEALS

Description: This opening brief from a Fifth Circuit case presents basic issues regarding the appeal of a denial by an immigration judge and the Board of Immigration Appeals (BIA) of a request for Asylum and Withholding of Removal.

Advantages: The purpose of this brief is NOT to serve as a cut and paste brief for any individual appeal, but rather, to provide practitioners an example of the style, scope, format, and content of an opening brief.

Limitations: Every case is different, and thus, each brief is necessarily different. Make sure to make the necessary factual and legal arguments that apply to the individual client's case.

IN THE
UNITED STATES COURT OF APPEALS
FOR THE FIFTH CIRCUIT

CASE NO. ____________

[Alien],

A[Number]

Petitioner,

v.

ALBERTO R. GONZALES,

U.S. ATTORNEY GENERAL

Respondent.

APPEAL FROM THE BOARD OF IMMIGRATION APPEALS
BRIEF FOR PETITIONER

[Attorney]
Attorney for Petitioner

IN THE UNITED STATES COURT OF APPEALS
FOR THE FIFTH CIRCUIT

No._____

	)
Petitioner	)
	)
vs.	)
	)
ALBERTO R. GONZALES	)
U.S. ATTORNEY GENERAL,	)
	)
Respondent.	)
______________________________	)

CERTIFICATE OF INTERESTED PERSONS AND CORPORATE DISCLOSURE STATEMENT

Pursuant to Rule 28.2.1 of the Rules of the United States Court of Appeals for the Fifth Circuit, the undersigned counsel of record certifies that the following listed persons have an interest in the outcome of this case. These representations are made in order that the judges of this court may evaluate possible disqualification or recusal:

Board of Immigration Appeals

Bureau of Customs and Immigration Enforcement

Department of Homeland Security

[All other relevant individuals]

**IN THE UNITED STATES COURT OF APPEALS
FOR THE FIFTH CIRCUIT**

No. __________

	)
Petitioner	)
	)
vs.	)
	)
ALBERTO R. GONZALES	)
U.S. ATTORNEY GENERAL,	)
	)
Respondent.	)
______________________________	)

**CERTIFICATE OF INTERESTED PERSONS
AND CORPORATE DISCLOSURE STATEMENT (CONT'D)**

Pursuant to Rule 26.1 of the Federal Rules of Appellate Procedures, the undersigned counsel of record certifies that Petitioner is not a corporation and there is no parent corporation or public held owner of Petitioner.

Respectfully submitted this ____day of ______, 20__.

[Attorney]

STATEMENT REGARDING ORAL ARGUMENTS

Petitioner believes that the issues presented can be determined upon the record, and that oral argument would not benefit the panel. However, if the Court finds that oral argument would be of assistance, Petitioner would be more than happy to prepare and present oral arguments to the panel.

[Attorney]

TABLE OF CONTENTS

TABLE OF AUTHORITIES

Cases:

Statutes:

Regulations:

STATEMENT OF JURISDICTION

This is a Petition to Review the final order of removal entered against **[Alien]** (hereinafter referred to occasionally as "Petitioner") by the Board of Immigration Appeals on February 1, 2005. (A.R. 2)[1]. The instant appeal is taken pursuant to former Section 242 of the Immigration and Nationality Act ("I.N.A."), 8 U.S.C. §1252. As this case is a review of a final order of removal, jurisdiction is therefore proper in this case pursuant to I.N.A. §242.

STATEMENT OF THE ISSUE PRESENTED FOR REVIEW

Whether the Petitioner established that it is more likely than not that she would be subject to persecution if forced to return to Pakistan due to her religious beliefs.

STATEMENT OF THE CASE

The legacy Immigration and Naturalization Service ("legacy INS") issued a Notice to Appear (Form I-862) to **[Alien]**, charging her with removability under section 237(a)(1)(B) of the Immigration and Nationality Act, 8 U.S.C. §1227(a)(1)(B). (A.R. 546-47). **[Alien]** was charged with having remained in the United States beyond the period for which she was authorized as a nonimmigrant. **[Alien]** conceded removability and sought relief pursuant to I.N.A. §208(a), 8 U.S.C. §1158(a), and I.N.A. §241(b)(3), 8 U.S.C. §1231(b). (A.R. 504-14).

After a hearing on the merits, the Immigration Judge denied **[Alien]**'s application for asylum and withholding of removal on January 20, 2004. (A.R. 55-68). On February 10, 2004, Petitioner filed a Notice of Appeal with the Board of Immigration Appeals ("BIA"), pursuant to 8 C.F.R. §1240.15. (A.R. 34). After submission of briefs by both parties, the BIA summarily affirmed the decision of the Immigration Judge, without opinion on February 1, 2005. (A.R. 2). Petitioner filed a Petition for Review with this court on February 25, 2005, and the instant petition for review follows.

STATEMENT OF FACTS

Petitioner, **[Alien]**, is a native and citizen of Pakistan, and a Shia Ismali. Prior to her departure from Pakistan on July 7, 1999, **[Alien]** resided in Karachi, Pakistan. (A.R. 508). Pakistan is comprised of a population which is approximately 99% Islamic. (A.R. 171). Within the Islamic population, there is hostility and violence between the Sunni and Shia denominations, which has been, and is, escalating significantly. (A.R. 167-68).

Both the Sunni and Shia denominations of Islam have sub-denominations. The Sunni denominations of Islam comprise approximately 85% of the total population of Pakistan; whereas, the Shia denominations comprise only approximately 15% of the total population. (A.R. 165). Within the Shia denominations, approximately 33% of the practitioners are Shia Ismali; or in other words, Shia Ismali practitioners only comprise approximately 5% of the total population of Pakistan. (A.R. 165). Currently, extremist groups among the Sunnis, who are supporters of terrorist organizations such as the Taliban, al Qaeda, and Hezbollah, (A.R. 175), want to "wipe out and reduce the influence of the Shia community in Pakistan." (A.R. 171).

Violence and discrimination against Shias, specifically Shia Ismails, is a significant problem in Pakistan. (A.R. 144). Discord between the Sunnis and Shias has deep roots in Pakistani history. (A.R. 197). When **[Alien]** was only nine years old, Sunni extremists attacked the mosque where her family worshiped. (A.R. 116). During the attack, tear gas was shot into the mosque where Shia practitioners were engaged in prayer, followed by random shootings. (A.R. 117). When **[Alien]** was approximately sixteen years of age, Sunni ex-

[1] The abbreviation "A.R." followed by a number refers to a page of the Certified Administrative Record on file with this court.

tremists threatened to attack the mosque where her family worshiped, again. (A.R. 116-117). The mosque was subsequently closed, and **[Alien]** was not able to practice her religion in accord with her beliefs. (A.R. 116-117).

Although violence has historically occurred in many parts of the country, the violence inflicted upon the Shias by the Sunnis has significantly escalated recently. (A.R. 116-117). The recent increase in violence against Shias is the result of many converging factors. Of the many factors that have lead to the increase in violence against Shias, the most prominent are: Increase in terrorist activities in the region, (A.R. 168), Pervez Musharraf's support of Sunni extremist groups in order to maintain power, (A.R. 191-92), and the presence of the United States in the region. (A.R. 179).

Terrorist activities in and outside of Pakistan have increased. (A.R. 168). Since 2003, revolutionary Sunni groups have embraced terrorism as a means of conveying their message. (A.R. 172). According to Sunni extremists, Shias are "infidels," and the goal of these extremists groups is to completely rid Pakistan of any, and all, Shia influence. (A.R. 172). To this end, Sunni extremists view Shia Mosques and Shia practitioners as legitimate targets, and have no problems in attacking innocent Shia practitioners due to their religious and political beliefs. (A.R. 172).

In order to strengthen and fortify their position within Pakistan, Sunni extremist groups have aligned themselves with such international terrorist organizations as the Taliban, Hezbollah, and al Qaeda. (A.R. 172, 175). As of late, Pakistan has become a rallying point for international terrorist organizations, especially al Qaeda. (A.R. 197). When the United States deposed the Taliban in Afghanistan, much of the Taliban regime sought refuge by crossing the Afghan-Pakistan boarder, and then joining with Sunni extremist groups. (A.R. 175). Hezbollah has shifted its center of operation to Pakistan after being asked to leave Iran by the Iranian government, (A.R. 175), and al Qaeda has an inter-relationship with Sunni extremists in Pakistan. (A.R. 179). Although these terrorist organizations have significantly different views in many different regards, they all agree on one thing; Shia are infidels, and their influence must be eliminated from Pakistan so that they may impose their understanding of Islamic law upon the people of Pakistan. (A.R. 168).

In addition to increased terrorist activities within Pakistan, Pervez Musharraf has supported extremist groups in order to destabilize the government, thus allowing him to maintain power. (A.R. 191). Pervez Musharraf became the de facto Head of Government of Pakistan on October 12, 1999, following a coup d'ètat. Following the coup d'ètat, Pervez Musharraf assumed the office of President of Pakistan on June 20, 2001. Since his usurpation of power, President Musharraf has been actively involved in organizing extremists, sometimes referred to as "new Taliban," in efforts to destabilize the government. (A.R. 191). By destabilizing the government, Musharraf is then permitted to use military force to bring about stability in the country by denying Pakistanis their rights, and retaining power for himself. (A.R. 193). Thus, Masharraf looks upon extremist organizations as his allies, not his enemies, as instability in Pakistan is needed in order for him to maintain power. (A.R. 190-91).

Further, the presence of the United States has played a significant role leading to increased violence in Pakistan. According to extremist organizations and the Sunni majority, Americans are infidels and legitimate targets. (A.R. 172). Accordingly, the Shias are also legitimate targets because they are perceived as being pro American, due to their work and cooperation with the United States in Pakistan and Iraq. (A.R. 172, 194). Although there has historically been discord between the Sunni and Shia in Pakistan, the presence of the United States has caused an escalation in the violence against Shias by the Sunnis. (A.R. 197).

SUMMARY OF ARGUMENT

Petitioner has met the statutory requirements for withholding of removal, and the Immigration Judge failed to adequately articulate otherwise in his oral decision. (A.R. 55-68).[2] Petitioner established through testimony and documentary evidence that she has suffered past persecution, and that if she was forced to return to Pakistan, it would be more probable than not that she would be persecution based upon her religious beliefs and practices again.

The Immigration Judge failed to articulate adequately in his oral decision why **[Alien]** did not meet the burden of proof to qualify for withholding of removal. Instead, the Immigration Judge spoke at length about why **[Alien]** was not eligible for an exception to the one year statutory limit for filing her asylum application, and then in passing stated that she was not eligible for withholding of removal because he was not sure if **[Alien]** would be persecuted or tortured by the Pakistani government or others operating with the acquiescence of the government of Pakistan. (A.R. 67).

The appropriate standard in determining an applicant's eligibility for withholding of removal is not if the government persecutes, or permits the persecution of the applicant, but, rather, if forced to return to their country of origin will the applicant's life or freedom be threatened because of their religion. I.N.A. §241(b)(3)(A), 8 U.S.C. §1231(b).

Once a finding is made that it is more probable than not future persecution will occur, withholding of removal is mandatory, not discretionary. Thus, the Immigration Judge erred in not granting **[Alien]**'s application for withholding of removal because **[Alien]** proved that it is more probable than not she will be persecuted if forced to return to Pakistan.

The BIA erred in summarily upholding the denial of **[Alien]**'s application for withholding of removal when the corroborating evidence proved that **[Alien]** cannot safely return to Pakistan. The evidence demonstrates that **[Alien]** would be in great danger of attack by Sunni extremists if forced to return to Pakistan, and that the government of Pakistan not only fails to provide adequate protection, but that the government supports Sunni extremist groups and instability within Pakistan itself. Further, by summarily upholding the Immigration Judge's decision, the correct standard of proof was never applied to **[Alien]**'s application for withholding of removal.

ARGUMENT

I. THE IMMIGRATION JUDGE'S FINDING THAT [ALIEN] DOES NOT QUALIFY FOR WITHHOLDING OF REMOVAL IS NOT SUPPORTED BY SUBSTANTIAL EVIDENCE.

A. Standard of Review

When the BIA clearly adopts and incorporates the Immigration Judge's reasoning, the court reviews improper applications of legal standards of the Immigration Judge's decision *de novo*. *I.N.S v. Cardoza-Fonseca,* 480 U.S. 421 (1987); *Mikhael v. I.N.S.*, 115 F.3d 299, 302 (5th Cir. 1997). When the Immigration Judge has failed to follow proper legal standards, the factual findings of the Immigration Judge are subject to an abuse of discretion review. *Lopez-Gomez v. Ashcroft*, 263 F.3d 442, 444 (5th Cir. 2001); *Stankovic v. I.N.S.,* 94 F.3d 1117 (7th Cir. 1996). This court has also not hesitated to reverse the BIA, when the BIA's

[2] As the BIA has adopted for its decision in this matter the decision of the Immigration Judge, pursuant to *Chun v. I.N.S.*, 40 F.3d 76, 78 (5th Cir. 1994) and *Gomez-Mejia v. I.N.S.*, 56 F.3d 700, 702 (5th Cir. 1995), Petitioner will refer to the decision of the Immigration Judge as the controlling decision in this case.

decision has been based upon flawed reasoning or faulty assumptions. *Abdel-Masieh v. I.N.S.*, 73 F.3d 579, 585 (5th Cir. 1996); *Mikhael, supra*; *Rivas-Martinez v. I.N.S.*, 997 F.2d 1143 (5th Cir. 1993). Petitioner respectfully submits that the BIA's decision, as reflected in the Immigration Judge's decision, is patently flawed in this case.

B. The Court Should Review The Immigration Judge's Decision Because The Board Of Immigration Appeals Adopted The Immigration Judge's Decision.

This court must uphold the BIA's decision unless the petitioner can demonstrate that the BIA's findings were not supported by substantial evidence. *Lopez-Gomez,* 263 F.3d at 444. However, when the BIA clearly adopts and incorporates the Immigration Judge's reasoning, the court reviews the Immigration Judge's decision. *Mikhael,* 115 F.3d at 302. In the order rendered by the BIA on February 1, 2005, the BIA clearly adopted and incorporated the Immigration Judges decision. (A.R. 2). Thus, the court should review the decision of the Immigration Judge in reaching their decision.

C. The Legal Standard For Withholding Of Removal.

To qualify for withholding of removal, an alien must establish that it is more likely than not that they will be subject to persecution if returned to their home country.[3] *See generally I.N.S. v. Cardoza-Fonseca*, 480 U.S. 421 (1987). Thus, in order to qualify for withholding, the petitioner must show that there is a clear probability that they will be persecuted if forced to return. *Castillo-Rodriguez*, 929 F.2d 181, 185 (5th Cir. 1991). The applicant for withholding of removal carries the burden of proof that it is more reasonable than not they will be persecuted if forced to return. *Mikhael,* 115 F.3d at 306; *Castillo-Rodriguez,* 929 F.2d at 185. Once the applicant meets their burden of proof, withholding of removal is *mandatory*, not discretionary. I.N.A. §243(h)(1), 8 U.S.C. §1253(h)(1), *Mikhael,* 115 F.3d at 306.

Unlike the one year statutory time limit associated with filing an application for asylum, there are no time limits associated with filing an application for withholding of removal. 8 U.S.C. §1231(b)(3)(A), *Zhu v. Ashcroft,* 382 F.3d 521, 528 (5th Cir. 2004).

D. The Immigration Judge Erred By Denying Petitioner's Request For Withholding Of Removal.

Under the substantial evidence standard of review, if the evidence would compel a reasonable fact finder to reach a contrary result, then the judge's decision must be overturned. *Lopez-Reyes v. I.N.S.*, 79 F.3d 908, 911 (9th Cir. 1996). From the record, a reasonable fact finder would have determined that **[Alien]** fulfilled her burden of proof that there is a clear probability that she will be persecuted if forced to return to Pakistan due to her religious beliefs, and the Immigration Judge's decision is not based on substantial evidence. *See*, I.N.A. §241(b)(3); *Castillo-Rodriguez,* 929 F.2d 181, 185 (5th Cir. 1991). The undisputed direct testimony of **[Alien]**'s expert witness, Dr. Hamed Madani, was that violence between the Sunni and Shia has escalated significantly in Karachi, Pakistan within the past few years. (A.R. 178). The escalation in violence has manifested itself in the form of more attacks on religious sanctuaries, political assassinations, drive by shootings, and the use of planted explosive devices. (A.R. 178). One specific attack, which the Immigration Judge even references in his oral order, left more than 40 Shia Ismalis dead. (A.R. 63).

Dr. Madani further testified that the threat level for Shias has dramatically increased, as not only has the violence increased, it has changed. (A.R. 174). Sunni extremists have aligned with international terrorist or-

[3] Pursuant to I.N.A. §208(a)(3), 8 U.S.C. §1158(a)(3) this court does not possess the jurisdiction to review the BIA's refusal to grant Petitioner an exception to the requirement that asylum applications be filed within one year from the date of entry, and Petitioner does not raise the issue at this time.

ganizations, (A.R. 172), and the threat to Shia Ismalis will only increase with time. (A.R. 181). Further, Dr. Madani was accepted as an expert in this area. (A.R. 62).

[Alien] testified that she has been subjected to persecution due to her religious beliefs in Karachi, Pakistan, in the past. **[Alien]** testified that when she was nine years old, Sunni extremists attacked the mosque where her family worshiped, due to their religious beliefs. (A.R. 116). During the attack, tear gas was shot into the mosque as Shia Ismali practitioners were engaged in prayer, followed by random shootings. (A.R. 117).

When **[Alien]** was approximately sixteen years of age, she was subjected to persecution due to her religious beliefs once again. In this instance, **[Alien]** testified that Sunni extremists used violence and terrorism to force the closure of the mosque where her family worshiped, because the Sunni extremists did not believe that women should be allowed to worship within the mosque, and that men and women should be segregated. (A.R. 116-117). The mosque was subsequently closed for a period of time to all Shia Ismalis, followed by a period of time in which the mosque was opened, but only to men, as women were not allowed to enter for safety reasons. (A.R. 116-17).

Instead of focusing on what the probability that **[Alien]** would be subjected to persecution if forced returned to Karachi, Pakistan, the Immigration Judge focused on the likelihood of complete extermination of Shias in Pakistan by Sunni extremists. (A.R. 195-96). Specifically, the Immigration Judge asked **[Alien]**'s expert, Dr. Madani, questions such as "Do you think it's a 50/50 that it's more likely that their going to be wiped out?" and "You think the Shias are going to be exterminated?" (A.R. 195). Dr. Madani's response to these questions was that it is the goal of the Sunni extremists to completely eliminate Shias in Pakistan, and that with the way activities have been escalating, there may be a 50/50 chance that Sunnis will eliminate Shias in Pakistan. (A.R. 195-96).

The Immigration Judge's factual findings must be overturned because they are not supported by the evidence. Immigration Judges are given significant discretion; however, they "cannot reach their decisions capriciously" and "must indicate 'how [they] weighed the factors involved' and 'how [they] arrived at [their] conclusion.'" *Yepes-Padro v. I.N.S.*, 10 F.3d 1363, 1370 (9th Cir. 1993) (quoting *Dragon v. I.N.S.*, 748 F.2d 1304, 1307 (9th Cir. 1984)).

[Alien] offered evidence through direct testimony and through expert testimony that her life and liberty would be placed in jeopardy if forced to return to Pakistan. At no place in the Immigration Judge's order did the Immigration Judge find that **[Alien]**'s testimony was not credible, but instead focused almost entirely upon **[Alien]**'s failure to file for asylum within the requisite one year time restraints. *See* (A.R. 55-68). However, it is implicit in the Immigration Judge's order that the Immigration Judge found **[Alien]**'s testimony to be credible, as the Immigration Judge made comments such as **[Alien]** had "argue[d] persuasively," (A.R. 64), and "respondent recalls what I believe would be significant problems of strife between religious groups," (A.R. 64), which the Immigration Judge then used as a basis for denying **[Alien]** an exception to the one year time restraint associated with the filing of asylum applications.

Although the evidence **[Alien]** presented clearly demonstrates that **[Alien]** has been subjected to past persecution, including having been shot at while worshiping in her mosque, and that she will be subjected to future persecutions due to her religious beliefs if forced to return to Pakistan, the Immigration Judge simply stated that "its not clear from the evidence here that she would be persecuted on account of any protected reason." (A.R. 67). The most ironic aspect of the Immigration Judge's declaration that "he didn't believe" there was evidence that **[Alien]** would be subject to persecution if forced to return to Pakistan is that the Immigration Judge had just finished stating that "the respondent recalls what I believe would be significant problems of strife between religious groups," (A.R. 64), and "while the events last year my been more dramatic than in earlier years the circumstances are still such that it must be said that *that there is violence*. (A.R. 65) (emphasis added). At no point does the Immigration Judge state how he weighed the testimony of **[Alien]** or Dr. Madani, which clearly proved she would be subject to persecution due to her religious beliefs if forced to return to Pakistan, nor does the Immigration Judge ever comment on how he reached his conclusion, other than to say "it's not clear from the evidence here that she would be persecuted on account of any protected reason." (A.R. 67).

The Immigration Judge denied **[Alien]**'s application for withholding of removal after having admitted that Shias are subjected to violence at the hands of Sunnis, (A.R. 65), and that **[Alien]** has already faced persecution for her religious beliefs, (A.R. 64). Further, implicit in the Immigration Judge's order is that **[Alien]**'s and Dr. Madani's testimony was credible. As **[Alien]** has proven that it is more likely than not she would be subjected to persecution if forced to return to Pakistan, and that her testimony was credible, **[Alien]** has proven that not only is the Immigration Judge's decision capricious, but that it is also illogical, and therefore the decision of the BIA and the Immigration Judge must be overturned. *See generally, Yepes-Padro v.* I.N.S., 10 F.3d 1363, 1370 (9th Cir. 1993); *Dragon v. I.N.S.*, 748 F.2d 1304, 1307 (9th Cir. 1984).

According to I.N.A. §241(b)(3) and 8 U.S.C. §1231(b) the Attorney General *may not* remove an alien to a country where their life or freedom may be put into jeopardy due to their religious beliefs. Specifically, I.N.A. §241(b)(3) states:

> [T]he Attorney General may not remove an alien to a country if the Attorney General decides that the alien's life or freedom would be threatened in that country because of the alien's race, religion, nationality, membership in a particular social group, or political opinion.

As the Immigration Judge's decision to deny **[Alien]**'s application for withholding of removal was incorrect based upon the articulated and accepted facts which illustrate that **[Alien]** would be subjected to persecution if forced to return to Pakistan, I.N.A. §241(b)(3) requires that **[Alien]**'s application for withholding of removal be granted.

II. THE BOARD OF IMMIGRATION APPEALS ERRED IN AFFIRMING THE DECISION OF THE IMMIGRATION JUDGE WHEN THE RESULTS WERE INCORRECT.

Because the Immigration Judge made legal errors in his decision by not properly weighing all of the evidence, the BIA erred in affirming the Immigration Judge's decision. The BIA was required to give this case full consideration, and failed to do so. 8 C.F.R. §1003.1(e)(4).

It is incumbent upon agencies to follow their own procedures, especially when individual's rights are involved. *Morton v. Ruiz*, 415 U.S. 199, 235 (1974). Failure to act fairly and consistently constitutes an abuse by the agency. *N. Am. Indus. v. Feldman*, 722 F. 2d 893, 898-99 (1st Cir. 1983) (decisions based on misunderstandings of the law are considered an abuse); *Green Co. Mobilphone, Inc. v. F.C.C.*, 765 F.2d 235, 237-38 (D.C. Cir 1985) (agency must make reasonable distraction between given case and past cases that appear similar). The failure to consider and weigh even a single pertinent factor can distort the Immigration Judge's evaluation and compromise the result of the outcome reached. *Jen Jung Ng v. I.N.S.*, 804 F.2d 534 (9th Cir. 1986). Thus, when the BIA failed to consider all the evidence **[Alien]** presented in support of her application for withholding of removal, and failed to recognize that the Immigration Judge had applied an inappropriate standard of proof to **[Alien]**'s application for withholding of removal, the BIA erred in affirming the Immigration Judge's holdings.

In this case, the BIA did not have the legal authority to affirm the Immigration Judge's decision without a review of the file and a measured decision of its own. This error was neither harmless nor immaterial because it resulted in an order of removal against the Petitioner. Because the result by the Immigration Judge was incorrect, based on articulated and accepted facts, the errors were neither harmless nor immaterial; resulting in the decision of the BIA not being supported by the evidence, and should be reversed.

CONCLUSION

Based upon the foregoing facts and law, Petitioner **[Alien]** respectfully requests that this court reverse the decision of the Board of Immigration Appeals and the Immigration Judge and grant her application for withholding of removal pursuant to I.N.A. §241(b)(3) and 8 U.S.C. §1231(b).

Respectfully submitted this ____ day of ____, 20__.

[Attorney]

[ADD CERTIFICATE OF SERVICE]

[Document Nos. 608–09]

PETITION FOR REHEARING AND SUGGESTION FOR REHEARING *EN BANC*

Description: These are samples of petitions requesting a panel rehearing and a rehearing en banc on an unfavorable decision before the U.S. Court of Appeals. A request for a panel rehearing is a request for the panel that heard the case to rehear it. A suggestion for rehearing en banc is a request to have the entire circuit rehear the case.

Advantages: These requests are made when it is believed the court did not consider something in its first decision, either based on the law or the facts. They are not to be used for the court to reconsider the merits of the case. They are used when the panel decision conflicts with law or the facts.

Notes; Citations: A petition for a rehearing en banc is covered by Fed. R. App. P. 35. A petition for panel rehearing is covered by Fed. R. App. P. 40. If a petitioner files them separately, the court will consider them to be one document. It is important to review the local rules as well. The local rules provide such information as the number of copies to be filed. *See* Fed. R. App. P. 35(d). Before filing, review Fed. R. App. P. 32(c)(2), which outlines the form of the petition for rehearing and suggestion for rehearing en banc. In a civil case, if the United States or its officer or agency is a party, the party seeking rehearing may do so 45 days after entry of judgment.

The first petition challenges the panel's decision based on the law. The second sample challenges the panel's decision on its interpretation of the facts.

Pursuant to Fed. R. App. P. 35, a petition for rehearing en banc must have a statement that explains that (1) the decision conflicts with the U.S. Supreme Court or the court to which the petition is addressed and consideration is necessary to maintain uniformity with the court's decisions; or (2) the case involves questions of exceptional importance.

Pursuant to Fed R. App. P. 40, a petition for panel rehearing must state with particularity each point of law or fact that the petitioner believes the court has overlooked or misinterpreted and must argue in support of the petition. Oral argument is not permitted in support of the petition. Unless the court requests, no answer to a petition for panel rehearing is permitted. But, ordinarily, a rehearing will not be granted in the absence of such a request.

If a petition for panel rehearing is granted, the court may (1) make a final disposition of the case without reargument; (2) resolve the case to the calendar for reargument or resubmission; or (3) issue any other appropriate order.

UNITED STATES COURT OF APPEALS
FOR THE FOURTH CIRCUIT

No. ______

____

Petitioner-Appellant,

v.

ALBERTO R. GONZALES
U.S. ATTORNEY GENERAL

Respondent-Appellee

Review of Decision of the Board of Immigration Appeals

PETITIONER'S PETITION FOR REHEARING AND SUGGESTION FOR REHEARING EN BANC

[Attorney]
Counsel for Petitioner

PETITIONER'S PETITION FOR REHEARING AND SUGGESTION FOR REHEARING EN BANC

COUNSEL'S STATEMENT OF PURPOSE PURSUANT TO LOCAL RULE 40(B)

In the judgment of undersigned counsel, the Petitioner's appeal merits rehearing for the following reasons:

1. The Panel overlooked a material principle of law in its decision. Specifically, it completely ignored longstanding United States Supreme Court precedent holding that ICE bears the burden of establishing an alien's deportability by clear and convincing evidence. *See Woodby v. INS*, 385 U.S. 276 (1966).
2. The Panel's decision is in conflict with other courts of appeal in that it affirms an order of deportation based on a ground of deportability not charged against the Petitioner.
3. The Panel's decision is in conflict with decisions of the United States Supreme Court and this circuit, in that it violates applicable canons of statutory construction. First, it failed to interpret the statute at issue, §241(a)(2)(C) of the Immigration and Nationality Act, in accordance with its plain meaning. In addition, it failed to apply the principle of "expressio unius est exclusio alterius," which dictates that the enumeration of particular things in the language of a statute excludes the idea of something else not mentioned. Finally, it ignored the principle that statutes regarding deportability are to be strictly construed in favor of the alien.
4. The proceeding involves two issues of exceptional importance:

   a) The proper application of the government's burden of proof in establishing the deportability of a lawful permanent resident of the United States. The Panel's decision, if left undisturbed, presents a substantial risk that decisions within this Circuit regarding deportability from the United States will be made or reviewed pursuant to the wrong legal standard.

   b) The proper role of the judiciary in interpreting statutes. Here, the Panel failed to interpret the statute at issue according to three longstanding canons of statutory construction: the plain meaning doctrine, the doctrine of "expressio unius est exclusio alterius," and the doctrine requiring narrow construction of deportation statutes. By doing so, it impermissibly included within the scope of the deportability statute a crime not expressly enumerated therein by Congress.

SUGGESTION FOR REHEARING EN BANC

Because the Panel's decision ignored the applicable burden of proof upheld a finding of deportability based on a ground not even charged, and violated applicable canons of statutory construction, Petitioner requests rehearing *en banc*.

BACKGROUND FACTS

Petitioner **[Alien]** is a native and citizen of Jamaica, who has been a lawful permanent resident of the United States since 1974. He lives with and contributes to the support of his fourteen year old daughter who is a United States citizen. Mr. **[Alien]** had no criminal record of any kind until he was convicted in 1991 of making a false statement to a firearms dealer in violation of 18 USC §922(a)(6). That conviction gives rise to the issues presented in this appeal.

Mr. **[Alien]** was placed in deportation proceedings on **[date]**. ICE issued an Order to Show Cause (OSC or "charging document") on that date, which alleged in pertinent part that Mr. **[Alien]** was deportable pursuant to §241(a)(2)(C) of the Immigration and Nationality Act (INA). At the time Mr. **[Alien]**'s OSC was issued, §241(a)(2)(C) provided that

> [a]ny alien who at any time after admission is convicted under any law of purchasing, selling, offering for sale, exchanging, using, owning, possessing, carrying, *or of attempting or conspiring to* purchase, sell, offer for sale, exchange, use, own, possess, or carry any weapon, part, or accessory which is a firearm or destructive device (as defined in section 921 (a) of Title 18) in violation of any law is deportable. (Emphasis added.)

However, the OSC lodged by ICE against Mr. **[Alien]** did *not* include the language establishing deportability for any conviction for "attempting or conspiring to" do any of the enumerated acts listed above.

The Immigration Judge and the Board of Immigration Appeals found Petitioner deportable as charged. He sought review in this Court, arguing, *inter alia*, (1) that he could not be found deportable on the basis of a ground of deportability with which ICE had not even charged him; and (2) that the crime of making a false statement to a firearms dealer is not a conviction within the scope of *either* version of INA §241(a)(2)(C). In other words, Mr. **[Alien]**'s conviction for making a false statement was not a conviction for any of the acts enumerated in the pre-1994 version of §241(a)(2)(C), *nor* was it a conviction for an attempt or conspiracy to do any of the enumerated acts.

RELEVANT ASPECTS OF THE PANEL'S DECISION

Nowhere in the Panel's decision does it even address the burden of proof ICE must satisfy to establish an alien's deportability. Obviously, it never determined whether ICE had satisfied that standard.

With regard to the specific issues raised by Mr. **[Alien]**, the Panel's decision was in error in a number of respects. First, the Panel dismissed the issue concerning the propriety of finding Mr. **[Alien]** deportable on a ground not charged against him with only a footnote. The Panel stated that the OSC "did cite the statutory authority for his deportationCINA §241(a)(2)(C)" and that this was sufficient to give Mr. **[Alien]** notice of the charge he faced. (Slip op. at 8 n. 4.) This conclusory ruling did not address, much less distinguish, cases in the First and Ninth Circuits (as well as the BIA) holding that such action is impermissible.

On the statutory interpretation questions, the Panel's decision was similarly deficient. Although stating that it was construing the statute in accordance with its plain meaning (slip op. at 6), surrounding language in the Panel's decision reveals that it significantly enlarged the scope of the statute by its interpretation.

> [The statute's] list of gerunds captures *all varieties of conduct* relating to firearms transactions. . . . This wide ranging text envices an expansive purposeCto render deportable those aliens that commit firearms offenses *of any type*. (Emphasis added.) (Slip op. at 6.)

This elaboration in the statute's scope appears in the decision yet again. Addressing Petitioner's argument that he did *not* have a conviction for an attempt to purchase a firearm, the Panel stated:

> [Petitioner] participated in and enabled an unlawful purchase of a firearm. Section 241(a)(2)(C) does not exclude the mode of participation in which [petitioner] indisputably engaged. (Slip op. at 7.)

This language illustrates the Panel's error. Rather than reading the statute to determine what type of convictions it actually included, it read it to encompass a "mode of participation" and not to require a conviction at all.

Similarly, the Court failed to directly address the canon of statutory construction adopted by this and other circuits providing that "expressio unius est exclusio alterius." The language set forth above demonstrates that it failed to abide by that controlling principle.

ARGUMENT

I. THE PANEL COMPLETELY IGNORED THE STANDARD OF PROOF, IDENTIFIED BY THE UNITED STATES SUPREME COURT, BY WHICH IMMIGRATION AND CUSTOMS ENFORCEMENT MUST ESTABLISH DEPORTABILITY.

The seminal case regarding the burden ICE must satisfy in establishing an individual alien's deportability from the United States is *Woodby v. INS*, 385 U.S. 276 (1966). In *Woodby*, which also involved a lawful permanent resident alien, the Supreme Court specifically analyzed the burden legacy INS/ICE must satisfy, recognizing "the drastic deprivations that may follow when a resident of this country is compelled by our Government to forsake all bonds formed here. . ." *Id.* at 285. The Court rejected the preponderance of the evidence standard urged by INS, and held instead that the agency must meet the same high standard of proof required in denaturalization and expatriation causes; *i.e.*, the INS must establish its allegations by clear, unequivocal, and convincing evidence. *Id.* The Supreme Court based its ruling on the fact that deportation sometimes imposes even greater hardship than denaturalization, because it necessarily results in expulsion from our shores. Moreover, the Court recognized that in some cases, permanent residents have lived in the United States longer than some who have become citizens, and as a result, have established stronger family, social and economic ties. *Id.*

This is precisely the situation in the instant case. Mr. **[Alien]** has been a permanent resident for a period now exceeding 25 years. He has virtually no ties to Jamaica, but lives here in an intact nuclear family unit with a U.S. citizen child. His social and economic support system is exclusively in the United States. Supreme Court precedent demands that his deportability be established by clear, unequivocal and convincing evidence. ICE has failed to meet that burden in this case. To the contrary, Mr. **[Alien]** has been found deportable on a ground of deportability ICE did not even allege against him. To make matters worse, the BIA and this Court's Panel have interpreted the statute in an expansive manner inconsistent with the principles established by the Supreme Court.

II. THE PANEL ERRONEOUSLY UPHELD THE BOARD OF IMMIGRATION APPEALS' FINDING OF DEPORTABILITY ON A GROUND THAT IMMIGRATION AND CUSTOMS ENFORCEMENT DID NOT EVEN ASSERT AGAINST PETITIONER [ALIEN].

Petitioner has consistently argued that he cannot properly be found deportable on the basis of a charge *not even* included in the OSC alleging his deportability; *i.e.*, that he is deportable for having a conviction for an *attempt or conspiracy* to do any of the acts enumerated in INA §241(a)(2)(C). This point now has taken on critical importance, because at oral argument, ICE counsel identified in response to a question from Judge Motz *exactly what the basis of Mr.* ***[Alien]****'s deportability was.* The answer was clear: an attempt to purchase a firearm.

There can be no dispute that the OSC forming the basis for Petitioner's deportation proceedings reflects no such charge. (R. 337-41.) Case law from the First and Ninth Circuits confirms that ICE cannot deport an alien on uncharged grounds, *even if it could have amended the charging documents to include those other charges.*

In *Hirsch v. INS*, 308 F.2d 562 (9th Cir. 1962), the Court confronted a situation in which the BIA found the respondent not deportable under the charges actually made against her, but deportable "by reason of matters never charged." *Id.* at 566. As the Court stated in setting aside the deportation order, "This will not do." *Id.* Similarly, in *Choeum v. INS*, 129 F.3d 29 (1st Cir. 1997), the Court held that the INS could not substitute grounds of deportability (even legitimate ones) during review of an Immigration Judge's decision. Despite the fact that its regulations would have permitted the INS to lodge additional charges of deportability at any time, the Court found that the INS had failed to comply with those necessary formalities, including submitting the charges in writing and serving them on the alien, and therefore it did not permit the new grounds of deportability to be considered. *Id.* at 40; *see also Matter of Pichardo-Sufren*, Int. Dec. 3275 (BIA 1996). The Panel's decision did not address, much less distinguish, the decisions in other circuits on this issue.

III. THE PANEL EXCEEDED ITS AUTHORITY BY EFFECTIVELY BROADENING THE LIST OF FIREARMS-RELATED GROUNDS OF DEPORTABILITY TO INCLUDE AN OFFENSE NOT EXPRESSLY ENUMERATED BY CONGRESS EVEN WHEN CONGRESS INTENTIONALLY EXPANDED THE LIST OF DEPORTABLE FIREARMS OFFENSES.

A. The Plain Meaning Doctrine

The principal canon of statutory construction is that a statute must first be interpreted by giving its language its plain and ordinary meaning. *K-Mart Corp. v. Cartier, Inc.,* 486 U.S. 281 (1988); *Park 'N Fly Inc. v. Dollar Park and Fly,* 469 U.S. 189 (1985); *CBS, Inc. v. FCC,* 453 U.S. 367 (1981). Therefore, in determining whether Mr. **[Alien]** was deportable, the Panel should have looked at the specific language of §241(a)(2)(C) and asked itself whether Mr. **[Alien]** had been convicted of any of the specific crimes listed therein. If it had done so, it would have determined that Mr. **[Alien]** is not deportable. It failed to do so, completely ignoring the plain meaning rule.

Although invoking the plain meaning doctrine (slip op. at 6), the Panel actually engaged in a complete rewrite of the statute. The Panel relied on the fact that both the Immigration Act of 1990 and the Immigration and Technical Corrections Act of 1994 successively expanded the definition of a deportable firearms offense to reach the conclusion that the current version of §241(a)(2)(C) intended "to render deportable those aliens that commit firearms offenses *of any type*." (Emphasis added). (Slip op. at 6.)

This conclusion is completely unsupported. In fact, exactly the opposite is apparent. The simple fact that Congress did *not* say in §241(a)(2)(C) that any alien who had a conviction for any offense in Chapter 44 of 18 USC (the firearms title), or even in all of §922 is evidence that it did not intend to go that far.

B. Expressio Unius Est Exclusio Alterius

The same conclusion is compelled by the other applicable canon of statutory construction, "expressio unius est exclusio alterius," dictating that the enumeration of particular things in the language of a statute excludes the idea of something else not mentioned. *Adams v. Dole*, 927 F.2d 771 (4th Cir.) *cert. denied*, 502 U.S. 837 (1991); *Allstate Ins. Co. v. Skeeters*, 846 F.2d 932 (4th Cir. 1988).

Congress clearly chose to enumerate a laundry list of specific acts that are included in various parts of §922, but making a false statement under §922(a)(6) is simply not among them. The error was compounded by the way the Panel dispensed with the requirement for a conviction. It found only that Mr. **[Alien]** had "participated in and enabled an unlawful purchase of a firearm," and found him deportable as a result. By doing so, it read the requirement for a conviction right out of the statute.

C. Narrow Construction of Deportation Statutes

The Panel's decision also ignored the longstanding principle that deportation statutes must be narrowly construed, and construed in favor of aliens. The Supreme Court has consistently applied this rule. *INS v. Errico*, 385 U.S. 214, 225 (1996); *INS v. Cardoza-Fonseca*, 480 U.S. 421, 449 (1987); *Rosenberg v. Fleuti*, 374

U.S. 449, 459 (1963); *Bonetti v. Rogers*, 356 U.S. 691, 699 (1956); *Barber v. Gonzalez*, 347 U.S. 637, 642-433 (1954); *Fong Haw Tan v. Phelan*, 333 U.S. 6 (1948).

The discussion above illustrates that the approach taken by the Panel was repeatedly at odds with this aspect of Supreme Court precedent. At every turn, the Panel interpreted §241(a)(2)(C) as broadly as possible, rather than narrowly. It cannot be disputed that this worked to the detriment of Mr. **[Alien]**. If the statute had been read narrowly, according to its plain meaning, and without reading into the statute a firearms-related conviction that was *not expressly enumerated therein*, the Panel would have been compelled to reach a different result.

A re-examination of the Panel's decision reveals a decision made too hastily. A closer examination of the record and applicable law, including canons of statutory construction, shows that the Panel's decision ignored the burden of proof and the law, and in so doing, reached an incorrect decision on an issue of the highest importance, the deportation of a lawful permanent resident from the United States.

CONCLUSION

A decision regarding deportability is extremely serious. Indeed, the Supreme Court has recognized that deportation implicates "issues basic to human liberty and happiness." *Wong Yang Sung v. McGrath*, 339 U.S. 33 (1950). When a lawful permanent resident is involved, deportation is the equivalent of banishment or exile. *Delgadillo v. Carmichael*, 332 U.S. 388 (1947). With this degree of constitutionally protected interests at stake, and the requirement that this Court should construe statutes establishing deportability narrowly, rather than broadly, the cumulative impact of errors in the Panel's decision are obvious. This is particularly true in light of the burden of proof ICE must bear in establishing deportability.

For all of the reasons set forth above, Petitioner respectfully urges this Court to vacate its decision dated **[date]** and schedule the case for rehearing *en banc*.

Respectfully submitted,

[Attorney]

[ADD CERTIFICATE OF SERVICE]

UNITED STATES COURT OF APPEALS
FOR THE FOURTH CIRCUIT

No. ______

____

Petitioner-Appellant,

v.

ALBERTO R. GONZALES
U.S. ATTORNEY GENERAL

Respondent-Appellee

Appeal from the United States District Court for the Eastern District of Virginia at Alexandria (Hon. [Judge])

PETITIONER'S PETITION FOR REHEARING AND SUGGESTION FOR REHEARING EN BANC

[Attorney]
Counsel for Petitioner

TABLE OF CONTENTS

TABLE OF AUTHORITIES

Cases

Bolanos-Hernandez v. INS, 767 F.2d 1277 (9th Cir. 1984)

Borca v. INS, 77 F.3d 210 (7th Cir. 1996)

Bueno Carillo v. Landon, 682 F.2d 143 (7th Cir. 1982)

Carranza-Hernandez v. INS, 12 F.3d 4 (2d Cir. 1994)

Castillo-Villagra v. INS, 972 F.2d 1017 (9th Cir. 1992)

de la Llana-Castellon v. INS, 16 F.3d 1093 (10th Cir.1994)

Desir v. Ilchert, 840 F.2d 723 (9th Cir. 1988)

Doe v INS, 857 F.2d 285 (6th Cir. 1989)

Draganova v INS, 82 F.3d 716, 1996 U.S. App. LEXIS 9870 (7th Cir. 1996)

Gebremichael v. INS, 10 F.3d 28 (1st Cir. 1993)

Ghebllawi v. INS, 28 F.3d 83 (9th Cir. 1994)

Hernandez Cordero v. INS, 819 F.2d 558 (5th Cir. 1987)

Herrera v INS, (1996 U.S. App. LEXIS 3553, Feb. 7, 1996)

INS v. Cardoza-Fonseca, 480 U.S. 421(1987)

INS v. Elias-Zacarias, 502 U.S. 478 (1992)

Kapcia v. INS, 944 F.2d 702 (10th Cir. 1991)

Kovac v. INS, 407 F.2d 102 (9th Cir. 1969)

Osorio v. INS, 18 F.3d 1017 (2d Cir. 1994)

Perez Alvarez v. INS, 857 F.2d 23 (1st Cir. 1988)

Ramos v. INS, 695 F.2d 181 (5th Cir. 1983)

Santana-Figueroa v. INS, 644 F.2d 1354 (9th Cir. 1981)

Shirazi-Parsa v. INS, 14 F.3d 1424 (9th Cir. 1994)

Sotelo-Aquije v. INS, 17 F.3d 33 (2d Cir. 1994)

Tarvand v. INS, 937 F.2d. 973 (4th Cir. 1991)

Youssefina v. INS, 784 F.2d 1254 (5th Cir. 1986)

SEC v. Chenery Corp., 318 U.S. 80 (1943)

Administrative Decisions

In re B, Interim Dec. 3251, 1995 BIA Lexis 15 (BIA May 19, 1995)

Matter of Mogharrabi, 19 I & N Dec. 439 (BIA 1987)

Statutes

8 USC §1101 *et seq.* (INA)

8 USC §1105(a)(4)

PETITIONER'S PETITION FOR REHEARING AND SUGGESTION FOR REHEARING EN BANC

COUNSEL'S STATEMENT OF PURPOSE PURSUANT TO IOP 40.5

It is the opinion of undersigned counsel that the petitioner's appeal merits rehearing for the following reasons:

1. The Panel misstated the findings on which the Board based its opinion in Mr. **[Alien]**'s case. The restatement of those findings and the process whereby they were formulated by the Board obscured the basis of **[Alien]**'s appeal and denied him an opportunity of judicial review of the Board's actual findings and procedures. As a result, the Panel has upheld a decision which improperly denies eligibility for asylum without having considered the evidence that supports Mr. **[Alien]**'s claim. Sound and well established principles of administrative law, which operate to avoid such arbitrary results, were overlooked and therefore not enforced by the Panel. These include:

    a) a quasi-judicial agency's prerogative and duty to make factual determinations in the first instance, subject to review by the courts;

    b) the agency's duty to articulate the basis of its decision and the Court's duty to review a decision based on the agency's stated findings; and

    c) the agency's duty to develop an evidentiary record subject to procedural safeguards and the court's duty to remand cases to the agency rather than review factual determinations in the absence of an adequate record.

2. The Board's interpretation of the asylum applicant's burden of proof with regard to the persecutor's motives, as upheld by the Panel, is in conflict with the decisions of other Circuits where, as in this case, there was evidence of "mixed motives on the part of the persecutors." The Panel affirmed the manner in which **[Alien]**'s claim was disposed of, without regard to ample evidence in the record supporting his claim. They failed to evaluate whether a reasonable person in his circumstances would fear persecution based on his religion, political opinion and social group, merely because there was some evidence that his persecutors had also engaged in attempts to extort money from him. Other Circuits have held that evidence of extortion or other financial hardship does not preclude a finding of "persecution." The facts of each individual case should be evaluated to determine whether the economically related measures were imposed for punitive reasons amounting to persecution; or whether the evidence shows additional motives of the persecutor which do amount to persecution.

3. Rehearing would also afford the Panel the opportunity to consider certain issues raised in the appeal but not addressed in the decision.

SUGGESTION FOR REHEARING EN BANC

Due to the departure of the Panel's decision from established principles of administrative law and the conflicts that this decision presents with cases decided in other Circuits, Petitioner requests rehearing en banc.

RELEVANT ASPECTS OF THE PANEL'S DECISON

[Alien]'s initial application for asylum was based on his fear of persecution in Afghanistan both from that country's Soviet-backed government and Mujaheddin factions in conflict with his own. It has long been conceded that the first claim is now moot, due to the subsequent change in country conditions.

The central issue in this appeal was whether the Board had applied the proper standard of eligibility for asylum to Mr. **[Alien]**'s second claim: fear of persecution from the rival Mujaheddin factions. To establish eligibility for asylum, an applicant must show that a reasonable person in his circumstances would fear harm based on one of the grounds enumerated in the Statutes: Immigration and Nationality Act (Immigration and Nationality Act, 8 USC §1101 *et seq.* (INA or the "Act"). It is clear from the Board's decision that **[Alien]** was required to show *with certainty* that his persecutors where motivated by one of those grounds, *to the exclusion of any other reason.*

> They have not shown that any action the members of the Hezb-i-Islami and the Harrakat-Islami might take against each other would be one of the five grounds specified in the Act [or that the Hezb-i-Islami's acts were intended to] punish him for one of the five grounds specified in the Act *rather than* to extort from him money needed by the Hezb-i-Islami to conduct its militant activities against the government (emphasis added). (JA 166).

The Panel's opinion restates the Board's finding on the motive issue by using language that obscures the Board's error:

> Based on testimony in the record the BIA found . . . the Hezb-i-Islami sent threatening letters to **[Alien]** while he was in Pakistan merely to extort money from **[Alien]** to finance its operations, and not to persecute **[Alien]** based on one of the five enumerated categories. (***[Alien]*** *v. Carroll*, No. 95-6480, slip op. at 5 (hereinafter "Panel Op.")).

The Board's exact language indicated clearly that it did not apply the "reasonable person" standard in weighing the evidence of persecutor's motive in this case. Its use of the term "rather than" indicates that the mere possibility of an extortionist motive precluded its weighing of any other evidence regarding motive.

The Panel also misinterpreted the process whereby the BIA reached its decision.

> The BIA did not agree that **[Alien]**'s evidence satisfied the objective part of the analysis because a reasonable person would not fear persecution as a result of race, religion, nationality, membership in a particular social group or political opinion. (Panel Op. at 4-5.)

The BIA did not engage in such analysis. Instead it held that **[Alien]** did not prove that his persecutors did not have a motive unrelated to the Act, and ended its deliberation right there. In overlooking this distinction, the Panel failed to address the Board's errors and the basis for this appeal.

ARGUMENT

1. The Panel's Decision Overlooks Fundamental Principles of Administrative Law and Conflicts With Decisions of This Circuit and Other Circuits on This Issue

The Panel's decision is in conflict with a long-established principle of administrative law, that the administrative agency's decision must be upheld, if at all, on the same basis that the agency decided it. *SEC v. Chenery Corp.*, 318 U.S. 80 (1943). The panel's interpretation of the Board's decision enunciates a standard of proof that was not applied in the Board's decision and assumes that the Board weighed facts when in fact it did not. The "orderly functioning of the process of review requires that the grounds upon which the administrative agency acted *be clearly disclosed and adequately sustained* (emphasis added)." *Id.* at 94. By interpreting the Board's decision to have a different meaning than that which it actually has, the panel substituted its judgment for the Board's. Under the INA, it is the Attorney General and his delegates that are to make the decision in the first instance, not a panel of this Court. 8 USC §1158(a)(1988).

As discussed in Petitioner's brief, and noted by the district court[1], the Board did not explain the basis for its findings. In *Hernandez Cordero v. INS,* 819 F.2d 558, 563(5th Cir. 1987) the court held that "the Board must consider the issues raised and announce its decision in terms sufficient to enable a reviewing court to perceive that it has heard and thought and not merely reacted."

The Ninth Circuit in *Santana-Figueroa v. INS,* 644 F. 2d 1354, 1357 held that:

> When allegations are specific and supported by evidentiary material, and the Board denies eligibility for relief, it must give reasons for its decisions showing that it has properly considered the circumstances. *To affirm on the theory that the Board necessarily considered whatever the petitioner asserted would free the Board of the obligation to articulate a reasoned basis for its decisions, eliminating any guaranty of rationality* . . .(Emphasis added).

See also Bueno Carillo v. Landon, 682 F.2d 143 (7th Cir. 1982) and *Ramos v. INS,* 695 F.2d 181 (5th Cir. 1983). The relief sought in those cases was suspension of deportation rather than asylum. However, while suspension permits the Attorney General, acting through his agents, to grant relief in the exercise of discretion, the determination of eligibility for asylum is a matter of law. *INS v. Cardoza-Fonseca,* 480 U.S. 421 (1987). Therefore, the need for the Board to articulate its reasons for finding an applicant ineligible for asylum is even greater than in the context of suspension cases.

Furthermore, the Panel's application of the substantial evidence standard employed in *INS v. Elias-Zacarias,* 502 U.S. 478 (1992), is inappropriate where, as in this case, the Board's misapplication of law precluded its proper consideration of the evidence. In *Elias,* the Board's decision was not being challenged on legal and procedural grounds. When, as in this case, it is clear that ". . . an alien's request for asylum has been erroneously evaluated by application of the standard for withholding of deportation, remand is appropriate." *See Doe v INS,* 857 F.2d 285, 290-91 (6th Cir. 1989); *Perez Alvarez v. INS,* 857 F.2d 23, 24-25 (1st Cir.) 1988; *Tarvand v. INS,* 937 F. 2d. 973, 975 (4th Cir. 1991).

The court's ruling in *Elias* does not negate the fact that the Board's decisions are subject to the principles of administrative law, *Ghebllawi v. INS,* 28 F.3d 83 (9th Cir. 1994). The Board's findings are the only indicators of their adherence to those principles. The Panel's mischaracterization of the Board's findings precluded proper scrutiny of the Board's decision.

2. The Panel's Formulation of the Asylum Applicant's Burden of Proof Regarding the Motivations of his Persecutors Conflicts with Decisions of Other Circuits

The BIA's decision demonstrates that it considered evidence of an extortionist motive to preclude consideration of any other motive evidence.

> They have not shown that any action the members of the Hezb-i-Islami and the Harrakat-Islami might take against each other would be one of the five grounds specified in the Act . . . [or that the Hezb-i-Islami's acts were intended to] punish him for one of the five grounds specified in the Act *rather than* to extort from him money needed by the Hezb-i-Islami to conduct its militant activities against the government. (Emphasis added). (JA 166).

Its use of the words "rather than" illustrates the Board's belief that an applicant can only be eligible for aslyum if his persecutor had but a single motive. In reality, this is often not the case, nor is it the law.

Other circuits have found applicants to be eligible for asylum in the presence of mixed motives. *Osorio v. INS,* 18 F.3d 1017 (2d Cir. 1994); *Sotelo-Aquije v. INS,* 17 F.3d 33 (2d Cir. 1994); *Carranza-Hernandez v.*

[1] In the words of the District Court, the Board's decision consists of "fairly conclusory language" that "hampers a considered review of their own statements." (JA 196).

INS, 12 F.3d 4 (2d Cir. 1994); *Shirazi-Parsa v. INS*, 14 F.3d 1424 (9th Cir. 1994); *Desir v. Ilchert*, 840 F.2d 723 (9th Cir. 1988). The same basis used by the Board to reject **[Alien]**'s claimCthat he had failed to prove persecution based on one of the five grounds specified in the ActC*rather than* to extort money from himCwas used by the Board in a case recently reversed by the Ninth Circuit. *Herrera v INS,* 1996 U.S. App. LEXIS 355 (Feb. 7, 1996). There, the Board held that Herrera failed to establish that his mistreatment at the hands of the Nicaraguan Sandinistas had been "for an imputed political opinion *rather than* for his desertion or failure to divulge information that the Sandinistas believed he possessed" (emphasis added). *Id.* at *13. In granting a remand, the court stated:

> Where more than one motive exists for persecutory conduct, however, it is sufficient if the applicant shows that "one motive is [on account of] one of the statutorily enumerated grounds." *Ilchert*, 63 F.3d at 1509.

The Panel's affirmance of the Board's decision in a mixed motive case clearly conflicts with other circuits on the issue of mixed motive. In the instant case, the Panel held that evidence **[Alien]** presented regarding his persecutor's motives "*was not concrete enough* to establish **[Alien]**'s well founded fear of persecution 'with the degree of clarity necessary to permit reversal of a BIA finding to the contrary.' *Elias-Zacarias*, 502 U.S. at 483." (Emphasis added) (Panel Op. at 6.)

Whether or not evidence of motive is sufficiently "concrete" to establish eligibility for asylum is a matter of law. Accordingly, in *Draganova v INS,* 82 F.3d 716 (7th Cir. 1996), the Court, reviewing *de novo* for legal error, found that the Board erred in requiring "conclusive" evidence of the persecutor's motive.

> . . . the IJ stated in considering the father's situation, that (there is insufficient evidence to conclusively determine) the motivation of their mistreatment. [C]ontrary to the IJ's statement, the evidence presented need not conclusively prove that an applicant has a well founded fear of persecution.

Draganova, 82 F.3d __ 1996 U.S. App. LEXIS 9870 at *12; *See I.N.S. v. Cardoza-Fonseca,* 480 U.S. 421(1987) (parallel citations omitted).

The Court applied the same analysis to the asylum applicant's claim of past persecution, also a question of law. "We see no reason to set a greater burden of proofCsuch as conclusive proofCfor a claim of past persecution than for a claim that persecution would occur in the future." *Id.*

In the instant case, the Board did not even reach the question of whether **[Alien]**'s evidence regarding the persecutor's motive was "conclusive." Instead, it regarded the presence of evidence of any supposedly non-related motive (in this case, extortion) to preclude a showing of eligibility. The Supreme Court has held that the term of "well founded fear" can be given concrete meaning only through a process of "case by case adjudication." *INS v. Cardoza-Fonseca*, 480 U.S. at 421. Such generalizations deny an applicant's right to have his case decided according to his particular circumstances.

Conceivably, any type of harm could be related to one of the protected grounds *depending on the particular circumstances of the case.* Indeed, extortion and other forms of economic deprivation have been found to constitute persecution in some cases. *See Desir v. Ilchert*, 840 F.2d 723, 727 (9th Cir. 1988); *Youssefina v. INS*, 784 F.2d 1254 (5th Cir. 1986); *Kovac v. INS*, 407 F.2d 102 (9th Cir. 1969). The economic harm must be deliberately imposed as a form of punishment, as opposed to natural, non-primitive measures with economic effects. *Borca v. INS*, 77 F.3d 210, 215 (7th Cir. 1996).

3. Even Assuming That the Panel Was Correct In Applying the "Substantial Evidence" Test of *Elias-Zacarias* to This Case, It Overlooked Evidence Regarding [Alien]'s Inclusion in a Protected Class and the Motivations of His Persecutors

As discussed at length in Petitioner's brief (pp. 15–20), **[Alien]** is a Shi'a Muslim and ex-militant of the Harrakat-Islami. The threatening letters that he received in Pakistan from members of a rival Mujaheddin faction (Hezb-i-Islami) were but one chapter in a history of aggression by that group against his own. That history began before he left Afghanistan and it continues to this date. The unrefuted testimony of **[Alien]**, corroborated by his father and the stipulated testimony of his wife, indicated that the harm threatened against him was due to the religious and political differences between the two groups. Documentary evidence presented by **[Alien]** as well as in the State Department Report[2] introduced into the record by the BIA also attested to ongoing violence rooted in their differences.

In determining whether the requisite motive of the persecutors had been shown, the Board did not consider any of that evidence. As discussed below, the Board applied an improper standard of proof with regard to the persecutors' motive. Having required **[Alien]** to prove a negative (that the threats against him were not for purposes of extortion) the Board ended its inquiry without examining the evidence of motive linked to the grounds stated in the Act.

The Board's failure to consider evidence regarding the motives of **[Alien]**'s persecutors was not addressed by the Panel. While the decision indicates that **[Alien]**'s eligibility was reviewed *de novo*, the Panel, like the Board, omitted from its review all the record evidence showing a link between the persecutors' motives and **[Alien]**'s religious and political affiliations. Citing *Elias-Zacarias,* the Panel's decision states that "the mere existence of a political or religious motive underlying the Hezb-i-Islami's actions does not *necessarily* render those acts persecution on account of **[Alien]**'s political or religious views (Emphasis added)." (Panel Op. at 6). However, the decision fails to contemplate when it is that such circumstances *may* indicate persecution, as suggested by the use of the term "*necessarily*" in *Elias*. Specifically, it failed to consider whether the circumstances faced by **[Alien]** may fall within that possibility.

The Supreme Court used the language quoted by the Panel directly following its thorough review of the facts of the case. The Court then that there was no evidence that Elias belonged to one of the protected categories. Like **[Alien]**, Elias showed likelihood of future harm, but without his inclusion in a protected class the Court could not find that such harm amounted to persecution. **[Alien]**, however, presented ample evidence of his inclusion in three of the protected categories: religion, social group and political opinion, and evidence that the threats against him and his family were made on that basis. The Panel's *de novo* review of his case included no discussion of **[Alien]**'s inclusion in a protected class.

Also, *Elias* does not require "concrete" evidence of a persecutor's motive but rather "some" evidence.[3] **[Alien]** presented more than "some" evidence of the persecutor's motivations in bringing him harm. However, the Panel, not having reviewed the record as a whole, failed to give proper weight to the evidence presented. Proper review of the Board's decision requires review of the record "as a whole." *See* 8 USC §1105(a)(4). Indeed the only discussion of the evidence in the Panel's decision is a reference to evidence that **[Alien]** did *not* presentCthe letters he received from the Hezb-i-Islami. The Panel relied solely on the fact that **[Alien]** did not present the threatening letters in evidence, to state that his claim had not been established "with the degree of clarity necessary to permit reversal. . ." (Panel Op. at 6.) It is well established asylum law that "the alien's own testimony may in some cases be the only evidence available, and it can suffice where the testimony is believable, consistent, and sufficiently detailed to provide a plausible and coherent account

---

[2] Committees on Foreign Relations and Foreign Affairs, 103d Cong., 1st Sess., *Country Reports on Human Rights Practices for 1992*, 1115 (Joint Comm. Print 1993).

[3] The Supreme Court specifically stated: "he cannot be expected to provide direct proof of his persecutors' motives. We do not require that." *Elias-Zacarias*, 502 U.S. at 816–17.

of the basis for his fear." *Matter of Mogharrabi*, 19 I&N Dec. 439 (BIA 1987).

As indicated by the Ninth Circuit, "Persecutors are hardly likely to provide their victims with affidavits attesting to their acts of persecution," *Bolanos-Hernandez v. INS*, 767 F.2d 1277, 1285 (9th Cir. 1984), including, of course, their motives.

Mr. **[Alien]**'s testimony was found to be detailed, credible and consistent by the Immigration Judge (JA 153), and that finding was not disturbed by the BIA. Thus, his testimony established the existence of the letters and their content, and the fact that they were never physically made part of the record was not relevant to the Panel's review of the BIA decision.

4. The Panel Overlooked the Board's Legal Error in Taking Selective Administrative Notice of Change in Country Conditions

It is common for the Board to take administrative notice of changes in country conditions in the context of asylum applications. The courts have approved this method for the Board to consider "current events bearing on an applicant's well founded fear of persecution." *Kapcia v. INS*, 944 F.2d 702, 705 (10th Cir. 1991). However, "an agency's discretion to take administrative notice depends on the particular case before it." *Castillo-Villagra*, 972 F.2d at 1028; *see also Gebremichael v. INS*, 10 F.3d 28, 39 (1st Cir. 1993) (noting that in the context of administrative notice-taking, the demands of due process ultimately depend on the circumstances); *de la Llana-Castellon v. INS,* 16 F.3d 1093, 1097 (10th Cir. 1994).

The circumstances in this case are such that the principal source of **[Alien]**'s fear of persecution changed from the Soviet-backed Afghani government to the Hezb-i-Islami, while his appeal was pending before the BIA. Hence, the BIA appropriately took notice of this aspect of the changed country conditions. However, the intensification of the conflict between rival Mujaheddin forces was, by the time of the Board's consideration, even more relevant to his claim. However, this fact was not administratively noticed by the Board. In the opinion of the Panel, there was no need for the Board to acknowledge this fact since "it clearly stated that it considered evidence that the Mujaheddin groups were fighting among each other." (Panel Op. at 5, fn.) The Board's conclusory statement about the infighting hardly reflects the magnitude and quality of the facts bearing upon **[Alien]**'s eligibility for asylum which were "current" *at the time the Board decided his appeal.* In citing the State Department Country Reports[4] as support for its finding that the government **[Alien]** feared had been overthrown, the Board established the need to open up the record to all the evidence in that Report, as well as the contemporaneous newspaper article submitted by the Petitioner with his appeal brief. (JA 163). The evidence supporting **[Alien]**'s claim in the Country Reports was that the fighting between Mujaheddin factions had reached a major scale; and included conduct which amounted to human rights violations, i.e. "mass hangings on both sides."[5] The newspaper article attested to the fact that the Superpowers were giving up on trying to bring an end to the conflict between Mujaheddin factions by peaceful means and that "the [then] recent pattern of sporadic battles might evolve into open, bloody chaos." (JA 163).

Both reports also contained information which further corroborated the political and religious bases for the conflict between Mujaheddin forces upon which **[Alien]**'s claim was based. Yet the Board found and the

---

[4] Committees on Foreign Relations and Foreign Affairs, 103d Cong., 1st Sess., Country Reports on Human Rights Practices for 1992, 1115 (Joint Comm. Print 1993).

[5] In reference to the fighting between the Mujaheddin factions, the Report stated:

> In June and July, intense fighting between Shi'a and Sunni forces provoked reprisal attacks against civilians including kidnapping, beatings and indiscriminate shelling and rocket attacks in residential areas. The fighting left more than 100 dead and 400 wounded in the streets of Kabul. There were reports of mass hangings of captured prisoners by both sides... In August the Hezbi-Islami group of Gulbuddin Hetmakyar began a three week rocket and artillery attack on Kabul that killed as many as 2,000 people.

Panel upheld the finding that . . . "[T]hey have not shown that any action the members of the Hezb-i-Islami and the Harakat-Islami might take against each other would be one of the five grounds specified in the Act."

A similar instance of "selective administrative notice" was made by the Board in *de la Llana-Castellon v. INS*, and rejected on appeal by the Tenth Circuit. 16 F.3d at 1093. There the Board took administrative notice of the fact that the Nicaraguan Sandinistas had been removed from the government by popular vote. However it failed to take notice of evidence that they still maintained a certain amount of "control" in the country which in the court's opinion had a bearing on the asylum claim. Therefore, it should not have been ignored by the Board. In fact, the court held that the petitioner had a right to "notice and an opportunity to rebut the facts so noted" when the Board used the mechanism of administrative notice to admit new evidence in his case. *Id.* at 1100, *citing Castillo-Villagra,* 972 F.2d at 1029-30.

The manner in which the Board took selective notice of political changes in Afghanistan in this case is also in direct conflict with its own more recent decision in *In Re B,* Int. Dec. 3251, 1995 BIA LEXIS 15 (May 19, 1995). There, based solely on the applicant's fear of the then-overthrown Soviet-backed government, the Board acknowledged the severity of the conflict between Mujaheddin factions as a valid reason for the applicant's refusal to return to his country. It did so by taking administrative notice of the very same Country Report of which it took only partial administrative notice in **[Alien]**'s case. It also took notice of news articles providing evidence similar to those **[Alien]** submitted in support of his appeal. The Board ignored the *same* evidence in **[Alien]**'s case, despite the fact that it was more relevant to his claim than it was to B's. This conflict was brought to the attention of the panel in the brief of Amicus Curiae, as well as at oral argument, but the issue was not addressed in its decision.

CONCLUSION

For all of the reasons set forth herein, Petitioner respectfully urges this Court to rehear this case en banc, and upon rehearing remand it to the administrative agency for proper consideration of his claim.

Respectfully submitted,

[Attorney]

[ADD CERTIFICATE OF SERVICE]

CHAPTER 7
REAL ID ACT MATERIAL

Caveat: These materials were developed after the REAL ID Act was enacted and before much case law on the Act has developed. Practitioners should research case law in their own circuit to see what, if any, position the circuit has taken on how the REAL ID Act is to be implemented.

UNITED STATES COURT OF APPEALS
FOR THE SECOND CIRCUIT

June 8, 2005

SPECIAL NOTICE

Re: **Real ID Act of 2005.** Pub. L. No. 109-13, 119 Stat. 231 (May 11, 2005)

This notice is to the district courts within the Second Circuit. It outlines the preferred procedures for transferring cases from the district courts to the Court of Appeals pursuant to the Real ID Act of 2005.

1. Please provide the parties with the opportunity to stipulate to, or to brief the propriety of, the transfer.

2. If the district court agrees that the case is appropriate for transfer under the Real ID Act, the district court should issue an order of transfer and send the case to the Court of Appeals as a **Petition for Review.**

3. In its transfer order, the district court should stay the petitioner's removal or deportation pending further order from the Court of Appeals. The Government may move, in the Court of Appeals, to vacate the stay.

4. The transfer order must clearly indicate that the transfer is made pursuant to the Real ID Act. The transfer order must also include the petitioner's Alien Number (the eight-digit number preceded by the letter "A").

5. The district court clerks are requested to transmit the entire record to the Court of Appeals at the same time they transmit the transfer order. If only a portion of the district court case is being transferred to the Court of Appeals as a Petition for Review, that portion of the district court record which relates to the Petition for Review should be forwarded. The Court of Appeals will accept paper documents or electronic documents.

John M. Walker, Jr.
Chief Judge

UNITED STATES COURT OF APPEALS FOR THE THIRD CIRCUIT

June 16, 2005

SPECIAL NOTICE

RE: Real ID Act of 2005, Pub. L. No. 109-13, 119 Stat 231 (May 11, 2005)

This notice is to the District Courts and litigants within the Third Circuit. It outlines the preferred procedures for transferring cases from District Courts to the Court of Appeals pursuant to the Real ID Act of 2005.

1. Because not all petitions for habeas corpus are subject to transfer and because cases to be heard as a petition for review must be transferred to the Circuit Court of Appeals where the Immigration Judge concluded proceedings, it is suggested that District Judges provide the parties an opportunity to stipulate to or brief the propriety of the transfer order.

2. If the District Court agrees that the case is appropriate for transfer under the Real ID Act, the District Court should issue an order of transfer and send the case to the appropriate Court of Appeals as a petition for review.

3. The transfer order should indicate that the transfer is made pursuant to the Real ID Act. The transfer order should also indicate where the Immigration Judge concluded the proceedings, which Court of Appeals the case should be transferred to, and include the petitioner's Alien Number (the eight-digit number preceded by the letter A).

4. Any stay previously issued by the District Court shall remain in place during and after transfer. The Government may move in the Court of Appeals to vacate the stay if appropriate.

5. The District Court clerks are requested to transmit the entire record to the Court of Appeals at the same time they transmit the transfer order. If only a portion of the District Court case is being transferred to the Court of Appeals as a petition for review, that portion of the District Court record which relates to the petition for review should be forwarded to the Court of Appeals. The Court of Appeals will accept paper documents or electronic documents.

6. Within ten days of the case being opened in the Court of Appeals, the parties shall inform the clerk whether the record transmitted by the District Court is sufficient for purposes of the petition for review or whether additional documents are necessary.

/s/ Anthony J. Scirica
Chief Judge

UNITED STATES COURT OF APPEALS FOR THE FIFTH CIRCUIT

Memorandum

To: District Court Clerks

From: Charles R. Fulbruge III

Date: May 31, 2005

Re: Real ID Act

On May 11, 2005, "The Emergency Supplemental Appropriations Act for Defense, the Global War on Terror, and Tsunami Relief Act, 2005," also known as The Real ID Act, became law. Section 106 of the act has a major impact on courts of appeals. It provides as follows:

> (c) TRANSFER OF CASES. If an alien's case, brought under section 2241 of title 28, United States Code, and challenging a final administrative order of removal, deportation, or exclusion, is pending in a district court on the date of the enactment of this division, then the district court shall transfer the case (or the part of the case that challenges the order of removal, deportation, or exclusion) to the court of appeals for the circuit in which a petition for review could have been properly filed under section 242(b)(2) of the Immigration and Nationality Act (8 U.S.C. § 1252), as amended by this section, or under section 309 (c)(4)(D) of the Illegal Immigration Reform and Immigrant Responsibility Act of 1996 (8 U.S. C. § 1101 note). The court of appeals shall treat the transferred case as if it had been filed pursuant to a petition for review under such section 242. . . .

This section raises numerous questions of both substance and procedure which we bring to your attention in the discussion below.

I. Transferring Cases

After reviewing the AO's May 25, 2005 memo, and participating in a conference call on May 25, there is a general consensus district courts will transfer cases under the act after review by a district or magistrate judge. Individual district courts will determine whether transfer review will be undertaken *sua sponte* by the court, or on motion by the U.S. Attorney or the petitioner's attorney. Current record keeping does not identify this specific type of case, so we do not know how many case might be involved. To date we have received four transfers, one from the Eastern District of Louisiana and three from the Western District of Texas, El Paso.

II. Court to Which Transfer is Made

The act provides the cases shall be transferred "to the court of appeals for the circuit in which a petition for review could have been properly filed. . . ." Habeas corpus challenges to an order of removal, exclusion, or deportation are filed in the district court where the alien is located; petitions for review of such orders are filed in the district court where the final administrative order was issued. Thus, we expect there are some cases in the district courts in this circuit that should be transferred to another court of appeals, and *vice versa*. We ask our district courts to review the cases thoroughly enough to determine the proper court of appeals.

III. The Record

In most cases, the record in the district court will consist of little more than the Immigration Judge's decision and the BIA order affirming it. Our court will want more than what likely is available at the district court. The Justice Department will provide the necessary records but there will be a substantial delay. We ask that the district court send everything it has when the case is transferred. After we have reviewed the case, we will determine whether the administrative record is necessary and, if so, order it from DOJ.

IV. Stay of Removal

Often, habeas petitions are not filed until there is an order of imminent removal or deportation. The petitioner then also submits an application for stay of deportation. There is some sentiment that the district court should grant at least a temporary stay to prevent the issue from becoming moot during the transfer process. In most cases, it should not be necessary to do this as a routine matter. This court has recently adopted the four-factor test applied to preliminary injunctions, which is decidedly more favorable to petitioners. *Tesfamichael v. Gonzales*, — F.3d —, 2005 WL 1220939 (5th Cir. May 24, 2005). It should be relatively easy for the district courts to determine whether a stay is warranted on the merits without having to grant a stay automatically in every case.

V. Limited Transfer

The act specifies that, if a habeas petition in the district court attacks both the order of removal, exclusion, or deportation and the fact of detention, only the portion dealing with the order of removal, etc. can be transferred. The detention challenge will remain with the district court to be decided separately and the court of appeals will have no jurisdiction over that portion of the case unless and until the district court has entered a final judgment that has been appealed.

As we get more information and experience, we may supplement this memo. If you have questions, please contact Bill Zapalac, Counsel to the Clerk at (504) 310-7660.

Sincerely,

Fritz Fulbruge

cc: Bill Zapalac

UNITED STATES COURT OF APPEALS
FOR THE NINTH CIRCUIT

June 2, 2005

SPECIAL NOTICE

Re: Real ID Act of 2005, Pub. L. No. 109-13, 119 Stat. 231 (May 11, 2005)

This is a notice to the District Courts within the Circuit, as well as to concerned parties, regarding the preferred procedure for transferring cases from the district courts to the court of appeals in the aftermath of the Real ID Act of 2005, enacted May 11, 2005. It is suggested that the district courts:

1. Allow the parties the opportunity to stipulate to, or brief the propriety of, transfer.

2. If the district court agrees that the case is appropriate for transfer, the district court should issue an order expressly transferring appropriate cases, or portions of them, to the Ninth Circuit Court of Appeals as a ***Petition for Review***.

3. In its transfer order, the district court should inform this court whether the petitioner ever sought a stay of removal from the district court and what the district court's decision was, if any, on the stay request.

4. The district court clerks are requested to transmit the entire case file to the Court of Appeals, simultaneous with the transfer order. If only a portion of the case is transferred, the parties should notify the district court clerk's office as to which portions of the file should be transmitted to the Court of Appeals.

5. If a stay of removal had been requested in the district court at any time during the proceedings, then, absent further order of this Court, the district court's order transferring a case to this court as a petition for review shall trigger the temporary stay of removal contemplated by this court's General Order 6.4. This court will then issue an order directing the transferred parties on how to proceed further.

By direction of the Court Executive Committee:

Cathy A. Catterson
Clerk of Court

LEONIDAS RALPH MECHAM
Director

CLARENCE A. LEE, JR.
Associate Director

ADMINISTRATIVE OFFICE OF THE UNITED STATES COURTS

WASHINGTON, D.C. 20544

NOEL J. AUGUSTYN
Assistant Director

Office of Court Administration

May 25, 2005

TO: CLERKS, UNITED STATES COURTS OF APPEALS
CLERKS, UNITED STATES DISTRICT COURTS

SUBJECT: REAL ID ACT OF 2005: Aliens Challenging Removal, Deportation Or Exclusion

As some of you may know, the "Real ID Act of 2005" was signed into law (Pub. Law No. 109-13) on May 11, 2005, as Division B of the *Emergency Supplemental Appropriations Act for Defense, the Global War on Terror, and Tsunami Relief, 2005*, and became effective on the date of enactment. Though there are a number of important provisions that courts may wish to review, the Real ID Act has a specific impact upon both district and appellate clerks' offices with respect to "cases in which the final administrative order of removal, deportation, or exclusion was issued before, on, or after the date of enactment." Title I, Section 106(c) of the Act states:

> TRANSFER OF CASES.– If an alien's case, brought under section 2241 of title 28, United States Code, and challenging a final administrative order of removal, deportation, or exclusion, is pending in a district court on the date of the enactment of this division, then the district court shall transfer the case (or the part of the case that challenges the order of removal, deportation, or exclusion) to the court of appeals for the circuit in which a petition for review could have been properly filed under section 242(b)(2) of the Immigration and Nationality Act (8 U.S.C. 1252), as amended by this section, or under section 309(c)(4)(D) of the Illegal Immigration Reform and Immigrant Responsibility Act of 1996 (8 U.S.C. 1101 note). The court of appeals shall treat the transferred case as if it had been filed pursuant to a petition for review under section 242, except that subsection (b)(1) of such

section shall not apply.

This new law applies only to cases brought under Section 2241 by aliens challenging removal, deportation, or exclusion. It does not apply to those cases challenging detention.

The courts will need to develop procedures to implement the Act's requirement that "...the district court shall transfer the case". Certainly, one option for the district courts is for judges to initiate a review of all of these cases and prepare the transfer orders when appropriate. As an alternative, courts could require counsel to initiate the process. Administrative Office staff have been advised by Department of Justice personnel that some U.S. Attorneys' offices already have begun preparing transfer order motions in these cases. If this is occurring, the district courts should coordinate with the local U.S. Attorney regarding the process to be followed for transferring these cases, including how these cases will be identified and how and when the transfer will be initiated. In addition, the courts will need to determine how to proceed if only part of the case is transferred, and how the court of appeals would handle a stay of deportation or removal entered by the district court.

At the same time, the district courts should coordinate with the clerk of the appropriate appellate court regarding transmittal of all case-related records and the process for providing a complete certified record of these cases. District clerks also should note that the Section 106(c) requirement to transfer the case "to the court of appeals in the circuit in which a petition for review could have been properly filed" raises an issue of venue, since the case may need to be transferred to another circuit. Many district courts have not required the full certified agency record in these cases, but instead they have relied on the Board of Immigration Appeals order and supporting documents. The process for obtaining and transmitting the full certified record to the court of appeals must be worked out with the Department of Justice, since the appellate courts will likely require the full certified record. This is particularly important, as it may take Department of Justice offices several weeks or more to compile their records.

Finally, please note that the Act does not impose the collection of any new fees for the transferred petitions for review.

If appellate clerks have questions regarding the content of this memorandum, they should contact Gary Bowden, Chief, or Gloria Malkin, Attorney Advisor, Appellate Court and Circuit Administration Division.

If district courts have questions regarding the content of this memorandum, they should contact their regional administrator in the District Court Administration Division: James L. Caldwell (2nd, 9th Circuits); Steven Gallagher (1st, 5th, 10th, DC Circuits); David Mercanti (3rd, 4th, 7th Circuits); or, Thomas S. Russell (6th, 8th, 11th Circuits).

Noel J. Augustyn

cc: Circuit Executives
District Court Executives
Senior Staff Attorneys

NAVIGATING THE REAL ID ACT

by the AILF Legal Action Center and Anwen Hughes[*]

In spite of the valiant efforts of many organizations and individuals who opposed it, on May 11, 2005, President George W. Bush signed into law the REAL ID Act as part of an emergency spending bill on Iraq and Tsunami aid. In practice and to date, the REAL ID Act fortunately has not produced the draconian results that had been feared. In the judicial review context, for example, the Act actually expands the court of appeals' jurisdiction to hear legal and constitutional challenges in some contexts. To date, the district courts appear to be transferring pending habeas corpus cases to the courts of appeals without causing disruptions or putting the petitioners at greater risk of imminent deportation.

This article offers practical advice to the immigration practitioner on how to navigate the REAL ID Act provisions. First, it will discuss the provisions of the REAL ID Act that affect judicial review of immigration decisions under the INA. Second, this article will discuss the Act's amendments to the INA relating to burdens of proof; procedures for seeking asylum and other forms of relief from removal; and the definition of and removability provisions for terrorism and terrorist-related activities. The information contained in this article is not legal advice and does not substitute for advice supplied by a lawyer familiar with a client's case. Moreover, suggestions and strategies relating to the REAL ID Act are likely to evolve as the law is implemented.

JUDICIAL REVIEW

What changes to judicial review are included in the REAL ID Act?

The new provisions apply to final orders of removal, deportation, and exclusion issued before, on, or after the enactment date. Significantly, the amendments to INA §242 expand the courts of appeals' jurisdiction so that many individuals who were barred from bringing petitions for review prior to the REAL ID Act (including individuals with certain criminal convictions) now may file petitions for review in the court of appeals.

Specifically, the REAL ID Act amends the judicial review provisions relating to immigration cases in the following ways:

- It purports to eliminate all habeas corpus review of final orders of removal, deportation, and exclusion;
- It expands judicial review of final orders of removal, deportation, and exclusion via a petition for review in place of habeas corpus review, allowing some review of previously nonreviewable cases and issues; and
- It expands the bar on judicial review of discretionary decisions and actions to include certain agency decisions and actions outside of the removal context.

The REAL ID Act purports to eliminate all habeas corpus review of final orders of removal, deportation, and exclusion under 28 USC §2241. Congress has amended and/or created seven subsections of INA §242 to include a specific restriction on review by habeas corpus: INA §§242(a)(2)(A), (B) and (C); §242(a)(4) and (a)(5); §242(b)(9); and §242(g). These amendments will affect what issues, if any, may be reviewed via habeas corpus. They also will affect what happens to a habeas corpus petition that is already pending. These amendments, however, do not eliminate habeas corpus jurisdiction over detention challenges.

The Act's amendments to INA §242(a)(2)(B), which limit judicial review of certain discretionary decisions and actions, purport to eliminate review by habeas corpus and mandamus. A mandamus action is only appropriate where the challenged action is nondiscretionary. Because of this, it is unclear how significant this restriction on mandamus will actually be.

This section also states that judicial review is eliminated "regardless of whether the judgment, decision, or action is made in removal proceedings." It is not yet clear what impact this change will have on the jurisdiction of the courts to review immigration cases outside of the removal context, such as cases challenging the denial of family- or employment-based applications and petitions. In the removal con-

---

[*] **The Legal Action Center** (LAC) is the litigation arm of the American Immigration Law Foundation. **Anwen Hughes** helps oversee Human Rights First's pro bono representation program for indigent asylum-seekers. This article was published in 24 *AILA's Immigration Law Today* 12 (July/Aug. 2005).

text, a number of courts have narrowly construed the scope of this provision in accordance with the specific language chosen by Congress. These decisions should help define exactly what type of discretionary decisions, or action in the nonremoval context, are covered by this amendment.

Can I file a new habeas petition challenging a final removal order for my client?

No. The amendments eliminating habeas corpus review of final orders of removal, deportation, or exclusion apply upon enactment and apply to *all* final orders of removal, deportation, or exclusion issued before, on, or after the enactment date. Thus, as of May 11, 2005, the REAL ID Act provides that challenges to final orders of removal, deportation, or exclusion must be filed in the appropriate court of appeals via a petition for review.

The REAL ID Act expands the jurisdiction of the courts of appeals so that they may review certain issues previously precluded by IIRAIRA. *See Fernandez-Ruiz v. Gonzalez*, No. 03-74533, __ F.3d __ (9th Cir. May 31, 2005). A new INA §242(a)(2)(D) states that nothing in the INA "which limits or eliminates judicial review, shall be construed as precluding review of constitutional claims or questions of law raised upon a petition for review filed with the appropriate court in accordance with this section."

Thus, courts of appeals now have jurisdiction to review *all* constitutional issues and questions of law related to a final order of removal. In a case involving removal based on a criminal offense or a discretionary decision, review of legal issues will be in the federal appellate court rather than in the district court by habeas corpus. Consequently, while habeas corpus review has been eliminated, review over most—if not all—of the issues that would have been available in habeas corpus proceedings under IIRAIRA now should be available via petition for review in the courts of appeals.

What happens to habeas petitions filed prior to the REAL ID Act that are still pending?

The new law provides that district courts "shall" transfer pending habeas corpus petitions (or the part of the case challenging a final removal, deportation, or exclusion order) to the court of appeals in which a petition for review could have been filed (*i.e.*, the circuit court having jurisdiction over the place the immigration judge completed proceedings). The courts of appeals must treat the transferred case as if it were filed as a petition for review, with one exception: The requirement that a petition for review must be filed within 30 days of the final removal order does not apply to these transferred cases. This means that a habeas corpus petition challenging a final order that was pending in district court on May 11, 2005, will be transferred to the court of appeals even if the habeas corpus petition was not filed within 30 days of the final removal order. However, the 30-day deadline continues to apply to all other petitions for review.

This potentially can create a serious problem for some individuals. Prior to the REAL ID Act, an individual barred from filing a petition for review might have been able to get review through a habeas corpus petition. For example, many individuals with criminal convictions were barred from filing a petition for review under INA §242(a)(2)(C). However, these individuals could have filed a habeas corpus petition. There are individuals who did not file a petition for review within 30 days of their final order because there was no jurisdiction under pre–REAL ID Act law. If, as of May 11, 2005, they had not filed a habeas corpus petition, they now may be barred from any judicial review under the Act. They will no longer be able to file a habeas corpus petition and will have missed the 30-day deadline for filing a petition for review. Practitioners with clients in this situation may want to consult AILF's practice advisory that focuses on late-filed petitions for review. *See* "Suggested Strategies for Remedying Missed Petition for Review Deadlines or Filings in the Wrong Court" (AILA InfoNet Doc. No. 05042068).

Can I file a habeas corpus petition challenging my client's detention?

The REAL ID Act does not address detention challenges. Individuals may continue to challenge their detention by filing a habeas corpus petition in district court. In cases where a petitioner had a habeas corpus petition pending on May 11, 2005, challenging both removability and detention, the transfer provision of the Act says that the district courts shall transfer only "the part of the case that challenges the order of removal, deportation, or exclusion" to the appropriate court of appeals. Thus, to the extent that a petitioner is challenging his or her detention, that part of the case should remain at the district court.

If I could have filed a petition for review prior to REAL ID, can I still file a petition for review?

Yes. Thus, in all cases in which—prior to the passage of the REAL ID Act—you would have filed a petition for review under INA §242, you will continue to do so in the future. The general rules regarding when and where to file the petition for review remain unchanged, with one exception: The REAL ID Act states that a petition for review filed under IIRAIRA's transitional rules (IIRAIRA §309) shall be treated as if it had been filed under INA §242.

If I could have filed a habeas petition prior to REAL ID, do I file a petition for review now?

Yes, at least in the majority of cases. The REAL ID Act expands the jurisdiction of the courts of appeals to cover much—if not all—of the habeas corpus review that is being eliminated. The Act adds a new section (a)(5) to INA §242 stating, "a petition for review filed with the appropriate court of appeals in accordance with this section shall be the sole and exclusive means for judicial review of an order of removal entered or issued under any provision of this Act." The only exception to this pertains to review of an order of expedited removal under INA §242(e). Keep in mind that the petition for review, unlike the habeas corpus petition, must be filed within 30 days of the final removal order.

The Act also adds INA §242(a)(2)(D), which clarifies that review of all constitutional claims or "questions of law" shall be by petition for review. The courts of appeals retain jurisdiction over constitutional questions and questions of law regardless of any other restrictions on review contained in INA §242. *See Fernandez-Ruiz v. Gonzalez*, *supra*. Thus, the following are examples of individuals who now may bring legal or constitutional claims in the courts of appeals:

- Petitioners who were found removable based on a criminal conviction and also were denied relief from removal, such as a §212(c) waiver, withholding of removal, or CAT. Under pre–REAL ID law, these petitioners could not challenge the denial of relief in a petition for review (INA §242(a)(2)(C)).
- Asylum applicants whose applications were denied because they did not file their applications within one year of entering the United States. Under pre-REAL ID law, these petitioners could not seek judicial review of the decision to deny asylum based on the one-year filing deadline (INA §208(a)(3)).

The final bill deleted an amendment that would have qualified the phrase "questions of law" with the word "pure." Because Congress deleted the term "pure" from the final law, it can be argued that its intent was to ensure that *all* questions of law remain subject to review, even in situations where the decision-maker has to apply fact to law to reach a decision. AILF encourages practitioners to become familiar with existing case law on what constitutes a question of law; to note differences in how courts interpret the phrase depending on the context in which the term is being used; and to propose a broad definition to suit the context of the REAL ID Act.

In addition, courts retain authority to determine whether they have jurisdiction over the petition for review. Such issues may include, but are not limited to: (1) whether petitioner has been charged with and found deportable for a criminal offense; (2) whether the offense constitutes an aggravated felony or a crime involving moral turpitude; and (3) whether petitioner meets certain nondiscretionary statutory eligibility requirements for discretionary relief. AILF believes that such questions are reviewable regardless of how the courts ultimately construe the phrase "questions of law" in new §242(a)(2)(D).

How can I challenge the denial of a CAT claim?

The REAL ID Act eliminates review of Convention Against Torture claims by habeas corpus and amends INA §242 by adding a new section (a)(4). This section provides that a petition for review will be the sole and exclusive means for reviewing a CAT claim.

Has there been any change to the standard for getting a stay of removal?

No. While amendments to the standard for a stay were proposed in the Act, those were deleted from the final law.

Have the courts of appeal provided information on how transferred cases should be handled?

Yes. The Second, Third, Fifth and Ninth Circuit Courts of Appeals have issued "Special Notices" or memoranda setting out some limited instructions for lower courts and litigants for the transfer of habeas corpus cases and stays of removal. Those memoranda and other REAL ID Act resources can be found on AILF's REAL ID Act Resource Web page, at *www.ailf.org/lac/lac_realidresources.htm*.

ASYLUM & WITHHOLDING OF REMOVAL

How does the Act change the standards for asylum eligibility and other forms of removal relief?

The REAL ID Act makes four changes to INA §208:

- It requires asylum applicants to show that their race, religion, nationality, membership in a particular social group, or political opinion is "at least one central reason" for their past or feared persecution;
- It allows adjudicators to require applicants to provide corroboration of otherwise credible testimony;
- It allows adjudicators to base an adverse credibility determination on any of a long list of factors (including the "demeanor, candor, or responsiveness" of an applicant or witness, the inherent plausibility of his or her account, and any inconsistencies or falsehoods within an applicant or witnesses' current or prior statements or between those statements and other evidence in the record, "without regard to whether an inconsistency, inaccuracy, or falsehood goes to the heart of the applicant's claim); and
- It broadens the bars to asylum related to terrorism; taken together with the parallel expansions of the terrorist-related grounds of inadmissibility and deportability in §§212 and 237 (discussed below), this change purports to bar from asylum anyone who is described in *any* of the terrorism-related grounds of inadmissibility in §212(a)(3)(B), as further expanded by the REAL ID Act.

Amendments to §241(b)(3) make all four of these changes applicable to withholding of removal as well. The Act amends INA §240 to impose the corroboration and credibility provisions described above on applicants for all other forms of relief from removal.

On a positive note, the Act, through amendments to INA §§207 and 209, eliminates the annual statutory caps on grants of asylum based on resistance to coercive population control measures and on the adjustment of status of asylees.

The very recent passage of the REAL ID Act means that many of the questions it raises have yet to be answered through DHS and DOJ regulations and policy decisions, judicial interpretation, or both. This portion of the article attempts to flag some of these questions and suggest arguments and strategies attorneys may consider in representing clients affected by these changes.

When did the changes to standards of eligibility go into effect?

These changes—specifically, the "central reason" requirement for asylum applications, and credibility and corroboration provisions applicable to all forms of relief from removal—apply to applications for asylum or relief from removal made on or after May 11, 2005 (the date of enactment). Applications "made" on or after May 11 should mean applications "filed" on or after that date. Language in the conference report supports this interpretation. *See* H.R. Conf. Rep. No. 109-72, at 2871 (2005). Although the expansion of the terrorism bar to asylum in §208 also takes effect on May 11, the expansion of the parts of §§212 and 237 referred to in that portion of §208 purports to be extremely retroactive.

Where does the language "at least one central reason" come from?

The refugee definition at INA §101(a)(42) requires that persecution be "on account of" a person's race, religion, nationality, political opinion, or membership in a particular social group. The December 7, 2000, proposed regulation (65 Fed. Reg. 76588) interpreted this to require a showing that "the applicant's protected characteristic is central to the persecutor's motivation to act against the applicant." (AILA InfoNet Doc. No. 00120701). Language in the conference report to the Act cites to this proposed regulation as support for the Act's centrality requirement.

However, the December 2000 regulations were never issued in final form, and DHS, in its subsequent brief to the Attorney General in *Matter of R–A–*, 22 I&N Dec. 906 (BIA 1999), backed away from the "centrality" requirement.

It is important to note that the exact language of the REAL ID Act's "centrality" requirement arguably represents something of a dilution of that proposed by the December 2000 regulations, in the sense that it explicitly allows for the possibility that several reasons (some related to the protected grounds of the refugee definition, some not) could give rise to persecution that could make a person eligible for asylum or withholding of removal, and that its focus on the "reason" rather than the "motive" of the persecution may suggest an objective focus on the causes of the persecution rather than on the subjective motivation of the persecutor. (This may be helpful, for example, in cases of persecution by nongovernmental actors where the motivation of the persecutor may be mixed and murky, but the failure of protection on the part of the state is more easily tied to one or more of the protected grounds for asylum.)

What can I do to meet this corroboration requirement?

To start with, note that the Act sees itself as codifying the BIA's corroboration standards expressed in *Matter of S–M–J–*, 21 I&N Dec. 722 (BIA 1997), so that for attorneys practicing outside of the Ninth Circuit, REAL ID should represent an enactment of existing case law. The Act provides that if an adjudicator decides that the applicant should provide corroborating evidence, such evidence must be provided "unless the applicant does not have the evidence and cannot reasonably obtain" it.

Proactively, attorneys should make every effort to review all the facts and statements in their clients' cases, think through what forms of corroborating evidence an adjudicator might reasonably expect, and with respect to each such item, either obtain it, or, if it is not obtainable, build a record as to why it cannot be obtained. Defensively, advocates can look to case law from circuits that have upheld the BIA's corroboration requirements while insisting that the BIA follow its own standards of reasonableness in this regard. This case law provides useful guidance and authority on what is reasonable for adjudicators to expect, on the need for them to consider explanations as to the impossibility of obtaining particular forms of corroboration, and on the need not to "ambush" applicants with demands for certain specific forms of evidence. *See Diallo v. INS*, 232 F.3d 279 (2d Cir. 2000); *Qui v. Ashcroft*, 329 F.3d 140 (2d Cir. 2003); *Abdulai v. Ashcroft*, 239 F.3d 542 (3d Cir. 2001); *Mulanga v. Ashcroft*, 349 F.3d 123 (3d Cir. 2003).

Are there arguments to defend clients denied relief on credibility grounds under the Act?

The REAL ID Act's provisions on credibility determinations include a list of factors whose reliability as actual indicators of credibility varies widely, particularly in evaluating the testimony of people who may be testifying through poor-quality interpretation, with a limited understanding of and trust in the forum where they find themselves, and often with the added distortion of post-traumatic symptoms. In addition, these changes allow adjudicators to base an adverse credibility determination on inconsistencies, inaccuracies, or falsehoods that do not go to the heart of the applicant's claim.

There are, however, a few helpful points to be derived from the exact language of new INA §208(b)(1)(B)(iii). First, the language requires the adjudicator to consider the "totality of the circumstances, and all relevant factors" in basing a credibility determination on any of the enumerated list of factors (which is not exhaustive). This provides an argument against an adverse credibility determination that is based, for example, on one immaterial inconsistency that is part of an overall picture of consistent and plausible testimony, or that is adequately explained by surrounding circumstances. The same is true of inconsistencies with prior statements. Although these may be considered regardless of whether the prior statement was made under oath, the adjudicator is required to consider the circumstances under which such a statement was made.

Second, based on the references to "all relevant factors" and "any other relevant factor" at the beginning and end of this subsection—and on basic principles of due process—one can argue that in order to provide a valid basis for an adverse credibility determination, an inconsistency, inaccuracy, or falsehood must be *relevant* to the applicant's claim, even though it may not go to the heart of it.

Third, in order for any of this to be determinative of an applicant's claim for relief from removal, the applicant's credibility or lack thereof must still itself be material to his or her eligibility for the form of relief in question. *Example*: A woman applies for relief under CAT based on the fact that the country to which she faces removal systematically detains persons returned as deportees under terrible conditions, where detainees are routinely subjected to severe beatings, and a high proportion of women in that situation become victims of rape. If these facts are substantiated by independent evidence, then the fact that the person's testimony about her reasons for leaving her country originally, along with her method of entry into the United States and other facts of her life are deemed not to be credible, should not make her ineligible for relief under CAT—even under the REAL ID Act.

TERRORISM PROVISIONS

How does the Act alter the terrorism-related grounds of inadmissibility and deportability?

The Act works as a massive expansion of the terrorism-related grounds for removal. It does this in two ways. First, REAL ID expands the grounds of inadmissibility in INA §212(a)(3)(B). Second, and most radically, it amends §237(a)(4)(B) (which previously made engaging in terrorist activity grounds for deportability) to provide that anyone *described in any* of the (expanded) grounds of inadmissibility related to terrorism *is now deportable.*

How does the REAL ID Act make them broader?

With respect to the grounds of inadmissibility, the Act makes inadmissible, for example, anyone who "endorses or espouses" terrorist activity; anyone who has received "military-type training" from a terrorist organization; anyone who is a member of a terrorist organization or has provided material support to a terrorist organization or to a member of a terrorist organization, unless he or she can show by clear and convincing evidence that he or she did not know and should not reasonably have known that the organization was a terrorist organization. In parallel to this, the Act expands the definition of a "non-designated" terrorist organization (*i.e.*, one defined by §212(a)(3)(B)(vi)(III)) to include any "group of two or more individuals, whether organized or not, which engages in, or has a subgroup which engages in" any form of "terrorist activity" as defined at §212(a)(3)(B)(iv).

With respect to the grounds of deportability, whereas previously a person needed to have engaged in terrorist activity (however broadly defined) in order to be deportable under §237(a)(4)(B), the REAL ID Act makes the grounds of deportability related to terrorism coextensive with the grounds of inadmissibility. These provisions raise serious constitutional concerns, as well as issues of conflict with U.S. obligations under the Refugee Convention.

How does this affect the bars to asylum and withholding of removal?

The bar to asylum based on terrorism at §208(b)(2)(A)(v) excludes from asylum anyone described in specific grounds of inadmissibility within §212(a)(3)(B), or under §237(a)(4)(B). Since §237(a)(4)(B) now includes *all* of §212(a)(3)(B), this means that anyone who is inadmissible under any of terrorism-related grounds of inadmissibility in §212(a)(3)(B) would appear to be barred from asylum. The bar to withholding of removal at §241(b)(3)(B) excludes from withholding anyone described in §237(a)(4)(B), which, in turn, now includes anyone described in any subsection of §212(a)(3)(B).

When do these changes become effective and to what cases do they apply?

These changes went into effect on May 11, 2005, and purport to be extremely retroactive, applying to "removal proceedings instituted before, on, or after that date," and to "acts and conditions constituting a ground for inadmissibility, excludability, deportation, or removal occurring or existing before, on, or after such date." The retroactive application of these changes to make people (including lawful permanent residents) deportable with no opportunity for relief for conduct, speech, or associations that would not have subjected them to any immigration consequences at all at the time when they engaged in them, would raise serious legal concerns.

But given the extreme facial retroactivity of these provisions, it becomes doubly important to screen clients for any facts that could bring them within the scope of these bars. Form I-485 asks about any past or present organizational affiliations. It is very important to make sure that these questions are answered accurately and consistently with any past applications the person may have filed—*e.g.*, an I-589—that ask similar questions, and that you identify any associations that might raise red flags under these expanded inadmissibility/deportability grounds.

Are there any exceptions to the application of these provisions?

Yes, there are two. First, although §212(a)(3)(B)(i)(IX) makes inadmissible (and therefore deportable) the spouse or child of anyone who is inadmissible (and therefore deportable) under §212(a)(3)(B), the "innocent spouse or child" exception, eliminated in earlier drafts of this law, was restored in the final version. Second, although the final draft of the REAL ID Act eliminated language at the end of §212(a)(3)(B)(iv) giving the Attorney General and the Secretary of Homeland Security discretionary authority to waive the application of the "material support" provisions in particular cases, different waiver language was inserted into §212(d)(3). There are arguments that this new waiver authority allows DOS, DOJ, and DHS to create a solution to avoid the application of these bars to particular cases. There were never regulations implementing the old waiver language. Implementation of a solution under this new waiver language would require coordinated action by the three agencies, and the extent to which it would remedy the problems created by the Act would depend on the details of whatever procedures were agreed upon.

In addition to these explicit waiver provisions, people covered by a literal reading of these bars should continue to assert whatever defenses they have (*e.g.*, duress, lack of knowledge) and scrutinize the very complicated structure of this statute for any arguments that their actions or associations do not in fact fall under its scope.

[Document Nos. 701–06]

REAL ID ACT MOTIONS

Description: The attached are sample motions related to the impact of the REAL ID Act on a case. The first two (the motion to reissue and the motion to reopen and reissue) seek to have the BIA reissue a decision so that the individual can file a petition for review under the REAL ID Act. These are to be used in a case in which: the individual was previously barred from filing a petition for review; no habeas petition was ever filed; and, although a petition for review is now possible under the REAL ID Act, the individual is time-barred from filing a petition for review.

The third document is a motion to the district court seeking more time to brief the impact of the REAL ID Act on a pending habeas case. The final three documents are sample responses to a government motion to transfer a pending habeas case to the circuit court under the REAL ID Act.

Advantages: These sample documents illustrate various initial strategies that a practitioner can take to respond to the impact of the REAL ID Act on a case.

Limitations: These materials were developed immediately after the REAL ID Act was enacted and before much case law on the Act had developed. Practitioners should research case law in their own circuit to see what, if any, position the circuit has taken on how the REAL ID Act is to be implemented.

UNITED STATES DEPARTMENT OF JUSTICE
EXECUTIVE OFFICE FOR IMMIGRATION REVIEW
BOARD OF IMMIGRATION APPEALS
FALLS CHURCH, VIRGINIA

In re	)	
	)	
[Alien],	)	No. **[Case Number]**
	)	
Respondent.	)	
	)	
In **[Deportation or Removal]** Proceedings	)	
	)	
______________________________	)	

MOTION TO REISSUE THE BIA'S DECISION IN LIGHT OF THE REAL ID ACT

I. INTRODUCTION

Respondent asks the BIA to reissue the **[enter date]** order in this case in light of the recent enactment of the REAL ID Act of 2005, P. L. 109-13, 119 Stat. 231 (May 11, 2005). Prior to the REAL ID Act, Respondent was barred from filing a petition for review in the court of appeals because **[he/she]** was found removable based on one of the criminal grounds enumerated in INA § 242(a)(2)(C). The INA, as amended by the REAL ID Act, now provides Respondent with the opportunity to seek court of appeals review; however, because the BIA issued the order in this case more than 30 days ago, Respondent may be barred from review. *See* INA § 242(b)(1) (petition must be filed within 30 days of final order). Respondent also may be unable to seek review in the district court through a habeas petition, though **[he/she]** could have done so prior to the REAL ID Act. In order to remedy this unintended adverse effect of the enactment of the REAL ID Act, Respondent requests that the Board, in the interest of justice, reissue its order.

II. RELEVANT PROCEDURAL HISTORY

[Insert]

III. STATUTORY AND LEGISLATIVE BACKGROUND

In 1996, Congress barred respondents with certain criminal convictions from seeking judicial review in the court of appeals. *See* Anti-Terrorism and Effective Death Penalty Act (AEDPA), § 440(a), Pub. L. 104-207, 110 Stat. 3009 (April 24, 1996); Illegal Immigration Reform and Immigrant Responsibility Act of 1996 (IIRIRA), § 306, § 309 Pub. L. 104-208, 110 Stat. 3009 (Sept. 30, 1996), *codified* at INA § 242(a)(2)(C) and IIRIRA § 309(c)(4)(G). However, respondents with criminal convictions were not precluded from federal court review entirely. The Supreme Court, in *INS v. St. Cyr*, 533 U.S. 289 (2001), held that respondents barred from filing a petition for review in the court of appeals could seek review of their cases through habeas petitions, 28 U.S.C. § 2241, filed in the U.S. district court.

On May 11, 2005, the REAL ID Act of 2005, Pub. L. 109-13, 119 Stat. 231, was enacted. Section 106(a) of this new law purports to eliminate habeas corpus jurisdiction over challenges to final orders of removal, deportation, or exclusion. Congress, however, expanded the availability of court of appeals review. Specifically, section 106(a)(1) of the REAL ID Act amended INA § 242 to include a new section INA § 242(a)(2)(D), which says,

> Nothing in subparagraph (B) or (C), or any other provision of this Act (other than this section) which limits or eliminates judicial review, shall be construed as precluding review of constitutional or questions of law raised upon a petition for review filed with an appropriate court of appeals in accordance with this section.

As a result, respondents with criminal convictions who previously would have filed habeas petitions now may file petitions for review in the court of appeals. The legislative history confirms that this provision was intended to concentrate federal court review of all removal proceedings in the courts of appeals. *See* H.R. Conf. Rep. 109-72, at 2873 (2005).[1] ("By placing all review in the court of appeals, Division B would provide an 'adequate and effective' alternative to habeas corpus." (quoting *St. Cyr*, 533 U.S. at 314 n. 38)).

IV. ARGUMENT

A. The BIA Has Authority to Reissue Its Decision in the Interest of Justice.

Pursuant to 8 C.F.R. § 1003.1(d)(ii), the BIA is authorized to "take any action consistent with their authorities under the Act and the regulations as is appropriate and necessary for the disposition of the case." 8 C.F.R. § 1003.1(d)(ii). In addition, the Board has discretionary equitable powers to serve the interest of justice. *See e.g., Matter of G-D-*, 22 I&N Dec. 1132 (BIA 1999) (stating that as long as the Board has jurisdiction, its "discretionary powers are not limited, restricted, or qualified."); *Matter of X-G-W-*, 22 I&N Dec. 71 (BIA 1998) (exercising *sua sponte* authority to reopen proceedings to pursue certain asylum claims based on coerced population control policies to "serve the interest of justice"). In fact, on numerous occasions, the Board has reissued prior decisions in the interest of justice. *See Etchu-Njang v. Gonzales*, 403 F.3d 577 (8th Cir. 2004); *Roy v. Ashcroft*, 389 F.3d 132, 135 (5th Cir. 2004); *Lara-Torres v. Ashcroft*, 383 F.3d 968, 972 (9th Cir. 2004); *Firmansjah v. Ashcroft,* 347 F.3d 625, 626 (7th Cir. 2003); *Lonyem v. U.S. Atty. Gen.*, 352 F.3d 1338, 1340 n.3 (11th Cir. 2003).

In *Firmansjah*, the Seventh Circuit considered the BIA's authority to reissue decisions and the impact on the court's jurisdiction to review the underlying order. *See* 347 F.3d 626–27. The court held that "[b]ecause nothing prevents the Board from entering a new removal order, which is subject to a fresh petition for review, we have jurisdiction over the case and will proceed to briefing." *Id.* at 627.

---

[1] This report is available at *http://frwebgate.access.gpo.gov/cgi-bin/getpage.cgi?dbname=2005_record&page=H2813&position=all.*

B. Reissuing the Order in Respondent's Case Satisfies the Interest of Justice and Effectuates Congressional Intent.

Respondent now finds **[himself/herself]** subject to an adverse, and unintended, effect of the REAL ID Act. *See* H.R. Conf. Rep. 109-72, at 2873.[2] Prior to the REAL ID Act, Respondent would have been barred from filing a petition for review, but **[he/she]** could have filed a habeas corpus petition. Unlike a petition for review, there is no filing deadline for a habeas petition. *Compare* INA § 242(b)(1) *with* 28 U.S.C. § 2241. Although Congress has said that individuals such as Respondent now must seek review in the court of appeals, as opposed to the district court, Respondent may be barred from filing a petition for review because more than thirty days have passed from the date of the BIA's decision. *See* INA § 242(b)(1). This result would undermine the intent of Congress "to give every alien a fair opportunity to obtain judicial review while restoring order and common sense to the judicial review process." *See* H.R. Conf. Rep. 109-72, at 2873. By reissuing Respondent's order, the BIA would provide Respondent a "fair opportunity" to seek judicial review in the court of appeals. *See Firmansjah*, 347 F.3d at 627.

The BIA's caselaw supports Respondent's request. The Board—in extraordinary circumstances—exercises equitable power to *sua sponte* reopen or reconsider cases. The BIA has held that such exceptional circumstances exist where there has been a significant development in the law. *See, e.g., Matter of Muniz*, 23 I&N Dec. at 207–08 (sua sponte reopening a case where Ninth Circuit interpreted meaning of crime of violence differently from BIA); *Matter of G-D-*, 22 I&N Dec. 1132 1135-36 (BIA 1999) (declining to reopen or reconsider sua sponte where caselaw represented only "incremental development" of the law and respondent's case did not turn on cited authority); *Matter of X-G-W-*, 22 I&N Dec. 71, 73 (BIA 1998) (statutory change in definition of "refugee" warranted sua sponte reopening).

Although here Respondent is asking the Board to reissue the order, as opposed to reopen or reconsider the case, the principles involved in the cases cited above are applicable. The REAL ID Act's purported elimination of habeas corpus review of certain cases is a monumental change in immigration law and a dramatic departure from the historical role of habeas corpus in reviewing the legality of deportation. By reissuing the order in Respondent's case, the Board will prevent unnecessary and potentially irreparable harm to the Respondent. Otherwise, the Respondent may be deprived of all federal court review. Reissuing the decision will effectuate Congress' intent that Respondent have an "'adequate and effective' alternative to habeas corpus."

V. CONCLUSION

For the reasons stated above, Respondent requests that the BIA reissue the **[deportation** or **removal]** order dated **[date]**.

[Date]

Respectfully submitted,

[Attorney]

[ADD CERTIFICATE OF SERVICE]

[2] The legislative history of the REAL ID Act confirms that Congress did not intend that any person be deprived of judicial review: under section 106, "*all* aliens who are ordered removed by an immigration judge will be able to appeal to the BIA and then raise constitutional and legal challenges in the courts of appeals. *No* alien, not even criminal aliens, will be deprived of judicial review of such claims." H.R. Conf. Rep. 109-72, at 2873 (emphasis added).

UNITED STATES DEPARTMENT OF JUSTICE
EXECUTIVE OFFICE FOR IMMIGRATION REVIEW
BOARD OF IMMIGRATION APPEALS
FALLS CHURCH, VIRGINIA

In re **[Alien]**, Respondent. In **[Deportation or Removal]** Proceedings	))))))))	No. **[Case Number]**

MOTION TO REOPEN AND REISSUE THE BIA'S DECISION IN LIGHT OF THE REAL ID ACT

I. INTRODUCTION

Respondent asks the BIA to reopen and reissue the **[enter date]** order in this case in light of the recent enactment of the REAL ID Act of 2005, P. L. 109-13, 119 Stat. 231 (May 11, 2005). Prior to the REAL ID Act, Respondent was barred from filing a petition for review in the court of appeals because **[he/she]** was found removable based on one of the criminal grounds enumerated in INA § 242(a)(2)(C). The INA, as amended by the REAL ID Act, now provides Respondent with the opportunity to seek court of appeals review; however, because the BIA issued the order in this case more than 30 days ago, Respondent may be barred from review. *See* INA § 242(b)(1) (petition must be filed within 30 days of final order). Respondent also may be unable to seek review in the district court through a habeas petition, though **[he/she]** could have done so prior to the REAL ID Act. In order to remedy this unintended adverse effect of the enactment of the REAL ID Act, Respondent requests that the Board, in the interest of justice, reissue its order.

II. RELEVANT PROCEDURAL HISTORY

[Insert]

III. STATUTORY AND LEGISLATIVE BACKGROUND

In 1996, Congress barred respondents with certain criminal convictions from seeking judicial review in the court of appeals. *See* Anti-Terrorism and Effective Death Penalty Act (AEDPA), § 440(a), Pub. L. 104-207, 110 Stat. 3009 (April 24, 1996); Illegal Immigration Reform and Immigrant Responsibility Act of 1996 (IIRIRA), § 306, § 309 Pub. L. 104-208, 110 Stat. 3009 (Sept. 30, 1996) *codified* at INA § 242(a)(2)(C) and IIRIRA § 309(c)(4)(G). However, respondents with criminal convictions were not precluded from federal court review entirely. The Supreme Court, in *INS v. St. Cyr*, 533 U.S. 289 (2001), held that respondents barred from filing a petition for review in the court of appeals could seek review of their cases through habeas petitions, 28 U.S.C. § 2241, filed in the U.S. district court.

On May 11, 2005, the REAL ID Act of 2005, Pub. L. 109-13, 119 Stat. 231, was enacted. Section 106(a) of this new law purports to eliminate habeas corpus jurisdiction over challenges to final orders of removal, deportation, or exclusion. Congress, however, expanded the availability of court of appeals review. Specifically, section 106(a)(1) of the REAL ID Act amended INA § 242 to include a new section INA § 242(a)(2)(D), which says,

> Nothing in subparagraph (B) or (C), or any other provision of this Act (other than this section) which limits or eliminates judicial review, shall be construed as precluding review of constitutional or questions of law raised upon a petition for review filed with an appropriate court of appeals in accordance with this section.

As a result, respondents with criminal convictions who previously would have filed habeas petitions now may file petitions for review in the court of appeals. The legislative history confirms that this provision was intended to concentrate federal court review of all removal proceedings in the courts of appeals. *See* H.R. Conf. Rep. 109-72, at 2873 (2005).[1] ("By placing all review in the court of appeals, Division B would provide an 'adequate and effective' alternative to habeas corpus." (quoting *St. Cyr*, 533 U.S. at 314 n. 38)).

IV. ARGUMENT

A. The BIA Has Authority to Reopen and Reissue Its Decision.

Pursuant to INA § 240(c)(6) and 8 C.F.R. § 1003.2, respondents may file one motion to reopen within 90 days of the BIA's decision. The motion "shall state the new facts that will be proven at the hearing to be held if the motion is granted." INA § 240(c)(6)(B). "A motion to reopen shall not be granted unless it appears to the Board that evidence sought to be offered is material and was not available and could not have been discovered or presented at the former hearing." 8 C.F.R. § 1003.2(c)(1).

Here, the new evidence Respondent offers is the enactment of the REAL ID Act. Given that the BIA issued a decision in Respondent's case on **[enter date], [he/she]** could not have presented this evidence prior to the Board's decision. This evidence is material because it impacts whether the Respondent can file a petition for review in the court of appeals.

Moreover, the BIA is authorized to "take any action consistent with their authorities under the Act and the regulations as is appropriate and necessary for the disposition of the case." 8 C.F.R. § 1003.1(d)(ii). In addition, the Board has discretionary equitable powers to serve the interest of justice. *See e.g., Matter of G-D-*, 22 I&N Dec. 1132 (BIA 1999) (stating that as long as the Board has jurisdiction, its "discretionary powers are not limited, restricted, or qualified."); *Matter of X-G-W-*, 22 I&N Dec. 71 (BIA 1998) (exercising *sua sponte* authority to reopen proceedings to pursue certain asylum claims based on coerced population control policies to "serve the interest of justice"). In fact, on numerous occasions, the Board has reissued prior decisions in the interest of justice. *See Etchu-Njang v. Gonzales*, 403 F.3d 577 (8th Cir. 2004); *Roy v. Ashcroft*, 389 F.3d 132, 135 (5th Cir. 2004); *Lara-Torres v. Ashcroft*, 383 F.3d 968, 972 (9th Cir. 2004); *Firmansjah v. Ashcroft*, 347 F.3d 625, 626 (7th Cir. 2003); *Lonyem v. U.S. Atty. Gen.*, 352 F.3d 1338, 1340 n.3 (11th Cir. 2003).

In *Firmansjah*, the Seventh Circuit considered the BIA's authority to reissue decisions and the impact on the court's jurisdiction to review the underlying order. *See* 347 F.3d 626–27. The court held that "[b]ecause nothing prevents the Board from entering a new removal order, which is subject to a fresh petition for review, we have jurisdiction over the case and will proceed to briefing." *Id.* at 627.

[1] Available at *http://frwebgate.access.gpo.gov/cgibin/getpage.cgi?dbname=2005_record&page=H2813&position=all.*

B. Reopening and Reissuing the Order in Respondent's Case Satisfies the Interest of Justice and Effectuates Congressional Intent.

Respondent now finds **[himself/herself]** subject to an adverse, and unintended, effect of the REAL ID Act. *See* H.R. Conf. Rep. 109-72, at 2873.[2] Prior to the REAL ID Act, Respondent would have been barred from filing a petition for review, but **[he/she]** could have filed a habeas corpus petition. Unlike a petition for review, there is no filing deadline for a habeas petition. *Compare* INA § 242(b)(1) *with* 28 U.S.C. § 2241. Although Congress has said that individuals such as Respondent now must seek review in the court of appeals, as opposed to the district court, Respondent may be barred from filing a petition for review because more than thirty days have passed from the date of the BIA's decision. *See* INA § 242(b)(1). This result would undermine the intent of Congress "to give every alien a fair opportunity to obtain judicial review while restoring order and common sense to the judicial review process." *See* H.R. Conf. Rep. 109-72, at 2873. By reopening and reissuing Respondent's order, the BIA would provide Respondent a "fair opportunity" to seek judicial review in the court of appeals.

Even where a person did not file a motion to reopen within the statutory deadline, the BIA has reopened cases in extraordinary cases where there has been a significant development in the law. *See, e.g., Matter of Muniz*, 23 I&N Dec. at 207-08 (sua sponte reopening a case where Ninth Circuit interpreted meaning of crime of violence differently from BIA); *Matter of G-D-*, 22 I&N Dec. 1132 1135-36 (BIA 1999) (declining to reopen or reconsider sua sponte where caselaw represented only "incremental development" of the law and respondent's case did not turn on cited authority); *Matter of X-G-W-*, 22 I&N Dec. 71, 73 (BIA 1998) (statutory change in definition of "refugee" warranted sua sponte reopening).

The REAL ID Act's purported elimination of habeas corpus review of certain cases is a monumental change in immigration law and a dramatic departure from the historical role of habeas corpus in reviewing the legality of deportation. By reopening and reissuing the order in Respondent's case, the Board will prevent unnecessary and potentially irreparable harm to the Respondent. Otherwise, the Respondent may be deprived of all federal court review. Reissuing the decision will effectuate Congress' intent that Respondent have an "'adequate and effective' alternative to habeas corpus."

V. CONCLUSION

For the reasons stated above, Respondent requests that the BIA reopen and reissue the **[deportation** or **removal]** order dated **[date]**.

[Date]

Respectfully submitted,

[Attorney]

[ADD CERTIFICATE OF SERVICE]

[2] The legislative history of the REAL ID Act confirms that Congress did not intend that any person be deprived of judicial review: under section 106, "*all* aliens who are ordered removed by an immigration judge will be able to appeal to the BIA and then raise constitutional and legal challenges in the courts of appeals. *No* alien, not even criminal aliens, will be deprived of judicial review of such claims." H.R. Conf. Rep. 109-72, at 2873 (emphasis added).

UNITED STATES DISTRICT COURT FOR THE
[__________ DISTRICT OF __________]

[PETITIONER'S LAST NAME, First Name]	)	No. __________
	)	
Petitioner,	)	
	)	
v.	)	
	)	
[RESPONDENTS' NAMES]	)	
	)	
Respondents.	)	
	)	

MOTION FOR EXTENSION OF TIME TO RESPOND TO RESPONDENTS' MOTION TO TRANSFER

I. INTRODUCTION

On May 11, 2005, the REAL ID Act of 2005, Pub. L. 109-13, 119 Stat. 231 was enacted into law. Section 106(a) of the new law purports to eliminate habeas corpus jurisdiction over challenges to final orders of removal, deportation, or exclusion.[1] The REAL ID Act further provides that district courts must transfer pending habeas corpus petitions challenging final orders of removal, deportation, or exclusion (or the part of the case challenging a final removal, deportation or exclusion order) to the court of appeals in which a petition for review could have been filed. REAL ID § 106(c). Thus, by its express terms, the REAL ID Act provides that transfer is *not* appropriate in certain cases (or parts of certain cases). In addition, there may be other statutory and/or constitutional reasons why transfer is not appropriate in certain cases.

II. MOTION FOR EXTENSION OF TIME

On **[date]**, Respondents filed a motion to transfer the instant case to the U.S. Court of Appeals for the _____ Circuit. The basis of Respondents' motion is that such transfer is required by § 106(c) of the REAL ID Act.

Pursuant to Local Rule ______, Petitioner's response to Respondents' motion is due ___ days after the motion was **[served on Petitioner and/or filed with the court—check local rules]**. Thus, Petitioner's response is currently due on **[date]**.

The Local Rules further provided that a party may file a motion to extend time to file a responsive pleading and that the motion **[may/shall]** be granted upon a showing of ___________ **[good cause—check local rules]**. An extension of time to respond to Respondents' motion to transfer is warranted in this case for the following reason(s).

[1] The newly enacted provisions of the REAL ID Act became effective upon enactment and apply to final orders of removal, deportation, or exclusion issued before, on, or after enactment. REAL ID Act § 106(b).

The REAL ID Act's purported elimination of habeas corpus review of final orders of removal, deportation, and exclusion is a monumental change in immigration law and a dramatic departure from the historical role of habeas corpus in reviewing the legality of executive detention. As the Supreme Court has stated, "[t]he writ of habeas corpus has *always* been available to review the legality of executive detention." *INS v. St. Cyr*, 533 U.S. 289, 364-65 (2001). Emphasis added.

The issues presented in Respondents motion, including whether and, if so, how the REAL ID Act's provisions impact the instant case (specifically, whether transfer is appropriate and, if so, to which court of appeals the case should be transferred) are issues of first impression. A reasonable extension of time is warranted to allow undersigned counsel to adequately consider and address the new law's application to the instant case. Moreover, because any transfer order the court of appeals later determines was issued in error would significantly delay the instant litigation, permitting undersigned counsel a reasonable extension of time at this juncture may also further the interests of judicial economy.

[IF APPLICABLE, INCLUDE ADDITIONAL REASONS]

[In addition, Petitioner further warrants additional time to file a response to Respondents' motion due to counsel's extremely heavy case load and other previously scheduled commitments. *Explain*.]

II. RESPONDENTS' POSITION [IF APPLICABLE]

[*Note*: Some local rules may require a statement of opposing counsel's position on the motion. Check local rules.]

III. CONCLUSION

For the foregoing reasons, Petitioner respectfully requests that this Court grant a ___ day extension of time in which to file a response to Respondents' motion to transfer, such that the brief would be due on **[date]**.

[Dated:]

Respectfully submitted,

[Attorney]

[ADD CERTIFICATE OF SERVICE]

UNITED STATES DISTRICT COURT FOR THE
[__________ DISTRICT OF __________]

[PETITIONER'S LAST NAME, First Name]	)	No. __________
	)	
Petitioner,	)	
	)	
v.	)	
	)	
[RESPONDENTS' NAMES]	)	
	)	
Respondents.	)	
	)	

MOTION TO PERMIT BRIEFING ON THE IMPACT OF THE NEWLY ENACTED REAL ID ACT OF 2005

I. INTRODUCTION AND MOTION

On May 11, 2005, the REAL ID Act of 2005, Pub. L. 109-13, 119 Stat. 231 was enacted into law. Section 106(a) of the new law purports to eliminate habeas corpus jurisdiction over challenges to final orders of removal, deportation, or exclusion.[1] The REAL ID Act's purported elimination of habeas corpus review of final orders of removal, deportation, and exclusion is a monumental change in immigration law and a dramatic departure from the historical role of habeas corpus in reviewing the legality of executive detention and decisions. As the Supreme Court has stated, "[t]he writ of habeas corpus has *always* been available to review the legality of executive detention." *INS v. St. Cyr*, 533 U.S. 289, 364–65 (2001). Emphasis added.

The REAL ID Act further provides that district courts must transfer pending habeas corpus petitions challenging final orders of removal, deportation, or exclusion (or the part of the case challenging a final removal, deportation, or exclusion order) to the court of appeals in which a petition for review could have been filed. REAL ID § 106(c). Thus, by its express terms, the REAL ID Act provides that transfer is *not* appropriate in certain cases (or parts of certain cases). In addition, there may be other statutory and/or constitutional reasons why transfer is not appropriate in certain cases.

By this motion, Petitioner requests this Court's permission to brief whether and, if so, how the REAL ID Act's provisions impact the instant case; specifically, whether transfer is appropriate and, if so, to which court of appeals the case should be transferred. Such briefing is warranted to address any novel and complex issues presented by the new law's application to this case and to provide the Court with the benefit of the parties' briefing in deciding whether transfer is appropriate. Moreover, because any transfer order the court of appeals later determines was issued in error would significantly delay the instant litigation, permitting the parties to brief the issues at this juncture also furthers the interests of judicial economy.

---

[1] The newly enacted provisions of the REAL ID Act became effective upon enactment and apply to final orders of removal, deportation, or exclusion issued before, on, or after enactment. REAL ID Act § 106(b).

II. RESPONDENTS' POSITION [IF APPLICABLE]

[*Note*: Some local rules may require a statement of opposing counsel's position on the motion. Check local rules.]

III. CONCLUSION

For the foregoing reasons, the Court should set a reasonable briefing schedule to permit the parties to brief the impact of the REAL ID of 2005 on the instant case.

[Dated:]

Respectfully submitted,

[Attorney]

[ADD CERTIFICATE OF SERVICE]

UNITED STATES DISTRICT COURT
FOR THE DISTRICT OF COLORADO
DENVER, COLORADO

[Alien]	)	
Petitioner,	)	
vs.	)	
	)	Civil Action No. ______________
Douglas **MAURER** Interim Field Director, U.S. Immigration and Customs Enforcement	)	Agency Docket: ______________
U.S. IMMIGRATION AND CUSTOMS ENFORCEMENT	)	
Respondents.	)	

PETITIONER'S NON-OPPOSITION TO RESPONDENTS' MOTION TO TRANSFER HABEAS PETITION TO COURT OF APPEALS

COMES NOW the Petitioner, by and through **[his/her]** attorney, to reply to the Motion of Respondents seeking to transfer the instant petition to the U.S. Circuit Court of Appeals.

Although Petitioner does not necessarily concede that provisions of the REAL ID Act of 2005, Pub. L. No. 109-13, Div. B, § 106(a), 119 Stat. 231 (2005), serve to divest this Court of jurisdiction over all of the issues raised in **[his/her]** petition, Petitioner concedes that the interests of judicial efficiency would best be served by transferring **[his/her]** petition to the Circuit Court because it appears inevitable that the legal issues raised in **[his/her]** petition will need to be resolved by the Circuit Court.

Accordingly, Petitioner does not oppose the motion submitted by Respondents to transfer **[his/her]** petition to the court of appeals.

Respectfully submitted this ___day of __________, 20__.

[Attorney]

[ADD CERTIFICATE OF SERVICE]

UNITED STATES DISTRICT COURT
FOR THE DISTRICT OF NEW JERSEY

[Alien]	)	
	)	
Petitioner – Plaintiff	)	
	)	
v.	)	
	)	Civil Action No. __________
DOUGLAS **MAURER**,	)	
	)	Hon. **[Judge]**
Field Director, Immigration & Customs Enforcement, DHS	)	
	)	
DEPARTMENT OF HOMELAND SECURITY	)	
	)	
Respondents – Defendants.	)	

PETITIONER'S REPLY TO RESPONDENTS' MOTION TO TRANSFER

COMES NOW THE PETITIONER, by and through **[his/her]** attorney, to reply to the motion submitted by Respondents seeking to transfer this matter to the U.S. Circuit Court of Appeals for the Second Circuit.

1. Petitioner concedes that, because **[his/her]** initial removal proceedings were conducted in New York, the Second Circuit Court of Appeals is the appropriate venue for resolution of the issues surrounding the propriety of the order of removal entered against **[him/her]**.

2. Petitioner contends, however, that because Petitioner remains incarcerated at a facility located within the State of New Jersey, this Court retains jurisdiction to resolve the issues surrounding the duration, terms, and propriety of **[his/her]** incarceration.

3. Although the REAL ID Act, Div. B, 109 P.L. 13, 119 Stat. 231 (May 11, 2005), contemplates that judicial review of removal orders will be consolidated within the circuit courts of appeal, the Act does not divest the district courts of jurisdiction over petitions which challenge the terms and circumstances of an individual's detention. Indeed, the House Committee Report specifically acknowledged that "section 106 would not preclude habeas review over challenges to detention that are independent of challenges to removal orders. Instead, the bill would eliminate habeas review only over challenges to removal orders." Committee Report to accompany H.R. 1268, No. 20-930, May 3, 2005.

4. Although Petitioner's claim presently involves only issues surrounding the propriety of the order of removal entered against **[him/her]**, issues surrounding **[his/her]** detention are quite likely to arise in the foreseeable future.

5. Petitioner is currently protected under a stay of removal entered originally by the District Court for the District of Colorado after hearing on **[his/her]** Motion for a Temporary Restraining Order. In the Joint

Petition for Transfer to the jurisdiction of this court, the parties previously agreed to leave the stay in place until the merits of the case could be fully heard.

6. Accordingly, Petitioner would urge the Court to bifurcate the proceedings, transfer **[his/her]** request for judicial review to the Second Circuit of Appeals, hold in abeyance that portion of **[his/her]** claim seeking review of the terms of **[his/her]** physical incarceration and retain the stay of removal previously entered.

Respectfully submitted this ____ day of ____________, 20__.

[Attorney]

[ADD CERTIFICATE OF SERVICE]